The Russian Landed Gentry and the
Peasant Emancipation of 1861

To
VICTORIA

THE RUSSIAN LANDED GENTRY AND THE PEASANT EMANCIPATION OF 1861

TERENCE EMMONS
Assistant Professor of History
Stanford University

CAMBRIDGE
AT THE UNIVERSITY PRESS
1968

Published by the Syndics of the Cambridge University Press
Bentley House, 200 Euston Road, London N.W.1
American Branch: 32 East 57th Street, New York, N.Y. 10022

Library of Congress Catalog Card Number: 68-29654

Standard Book Number: 521 07340 5

Printed in Great Britain
at the University Printing House, Cambridge
(Brooke Crutchley, University Printer)

Contents

Contents

Preface

In a speech to the assembled gentry of Moscow province on 30 March 1856 shortly after the signing of the Treaty of Paris that had ended the Crimean War, Emperor Alexander II publicly declared his intention to proceed with the emancipation of Russia's 22,000,000 serfs. Thereupon began the 'Epoch of Great Reforms', productive of a series of changes in the civil and legal order which, measured by their collective impact on Russian life, constituted the most important episode in Russian history between the reign of Peter the Great and the Revolution of 1905. Although the 'Epoch' can be extended chronologically to include the last of the 'Great Reforms', the military reorganization of 1874, its central core encompassed the years 1856–62, during which time the primary and fundamental reform, the emancipation of the serfs, was prepared and carried out and the terms of two other important reforms—the *zemstvo* and judicial reforms—were publicly announced (although promulgated only in 1864). These years constitute the crucial period of the 'Epoch of Great Reforms' and a period in which there occurred a political crisis of great significance in the life of the state.

The central importance of the emancipation in Russia's modern history has always been recognized. Most scholars have been concerned either with its impact on the peasantry, or (especially since 1917) with its impact on the development of the revolutionary movement. In a phrase, the peasant and the 'revolutionary democrat' have received the lion's share of attention. Another intimate party to the emancipation—the landed gentry—has received scant attention. Yet it is hardly possible to understand either the character of the emancipation and succeeding reforms, or the political atmosphere in which they were devised, without coming to terms with the problem of the gentry. That problem is the subject of this book.

Chto takoe dvorianstvo?—What is the *dvorianstvo*? In nineteenth-century Russia the *dvorianstvo* was an official class which encompassed the Russian equivalents of the European social groups usually called 'gentry' and 'nobility' in English. It is inconvenient, for purposes of consistency in translation, to use both terms. I have chosen 'gentry' as the translation of the word, because this study is concerned primarily with the land- and serf-owners and their corporate life in the provinces; that is, with the *dvorianstvo* as 'landed gentry'.

In 1962 I began a study of the involvement of the gentry of Tver province in the peasant emancipation. Tver was a well-known center of abolitionist opinion in the 1850s and the scene of extensive political activity among the gentry in the early 1860s. Who were the gentry abolitionists and political reformers? What 'interests' did they represent? In whose interest was the emancipation carried out? These were some of the questions that led to a study of the Tver gentry. The discovery that the Tver gentry were not an isolated group, but were participating in a widespread movement, led me to a broader investigation of gentry involvement in the reform and of gentry politics. These studies were made possible by access to published and, especially, unpublished materials in the Soviet Union. I was able to work in the central state archives of Moscow and Leningrad, and in the provincial archives of Tver (present-day Kalinin).

As the study progressed, it also became clear that the views and activities of the gentry could not be evaluated properly without reference to certain economic problems; to the development of the state's plans for reform; and to broader currents of thought and politics. The result is neither an economic history of the emancipation, nor a study of state policy, politics or public opinion. It is, rather, a mixture of all these—with emphasis on the gentry—which, if it had to be labelled, might be called 'a social history of the emancipation'.

Particular attention has been paid to two areas of gentry activity: Involvement in the preparation of the reform between 1857 and 1861; and the political activities of the gentry—primarily in their provincial assemblies—in 1861-2. Greatest consideration has been given to the gentry liberals. Conservative gentry attitudes are relatively easy to understand. Gentry liberalism, which has been the subject of considerable historiographical controversy, is more in need of study and explanation, if only because the political program elaborated by the gentry liberals at this time was to a large extent the genesis of all subsequent efforts to reform the autocratic regime.

These comments should be of some help in approaching the organization of the study. The subject is large and complex, and the usual apologies for having neglected or failed to render justice to many important questions are more than usually in order. In particular, less attention has been paid to journalistic debates than would be desirable for a full consideration of contemporary currents of opinion. To have done so would have carried the study far beyond the limits of a single volume. Fortunately, the publicism of this period—in marked contrast to the corporate activities of the gentry—has been the subject of several important contributions by such scholars as Ivaniukov, Dzhanshiev, Kornilov, and Druzhinin. Still other limitations have been dictated, of course, by the availability and character of the sources.

I have received an almost embarrassing amount of support and encouragement in this undertaking. I am indebted to the Inter-University Committee on Travel Grants and to the Soviet Ministry of Higher Education for making possible nearly two years of uninterrupted research in the Soviet Union. To the Center for Slavic and East European Studies at the University of California, Berkeley; the Committee on International Studies, Stanford University; the Hoover Institution on War, Revolution, and Peace; and the American Philosophical Society, I am grateful for financial support at various junctures. I would like to record heartfelt thanks to the library staffs of the University of California, Stanford University, and the Hoover Institution; and to the many archivists and librarians of Moscow, Leningrad, and Kalinin, who worked hard and cheerfully to help me.

I owe a great deal more than this conventional nod to Miss Erica Brendel, Professor Ivo J. Lederer, and Professor Wayne S. Vucinich, for much help and kindness. I am deeply grateful to Professor Nicholas V. Riasanovsky and Professor Martin E. Malia

Preface

for reading the manuscript at various stages in its evolution, for many constructive comments, and especially for the privilege of being their student. My greatest debt in the preparation of this study is to the generous help, wisdom, and inspiration of Professor Petr Andreevich Zaionchkovskii. All errors and faulty judgments in this book are, of course, my own.

TERENCE EMMONS

Stanford University

NOTE. All dates are in the old style; that is, twelve days behind the Western calendar in the nineteenth century.

Key to Abbreviations

GAKO   Gosudarstvennyi arkhiv Kalininskoi oblasti (State Archive of Kalinin *Oblast'*).

TsGAOR   Tsentralnyi gosudarstvennyi arkhiv Oktiabr'skoi revoliutsii, vysshikh organov gosudarstvennoi vlasti i gosudarstvennogo upravleniia SSSR, g. Moskva (Central State Archive of the October Revolution, Higher Organs of State Authority and State Administration of the USSR, Moscow).

TsGIAL   Tsentralnyi gosudarstvennyi istoricheskii arkhiv SSSR, g. Leningrad (Central State Historical Archive of the USSR, Leningrad).

TsGALI   Tsentralnyi gosudarstvennyi arkhiv literatury i iskusstva SSSR, g. Moskva (Central State Archive of Literature and Art, Moscow).

PD   Institut russkoi literatury (Pushkinskii dom) Akademii nauk SSSR, g. Leningrad (Institute of Russian Literature [*Pushkinskii dom*], Leningrad).

ORLB   Gosudarstvennaia biblioteka SSSR im. V.I. Lenina, Otdel rukopisei, g. Moskva (State Lenin Library of the USSR, Manuscript Division, Moscow).

GPB   Gosudarstvennaia publichnaia biblioteka im. M.E. Saltykova-Shchedrina, Otdel rukopisei, g. Leningrad (State Public Saltykov-Shchedrin Library, Manuscript Division, Leningrad).

The use of page numbers followed by lower case 'a' (pp. 1–1a, etc.) in reference to materials from these archives corresponds to the reverse sides of the *leaves* that are the numerical units by which the materials are arranged.

The use of the abbreviation '*f.*' in reference to archival materials indicates the *fond* (collection) in which the materials are arranged (thus: *GAKO, f.* 59). Since archival materials are subject to reorganization, the titles—or lacking that, brief descriptions—of the *fondy* referred to are included in the bibliography.

PART I

THE LANDED GENTRY, SERFDOM, AND FIRST STEPS TOWARD EMANCIPATION

Non, Monsieur, soyez-en bien persuadé, il n'y a pas d'aristocrates, il n'y a que des serviteurs à Saint Pétersbourg.

Il faut dire cependant que, parmi ces nobles russe et surtout parmi les jeunes gens, il y en a déjà un assez grand nombre qui ont des tendances plus élevées . . . Ceux-la suivent avec amour les progrès de la civilisation et de la liberté en Europe, et se donnent toutes les peines du monde pour se rapprocher du peuple, chose extrêmement difficile, parce qu'ils en sont separés par un abîme. Ils tâchent de conserver et de cultiver en eux-mêmes, et d'allumer dans les autres le feu sacré des grands et des nobles instincts.

MICHAEL BAKUNIN, JANUARY 1845

I

Introduction. Some Social and Institutional Characteristics of the Landed Gentry before 1861

By the mid-nineteenth century, the hereditary gentry of European Russia numbered as an official estate (*soslovie*) nearly 610,000 persons—men, women and children.[1] According to the Tenth Revision (1857–8), there were within this class 106,391 gentry proprietors whose lands were populated by 10,694,445 'revision souls' (male serfs), or a total serf population of about 22,000,000.[2] In European Russia, in the central black soil and non-black soil provinces of the greatest population density, serfs represented well over half the total population.[3]

According to the figures compiled by Troinitskii from the Tenth Revision, serf-holding among the gentry proprietors was distributed as shown in table 1.[4]

Thus, 81 per cent of the serfs were owned by 22 per cent of the

---

[1] 'European Russia' included the fifty established provinces, or that territory of the Empire excluding Poland, Finland, the Caucasus and Siberia. A. Romanovich-Slavatinskii, *Dvorianstvo v Rossii ot nachala XVIII veka do otmeny krepostnogo prava* (St Petersburg, 1870), p. 509. On the peculiarities and insufficiencies of Russian population statistics in the first half of the nineteenth century, see V. M. Kabuzan, *Narodonaselenie Rossii v XVIII-pervoi polovine XIX v.* (Moscow, 1963).

[2] P. A. Zaionchkovskii, *Otmena krepostnogo prava v Rossii* (2nd ed. Moscow, 1960), p. 18. The more than 25,000,000 additional peasants who were 'serfs' of the state and Imperial family were emancipated by legislation based on the Act of February 19 and promulgated in 1863 and 1866. The civil and administrative status of these latter groups was thereby fused with that of the former landlords' serfs. The total population of the Empire *c.* 1861 was about 74,000,000.

[3] I. I. Ignatovich, *Pomeshchich'i krest'iane nakanune osvobozhdeniia* (2nd ed. Moscow, 1910), p. 46.

[4] *Ibid.*, p. 62. It should be noted that the actual number of estate owners was probably considerably smaller than indicated by these figures, since they are not corrected to allow for the frequent ownership of more than one estate by an individual *pomeshchik*. They come nearer to representing the number of estates, rather than of estate-owners.

gentry land-holders—those with estates of more than 100 souls. Nearly half (44 per cent) of the serf-owners had estates of less than 21 souls, while a mere one per cent of them—those with estates of more than 1,000 souls—owned 29 per cent of the total serf population.

TABLE I

	No. of gentry	Percentage of gentry	No. of souls	Percentage of souls
Gentry without estates but serf-owning	3,633	3·5	12,045	0·1
Gentry owning land inhabited by serfs:				
Less than 21 souls	41,016	39·5	327,534	3·1
From 21–100 souls	35,498	34·2	1,666,073	15·8
From 101–500 souls	19,930	19·2	3,925,102	37·1
From 501–1000 souls	2,421	2·3	1,569,888	14·9
More than 1000 souls	1,382	1·3	3,050,540	29·0

These figures show that the gentry was, in terms of economic circumstances, an extremely varied class with a large predominance of petty smallholders. (Granting regional variations, it is clear from state legislation that estates of less than 21 souls were completely insufficient to support a gentry family, and that an estate of less than 100 souls was generally considered inadequate.) Prince Vasil'chikov,[1] one of the earliest investigators of gentry landholding in Russia, came to the conclusion—based partly on the statistical information of the Eighth Revision (1834) and partly on his personal experiences as a provincial gentry official in the 1850s—that the gentry constituted not one, but three socio-economic classes. He noted that the 1,453 great serfholders who owned, in 1834, more than 1,000 souls each, together with the owners of more than 500 souls, numbered in all 3,276 persons and owned about half the total serf population.[2] According to Vasil'chikov's observations, many of these people had virtually nothing to do with the provincial life of the gentry: From their

[1] A. Vasil'chikov, *Zemlevladenie i zemledelie v Rossii i drugikh evropeiskikh gosudarstvakh*, 1 (2nd ed. St Petersburg, 1881), 422–5.
[2] Vasil'chikov's observations were made, of course, within the framework of quantitative groupings used in the official Revisions.

ranks came the high dignitaries of state and court; they lived in the capitals or abroad and rarely visited their estates.

The second 'class' of gentry, according to Vasil'chikov, was formed primarily from among the owners of 100–500 souls. In 1834 there were 16,740 of them, owning some 3,634,000 souls. These, he observed, were the *gentry (pomeshchiki)* properly speaking, who generally had provincial ties and at the same time service connections, an education in one or another of the cadet schools and, increasingly in the last decades before emancipation, in universities. The differences between this group and the first were not differences of blood: Many a provincial *pomeshchik* was of ancient lineage and princely origin, while many of the great landholders owed their circumstances primarily to the favor—expressed in huge grants of 'populated land' or access to the state treasury—that had been shown their fathers or grandfathers by Elizabeth I, Catherine II or Paul I.[1] Rather, these were the differences between the great *sanovniki* (courtiers) and high nobility of the capitals, and the ordinary *pomeshchiki* who had no entrance at court.

The third group designated by Vasil'chikov were 'gentry' by official designation only. These were the smallholders, those owners of less than 100 souls who constituted 84 per cent of the total number of serf owners in 1834. Of these 106,000 smallholders, 17,000 had no land at all, but only a few serfs ascribed to their households; 31,000 had holdings averaging 49 souls each; while 58,000 owned an average of 77 souls each. For many of this group who lived on the land, the manner of life was often nearer to that of the peasants than to the great landholders who were their legal peers. But most of them, Vasil'chikov observed, pursued careers, serving in the civil administration or the army.[2]

Vasil'chikov's conclusions find remarkable confirmation in a study of gentry involvement in the peasant emancipation. The

[1] Cf. J. Blum, *Lord and peasant in Russia from the ninth to the nineteenth century* (Princeton, 1961), pp. 355–8. Between 1740 and 1801 the Russian rulers turned over to private proprietors more than 1,304,000 adult male peasants with their families. These peasants came from the lands of the state and the holdings of the Imperial family. Catherine and Paul were the most generous, giving away between them some 1,400,000 peasants. This prodigality, though not the practice itself, ceased with the ascension to the throne of Alexander I. [2] Vasil'chikov, *Zemlevladenie*, I, 424–5.

owners of less than 100 serfs especially stand out as a distinct group, for since the major review and revision of the legal status of the gentry in 1831–2 these petty-holders had suffered certain corporate disabilities in relation to their wealthier peers: In particular, they had lost the right of direct participation in the local assemblies of gentry.[1] For this reason, and as a result of very widespread absentee ownership,[2] virtually nothing in the provincial gentry assemblies and committees of the time is heard from these petty gentry who made up the large majority of the official gentry class. Thus they took little, if any, part in the gentry's discussion of peasant emancipation.

Vasil'chikov's distinction between the middling gentry of the provinces and the great landholders is also confirmed in the study of the gentry in the reform period, although it is impossible to draw a firm line between them on the basis of estate-size. The 'active' gentry of a province, those who both possessed and exercised the right to participation in class affairs, usually numbered a few hundred individuals.[3] In most gentry assemblies and

---

[1] See below, pp. 14–15.

[2] No general figures are available on this question, but absentee ownership of estates was extremely common in this period, and was probably the practice of the majority of landowners. In some provinces (e.g. Tver, Vladimir, Nizhnii Novgorod), contemporary sources indicate that rarely did more than a quarter of the gentry (and sometimes a much smaller proportion) maintain residence on their estates for even part of the year. (See the detailed discussion of these provinces in the text.) There were regional variations in the pattern, usually related to the extensiveness of demesne holdings (the more demesne, the less absentee ownership) and estate size. If a sizeable majority of the gentry did not live on their estates, meaning that most smallholders did not, probably it can be assumed that most of them were in state service since only large landowners could maintain residences in town with their estate incomes. This supposition is supported by figures on the noble contingent in urban population, as well as by what is known of the extent of noble participation in the civil administration and the officers' corps. (See the immediately following pages and: A. Povalishin, *Riazanskie pomeshchiki i ikh krepostnye* (Riazan, 1903), pp. 26–8; Ignatovich, *Pomeshchich'i krest'iane*, pp. 64–6.)

[3] The right of direct, individual voting in gentry assemblies was restricted by a property qualification (100 serfs or 3,000 *desiatiny* of unpopulated land). As the figures introduced by Blum indicate, this qualification severely restricted the number of active participants in gentry affairs: In 1858, only 635 out of 3,926 registered *pomeshchiki* of Riazan province had the right to vote; in Chernigov, 476 out of 6,268; in Kaluga, 463 out of 3,406. (*Lord and peasant*, p. 354.) As a rule the number of 'active' gentry was further reduced by widespread absenteeism. Thus in Tver province, a highly important provincial assembly meeting called in the midst of a period of heightened gentry interest in corporate affairs (1862) was attended by only 140 persons, although the number of qualified estate-holders in the province was in excess of 900 (and the total number of gentry registered as landholders in the province exceeded 3,500!). (See below, pp. 340–4.)

committees these were the middling gentry, owners of several hundred serfs, and only in a relatively few cases—primarily in the capital provinces of St Petersburg and Moscow—were great landholders heard from.

State dignitaries and great landholders in general tended to congregate in the gentry assemblies of Moscow and Petersburg because they preferred to participate in gentry affairs, if at all, in the capitals where they resided, although their landed wealth often lay mainly elsewhere.[1] In these assemblies they exercized an important though not always predominant influence, and it is for this reason that the assemblies of the capitals acquired, as will be seen, much more than a 'provincial' significance.[2]

For the most part, therefore, the 'provincial gentry' were the middling gentry, and it was they who in most provinces carried on the debates and issued the declarations in the committees and assemblies which will be referred to in this study.

It is well known that the Russian gentry did not have the ties to the land, and lacked, in particular, the regional orientation of their western European counterparts: Permanent habitation in the country was relatively rare, and few were the Russian gentry families that had maintained a fixed domain for more than two or three generations.[3] These circumstances were related to the recent service origins and continuing service-orientation of large numbers of the Russian gentry.

As a legally defined 'estate', the Russian gentry of the nineteenth century was of very recent origin: It had, in fact, been created by Peter the Great, or, more exactly, by the Table of Ranks established by Peter in 1722. To be sure, it was not created from nothing: The framework constructed by the Table of Ranks (a hierarchy of 14 ranks each for the military services and the civil administration) was at first filled primarily by the *sluzhilye*

---

[1] A nobleman could participate in the assemblies of any province where he could fulfill the standard property requirements.

[2] See the comments of Bismarck, who was Prussian ambassador in Petersburg from 1859 to 1862; cited in B. Nol'de, *Petersburgskaia missiia Bismarka, 1859–1862* (Prague, 1925), p. 256.

[3] See the comparative comments by Marc Raeff: *Origins of the Russian intelligentsia. The eighteenth century nobility* (New York, 1966), ch. 3.

liudi, the numerous group of state servitors which had emerged as Russia's 'upper class' in the course of the sixteenth and seventeenth centuries.[1]

With the Table of Ranks, gentry status had been made directly dependent on service, either in the military or in the civil administration: Status was obtained by the acquisition of rank and, until the 'emancipation' of the gentry from obligatory service in 1762, had to be maintained the same way. After 1762, families possessing gentry status at that time retained it regardless of service, but the Table remained operative for entrance into the gentry (with certain modifications, until 1917). The Russian gentry remained a class that was 'open-ended' at the bottom. (Ennoblement through service was, of course, practiced in other European states, but only in Russia was it organized into a formal system in which nobility was granted automatically by attainment of relatively low rank in the administrative or military hierarchies.)[2]

Despite its hierarchial arrangement, the new system gave to the holders of rank as a group the shared attribute of gentry status and attendant privileges, a circumstance contributing to the development, for the first time in Russia, of a sense of cohesiveness or corporate self-awareness within the privileged serving class. (The pre-Petrine 'nobility' had been atomized in an infinite hierachy of privilege and social status according to the curious combination of family origins and service records embodied in the *mestnichestvo* system.)[3] The results of this new corporate consciousness were abundantly apparent in the post-Petrine eighteenth century, which saw the steady increment and growing exclusivity of gentry privilege, culminating in the emancipation of the gentry from service in 1762, its monopoly on serf-holding and greatly increased authority over the serfs, and the creation in 1785 of gentry 'estates' in the newly-established provinces.[4]

[1] Cf. N. Pavlov-Sil'vanskii, *Gosudarevy sluzhilye liudi. Proiskhozhdenie russkogo dvorianstva* (St Petersburg, 1898).

[2] Cf. H. Rosenberg, *Bureaucracy, aristocracy and autocracy. The Prussian experience, 1660–1815* (Cambridge, Mass. 1958), pp. 142–3.

[3] Cf. V. O. Kliuchevskii, *Kurs russkoi istorii*, II (Moscow, 1957), 145–56.

[4] The frequent tendency of historians to refer to the events of Russia's 'golden age of the nobility' as part of the eighteenth-century pan-European noble resurgence or 'feudal reaction' should be viewed with some reservation. There were in Russia, after all, no

Social and institutional characteristics of the gentry

At the same time, the Table of Ranks helped to prevent the development of a tight-knit hereditary aristocracy with all the political and social attributes thereof, for the gentry was constantly subjected to infusions of parvenus who had climbed up the ladder of rank. Particularly in the first half of the nineteenth century, under Alexander I and Nicholas I, this process advanced at an accelerating rate: The creation of the ministerial system of state administration (1803, modified and expanded in 1811) marked the beginning of a period of rapid expansion in the size and functions of the civil and military bureaucracies which continued throughout the reign of Nicholas I. In this period, Russia acquired a huge 'civil service'[1] and the largest standing army in Europe.[2] Since officer status and all but menial administrative posts automatically granted ennobling rank (until 1845), this process resulted in a considerable numerical growth in the gentry, over and beyond its natural increase or the incorporation of the Polish *szlachta* in those regions acquired by the partitioning of Poland during the reign of Catherine II.[3] Entrance into the

'estates' (*Stände*, *états*) to be revived, and the historical continuity between the old territorial princelings and boyars (whose power had been destroyed by the centralizing grand princes of the fifteenth–sixteenth centuries) and the eighteenth-century gentry was exceedingly tenuous, if existent at all in any useful sense.

[1] The first modern census in Russia (1897) revealed that approximately 260,000 persons served in the state civil administration (including police and judiciary). According to some rough calculations, there were 195,300 'civil servants' of gentry status (including dependents) living in the towns of the Empire in 1811. In 1843, in Petersburg alone, there were 32,467 active 'civil servants' of gentry status (also including dependents). (Both estimates apparently included 'personal gentry', the status of civil servants occupying the lowest five of the fourteen ranks of the Table.) In 1858, 291,700 persons ascribed to the category 'gentry and [gentry] civil servants' (families included) were living in the cities of European Russia. A. Edeen, 'The civil service: its composition and status', in C. Black (ed.), *The transformation of Russian society. Aspects of social change since 1861* (Cambridge, Mass. 1960), (pp. 274–91), p. 276; A. Rashin, *Naselenie Rossii za sto let (1811–1913 gg.)*. *Statisticheskie ocherki* (Moscow, 1956), pp. 119, 121, 127–8.

[2] At the end of 1852, before its considerable expansion during the Crimean War, the Russian army stood nearly a million strong, including 27,716 'officers and generals'. *Entsiklopedicheskii slovar'* (Brokgauz-Efron), xxviiia (St Petersburg, 1899), 173.

[3] According to the figures introduced by Kabuzan, the gentry population of the old state territory (excluding left-bank Ukraine, the Baltic provinces and the territories acquired during the partitioning of Poland) nearly quadrupled from the Second (1744) Revision to the 10th Revision, rising at the same time from 0·50% to 0·76% of the population in that territory (from 37,326 males to 142,118 males). Kabuzan notes a particularly rapid increase in the relative weight of the gentry population in the first thirty years of the nineteenth century, i.e. roughly the years of the establishment and elaboration of the ministerial system. Kabuzan, *Narodonaselenie Rossii*, p. 154. (See notes immediately preceding.)

9

gentry was opened to increasing numbers of commoners, *raznochintsy*, and especially to the seminary-educated sons of priests to whom the state so frequently turned in its search for literate servants.[1] The ranks of the gentry proprietors were swollen from this source, too, for the acquisition of gentry status brought with it the right to purchase 'populated lands', and many newcomers apparently availed themselves of this right.[2]

The standard histories of the gentry[3] demonstrate, with frequent reference to contemporary opinion, that the gentry as a group, even after their 'emancipation' in 1762, continued to think of themselves as members of a serving class and, in fact, regularly continued to serve, either in the military or in the civil administration. Most gentry continued to measure individual achievement and social status in terms of rank and office, and it was generally accepted that every nobleman, upon completion of his education, bore the obligation to serve for at least a few years.[4] This outlook was, of course, encouraged by the state, especially during the reign of Nicholas I, whose emphasis on the ideal of 'service' for all inhabitants became legend.

By all evidence, the majority of the gentry preferred life in town (in the capitals if possible) and/or in state service to the life of the country squire. Although a sizeable minority of the gentry apparently could afford to maintain residence in town (at least in the provincial towns) without serving,[5] for the majority

[1] S. Korf, *Dvorianstvo i ego soslovnoe upravlenie za stoletie 1762–1855 godov* (St Petersburg, 1906), pp. 362–3 *et passim*; M. Raeff 'The Russian Autocracy and its Officials', *Harvard Slavic Studies*, IV (Cambridge, 1957), 77–92.

[2] See Haxthausen's remarks on this subject: Baron A. von Haxthausen, *Études sur la situation intérieure, la vie nationale et les institutions rurales de la Russie*, I (Paris, 1847), 103.

[3] That is, Romanovich-Slavatinskii, *Dvorianstvo*; and Korf, *Dvorianstvo*. Both large books, being the work of juridical scholars, are devoted largely to the history of legislation pertaining to the gentry. Nevertheless, both are generous, if not replete, with reference to contemporary testimony on the gentry's 'style of life'.

[4] For a recent discussion which places much emphasis on the service-orientation of the nobility (applicable to the nineteenth century, although its general focus is on the eighteenth), see Raeff, *Origins*.

[5] A German observer at the end of the eighteenth century noted the considerable winter–summer fluctuations in the population of Moscow produced by the summer exodus of 5,000 gentry families. M. Beloff, 'Russia', in A. Goodwin (ed.), *The European nobility in the eighteenth century* (1953), p. 182. As early as 1811, more than 112,000 members of the gentry class apparently lived in the towns without serving. Rashin, *Naselenie Rossii*, p. 119.

the escape from the country was coupled with service to the state. Thus, in addition to the force of inclination and prestige, the preponderance of smallholdings (not to mention the situation of those newly-ennobled persons who may have lacked either serfs or land) apparently made service a practical necessity—or at least the only opportunity to escape the 'idiocy of rural life'—for a great many gentry.[1] The high rate of absentee proprietorship indicates that this alternative was not considered an unattractive one.

These general characteristics of Russia's 'first estate' must be kept in mind when considering the gentry, both in their corporate affairs and in their activities as land and serf-owners.

In 1785 Catherine II had granted the 'Charter to the Gentry'. Modeled in part after the corporate institutions of the Baltic nobility and certain English institutions,[2] the Charter granted to

[1] It would be useful to have some studies of income and budgets among the smallholding gentry, but such do not, apparently, exist. As noted earlier, it is clear from state legislation that estates of less than 21 souls were completely insufficient to support a gentry family, and that anything less than 100 souls was generally considered inadequate. Since the average annual *obrok* per *tiaglo* (peasant man and wife, usually) was in the neighborhood of 20 silver rubles at mid-century, it may be assumed that the gross income from the estates of the majority of gentry (and most smallholders collected *obrok* from peasants) was below 2,000 rubles. The more than 40% of gentry proprietors whose holdings were less than 21 serfs in 1858 must have had gross annual incomes from their estates of less than 400 rubles. (Neither additional peasant obligations nor the problem of arrears are considered in such a calculation, of course.)

Service salaries were not large except, of course, at the highest levels, but ranking civil servants and officers generally received considerable additional allowances for food, lodging and other expenses. Moreover, there were periodic raise scales and retirement pensions. Some idea of the importance of service salaries in the life of the gentry can be gotten from the following information, taken from the *kniga shtatov*: In 1824, 1,137 persons were employed in the chanceries of the various departments of the Ruling Senate. Salaries ranged from 4,000 rubles *per annum* for the Procurator-General, 3,000 rubles for each of 36 senior department secretaries, 1,500 rubles for each of 78 department secretaries down to much smaller sums for menial posts. The total annual salary budget was 934,880 rubles. *Polnoe sobranie zakonov Rossiiskoi imperii*, XLIV, *chast'* 2. *Kniga shtatov. Otdelenie* III *i* IV (St Petersburg, 1830), 117–19. On military salaries and allowances at mid-century, see J. S. Curtiss, *The Russian Army under Nicholas I, 1825–1855* (Durham, N.C., 1965), pp. 192–4.

[2] A detailed account of the origins and early development of the gentry institutions can be found in Korf, *Dvorianstvo*. As Korf shows, the Charter in fact gave formal recognition and some elaboration to already existing institutions. The first local assemblies of gentry and the appearance of gentry marshals can be traced to the preparation by the gentry for representation in the great legislative commissions of 1767–8.

the gentry—in addition to reaffirming the various privileges of the individual nobleman—provincial and district (*uezd*) assemblies, which were to convene periodically for discussion of gentry affairs and to elect their marshals (*predvoditeli dvorianstva*) and other officials.

As originally established, these class institutions were involved largely (though never exclusively) with the corporate affairs of the local gentry; maintenance of the rolls of the gentry in each province, certain intra-class judicial functions, guardianship over the estates of gentry minors and incompetents, and the like. With the passage of time and the constant expansion of the state administration into rural Russia after the creation of the provinces (1775), the gentry came to be burdened with ever-increasing responsibilities in the field of general administration: The state, in short, turned to the landed gentry as the main source of administrative talent in the countryside. Gradually, the gentry were invested with nearly total responsibility in administrative, police and judicial affairs at the *uezd* level and with considerable responsibilities in organs functioning at the provincial level.[1] These functions were performed by officials elected by the gentry but at the same time fulfilling the tasks and receiving the ranks and rewards of ordinary civil servants. The provincial gentry marshal in particular had, by the mid-nineteenth century, become an important government official, second only to the governor in rank and protocol and participating *ex officio* in innumerable committees and bureaus of the provincial administration (itself an extension of the Ministry of Interior). He represented the local gentry before the government, and in general acted as a liaison between the local gentry and central authorities; he was charged with control over gentry corporate funds,

---

[1] Among the posts filled by elected gentry officials (other than marshals) after the revision of the gentry's legal status in 1831 were: Presidents of the provincial criminal and civil courts and associate judges of the same; judges of the 'conscience courts' (low, informal courts of mediation, participated in by representatives of other classes as well); *uezd* judges and associate judges of the *uezd* court; *zemskie ispravniki* (until 1837 the general police and judicial authority in the *uezdy*, standing at the head of the *zemskii* courts); the honorary directors of secondary schools; and members of numerous commissions dealing with the maintenance of emergency grain stores, resources and the like. Korf *Dvorianstvo*, pp. 563–7.

presided at gentry assemblies, and intervened in 'disputes' between landlords and their peasants. In addition to these and a multitude of other affairs of the gentry corporation, he participated in numerous general-administrative institutions involved with the gathering of army recruits, the production of horses for the army; the maintenance of roads, posts, fire protection and supply-stores; the levying and expenditure of local taxes and many other functions.[1]

Except for the fact that the provincial marshal was not salaried and was the official head of the gentry, his social position and responsibilities were almost identical to those of the Prussian *Landrat* under Frederick II.[2] The marshals appear to have come consistently from the wealthier strata of *pomeshchiki*, a circumstance no doubt related to the importance and prestige of the office (it gave fourth rank in the Table of Ranks and provided direct access to the Emperor's ear), but also to the fact that it was not a remunerative position: On the contrary, it generally entailed numerous expenses that had to be met from the personal funds of its holder. As a result, suitable and willing takers of this office, especially during the reign of Nicholas I when its responsibilities were greatly extended, appear to have been few and far between. The office consequently changed hands rarely, although the term was only three years. As a general rule, it would appear that this was, in the pre-reform era, the preserve of rich and elderly *pomeshchiki* who had time to spare, some contacts, preferably, in the court or ministries, and the generosity to set a good table for their peers at the time of the gentry assemblies.[3]

The growing dependence of the state on gentry-elected officials in local administration was the major consideration which led the government in the first half of the nineteenth century to attempt to elevate the prestige and independence of the gentry's corporate institutions. And for the same reason it sought to make the elected offices more appealing by assimilating them into the

[1] *Ibid.*, pp. 558–63. The *uezd* marshals occupied much the same position *vis-à-vis* the *uezd* gentry assemblies and the *uezd* administration. They were not the subordinates of the provincial marshals, but were independent elected representatives of the *uezd* assemblies of gentry. [2] Rosenberg, *Bureaucracy*, p. 166.
[3] Romanovich-Slavatinskii, *Dvorianstvo*, pp. 456–62.

general system of rank and reward; to make acceptance of elective posts a legal obligation; and to raise the general 'quality' of the gentry institutions by efforts to reduce the influence of the smallholding gentry in them.

By legislation of 1831-2, the assemblies were given some new prerogatives designed to enhance their independence and thus, it was hoped, their appeal to the gentry: Officials of the provincial administration were definitely barred from participation or presence in the gentry's assemblies; these were given the right to petition the Emperor directly about their needs; and the marshals were to be confirmed in office by the Emperor personally, rather than by the governors as had been the practice previously.

State legislation throughout the first half of the nineteenth century had led toward assimilation of the elective offices of the gentry into the bureaucratic hierarchy. Under Nicholas I, this process was completed: Both the 'class' posts and gentry-elected offices of general administration were adorned with the bureaucratic encumbrances of rank and uniform, awards and in some cases, retirement pensions, although the strictly 'class' offices remained unsalaried (except for full-time clerical jobs). In the government's communications with the local administrations, the holders of these offices were regularly referred to as *chinovniki sluzhashchie po vyboram* ('elected civil servants'), as *statskii sovetnik* or *kollezhskii assesor*.[1] By the legislation of 1831-2, the tie between service and corporate life was reinforced by making active participation in gentry assemblies dependent on previous acquisition of rank through service.[2]

By the same legislation the right of active participation (individual voting) was also restricted to gentry owners of more than 100 serfs or 3,000 *desiatiny* of uninhabited land.[3] But this was not

---

[1] G. Evreinov, *Proshloe i nastoiashchee znachenie russkogo dvorianstva* (St Petersburg, 1898), p. 49.

[2] Romanovich-Slavatinskii, *Dvorianstvo*, p. 435. The individual had either to have acquired the lowest, fourteenth rank 'by actual service', to have served for three years as an elected gentry official, or to have received an order.

[3] Smallholders could pool their holdings and appoint one representative with full rights in the assemblies for each 100 serfs or 3,000 *desiatiny*. Certain honors, ranks and service records also allowed participation without the standard property qualifications. Korf, *Dvorianstvo*, pp. 540-3 *et passim*.

the only way in which the state attempted to limit participation in corporate affairs to the wealthier gentry: Under Nicholas I, legislation was passed to limit the influx into the gentry from below, and even to reduce the existing number of smallholders. Early in his reign, plans were discussed by the high-level secret committee of 6 December 1826 for reducing the number of smallholders by removing their right to own serfs, and by transforming the poorest among them into freeholding peasants (*odnodvortsy*). The Committee of Ministers discussed plans for resettling impoverished and landless gentry in Siberia or Trans-caucasia,[1] and a law of 1841 removed from gentry without land the right to own serfs. In 1845, entrance requirements into the hereditary gentry were raised: To fifth rank in the civil bureau-cracy, and to the rank of staff officer (No. 8) in the military. (Ranks 9–5 in the civil administration, and junior-officer rank in the military gave 'personal nobility', which did not include the right to own serfs.)[2]

Finally, the government frequently reiterated, throughout the first half of the century, the legal obligation of the qualified land-owners to attend their assemblies and to accept election to offices, although the attendant penalties were, apparently, rarely enforced.[3]

The government thus aimed to reinvigorate the gentry 'estates' by enhancing their privileges and limiting them to the wealthier and 'established' gentry. In so doing, it hoped to raise the quality of local administration (or that part of it which was in the hands of 'elected civil servants') and in general to improve the situation of the landed gentry: The large numbers of impoverished gentry had become a problem and a source of considerable expense to the state, which was also not unaware that the poorer serf-owners tended to treat their peasants in worse fashion than did their peers of easier circumstances.[4] It did not go so far, however, as

---

[1] *Ibid.*, pp. 452 ff., 482–3. Of these plans, only the resettlement scheme was implemented, and that apparently on a small scale.

[2] M. Iablochkov, *Istoriia dvorianskogo sosloviia v Rossii* (St Petersburg, 1876), p. 625.

[3] Korf, *Dvorianstvo*, pp. 555–6. The levying of fines and other sanctions for these trans-gressions was left up to decision of the assemblies themselves.

[4] *Ibid.*, pp. 482–3. See also, Ignatovich, *Pomeshchich'i krest'iane*, pp. 60–5; A. Koshelev, *Zapiski (1812–1883 gg.)* (Berlin, 1884), pp. 57 ff.; A. Levshin, 'Dostopamiatnye Minuty v moei zhizni', *Russkii arkhiv*, no. 2 (1885), pp. 478–80.

to close off entrance into the gentry altogether: The government was well aware that acquisition of gentry status was one of the main rewards and incentives for good service.[1]

As Korf perceptively remarked, the government's aims were mutually contradictory and incapable of realization: It could not impose upon the gentry a greater sense of pride and involvement in their local institutions at the same time that it insisted, and with increasing persistence, on regarding these institutions as mere extensions of the bureaucratic administration. (The nature of the paradox was best displayed by the government's efforts to increase the independence of the gentry assemblies at the same time it was repeating that service in elective offices was a state obligation.) In any case, the government's granting of greater independence to the gentry assemblies was almost entirely illusory. The power of the governors over the local gentry steadily increased with the general expansion of the provincial administrations. They had the power of interference in gentry affairs on a wide scale, including the authority to reject candidates to elected gentry offices, even (in practice, though not in law) the gentry marshal. In the relatively rare cases of conflict between the assemblies and the provincial administrations, the central government apparently generally backed up the governors, for fear of undermining their authority. It could hardly have done otherwise, since it held the governors responsible for the correct conduct of gentry affairs in their respective provinces![2]

The results of the government's legislation were apparently negligible so far as the quality of gentry 'elective service' and the importance attached by the gentry to their corporate institutions were concerned. (It may have played some part in curtailing the proportion of smallholders among the gentry. Between 1834 and 1858 the percentage of owners of less than 101 serfs among the gentry dropped from 84 to 78.)[3] The expanding administrative,

---

[1] The possibility of making the gentry into a closed corporation was discussed in high governmental circles early in Nicholas' reign, and rejected on these grounds explicitly. See Korf, *Dvorianstvo*, pp. 461–72.   [2] *Ibid.*, pp. 579–83.

[3] Especially marked was the drop in the number of serfowners without land—from 17,763 to 3,633 (the result, apparently, of the law forbidding ownership of serfs without land), and the decline in the number of *pomeshchiki* with less than 21 souls—from 58,457 proprietors to 41,016. The primary factor in the shrinking of the latter group was

judicial and police authority vested in the elective offices of the assemblies did not serve to make them widely sought after by 'responsible' members of the local gentry. On the contrary, the history of legislation pertaining to the gentry institutions prior to the emancipation testifies to a progressive decline in the quality of personnel and to the problems ensuing from the frequent lack of takers for these offices, so that the state had often to fill them by appointment.[1]

The apparent fact was that the Russian gentry, on the whole, showed little interest in their corporate institutions, and tended to regard their elective functions not as privileges, but simply as 'service', and, moreover, as the least desirable form of service. A position in the military or civil administration of the capital, or at least in the 'real' administration of the provinces, was generally to be preferred to this sort of service—for reasons of prestige, location, rank, salary, and the possibilities of advancement. And the rapid expansion of the military and administrative apparatuses gave ample opportunity for the exercising of these preferences, at least to the able.[2] The elective offices were filled grudgingly,

probably economic pressure, which forced many petty proprietors to sell their holdings for debts. (This traffic in estates was probably frequent among larger holders as well, but it adversely affected the number of smallholders in particular because, as Povalishin noticed, small estates tended to be purchased by proprietors whose holdings were already of some size.) As a result of this situation and the general tendency toward subdivision of very large holdings because of the absence among the Russian gentry of the practice of primogeniture or entail (with few exceptions), the numbers of middling *pomeshchiki* increased over the first half of the nineteenth century, while the two extreme groups shrank somewhat. The predominance of small-holding among the gentry continued, however, to be the rule as it had been since the beginning of the eighteenth century. Blum, *Lord and peasant*, pp. 367–9; Povalishin, *Riazanskie pomeshchiki*, p. 27; N. Shepukova, 'Ob izmenenii razmerov dushevladeniia pomeshchikov evropeiskoi Rossii v pervoi chetverti XVIII–pervoi polovine XIX v', *Ezhegodnik po agrarnoi istorii vostochnoi Evropy. 1963 g.* (Vilnius, 1964), pp. 380–419.

[1] This problem doomed attempts to limit the participation of the small-holding gentry in gentry affairs: The state, at the same time that it restricted voting rights in the assemblies to the wealthier members of the local gentry, had to leave access to elective positions almost entirely free of qualifications: No property qualifications were required; even personal gentry and in some cases non-gentry could be elected to these posts. Korf, *Dvorianstvo*, pp. 548–50.

[2] Indeed, such were the opportunities and desire for service in the army and the central administration during Nicholas' reign that the government was hard-pressed even to find persons willing to serve in the 'real' administration of the provinces. Nicholas attempted to remedy this situation by ordering, in 1837, that all young gentry desirous of serving in the ministries at Petersburg had first to spend three years of service in the provinces. Korf, *Dvorianstvo*, pp. 474–5.

most often by impoverished gentry who, in the words of one historian of the gentry, 'either did not wish to serve but had not the means to avoid it [that is, could not pay the fines or bribes to be excused] or were quite unfit for service, but, having no fortune at all, sought some kind of position.'[1] (The gentry marshals, perhaps, generally excepted.) Judging from official discussions of the subject and the testimony of numerous contemporaries, these offices were very often the sources of considerable corruption and graft.[2]

Reflecting on all these circumstances, it is not surprising that the 'estates' showed little sign, in the first half of the nineteenth century, of becoming centers for the organized expression of gentry interests. They had certainly not served as schools of political experience for the gentry, and there were no others. The Russian 'estates' were not the emasculated survivors of an earlier onslaught carried out against the political independence of the nobility by the centralizing monarchy. They were more nearly its creatures than aged invalids who might have been expected, conditions permitting, to undergo rapid revival. Nevertheless, when the 'rights' and privileges of the gentry came under unprecedented attack by the state early in the reign of Alexander II, these institutions displayed an equally unprecedented vitality and were vested, often to the accompaniment of eloquent references to a largely fictitious past, with an importance they had never previously known.

[1] Evreinov, *Proshloe i nastoiashchee*, p. 49.
[2] Korf, *Dvorianstvo*, pp. 442–4. Also see chapter 4, below.

2

The Gentry as Serf-owner and First Steps toward Emancipation

THE LANDED ESTATES UNDER SERFDOM

As a legal order and as an economic system,[1] serfdom in Russia on the eve of its abolition was far from a mere shadow of a once viable institution: it remained to the very end a rigid system of personal dependency that very nearly approached the 'peculiar institution' of the American South so far as the legal status of the serf was concerned. Moreover, this system had become more, not less, rigid during the last century or so of its existence. Although the state had stopped the expansion of serfdom to ever wider circles of the peasant population by the turn of the century and had acted, in succeeding decades, to remove some of the more flagrant slavery-like practices (such as the advertised public sale of serfs taken from the land and the splitting up of peasant families at auction), the overall result of state legislation and the expansion of the bureaucratic administration over this period had been to make gentry domination over the peasants ever more encompassing. The landowner could generally deal with his serf as he saw fit, short of murdering him, and was provided by the state with powerful instruments of coercion, including the right to send recalcitrant serfs into the army or to Siberian resettlement. And, as a result of the new authority vested in elected gentry officials, the landowners had also become the state-supported judges and police-masters over the peasants.[2] Serfdom was, in fact, the 'law of the land', and all state institutions—the courts, the schools,

[1] In Russian scholarship, the distinction is drawn traditionally between 'serf law' (*krepost-noe pravo*) and 'serf economy' (*krepostnoe khoziaistvo*).
[2] The nature of *pomeshchik* authority over the peasants and the record of the abuses of this authority are too well known to merit detailed recounting here. For an account in English, see Blum, *Lord and peasant*, especially chapters 21–2.

the army, the tax system—were organized in accordance with it. As Tsagolov and other scholars have remarked, such a system could be abolished (barring revolution) only by an act of the state.[1]

The same was true of the 'serf economy'. Land relations on the gentry estates remained, as traditionally, extremely complicated, with the peasant and gentry enterprises intimately intertwined. Although demesne cultivation was extensive (it has been estimated that 58 per cent of the arable on gentry estates for Russia as a whole was demesne land cultivated with peasant labor at mid-century),[2] there was, with relatively few exceptions, no such thing as 'gentry farming' in most of Russia before 1861; there was only peasant farming. All the land, both demesne and peasant allotments proper, was parcelled in strips and worked according to the traditional three-field system by the peasants, who also furnished equipment and draft animals. Most estates, whether small or large, were worked in this manner, so that there was (again with relatively few exceptions) no large farming in Russia, but only greater or smaller agglomerations of peasant operations.[3]

Russia was not, however, totally lacking in 'improving gentry' or commercial agriculture. Gentry interest in commercial farming, and along with it an interest in what was generally called the 'rationalization of agriculture' developed in the years following the emancipation of the gentry from obligatory service

[1] N. Tsagolov, *Ocherki russkoi ekonomicheskoi mysli perioda padeniia krepostnogo prava* (Moscow, 1956), pp. 27–8. It is often noted that the Russian emancipation legislation, despite manifold flaws, had no rivals in Europe for thoroughness and universality. That this was so may be in some sense admirable, but it was also an absolute necessity, because the institution that was being abolished had far broader ramifications in the structure of state and society than had been the case in any of the other states which had legislated emancipation.

[2] There were of course wide variations in the pattern of landholding, both among individual estates and regionally. In the 'central-industrial region' to which Moscow belonged, the peasants held 51·9% of the estate-lands at mid-century; in the mid-Volga region, 38·3%; in the black soil provinces, 27·7%. V. Picheta, 'Pomeshchich'e khoziaistvo nakanune reformy', in *Velikaia reforma. Russkoe obshchestvo i krest'ianskii vopros v proshlom i nastoiashchem*, III (Moscow, 1911) (105–38), 126–7.

[3] For a detailed analysis of the structure and functioning of the Russian gentry estates in the pre-reform period see M. Confino, *Domaines et seigneurs en Russie vers la fin du XVIIIe siècle. Etude de structures agraires et de mentalités économiques* (Paris, 1963).

in 1762, an act which for the first time permitted the gentry in significant numbers to turn their attention to the exploitation of their estates. The second half of the eighteenth century also saw a 'clearing of the decks' for commercial production: abolition of internal tariffs (1754), state permission to export grain (1766), and acquisition of the fertile southern steppes and the Black Sea ports following the wars with Turkey.[1] As a result of population growth and the expansion of the non-agricultural sector of the economy in the north-central region of the country, this area became, in the course of the eighteenth century, dependent for at least a portion of its foodstuffs on the fertile area to the south. This regional differentiation and more general processes of population growth and expansion of the non-agricultural economy gave rise to an extensive internal grain market, augmented by growth of production for the European market, especially after Russia's southern acquisitions.[2] As a result of the expanding agricultural market, the gentry (whose demesne holdings produced the biggest share of grain for the market)[3] were able to see a large growth in grain prices over the late eighteenth and first half of the nineteenth century (albeit with great periodic fluctuations and regional differences due to poorly developed transport facilities).

These developments were accompanied by considerable interest in agricultural improvements. In 1765 the renowned Free Economic Society was founded by a group of aristocratic landowners with the original aim of studying and publicizing the conditions of agriculture and animal husbandry in Russia.[4] It was

[1] Confino, *Domaines et seigneurs*, pp. 21–2.
[2] It has been estimated that the average yearly export of grain increased from 19,873 *pudy* at the beginning of the nineteenth century (1801–5) to 69,254,000 in the late 1850s. Some 320,000,000 *pudy* of grain were sold annually on the internal market at mid-century. (One *pud* equals 36 pounds.) P. A. Zaionchkovskii, *Otmena krepostnogo prava v Rossii* (Moscow, 1954), p. 44; M. K. Rozhkova (ed.), *Ocherki ekonomicheskoi istorii Rossii pervoi poloviny XIX veka* (Moscow, 1959), p. 263.
[3] The traditional estimate is that about 90% of marketed grain came from the gentry demesne lands in the years immediately preceding emancipation. Koval'chenko has recently challenged this estimate, producing figures indicating that demesne production never exceeded 55% of total commercial output in this period. I. D. Koval'chenko, 'O tovarnosti zemledeliia v Rossii v pervoi polovine XIX v.', in *Ezhegodnik po agrarnoi istorii vostochnoi Evropy, 1963 g.* (Vilnius, 1964), pp. 481–3.
[4] V. I. Semevskii, *Krest'ianskii vopros v Rossii v XVIII i pervoi polovine XIX veka*, 1 (St Petersburg, 1888), 19–20.

followed by the foundation of similar organizations with regional orientations, beginning about the turn of the century in the Baltic Provinces where the production of grain for export had first gotten underway. The first society of this sort in central Russia— the Moscow Agricultural Society—was founded in 1818, and by the time of the emancipation twenty-nine such organizations existed in Russia.[1] Truly widespread propagandizing of farming improvements was gotten underway during the reign of Nicholas I. In these years, in addition to the establishment of numerous agricultural societies, there was begun the large-scale organization of agricultural fairs and exhibitions,[2] and a large number of books —mainly practical guides to agricultural improvements and estate-organization—were published.[3]

However, despite the growing importance of commercial production in agriculture over the last three-quarters of a century of serfdom (to about 20 per cent of the country's gross annual grain production), the structural characteristics of the gentry estates changed very little over this period. The landed estate remained essentially an organization for the exploitation of the peasants ('a cow to be milked' as Korf put it), and the modes of exploitation remained the same—the acquittal of peasant obliga-tions either in *obrok* (quitrent) or in *barshchina* (*corvée*, labor dues). The mass of gentry proprietors took no steps to interfere in the widespread peasant practices of communal tenure and periodic redistribution of the land. Few anywhere, except in the southern steppes (which were only recently opened to agriculture and were from the beginning partly given over to large-scale commercial production), introduced crop rotation or other innovations of a technological nature, as indicated by the fact that the (very low) agricultural yield rates in Russia remained almost stationary

---

[1] Blum, *Lord and peasant*, p. 405.

[2] S. S. Dmitriev, 'Vozniknovenie sel'skokhoziaistvennykh vystavok v Rossii', in *Voprosy istorii sel'skogo khoziaistva, krest'ianstva i revoliutsionnogo dvizheniia v Rossii. Sbornik statei k 75-letiu Akademika Nikolaia Mikhailovicha Druzhinina* (Moscow, 1961), pp. 172–80.

[3] These books bore such titles as: *What does the barshchina peasant need to maintain a viable economy in the non-black soil provinces. Thoughts and observations on the conditions of agri-cultural production. Thirty years' farming experience, or rules for managing an estate. Notes of a Penza pomeshchik on the theory and practice of agriculture. How to conduct Russian agriculture efficiently, successfully, and profitably, or talks on private profits.*

throughout the first half of the nineteenth century.[1] Most *pomeshchiki* had no capital for investment in agricultural improvements, however these may have been urged upon them by the propagandists; there was no question for them of 'rationalizing' their operations through introduction of new techniques and machinery, or through experimentation with expensive hired labor.[2] Some success was had with the introduction of new cultures, especially sugar beets, and with the establishment of processing plants, such as sugar refineries and distilleries, but these enterprises involved a small minority of gentry estates.[3]

In his remarkable study of gentry agriculture, Professor Confino noted a trend already underway in the late eighteenth century. The gentry, provided with the two modes of exploiting their peasants—*obrok* and *barshchina*—were tending in practice toward an elastic employment of the two as local conditions permitted.[4] In this manner, and for the most part only in this manner, the gentry continued to adapt to changing conditions and opportunities throughout the first half of the nineteenth century. In areas with ready access to markets, many gentry landholders concentrated on the production of grain. This involved expanding their demesne holdings where possible,[5] and

---

[1] Liashchenko, *History of the national economy*, p. 324.

[2] As Alexander Gerschenkron has remarked, the relative profitability of hired labor would have had to have been very great and very obvious before the *pomeshchiki* could have been prompted to discard serf labor, which was 'free'. A. Gerschenkron, 'Agrarian policies and industrialization, Russia 1861–1917', in *Cambridge economic history of Europe*, VI, part 2 (Cambridge, 1965), 707. Very few *pomeshchiki* found it so before 1861. Extensive employment of supplementary hired agricultural labor was common only where serfs were few but soil conditions and transport facilities were favorable to commercial production; that is, especially in the southern steppes and the Volga region.

[3] Blum, *Lord and peasant*, pp. 401–4.   [4] Confino, *Domaines et seigneurs*, pp. 194–201.

[5] The nature and extent of this process is very imperfectly understood. The general observation that demesne land constituted a larger proportion of total estate-holdings at mid-nineteenth century than at the end of the eighteenth century, together with some evidence that individual peasant allotments were generally smaller at the end of this period than earlier, has led many historians to conclude that a considerable expansion of demesne took place over this period, particularly in the fertile, *barshchina*-dominated regions, and that this was accomplished primarily at the expense of peasant holdings— in other words by a process similar (in character, if not in scope) to the English or East Elbian experiences. However, Ignatovich (who provided the calculations on allotment sizes generally employed by later scholars) concluded only that the decrease in size of individual peasant allotments prior to emancipation was due primarily to peasant population growth 'in the presence of little or no increase in land'. This view is confirmed by the recent study of B. G. Litvak who argues further (on the basis of evidence

increasing the application of *barshchina* labor to these holdings by raising the level of obligations and by transferring formerly *obrok* peasants to *barshchina*. In other areas, the expanding labor market led many landowners in search of increased revenues to transfer formerly *barshchina* peasants to *obrok* and to increase the *obrok* obligations in general.[1] The composite of local conditions and the responses provoked by them among landowners had produced, before the end of the eighteenth century, a relative prevalence of *obrok* in the non-black soil provinces and a clear predominance of *barshchina* in the black soil areas.[2] Although there is no general agreement on this subject among scholars, it appears that *barshchina* continued to expand at the expense of *obrok* up to the time of emancipation in connection with the growing agricultural market, and that this expansion took place by the increasing tendency of landowners to employ 'mixed obligations' (*smeshannye povinnosti*) on their estates, which, considering the country as a whole, most frequently involved the partial displacement of *obrok* by *barshchina*.[3] According to Confino's calculations, 17·2 per cent of the peasants in twenty provinces of 'Great Russia' acquitted 'mixed obligations' in 1858, 37·07 per cent

from several black soil provinces) that reduction in the size of individual allotments was much less extensive than is generally accepted; that total land area in peasant hands probably increased; and that the expansion of demesne holdings was, accordingly, accomplished primarily by bringing new lands into cultivation, especially forest, and to some extent by encroachment on state lands. Cf. Ignatovich, *Pomeshchich'i krest'iane*, pp. 68–71; B. G. Litvak, 'Ob izmeneniiakh zemel'nogo nadela pomeshchich'ikh krest'ian v pervoi polovine XIX v', in *Ezhegodnik po agrarnoi istorii, 1963 g.*, pp. 523–34.

[1] The dynamics of *obrok* obligations constitute another subject of controversy among historians. Although the evidence shows that *obrok* rates generally increased in Russia several times over from the end of the eighteenth century (to an average of more than 20 rubles annually per *tiaglo* by mid-century), some scholars have argued that inflation of the ruble and changing prices over this period produced little if any augmentation in the real value of *obrok*. Most Russian scholars are persuaded, however, that *obrok* was indeed becoming more burdensome for the peasants over this period, a view given new substantiation in a recent study of peasant incomes, budgets and obligations in four central provinces: I. D. Koval'chenko and L. V. Milov, 'Ob intensivnosti obrochnoi ekspluatatsii krest'ian tsentral'noi Rossii v kontse XVIII–pervoi polovine XIX v.', *Istoriia SSSR*, 1966, no. 4, pp. 55–80.

[2] According to the generally-employed calculations of Semevskii, 55% of the serfs were on *obrok* at that time in the 13 non-black soil provinces, in contrast to only 26% in seven black soil provinces. The average for the twenty Russian provinces included in his calculations was 44% of the serfs on *obrok*, 56% on *barshchina*. V. I. Semevskii, *Krest'iane v tsarstvovanie Imperatritsy Ekateriny II*, I (2nd ed., St Petersburg, 1903), xi.

[3] See the analysis of the evidence by Confino, *Domaines et seigneurs*, pp. 194–201.

were on *obrok* and 45·8 per cent were on *barshchina*.[1] (If Belorussia, the Ukraine, and the extreme south are added, in all of which areas *barshchina* obligations were acquitted by more than 90 per cent of the serfs, well over 70 per cent of the serfs in European Russia were probably on *barshchina* at this time.[2] If *obrok* tended to hold its own in areas of general backwardness or even to be expanded in some areas by *pomeshchiki* seeking to take advantage of the labor market, the tendency toward increased application of *barshchina* labor to *agriculture* was marked.[3]

Thus the changing economy and the gentry's efforts to increase their estate-incomes resulted not in the deterioration of servile relations, but in their intensification and in the landowners' increased dependence on them. Here one might handily paraphrase Barrington Moore's recent observation about eighteenth-century France: In contrast to England, commercial influences as they penetrated the Russian countryside did not undermine and destroy the feudal framework. If anything, they infused new life into old arrangements.[4] For the gentry it was primarily a matter of the continuing exploitation of privileges supported by the power of the state, for their active or 'entrepreneurial' contribution to the economic system was slight, restricted for the most part to their role in putting grain on the market.

Consequently, the mass of landed proprietors remained unwilling to part with the privileges which gave them free labor and quitrent, at least so long as they had no idea of if and how the state intended to guarantee their welfare and remunerate them for the loss of these privileges. The majority of *pomeshchiki* were smallholders, many of whom simply collected *obrok* because their estates were too small to afford division into demesne and peasant allotments; while the demesne lands of many others probably sufficed only to produce enough for domestic consumption. Serfdom afforded these people simple privileges, and its abolition alone promised them nothing. The better-endowed minority of *pomeshchiki* were equally dependent on the existing

[1] *Ibid.*, p. 196, fn.   [2] *Ibid.*, p. 197, fn.
[3] Cf. Tsagolov, *Ocherki*, pp. 41–2.
[4] Cf. Barrington Moore, Jr., *Social origins of dictatorship and democracy. Lord and peasant in the making of the modern world* (Boston, 1966), p. 55.

system and were generally as short of cash as their poorer relations. (And for many of them as well, much of demesne production must have gone to domestic consumption, considering the very low yield-rates and the widespread practice of maintaining large quantities of unproductive household serfs and extensive stables.)[1] There was no significant number of gentry whose estates had been transformed to the point where serfdom represented an obvious hindrance that could have been cast off with certain assurance of gain. There were those, it will be seen, who anticipated positive results for the landowners from emancipation, but this anticipation was based on a variety of ideas, not on a previous 'retooling' of their estates that had made them independent of servile relations.

It would be wrong, however, to conclude from these circumstances that the Russian landed proprietors were generally content with their lot. For despite increasing, and increasingly flexible, exploitation of the peasantry and growing participation in commercial production during a period of rising agricultural prices, most gentry proprietors, far from prospering, were sinking ever more deeply into debt. Since the creation of state credit institutions for the purpose of making loans available to gentry landowners (the first was the State Loan Bank founded in 1754), gentry indebtedness to these institutions had steadily and rapidly increased. The figures in table 2 indicate this process over the last forty years of serfdom:[2]

TABLE 2

Year	No. of souls mortgaged (in millions)	Percentage of all serf souls	Amount owed state credit institutions (millions of rubles)
1820	1·8	20	110 (assignat)
1833	4·5	37	950 ,,
1842	5·6	50	
1855	6·6	61	398 (credit rubles)
1859	7·1	66	425 ,, ,,

[1] This practice provoked Haxthausen to describe the life of the Russian gentry as 'half European, half oriental': 'Son genre de vie moitié européen et moitié oriental se distinguait surtout par un grand luxe de dvoroviés et de chevaux.' *Etudes*, I, 41.
[2] Blum, *Lord and peasant*, p. 380.

The gentry as serf-owners

In 1856, the average debt on a mortgaged serf (for the serfs, not the land, were mortgaged to the credit institutions) was about 69 rubles. In addition many *pomeshchiki* must have had extensive private debts.

Why were the landed gentry as a group sinking into debt? (As the above figures show, it was by no means only the small-holding proprietors who had contracted extensive mortgages.) There is no tidy answer to this question, if only because the circumstances of the gentry varied widely from estate to estate.

The ready availability of state loans was itself partly responsible. Despite P. B. Struve's well-known contention, there is no evidence to suggest that any significant proportion of the capital borrowed from the state was used to constructive ends, such as investment in agricultural expansion and improvements.[1] The great majority of gentry loans were apparently used simply for everyday expenditures and what at a later date came to be called conspicuous consumption.[2] The deleterious effect of the gentry's growing dependence on credit simply to make ends meet was widely remarked by the Decembrists, who testified after their arrest in 1825 (according to the compendium of their testimonies

---

[1] In his famous study of *The serf economy*, Struve argued that the growth of gentry indebtedness was a positive phenomenon reflecting investment borrowing for the purchase of land and for various improvements. Struve agreed with many other investigators in concluding that 'serfdom was abolished against the interests of the *pomeshchik* class', but maintained that this was because the gentry were engaged before 1861 in successful capitalist agriculture based on *barshchina* labor. Although Struve's work is often referred to as if it were a comprehensive study of the 'serf economy', it was in fact a polemical essay written to combat the traditional view (then recently reinvigorated by Marxist historians) which held that successful 'capitalist' agriculture was impossible under serfdom (or, corollarily, that the development of capitalism in Russia 'necessitated' the emancipation at that time). While he argued his theoretical case persuasively, and was able to find examples from Russian agrarian history to exemplify it, he certainly did not provide an analysis of the general evolution of Russia's 'serf economy'. P. B. Struve, *Krepostnoe khoziaistvo. Issledovaniia po ekonomicheskoi istorii Rossii v XVIII i XIX vv.* (St Petersburg, 1913), especially pp. 140, 142. Struve's book was based on an article first published in the journal *Mir Bozhii* in 1900.

[2] Cf. Haxthausen, *Etudes*, III, 53; Romanovich-Slavatinskii, *Dvorianstvo*, pp. 334–7; Evreinov, *Proshloe i nastoiashchee*, p. 78. The state was aware of the uses to which these loans were generally put, as Nicholas I revealed when, in making provisions for the enlarging of state credit, he chided the gentry that the loans should be applied 'not to the whims of luxury nor to increasing debts of extravagance, but to the better organization of the gentry estates, to the further development of agriculture, and to the expansion of agricultural and other industries'. Evreinov, *Proshloe i nastoiashchee*, p. 78.

made for Nicholas I) that the gentry 'had been completely ruined by loans from the credit institutions'.[1] At the very least this practice meant that an increasingly large proportion of the gentry's annual estate-income went to making payment on these debts. Nor did the ready availability of state credit encourage frugal habits.

Haxthausen, who toured the Russian provinces in 1843, thought that Napoleon's invasion of 1812 had ruined large numbers of the gentry. There is some evidence that the Russian 'scorched-earth' policy at that time, as well as extensive levies of men and matériel and the general social and economic dislocations of the war, injured gentry estates far beyond the immediate arena in which the war was actually waged.[2]

In addition to these specific circumstances, the gentry estates were having to support increasing numbers of individuals, the result of the gentry's natural increase and of cooptation into the class of landed proprietors through the Table of Ranks. In particular, the common practice by which the sons of a father shared equally in the family inheritance resulted in a steady increase in the number of persons dependent on the income of a single estate, and often in its physical subdivision.[3]

At the same time that the gentry's needs as a group were steadily expanding, so too were their needs as individuals. The growing Europeanization and sophistication of the tastes and requirements of the gentry since their emancipation has often been remarked. Although it is probably an exaggeration to claim this as the main cause for their financial distress,[4] certainly their newly acquired taste for things European did significantly increase their need for cash.[5] And in a more general sense, the growth of the exchange money economy in Russia over this

---

[1] Quoted in A. Kizevetter, *Istoricheskie ocherki* (Moscow, 1912), p. 425.

[2] Cf. B. Kafengauz, 'Voina 1812 goda i ee vliianie na sotsial'no-ekonomicheskuiu zhizn' Rossii', *Voprosy istorii*, no. 7 (1962) pp. 69–80. (Following the war the government gave eight-year postponements on debt payments for estates in provinces where fighting had been carried on.)

[3] The Russian gentry had never practiced primogeniture or unified inheritance. The sole attempt to legislate the practice (Peter I's law on the *Majorat*, 1714) was never successful and was abolished in 1731.

[4] See Confino's sober comment on this subject, *Domaines et seigneurs*, p. 180.

[5] Cf. Haxthausen, *Etudes*, I, 103.

period put increasing pressure on the gentry for new sources of cash revenues. The *pomeshchiki* were having to buy things their fathers had gone without or had, in some cases, produced on their own estates before these had become specialized for the acquisition of cash revenues.

In general, the gentry's needs grew faster than their incomes.[1] Without dwelling on the question of whether successful capitalist agriculture is by definition impossible with an enserfed peasantry (a proposition to which most Russian historians have subscribed), it is clear that economic developments were not creating a prosperous landed gentry in Russia before 1861.

ABOLITIONIST SENTIMENT

Considering the economic plight of the *pomeshchiki*, it is perhaps not surprising that abolitionist sentiment was in fact gaining ground with fair rapidity among the landed gentry in the years preceding the Crimean War.[2] Despite their dependence on it, increasing numbers of *pomeshchiki* were coming to believe that serfdom was indeed a hindrance to their continued welfare. In the early 1840s, A. P. Zablotskii-Desiatovskii, the liberal bureaucrat and biographer of Count Kiselev, described gentry opinion toward serfdom in the following way: The less educated *pomeshchiki*, he wrote, continued to look on serfdom as 'a necessary condition of their existence. They do not penetrate the essence of the question, but only know that they control people who are compelled to work for them for nothing'. All the same, he concluded,

It is impossible not to notice that the question of the abolition of serfdom, which several years ago seemed extraordinarily rash, now

---

[1] The plight of the gentry was succinctly described by Nicholas Turgenev in 1847: '... Pour tous le besoin d' accroître leurs revenus devient de plus en plus pressant; car, quelle que soit la diminution de leurs ressources, chez eux l'amour du luxe est resté le même, et le pouvoir des maîtres, tout exorbitant qu'il soit, ne suffit pas à tirer des esclaves de quoi satisfaire à des exigences sans nombre, que leurs pères ne connaissaient point.' N. Turgenev, *La Russie et les russes*, III (Paris, 1847), 39.

[2] The history of 'the peasant question' has received its classic treatment in the work of V. I. Semevskii, *Krest'ianskii vopros v Rossii* (the second volume is devoted to the reign of Nicholas I).

astonishes no one. Everybody in one way or another is prepared to discuss it . . . In general, this thought is not considered rash by anybody now. It is talked about not only by professors, but is discussed, in one way or another, by the *pomeshchiki* as well.[1]

Baron Haxthausen confirmed this observation during his 1843 tour, adding that 'all sensible people agree that it is impossible to long maintain [serfdom] in its present state'.[2]

Most contemporary observers agreed that growing fear of peasant revolt played an important role in the rise of abolitionist sentiment among the gentry, and in explanation of this pheno- menon historians have remarked both the increasing frequency of peasant disorders in Russia[3] and the impression produced on gentry minds by certain dramatic events, particularly the bloody peasant rebellion against the landlords of neighboring Galicia in 1846.[4]

Another clearly observable factor leading to abolitionist senti- ment among the gentry was the specific desire to escape from indebtedness: mortgage payments had by this time obviously become a heavy burden for many *pomeshchiki*.[5] This desire was expressed in advocacy of an emancipation that would provide significant remuneration for the gentry, and in particular liquida- tion of their debts to the state credit institutions. By the late

---

[1] *Ibid.*, II, 468–9. [2] Haxthausen, *Etudes*, I, 103.
[3] According to data collected by the Ministry of Interior in the second quarter of the nineteenth century, peasant 'disturbances' of sufficient gravity to attract the attention of the government occurred in the following quantities over five-year periods between 1826–54:

Years	Number of disturbances
1826–9	85
1830–4	60
1835–9	78
1840–4	138
1845–9	207
1850–4	141

Zaionchkovskii, *Otmena krepostnogo prava*, p. 45. On the character of these 'dis- turbances', see I. Ignatovich, 'Krest'ianskie volneniia', *Velikaia reforma*, III, 41–65.
[4] I. Ignatovich, 'Otrazhenie v Rossii krest'ianskogo dvizheniia v Galitsii 1846 goda', in *Sbornik trudov professorov i prepodavatelei gos. Irkutskogo universiteta. Vypusk* V (1923), pp. 161–208.
[5] Semevskii, *Krest'ianskii vopros*, II, 617.

1840s numerous memoirs written by *pomeshchiki* advocating emancipation of the peasants had reached the government's attention, and of these a significant number addressed themselves directly to the problem of growing gentry indebtedness and the prospect of escaping from it.[1] One of the earliest of these was elaborated (in 1844) by nine *pomeshchiki* in the gentry assembly of Tula province. They proposed emancipation of their peasants with one *desiatina* of land per soul. In return they asked that their debts to the state credit institutions be transferred to these peasants, at the rate of 45 rubles per peasant.[2] Similar projects were conceived in following years by these and other landowners of the province.[3] In 1847, the Penza *pomeshchik* Zheltukhin (and later, in 1858–60, editor of the journal *Zhurnal zemlevladel'tsev*) presented to the Minister of Interior a project for emancipation of the serfs with land which was designed specifically to eliminate gentry indebtedness.[4] Another memoir of this kind was presented about the same time by A. Vonliarliarskii, a *pomeshchik* of Smolensk province where discussion of peasant reform among the gentry had been particularly widespread in the late 1840s. (The Smolensk gentry, as a group, were reputed to be among the poorest in the Empire.)[5] Vonliarliarskii proposed full emancipation of the peasants with all the land they currently possessed. This they were to receive in property in return for redemption to be carried out by a state-sponsored financial operation extending over a thirty-seven-year period. The total sum for such an operation, according to Vonliarliarskii's calculations, would amount to 650,000,000 rubles, part of which was to be paid out immediately to the gentry as working capital. The peasants could make annual payments to the state credit institutions.[6]

[1] *Ibid.*, ch. xv.

[2] O. Trubetskaia, *Materialy dlia biografii kn. V. A. Cherkasskogo*, I (Moscow, 1901), 10.

[3] V. Semevskii, 'Krest'ianskii vopros vo vtoroi polovine XVIII-go i pervoi polovine XIX veka', in *Krest'ianskii stroi* (P. D. Dolgorukov and S. L. Tolstoi, editors) (St Petersburg, 1905) (pp. 157–295), pp. 271–6.

[4] 'Proekt osvobozhdeniia krest'ian', *Zhurnal zemlevladel'tsev*, vol. VI (1860), *prilozhenie* 6.

[5] A detailed statistical study of the plight of the peasants and gentry of Smolensk province, published in 1855, became a main weapon in the abolitionist arsenal: Ia. Solov'ev, *Sel'sko-khoziaistvennaia statistika Smolenskoi gubernii* (Moscow, 1855).

[6] V. Bochkarev, 'Dvorianskie proekty po krest'ianskomu voprosu pri Nikolae I', in *Velikaia reforma*, III, 167–8.

It is noteworthy that these and other projects advocating emancipation of the peasants with land in return for remuneration appear to have first been provoked by the publication of the 1842 law on 'obligated peasants', which offered no compensation to the gentry, but only the right to voluntarily submit to state regulation of peasant holdings and obligations on their estates.[1] Similar responses were provoked in the western provinces annexed from Poland after the state in 1847 began the introduction of the 'inventory rules' there, i.e. state regulation of peasant obligations.[2] By the late 1840s, groups of gentry in several provinces had petitioned the government to be allowed to summon committees for the discussion of the best means for emancipating their peasants.[3] These were, to be sure, minority voices, and the state left them unacted upon, usually referring their authors to their right to avail themselves of Alexander I's 'law on free cultivators' (1803) or Nicholas' law on 'obligated peasants'.

The character of these gentry proposals and the circumstances in which they were produced makes it clear that the idea of escaping from indebtedness and obtaining some capital from emancipation was spreading among the landed proprietors. And this idea was linked with the idea of emancipating the peasants with land—payment for which would provide the one and the other. (Tsagolov accordingly wrote of Zheltukhin's project that its basic point was 'not the question... of providing [the peasants] with land, but the question of providing the *pomeshchiki* with capital'.)[4] It was surely the absence of such a provision that had prevented any significant number of *pomeshchiki* from taking advantage of the government's legislation providing for voluntary emancipation or regulated peasant status.[5] And the piecemeal

---

[1] Semevskii, *Krest'ianskii vopros*, II, 450 ff.

[2] Cf. Semevskii, *Krest'ianskii vopros*, II, 481–513; Semevskii, 'Krest'ianskii vopros', 275–6.

[3] Semevskii, *Krest'ianskii vopros*, II, 254; and A. Kornilov, 'Gubernskie komitety po krest'ianskomu delu v 1858–1859 gg.', in *Russkoe bogatstvo* (1904, nos. 1–5), no. 1, pp. 123–4.

[4] Tsagolov, *Ocherki*, p. 173.

[5] Under Nicholas I, 250 landowners had taken advantage of the 1803 law to free 67,491 souls; three great landowners applied the 1842 law to 24,708 souls. Semevskii, 'Krest'-ianskii vopros', pp. 279–80. In a more general way, it would appear extremely unlikely that any significant number of *pomeshchiki* would have availed themselves of these laws so long as serfdom remained the 'law of the land' and the mass of the peasant

moves in the direction of emancipation under Nicholas I, such as the 1842 law and the inventories, which provided no arrangements for the removal of gentry indebtedness or the furnishing of capital, provoked the proposals demanding just these things.

Gentry abolitionist opinion was, then, related to various expectations, but these were not the certain expectations of a group of successful agrarian entrepreneurs. Moreover, these expectations were only part of a body of ideas which could not simply be deduced from their immediate situations as landowners.

It would be a mistake to attempt to consider gentry opinion, especially abolitionist opinion, in mid-nineteenth-century Russia apart from 'public opinion' (*obshchestvennoe mnenie*) in general. By the middle of the nineteenth century, educated, or 'enlightened' public opinion was, almost by definition, abolitionist opinion. Contemporaries and early students of the emancipation generally attributed the rise of abolitionist sentiment in society at large and among the gentry in particular to the spread of 'enlightenment'. And the spread of 'enlightenment' among the gentry was in turn attributed to the influence of the universities, where the sons of landed proprietors began to seek their education in significant numbers especially in the 1830s and 1840s.[1] Here they received a 'European education' which led them, in increasing numbers, to look upon the existence of serfdom in Russia as a moral scandal. This was, indeed, the attitude of most educated Russians at the time. By the mid-1850s, defense of serfdom was neither fashionable nor respectable in educated society, and

population remained unfree. For one thing, these proprietors, if they had wished to continue operating their estates, would have had difficulty finding hired labor in many areas.

[1] Cf. Ia. Solov'ev, 'Zapiski senatora Ia. A. Solov'eva o krest'ianskom dele', *Russkaia starina*, XXX, 607; XXIV; 128–9; and I. Ivaniukov, *Padenie krepostnogo prava v Rossii*, 2nd ed. (St Petersburg, 1903), ch. 4, *passim*.

In a broad sense the product of the cultural Europeanization of the gentry, the new importance of university education was immediately related to developments begun in the early reign of Alexander I: the expansion of the university system (until the reign of Alexander there had been only one university in Russia, the University of Moscow, founded in 1755), which by Nicholas' reign had created several universities resembling their European models and largely staffed by foreign professors; and the Examination Act of 1809, which linked successful pursuit of a bureaucratic career to formal education, including the acquisition of university diplomas. In 1848, 43% of the 1,329 students enrolled in Moscow university were sons of noblemen.

scarcely anyone, it was said, could be found who was willing to argue in behalf of its preservation.[1]

The moral argument against serfdom in educated society was, of course, an old one. In the liberal tradition of Russian thought and historiography, the origins of the abolitionist movement and emancipation are traced to the late eighteenth century. With the expansion of the Russian state to its 'natural limits' and the emancipation of the gentry from obligatory service, there began, in this view, the historical trend toward the 'unbinding' (*raskreposhchenie*) of all society; and under the influence of the Enlightenment there appeared the first eloquent opponents of serfdom: men like Novikov and Radishchev. This movement was broadened subsequently, especially during the reign of Alexander I, when it penetrated into the higher levels of government and to the Emperor himself, with the result that the expansion of serfdom was brought to an end and the state took the first cautious steps towards emancipation, consisting in Alexander's reign of the Law on Free Cultivators (1803) and the emancipation of the Baltic peasants (1817–19). At the end of that reign, following gradual abandonment by the Emperor of his original goals, the Decembrist Rebellion marked (among other things) the first concerted opposition to serfdom by a significant group in Russian society, and moreover by a group of gentry origin.[2] This 'moral tradition' reached its pre-emancipation height in the 1840s with the 'discovery' and idealization of the peasantry and peasant institutions (primarily the commune) by Russian intellectuals under the influence of German Romanticism, a development prompted in part by Baron Haxthausen, whose writings have been referred to

[1] Ivaniukov, *Padenie*, pp. 104–5. When A. Koshelev presented a memoir with a plan of emancipation to the Emperor in 1857, he began by declaring: 'There are few people now who categorically deny the justice and necessity of abolishing serfdom in Russia.' A. I. Koshelev, *Zapiski (1812–1883)* (Berlin, 1884), *prilozhenie 5*, p. 57. (To be sure, such a statement clearly implied that this was not true, but its use reflects well enough the prevailing current of opinion.) Cf. also, A. G. Dement'ev, *Ocherki po istorii russkoi zhurnalistiki 1840–1850 gg.* (Moscow-Leningrad, 1950), p. 368.

[2] This general view of gradual expansion of civil freedoms as the central theme in modern Russian historical development was already well-established by the 1850s, when it was expounded by such writers as Boris Chicherin, and was subsequently taken over by most liberal historians. It has had a powerful influence on historical writing in the West down to the present day. See, for example, V. Leontovitsch, *Geschichte des Liberalismus in Russland* (Frankfurt/Main, 1957).

here. This was the source of some of the ideological configurations of Slavophilism, of early theories of 'Russian socialism' (Herzen), and of later Populism. The culmination of this tradition before emancipation may be said to have been the appearance, in 1847, of Ivan Turgenev's *A Sportsman's Sketches*, which were of enormous significance in bringing the educated public to an awareness of the Russian peasant as a human being, indeed as a noble human being.

There had thus occurred in Russian educated society by the mid-nineteenth century a very complex process which in the language of modern social science might be called 'exogenously-influenced value-changes productive of a conflict between the existing division of labor and the value structure'—or what has traditionally been referred to in Russian scholarship as the 'Europeanization' of social thought, leading educated Russians (who in their large majority were members of the gentry class) to look upon serfdom as a moral scandal and a social anachronism. The belief among the landed gentry that they had the 'right' to rule over other human beings was in a process of serious decay.[1] It is only against the background of this expanding belief that the apparent increase in the frequency of peasant disturbances in the last quarter-century before emancipation takes on meaning. Even if one accepts at face value the government-recorded increases (they may well have been primarily the statistical reflection of the government's growing nervousness about peasant unrest), their total number seems slight considering the size and population of the country. It seems reasonably clear that the gentry were growing increasingly apprehensive about peasant unrest not primarily because of changing peasant conditions but as a result of their own changing values.

By the late 1840s, the moral case against serfdom was increasingly becoming supplemented by economic arguments, for the most part also drawn from the Western intellectual arsenal. In government circles and in educated society at large, the conviction had by that time become very widespread that serfdom was retarding Russia's economic development. And it was another

[1] On the development of the liberal culture under Nicholas I, see A. Netting, *Russian liberalism: The years of promise, 1842–1855* (Columbia University dissertation, 1967).

Turgenev, Nicholas, who—living in European exile as an ex-participant in the Decembrist movement—gave the most explicit, if somewhat peripheral, voice to this conviction in the same year that *A Sportsman's Sketches* appeared. Writing in Paris, Turgenev argued the economic necessity of peasant emancipation. For the gentry, he wrote, it was not so much a matter of the degeneration of serfdom as it was the need to increase their revenues: 'Les propriétaires fonciers se convainquent chaque jour davantage que l'esclavage n'est guère profitable aux maîtres, et que leurs propriétés sont loins de rapporter ce qu'elles devraient rapporter . . .'[1] As for the state, Turgenev prophetically warned that as a result of serfdom the national economy was stagnating and Russia was consequently falling behind the western nations in the technology of war.[2]

There was, in fact, nothing new in this argument against serfdom—Turgenev himself, along with other future Decembrists, had condemned serfdom on the basis of liberal economic doctrine even before 1825[3]—but its appeal to significant numbers of *pomeshchiki* probably dates only from the 1840s. There is no need to dwell at length on this aspect of the abolitionist tradition, for it has been on the whole thoroughly explored by Semevskii and more recent students of the history of Russian economic thought.[4]

It may be that the questioning of serfdom on economic grounds became inevitable as soon as the landed gentry began to think of their estates in terms of profits. To be sure, the practical results of this activity were minimal in terms of actual changes made on *pomeshchik* estates, for the reasons already mentioned. Nevertheless, the discussion was gotten underway, in the Free Economic Society and elsewhere, and within it the question of labor—how it was to be best exploited—came to occupy a central position.

---

[1] N. Turgenev, *La Russie et les russes*, III (Paris 1847), 39.   [2] *Ibid.*, pp. 29–30.

[3] Cf. I. Bliumin, 'Ekonomicheskie vozzreniia dekabristov', *Problemy ekonomiki*, 1940, no. 5–6, pp. 204–20.

[4] I. Bliumin, *Ocherki ekonomicheskoi mysli v Rossii v pervoi polovine XIX veka* (Moscow-Leningrad, 1940); V. Shtein, *Ocherki razvitiia russkoi obshchestvenno-ekonomicheskoi mysli XIX–XX vekov* (Leningrad, 1948); *Istoriia russkoi ekonomicheskoi mysli*, vol. I, pt. 2 (Moscow, 1958); A. Skerpan, 'The Russian national economy and emancipation', in A. Ferguson and A. Levin (eds.) *Essays in Russian history. A collection dedicated to George Vernadsky* (Hamden, Conn., 1964), pp. 161–230.

The gentry as serf-owners

Beginning with a discussion over the relative merits of *obrok* and *barshchina*, the debate had entered a new phase by 1812, when the Free Economic Society proposed a competition, approved by Alexander I, on the respective merits of hired and serf labor.[1] This event brought the question of the economic justifiability of serfdom into the open. As much as the 1803 law on free cultivators which demonstrated for the first time the government's negative attitude toward serfdom, the granting of first prize in the competition to Professor Jakob (then employed in the Ministry of Finance) marked the end of an era. His essay, published in 1814, argued the superiority of free labor in agriculture from the land-owners' point of view.[2]

The spread of this conviction in Russian state and society was connected, throughout the first half of the nineteenth century, with the teachings of Adam Smith on the virtues of free labor and free trade.[3] Smith's influence on Russian economic thought extended back to the late eighteenth century when his ideas were first introduced in academic circles. *The wealth of nations*, first published in a government-sponsored translation in 1802–6, exercised a deep influence on Russian thought throughout the reign of Alexander I, to the extent that its reading became 'mandatory for an educated person'.[4] Numerous précis and vulgarizations of Smith's works were published in these years. Public discussion of political economy underwent an eclipse in the 1820s and 1830s, at least partially under the influence of the prevailing conservative political atmosphere,[5] but entered a new

---

[1] Semevskii, *Krest'ianskii vopros*, I, 317–33.   [2] *Ibid.*, pp. 317–20.

[3] Cf. A. Skerpan, 'The Russian national economy'. These and the immediately following comments owe much to the penetrating study of Professor Skerpan.

[4] To quote Professor Bliumin on Adam Smith: 'Interest in political economy in Russia was associated primarily with his name. . . . The study of Adam Smith in the first two decades of the nineteenth century was mandatory for an educated person. It is interesting that the Empress Maria Fedorovna decided on the feat of hearing a full course of lectures on political economy and introduced political economy as a required subject not only for her sons, but for her numerous daughters as well.' Bliumin, *Ocherki*, p. 50.

Pushkin 'celebrated' Smith in *Evgenii Onegin*:

Branil Gomera, Feokrita	I chem zhivet, i pochemu
Zato chital Adama Smita	Ne nuzhno zolota emu,
I byl glubokii ekonom,	Kogda prostoi produkt imeet.
To est' umel sudit' o tom,	Otets poniat' ego ne mog
Kad gosudarstvo bogateet	I zemli otdaval v zalog.

[5] Cf. Bliumin, *Ocherki*, pp. 67–9.

37

period of influence in the late 1840s when the centrality of the
labor question and the idea of the superiority of free labor was
widely propagated in academic circles and in journalism.[1]

On the eve of emancipation, liberal economic views regarding
serfdom and labor apparently prevailed in government circles
and among the educated public. As summarized in a recent study
of Russian economic thought, these views included the following
basic propositions:

First, labor in bondage meant both an absence of adequate free labor
supply and high labor costs and thus was a restraint on a more rapid
economic development. Second, a serf population exploited for the
private benefit of the landlord was kept impoverished and thus incapable of creating an adequate demand for commerce and the products
of machine-age industry. And, third, serf labor, i.e. on corvee, was
basically forced labor, and forced labor, denied the enjoyments of its
fruits, was unproductive.[2]

The broad appeal of political economy in educated society as
well as the government's unhospitable attitude toward this subject in the 1820s and 1830s indicate that an importance was
attached to it which far transcended purely 'economic' considerations. Smith's teachings on labor, trade and non-inter-
ference of the state in economic life received an enthusiastic
reception in Russian educated society because of the obvious
political connotations they bore in an autocratic state and,
specifically, because they permitted indirect expression of abolitionist sentiment when direct public discussion of this subject
was not allowed. As Bliumin has remarked: 'This work excited
not only purely economic, but political interest. The strong
interest in Smithism was one of the forms of demonstration of

---

[1] Skerpan, 'Russian national economy', pp. 169–73. The author suggests that the revival
of interest in free labor resulted from an upswing of social and economic stresses—
primarily crop failures and increasing peasant disturbances in this period—and also
from new interest in industrial development and new social and economic thought in
western Europe. This suggestion is indirectly supported by Liashchenko who points
out that the literature on serf-based agricultural improvement declined after 1840 for
the same reasons: It had been related to the expansion of commercial production based
on serfdom which, he argues, enjoyed success only until about 1840 (the approximate
point at which Soviet historiography marks the beginning of the 'crisis of *barshchina*'
that, in this view, necessitated the emancipation). Liashchenko, *History*, p. 317.
[2] Skerpan, 'Russian national economy', p. 176.

the growing liberal attitudes among the Russian gentry.'[1] Without claiming that liberal economic thought in Russia before 1861 was simply subsidiary to political considerations, the employment of the former in the service of the latter cannot be denied. The nature of this connection was made obvious in the debate surrounding the preparation of the emancipation, when it became clear that abolitionist opinion generally employed the language of economic liberalism, but that abolitionist opinion was not the sole property of a group or groups in Russian society whose 'economic self-interest' clearly dictated identification with liberal economics.[2]

THE LIBERAL REFORM PROGRAM

As a result of the conjuncture of experience, values and economic doctrine, most of educated Russian society fully subscribed to the liberal propositions mentioned above. And a liberal reform program, founded in part on these propositions, was elaborated and publicized (in manuscript and in the émigré press) before the government came to announce its decision to emancipate the serfs. The fundamental points of this program, as it applied to the 'peasant question', were: Emancipation of the serfs with land in full property in return for redemption payment to the gentry; government financing of this redemption; and complete cessation of all obligatory relations between the *pomeshchiki* and their peasants.

As remarked earlier, gentry memoirs advocating emancipation with land in return for redemption to the *pomeshchiki* had been presented to the government before the Crimean War. Essentially the same solution proposed by the Smolensk *pomeshchik* Vonliarliarskii was elaborated by the professor of law (and at that time tutor to the tsarevich) K. D. Kavelin,[3] in a memoir

---

[1] Bliumin, *Ocherki*, p. 55.

[2] Evidence of the predominantly political significance of political economy in Russia was the general disregard there for the theoretical intricacies of that subject, and the general lack of influence of the more 'academic' economists such as Ricardo. Cf. Bliumin, *Ocherki*, pp. 57–9.

[3] Kavelin (1818–85), had been a professor in Moscow University until 1848, when he moved to Petersburg and entered state service in the Ministry of Interior, and subsequently became tutor to the heir to the throne. In 1857, Kavelin was dismissed from this

which was widely circulated during the first months of the new reign, by which time the subject of emancipation had become the general topic of conversation in Russian society. Kavelin proposed emancipation of the peasants with all the land currently in their use and with remuneration to the gentry for both land and the person of the peasants (that is for the loss of *obrok* payments and labor value). This was to be effected by a state-sponsored financial operation, which could be carried out gradually, by regions, to avoid excessive burden on the state finances. Kavelin further proposed that the debts of the gentry to the state should not be retired in connection with this operation, since this would deprive the gentry of the working capital necessary for adapting their farms to the new conditions.[1]

Another influential proposal on emancipation was written and circulated somewhat later by the 'rational farmer' and Slavophile publicist A. I. Koshelev. He proposed a more detailed and radical plan than Kavelin, insisting that the peasants be liberated simultaneously in all provinces, but his basic proposals—emancipation with land for government-financed redemption—were the same.[2]

There is no need to digress here with summaries of the details of these lengthy memoirs. They are well known in the historical literature and their arguments will be met many times in the course of this study. There is, however, one point that should be made at the outset. These well-known memoirs, like all abolitionist publicism of the period, were of course written with a purpose: Partly in an effort to persuade the government of the necessity of one or another sort of emancipation, but especially with the intention of influencing the opinion of the landed gentry proprietors. It is for this reason—the attempt to persuade the gentry of the rightness of the abolitionist case—that such statements generally dwelt at length on the positive benefits to be had from emancipation by the gentry, often with minute calculations of

post because of a scandal provoked by the publication of part of his memoir in *Sovremennik* (before discussion of emancipation was officially allowed in the press), at which point he returned to academic life, taking a professorship at Petersburg University.

[1] K. D. Kavelin, *Sobranie sochinenii*, II (St Petersburg, 1898), 9–87.

[2] A. I. Koshelev, *Zapiski, prilozhenie* 5 (especially p. 128).

projected estate-incomes, frequent reference to the capital the gentry would receive from the redemption operation, and with reassurance about the future presence of a cheap labor force in the countryside (since the peasants would be forced to work because of their redemption obligations, etc.). The axis around which these arguments revolved was the fundamental postulate that free labor is more productive than serf labor. Unfortunately, historians have more often than not tended to look upon abolitionist publicism simply as 'expressions of gentry interests', rather than as propaganda directed toward the landed gentry.[1]

The agreement between the 'Westerner' professor Kavelin and the 'Slavophile' wealthy landlord Koshelev on the fundamental requirements of emancipation reflected widespread agreement on this issue in educated society. When a measure of free discussion of the 'peasant question' was granted to Russian journalism after publication of the government's Nazimov Rescript in November, 1857, this solution was universally propagated in the periodical press.[2]

For educated Russian society of the 1850s, however, emancipation was only one, although the most pressing, goal of a general program of reforms. The profoundly reactionary course taken by the government of Nicholas I after the outbreak of the February Revolution had driven all of educated society into one or

---

[1] As examples of otherwise valuable studies of contemporary publicism which fail to ask the basic question 'to whom was this statement addressed, and for what purpose?' see: N. M. Druzhinin, 'Zhurnal zemlevladel'tsev, 1858–1860', *RANION, Sbornik statei*, I (1926); *Uchenye zapiski*, II (1927); and N. G. Sladkevich, *Ocherki istorii obshchestvennoi mysli Rossii v kontse 50-nachale 60-kh godov XIX veka* (Leningrad, 1962).

[2] Cf. Ivaniukov, *Padenie*, ch. IV (especially pp. 97–9, 122–9). There were, to be sure, considerable differences of opinion expressed in the press on specific questions concerning emancipation—differences over quantitative aspects of the proposed economic settlement, and especially the question of the peasant commune. Although this latter issue will be treated at greater length in the text, it can be noted here that there were essentially three positions on the question of the commune: The Slavophiles and the 'proto-Populists' (most effectively represented by Chernyshevskii, writing in *Sovremennik*), defended permanent retention of the commune, if for quite different reasons; a majority of abolitionist opinion proposed temporary retention of the commune for reasons of social and fiscal stability, but as adherents to liberal economic doctrine considered it a necessary evil; the doctrinaire 'economic liberals' (led by Vernadskii's journal, *Ekonomicheskii ukazatel'*) demanded immediate elimination of the peasant commune.

another degree of opposition. Their own cultural growth, the long history of autocratic arbitrariness and especially the great expansion of the bureaucratic administration under Nicholas I had made the *Rechtsstaat* the political ideal of much of educated Russian society as a whole. In the view of its representatives, lack of success in the Crimean War had deprived 'bureaucratic absolutism' of its central *raison d'être*, and on the eve of the final defeat, in conditions of somewhat relaxed internal political circumstances, there began a campaign of manuscript pamphleteering based on hopes of basic reforms in the bureaucratic administration. The manuscript literature of this campaign was directed, from whatever its source—the Slavophile Koshelev, the professional bureaucrat P. A. Valuev, the conservative nationalist historian M. P. Pogodin—against bureaucratic corruption, political reaction, and the stifling of the press, education and other public institutions.[1] The key to the necessary changes, it was generally recognized, lay in the reform of the bureaucratic administration which in its recent great expansion had become the *bête noire* of all articulate Russians. The outstanding characteristics of the bureaucratic administration, as Valuev defined them in a famous memoir of the time, consisted of:

... Universal lack of truth, mistrust by the government toward its own instruments, and disregard for everything else. The multiplicity of forms smothers the essence of administrative activity and assures universal official falsehood . . On the surface—luster; beneath—decay.[2]

In the first years of the new reign, the most detailed critique of the existing political and administrative system and a detailed program of reforms, beginning with emancipation, were elaborated by the liberals K. D. Kavelin and Boris Chicherin.[3] These were originally circulated in manuscript and then pub-

[1] A. A. Kornilov, *Obshchestvennoe dvizhenie pri Aleksandre II.* (*1855–81.*) *Istoricheskie ocherki* (Moscow, 1909), pp. 6–16.

[2] Quoted in Zaionchkovskii, *Otmena krepostnogo prava*, p. 73.

[3] The fame of Chicherin (1828–1904) as a historian, philosopher, and 'conservative liberal' political man, lay still in the future at this time, when he was a 'graduate student' in his late twenties, working on his dissertation *The local institutions in Russia in the seventeenth century*. Chicherin, whose biography is well-known through his memoirs, was born into a wealthy gentry family of Tambov province, in circumstances, material and intellectual, as near to being 'aristocratic' as then existed in Russia.

lished abroad in Alexander Herzen's *Voices from Russia*.[1] With the new Emperor's accession to the throne, Kavelin and Chicherin decided to elaborate a political program 'which could unite the broadest levels of the gentry intelligentsia around the reforming activities of the new Emperor.'[2] With this aim in mind, the articles were sent to Herzen for publication.[3]

The first collection of articles was published in 1856. In an introduction, the authors declared their general aims:

We are thinking of how to free the peasants without upsetting the whole social organism; we dream of the introduction of freedom of conscience in the state, of the revocation or at least the weakening of the censorship ... We are prepared to rally around any even slightly liberal government and support it with all our strength for we are firmly convinced that in Russia it is possible to act and achieve any kind of results only through the government.[4]

The articles in the first volume were devoted to chronicling the evils of the Nicolaetian system: Serfdom and backward agriculture; the huge army and the recruiting system; internal reaction and the bureaucracy (the 'writing army'); secret police and censorship; religious persecution and national persecution of the Poles; the reactionary international politics which had resulted in Russia's isolation in the Crimean War; the internal passport system and restrictions against freedom to travel abroad; the educational system and the corps-schools.

The second volume of articles, also published in 1856, contained most notably Chicherin's essay 'On Serfdom'. Here he ex-

[1] *Golosa iz Rossii*, vols. I–IV (London, 1856–8). The idea of elaborating a liberal political platform belonged to Kavelin, who in January 1855 invited the cooperation of Chicherin. They were joined subsequently in the effort by N. A. Mel'gunov (d. 1867, a writer and essayist of gentry origin). For the history of this undertaking, see V. N. Rozental', 'Pervoe otkrytoe vystuplenie russkikh liberalov v 1855–56 gg.', *Istoriia SSSR*, no. 2, 1958, pp. 113–30.

[2] Rozental', 'Pervoe otkrytoe vystuplenie', p. 118.

[3] B. N. Chicherin, *Vospominaniia. Moskva 40-kh godov* (Moscow, 1929), p. 172.

[4] *Golosa iz Rossii*, I, 22. This introduction began with a critique of Herzen's 'Russian socialism' from the point of view of what might be called 'pure Westernism', with the object of demonstrating independence from Herzen's outlook. Herzen, its authors claimed, was negating history by placing his faith in the peasant commune as the kernel of a future society. The commune, they argued, equalled backwardness, and nothing more. (*Ibid.*, pp. 22–4.)

pounded the liberal arguments against serfdom. It had to be abolished for moral and economic reasons, as well as for reasons of state interest. Free labor was more profitable than serf labor; it was necessary for the advance of Russian agriculture and industry. Serfdom had immoral effects on the gentry, and was, moreover, dangerous ('Who knows,' Chicherin rhetorically asked, 'may not the Pugachev era be resurrected?'). From the state's point of view, therefore, the historical need of serfdom had passed; Russia was in an epoch of 'disenserfment' (*raskreposh-chenie*), which had begun with the emancipation of the gentry from compulsory service in 1762.[1]

How then were the peasants to be emancipated? Emancipation without land, Chicherin argued, was impossible: It would constitute a return to the vagabondage which serfdom itself had been instituted to stop. A regulated system of 'inventories' or obligatory rents would be no better: The peasant would not treat the land properly, the gentry would have no investment or operating capital, and a constant struggle between the classes would ensue. Real emancipation, Chicherin concluded, 'consists of redemption by the peasants of those lands which they now hold'.[2] But what of the gentry. Would this alienation of land be fair to them? In the first place, Chicherin argued, the land had never belonged fully to the *pomeshchiki*; it had always been considered the peasants' land as well. Moreover, he claimed, 'the right of property always gives way before the state welfare'.[3] In the second place, the *pomeshchik* would in fact lose nothing: In return for loss of land he would gain fluid capital, the lack of which had always prevented him from improving his lands. The solution was simple:

[1] The same arguments were used in the memoirs of Kavelin and Koshelev. (In his memoir, written somewhat later, Koshelev in addition to pointing to growing peasant discontent as a factor impelling emancipation for state interests, also remarked the potential danger of enemy forces reaching the interior and proclaiming emancipation—a remark which was related to rumors current in Russia during the Crimean War that the English and French wanted to emancipate the Russian serfs.)

[2] 'If the peasant', Chicherin summarized, 'is unjustly oppressed, it is necessary to free him; if he is happy and peaceable only when he has his plot of land, it is necessary to give him land. This is demanded by moral sensibility, state interest, and national welfare'. *Golosa iz Rossii*, II (1856), 198, 215.

[3] *Ibid.*, pp. 200–1.

... It is necessary to undertake a quite simple operation, namely emancipation of the peasants; to sell that part of the land which presently is in their use and remains without benefit for the *pomeshchik*; and with the capital received to turn to the improvement of the farm and to the hiring of free laborers, whose labor is enormously more productive than the labor of serfs, and who will spare the *pomeshchik* from all unnecessary troubles and losses.[1]

The gentry, Chicherin concluded, would be better off: As a result of the emancipation, which would create a great new land market and would flood the labor market with hands, land values would go up and agricultural labor would become cheaper.

The remainder of Chicherin's writings—in the third and fourth volumes of *Voices from Russia*—were devoted in particular to encouraging the government to undertake the needed reforms without fear of any political threat to the autocracy, and in general to defining the meaning and requirements of liberalism in the Russian context. The hero of Russian history, he affirmed, was the state:

The government has always stood in Russia at the head of development and change. With its passive character, the Russian people has not been in a condition to produce varied forms of life by its own forces. The government has led it by the hand, and the people has blindly submitted to its guide.[2]

But why, Chicherin asked, had the government in recent times failed to play a progressive role? The answer was one that all Russians knew by heart: Because the bureaucracy had separated the tsar from the people and had muted all attempts to make popular needs known to him.[3] Only now the need for reform

---

[1] *Ibid.*, pp. 204–5.　　　　　　　　[2] *Ibid.*, IV, 64–5.

[3] This belief in Russia before 1861 comes close to deserving the status of a 'social fact'. It was shared by conservatives, by many radicals (at least in their weaker moments), by the peasants (who on a few occasions were able to express it in quite modern terms and not only in *poslovitsy* and *pogovorki*), and even by many liberals with bureaucratic experience who might have been expected to look at domestic politics in different terms. The strength of this belief is evidence, as Marc Raeff has recently noted, of the enduring personal character of political authority in Russia. It would appear that the idea was actually reinforced as a result of the expansion of the bureaucracy in the first half of the nineteenth century. Cf. M. Raeff (ed.), *Plans for political reform in imperial Russia, 1730–1905* (Englewood Cliffs, N.J., 1966), pp. 6–11. On the 'ruler myth', see M. Cherniavsky, *Tsar and people. Studies in Russian myths* (New Haven and London, 1961).

had become so great, especially since the loss of the war, that it had become obvious for all to see. What then was needed?

We do not need either class privileges or limitation of the power of the tsar ... We need freedom. We desire that all that is within us might be freely expressed and developed; that the tsar know what Russia is doing and thinking and can thereby rule us with a clear understanding of affairs ...

Liberalism! This is the slogan of every educated and sensible person in Russia. This is the banner which can unite around it people of all spheres, all classes, all tendencies ... In liberalism lies the whole future of Russia ...

But what should be understood by the term liberalism ... ? In a word, what measures should be taken by a liberal government and what should be desired by the liberal party in society?

1. Freedom of conscience.
2. Freedom from serfdom ...
3. Freedom of public opinion ...
4. Freedom of the press ...
5. Freedom of teaching.
6. Publicity of all government activities whose exposure is not harmful to the state, and especially of the budget of state revenues and expenditures.
7. Publicity and public conduct of legal procedures.

... Everyone who sincerely loves his homeland, every enlightened citizen, must adhere to this banner.[1]

A large number of 'enlightened citizens' did in fact adhere to this banner, including an influential and articulate minority of the landed gentry proprietors who were subsequently called upon to participate in the preparation of emancipation. The initiative, however, lay with the government. And the government's intentions regarding emancipation and other reforms called for in this program remained as yet unrevealed.

[1] *Golosa iz Rossii*, II, 110–13, 126.

3

The Government's First Steps and the Gentry

THE NEW REIGN

Nicholas I had long been convinced of the necessity of abolishing serfdom, an idea which perhaps first came to him from his acquaintance with the testimonies of the Decembrists. With this aim in mind he had ordered a series of secret committees to discuss the 'peasant question'; and he had seen to the passage—in 1842 and 1847—of two laws which allowed, respectively, the voluntary limitation by the *pomeshchiki* of their authority over their peasants, and the purchase of freedom and land by peasants on estates sold at auction.[1] He did not, however, take the final step, for a variety of reasons—including, primarily, uncertainty about how emancipation ought to be effected, and fear (especially after 1848) of the possible social and political consequences of such an undertaking.

The loss of the Crimean War and assumption of power by a new Emperor sufficed to overcome this hesitancy. A great deal has been written about the psychological shock produced in Russian ruling circles by the defeat in 1856, which rudely forced recognition that the period of Russia's self-assured military predominance on the continent—firmly established in 1815 and reinforced as recently as 1848–9—was at an end. The parallel between Prussia's great era of reforms beginning in 1806 and the situation in Russia exactly fifty years later has often been drawn. While most historians agree on the great importance of the defeat

---

[1] This second law was annulled under the impact of the revolutions of 1848 in Western Europe. The introduction of the 'inventories' in the western provinces beginning in 1846 and the reform of the state peasants' status carried out under the direction of Count Kiselev between 1837 and 1842 can be considered at least tangential products of the same general impulse. The history of the 'peasant question' in the reign of Nicholas I is related in the second volume of Semevskii, *Krest'ianskii vopros*.

First steps toward emancipation

as a factor impelling the government at last to undertake reform, the specific lessons drawn from this experience in the government constitute a subject of considerable controversy.[1]

While no definitive assessment of this question is going to be attempted here, a few statements can be made with relative assurance. There are two overriding considerations to be perceived in the state's motivations for undertaking emancipation: concern for economic development, and a desire to ensure social and political stability. Both were directly related to the experience of Russia's defeat in the Crimean War.

It was clearly understood by Alexander II and the 'enlightened bureaucrats' who were the actual architects of the reform[2] that the Crimean defeat, that is, Russia's military backwardness, was directly related to Russia's general economic and technological backwardness,[3] and it was believed that the main obstacle to overcoming this situation was the existence of serfdom. To be sure, it has often been pointed out that the government's attitude at that time toward 'industrialization'—in particular the creation of large factory centers—was at best ambiguous, because of the fear of creating a 'rootless proletariat' (the danger of which had

[1] See the judicious comments on this controversy, and a new interpretation of the evidence, by Alfred J. Rieber (ed.), *The politics of autocracy. Letters of Alexander II to Prince A. I. Bariatinskii, 1857–1864* (Paris–The Hague, 1966), pp. 15–58.

[2] Until 1857, when they became involved in the government's formal elaboration of reform plans, some of the outstanding 'enlightened bureaucrats' generally shared the views of the authors of the liberal reform program and were intimately involved in its composition: From the late 40s to 1857, the 'hommes d'état par excellence' N. A. and D. A. Miliutin, A. P. Zablotskii-Desiatovskii, K. K. Grot, V. P. Bezobrazov and others then occupying or destined to occupy high posts in the administration were participants along with Kavelin, in a liberal Petersburg *kruzhok* (circle) where the initiative for the liberal programmatic statements published by Herzen was taken. The extent to which the government legislation ultimately resembled the liberal reform program may have been in large measure due to the views developed by these 'enlightened bureaucrats' in this circle. Cf. V. N. Rozental' 'Ideinye tsentry liberal 'nogo dvizheniia v Rossii nakanune revoliutsionnoi situatsii', in *Revoliutsionnaia situatsiia v Rossii v 1859–1861 gg.* (Moscow, 1963), pp. 372–98.

[3] Russia's difficulties in the war were generally ascribed to the technological superiority of the enemy even before the final defeat, a theme which was the subject of numerous memoirs presented to the throne. Koshelev's comments, presented to the new Emperor in April 1855, were typical: 'The French and English weapons are distinctly superior to ours; the French weapons destroy ours and confuse our columns. And the English and French navies, having taken advantage of the latest improvements, walk on the sea as men formerly walked on land.' *Zapiski, prilozhenie,* p. 44.

been demonstrated most recently in the European events of 1848),[1] And it has further been noted that government officials in general, and Alexander II in particular, were apparently totally innocent of any modern notion of state direction of economic development of the sort that came to the fore with Count Witte at the end of the century.[2] The fact remains that the Russian state had a very long experience—extending backward in time well beyond the reign of Peter the Great—in manipulating the social and economic resources of the country in the search for the wherewithal to undertake military improvements. In other words, it was not, in the government's view, specifically industrial development alone which presented the possibility of strengthening the material basis of state power, and ultimately its ability to wage war. As always, the government was seeking new sources of state revenues, and here improvement of Russia's predominantly agrarian economy was a major concern, and this in prevailing thought was predicated on the abolition of serfdom.[3]

It was, however, concern for the maintenance of social and political stability that was uppermost in the minds of the Emperor and his advisors. There was the ever-present fear of a peasant *jacquerie*, a *Pugachevshchina*, which had haunted Nicholas I throughout his reign.[4] And serious peasant disorders during the Crimean War, necessitating the redeployment of troops much needed at the front, had impressed the government with the debilitating effects of serfdom on the waging of military campaigns.[5] From the beginning to the end of the reform's preparation, the official explanation for the emancipation was that it had been made necessary by the deterioration of relations between the peasants and their gentry masters.[6] The extent to which these

---

[1] Cf. M. Tugan-Baranovskii, *Russkaia fabrika v proshlom i nastoiashchem* (7th ed., Moscow, 1938), pp. 423–5; and Gerschenkron, 'Agrarian policies', pp. 712–13. (Aversion to a 'proletariat' was another of those 'Russian ideas' uniting many thinkers, from socialists to conservative government bureaucrats.)

[2] Cf. Rieber, *The politics of autocracy*, pp. 37–8.

[3] Skerpan, 'Russian national economy', pp. 165–8.

[4] Cf. P. Pechoux, 'L'ombre de Pugačev', in R. Portal (ed.), *Le statut des paysans libérés du servage, 1861–1961* (Paris–The Hague, 1962), pp. 128–52.

[5] Cf. Ignatovich, 'Krest'ianskie volneniia'.

[6] This was mentioned in Alexander's speech to the Moscow gentry which opened the preparation of the reform, and in the manifesto of emancipation which closed it in 1861.

relations had actually deteriorated in the recent past is a debatable matter,[1] and the official explanation was certainly, to some extent at least, a 'veiled form of blackmail' directed toward the gentry.[2] Nevertheless, the very fact that such 'blackmail' could be used was indicative of the prevailing state of mind both in the government and among the landed gentry.

Moreover, it was generally understood by Russian military experts, including D. A. Miliutin (soon to become Minister of War) and, apparently, Alexander himself, that the possibility (in their view a necessity) of transforming Russia's huge standing army into a less costly and more efficient 'citizen army' backed by a large body of trained reserves (in a word, the sort of army which had defeated Russia in 1856) depended on the abolition of serfdom. Whether, as Rieber has argued,[3] it was precisely this idea, or whether it was broader considerations which impelled Alexander II to proceed with the emancipation, it is clear that concern for the future maintenance of social and political stability decisively shaped the reform legislation. In this respect the emancipation was looked upon as a conservative measure above all.

The beginning of the reign of Alexander II offered little encouragement to abolitionist sentiment, for it was marked by several acts and utterances on the part of the government designed, apparently, to reassure the landed gentry of the inviolability of their privileges and material welfare.[4] From the very first days of Alexander's reign, however, rumors were rampant, in Peters-

---

[1] Cf. the author's 'The peasant and the emancipation', in W. S. Vucinich, editor, *The peasant in nineteenth century Russia* (Stanford, 1968), pp. 41–71.

[2] Rieber, *The politics of autocracy*, p. 36.

[3] *Ibid.*, pp. 24–9.

[4] Chief among these were the removal of D. G. Bibikov from the post of Minister of the Interior, and the circular to the provincial gentry marshals in the name of his successor, S. S. Lanskoi. (Bibikov, in the last years of the reign of Nicholas I, had aroused the animosity of conservative gentry by his energetic introduction of the 'inventory rules' in the western provinces which had been incorporated from Poland. Cf. Semevskii, *Krest'ianskii vopros*, II, 481–513.) Lanskoi's circular, dated 28 August 1855, declared the new Minister to be 'the representative before the throne of His Imperial Majesty's worthy Russian gentry'. 'Our most gracious Sovereign', the circular continued, 'has ordered me to preserve undisturbed the rights granted the gentry by his Imperial predecessors.' Although this circular contained nothing more than the assurances usually put forth at the beginning of a new reign, it was evidently understood by many gentry to refer specifically to the preservation of serfdom. *Materialy*, I (Berlin, 1860), 103–4.

burg, Moscow and wherever the gentry gathered, that the Emperor nevertheless intended to proceed with the abolition of serfdom.[1] And, indeed, these rumors appeared to be justified by Alexander's speech to the Moscow gentry on 30 March 1856, soon after the signing of the treaty ending the Crimean War. In response to the request of the Moscow Governor-General, Count Zakrevskii, that he 'calm the gentry' who were agitated by rumors that the government intended to emancipate the peasants, Alexander pronounced the historic words:

I have heard, gentlemen, that rumors have spread among you to the effect that I intend to abolish serfdom. In order to dispel various unfounded rumors about a subject of such importance, I consider it necessary to inform you that I do not have the intention of doing that at this time. But of course, you yourselves know that the existing order of ruling over living souls cannot remain unchanged. It is better to abolish serfdom from above than to await the day when it will begin to abolish itself from below. I ask you, gentlemen, to consider how this is to be accomplished. Convey my words to the gentry for their consideration.[2]

The Emperor was not being entirely frank with the Moscow gentry, for upon returning to Petersburg he immediately entrusted to the Ministry of Interior the task of elaborating the principles of reform and the manner in which they were to be implemented.[3] From this time until the publication of the famous Nazimov Rescript on 24 November 1857—the first public announcement of the government's plans for emancipation[4] —initiative in the preparation of the reform remained a virtual monopoly of the Ministry of Interior. The Secret Committee

---

[1] One of the most persistent rumors at that time was that Napoleon III had made Alexander agree to emancipate the peasants as one of the conditions of the peace treaty. 'Na zare krest'ianskoi svobody', *Russkaia starina*, XCII, pp. 7–8.

[2] *Materialy*, I, 114. [3] *Ibid.*, pp. 116–18.

[4] Strictly speaking, the Nazimov Rescript and accompanying 'instructions' from the Minister of Interior (signed by the Emperor on 20 November) were not 'published' on 24 November, but only printed in limited quantity and sent out to provincial governors and gentry marshals, 'for consideration and, in some cases, for guidance of local governors, and for the greater reassurance of the gentry against the misunderstandings which arise from unclear understanding of the good intentions of the Sovereign' (the words of Lanskoi, who proposed this action to the Emperor on 22 November). A. Popel'nitskii, 'Sekretnyi komitet v dele osvobozhdeniia krest'ian ot krepostnoi zavisimosti', *Vestnik Evropy*, March 1911, p. 142.

on Peasant Affairs, convened on 3 January 1857 after the model of the numerous secret committees of Nicholas' reign, was itself created by recommendation of Lanskoi, the Minister of Interior.[1] Although formal discussion of emancipation subsequently took place in this committee, it was composed of highly-placed state dignitaries, the majority of whom repeatedly proved their hostility to any substantive reform plans, and the initiative continued to lie with the Ministry of Interior.[2]

THE NAZIMOV RESCRIPT AND ITS ORIGINS

The Nazimov Rescript was a directive from the Emperor to V. I. Nazimov, Governor-General of the Lithuanian provinces (Kovno, Vilno and Grodno), providing that the gentry of these provinces be allowed to form provincial committees for the purpose of drawing up projects of emancipation for their peasants, on the basis of principles included in the Rescript and in accompanying instructions of the Minister of Interior. With certain modifications, the Nazimov Rescript served as the model for rescripts subsequently sent to the gentry of all the Russian provinces. The exact prototype of all subsequent rescripts was presented to the gentry of Petersburg province on 5 December 1857.[3]

---

[1] In a memoir to the Emperor dated 20 December 1856, Lanskoi had proposed the summoning of a committee for consideration of certain reform proposals. Lanskoi's memoir, however, had proposed a committee composed of 'several persons convinced of the necessity of progressing to a new order', as well as a number of temporary 'technical committees' composed of experts, 'well-intentioned *pomeshchiki* and several representatives of the gentry'. P. I. Liashchenko, *Poslednii sekretnyi komitet po krest'-ianskomu delu. 3 ianvaria 1857 g.—16 fevralia 1858 g. (Po materialam arkhiva gosudarst-vennogo soveta)* (St Petersburg, 1911), pp. 7–8.

[2] The original members of the committee, personally appointed by Alexander II, were: Prince A. F. Orlov (Chairman of the State Council and Committee of Ministers), S. S. Lanskoi, Count D. N. Bludov (President of the Academy of Sciences), M. N. Murav'ev (Minister of State Properties), K. V. Chevkin (Minister of Communications), Ia. I. Rostovtsev (Director of Military Schools), Baron M. A. Korf (member of the State Council), Prince P. P. Gagarin (member of the State Council), Count V. F. Adlerberg (Minister of Court), Prince V. A. Dolgorukov (Head of the Third Section), and P. F. Brok (Minister of Finances). The Emperor himself was official chairman of the committee, with Orlov chairing in his absence.

[3] Essentially, the difference between the Nazimov Rescript and the subsequent rescripts was necessitated by the peculiar situation prevailing in the Lithuanian provinces. There,

This rescript provided for the creation of provincial gentry committees, under the chairmanship of the provincial gentry marshals, to be formed from two elected gentry representatives from each *uezd* plus two 'experienced *pomeshchiki*' to be appointed by the provincial governors. These committees were to draw up draft statutes 'on the organization and improvement of the condition of the landlords' peasants', in accordance with principles included in the rescript and appended instructions. 'The development of these principles and their application to the local areas of the province', the rescript stated, 'is the responsibility of the committee'.[1] Upon completion of their draft statutes, the committees were to present them to the Emperor through the Ministry of Interior.

Judging from these principles and directives, it is obvious that the government had not yet gotten very far along the way toward the elaboration of a finished plan of peasant emancipation. They left many crucial questions undecided, and they were on

unlike the Russian provinces, special inventory rules had been introduced (though not yet implemented) and gentry 'inventory committees' were already in existence. Aside from changes related to this situation, the most noticeable modifications were two: The word 'emancipation' or 'liberation' (*osvobozhdenie*), which had been used in the instructions of the Ministry of Interior accompanying the Nazimov Rescript was removed from subsequent instructions and replaced with the term 'improvement of peasant conditions'. Secondly, the Lithuanian gentry had been instructed that the redemption price of the peasant *usad'ba* (that is, the peasants' dwellings, outbuildings and the land immediately under and around them) was 'not to exceed the value of the *usad'ba* homestead'; while subsequent instructions allowed for what was in effect veiled redemption of peasant labor as well. These changes led many contemporaries and some later commentators to believe that the Secret Committee had put pressure on the Ministry to revise the rescripts in favor of gentry interests and in a generally conservative direction. (Cf. S. S. Tatishchev, *Imperator Aleksandr II. Ego zhizn' i tsarstvovanie*, I (St Petersburg, 1911), 294–5.) It would appear, however, that the Secret Committee had little to do with these changes: The draft of the Petersburg Rescript was drawn up in the Ministry of Interior with the cooperation of the Petersburg Governor-General, Ignat'ev; the omission of the word 'liberation' (and also 'abolition of serfdom') in the rescript to the Petersburg gentry was the result of the specific conditions in which it was produced (it was presented in answer to a request from the Petersburg gentry which had made no mention of emancipation but only asked permission to draw up a 'project for the ... administration of *pomeshchik* peasants'); and the ruling on evaluation of the peasant *usad'ba* was based on a scheme worked out earlier in the Ministry of Interior. (A. I. Levshin, 'Dostopamiatnye minuty v moei zhizni', *Russkii arkhiv*, no. 2 (1885), pp. 535–6; Liashchenko, *Poslednii sekretnyi komitet*, p. 55; A. Skrebitskii, *Krest'ianskoe delo v tsarstvovanie Imperatora Aleksandra II*, I (Bonn, 1862), iii–xiv (the texts).)

[1] Skrebitskii, *Krest'ianskoe delo*, I, x.

several important matters mutually contradictory. Nothing was said about when the government intended to proceed to emancipation, nor was anything specific mentioned about the final solution of emancipation after a 'transition period' (not to exceed twelve years) projected in the rescript. It was at once proposed that the gentry were to retain property-rights to all the land, and that the peasants were to purchase their *usad'by* and to receive in usage a certain amount of field land in addition. 'Patrimonial police authority' was presumably to be retained by the *pomeshchiki* during the course of the proposed transition period, but the creation of a special '*uezd* commission' for intervention in disputes between peasants and *pomeshchiki* was also mentioned. The arrangement of peasant allotments in field land, and of peasant obligations, was apparently left to the gentry committees with only vague indications about their proper determination.

Nevertheless, the government had arrived at a few fundamental decisions: The peasants were to be freed with their *usad'by*, which were to be redeemed by them (by valuation 'not only of the *usad'ba* land and buildings, but also of productive benefits and local advantages'). The peasants were to have the right to use some further amount of field land. They were to pass through a transition status, during which they were to remain tied to the land. And when freed they were to remain in their communes. Finally, the gentry were to be given apparently substantial participation in the preparation of the reform.

The Rescripts and the decisions leading up to them show clearly that from the government's point of view the alternative means of effecting emancipation were restricted within certain definite limits. On the one extreme, total expropriation of gentry lands was out of the question; on the other, a simple abolition of personal bondage—a landless emancipation of the peasantry—was equally excluded from the range of possibilities.

Expropriation of the landed gentry was never considered. Theoretically, this would have entailed the disintegration of the landowning class which was the social basis of the civil and military bureaucracy, not to speak of the probable collapse of the agricultural market which was supplied largely by that class.

Even if the government had been inclined to follow such a policy, it was ruled out by immediate political considerations: Quite aside from the very great likelihood of provoking a *coup d'état* by such a policy, the government could not have implemented any kind of significant reform in rural Russia without the cooperation of the landed gentry, who would necessarily have to provide the personnel for such an undertaking. Political realities were such that even the partial alienation of gentry lands (more exactly, of a part of the lands in fact held by the peasantry) subsequently met with such opposition from the gentry that the government was compelled to reduce significantly the amount of land it had originally intended for peasant usage.

A landless emancipation of the peasantry was equally unacceptable to the Emperor and his advisors. Emancipation with land had been a recognized principle in the government since long before the reign of Alexander II. This principle had been incorporated into the earlier laws that had provided for voluntary emancipation of peasants by gentry landowners. The government's one effort at landless emancipation—in the Baltic Provinces in 1817–19—had produced conditions among the peasants there that were notorious in Russian society. This was clearly recognized by Nicholas I, who in 1842 had explicitly declared that freed peasants must be allowed to keep their land 'in order to avoid the unsatisfactory situation that now exists in the Baltic provinces —a situation which has brought the peasants there to a most pitiable condition'.[1] The government recognized the necessity of emancipation with land primarily out of a concern for social stability: It feared that a landless emancipation would result in 'vagabondage' among the peasantry, if not in peasant rebellion.[2]

---

[1] Quoted in Blum, *Lord and peasant*, p. 544.

[2] Skrebitskii, *Krest'ianskoe delo*, I, v. The necessity of emancipation with land for these reasons was the message of an important memorandum presented to Alexander II in October 1856, by one of the chief architects of the later reform legislation, Nicholas Miliutin. (*TsGIAL, f.* 1180, no. 85, pp. 437–57). This warning was repeated to Alexander in the summer of 1857 by one of his most influential and respected advisors, Count Kiselev (former Minister of State Properties, then Ambassador in Paris), who wrote that 'cultivators without land would end up in the most burdensome dependence on the landlords and would be their complete slaves, or would constitute a proletariat, undesirable for themselves and dangerous for the state.' Popel'nitskii, 'Sekretnyi komitet' (Feb.), p. 64.

It was also concerned to keep the peasants tied to the land for immediate reasons of fiscal stability.[1]

The government was, therefore, faced with the necessity of working out some sort of compromise solution within the framework dictated by these fundamental considerations.[2] When Alexander II first informed the Minister of Interior that he intended to proceed with emancipation,[3] nobody in the government was prepared to come forth with a comprehensive plan. The task of elaborating such a plan was begun in the Ministry of Interior: The ideas which produced the Nazimov Rescript, the decision to call the gentry to participation in the reform, the decision to publicize the government's reform plans and the first principles of reform, were all developed there—primarily by A. I. Levshin, who occupied the post of Assistant Minister until April 1859.[4] But because of the magnitude of the task and the lack of legislative precedents in Russia or elsewhere in Europe,[5]

[1] Cf. Skerpan, 'The Russian national economy,' pp. 181–2.

[2] This situation, as well as the general framework of alternatives open to the government, has been described by Gerschenkron, 'Agrarian policies', pp. 722–7. He overstates the case, however, in concluding that Russia avoided a landless emancipation for the peasantry only by a change of mind on the part of Alexander II in 1858 which led to explicit affirmation that the peasants were to retain permanent use of their field lands. While it is true that this issue was publicly resolved only at that time, the planners of the reform had in fact decided the issue long before. The government got around to announcing that the final goal of the reform was redemption of their lands by the peasants only in mid-1858 for a number of reasons—among them: fear of alienating the gentry, general ill-preparedness, and an intense fear of committing the government to a financial operation. (See the immediately adjacent comments and chapter 6 below.)

[3] Lanskoi had probably been informed of the Emperor's intention before the end of 1855. Cf. Ia. Solov'ev, 'Zapiski senatora Ia. A. Solov'eva', *Russkaia starina*, xxx, 229 (see bibliography for inclusive page numbers).

[4] Levshin was responsible for most of the Ministry's protocols (including the personal reports of Lanskoi) on reform from the beginning of Alexander's reign until the publication of the Nazimov Rescript. (He was transferred from the Ministry of State Properties to the Ministry of Interior in late 1855, and immediately was set to work on the 'peasant question'. Levshin, a bureaucrat of gentry origin, had worked under Kiselev and thus provided a certain continuity between the government circle which had discussed the reform during the reign of Nicholas and the new center of discussion in the Ministry of Interior.) Shortly after that event, Levshin was removed from active participation in the preparation of reform, evidently as a result of his objection to the rapidity with which the Minister, Lanskoi, and others in the Ministry—primarily Nicholas Miliutin and Ia. Solov'ev—wished to effect emancipation. His place as effective formulator of the Ministry's policies was taken by Miliutin. Levshin, 'Dostopamiatnye minuty', pp. 475–557.

[5] The history of agrarian reform in Central Europe was well known in Russian governmental circles. The Editing Commissions (the body, created in 1859, to which the final

many of the basic principles of the reform as it was eventually promulgated took shape only very late in its preparation. This fundamental circumstance of the reform's preparation exercised, as will be seen, a profound influence on relations between the government and the landed gentry.[1]

In their first effort to elaborate some of the basic principles of reform for the Emperor, in December 1856, the officials of the Ministry definitely concluded that the peasants were to be emancipated with land. Ideally, the Minister wrote in a memorandum to Alexander, the obvious solution would be a state-sponsored financial operation for redemption of the peasant lands. But this was out of the question:

> The allotment [in property] to the emancipated peasants of all the land necessary for their welfare cannot be accomplished except by redemption of the land from the gentry by means of a financial operation of the greatest proportions; but these means could disarray state finances to such a degree as to produce another pernicious cataclysm in the State.[2]

This fear of committing the government to a financial operation —a fear generally shared in government circles—was expressed at the nadir of a thirty-year-period of ever-growing state budgetary deficits. The first post-war years, the very years of the preparation of the peasant reform, was a time of grave concern in the government about the situation of the state finances. A series of commissions were formed to consider the problem of

---

reform legislation was entrusted) possessed a large library on agrarian reform, including 32 works on the 'peasant question' in Austria and Prussia, which had been collected and donated by the Grand Duchess Elena Pavlovna (Alexander's aunt), one of the foremost advocates of emancipation at court. But Austria and Prussia offered no models for positive legislation, especially on the crucial subject of a universal land settlement. The main lesson learned from these examples was apparently that the state must avoid the creation of a rural proletariat.

[1] Alexander was perfectly aware of the dangers involved in opening the question of reform without first elaborating a finished plan. In the summer of 1857, he was presented a memorandum by Baron Haxthausen, which declared in part that 'the government must take part [in the preparation of reform], lest events, overtaking it, not force concessions from it which would lead to decline or disaster'. Opposite this statement, Alexander wrote in the margin: 'Completely just, and this is my main concern.' Popel'nitskii, 'Sekretnyi komitet', (Feb.), p. 65.

[2] *ORLB, Arkhiv Cherkasskikh, kn. V. A. Cherkasskogo i kn. E. I. Cherkasskoi*, 1 16/9, 2–2a. (Reference was, evidently, to the loss of the Crimean War.)

growing state deficits, all of which pronounced the state finances to be in a dire condition.[1] In this context the government's apprehension at committing state resources to a financial operation for redemption of the peasant lands, which was nevertheless recognized—in the Ministry of Interior at least—to be the best solution in principle, seems understandable. The government steadfastly refused to commit itself to a general redemption operation, although later—in 1858—it agreed to financial redemption of peasant lands on estates where redemption had been voluntarily agreed to by peasants and *pomeshchiki*, or by request of the *pomeshchiki* alone.

The government's decision on this point—on the unavailability or limited availability of state capital for effecting a land settlement between the *pomeshchiki* and the peasants—influenced all further decisions about emancipation. For the Ministry of Interior, the first problem was how to formulate the principle of emancipation with land without a large-scale redemption operation. The first decision on this question, also taken at the end of December 1856, was that it would be possible for the time being to restrict the reform plans to 'granting the peasants personal freedom and the right of communal ownership of the [*usad'ba*] land:'

This arrangement [Lanskoi wrote in a memorandum to the Emperor] gives the peasant, so to speak, a permanent nest and will protect him at the outset from the possibility of being driven from [the land] by the arbitrariness of the *pomeshchik*.[2]

The peasants could redeem their *usad'by* without any complicated financial operation. And the obtaining from the *pomeshchiki* of field land in property by the peasants could be left to 'time and their mutual agreement'.[3]

The next problem was how to define the relationship of the peasants to the land pending such mutual agreement. This task was accomplished in a Ministry memorandum presented for the guidance of the Secret Committee in July 1857: 'The property-

---

[1] P. L. Kovan'ko, *Reforma 19 fevralia 1861 goda i ee posledstviia s finansovoi tochki zreniia. (Vykupnaia operatsiia 1861 g.–1907 g.)* (Kiev, 1914), pp. 24–31.
[2] *ORLB, Arkhiv Cherkasskikh,* I 16/10, 1.   [3] *Ibid.*

right to the land remains with the *pomeshchik*, but the peasants retain the right to use the land, with the indispensable condition of paying for it with money or labor.'[1] This was essentially as far as the government had progressed toward the solution of the land question by the time of the publication of the Rescripts in November–December 1857. Although neither the Ministry memoranda nor the Rescripts specifically stated that the lands left in peasant usage were never to revert to the *pomeshchiki*, this was clearly the government's intention. No mention had been made anywhere of temporary usage of the land by the peasants.

The remainder of the principles relating to the peasants' status and obligations published in the Rescripts were also gradually elaborated in the Ministry of Interior in the course of 1856–7.

Alexander II had apparently decided at the very beginning to call the gentry to participation in preparation of the reform. It was clearly this idea which had prompted him, in March 1856, to ask the Moscow gentry 'to consider how [emancipation] is to be accomplished'.[2] The summoning of provincial gentry committees had been recommended in Lanskoi's first memorandum to the Emperor on the principles of reform in December 1856:

... The expression of the government's views should be such that they produce results in keeping with the aim, and should be made only to the gentry, who should be made to discuss the details of the new and future order. The principles of the matter should be pointed out by the central government; their elaboration can be accomplished only by provincial committees of the gentry. The supreme central authority will never untie the small knots in this matter, which are known only to practicing landowners.[3]

The creation of provincial gentry committees had also been advocated by several members of the Secret Committee (especially by General Rostovtsev and Baron Korf), and the same had

[1] Levshin, 'Dostopamiatnye minuty', p. 504.
[2] 'It seems,' Solov'ev wrote in his memoirs, 'that the idea of the Emperor consisted of attracting the gentry to him by gracious expression of full faith in the gentry, and of carrying out the emancipation of the peasants through the gentry.' (*Russkaia starina*, xxx, p. 226.) These memoirs were read by Alexander II (apparently a few days before his assassination), who marked off this passage and indicated his confirmation of Solov'ev's surmise in the margin (*Russkaia starina*, xxx, pp. 903–5).
[3] ORLB, *Arkhiv Cherkasskikh*, 1 16/9, 2–2a.

been urged upon the Emperor by Baron Haxthausen, during Alexander's trip abroad in the spring of 1857.[1]

With the approval of the Emperor, the Ministry of Interior had in fact begun to lay plans to involve the gentry in the preparation of reform as early as August 1856. The aim of these plans was to arrange things so that the gentry 'would take the first step and be the first to pronounce the word *freedom*'.[2] In these plans lay the origin of the Nazimov Rescript. Contrary to the official myth that the Nazimov Rescript was issued in answer to a voluntary request from the Lithuanian gentry asking that they be allowed to liberate their peasants,[3] the whole affair was arranged in the Ministry of Interior. It was so arranged for the explicit purpose of creating an impression that the gentry themselves were anxious to cooperate in the government's undertaking.

The Ministry chose the Lithuanian gentry for the following reasons: It was thought that these gentry, being in close proximity to regions inhabited by free peasants (Poland and the Baltic provinces), were more favorably disposed to emancipation than the gentry of most other provinces. Moreover, there were already in existence in these provinces gentry committees, working (since 1854) on the review of the 'inventory rules'. The fact that these rules were currently under review made it particularly easy for the government to persuade the gentry there to 'pronounce the word freedom:' Pressure was put upon the local governors and gentry marshals of the Lithuanian provinces through Nazimov, beginning in August 1856, to forward a request to the government asking permission to form provincial committees for the purpose of drafting projects of emancipation for their peasants. This was done by letting these gentry know unmistakably that if they failed to cooperate there would be a revision of the inventory rules that would likely lessen the rights and benefits of the *pomeshchiki*.[4]

---

[1] Popel'nitskii, 'Sekretnyi komitet', (Feb.), p. 65.

[2] Levshin, 'Dostopamiatnye minuty', p. 484.

[3] For an example of the official version of this episode, see Tatishchev, *Imperator Aleksandr II*, I, 286.

[4] Levshin, 'Dostopamiatnye minuty', pp. 483–6; Liashchenko, *Poslednii sekretnyi komitet*, pp. 52–4. These plans were begun in talks with Nazimov at the time of the Emperor's

The government's first steps

In the end, all the government was able to obtain from the Lithuanian gentry was a rather feeble agreement to emancipation of the peasantry without land, on the model of the Baltic provinces. But this was sufficient for the government's purposes, and when Nazimov arrived in Petersburg with this request in late October 1857, a rescript to the Lithuanian gentry based on the recent memoranda of the Ministry of Interior was composed —without any reference to the terms of the Lithuanian gentry's request (or for that matter, to the views of the majority in the Secret Committee).[1]

Thus Alexander II and the 'reforming bureaucrats', realizing the need to rely on the gentry for the implementation of emancipation, sought the cooperation of the gentry, or at least its appearance, from the beginning, by actively soliciting gentry participation in the preparation of the reform. So too, they had sought the cooperation of the high state dignitaries—Russia's approximation of the representatives of aristocratic interests—by involving them in their plans through the creation of the Secret Committee.[2] But just as the reformers had shown no willingness

coronation in Moscow in August 1856. (A rather exaggerated version of Nazimov's role is given by A. S. Pavlov, 'V. I. Nazimov. Ocherki iz noveishei letopisi severo-zapadnoi Rossii', *Russkaia starina*, XLV, pp. 578–80.)

[1] Cf. Levshin, 'Dostopamiatnye minuty', pp. 527–35. Alexander demanded a reply to the Lithuanian request from the Secret Committee within eight days. The Committee turned the task over to Lanskoi and Murav'ev (Minister of State Properties), with the cooperation of Nazimov. From there the work devolved upon Levshin, who drew up the rescript on the basis of Lanskoi's (that is, his own) memoranda, primarily the Minister's report of 26 July 1857, to the Secret Committee.

The decision to generalize the Nazimov Rescript, that is to apply it to all provinces and to send it to all governors and gentry marshals, apparently belonged to Lanskoi and Alexander's brother the Grand Duke Konstantin Nikolaevich, whom Alexander had put in charge of the Secret Committee in August 1857, as a result of dissatisfaction with the Committee's inconclusive deliberations. With Alexander's previous approval, they succeeded in getting the Committee's approval for these measures, apparently against the wishes of the majority. Cf. *ibid.*, pp. 534–5; Popel'nitskii, 'Sekretnyi komitet', (March), pp. 138–42; *Materialy*, I, 155–6.

[2] According to Levshin, Lanskoi was at first reluctant to create a committee, and wanted to process reform plans exclusively in the Ministry, but was persuaded by Levshin (as he argued in the Minister's report for 20 December 1856) that the Ministry alone could not hope to get a project through the State Council. (Levshin, 'Dostopamiatnye minuty', pp. 490–3.) Alexander's motive, in appointing to the Committee dignitaries whom he well knew to be unfavorably disposed toward reform, clearly appears to have been the hope of neutralizing their opposition to his plans.

to grant real authority to the Secret Committee, neither did they intend to have their plans thwarted by the provincial committees they had been responsible for creating.

FURTHER GOVERNMENT INSTRUCTIONS:
THE PROGRAM OF 21 APRIL 1858

After the publication of the Rescripts to Nazimov and the Governor-General of Petersburg province, the first really voluntary request to create a provincial committee came from the province of Nizhnii Novgorod on 17 December 1857.[1] Other requests followed shortly afterward. 'These were', Levshin recalled, 'already normal actions, and more or less tardy. They had as their sources not enthusiasm, but the impossibility of any province to fall behind the others, and reminders to the governors from the Ministry.'[2] By July 1858, most of the provincial gentry had requested and received the Rescript allowing them to open provincial committees.[3]

According to the Rescripts, the government apparently intended to grant considerable initiative to the gentry committees. They were given the responsibility of determining, within general limits, the redemption price of the *usad'ba*, the amount of field land to be left in peasant usage, and the amount of rent to be received from it. It also appeared that, within the maximum limit of twelve years, they would be allowed to define the length of the peasants' transition status. The government, however, in seeking gentry approbation and commitment to the reform through involvement in its preparation, wanted to have

[1] The Petersburg Rescript had not in fact been requested by the local gentry, but was sent out 'in reply' to a request by a group of Petersburg gentry for something quite different. Similarly, the Moscow gentry (the third group to receive a rescript) had had pressure applied from Petersburg to make the request. The government was concerned to have these two most important provincial corporations set the example for their peers in other provinces. Cf. Kornilov, *Ocherki po istorii obshchestvennogo dvizheniia i krest'-ianskogo dela v Rossii* (St Petersburg, 1905), pp. 175, 196.

[2] Levshin, 'Dostopamiatnye minuty', p. 537. 'It was impossible,' Solov'ev wrote in his memoirs, 'to openly and steadfastly be in opposition in some provinces after the peasants had learned from the newspapers that emancipation of the peasants was proceeding in other provinces in accordance with the wishes of the gentry themselves.' Solov'ev, 'Zapiski', xxxi, 5.   [3] Skrebitskii, *Krest'ianskoe delo*, I, xxiv–xxv.

its proverbial cake and eat it, too. That is, it wanted gentry commitment, but did not in fact want to relinquish any real initiative to the gentry committees. The appearance to the contrary was, as subsequent events showed, more the result of confusion and uncertainty about major questions of reform on the part of the government than of any desire to grant such initiative.

The first fruit of this situation was a confrontation with several gentry committees over the fate of the peasant *usad'ba*. The Petersburg committee objected, soon after its convocation early in 1858, that the Minister's instructions on the *usad'ba* violated the words of the Imperial rescript to the effect that the gentry were to retain 'the property-right to all the land'.[1] Besides such protests against any alienation of property, there appeared other questions, also mostly related to the failure of the Rescripts to define the final solution of the land question.[2]

Generally speaking, government officials tended to interpret these responses as evidence that most gentry were simply opposed to emancipation.[3] From the beginning of Alexander's reign, attempts to find signs of approval for emancipation among the gentry had been poorly rewarded. Levshin, who had been dispatched to raise the question among the gentry assembled for Alexander's coronation in August 1856, had reported that:

The majority of the representatives of the landholders was completely unprepared to set out on a new path, had never discussed serfdom from the point of view of emancipation; and therefore at the first hint of this displayed amazement, and at times genuine terror...[4]

Later, the government had had to arrange secretly for a request from the Lithuanian gentry in order to perpetrate the fiction that the gentry themselves had asked to emancipate their peasants, and the same sort of subterfuge was resorted to with the Petersburg gentry. When, after publication of the Nazimov Rescript, the Minister of Interior solicited information about the impression produced on the gentry by the Rescript, the response was not

---

[1] *Materialy*, I, 323.   [2] Solov'ev, 'Zapiski', XXXI, 18–22.
[3] Cf. Kornilov, 'Gubernskie komitety', no. 2, pp. 208–9.
[4] Levshin, 'Dostopamiatnye minuty', pp. 483–4.

encouraging: Most of the 'impressions' sent into the Ministry in December 1857 by the governors and gentry marshals were critical of the Rescript, expressing either a general lack of sympathy with the idea of emancipation or dissatisfaction with the specific course chosen by the government.[1]

The state of gentry opinion involved more, however, than simple opposition to emancipation, a fact which had been observed in the Ministry's own report. In response to the advice that they pursue the Emperor's suggestion to consider how to go about abolishing serfdom, the gentry marshals gathered for the coronation had answered, Lanskoi (actually Levshin) wrote in December 1856:

Firstly, that they do not consider themselves to have the right to set an example for their fellows. Secondly, that they do not know the principles on which the government proposes to carry out this reform, and without this they cannot decide to do anything, although they remain convinced that emancipation of their peasants is necessary.[2]

This description of the gentry's response has a ring of truth to it. The gentry had never had an opportunity to display initiative in important state questions, and it would have been surprising if they had suddenly begun to do so. Many, perhaps most, gentry carried the intellectual conviction that emancipation was necessary but few showed any inclination to test their immediate privileges and economic circumstances against this conviction so long as there were no definite assurances from the government about their welfare. It may be, as Kornilov argued, that most *pomeshchiki* would have had nothing against an emancipation which left them the bulk of their lands and guaranteed them a good sum of money.[3] The Rescripts, of course, had promised neither of these. In any case, as soon as the government announced its intention to proceed with emancipation, the question for most gentry ceased to be one of simple acceptance or rejection of emancipation, but a question of the exact nature of the settlement to be effected. Many gentry at first opposed the government's plans from a conservative position: They were opposed to the

[1] Solov'ev, 'Zapiski', xxx, 745–9.   [2] *ORLB, Arkhiv Cherkasskikh*, I, 16/9, 2.
[3] Kornilov, 'Gubernskie komitety', no. I, p. 123.

alienation of land, especially when the government displayed no intention of otherwise guaranteeing their economic welfare.

But this was not the only source of gentry opposition. A minority among the gentry responses to the Rescripts—including a letter from the marshal of Tver province, the addresses of four *uezdy* of Tver, one *uezd* of Kharkov province and the address of the Nizhnii Novgorod gentry—criticized the government's plans from the point of view of the liberal reform program described earlier in chapter two.[1] This minority went beyond the government's plans, calling for full and immediate emancipation of the peasants with land, and summoned the government to assume the responsibility of a financial operation to effect redemption of these lands. The most forceful presentation of this view was made by A. M. Unkovskii, gentry marshal of Tver province. He wrote:

Although it was impossible as yet to define accurately the impression which the circulars may have on the whole mass of the gentry, one can almost be certain that the gentry [of Tver province] will fully understand the necessity of abolishing serfdom. At the same time, I cannot but remark the fact that when reading the circulars . . . and the copies of the Imperial Rescript . . . [the gentry] expressed the opinion that the principles outlined in them are completely inapplicable to the conditions of the Great Russian peasants, who will never comprehend a middle way between servile labor and free labor; and they consider possible only one method of freeing the peasants—by means of their redemption of a certain part of the land.[2]

At that time, the government was plainly unwilling to accept the responsibility for such an operation, and it may be that the desire to avoid a proliferation of gentry demands for this solution from the provincial committees was a major factor leading to the rapid adoption of more explicit directives for the committees.[3]

---

[1] Solov'ev, 'Zapiski', XXXI, 18–19.

[2] Kornilov, 'Gubernskie komitety', no. 2, p. 207. In their address, the gentry of Sumy *uezd* (Kharkov province) added the specific request that 'the proper remittance of redemption by the peasants be guaranteed by the participation of the government itself'. Solov'ev, 'Zapiski', XXXI, 18–19.

[3] Herzen, writing in *Kolokol*, claimed that the government's desire to avoid such an operation at all costs was the one main reason for adoption of the 'April Program' (see below). Herzen advocated acceptance of the liberal proposal, arguing that only by

The government's initial response to the conflicting gentry views was Lanskoi's circular of 17 February 1858, to the Governor-General of Petersburg. Here Lanskoi on the one hand assured the committees that 'it is not necessary to seek in my instructions . . . a detailed program for the deliberations of the committees', while on the other hand he affirmed that the *usad'ba* was to become, irrevocably, the property of the peasants, even if its redemption were not completed within the transition period.[1] This left the question of the significance of the instructions wide open, and did nothing to restrict the proliferation of misunderstandings and inquiries as time passed and new committees were convened. Some committees proceeded to draw up plans for emancipation based on the idea that all lands would revert to the *pomeshchiki* after expiration of the transition status. A few, like the committee of the Tver gentry, began to elaborate plans for the redemption by the peasants of *usad'ba* and field lands alike.

The government soon began to fear that the projects of the gentry committees would significantly depart from the desired goal. It realized that it could not itself leave major questions unresolved and be able to expect anything but confusion from the committees. In short, by creating the gentry committees, the government forced itself to proceed quickly to an elaboration of more detailed reform plans.[2]

The government's next step was to compose a detailed program, issued on 21 April 1858, for the guidance of the provincial gentry committees. This program, composed in the Main Committee (the Secret Committee was so renamed in January 1858, since the subject of its deliberations was no longer secret),[3] at once dispensed with the *laissez faire* attitude toward the provincial committees that had so far been displayed in the Ministry of Interior, and threatened to reduce the provincial committees to a series of

obligating itself to reimburse the gentry properly could the government be assured of the gentry's support for emancipation with land. (*Kolokol*, no. 19, 15 July 1858, pp. 153–60).

[1] *Materialy*, I, 325–8. [2] *Ibid.*, p. 329.

[3] Once the government had publicly announced its intention of emancipating the peasants, the Ministry of Interior lost the monopoly of initiative which it had held to that time, and the Main Committee—of which Lanskoi was, of course, a member—began to play a more active role in decision-making on questions of reform.

information-gathering agencies with no right whatever to consider basic questions of reform.

The 'April Program' introduced nothing new in the way of principles: It reaffirmed the government's position on the *usad'ba* —it was to be redeemed in any case, whether or not redemption were completed during the transition period. It reaffirmed that field land as well was to be left in peasant usage. And it repeated that the peasants were to receive 'civil rights' at the end of the transition period, whether or not they had by then redeemed their *usad'by*. But it also repeated the apparently contradictory principles of the 'inviolability of the property-rights of the *pomeshchiki* to all land', and the retention for the *pomeshchiki* of 'patrimonial police authority'.

The primary purpose of the program was to restrict severely the field of initiative open to the provincial committees. This was done by dividing the activities of the committees into three periods: In the first period (of six months), the committees were to draw up reform projects for the transition status only; in the second period these projects, as approved by the government, were to be implemented; in the third period only were the committees to take up the 'final arrangement of the peasantry', that is the final solution of the emancipation. No dates were set for the second and third periods. The committees were thus prohibited from considering for the time being (that is, for the duration of the 'first period') any ultimate solution to the emancipation. In addition they were given the task of gathering during the 'first period' a huge amount of statistical material about the state of peasant landholding, and were also provided with a detailed model of a statute for the transition status, to which they were to adhere strictly in composing their own statutes.[1]

The 'April Program' was essentially a stop-gap measure designed to allow the government time to develop its own reform plans without having those of the gentry forced upon it in the meantime.[2] The government later made several tactical

---

[1] Skrebitskii, *Krest'ianskoe delo*, I, xxvi–xxxii.

[2] The program was written by M. P. Pozen and sponsored in the Main Committee by General Rostovtsev. Pozen's aim, in writing the program, has generally been considered a reactionary one—to prevent government acceptance of the alienation of gentry lands,

retreats from the terms of the program, but its basic decision—to disallow any wide-ranging initiative by the provincial committees—was never reversed. The program was a fateful step in the evolution of government–gentry relations during the period of reform preparation. The government could have made its position on gentry participation in the reform through the committees clear and unequivocal in one of two ways—either by giving the provincial committees a free hand in their deliberations from the outset, or by explicitly restricting them to the status of information-gathering agencies for supplying the government with the raw material for its legislation. Doing neither, the government continued to encroach upon the field of initiative left to the gentry in the preparation of the reform.

and to postpone any final solution to the question by restricting legislation to the transition status. Pozen was, however, always careful to insist on his devotion to emancipation. Whatever his aims, the program was accepted by Rostovtsev and the majority of the Main Committee as a progressive measure designed to keep the uncooperative provincial committee in line. Cf. Kornilov, 'Gubernskie komitety', no. 3, pp. 110–11, 115–16; M. P. Pozen, *Bumagi po krest'ianskomu delu* (Dresden, 1864).

PART II

THE PROVINCIAL GENTRY COMMITTEES, 1858-9

The transitional status which the government proposes to introduce will provoke everywhere what now occurs in rare instances, and will lead to complete anarchy. Hatred between the two classes, which are obliged to live together and on whose mutual cooperation the entire welfare of the state must be based, will take firm root. To reconcile freedom and slavery, the police and administrative authority of the *pomeshchik* and the independence of the peasant—this is an utterly impossible task. And it is this task which lies at the base of the idea of a gradual transition from dependency to freedom . . .

Moreover, rumors have long been circulating among the people that they are to be freed. They sense that the time has come when they can hope for a better lot . . . Place them now in a state of semi-dependency, . . . and they will not believe that this has Imperial sanction. They will be disappointed in their expectations and their dissatisfaction . . . will be turned once again against the *pomeshchiki*, whom they will regard as their persecutors. The result of such a state of affairs will inevitably be the destruction of the entire economic order—the very thing [the government] wanted to strengthen by effecting gradual emancipation . . .

From all this it is clear that gradual emancipation presents dangers which should not be risked. An entirely different matter would be a decisive transition that would leave no relations between the peasant and the *pomeshchik* except those that could be established by means of mutual agreement.

A. A. GOLOVACHEV, January 1858

These pages devoted to the provincial gentry committees in no way constitute an exhaustive study of the gentry's organized discussion of peasant reform. A general study of the formal projects of the committees has been made—by A. A. Kornilov in 1904[1]—but an analysis of the official projects alone is of limited value for a study of those broad issues of gentry concern which are the subject of this section, and of this book in general. Such an analysis is of limited value because the official committee projects, being restricted, to a greater or lesser degree, to the framework dictated by the government's instructions, afford only a dim, at best an indirect, view of the gentry's real concerns.

There do exist more extensive sources for the study of the gentry debate—the records (comprising the committee minutes, written opinions, and various other documents) which were kept by most of the committees, and many of which have survived. But it would be out of the question for one scholar to undertake a study of the massive records of the forty-six provincial committees.[2] A compromise is therefore in order, and in the present case it is the following:

It has been decided, in approaching the study of the provincial committees, to focus primary attention on the fortunes of the liberal reform program. Several considerations have prompted this decision: (1) Because this was an identifiable program, it provides a convenient point of reference from which the variety of opinions expressed in the gentry committees can be approached; (2) Generally speaking, it was in those committees where some adherents of the liberal program were to be found where the debate was the liveliest—in short, where the issues were most clearly defined; (3) For the same reason, focus on the liberal program provides an efficacious device for judging the relationship between such factors as nation-wide or 'class-wide' concerns and local economic conditions in gentry opinion; (4) It

---

[1] 'Gubernskie komitety po krest'ianskomu delu v 1858–9 gg.' *Russkoe bogatstvo*, nos. 1–5 (1904). (The official projects of all the committees were published by the government soon after their completion.)

[2] In his study, the only general survey of the provincial committees, Kornilov studied first-hand the records of only two committees—Kaluga and Saratov.

71

is of particular importance to consider the liberal program because, as will be seen later, it was subsequently adopted by the large majority of gentry proprietors as their alternative to the government's solution; (5) Finally, as a general observation, it can be said that the liberal position was intrinsically the most interesting, because it was the most creative and 'positive', in contrast to most, though not all, opposing views, which were essentially negative reactions forced by the government's initiative in peasant reform.

With these considerations in mind, Part II begins with an account, based on first-hand study of the records, of the provincial committee of Tver province. This committee was chosen because it was the committee in which the liberal program found its most articulate and most numerous adherents. A detailed study of the Tver committee permits, at the same time, an understanding of the workings of a provincial committee, the nature of the issues discussed, and the variety of opinions expressed—in a phrase, the 'politics of a provincial committee'— which can, with due caution, be generalized for all the provincial committees. Following this study (Chapter 4), an attempt has been made to consider, in much briefer fashion, several other committees in which the debate between the adherents of the liberal solution and their opponents, within the context of local conditions, contribute to an understanding of the issues (Chapter 5). The specific choice of committees has been determined, in addition to this primary consideration, by essentially two factors: (1) Regional distribution—in an attempt to represent each of the traditionally-defined major economic-geographic regions of European Russia; (2) the availability of monographic studies or published documents (correspondence, memoirs, etc.) allowing a reasonably close acquaintance with the activities of these committees and the views of their members.[1]

[1] A considerable number of monographic studies of the reform in various provinces exist, but the majority of these (especially those produced in recent years) do not deal with the 'politics of reform' in the provincial gentry committees. See the bibliography for references.

4

The Tver Landed Gentry Prepare for Peasant Emancipation

TVER PROVINCE ON THE EVE OF EMANCIPATION

Tver province under the old regime occupied about the same territory as the present Kalinin *oblast'* in the Russian Federation of the USSR. Located in the Russian heartland between Petersburg and Moscow, Tver was one of the largest Great Russian 'non-black soil' provinces in the so-called 'Central-Industrial Region'.[1] With approximately 1,500,000 inhabitants, Tver was exceeded in population in this region only by Moscow province.[2] Though blessed with extensive hydraulic and some forest resources, this region is a forbidding land for the sower.

Two factors predominated in shaping the economic character of mid-nineteenth-century Tver province: extreme poverty of the soil, and the location of the province between the two great centers of Russian commercial and industrial life, Petersburg and

---

[1] This region included the provinces of Moscow, Tver, Iaroslavl, Kostroma, Nizhnii Novgorod and Vladimir.

[2] A break-down of the mid-nineteenth-century population total for Tver province yields these approximate figures:

Hereditary Gentry (both sexes)	7,000
Non-Hereditary Gentry (both sexes)	3,500
Peasants, belonging to the Hereditary Gentry (including approx. 20,000 'household serfs')	755,000
State Peasants (peasants living on state lands administered by the Ministry of State Properties)	500,000
Udel Peasants (primarily peasants living on lands owned by the Imperial family)	62,000
Clergy (including priests' families and women in convents)	24,000
Merchants and Townspeople	93,000

These figures have been compiled from the following sources: *Pamiatnaia knizhka Tverskoi gubernii za 1861g.* (Tver, 1862), pp. 61–2; V. Preobrazhenskii, *Opisanie Tverskoi gubernii v sel'skohoziaistvennom otnoshenii* (St Petersburg, 1854); *Voenno-statisticheskoe obozrenie Tverskoi gubernii* (St Petersburg, 1848); A. Troinitskii, *Krepostnoe naselenie v Rossii po X narodnoi perepisi* (St Petersburg, 1861), p. 49.

Moscow. Practices conducive to improvement of soil conditions, such as crop rotation and the use of cover crops, were virtually unknown in Tver, as elsewhere in Central Russia. The three-field system remained the rule, and modern agricultural practices were extremely rare, even on demesne lands.[1] These conditions, together with a harsh continental climate, allowed for a very low level of agricultural productivity. For the peasantry, the accumulation of animal fertilizer, and of night soil which was used extensively in garden plots, was a matter of primary significance. Without extensive use of fertilizer the land yielded almost nothing. The welfare of a peasant village therefore depended upon the size of the herd it possessed, which in turn was determined largely by the amount of grazing lands at its disposal. After these considerations, the most pressing problem for the peasantry was the obtaining of fuel in a land largely denuded of forests.

Most of the arable land in Tver province was devoted to two crops: rye and oats. The yield on these crops was extraordinarily meager: for rye an average yield of four-fold; for oats, from three to four-fold.[2] In the years before the Crimean War, the province at best managed to produce enough of these grains for its own needs and in an occasional good year a small surplus could be marketed outside the province.[3]

Despite its grudging rewards, agriculture remained the predominant source of peasant welfare in pre-reform Tver province, probably the least 'industrialized' of the 'industrial' provinces. Petty craft industry occupied a small part of peasant labor, and manufacturing enterprises were extremely rare on gentry estates.[4] Most manufacturing in Tver province was in the hands

[1] A study of pre-reform agriculture in Tver province has recently revealed that out of 1,960 gentry estates, crop-rotation was practiced on only 78 (roughly 4 per cent). The use of grasses and of agricultural machinery were virtually unknown in the province. V. A. Federov, 'Mezhevye opisaniia 1850kh godov kak istochniki po istorii krest'ianskogo khoziaistva v Rossii (po materialam Tverskoi gubernii)' (unpublished paper presented at the History Faculty of Moscow State University, 31 October 1962), p. 27.   [2] Preobrazhenskii, *Opisanie*, pp. 270–2.

[3] Lack of self-sufficiency in grain was frequent in Tver, as indicated by the price of grain, which was generally somewhat higher than in surrounding areas before the emancipation. *Ibid.*, p. 131.

[4] Modest enterprises for the processing of agricultural products seem to have been fairly common on the *pomeshchik* estates. These were generally run with *barshchina* labor or

of the *kuptsy* (merchants), who built their factories in towns and relied almost exclusively on the urban classes for labor.[1]

Tver province's relative 'backwardness' and its geographic location contributed to the proliferation of *otkhodnichestvo* there, the hiring out by peasants as laborers in other provinces in addition to or in lieu of cultivating the land. Although precise figures are lacking, it is clear that *otkhodnichestvo* gradually became one of the outstanding characteristics in the economic life of the Tver peasantry as, in the first half of the nineteenth century, the development of commerce and industry—especially in Petersburg and Moscow—provided increasing numbers of jobs. It would appear that in the years just prior to the Crimean War (1847–9) about 30 per cent of all adult male peasants 'went out' to work at some time during the year, the large majority for less than six months. Probably more than half of them went to Petersburg or Moscow.[2]

It was remarked long ago that the percentage of peasant households on *obrok* in Tver province before the emancipation was significantly lower than in the other provinces of the 'central-industrial' region. According to Ignatovich, the standard authority on pre-emancipation peasant conditions, 41 per cent of the landlords' peasants were on *obrok*, 59 per cent on *barshchina* or:

On *obrok* alone ... ...   33·65 per cent
On *barshchina* alone ... ...   31·59 per cent
On 'mixed obligations' ... ...   34·76 per cent[3]

by household serfs. Of the four or five per cent of the peasant population engaged in crafts, about half (eight or nine thousand) were occupied with shoemaking and blacksmithing. The majority of peasants so employed were state peasants. Federov, 'Mezhevye opisaniia', pp. 41–2; *Sostoianie promyshlennosti Tverskoi gubernii za 1850g.* (Tver, 1851), p. 51.

[1] *Voenno-statisticheskoe obozrenie*, p. 197.

[2] The first market for this labor force was the transport industry: work on ships and barges plying the inland routes from Petersburg to Moscow, on-land hauling, and in the late 40s work on the construction of the Petersburg-Moscow railway. Next came work in factories of the capitals, then forestry and general construction. Federov, 'Mezhevye opisaniia,' pp. 44–7. See also the article by E. K. Rozov, which gives a higher estimate on the number of *otkhodniki*: 'K voprosu o razlozhenii feodal'no-krepostnicheskoi sistemy khoziaistva i dvizhenii pomeshchich'ikh krest'ian v pervoi polovine XIX veka (po materialam Tverskoi gubernii)', *Smolenskii Gos. Pedagogicheskii Institut. Uchenye zapiski*, V (1957), 152.

[3] Ignatovich, *Pomeshchich'i krest'iane*, pp. 52–3; 290–1. In the other provinces of the region, according to Ignatovich's calculations, the percentage of peasants on *obrok*

Recent studies of 'mixed obligations' in Tver province have indicated that the number of peasants who were, for all practical purposes, paying *obrok* was considerably higher than Ignatovich's estimate.[1] Their authors have accordingly asserted that in Tver as in all the 'non-black soil' provinces, *barshchina* was less widespread than *obrok* and was on the decline in the first half of the nineteenth century. Moreover, if *obrok* was more widespread than *barshchina* in Tver province, it was in a peculiar way: Many peasant households retained *barshchina* obligations at the same time that some of their members went out of the province to seek non-agricultural wage work. The observation of Ignatovich and other early scholars had been correct: The economy of Tver province remained more strictly agrarian and 'feudal', less diversified than in neighboring provinces.

The patterns of landholding and obligations on the gentry estates of Tver province were roughly typical for the central Russian 'non-black soil' region as a whole. About three quarters of the tillable land owned by the gentry was in peasant usage.[2] The average land allotment for each peasant 'soul' was about four and one-half *desiatiny*.[3] Peasants on *barshchina* worked about 135 days a year for their gentry masters.[4] Most peasants who owned obligations exclusively in *obrok* paid about 17–21 silver rubles per *tiaglo* yearly.[5]

The pattern of serf-holding among the Tver gentry appears to have differed little from other central Russian provinces: A total of 3,507 estate-owners possessed 361,702 souls, or an average of 103·14 souls per serf-owner. But two-thirds of the serf-owners had less than 100 souls each, and nearly half this number had less than 21 souls each, a holding which, especially in Tver, signified

everywhere exceeded 70%, while the percentage of households fulfilling 'mixed obligations' was everywhere well below 30%.

[1] Rozov, 'K voprosu', p. 138; Rozov, 'O sushchnosti smeshannoi sistemy ekspluatatsii v Tverskoi gubernii nakanune reformy 1861g.', no. 1 (1958). *Istoricheskie nauki*.

[2] Ignatovich, *Pomeshchich'i krest iane*, pp. 294–7. Or somewhere between 40 and 50 percent of total gentry landholding, which constituted 3,500,000 *desiatiny* in the province.

[3] Rozov, 'K voprosu', p. 141.

[4] Preobrazhenskii, *Opisanie Tverskoi gubernii*, p. 103. (Rozov maintains that *barshchina* obligations had risen to four days for most peasants: 'K voprosu,' p. 139,

[5] Preobrazhenskii, *Opisanie*, p. 103; and Ignatovich, *Pomeshchich'i krest'iane*, p. 298. (The *tiaglo* in Tver province generally comprised three persons.)

acute hardship and inability to carry on a viable farming operation. Nearly half the estate-owners fell into the 21–100 soul
category.[1] Seven hundred-seventy-five gentry had estates of
100–500 souls, and this group, typically, produced the large
majority of politically and socially active *pomeshchiki* in the
province. They owned just about half the serf population. The
wealthy gentry, possessors of more than 500 serfs each, comprised a small group of 130, but owned more than a third of the
serfs in the province. The wealthiest of these, those with estates
of thousands of serfs, belonged to the salon aristocracy of the
empire and did not reside in the province. Generally owning
large holdings in other provinces as well, they had virtually no
contacts with the Tver gentry and played no role in the preparation of peasant reform in Tver.[2]

The large majority—perhaps three-fourths—of the registered
Tver *pomeshchiki* did not live on their estates permanently
or even during part of the year.[3] Although no general information is available on the whereabouts of Tver's absentee
landlords, it is probably safe to assume that these adhered to
the same pattern related to wealth and service as described in
Chapter 1.

The indebtedness of the Tver gentry to the state credit institutions was also typical, adhering to the national average in almost
every respect, save that the gentry's debt per soul was somewhat

	No. of gentry	No. of serfs
[1] Gentry without estates, but serf-owning	37	66
Gentry owning land inhabited by serfs:		
Less than 21 souls	1,105	11,498
From 21–100 souls	1,460	72,688
From 101–500 souls	775	148,413
From 501–1000 souls	91	60,635
More than 1000 souls	39	68,402

Troinitskii, *Krepostnoe naselenie v Rossii*, p. 45.

[2] Such were the Tver landowners: Count D. Mordvinov, owner of 245 villages and
7,188 souls in the province (a small part of his total holdings); General Zinov'ev,
Director of the Corps of Pages and owner of some 1,700 souls in Tver; Prince Golitsyn,
with 2,137 souls in Tver province, a small part of his holdings; Count Panin, Minister
of Justice, owner of an estate of 2,094 souls in the province and many thousands more
all over Russia. *Redaktsionnye komissii, Prilozhenie k trudam. Svedeniia o pomeshchich'ikh
imeniiakh*, IV (St Petersburg, 1860), no. XI, 6, 12.

[3] Preobrazhenskii, *Opisanie Tverskoi gubernii*, p. 103.

lower in Tver than the average. Two-thirds of the peasants of Tver province were mortgaged to the state institutions by the time of the emancipation.[1]

In most respects, then, conditions in Tver province were typical of the north-central 'non-black soil' region as a whole. The province's outstanding peculiarities were a comparatively low level of non-agricultural development, a high percentage of landlords' peasants on *barshchina*, and the widespread practice of *otkhodnichestvo* by the peasants.

Gentry Attitudes and Activities in Tver Province Before the Founding of the Provincial Gentry Committee

Little evidence remains on what was being said and done about the question of peasant reform among the landed gentry of Tver province before the publication of the Nazimov Rescript in November 1857. Of the growing number of gentry reform projects sent to the central government in the course of the 1840s and early 1850s there are none to be found from Tver province.[2] The Tver gentry, in assembly, presented no petitions for peasant reform to Nicholas I, as had the Tula gentry in 1844, nor is there

[1] Skrebitskii, *Krest'ianskoe delo*, IV, 1248–9.

Number of souls belonging to gentry of Tver province	359,759
Number of souls on mortgaged estates	
in 1855	227,010
in 1859	240,155
Amount of debts (to government credit institutions) on gentry estates	
in 1855	12,861,782 rubles
in 1859	13,684,583 rubles
Average debt per soul on these estates	
in 1855	56 rubles
in 1859	57 rubles
Mortgaged souls, per 100 souls	
in 1855	63
in 1859	66

[2] None of the numerous gentry reform projects collected by the government during the reign of Nicholas I and preserved in the Central State Archive in Leningrad appear to have been the work of Tver gentry. (These projects are to be found in the archives of the *Zemskii otdel* of the Ministry of Interior, No. 1291, and in the archives of the Main Committee on Peasant Affairs. No. 1180).

any record that the question of peasant reform had dominated the proceedings of the Tver gentry assemblies, as it had in Riazan, Smolensk and several other provinces in the late 1840s.[1] Nevertheless, it is reasonable to assume that these questions were much on the minds of the Tver gentry, in a province where the problems of gentry indebtedness and a stagnating agrarian economy were as serious as anywhere else in the Empire. The first identifiable impetus to reform in Tver province came in the 1850s and was provided by a group of young, well-educated members of the gentry class who had retired from service at an early age to occupy themselves with the improvement of their estates and with local gentry self-government. The outstanding figures in this group were A. M. Unkovskii and A. A. Golovachev.

Aleksei Mikhailovich Unkovskii (1828–93) came from a rather old and enlightened, but not wealthy gentry family,[2] which had long been one of real *pomeshchiki*, rooted to the land. No one in the family seems to have served for any length of time after the gentry's emancipation from obligatory service in 1762. Unkovskii's father had held several posts in local gentry administration, including that of gentry marshal. Aleksei Mikhailovich's early education was supervised at home by one of those ubiquitous officers from Napoleon's army who had been stranded in Russia after 1812, a Saxon named Englehardt. From his tutor Unkovskii perhaps imbibed some of the principles of French Liberalism of the revolutionary period.[3] From home in the late 1830s Unkovskii was sent to study at the Moscow Gentry Institute (*Moskovskii dvorianskii institut*), where he finished first in his class in 1843. From there he went to the famous *lycée* in Tsarskoe Selo. At the end of 1844 Unkovskii was expelled from the *lycée* after a search by

---

[1] Cf. Semevskii, *Krest'ianskii vopros v Rossii*, vol. II, ch. xv.

[2] According to Unkovskii's biographer, his ancestor Bogdan Gavrilovich Boush-Unkovskii had been granted the *votchina Dmitriukovo* in Tver province by Tsar Vasilii Shuiskii (1606–10). (At the time of emancipation, 1861, the Unkovskii estate numbered some 228 souls.) The family either came from Poland or was of the same stock as the Unkovskii line in Kaluga, which was of Tatar origin. G. Dzhanshiev, *A. M. Unkovskii i osvobozhdenie krest'ian* (Moscow, 1894), pp. 1–3.

[3] Unkovskii claimed in his recollections, in any case, that his tutor instilled in him a hatred of serfdom. A. M. Unkovskii, 'Zapiski', *Russkaia mysl'*, no. 6 (1906), p. 187.

the gendarmes uncovered a notebook in which he had written a satirical libretto (with political overtones) to a popular *opera-bouffe* called 'The Trek to Khiva'.[1]

Leaving Petersburg, Unkovskii went to Moscow where he entered the juridical faculty of Moscow University. At the university he attended lectures by Granovskii and Kavelin, and was in particularly close contact with the latter as a regular participant along with F. M. Dmitriev, Boris Chicherin and others at Kavelin's famous Sunday-morning discussions with students, where the peasant question was the continuing topic of discussion.[2] According to his biographer, Unkovskii supplemented his studies with wide reading in German, French and English jurisprudence and political economy.[3]

Finishing the university in 1850, Unkovskii took a position in the Foreign Ministry, where he assisted his uncle, M. A. Obolenskii, director of the Ministry's archives, with the publication of diplomatic correspondence. After his father's death in 1852, Unkovskii, an only son, retired from service at the age of twenty-four and returned to Tver province to run the family estate and to begin a very active ten-year career as a member of the Tver gentry. Once back on the family estate Unkovskii, perhaps under the influence of Kavelin's impassioned protest against serfdom, immediately set about improving the lot of his peasants. His first act was to offer freedom to his household serfs, only a few of whom, however, accepted the offer, much to their master's amazement.[4]

---

[1] Dzhanshiev, *A. M. Unkovskii*, p. 12.

[2] N. Koliupanov, 'Pamiati K. D. Kavelina', *Russkie vedomosti*, no. 123, 7 May 1885, p. 1. Koliupanov recalled, in describing Kavelin's Sunday-morning talks that ' . . . the dominant place . . . was occupied by the question of serfdom. At that time (the late 1840s) the students were of a different sort: The majority of them were sons of *pomeshchiki*, of slaveowners, as Konstantin Dmitrievich did not hesitate to tell them to their faces. His sharp, merciless protest against serfdom had an enormous effect. Doubt crept into the minds of all his listeners to one degree or another. . . . Involuntarily this protest was assimilated by his listeners. It somehow became shameful to regard this phenomenon (serfdom) so calmly and passively as they had before their acquaintance with K. D.'

[3] Dzhanshiev, *A. M. Unkovskii*, pp. 12–15.

[4] Household serfs (*dvorovye liudi*) comprised a special legal class of landless peasants who subsisted on the bounty of their masters while working as household servants, stable-keepers, and in a host of other occupations. In some cases they supplied the labor force

Unkovskii then proceeded to give his other peasants more freedom in their affairs[1] and to put them all on an easy *obrok*, hiring laborers in their stead. He also introduced a system of crop-rotation on his lands.[2]

Unkovskii soon went to the capital city of Tver and became involved in local gentry affairs. In the first year of his residence in Tver he was elected as a gentry deputy from Tver *uezd* to the *revizionnaia komissiia*, or control commission, which had the job of checking the collection and expenditure of local tax moneys by the provincial administration.[3] It was as a member of this commission that Unkovskii began a period of intense activity

in manufacturing enterprises on estates, and also went out on *obrok* to work in other occupations. They numbered about ten per cent of the serf population ascribed to the gentry class.

[1] The most important privilege which Unkovskii granted his peasants was the right to choose the peasants who were to stand for recruiting into the army without his interference. Although the peasant commune traditionally allotted this obligation among the peasant households that belonged to it, the prerogative of the *pomeshchik* to choose recruits himself, as a form of punishment, was one of the most powerful implements of control that he held over his peasants. The period of obligatory military service for peasant recruits was twenty-five years! Dzhanshiev, *A. M. Unkovskii*, pp. 16–22.

[2] Unkovskii, 'Zapiski', *Russkaia mysl'*, no. 6, pp. 187–8; no. 7, p. 101. Unkovskii had put the farming of his lands on an entirely hired-labor basis before 1855.

[3] The general taxes (*zemskie povinnosti*) in pre-reform Russia were the source of enormous fiscal confusion and equally enormous abuse on the part of provincial administrations. Of ancient origins, these taxes came to be defined as those revenues collected from local property for the purpose of maintaining local (i.e., provincial and sub-provincial) institutions and services; e.g., the maintenance of local roads, the post, public buildings, local police and courts. They also included special taxes levied on landed estates for the maintenance of the local gentry administration. These taxes were levied on land, on trade and manufacturing, and on the peasantry as a class, which bore by far the greatest part of the tax burden. These tax sources were traditionally abused by the provincial administrations, chiefly by being inflated to cover all sorts of expenditures not included in 'local needs'. The landed gentry, through elected deputies and their elected marshals, had in theory very considerable rights of control over the distribution of the tax burden, on the setting of its value, and on the manner in which these tax moneys were to be spent by the provincial administration. Such had been the case since the beginning of the nineteenth century, and in 1851 the entire handling of these taxes came partially under the control of the gentry. Estimates, distributions of obligations and spending of revenues were all to be managed by a committee presided over by the provincial governor but including gentry marshals and deputies elected by the *uezd* gentry assemblies (as well as deputies from provincial towns). All questions were to be decided in this committee by simple majority vote. From the testimony of contemporaries, however, it would seem that the gentry in general did not take advantage of their rights of control, and their function almost everywhere turned into a mere formality. To such a committee Unkovskii was elected in 1852 (the first to be put into existence in Tver province). Cf. Romanovich-Slavatinskii, *Dvorianstvo v Rossii*, pp. 446–76; *Entsiklopedicheskii slovar'* (Brokgauz-Efron), XXIV (St Petersburg, 1894), 514–24.

as a liberal reformer and gained a reputation as such among the gentry of his province. Here too he met Aleksei Adrianovich Golovachev, deputy to the commission from Korcheva *uezd*. With Golovachev, Unkovskii began an acquaintanceship which was to have a profound influence on the progress of the peasant reform in Tver province.

Unkovskii was a 'liberal Westerner'. His adherence to the liberal reform program as it had been expounded by Kavelin, Chicherin and others was unequivocal, and reinforced, perhaps, by personal contacts with some of its foremost exponents. As an enemy of serfdom, his arguments showed the plain influence of liberal economic doctrine. As a liberal political reformer after the emancipation, he played a prominent role in the short-lived constitutionalist campaign of 1861–2, and then, as a lawyer, devoted himself to agitation for judicial reform. He was at the same time a man of harsh judgments, strong opinions, and little tolerance for the failings of others. In his personal relations, Unkovskii was rather stiff and distant; he was not given to sociability and (as the gendarme officer in Tver had occasion to remark in a report made in 1860) although he had wide acquaintances, he was on close terms with very few. In general, one receives the impression from his memoirs and from the recollections of others about him of an entirely honorable and principled man of rather severe bearing; a man of remarkable energy, perseverance and true devotion to the cause of liberal reform.

Unkovskii cherished few illusions—even in the period in which we find him here—about Russian politics and society. He was a long way from idealization of the peasantry (in contrast to some of his acquaintances among the liberal Slavophiles), and his general opinion of his own class was not high. But Unkovskii's special contempt was reserved for the bureaucracy, an attitude he shared with so many men of his generation, and one which he never hestitated to display.[1]

---

[1] Unfortunately, most of the direct information about Unkovskii's character comes from the later years of his life, when he was bitterly disillusioned with the outcome of the peasant reform and with the general course of state politics, and was in ill health. Dzhanshiev's book contains some interesting comments about Unkovskii's personality. Especially interesting are his own memoirs (partly published in *Russkaia mysl'*), and the

Little is known about Golovachev in the years preceding the reform era, though later he was to become an influential publicist, economist, historian of Russia's railway development, and government official.[1] Older than Unkovskii by nine years, Golovachev was born into a relatively wealthy gentry family of Korcheva *uezd* in Tver province. His father and grandfather before him had served as gentry marshals in that *uezd*. Golovachev graduated from the juridical faculty of Moscow University in 1839, and in the same year was elected *uezd* judge by the Korcheva gentry.[2] During the 1840s Golovachev held several civil posts, including one in the office of the Civil Governor of Moscow and in the Third Department of the Moscow City Court.

At the same time, Golovachev indulged a strong penchant for undertaking various entrepreneurial enterprises on his estate. Beginning with logging operations to supply wood for a great steamship trade which failed to materialize (and in connection with which he became involved in several law suits), he lost half his property. Turning next to a cigarette factory, he lost more. This was followed by a steam-powered flour mill and other schemes. Born into substantial means, Golovachev and his large family were left, by the time of the peasant emancipation, with only a small part of the inherited estate.[3]

Golovachev was known in local society for his intelligence, for his knowledge of financial affairs, for his gift of oratory, and for a harsh and acrimonious temper.[4] In his views on serfdom and emancipation, as in political matters generally, Golovachev

recollections of one of his daughters (S. A. Unkovskaia, 'Vospominaniia' and etc.), preserved in the manuscript collection of the Saltykov-Shchedrin Library in Leningrad (f. 1007) (Unkovskii married in 1865).

[1] His two most significant works were: *Desiat' let reform* (St Petersburg, 1872) (an influential liberal critique of the financial, *zemstvo*, and judicial reforms); and *Istoriia zheleznodorozhnogo dela v Rossii* (St Petersburg, 1881).

[2] The office of *uezd* judge (*uezdnyi sud'ia*), who together with two associates formed the *uezd* court, was elective by the gentry. A remunerative office which granted the holder eighth rank in the Table of Ranks, it was held for three years. A court of first instance, it was a strictly gentry tribunal and did not hear cases involving peasants or other estates. Romanovich-Slavatinskii, *Dvorianstvo v Rossii*, p. 465.

[3] PD. f. 265, opis' 2, no. 2911, *Arkhiv zhurnala Russkaia starina*, no. 6828. Unkovskii, A. M., *Materialy k ego biografii (rasskazy ego i o nem)* (1889), pp. 96–8a. On the eve of emancipation, Golovachev had an estate of about 140 souls.

[4] *TsGAOR, f.* 109, no. 11, part 14, pp. 159a–60.

occupied a position which was for all practical purposes identical to that of Unkovskii.

With Golovachev, an impulsive man given to violent argumentation (an inclination which was later, in 1859, to lead him into a libel suit with the provincial gentry marshal), Unkovskii, himself more subdued, but also strongly opinionated, found an immediate identity of aims. Together they set out to reform the bureaucratic administration, beginning with one of its most abused functions, the local tax administration. Exercising their rights as gentry deputies on the control commission, Unkovskii and Golovachev proceeded to challenge, loudly and insistently, the provincial administration's abuse of tax funds. Their outraged discovery that the other gentry deputies paid no serious attention to the financial responsibilities of the administration and winked at all manner of shady dealings only increased their zealousness, the result of which was to be expected: They succeeded in winning the enmity of the majority of the commission's members and of the provincial administration headed by the governor, A. P. Bakunin, an old-fashioned (that is, not very honest) bureaucrat whose lack of sympathy with the government's reform plans and lack of popularity among the Tver gentry led to his removal in November 1857.[1]

In 1853, Unkovskii was elected *uezd* judge in Tver *uezd*, a post evidently offered him by the local gentry out of sympathy with his attacks on the provincial administration.[2] This function occupied Unkovskii from 1854 to 1857, during which time he devoted himself to reforming the court, which was ridden with graft and accumulated neglect.[3] For his work there, as well as for his reputation as an opponent of serfdom, Unkovskii won wide recognition among the Tver gentry, recognition which lead to his election as provincial gentry marshal in 1857.

---

[1] Bakunin described the activities of Golovachev and Unkovskii on the control commission in a complaint written against the former in 1857: 'Golovachev . . ., from the very opening of the provincial committee on general taxes in 1852, in all its meetings and in all subsequent gentry assemblies, allowed himself, together with . . . Unkovskii, openly and brazenly to accuse the provincial administration of illegal use of funds . . .' *TsGAOR, f.* 109, no. 37, part 14, pp. 14–15.

[2] Dzhanshiev, *A. M. Unkovskii*, pp. 23–24.   [3] *Ibid.*

The Tver gentry prepare for emancipation

In February 1857, Unkovskii, a young man of twenty-eight, of no particular means and without influence in Petersburg, was nominated and confirmed in office as Tver provincial gentry marshal. His election to that office was to have great influence on the progress of the reform in Tver province, particularly on the work of the provincial gentry committee (where Unkovskii, as marshal, was to preside). The fact and circumstances of his election reveal much about the mood of the Tver gentry on the eve of the emancipation.

The direct sequence of events leading to Unkovskii's election as provincial marshal began early in 1856 when the current provincial marshal, Ozerov, made the mistake of offering the government—without consulting the gentry—a school building in Tver (the property of the gentry corporation) for the use of the Arakcheev Cadet Corps. In an extraordinary meeting held in the summer of 1856, the gentry, inspired by an impassioned speech from Unkovskii, condemned Ozerov's action.[1] Ozerov, a *pomeshchik* of reactionary views who had been elected marshal for the typical reason that he had once served as tutor to the Grand Duke Konstantin Nikolaevich and was thus supposed to have connections at court, was put in an awkward position vis-à-vis the government as a result of this affair: He was refused confirmation in office after having been duly reelected in December 1856.[2] Left without a marshal, the Tver gentry met in extraordinary assembly on 8 February 1857, to elect candidates for that office.

What happened at that extraordinary assembly was described in some detail by the gendarme officer in Tver in a report to the Third Section: It is worth quoting:

On 8 February of this year 1857 [the report stated] elections were held, in accordance with the Imperial wishes, for the selection of two candidates for the office of gentry marshal.

Gentry marshal of Tver *uezd* Balkashin, acting provincial gentry marshal, . . . having read a list of persons eligible to be candidates for

---

[1] The speech has not been preserved. Unkovskii evidently spoke against founding a military school, favoring an institution which would provide 'a general humanitarian education'. *Velikaia reforma*, v, 119; Unkovskii, 'Zapiski', no. 6, pp. 190–1.
[2] *Ibid.*

the office ... allowed a vote to be taken for Privy Councillor Doma-
lov, who failed to receive the required number of ballots ... After
this followed balloting on *Gospodin* Chasnikov, who received 99 votes
... After this the acting marshal appealed to all the gentry who were
eligible for election [to stand as second candidate; Chasnikov had
received the required number] ... No one responded to this appeal.
After long pleading from the gentry, Collegiate Assessor Prince
Golitsyn agreed to election as the second candidate, and received 109
positive votes against 85 negative, thus becoming the second candidate.
Balkashin, on the basis of Statute 151 and in accordance with Imperial
instructions, should have stopped all balloting after the election of
two candidates. But distracted by the convictions of a party of young
men, he decided to allow voting on a third candidate, Collegiate
Secretary Unkovskii. The election of this young man proceeded in a
strange fashion: There were three ballotings. The first time, when the
gentry of Kashinsk *uezd* refused to vote on Unkovskii after the election
of two candidates had already taken place, many young gentry of
Tver province, after protestations based exclusively on their opinions,
and quite mistaken opinions at that (evidence of which is that they
had been seduced by the spirit of the Unkovskii faction), announced
that although they had indeed elected two candidates, it was not
prohibited by law to elect still other candidates after that.

One *uezd* against a large number, and receiving, moreover, no support
from the acting marshal, could not quarrel and therefore the gentry
of Kashinsk *uezd*, though convinced of the correctness of their argument, decided to vote on the Unkovskii nomination. There followed
the second balloting, which ... resulted in 104 'for' votes, 91 'against'
... Then the third balloting was taken and Unkovskii this time
received 112 votes against 82, making him the first candidate.[1]

The three candidates' names, with Unkovskii's in first place,
were presented to the Ministry of Interior for confirmation. In
spite of the governor's protestations about the irregularity of
Unkovskii's election (laced, according to Unkovskii's memoirs,
with references to his expulsion from the *lycée* and his acquaintance, in 1844, with the notorious Petrashevskii),[2] Unkovskii
was duly confirmed as Tver gentry marshal.

[1] *TsGAOR, f.* 109, no. 37, pt. 14, pp. 8–9a.
[2] Unkovskii, 'Zapiski', no. 6, pp. 189–91.

The Tver gentry prepare for emancipation

That Unkovskii had come to the gentry assembly at the head of an organized 'faction' to capture the election for himself, as the above account seems to suggest, is unlikely.[1] But his election was hardly an accident, and it is revealing both about developments among the Tver gentry and in the Ministry of Interior. The actions of the Ministry in relation to the Tver gentry elections appear at first glance to be contradictory: The Ministry had overruled the recommendations of its own official, the governor of Tver, in favor of two private individuals who were intent on discrediting the provincial administration, an organ of the Ministry. In fact, the Ministry, where to that time all active government preparations for peasant reform were concentrated, was pursuing a definite plan: In preparation for reform it was conducting a sort of purge of provincial administrations, clearing the way for the appointment of people known to be favorably disposed to emancipation.[2] Unkovskii's friend Golovachev had had a similar experience at the time of the regular gentry elections in December 1856. Elected first candidate for the office of *uezd* marshal in Korcheva, Golovachev had been refused confirmation by the governor. Golovachev took the case before the provincial assembly, claiming that the governor had acted out of personal hostility because of his 'frequent discovery of improper procedures on the part of

[1] At least there is no mention of such an organized faction or party either in Unkovskii's memoirs or elsewhere in the archival records.

[2] The appointment of Count P. A. Baranov as Governor of Tver in November 1857, and of V. A. Artsimovich as Governor of Kaluga in August 1857 are two of the best-known examples of this policy. Both men are examples of a type of bureaucrat on which the government depended heavily in carrying out the reform. Baranov, who replaced Bakunin, a reactionary in bad odor with the local gentry, was a Lutheran nobleman from the Baltic Region (Estland) whose mother, a *Stats Dama* in the Court of the Empress Maria (wife of Nicholas I) had won the title of Count for her heirs. Of a military background (he was a major-general), Baranov was sympathetic to peasant reform, if not its active champion. As governor of Tver he gave his support to the efforts of Unkovskii as president of the provincial committee and was responsible for the appointments of two energetic opponents of serfdom to the provincial committee as 'members from the government'. Artsimovich, also of the Baltic nobility (Lithuanian), a Catholic from a family of bureaucrats in Russian service, was a typical 'enlightened bureaucrat' committed to reforming the bureaucracy from within. A man of firm principles and considerable ability, Artsimovich was more positively committed to reform than Baranov, and had a very great influence on the progress of the reform in Kaluga province. *GAKO, f.* 466, no. 917, pp. 1–15; A. A. Kornilov, 'Krest'ianskaia reforma v Kaluzhskoi gubernii pri V. A. Artsimoviche', *Sbornik, izd. v pamiati V. A. Artsimovicha* (St Petersburg, 1904), pp. 149–401.

the commission on general taxes', and proposed that a gentry deputation be formed to seek explanations from the governor. This was unanimously approved, and, when the governor refused to deal with the deputation, the assembly turned to the Ministry of Interior. The Ministry referred the case to the Committee of Ministers, which found Bakunin's action improper and ordered the confirmation of Golovachev as gentry marshal of Korcheva *uezd*.[1]

These were uncommon actions. The government, which at this point had no reason to expect anything but hostility from the mass of the gentry toward its abolitionist plans, was seeking supporters. The fact that Unkovskii and Golovachev enjoyed reputations as proponents of emancipation undoubtedly helped them secure government confirmation in their election as gentry marshals.

The activities of Unkovskii and Golovachev in these years and the support afforded them by the Tver gentry are exemplary of a movement among the Russian gentry in the last years of Nicholas' I's reign, and especially after the Russian defeat in the Crimean War: A new interest in the organs and functions of gentry self-administration, and the expression through them of strong criticism of the bureaucratic administration. The Russian gentry, called upon in November 1857 to participate in the 'improvement of peasant conditions', from the beginning spent a large portion of its efforts—in the provincial committees and elsewhere—attacking the bureaucratic administration and its provincial institutions in particular. This attack was, to be sure, composed of various currents of opinion. One of the strongest, undoubtedly, came from conservative groups hostile to peasant reform, which saw their main enemy in the *reforming* bureaucracy. But another current of gentry opinion, that represented by Unkovskii and Golovachev, composed a liberal opposition which, neither content with the government's reform plans, nor willing to restrict its demand to the question of emancipation alone, was to go on, after 1861, from a critique of the bureaucracy to elaboration of a semi-constitutionalist program which was to some

[1] *TsGAOR, f.* 109, no. 37, pt. 14, pp. 3–4, 14–17.

extent reflected in the *zemstvo* reform of 1 January 1864, and the judicial reform of the same year.[1] Golovachev, and especially Unkovskii, had gained wide support amongst their peers in Tver province in their battle against bureaucratic corruption. However, by no means all their supporters were of one mind with them on the question of peasant reform, a subject on which their views had not, as yet, been fully elaborated. The time for that was to come shortly.

THE TVER GENTRY DISCUSS EMANCIPATION: THE UNKOVSKII–GOLOVACHEV MEMORANDUM AND THE GENTRY ASSEMBLIES OF 1858

The Memorandum

In April 1857, the new gentry marshal of Tver province journeyed to Petersburg to pay his respects, according to custom, to the Emperor. Alexander II, in this period, when the government had not yet decided to proceed publicly with plans for emancipation, was intensely concerned about gentry attitudes on this question. He took Unkovskii aside and questioned him at length about the Tver gentry. Hearing from Unkovskii that the Tver gentry 'recognized the need for reform', Alexander confided that the time had come to put an end to the 'patriarchal relations between peasants and *pomeshchiki*', that they should, however, be done away with gradually, perhaps by regions, and that the peasants must be freed with land. He also told his listener that he could discuss reform and what he had been told with the Tver gentry, but 'on the quiet...in order to prepare public opinion'.[2]

Elated by this audience, Unkovskii returned to Tver and informed the gentry, not very quietly, of the government's intention to proceed with peasant reform. Unkovskii, Golovachev and several other *uezd* gentry marshals proposed to the gentry, gathering in the summer of 1857 for *uezd* assemblies, that they begin by voluntarily forfeiting various arbitrary powers

---

[1] The government was aware from the beginning that it was faced with a 'dual opposition', conservative and liberal, within the gentry. Solov'ev, 'Zapiski', xxx, 749–51.
[2] Unkovskii, 'Zapiski', no. 6, p. 193.

over their peasants (as Unkovskii had already done on his own estate).[1] Discussions, primarily with Golovachev, followed about the necessary principles of reform.

The publication of the Nazimov Rescript on 20 November 1857, found Unkovskii and Golovachev prepared to offer a detailed critique of this first attempt by the government to define publicly the fundamental principles on which it intended to carry out peasant emancipation. When the Rescript and accompanying circulars of the Ministry of Interior reached Tver, Unkovskii called a meeting of the *uezd* gentry marshals, to whom these documents were shown. They all joined with Unkovskii in objecting to various parts of the Rescript, particularly the statements affirming retention of certain aspects of *pomeshchik* control over the peasantry. At the request of the gentry marshals, Unkovskii and Golovachev set about writing a formal critique of the Rescript, including their own positive program for reform.[2]

The Unkovskii-Golovachev memorandum (*zapiska*), sent to Alexander II in December 1857,[3] was destined to become the basic document of the 'liberal gentry opposition' (it was, in fact, the first widely-circulated statement representing that position and can, therefore, be considered its 'birth-declaration'); and its positive program was incorporated, almost intact, in the project later presented to the government by the Tver provincial gentry committee. The document therefore demands careful examination.[4] It was written in two parts: The first, the work of Golovachev, criticized the government's reform plans. The second, by Unkovskii, presented a positive program of reform.[5]

Why was emancipation necessary? Because serfdom was in a process of rapid decline, as evidenced most particularly in the deterioration of relations between the *pomeshchiki* and the pea-

---

[1] *Ibid*. The gentry, as a body, did not act on this proposal.

[2] Unkovskii, 'Materialy k biografii', pp. 44–6a. In his unpublished memoirs Unkovskii claimed that he and Golovachev were instructed by the gentry marshals to compose this memorandum. Considering their activities at that time, it seems likely that he and Golovachev took the initiative and talked the gentry marshals into giving them their support. *Ibid*. [3] Dzhanshiev, *A. M. Unkovskii*, p. 41.

[4] The following analytical comments are supplemented by Appendix I, consisting of major statements from the text.

[5] *TsGAOR, f.* 109, no. 1960 (*Zapiska Golovacheva, A. A. i Unkovskogo, A. M.*, 1858).

sants (the authors of the *zapiska* summoned the specter of a *Pugachevshchina*). This situation had arisen from two fundamental causes, one economic in nature, the other of a moral or 'intellectual' order: On the one hand the advent of 'free labor', by which servitude had been tried and found wanting. The presence of servile labor in agriculture provided a security which stultified any interest in progress, whereas other industries, lacking this security, were compelled to constantly improve themselves. The contrast between the success of other branches of activity and agriculture naturally provoked thoughts about the harmfulness of serfdom to the economy. Alongside this objective progress of free labor in Russia there had also developed growing recognition of the evils of serfdom. This was the process of 'enlightenment' or 'civilization', which had separated the gentry from the people but had also ultimately led to a recognition among them of the injustice of serfdom. In other words, the development of domestic industry based on hired labor, the Europeanization of the landed gentry, and the progress of education were the fundamental causes for the weakening of the old order.

What was wrong with the government's plans for gradual emancipation as enunciated in the Rescripts? Virtually everything. To the provision that emancipation be carried out gradually, with a transition period of twelve years, Golovachev and Unkovskii replied that the result of such delay would be class war, the peasants being convinced that only the *pomeshchiki* stood between them and real freedom. Indeed, the piecemeal legislation with which the government had been groping toward emancipation over the preceding half-century had been largely responsible for the growing antagonism between the classes—for the simple reason that the peasants had come to the conclusion that the government wanted to free them but was prevented from doing so by their masters. The provision giving the peasantry only the *usad'ba* in property (in return for redemption payment) was denounced as imprisonment for the peasant, who would be unable to leave and thus forced to rent or buy immediately-surrounding lands on any terms the *pomeshchik* might devise. That all land, excluding the *usad'ba*, was to remain the property of the *pomeshchik*, yet with a portion of it in fact alienated to peasant usage (evidently forever), the authors called a fiction; and a fiction which would result in the ruination of the gentry who would be left without the capital necessary to undertake the exploitation of the land left to them and unable to count on the proper fulfillment of peasant obligations. For the same reasons, the retention of labor rent was out of the question—it was both incompatible with freedom for the peasants and would leave the gentry without capital. Retention of police and administrative authority for the *pomeshchik* was likewise denounced as incompatible with any idea of emancipation; it would lead to a situation worse than serfdom itself, since the *pomeshchik* would retain power over the peasants, but no responsibilities toward them. With one point only of the Rescripts did the authors concur: The peasant commune should be retained after the emancipation, for the sake of social stability and to insure proper payment of taxes and other obligations.

What, then, should be done? This was spelled out in great detail, particularly in the second part of the *zapiska* composed by Unkovskii. The solution was the liberal one advanced earlier by Chicherin, Kavelin, Koshelev and others: Complete elimination of *pomeshchik* authority over the peasants, and the supplying of the peasants with field land as well as the *usad'ba*, in return for the payment of redemption which was to be financed by the government. Golovachev and Unkovskii particularly stressed the necessity of instituting emancipation immediately, avoiding altogether or in so far as possible any 'transition period'. Unlike most earlier liberal proposals, the memoir, written as a response to the government's Rescripts and claiming to represent the best interests of the landed gentry, laid out a detailed program dealing with practical questions of ways and means.

The basic questions which Unkovskii sought to answer in the *zapiska* were three: Granting that the peasants would have to be emancipated with land and the gentry properly remunerated, what exactly were the peasants to receive, for what exactly were the *pomeshchiki* to be remunerated, and how was remuneration to be arranged.

The Tver gentry prepare for emancipation

The peasant was, of course, to receive land in property, in addition to the *usad'ba*. But how much land? Unkovskii's answer to this question was in effect: 'As much as necessary for subsistence but no more'. This amount could not be accurately determined either by setting up general figures for a given territory or by observing existing allotments: The first was impracticable because of the infinite variety of soils and other conditions: the second because the amount of land in peasant usage depended on the whim of the *pomeshchik*.[1] Unkovskii proposed 'voluntary agreement between the *pomeshchiki* and peasants, placed within certain limits for the control of arbitrariness',[2] namely by the establishing of a minimum quantity of land in each region as the amount the *pomeshchik* was *obliged* to give to the peasants.

To the second question, Unkovskii's answer was unequivocal: The *pomeshchiki* were to be renumerated both for the land removed from their control and for the freed peasants themselves. It was obvious, he argued, that the value of gentry estates consisted not only of land but of the people who lived on the land and worked it as well. This was especially true in certain areas (like Tver province) where uninhabited land was virtually worthless. It was an obvious fact that for the gentry the peasants represented a form of property, and it would be manifestly unjust to suddenly deprive them of this property without remuneration. The peasants, however, should not be obliged to shoulder this entire burden. They should pay for the land which they received, but they should not have to redeem their servitude, for which they were in no way responsible. This burden should be borne, then, by 'all classes in the State, and [by] all property without exception'.

The significance of this proposition was made clear in the discussion of the general question of how remuneration was to be arranged. 'Reimbursement', Unkovskii wrote, 'must be based on money capital and presented to the *pomeshchiki* in the form of fully guaranteed, interest-bearing bonds'.[3] Thus it was the state

[1] That is, essentially, on whether the *pomeshchik* had decided to cultivate demesne land with *barshchina* labor, or had 'opted out' of direct production and turned all the land over to *obrok*-paying peasants.

[2] *Ibid.*, p. 64a.   [3] *Ibid.*, pp. 64a–65.

which was to pay for the redemption of the peasants, covering this expenditure by revenues which would be drawn from 'all classes . . . and all property'. The state was also to finance the redemption of the peasant lands, by providing interest-bearing bonds immediately to the gentry—in effect, by floating a long-term loan to the peasant communes. In other words, the redemption operation, while financed entirely by state credit, was to consist of two distinct financial arrangements, the feasibility of which Unkovskii argued at great length: It was wrong, he insisted, to reject the only reasonable method of emancipation out of fear for the stability of the state finances. The redemption operation could be implemented without upsetting the state budget.[1] For redemption of the peasants (that is, of their labor value), Unkovskii proposed the issuing of four-percent bonds to the *pomeshchiki*, with annual payment of five percent (one percent going to capital reduction) covered by a tax levy on individuals and property in each province. The size of this payment could be based on the average sale-price of peasants without land, or about fifty or sixty rubles per peasant.

Reimbursement for the land was simply to be made by the peasants themselves, and would be guaranteed by the land which they held. The size of peasant obligations for the land should be determined by the provincial committees on the basis of existing land prices on gentry estates. Unkovskii estimated that the annual payment in Tver province would be about five rubles per soul, a light *obrok*. (No arrears would be forthcoming, he added, if failure to pay promptly were accompanied by the threat of loss of the land allotment and deportation to Siberia.) For the implementation of this dual operation, Unkovskii proposed the creation of circulating banks in each province, to be administered by publicly-elected officials, not by irresponsible *chinovniki*.

This last proposal was but one example of a fundamental point raised by the *zapiska*, and a harbinger of future conflict with the government: Unkovskii and Golovachev repeatedly argued that the question of emancipation went far beyond the bounds of merely 'improving peasant conditions' in which it had been

---

[1] For the details of Unkovskii's plan see the excerpt from the *zapiska*, Appendix I.

placed by the government Rescripts. 'All sides of the public life of the people,' Golovachev remarked in his opening statement, 'are connected, to one degree or another, with these questions and therefore will need reforming'.[1] The question was thus one of general reform and of public participation in the process. Unkovskii accordingly concluded his half of the *zapiska* with the demand that the role of the provincial gentry committees summoned by the government be as great, if not greater, than that of the government itself. The committees, he insisted, should not be bound by the framework of the government instructions, but should have the right 'to put forth and discuss all necessary matters with complete frankness', including provincial finances, the structure of the rural administration and the local police, and other institutions.[2]

In all its essentials, the Golovachev-Unkovskii *zapiska* was a restatement of the liberal reform program which had been in circulation in Russia since 1855.[3] It was at the same time an expansion of the liberal program to incorporate a critique of the newly-announced government plans and the elaboration of a much more detailed positive program, drawn up with particular attention paid to the gentry and their circumstances. The *zapiska* was addressed to the Emperor (that is, to the government), for whom the main message was the feasibility and desirability of a state-financed redemption operation. It had another major, though unnamed, addressee, the landed gentry, who were urged to understand that immediate emancipation with land was in their own best interest. In proposing that the gentry committees be given the right to discuss freely both emancipation and all other necessary reforms, its authors were obviously hoping to find support for the liberal reform program among the landed gentry. The extent to which their hopes were justified was revealed, in Tver province and elsewhere, in succeeding months.

[1] *Ibid.*, pp. 3–3a. [2] *Ibid.*, pp. 74a–75.
[3] In particular, the arguments of Golovachev and Unkovskii—especially those on the necessity of emancipation with land and on the justifiability of alienating gentry land— bore a striking resemblance to the arguments used by Chicherin in his 1856 article 'On Serfdom'. (See above, pp. 43–5.)

The Gentry Assemblies

The Unkovskii–Golovachev *zapiska* immediately received wide circulation all over Russia, and became one of the best-known projects for peasant reform of the day. It was known, certainly, by most of the gentry in Tver province.[1] In accordance with procedures provided in the Rescripts, the Tver gentry gathered in their *uezd* assemblies at the end of January 1858, to discuss the government's instructions and reform in general. The Unkovskii–Golovachev *zapiska* was presented at these meetings and widely discussed.[2] On 16 February 1858, the marshals and deputies from all the *uezdy* of the province gathered in Tver, where they heard the resolutions of the recent *uezd* assemblies and several individual opinions. Following its deliberations, the provincial gentry assembly composed a protocol of the following contents:

Fully supporting the noble design of His Majesty, and finding that the improvement of peasant conditions is possible only through the liquidation of serfdom, the gentry of Tver province have expressed complete readiness in their *uezd* assemblies to fulfill the Imperial will. In addition, the gentry of Zubtsov, Rzhev, Bezhetsk, and Kaliazin *uezdy* have expressed the desire to guarantee to the peasants the use of an adequate quantity of land, and to present to the peasants the redemption of their persons and of their *usad'ba* as property. The gentry of Tver, Korcheva, Torzhok, and Ves'egonsk *uezdy* have found it more suitable to present to the peasants the right and opportunity to redeem from the *pomeshchiki*, along with their person, not only the *usad'ba*, but parcels of land capable of fully guaranteeing their welfare as well. The *pomeshchiki* are to be reimbursed by means of public credit. The gentry of Staritsa, Kashinsk and Ostashkov *uezdy* have expressed the wish to free the peasants from servile dependency personally, with

---

[1] It was sent to all the gentry marshals of Tver province. Unkovskii later expressed regret that this *zapiska* was distributed in large quantities. According to him it was copied in a warped version. Unkovskii himself presented to the Grand Duchess Elena Pavlovna a fuller version with a 'very sharp' conclusion, which he had not dared send to the Emperor. Elena Pavlovna, the most outspoken proponent of emancipation in the Imperial Family, evidently made this version well-known, an action probably instrumental in creating Unkovskii's reputation as a radical in Petersburg government and court circles—a reputation which was soon to stand him in no good stead. Unkovskii, 'Materialy k biografii', pp. 69–69a.

[2] V. Pokrovskii, *Istoriko-statisticheskoe opisanie Tverskoi gubernii*, I (Tver, 1879), 161–2; Dzhanshiev, *A. M. Unkovskii*, pp. 71–2.

presentation to them in use, but not in property, of both *usad'ba* as well as field land, in a quantity sufficient for guaranteeing their welfare.[1]

Thus four *uezd* assemblies (Zubtsov, Rzhev, Bezhetsk, and Kaliazin) seem to have accepted the government's program as it was. Three assemblies (Staritsa, Kashinsk, and Ostashkov) refused to accept the idea of granting any land to the peasants, even the *usad'ba*. Four assemblies (Tver, Korcheva, Torzhok and Ves'egonsk) expressed fundamental agreement with the program of Unkovskii and Golovachev. The extent to which these latter groups of gentry were influenced by the Unkovskii-Golovachev *zapiska* can best be illustrated by quoting one of their resolutions, that of the Korcheva gentry:

... Any semi-dependency [of the peasants] will give birth to complete disorder in the relations of the two classes. [Real freedom will come] not in words, but in reality, when freedom of the peasant is guaranteed by property. [Emancipation with only the *usad'ba*] will not permit the peasant to retain his settled way of life nor will it provide any guarantee for the interests of the *pomeshchik*. Moreover, there is no way to assure the punctual receipt of state taxes and obligations. Therefore the peasants must of necessity be freed with field, meadow and pasture land in quantity required for their economic welfare and guarantee of all state obligations. Justice demands that the *pomeshchiki*, in such an emancipation of the peasants, be fully reimbursed both for the land removed from their control and for the people, for the value of each estate consists not of the land alone, but of the people as well; the more so because in certain areas unpopulated land does not have sufficient value. Reimbursement of the *pomeshchiki* can be arranged with the help of state credit, by means of fully guaranteed interest-bearing bonds.

For this purpose [arranging land allotments, prices, etc.] it will be necessary to expand the right granted the [provincial gentry] committees, and to allow them to demand necessary information from all

[1] Pokrovskii, *Istoriko-stat. opisanie Tverskoi gub.*, p. 162. (It should be noted that the version of this document published by Pokrovskii contains several errors in the naming of *uezdy* adhering to the three basic positions described. These errors have been corrected in the above translation, in accordance with other documents presented by Pokrovskii himself, and other sources.)

institutions and persons, to discuss the financial resources of the province, and those reforms which will be necessary for the organization of the courts, the police, and other institutions connected with them. The measures so compiled must be discussed and unified in a general meeting of deputies from the whole State, one deputy from each *uezd*. If the measures of the committees are considered in any other fashion, and are altered by administrative action, then the very purpose for the founding of the committees must inevitably perish.[1]

This resolution of the Korcheva gentry, whose marshal was none other than Golovachev, was written, not surprisingly, in the very language of the *zapiska*. It included all the major points of Unkovskii's program, plus the added demand that representatives from all the *uezdy* of the Russian provinces be called to Petersburg for the codification, based on the projects of the provincial gentry committees, of the reform legislation in its final form. In effect this was a demand that the work of legislating on peasant emancipation and various aspects of local administration be taken out of the hands of the central government and turned over to a 'council of deputies' (i.e., gentry deputies). All this was a far cry from the function assigned the provincial committees by the government.

The gentry of Torzhok *uezd*, led by their marshal N. A. Bakunin (brother of Michael Bakunin, once a 'nobleman of Torzhok *uezd*' himself), supported Unkovskii's program no less unequivocally. On 5 February 1858, they had presented Unkovskii a formal pledge of support, which concluded with these words:

Our descendants will pronounce the name of A. M. Unkovskii with respect, and we, expressing to you our sincere, heartfelt thanks for your efforts...are proud to be your contemporaries. We find in the representative of our class [i.e., the gentry marshal] a man fully aware of his high calling, and the defender *not only of our rights, but of our property as well*.[2]

[1] *ORLB, fond Pogodina, M. P.* III 25/52. *Dvorianstvo Korchevskogo uezda (Tverskoi gubernii). Postanovlenie dvorianskogo sobraniia po voprosu ob osvobozhdenii krest'ian ot krepostnoi zavisimosti*, 1–3.
[2] Dzhanshiev, *A. M. Unkovskii*, pp. 76–7.

Four of the twelve gentry assemblies of Tver province stood in full support of the Unkovskii-Golovachev program.[1] All of them agreed on the necessity of redemption for the person of the peasant as well as for his land.

The extraordinary provincial gentry assembly sent the resolutions of the *uezd* assemblies to Alexander II, together with a request for permission to found a committee . . .

For drafting a project for the [future] organization of the Tver peasantry, and for a survey of means to facilitate redemption of the peasants with the *usad'ba* alone or with field land also, and for the guaranteeing of *pomeshchik* interests.[2]

This petition was answered on 16 March 1858, in a rescript to the governor of Tver province. Following established protocol the gentry were called upon to form a committee under the chairmanship of the provincial gentry marshal consisting of two deputies from each *uezd*, to be elected by the gentry owning 'inhabited estates' in that *uezd*; plus 'two experienced *pomeshchiki*' of the province, to be appointed by the governor. The order reiterated the principles established in the government Rescripts of November–December 1857, but omitted reference to the demands of the four Tver *uezd* assemblies that the peasants be presented field lands for redemption in addition to the *usad'ba*.[3]

Another extraordinary gentry assembly was called on 3 June 1858, where the deputies to the committee (plus one reserve candidate from each *uezd*) were elected. The Tver Provincial Committee For the Improvement of Peasant Conditions opened for business on 7 August 1858.

[1] It is possible that the assemblies of Tver and Ves'egonsk were not so enthusiastically predisposed to the Unkovskii program as were their colleagues of Korcheva and Torzhok. Unfortunately, their resolutions do not appear to have survived.

[2] Pokrovskii, *Istoriko-stat. opisanie Tverskoi gub.*, p. 162.

[3] *Ibid.*, pp. 163–4.

The provincial gentry committees, 1858–9

THE TVER PROVINCIAL GENTRY COMMITTEE,
7 AUGUST 1858–19 JANUARY 1859:
ITS WORK AND ITS PROJECTS[1]

The following discussion of the activities of the Tver provincial committee has two aims: To describe the activities of the committee, leading up to the elaboration of the emancipation project for Tver province; and to outline the main trends of thought within the committee, paying special attention to the 'majority' and 'minority' positions there. (The Tver committee produced two reform projects: One, the majority, or official project, was signed by fifteen members led by Unkovskii; the other, the 'minority project' was signed by nine members.)[2]

Although in the historiography of the peasant emancipation and its preparation a good deal of attention has been paid to the activities of the Tver committee, and to the activities of Unkov-

[1] The Tver committee began its work relatively late, being the seventeenth committee to open. This tardiness, in a province whose gentry were more favorably disposed to emancipation than in most other provinces, had two causes: (1) The gentry assembly for the election of deputies to the committee was called only in June 1858, after long discussion among the gentry of Unkovskii's program and other questions surrounding emancipation; (2) The members of the committee, elected then, petitioned the governor to postpone the opening of the committee until August, because of their need to attend to their agricultural operations during the summer months. This request was granted by the Minister of Interior. It may be that the request, whose author was Unkovskii, was made on his initiative in order to give him time to organize support for his program among the committee membership. *GAKO, f.* 148, *opis'* 1, no. 1878, pp. 1–3a.

[2] The sources for the study of the Tver committee are the following: *Zhurnaly Tverskogo gubernskogo komiteta ob ustroistve i uluchshenii byta pomeshchich'ikh krest'ian* (*Journals of the Tver provincial committee for the organization and improvement of peasant conditions*), vols. 1–3 (Tver, 1858–9, lithographed); and *Proekt polozheniia Tverskogo komiteta ob uluchshenii byta pomeshchich'ikh krest'ian* (*Draft project of the Tver committee . . .*) (Tver, 1859). The journals, or minutes, of the Tver committee, which were compiled day-by-day by the committee secretary D. P. Tyrtov, comprise nearly 1,200 pages of tightly handwritten manuscript. To the author's knowledge, they were the only journals of a provincial committee to have been lithographed in full. (The lithographed copies of the journals, made on Unkovskii's initiative, were primarily for the use of the committee's members. But copies were also widely distributed by Unkovskii—to the gentry marshals of the province, to other committee chairmen, and to various public and government figures. Herzen also received regular copies in London, from which he frequently published excerpts in *Kolokol*. The activities of the Tver committee were thus widely known and, coming from the most 'progressive' of the gentry committees, carefully followed.) At least two copies of the committee's journals have been preserved, one in the archives of Kalinin *oblast'*, the other in the Lenin Library in Moscow. All references in the present discussion are to the latter copy.

skii in particular, only three writers have studied the journals of the Tver committee. The first to do so was V. Pokrovskii.[1] An agronomist interested in the history of agriculture in Tver province, Pokrovskii utilized those of the committee's materials which told something about the state of the *pomeshchik* economy. He also published a few speeches made by Alexander II, Unkovskii and others, but did not undertake a general study of the committee's activities. The second writer to study the materials of the Tver committee in some detail was Unkovskii's biographer, Dzhanshiev, who set himself the task of writing a praiseful account of Unkovskii as a great liberal leader in the reform.[2] Despite the inclusion in his book of several letters by Unkovskii testifying to the contrary, Dzhanshiev chose to interpret the work of the committee as a struggle between the 'selfless liberals' led by Unkovskii, and the 'reactionaries' (*krepostniki*) (that is, everyone opposed to the majority project written by Unkovskii). In fact, Dzhanshiev did not study the activities of the committee in detail, confining himself, chiefly, to a few of Unkovskii's speeches and commentaries.

The only historian to have made a systematic study of the Tver committee was M. A. Rozum, in an unpublished dissertation written in 1940.[3] While paying some attention to the importance of Unkovskii as a leader in the preparation of the peasant reform, Rozum was concerned mainly to show that the majority of the Tver committee was far from being a united group of 'selfless liberals'. He quite rightly demonstrated that the majority of the committee were not neglecting their own interests, but were convinced that their program was the best solution not only for the peasants but for the gentry as well. It may be said that Rozum was concerned to counteract both the idealist picture presented by Dzhanshiev and the distortions of the . . .

---

[1] *Istoriko-statisticheskoe opisanie Tverskoi gubernii*, vols. I–II (Tver, 1879).

[2] *A. M. Unkovskii i osvobozhdenie krest'ian* (St Petersburg, 1894).

[3] *Tverskie liberaly v reformakh 60kh godov XIX veka* (Moscow, 1940). (Professor Rozum was kind enough to show the author a copy of his dissertation. The chapter of this dissertation which deals with the activities of the Tver committee has been published in part: 'Podgotovka krest'ianskoi reformy v Tverskom komitete', *Uchenye zapiski Kalininskogo pedagogicheskogo instituta*, vol. 10, no. 1 (1945).

So-called 'Pokrovskii School' [which has] cheapened and distorted the reform and its many progressive leaders, one of whom was without doubt A. M. Unkovskii.[1]

However, Rozum paid attention primarily to those aspects of the committee's work which showed that the majority were concerned to win in the reform a profitable outcome for the *pomeshchiki*, thereby ignoring numerous other questions. Though characterizing the differences within the majority of the committee, he did not do the same for the minority, and presented them as a block of 'reactionaries'. This is not an accurate representation, as will be shown in the following pages.

The committee's first steps

The Tver committee was opened with all the ceremony available in a Russian provincial capital. Following a solemn service in the Tver cathedral, the members of the committee, together with notables from the local gentry and the provincial bureaucracy, repaired to the gentry assembly hall, where they were addressed by the governor and by Unkovskii, who concluded his speech with these words:

All that is unjust and false must give way to good and truth, and therefore unjust relations between men give way everywhere to just and free relations. There is no longer serfdom in Europe. Now the Sovereign, in accordance with the avowed wish of our class, and proclaiming new and better times for our Fatherland, has made us instruments of that invisible popular force which, by the mysterious fortunes of Divine Providence, will irrepressibly lead men to perfection on the road to goodness and truth. And we shall take this road, guided by historical experience . . . Having before us the experience of many countries . . . we hope to complete our task in accordance with the high designs of our Monarch, and to justify the faith of our electors and the strivings of the peasantry.[2]

On this moralizing note Unkovskii began his duties as chairman of the Tver provincial committee. However high-flown the

---

[1] 'Podgotovka krest'ianskoi reformy . . .', p. 2. (This reference is, of course, to M. N. Pokrovskii, The 'dean of Soviet historical studies' until his death in 1932.)

[2] Pokrovskii, *Istoriko-stat. opisanie Tverskoi gub.*, I, 165–6.

rhetoric in which his message was couched, the message itself and the understanding behind it were clear: Unkovskii knew, as did all gentry proponents of peasant emancipation, that one of the greatest obstacles to successful emancipation was the fear and greed of the Russian gentry. He knew that, in this question, there were two effective appeals to the gentry: The appeal to their economic self-interest as a class of agrarian landowners (which Unkovskii had made in his *zapiska* in spelling out carefully that the gentry must be fully reimbursed for their losses); and the appeal to them as educated and enlightened men.

Unkovskii immediately led the committee[1] into a discussion of procedural rules.[2] In the second session, 9 August, the problem

---

[1] The Provincial committee was composed of the following deputies (listed here by the *uezdy* they represented):

Tver: A. V. Verevkin	Kashinsk: P. P. Maksimovich
A. S. Balkashin	V. P. Zmeev
(A. I. Chagin, candidate)	(M. A. Miloradovich, cand.)
Kaliazin: L. A. Rakovskii (later	Bezhetsk: P. V. Betikov (later
replaced by F. A. Shakhonskii)	replaced by M. E. Vorob'ev)
M. V. Neronov	L. A. Doroshkevich
(P. N. Shubinskii, cand.)	(P. N. Obol'ianinov, cand.)
Ves'egonsk: A. A. Kaliteevskii	Vyshnii Volochek: N. P. Kharlamov
N. A. Ushakov	N. P. Miliukov
(P. A. Izmailov, cand.)	(V. F. Ott, cand.)
Ostashkov: E. A. Kardo-Sysoev	Rzhev: V. I. Litvinov
Ia. A. Korbutovskii	N. P. Semenov
(D. N. El'chaninov, cand.)	(S. V. Lutkovskii, cand.)
Zubtsov: A. D. Kudriavtsev	Staritsa: A. N. Vul'f
(replacing V. I. Chasnikov)	P. Z. Panafidin
N. A. Zubkov	(N. A. Vul'f, cand.)
(K. S. Karamyshev, cand.)	
Torzhok: K. N. Miachkov	Korcheva: A. N. Perukhov
P. D. Kashenskii	A. A. Golovachev
(I. F. Moskvin, cand.)	(M. P. Azanchevskii, cand.)

Members from the government: N. A. Bakunin
A. V. Vel'iashev (replacing
P. I. Skazin-Tormasov)

[2] The first problem solved by the committee was the matter of establishing strict rules of debate. The hours of meeting were to be Mondays, Wednesdays and Thursdays from 11 am to 3 pm, with fourteen members constituting a quorum. The rules of debate were established as follows: No speaker was to be interrupted, the members were to speak in strict order. A subject for discussion was to be announced one day in advance by the chairman, with those wishing to speak on a given subject registering beforehand. Decision to proceed to another subject was to be decided by roll-call. All members were to have the right to submit subjects for discussion to the chairman, who was to refer their possible discussion to the floor. When the committee had decided that a sufficient number of subjects had been discussed, an editing commission was to be

of gathering data about the landed estates of the province (one of the assigned tasks of the provincial committees) was solved by a large majority vote. It was decided that time was too scarce to allow dispersal of the committee for this purpose (a procedure nevertheless followed in many provinces). The information would be solicited from the *uezd* gentry marshals, and a sub-committee was appointed for compiling these data into a unified digest. At the same meeting the committee appointed, on Unkovskii's initiative, another special sub-committee, for the drawing up of a general plan of work for the committee.[1]

Various other procedural questions were raised in the immediately following meetings, including, on 13 August, the question of the resolutions of the *uezd* assemblies. Should these resolutions, it was asked, be read before the committee and accepted as instructions for the committee? It was unanimously decided, on the proposal of N. A. Zubkov, that these resolutions not be read and that they should not have any binding force on the committee. The burden of Zubkov's argument was that these resolutions, which had been made previous to the 16 March 1858 Rescript allowing the Tver gentry to form a provincial committee, were also previous to government instructions on the principles of reform, and therefore could not serve as directives for the committee. 'These resolutions', it was decided, 'should not hinder the free decisions of the committee.'[2]

Thus, at the outset the Tver committee successfully avoided two pitfalls which proved obstructive to the progress of the debate on reform in many provincial committees: A long dismissal of the committee to allow the gathering of data about the landed estates, and a long argument over the meaning of gentry resolutions. The committee, in deciding these questions, found itself in virtual unanimity.

In the meantime the Tver gentry had been paid a visit, on

formed to draw up the actual draft project, which would then be re-examined by the committee, each article to be accepted, rejected or modified by majority vote. *Zhurnaly*, I, 8.

[1] The following deputies were elected to the sub-committee: Bakunin, Verevkin, Kardo-Sysoev, Kishenskii, Chasnikov, Balkashin, Kharlamov, Vul'f, and Unkovskii as chairman. *Zhurnaly*, I, 9.

[2] *Ibid.*, p. 12.

11 August, by Alexander II, who was engaged that summer in travelling about the provinces (in most of which provincial committees were then at work) in a sort of morale-boosting campaign among the gentry.[1] At a reception attended by local notables and the members of the Tver committee the Emperor delivered a brief speech similar to those he had made before the assembled gentry of other provinces:

I am happy [he said] to have the opportunity to express personally my gratitude to the Tver gentry, which has already shown me its devotion and readiness to assist the general welfare many times ... Now I have given you a task, important for Me and for you, the task of peasant reform. I hope that you will justify my trust. Persons, elected from your midst, have been delegated to deal with this cause. Discuss it, give it your mature reflection, seek the means with which best to devise a new status for the peasantry. Decide [this matter] in accordance with local needs, in a way that will be beneficial for you, and for the peasants, on the basis of those main principles laid down in my Rescripts. You know that your welfare is close to my heart. I hope as well that the interests of your peasants are dear to you.[2]

But then the Emperor went on to state, for the first time publicly, the government's intention to call deputies from the provincial committees to St Petersburg:

When your work is finished, the project of the committee will be sent through the Minister [of Interior] for my approval. I have already ordered that a decree be made providing that two deputies be chosen from among your members for attendance and general discussion in St Petersburg during the review of the projects from all provinces in the Main Committee.[3]

---

[1] Tver was put in a terrible fluster by the Imperial visit. The 'Catherine palace' (built by the architect Kazakov for Catherine II, who had stopped there on trips between Petersburg and Moscow) had not been sufficiently prepared for the visit. The Imperial entourage was so huge that 'enough chairs for an army division' had to be commandeered about the city. The hordes of servants accompanying the Emperor were lodged in the townhouse of a member of the local gentry, where they did a great deal of drinking and fighting, to the terror of the local citizenry. Unkovskii, 'Materialy k biografii', p. 14.

[2] S. S. Tatishchev, *Imperator Aleksandr II. Ego zhizn' i tsarstvovanie*, 1 (St Petersburg, 1911), 308–9.

[3] *Ibid.* This decree was actually made on 15 July 1858. Its official wording promised less for these deputies than did Alexander's words in Tver (the first time that the gentry

It is possible that the Emperor chose to announce this plan before the Tver gentry because of the demands which had come from them for some sort of participation by local representatives in the final elaboration of the reform legislation. Such demands were implied in the Unkovskii–Golovachev *zapiska* and had been explicitly made in the resolution of the Korcheva gentry. And only a few days before the Emperor's visit, in the meeting of 8 August, a member of the Tver committee, E. A. Kardo-Sysoev, had proposed almost that which Alexander II announced in Tver, only asking that the deputies be given much more power than the central government intended.[1] Kardo-Sysoev wanted the committee to approve his proposal and to have Unkovskii present it to Alexander II upon his arrival in Tver. He found considerable sympathy for this proposal in the committee, but it was decided that it would be improper to petition the Emperor during such a visit, and that the Emperor should be approached about this matter only after completion of the committee's project.[2]

Unkovskii, as chairman of the Tver committee, made the most of the Imperial visit. Knowing that his goal of obligatory redemption of the whole peasant allotment was blocked by the government's program for the committees (which allowed projects to include only redemption of the *usad'ba*), Unkovskii had decided to circumvent the program. He approached the Emperor's confidant Count Adlerberg (Minister of Court) with the idea of 'calling the whole allotment . . . the *usad'ba*'. What, he asked, would the Emperor think of such a definition. Adlerberg discussed the question with Alexander II, who was, reportedly, 'delighted with the idea'.[3] At this time Unkovskii also asked for, and received, the Emperor's permission to lithograph the journals of the Tver committee.[4]

was told of this plan): 'Each provincial committee . . . upon completion of its project is to elect, at its own discretion, and send to St Petersburg, two members *for the purpose of furnishing the Central Government all information and explanations that it may need during the final discussion and review of each project*'. *Sbornik pravitel'stvennykh rasporiazhenii po ustroitstvu byta krest'ian*, vol. I (St Petersburg, 1857–60), section II, item 7.

[1] *Zhurnaly* I, 6.
[2] Unkovskii, 'Zapiski', no. 6, pp. 195–6.
[3] *Ibid.*   [4] *Ibid.*

The Tver gentry prepare for emancipation

Elaboration of fundamental principles of emancipation

Once again elated by his contact with Alexander II, Unkovskii returned to the committee and promptly set about implementing his plan for including obligatory redemption of field land in the Tver project. An end to the atmosphere of apparent unanimity which had so far predominated in the committee soon came. The real factional struggle had, in fact, been going on all along in the sub-committee charged with drawing up a plan of work for the committee. The majority of this sub-committee, under the leadership of Unkovskii, had more or less arrogated to itself the responsibility not only for the task of drawing up a program of work, but also for enunciating the fundamental principles of emancipation to be adhered to by the committee—on the grounds that the sub-committee could not know how to proceed until it knew the 'general view and aims of the committee'.[1] Or, as Unkovskii argued: '...It is imperative first of all to have a clear and precise idea of the situation to which the "temporary-obligatory status" merely leads.'[2] The object of this maneuver was clearly to circumvent the restriction prescribed in the government program that the provincial committees were to concern themselves with legislation applying only to the 'temporary-obligatory period'.[3] In a meeting of the sub-committee on 14 August, Unkovskii proposed the following definition of the committee's aims:

1. Granting to the peasants civil liberty, and therefore an end to obligatory labor and all natural obligations to the proprietors ...
2. Seeking means to guarantee to the peasants a sufficient homestead, and presenting this to them as their private property.
3. Since the *usad'ba* alone does not comprise this, ... the term peasant homestead [*krest'ianskaia osedlost'*] *should definitely be understood to include not only the so-called usad'ba lands, but the entire quantity of land necessary to guarantee peasant welfare.*[4]

This protocol was approved by a majority of five in the sub-committee,[5] and then presented to the full committee for dis-

[1] *Zhurnaly*, I, 15.   [2] *Ibid.*, p. 16.   [3] See above, ch. 3.   [4] *Zhurnaly*, I, 6–9.
[5] Voting for the protocol were: Bakunin, Kishenskii, Balkashin, Vul'f and Unkovskii.
  Voting against: Kardo-Sysoev, Verevkin and Chasnikov.

cussion on 18 August. With this act there began a protracted debate in the Tver committee, which continued for many weeks and was finally to produce a formal split resulting in the writing of a minority project signed by nine of the committee's twenty-seven members. The two crucial questions in the debate were: (1) The necessity of land-redemption, and (2) the possibility of according the Unkovskii definition of *usad'ba* with the government's instructions. As a result of the passing of the protocol in the sub-committee, one of the sub-committee's members, E. A. Kardo-Sysoev, resigned in objection to the attempt by Unkovskii and his followers to force on the committee their concept of the future relations of the peasants to the land. This question was, he declared, the crux of the entire problem of reform and should be discussed in full meeting of the committee, with each member expressing his views.[1] And, in fact, with this session there began a debate on each of the three propositions presented in the sub-committee protocol.

Defending the propriety of the protocol, Unkovskii and his followers assured their doubting colleagues that...

The Imperial Rescripts and the 21 April program are only general guides. The Emperor gave each committee the right to work out the project for its province, and to defend it before the Main Committee.[2]

Or, as one adherent of the protocol put it,

We have been called for the solution of a difficult problem. Will we not make it all the more difficult by adhering blindly to the letter of the program and the circular of the Minister [of Interior]? Will we be condemned for having overcome the difficulties without the program? The victor is not judged![3]

Actually, the decision of Unkovskii and his adherents to look upon the government's instructions as 'only general guides' was not so entirely arbitrary as their opponents insisted. In his circular of 7 February 1858, the Minister of Interior had recognized as much:

In my communications [he wrote] it is not necessary to seek a detailed program for the deliberations of the committees. These ideas should

---

[1] *Zhurnaly*, I, 17.   [2] *Ibid.*, p. 43.   [3] *Ibid.*, p. 157.

be taken only as indications ... The development of these questions and their adaption to local conditions has been presented, by Imperial Rescript, to the gentry itself, unhindered by the advice, so to speak, contained in my instructions. The measures for the means of deciding all individual questions are to depend upon the considerations of the committees themselves.[1]

This declaration, which did seem to promise a certain amount of freedom of interpretation to the individual committees, was, however, superseded by just such a 'detailed program'—the government program of 21 April 1858. This program, which originated outside the Ministry, really left very little room for 'interpretations'. If a committee wished to provide its own answers to the problems of reform, it had, to a considerable degree, simply to ignore the program, and that is what the majority of the Tver committee proceeded to do.

Supporters of the protocol in the committee argued at length on the economic necessity of land-redemption, and on the benefits to be gained from it by the gentry, dwelling on the progressive effects of reorganizing agriculture on the basis of hired labor. Their argument against the retention of obligatory labor (i.e. labor rent) was formulated at one point in the following manner:

1. Compulsory labor is immoral in itself ...
2. It is unprofitable compared to free labor.
3. Occupying many workers, it produces little, ... and is therefore harmful to the State.
4. Agriculture is not advancing with compulsory labor.
5. The impending reforms are going to be difficult for us. Why repeat these difficulties in the future—and they will be inevitable if compulsory labor is left intact.
6. [Compulsory labor] is hated by the peasants, and therefore in leaving compulsory labor intact ... we can surely count on great disorders in the land, disorders that can easily develop into disturbances greater than those of the terrible revolution of [17]89.[2]

They warned that a landless emancipation or any other conditional solution would bring the same threat of rebellion and

---

[1] *Ibid.*, p. 257. [2] *Ibid.*, p. 37.

revolution. In short, they repeated, and, to a certain extent, expanded upon the arguments already produced by Unkovskii and Golovachev in their memorandum.

Let us look at the major arguments of both the defenders and opponents of the protocol as they were developed in the course of the committee's work before going on to consider the fate of the protocol and of other important, but derivative, questions.

The leading defenders of the protocol were Unkovskii and Golovachev themselves. They continued in the committee the line of argument which they had pursued in the *zapiska* of January 1858, and, in fact, added relatively little to it.

Unkovskii himself gave perhaps the best account of the motives with which he approached reform in the Tver committee:

Do not imagine [he wrote to Dzhanshiev] that I dreamed only about the best and most profitable arrangements for the peasantry . . . I was not such an altruist, nor did I know any others. Nor could I be, as a representative of the gentry. [The majority of the Tver gentry] was prepared for considerable sacrifices, not only personal sacrifices, but sacrifices for their class, but only with abolition of serfdom not only for the peasantry alone, but for the people as a whole.[1]

This was the foundation of Unkovskii's approach both to the peasant reform and to general political and administrative reform ('the abolition of serfdom for the people as a whole'). In his arguments before the committee Unkovskii repeatedly stressed three points: That 'the idea of granting the peasants personal freedom without land is to the highest degree unjust and impossible of realization'; that emancipation of the peasants with land would be not only lacking in danger for the *pomeshchiki*, but positively advantageous for them; and that the *pomeshchiki*, in an emancipation of the peasants with land, need not fear default on peasant obligations or an exodus of the peasants from the land.[2] All these points had been developed by Unkovskii in

[1] *Ibid.*, p. 133.
[2] Unkovskii's views were most extensively developed in a long 'opinion' delivered on 21 August 1858. *Zhurnaly*, I, 50–66. This 'opinion' was later published, with minor changes, in Katkov's *Russkii vestnik. Sovremennaia letopis'*, XIX:2 (1859), pp. 112–25.

his *zapiska*, but in the committee he stressed certain aspects of his argument in order to combat the misgivings of his colleagues. Arguing the impossibility of a landless emancipation, he repeated the historical argument that ' . . . Hereditary usage and attachment to the land during the course of several centuries has led the peasants to believe in their right to the land, and nothing is capable of shaking this conviction of theirs'.[1] Nor had the *pomeshchik*, he pointed out, ever had unconditional rights to the land: He had had to care for the peasants, and could not freely sell the land under them. The advantages of redemption for the *pomeshchiki* Unkovskii described at length: Rent of land, he argued, is unfeasible, for there is no reliable guarantee of peasant obligations, nor of property: Peasants will not take proper care of rented land; not properly fertilized, it will soon be exhausted. Moreover, releasing land to peasant usage only would represent unjust alienation of the *pomeshchik's* property. Only in the case of redemption would he receive his property, which 'merely takes another form' (i.e., liquid capital). To the fear that the *pomeshchik* would be deprived of labor if the peasants were provided with their own lands (a special worry of the gentry in Tver province, where agriculture yielded small rewards and the habit of leaving the province to find work was widespread among the peasantry) Unkovskii paid a great deal of attention. It was, he argued, a groundless fear. One often hears that agriculture in Tver is not as profitable as other industries, 'that the peasants all try to seek other pursuits'. Unkovskii insisted that such was not the case. The peasants have had no choice in the past when seeking work, for no market for hired agricultural labor existed; but the peasants have never quit agriculture altogether, which is proof that they do not prefer other work. Their preference for *obrok* is not the dislike of agricultural work, but of *barshchina* and direct contact with the 'patrimonial authority':

Daily experience shows us that the value of land is everywhere increasing, and therefore there can be no doubt that the application of labor to the land is not only possible but even becomes more profitable with every year that passes . . .

[1] *Zhurnaly*, I, 50.

If we have seen hundreds of thousands of our peasants travelling hundreds of *versts* to find work, is it possible to conclude that they would refuse profitable wages offered them near their homes?[1]

Furthermore, non-agricultural production in Russia is not sufficiently developed to absorb more than a fraction of the freed peasants, and in any case the *pomeshchiki* will be able to operate with half the labor force when it will consist of hired workers.

Those were the lines of argument pursued by Unkovskii in the committee. Golovachev added his own. In addition to elaborating plans for administrative reforms (see below, pp. 134–7), Golovachev's special concern was to convince his 'less far-sighted colleagues' of the feasibility of a financial operation to effect redemption of peasant lands. Both he and Unkovskii were convinced that many of their colleagues in the committee were not opposed to redemption as such, but only feared bond-issues and other financial schemes. Golovachev began this work of enlightenment before the opening of the Tver committee, with an article in *Russkii vestnik*,[2] the aim of which was '. . . to show that the interests of the *pomeshchiki* cannot and need not suffer, and to refute those objections which are most frequently circulated in public against the reform now undertaken.'[3] Here Golovachev defined the character of the argument which both he and Unkovskii were to pursue in the Tver committee: It is wrong, he wrote, to argue for emancipation primarily on moral grounds, demanding sacrifices for the 'younger brother'. It is time to advocate emancipation on the grounds of 'justice, law, and economic interest'. Repeating many of the arguments already developed in his *zapiska*, Golovachev turned his attention to the fear of inflation in connection with redemption financed by government bond-issue. Many people in Russia, including Golovachev's colleagues in the Tver committee, had been aware of the fall in the course of the bonds which had been issued to the gentry in Austria in 1849–50 for the redemption of peasant dues and services there. The difficulties which had arisen in this

[1] *Ibid.*, p. 55.
[2] 'Po povodu voprosa ob uluchshenii byta pomeshchich'ikh krest'ian', *Russkii vestnik. Sovremennaia letopis'*, XIV:1 (1858), pp. 251–68.
[3] *Ibid.*, p. 253.

operation may have had a considerable influence on Russian thinking, both among the gentry and in the government, about the possibilities of undertaking a state bond-issue. The case was, at least, much discussed, and Golovachev found it necessary to indicate the causes of these difficulties and how they could be avoided in Russia. In the Austrian lands, he pointed out, indemnification was undertaken by the Crown on the grounds of political stability, and no attention was paid to real labor and land values. Therefore the bonds issued had no stable basis. The lesson for Russia was clear: The property and labor to be lost by the Russian gentry must not be evaluated too highly, but must be in keeping with real values.[1]

Golovachev cast his appeal to 'economic interest' in these terms:

[With serf labor] there are no gentry to be found ... who have grown rich through agricultural improvements. On the contrary we see that our gentry ... grows poorer every day ...
The one principle and basic cause of this is obligatory labor, which by its principle destroys any possibility of introducing any sort of agricultural improvements. Destroy this cancer of Russian agriculture and we, the *pomeshchiki*, will no longer envy our merchantry and commercial companies. We ourselves will grow rich as they have. Assured of our livelihoods by obligatory labor, we have prepared ourselves to be either officers or bureaucrats, but never to be landowners.[2]

In the committee, Unkovskii and Golovachev modified the program of their *zapiska* in essentially only two areas: In the first place they worked out the details of local administrative reform; these were presented in Golovachev's plan (discussed below), which was almost bodily incorporated into the majority project. Secondly, they evolved a plan for a redemption operation, which had been called for in the *zapiska* only in the most general terms. In the committee, plans were elaborated for the creation of credit institutions and financial operations on the provincial level. These plans underwent considerable changes during the course of the committee's activities, and found their final form in a detailed proposal made by Golovachev at the very

---

[1] *Ibid.*, pp. 259–60.   [2] *Ibid.*, pp. 267–8.

end of the committee's existence. Here Golovachev proposed the founding of a series of private banks in the province which would sell shares under the control of the local administration. Capital for the redemption of peasant lands would thus be privately accumulated, and the state would bear the responsibility only for the ultimate guarantee of the bonds issued by the banks.[1] This plan too was incorporated into the majority project. Earlier, Unkovskii and Golovachev had insisted on a financial operation financed by the state. The shift to local and semi-private institutions reflected their growing disbelief that the government would be willing to undertake such a general operation. Their disbelief was to be completely justified.

After Unkovskii and Golovachev, the most energetic supporters of the 'majority' position were:

N. A. Bakunin. Born in 1818 on the Bakunin family estate Premukhino in Torzhok *uezd*, Nicholas Bakunin had been educated at home until 1833, when he left that famous 'nobleman's nest' to study in the Petersburg Artillery Academy. Unlike Michael Bakunin, his elder brother by four years who had preceded him as a cadet there, Nicholas Bakunin finished the course of study and served for many years in the Russian Army, returning to the family estate only in the early 1850s. Once retired on the family estate (with 567 'souls'; Bakunin lived there with his aged mother, brothers and sisters), he, like Unkovskii and many other Tver *pomeshchiki* of his generation, busied himself with 'improvements', put his peasants on *obrok* and proceeded to take an active part in local gentry affairs. Bakunin was described in a contemporary gendarme report as 'intelligent, noble of thought, and an excellent master [of his serfs]'. Shortly after the end of the Crimean War, during which he and his brothers (excepting Michael) served in the volunteers, Bakunin was elected gentry marshal for Torzhok *uezd*, and held that office while serving in the Tver provincial committee as a 'member from the government', a position granted him as an educated and articulate advocate of emancipation. Bakunin was a close associate of Unkovskii and Golovachev in the committee, and

[1] *Zhurnaly*, III, 84–104.

supported their position unequivocally. His main service to the 'majority' was to throw his weight as a 'member from the government' behind the plan for obligatory redemption. Redemption, he argued, was indeed the general wish of the government.[1]

A deputy from Vyshnii Volochek *uezd*, N. P. Kharlamov was the committee's youngest member (b. 1831). A 'middle pomeshchik' with an estate of 385 souls, Kharlamov was, after Unkovskii and Golovachev, the committee's most outspoken advocate of free labor and 'free trade':

All attempts to initiate improved agricultural practices on a commercial basis [argued Kharlamov in a characteristic speech] have proved unsuccessful as a result of the competition by farms based on obligatory labor, and as a result of the high cost of hired laborers, who are extremely hard to find in a country where obligatory labor predominates. This same high cost of free labor retards the development of our factories, to support which against the strong competition of foreign production we are compelled to resort to protective tariffs; these force us to buy the poor products of our industry for three times the price for which we could buy the products of foreign industry. Thus, obligatory labor, killing the energy of our agricultural laborers, hinders the development of our agriculture and industry, and consequently decreases the national welfare to a significant degree.[2]

Kharlamov shared almost all the views of Unkovskii and Golovachev, disagreeing substantially with them only about their advocacy of immediate elimination of *barshchina*. Despite his glorification of free labor, Kharlamov maintained that it must be the goal of a gradual transition.[3]

Deputy from Korcheva *uezd*, owner of an estate of 250 souls, A. N. Perukhov was a middle-aged retired colonel, without any particular education, but widely-read. In the committee he was an outspoken advocate of emancipation, and a close adherent of Unkovskii. Perukhov's most significant contribution to the debate was his demand for immediate transition to full emancipation for the peasants without a preliminary 'temporary-obligatory' period. To persuade his colleagues of the feasibility of such a rapid transition, Perukhov presented an elaborate plan, in the

---

[1] *Ibid.*, pp. 142–4.   [2] *Ibid.*, pp. 31–2.   [3] *Ibid.*, II, 150–4.

spirit of the remarks made by Unkovskii in his *zapiska*, for the strict administrative control of the peasant commune. The obligations of the peasants, proposed Perukhov, should be the mutual responsibility of all members of the commune, and arrears incurred within the commune should be punished by compelling it to offer up recruits for the army by the casting of lots.[1]

Another young member of the committee, deputy from Kashin *uezd*, owner of an estate of 159 souls, P. P. Maksimovich had been actively engaged in gentry affairs in the province since 1848. In the committee Maksimovich joined with Unkovskii and Golovachev in enthusiastic support of a financial operation for the redemption of peasant lands. His special argument was that only land-redemption could save Russia from peasant rebellions similar to those that had occurred in Galicia and Germany in 1846–8. Summoning the ghosts of Pugachev and Stenka Razin, Maksimovich declared:

Pugachev and Stenka Razin found deep support among the peasants, arousing them not with the outrageous lie of the pretender, but with the promise of freedom . . . Why did [the peasants] exterminate their good masters who loved them . . . ? It follows that not blindness or malice dictated their actions, but calculation and self-interest, the desire to gain freedom and the property of others.

Does this not show that while serfdom exists the tranquillity of the State is in the hands of monsters, for whom all means are fair . . . in order to gain their goal, if need be over corpses and general ruin?[2]

On questions of allotment sizes and peasant obligations, however, Maksimovich was considerably less generous than Unkovskii, Golovachev and their more unequivocal supporters. In this he was followed by more than one member of the committee's majority.[3]

Opponents of the protocol, or some part of it, argued from various points of view. Some (a very few) were opposed to granting any lands whatever to the peasants, or were against the abolition of *barshchina* (primarily V. A. Verevkin, A. D.

---

[1] *Ibid.*, I, 215–17.   [2] *Ibid.*, pp. 69–71.
[3] *Ibid.*, II, 6.

Kudriavtsev and N. P. Miliukov). Many, perhaps the largest part of them, were opposed to obligatory redemption but were in general not opposed to selling land to the peasants (Sysoev, M. A. Vorob'ev, and others). Some of these were at least as insistent as the protocol's supporters about the necessity of abolishing labor rent (especially V. P. Zmeev). Several members of the committee seem to have objected to the protocol only because it overstepped the bounds established by the government orders, or because they genuinely feared the consequences of a financial operation on the state's finances. The minority's position was essentially a negative one, in opposition to the plan for obligatory land-redemption, and it is therefore not surprising that from within the minority there were mustered only two positive alternatives to counter the majority's views and the necessity of implementing them in accordance with the protocols. These arguments were presented by Zmeev and Kardo-Sysoev, respectively.

V. P. Zmeev, who owned an estate of 558 'souls' in Kashin *uezd*, was one of the very few Tver *pomeshchiki* who had introduced a system of crop-rotation on his lands. Although one of Unkovskii's most devoted opponents in the committee, Zmeev was described by Unkovskii himself as being one of the committee's most dedicated emancipationists.[1] Like Unkovskii and his followers, Zmeev favored an immediate transition to free status for the peasants without a temporary-obligatory period, and was especially opposed to the retention of *barshchina* in any form. (It was on a motion made by Zmeev that the committee voted for the immediate abolition of labor rent.[2]) Zmeev was, however, just as categorically opposed to the redemption of land by the peasants, proposing instead perpetual retention of peasant *usage* of *pomeshchik* lands, to which they were to remain permanently bound and for which they were to pay a money rent. Such an arrangement Zmeev called a special 'Russian property law'. His avowed aims were two: To provide a guaranteed income for the gentry, which must be preserved as the only educated class and the only link between the government and

---

[1] Dzhanshiev, *A. M. Unkovskii*, p. 96.   [2] *Zhurnaly*, I, 236–9; II, 55, 97.

'the people'; and to avoid the dissolution of the peasantry. Obligatory redemption would, he was convinced, lead inevitably to the destruction of the gentry as a class, and to the formation of a proletariat through the monopolization of the land by a few rich peasants, and thus to revolution.[1] Beware, Zmeev warned his colleagues, of wild ideas currently abroad in the educated world:

The appearance of various systems of new social organization, schemes for the destruction of private property, the family circle, even the individuality of man, these are ideas incompatible with human nature, but nonetheless they have distracted society, and have toppled one of the first thrones of Europe [France in 1848] . . . [They have] threatened with destruction the whole civilization of Europe, achieved by the centuries-long struggle and sufferings of the people. What would have happened to this civilization if Russia, by the will of Emperor Nicholas, had not . . . taken up arms to restore order in Europe . . . ?[2]

There are, Zmeev announced, two basic forms of socio-economic organization: The 'agrarian order' and the 'industrial order' (*khoziaistvennyi byt i promyshlennyi byt*). In order to preserve social peace and avoid the fate of Europe (which was on the road to socialism, the inevitable end of the 'industrial order'), Russia must retain her basically agrarian structure. But Russia must also progress economically. The question was, therefore, how to develop commerce and industry in Russia without producing frightening social changes. Zmeev's answer, lengthy and at times incoherent, can be reduced to a shorthand: The necessity to pay land rent will impel the peasantry to supply the work force for the growing industry (on a part-time basis, for the peasantry will remain tied to the land). The gentry will consume the products of the new industry and thus support the industrial class. The peasants will support the gentry, and the land will support the peasants. A proletariat will be avoided, a healthy division of labor for each man between agriculture and craft will be created, and the land will remain the basis of the economy. This state is called the 'agrarian-industrial order' (*khoziaistvenno-promyshlennyi byt*).[3] With these interesting, but highly doubtful,

[1] *Ibid.*, I, 92–8.   [2] *Ibid.*, pp. 91–2.   [3] *Ibid.*, pp. 92–7.

views Zmeev, evidently in all sincerity, countered the majority's demand for obligatory redemption, which would lead, in his belief, to revolution and socialism.

Zmeev's apprehensions about the 'industrial order' and a proletariat, his argument that Russia must retain her basically agrarian structure and other comments, reflected a persistent idea current in contemporary Russian thought. Many of these ideas had been expressed in the early 1840s in the influential writings of Baron Haxthausen. For obvious reasons, the belief that industrialization, at least in its European form, should be avoided in Russia became especially widespread after 1848. It was to be frequently met with in government circles and in the writings of such influential contemporary economists as Tengoborskii.[1] In intellectual circles, the idea that Russia must avoid the fate of Europe was to be found, of course, in an extraordinarily wide range of opinion: from the Slavophiles to Herzen, Chernyshevskii and the Populists. Zmeev's particular way of arguing—his distinction between 'Russia and the West' ('Russian principles' vs. 'European principles') and other paired opposites—seem to indicate the influence of formal Slavophile thought.

Zmeev was the most theoretically-minded of Unkovskii's opponents in the committee; no others formulated their objections in such a general manner. It is possible, however, that the influence of these ideas may have been a significant factor in the hostility of other members of the Tver committee toward the idea of land redemption.

E. A. Kardo-Sysoev (b. 1815), deputy from Ostashkov *uezd*, possessed remarkable knowledge about the agricultural economy of the province, and offered some of the most serious criticisms of Unkovskii's program. One of the majority's most active opponents, he was also the first to attack Unkovskii personally. Kardo-Sysoev objected to the protocols, and to the program which lay behind them, on four grounds: (1) Alienating land to the peasants immediately would demand means which the peasants did not possess; (2) a financial operation must be avoided, for it could lead to the destruction of state credit, 'already in a

[1] Cf. Tugan-Baranovskii, *Russkaia fabrika*, pp. 422–5.

doubtful condition'; (3) sudden transition to hired labor would result in an abrupt rise in the price of grain (because of higher production costs) and would thus lead to social unrest; (4) artificial retention of the peasant commune would 'retard the natural development of rational farming', and would lead to economic ruin and the formation of a proletariat.[1] Kardo-Sysoev proposed an alternative plan, for the gradual evolution to the 'farm-system of agriculture', via elimination of the peasant commune and its most pernicious feature, periodic redistribution of land:

One can say without error that the irrational conditions of communal landholding, which deaden efforts toward improvement, will leave peasant agriculture in the same routine and the same benighted condition in which it now finds itself.[2]

Even were redistribution to be eliminated, Kardo-Sysoev argued, the division of holdings into small strips would still make improvement impossible, and the common-lands would remain neglected. Deploring the tendency of peasants to occupy themselves with non-agricultural pursuits, Kardo-Sysoev saw this, and other deplorable conditions, as the inevitable fruit of communal practices:

Vagabondage and parasitism . . ., the gradual decline of morality . . ., the false communistic practice of living on another's efforts, growing indigence and other vices . . ., all these facts speak strongly against communal practices, and in general against the existing structure of the rural communes. [By contrast] we see among the *pomeshchik* holdings, or farms, those on which operations are conducted rationally, where harvests are in a flourishing state, and marked improvement in all branches of the economy [is observed].

These *pomeshchik* farms would serve, declared Kardo-Sysoev, as examples to the peasants. But how, in fact, were the peasants themselves to become 'farmers'?

The first step to family farming would be to round out the family plots and divide them among the heads of families, so that each of these could become a renter of his plot, and, gradually familiarizing himself with [individual farming], develop his farm . . .

[1] *Ibid.*, pp. 24–5.　　　　　　　　　　　　　　[2] *Ibid.*

The commune would be left intact during a transition period, in which the mentioned unification and redistribution would take place. After this period the peasant would have the option to pay either labor or money rent for the use of the land. He would subsequently be able to save money to buy his plot and to get out of the commune altogether.[1]

Kardo-Sysoev therefore questioned the whole approach to the reform of Unkovskii and his supporters. They were proposing that the solution to the peasant question and the key to sound agricultural practices lay in the abrupt separation of the two classes and the granting to the communes of land for redemption, via an altogether risky financial operation, one of the primary conditions of which would be the forced retention of the peasant commune. They were proposing thereby, declared Kardo-Sysoev, a misguided and dangerous solution to the problems, the only satisfactory solution to which was destruction of the peasant commune.

Kardo-Sysoev's general message was extreme gradualism. His proposal that the financial solution lay in waiting for the peasant to save money to buy his plot was obviously unrealistic. His comments on the peasant commune, however, were acute, radical, even, it may be said, prophetic. Kardo-Sysoev seemed to foresee with amazing clarity the agrarian crisis which awaited Russia, and to prescribe the solution which the state attempted to apply some forty-seven years later.

Faced with the protocol and the support it was receiving from the majority of the committee, several members soon sought to reverse the committee's unanimous decision to proceed in its deliberations without consulting the local gentry. Verevkin proposed a completely local solution to the peasant question: Let every *pomeshchik*, he proposed, draw up a 'project of re-organization' for his estate, on the general stipulation that peasant obligations should not be increased. The committee would act only as a 'checking commission', and each *pomeshchik* could decide for himself the questions of redemption, abolition of

[1] *Ibid.*, pp. 11–24.

barshchina, etc. To implement the 'reorganization', Verevkin proposed a temporary 'transition period' of ten years' duration.[1] Kardo-Sysoev, only recently one of the committee's most outspoken defenders of its independence from gentry instructions, now announced that he 'wished to know the opinions of [his] electors', and that for this purpose the committee should be temporarily adjourned. Both these proposals were rejected by a large majority vote.[2]

Voting on fundamental principles and the factional struggle

On 27 August the first point of the protocol was put to a ballot and approved by a vote of 21–5.[3] Kardo-Sysoev promptly left the committee and sent a letter containing an attack on Unkovskii to be read at the next meeting. Obligatory redemption, Kardo-Sysoev wrote, is wrong: It is contrary to the government's instructions, and is being forced on the committee by Unkovskii, who is holding back the legitimate activities of the committee (i.e., legislating for the 'temporary-obligatory period') until it will be accepted. Moreover, he declared, committee members are being threatened with a *Pugachevshchina* if they do not accept the idea of obligatory redemption:

> ... Not the just preservation of property rights, which are incompatible with obligatory land-redemption, but rather superfluous reminders of Pugachev rebellions, which might reach the ears of the unenlightened masses ..., will produce that anarchy on which the idea of land redemption here developed ... depends.[4]

Unkovskii defended himself against these accusations, reminding his colleagues that: ' ... Both the order and resolution of questions had always been a matter not of my decision alone, but of the will of the committee, expressed by vote ...'[5] Unkovskii was given a unanimous vote of confidence by the committee, and a letter of censure, expressing the 'collective dissatisfaction'

[1] *Ibid.*, p. 39. [2] *Ibid.*, p. 40.
[3] *Ibid.*, p. 121. Voting against its acceptance were Verevkin, F. A. Shakhonskii, N. A. Ushakov, N. P. Miliukov, and L. A. Doroshkevich.
[4] *Ibid.* [5] *Ibid.*, p. 129.

of the committee, was sent to Kardo-Sysoev.[1] The latter attempted to read an 'explanation' of his censured opinion at the next meeting of 1 September, but many of the members, fearing he would insult Unkovskii, left the hall, and Kardo-Sysoev declined to read the 'explanation'. Instead, accompanied by the other deputy from Ostashkov *uezd*, Ia. A. Korbutovskii, he presented his resignation from the committee. The resignations were sent to the governor, who refused to accept them, and the two deputies returned to the committee on 11 September.[2]

In the meantime, debate on the remaining two points of the protocol continued, with attention focused on the questions of redemption and the definition of the term 'homestead' (*osedlost'*) as offered by Unkovskii. Several attempts by individual members were made to prevent the committee from proceeding to a ballot on these points, but on 11 September they were put to a vote and approved by a majority of one, 14–13. On the basis of this vote on the two crucial points of the protocol were formed the 'majority' and 'minority' factions in the Tver committee.[3] In the following session several members of the newly-created minority made a serious attempt to nullify the vote just taken to accept as the basic aim of the committee the presentation of the peasants in property their *prochnaia osedlost'*, 'the entire quantity of land necessary to guarantee peasant welfare'. They continued to assert that these principles were contradictory to the government's instructions. Ushakov, Kardo-Sysoev, Verevkin and Kudriavtsev questioned the decisiveness of a majority of one in such an important question and demanded that the committee should turn to the government for a way out of the blind alley

---

[1] *Ibid.*, p. 130.　　　　　[2] *Ibid.*, pp. 139–40.

[3] *Ibid.*, pp. 186–7. The 'majority': Bakunin, Skazin-Tormasov (both members from the government), Maksimovich (Kashin *uezd*), Kharlamov (Vyshnii Volochek), Semenov (Rzhev), Vul'f, Panafidin (Staritsa), Perukhov, Golovachev (Korcheva), Kishenskii, Miachkov (Torzhok), Neronov (Kaliazin), Balkashin (Tver), and Unkovskii. The 'minority': Zmeev (Kashin), Doroshkevich, Vorob'ev (Bezhetsk), Ott (Vyshnii Volochek), Litvinov (Rzhev), Zubkov, Kudriavtsev (Zubtsov), Kardo-Sysoev, Korbutovskii (Ostashkov), Ushakov, Kaliteevskii (Ves'egonsk), Rakovskii (Kaliazin) and Verevkin (Tver). Ott and Kudriavtsev, both candidates, voted in place of N. P. Miliukov and V. A. Chasnikov, respectively. The latter were opponents of the majority position, also. Miliukov later returned to the committee, but Kudriavtsev replaced Chasnikov permanently.

into which the committee had wandered.[1] Unkovskii rejected this proposal. The government, he maintained, had been informed of the decisions taken by the committee, and could initiate any action it chose to.[2] Unkovskii's ruling was supported by a vote of 14–10.[3]

With six weeks of arguing about its 'basic aims' behind it, the committee now entered the second and longest phase of its activities: a discussion of the 'temporary-obligatory status' and elaboration of the draft-project as provided by the government program. This discussion was not, however, allowed to continue uninterrupted. On 29 September, in the middle of a debate on land-allotment, V. I. Litvinov (deputy from Rzhev *uezd* and member of the minority) proposed that the committee disperse for a time to gather relevant data about the landed estates of the province before deciding on the question of allotment. This proposal was put to a ballot and, despite the initial decision of the committee to the contrary, as well as several succeeding refusals by the committee majority to accept such an adjournment,[4] was approved by a vote of 15–9. Unkovskii, Bakunin, Maksimovich and several other members of the majority voted for approval of this proposal.[5] The committee then busied itself, in two following sessions (to 4 October), with the elaboration of methods for collection of data from the landed estates.

In the session of 4 October it became clear why Unkovskii and others of the majority had voted for adjournment: On that day the committee received a communication from the governor informing the committee that, as a result of misunderstandings there over the definition of the term 'homestead' (as reported to him in a petition from Kardo-Sysoev and others),[6] he had

---

[1] *Ibid.*, pp. 203–9.

[2] The chairmen of the provincial committees all made bi-weekly reports on the activities of their committees to the Minister of Interior.   [3] *Ibid.*, p. 210.

[4] This same proposal had been made most recently by Zmeev, on 18 September, at the very beginning of discussion on the question of land-allotment. This question of collecting data naturally arose once the committee had dispensed with the protocol and had gotten down to discussing concrete measures involving patterns of land-holding and obligations. *Ibid.*, p. 213.   [5] *Ibid.*, p. 257.

[6] In the meeting of 24 September, Kardo-Sysoev had declared that he and some other members (unnamed) had 'written to His Excellency the Governor requesting an interpretation of the correct definition of the "homestead" . . .' *Ibid.*, p. 233.

communicated with the Minister of Interior on that subject. The Minister's reply, wrote Baranov, was the following:

Although the majority of the [Tver] committee has proposed to join arable land [*polevaia zemlia*] to the homestead, [the Minister] does not feel justified in allowing any other interpretation of the term 'homestead' than that which was made by His Imperial Majesty in His communication to the St Petersburg Military Governor-General [Ignat'ev] on 5 December 1857 . . ., namely, that as 'homestead' or peasant *usad'ba* should be understood the peasants' dwellings and farm buildings with the land on which they stand, plus their garden plots. The words [of the Imperial Rescript] remove any possibility of confusing *usad'ba* lands . . . with arable lands, which the *pomeshchiki* have the right to present in use to the peasants in return for certain obligations. Therefore, the committee is obligated to examine the means for presenting to the peasants their *usad'ba* lands and arable lands separately, and not mixing them, to draw up separate legislation for each of them.[1]

Although several members of the committee were surprised by this communication, Unkovskii clearly was not. He immediately turned to A. D. Kudriavtsev (deputy from Zubtsov *uezd*) to demand an explanation, and Kudriavtsev admitted that on 24 September he had had an audience with Lanskoi as representative of those members of the Tver committee who chose to define the *usad'ba* in the narrow sense, and who 'protested redemption of all land necessary to the peasants'.[2] He had received from Lanskoi the definition just quoted. Unkovskii, obviously prepared for this offensive, presented for the committee's approval a long petition addressed to the governor of Tver. Its main points were the following:

In answer to Your Excellency's communication of 2 October . . ., the committee has the honor to inform you that in accepting a definition of the homestead contrary to the definition of the Minister of Interior it does not consider that it has departed from the fundamental principles put forth in the Imperial Rescripts. Decreeing that the peasant homestead, because of local conditions in Tver province, should constitute not only buildings and gardens, but arable plow, haying and pasture land as well, the committee has been guided by the following con-

[1] *Ibid.*, pp. 254–5.   [2] *Ibid.*, p. 255.

siderations: In the Rescript it is made the obligation of the gentry to present to the peasants their homesteads for redemption, but it is not positively defined of what this homestead is to consist. Therefore the committee considers itself justified in defining the homestead in accordance with local conditions, and has concluded that any decision furthering the faithful implementation of the just design of His Imperial Majesty, far from being contradictory to the Imperial Rescript, is full evidence of sincere readiness by the committee to fulfill His Majesty's sacred will. Restriction of the homestead to buildings and gardens alone will surely lead to a quite opposite result.

Going on to spell out the dire consequences of such a solution, and to reiterate the Minister's own words (of 7 February 1858) to the effect that the committees need not be restricted by the 'advice . . . contained in [his] instructions', the petition concluded

Having received Your Excellency's communication in which the definition of the homestead by the Minister of Interior is presented as obligatory . . . the committee finds itself in extreme confusion concerning the mandatory force of the opinion of the Minister . . . for the committee, and has therefore proposed by a majority vote: (1) To assure Your Excellency that, confined by the considerations of the Minister of Interior on the definition of the homestead, the committee can do nothing useful for the solution of the given question and requests Your Excellency to bring this confusion to the attention of His Imperial Majesty; (2) The committee also begs to be allowed to reconcile peasant and *pomeshchik* interests on the basis of the fundamental principles adopted by the committee as being in complete agreement with the principles elaborated in the Imperial Rescript, unhindered by the instructions of the Minister of Interior, which were declared without binding force.[1]

This petition in defense of the majority position in the committee was duly approved by a vote of 11–9, and it was further decided to send a deputation to Petersburg for personal explanations with the government. Unkovskii, A. N. Perukhov and P. D. Kishenskii were chosen for this task.[2] Then the committee adjourned,

[1] *Ibid.*, pp. 257–8.
[2] *Ibid.* Voting for the petition's approval were: Unkovskii, Bakunin, Golovachev, Maksimovich, Kharlamov, Semenov, Perukhov, Kishenskii, Miachkov, Izmailov, and Balkashin. Voting against: Litvinov, Zubkov, Kudriavtsev, Korbutovskii, Kardo-Sysoev, Rakovskii, Shakhonskii, Verevkin, and Zmeev.

as planned, until 27 October, for the gathering of data on the landed estates. It can be assumed that Unkovskii and his supporters knew of this impending crisis beforehand and therefore supported the move to adjourn, hoping to return at the end of the recess with governmental approval of their position.[1] Their hope was justified.

Arriving in Petersburg, the Tver deputation was warmly received in the Ministry of Interior, where Lanskoi promised to take their case before the Main Committee.[2] From the Ministry the deputation went on to see Ia. Rostovtsev, who by this time had become the Emperor's chief advisor on peasant emancipation. Rostovtsev expressed his full agreement with the Tver committee's reform plan.[3]

Reconvening the Tver committee on 27 October, Unkovskii explained the results achieved by the delegation to Petersburg. Lanskoi had told him, said Unkovskii, '... that his instructions in no way hinder the judgements of the committee, and he informed [us] that the petition of the Tver committee of 4 October had been given by Imperial order to the Main Committee'.[4] Therefore, Unkovskii proposed, the committee should proceed with its discussion of land-allotment 'on the basis of the adopted principles'. This the committee did, and on 10 November the

---

[1] Unkovskii had in fact talked with Lanskoi in Petersburg at the end of August about the Tver majority's proposals. According to a letter written by Unkovskii to Koshelev (18 Sept. 1858), '[Lanskoi] completely agreed with them and even willingly retreats from his proposals on the household plot'. Trubetskaia, *Materialy*, I, *prilozhenie*, 111–13.

[2] Dzhanshiev, *A. M. Unkovskii*, p. 92; Solov'ev, 'Zapiski', XXXVI, 245.

[3] Unkovskii has left this account of the visit to Petersburg: '[We] set out to speak with the Minister of Interior, arriving at the Ministry . . . at the time for the reception. We informed [Lanskoi] that we all refused to take any part in the peasant affair, so long as we would not be allowed to speak of those means of peasant emancipation which we considered the only ones possible. He was extremely embarrassed. "As you like", we said. "If it is ordered to write the project according to the program, then deputies [i.e. the provincial committees and their representatives to be sent to Petersburg] are not needed . . ." He said, "Wait, gentlemen, and I will see what can be done". . . . (Unkovskii, 'Materialy k biografii', p. 82.) 'Then we returned to the hotel, where we found an invitation from Rostovtsev to visit him that evening. We went, and Rostovtsev pronounced himself a defender of our ideas. On the next day we received permission to elaborate a plan of redemption.' (*Ibid.*, p. 19.)

[4] *Zhurnaly*, II, I.

committee received the ruling of the Main Committee, as communicated through the Ministry of Interior. The *usad'ba*, ruled the Main Committee, must be understood in the sense already defined by the government. But:

> As for the goal of the Tver committee, to replace redemption of the *usad'ba* with redemption of peasant lands in general: Although it is not true to the letter of the Imperial Rescript, it is in accord with its spirit, and with the goal of improving and securing peasant welfare.[1]

The government, Lanskoi reminded the Tver committee, could not reform its rules to follow any one committee, but must provide guidance for them all. General measures, such as a government-financed redemption operation, must be the responsibility of the government, and therefore decisions concerning them must remain the government's prerogative. The Main Committee had accordingly ruled:

> The Tver committee shall not be hindered in seeking means to present to the peasants field land in property, according to the wishes of the *pomeshchiki*, but the said committee must draw up provisions on *usad'ba* and arable lands *separately for each subject*.[2]

This ambiguous ruling retained the provision that *usad'ba* and arable land must be the subjects of separate clauses or provisions in the committee's project (as previously enunciated by the Minister of Interior). But it did remove the categorical prohibition against composing a project including redemption of field land, and it specifically gave the Tver committee majority permission to continue its work on the same foundations. However, it by no means gave the Tver committee the right to compose a project which would make such land-redemption *obligatory* for the *pomeshchiki*, providing as it did that the committee could 'seek means to present to the peasants field land in property, *according to the wishes of the pomeshchiki* . . .'[3] Just what was to be understood by making the *usad'ba* and field lands the subjects of 'separate provisions' was not explained. In fact, the

---

[1] *Ibid.*, pp. 61–2; Skrebitskii, *Krest'ianskoe delo*, I, XLV.
[2] *Ibid.* This ruling was subsequently generalized and sent to all committees.
[3] *Zhurnaly*, II, 61–2. Emphasis added.

ruling clearly reflected the state of indecision in which the government then found itself over the question of redemption. Its policy on the land question at this time had only two corner-stones: That *usad'ba* land should be sold to the peasants, and that some amount—as yet undetermined—of field land should be left, irrevocably, in their use. How land relations were to evolve beyond the 'temporary usage' stage had not been decided, mainly out of fear of instituting a government-sponsored financial operation for redemption. The question was not, in fact, finally settled until twenty years after the emancipation (as will be seen later), in spite of considerable support among influential persons in the administration, among them Rostovtsev and Lanskoi, for the idea of a government financial operation for redemption of peasant lands.[1]

The debate on secondary questions

Following the committee's temporary adjournment, it resumed discussion of the 'temporary-obligatory' status and elaboration of the draft-project as provided by the government program. The first problem to be raised in this context had been *the question of **barshchina** and **obrok** in the 'temporary-obligatory period'*. Here the line established in the struggle over the protocol began to be obscured. Several members of the majority took a position similar to that of their opponents on this question, advocating retention of labor rent for at least several years after emancipation. Most important for the *pomeshchik*, they argued, were obligatory labor and the agricultural implements and animals owned by the peasantry. In order to replace them some time should be allowed after emancipation.[2] Conversely, Zmeev and Kudriavtsev, among the most

---

[1] In a letter of 18 December 1858, to Unkovskii, Rostovtsev wrote: 'Your letter of 12 Dec. pleased me very much, first of all because you foresee the possibility of immediately abolishing obligatory labor . . . and secondly because you are convinced of the necessity . . . of land redemption.' Rostovtsev concluded this letter with a sketch of a plan to issue five-percent interest-bearing state bonds to the gentry in payment for the land. These were to be guaranteed by peasant obligations and the State Properties, a scheme, wrote Rostovtsev, 'to which the Minister of State Properties will agree'. Unkovskii, 'Materialy k biografii', pp. 131–3. Cf. also, Trubetskaia, *Materialy*, I, *prilozhenie*, III–13.

[2] Kharlamov was one of the most determined advocates of this from among the majority members. Another defendant from the majority of this point of view was Golovachev,

outspoken opponents of Unkovskii on the question of land-redemption, came forward as energetic advocates of an immediate cessation of *barshchina*. It was Zmeev who proposed the motion 'to abolish obligatory labor immediately upon completion of harvest work after 1 November, in the first autumn following Imperial approval of the committee's statute', which was passed by a vote of 16–30.[1]

On 25 September the committee had proceeded to *discussion of the peasant allotment*: its size, the lands it was to include, how it was to be delimited and evaluated. On this question began one of the longest discussions in the committee's brief history. Unkovskii, Bakunin, Golovachev, Balkashin, Kharlamov, and Kishenskii began by proposing the following rules for land-allotment:

1. In the homestead [*osedlost'*] to be redeemed there should be included: (a) all so-called *usad'ba* lands [buildings, gardens, etc.] at present in peasant usage; (b) special 'pasture lands' for grazing of peasant cattle when the meadows are closed; (c) 'field land, for crops and hay, which have been in peasant usage up to the present time' [including 'all those lands lying fallow which serve as pasture for cattle'.]
2. Where haying lands do not equal plowland, the difference is to be made up by attaching additional land to the homestead.
3. Determination of the allotment for peasants entirely on *obrok* at present should be the subject of other rules.[2]

At the same session a crucial question was decided, virtually without debate: On the proposal of N. P. Semenov, it was decided by a vote of 18–0 (six abstaining) . . .

though according to Unkovskii's memoirs, he was not sincere in his defense. Golovachev evidently arranged beforehand with Unkovskii to provoke Doroshkevich, one of their most determined opponents and a personal enemy of Golovachev, into supporting the measure to abolish compulsory labor. This they did, according to Unkovskii, by having Golovachev defend *barshchina* and vote for its provisional retention. Doroshkevich promptly voted against retention, after which, in a roll-call check of the balloting, Golovachev changed his vote. Outraged, Doroshkevich left the committee and never returned. His place was taken by P. N. Obol'ianinov. *Ibid.*; 'Materialy k biografii', pp. 19a–20.

[1] *Zhurnaly*, I, 234–6.
[2] *Ibid.*, pp. 239–40. This last measure was included in recognition of the fact that peasants whose obligations were entirely in *obrok* often had much larger holdings than peasants on *barshchina* or mixed obligations. In some cases all the land of an estate was worked by peasants on *obrok*.

To provide that land usage during the transition period and redemption of the homestead by the peasants shall be obligatory for both parties [i.e., peasants and *pomeshchiki*] and that the transition period is to be retained only until such time as credit institutions (for financing land redemption) shall be organized, *but in no case longer than three years*.[1]

The debate on the proper size of peasant allotments continued, now without any concerted opposition against inclusion of field land in the allotment. Most members agreed that retention of the existing peasant allotments should serve as the principle on which land-distribution would be effected in the emancipation, while at the same time they proposed various restrictions on this principle. The fundamental decisions on allotment were made in the sessions of 6 and 7 November. Approving the principle of retention of the existing allotments by a vote of 18–4, the committee unanimously agreed on the impossibility of simply continuing all existing peasant holdings. It was decided that a maximum allotment size would have to be established.[2] Lengthy debate on this crucial question was followed by balloting, in which the votes cast produced the following results: Fourteen members proposed a maximum allotment of four *desiatiny* for each peasant in the province. Nine members favored a maximum of three *desiatiny*. Two voted for an allotment of two *desiatiny*.[3] The majority which had supported Unkovskii in his advocacy of obligatory redemption disintegrated on this question. Only six deputies from this group joined Unkovskii in support of a maximum allotment of four *desiatiny* (Bakunin, Golovachev, Kharlamov, Balkashin, Miachkov, and Kishenskii). The other seven votes for a four-*desiatina* allotment came from the minority, and were cast by such otherwise outspoken critics of the majority as Kardo-Sysoev, Miliukov, Kaliteevskii and Zubkov. The rest of the majority's members voted for a maximum allotment figure of three *desiatiny*, except Vul'f, who voted for a maximum

[1] *Ibid.*, p. 241.　　　　　　　　　　　[2] *Zhurnaly*, II, 55.
[3] Voting for a four-*desiatina* maximum: Unkovskii, Miliukov, Kudriavtsev, Zubkov, Miachkov, Kishenskii, Bakunin, Golovachev, Kharlamov, Kaliteevskii, Ushakov, Kardo-Sysoev, Korbutovskii, and Balkashin.

　　　For a three-*desiatina* maximum: Maksimovich, Litvinov, Zmeev, Vorob'ev, Doroshkevich, Perukhov, Semenov, Panafidin, Neronov.

　　　For a two-*desiatina* maximum: Vul'f, Shakhonskii. *Ibid.*

peasant allotment of two *desiatiny*, less than half the average existing peasant holding in the province.

These decisions were, for the most part, consistent with the views expressed by Unkovskii in his *zapiska*, where he had argued against indiscriminate retention of existing peasant allotments. Recognition of the existing allotment as a *norm*, however, was insisted upon by Unkovskii in the committee as a means of avoiding a purely arithmetical solution to the question, a solution which he believed would involve an indefinite post-ponement of the reform. Retention of existing allotments, even with severe hedgings would, argued Unkovskii and others, leave the larger part of peasant holdings intact and facilitate rapid promulgation of emancipation including obligatory land-redemption. In general, the Tver committee's majority was not in favor of providing the peasantry with *generous* allotments. It maintained that the peasant should be provided with a just-sufficient, viable holding. In the opinion of Unkovskii such a modest, but adequate, holding amounted to about four *desiatiny*. Too-extensive allotments would, he believed, overburden the financial operation for land-redemption, and would thus make the government less willing to initiate such an operation. The peasants, provided with their basic holding, would always be able to rent or buy additional lands by free agreement.[1]

The following sessions were devoted to debate on *assessment of peasant obligations*. In this debate, Unkovskii and Golovachev proposed that the average *obrok* per *desiatina* of land in the province (that is the money obligations paid by peasants whose obligations for the land they worked were entirely of this kind) be taken as the basis for future peasant obligations. This method, they argued, would eliminate endless surveying, and would also recompense the *pomeshchik* for the peasants' labor as reflected in the value of the land. Simple land values alone would not repre-sent sufficient recompense.[2] But this proposal found little support

[1] *Ibid.*, pp. 32–3.
[2] Unkovskii had maintained all along that redemption of the land alone was not sufficient reward for the *pomeshchiki*, but he had declared in his *zapiska* that the peasants should bear the burden for redemption of land only, that the redemption of the labor value of the peasants should be the responsibility of 'all classes of the State'. He was unable to

in the committee, where virtually every member had his own ideas about the evaluation of peasant obligations.[1] After protracted discussion the committee compromised on a plan presented by M. A. Vorob'ev, which provided a somewhat higher remuneration for the *pomeshchiki* than the scheme advocated by Golovachev and Unkovskii. Vorob'ev's plan established general obligation figures for the whole of the province, based on a system of gradations: the largest yearly obligation was to be paid for the first *desiatina* of land, with descending obligations for the following *desiatiny*, up to the fourth (the largest possible holding), for which the smallest obligation was to be paid. This system was based on the frank recognition that the person of the peasant was to be compensated for in the high valuation placed on the first *desiatina*, which included the *usad'ba* and would thus be received by all peasants.[2] Vorob'ev proposed the following obligation rates for each *desiatina*:

For the first *desiatina* (including *usad'ba*) ....5·50 rubles
For the second   „   ....2·00 „
For the third   „   ....1·00 „
For the fourth   „   ....0·50 „

or 9 rubles in annual obligations for a peasant holding the maximum allotment of four *desiatiny*. A peasant with an allotment just half that size, two *desiatiny*, would be obliged to pay 7 rubles 50 kopecks, nearly four-fifths as much. Vorob'ev's plan was approved in the committee by a vote of 14–11.[3] Unkovskii, Golovachev, Bakunin and several other representatives of the majority voted for this plan while favoring lower obligation rates.[4] The rates were subsequently revised somewhat (to provide a maximum obligation of 8 rubles 70 kopecks), and capitalization of these obligation rates at six percent was agreed upon as the

find support for such a distinction in the Tver committee and therefore ceased to insist on it, perhaps also because he feared that it would make the chances of a state-wide redemption program more remote. *Ibid.*, pp. 101–6; 130–5.
[1] On the whole, these schemes tended to reflect the *obrok* rates prevailing in the *uezdy* represented by the various deputies.
[2] *Zhurnaly*, II, 152–62.   [3] *Ibid.*, p. 162.
[4] *Ibid.* Golovachev and Unkovskii also opposed the establishment of one set of rates for the whole province, favoring separate rates for each *uezd*. *Ibid.*, p. 161.

basis for *redemption* prices.[1] Vorob'ev's plan of descending
obligations was later adopted by the Finance Committee of the
Editing Commissions and served as the basis for the general
evaluation plan for all of Russia.[2]

The Question of Peasant Administration. The committee next proceeded, beginning 8 December 1858, to a discussion of peasant
administration. In the course of this discussion Golovachev
produced the 'liberal manifesto' on local administrative reform
which was to be embodied in the project of the Tver committee
and later echoed among the Tver gentry and elsewhere in Russia.
Golovachev presented an 'opinion' on the future administration
in general. Deep divisions within the committee on other
questions were erased in almost unanimous approval of Golovachev's demands for local reforms. His opinion was approved by
21 votes as the basis for administrative reform in Tver province,
and was turned over to the recently created 'editing commission'[3]
for its guidance in drawing up the administrative section of the
committee's project. This in spite of the fact that the Ministry
of Interior had expressly forbidden the provincial committees to
discuss general questions of local administration.[4]

Golovachev proposed five fundamental reforms:

1. Abolition of the departments [*vedomosti*][5] and creation of general
rural administration.
2. Autonomy of the peasant communes and communities [*obshchiny i
obshchestva*], both *uezd* and provincial, in the administrative sphere.[6]

---

[1] *Zhurnaly*, III, 58.
[2] Unkovskii, 'Materialy k biografii', pp. 46–46a.
[3] The 'editing commission' included Unkovskii, Bakunin, Golovachev and Kharlamov,
all members of the majority and close adherents of Unkovskii's position. The function
of the commission was to write the entire draft project on the basis of the measures
approved by the committee. *Zhurnaly*, II, 78.
[4] The government program of 21 April had reserved discussion of local administration
for the 'third period' of the committees' activities, which was to begin only *after*
emancipation; and the Ministry of Interior had informed the committee at the beginning
of its activities that such questions were not to be discussed. *Zhurnaly*, I, 2.
[5] Reference is to the separate bureaucratic administrations for each of the legal estates
(*sosloviia*).
[6] 'This autonomy', declared Golovachev, 'is expressed: (1) In the right of election
without the control of the local administration; (2) in the apportioning of revenues . . .;
(3) in the control over the use of revenues.' *Zhurnaly*, II, 179.

3. Separation of all administrative and judicial offices from the police.
4. Independence and autonomy of the courts and accountability before them of administrative and police functionaries in connection with complaints, and therefore institution of a jury-court system.
5. Abolition of secrecy in administrative and court procedures.[1]

Emancipation without complete reform of the administration, argued Golovachev, is impossible:

With the removal of *pomeshchik* control it will be necessary to create a new order, because the whole existing system has as its basis the principles of serfdom, which cannot continue ... [Serfdom] has penetrated all phases of life: What are our protective tariffs and customs if not the enserfment by several manufacturers of the whole of Russia ... All this evil comes from the fact that serfdom has developed in all spheres of our life and has planted deep roots there. If we do not propose measures for the reform of our bureaucratic system, if we leave it with the same rights and responsibilities, what will happen ...? Will not [the peasants] escape the control of one person, whose own interests forced him to consider their welfare, only to fall under the control of another, indifferent to that. If the character of our bureaucracy remains the same as before, then it is clear that this change will not abolish serfdom, but only transfer it and widen its limits, transforming not only the free classes, but even the gentry into serfs.

It will be objected that perhaps it is necessary first to abolish serfdom and then think about other improvements. I answer no, a thousand times no! The implementation of new bases of administration must at least accompany abolition of serfdom, if not precede it. You are abolishing the control of the *pomeshchiki*, therefore you must create a new control; but can this new control be based on the same foundations ..., that is on serfdom? Where then are the improvements? Where then will we, a newly-formed class of serfs, find justice if the peasants refuse to fulfill their obligations? Can it really be expected that we will carry our complaints to our courts or to our administrators and police officials? They will only tell you after a year has passed that you have not made your complaint according to the rules ... And what will the people say when they see that they have not been freed, but have only been sold by the *pomeshchiki* to the bureaucrats?[2]

---

[1] *Ibid.*, p. 175.   [2] *Ibid.*, pp. 177–8.

The abolition of serfdom, asserted Golovachev, meant that there was no longer any reason to maintain separate administrations for the various estates, which could only lead to increasing antagonism between the upper and lower classes. In advocating 'abolition of the departments and formation of a general rural administration', Golovachev and his colleagues of the majority called for creation of an 'all-class *volost*' (*vsesoslovnaia volost*') as the basic organ of local self-government. Their aim, declared N. A. Bakunin, was to 'replace the former, patriarchal ties ... with new ones, with ties of social benefit and mutual interest, and in the name of this significant principle, unite equally all inhabitants of the region'.[1] Some, however, were to be 'more equal than others': In the system of local self-administration as conceived by Golovachev, the gentry and the merchant-class were to have the right of individual participation. The peasantry was to provide its representatives.[2]

The attitude of Golovachev and most of his colleagues in the Tver committee toward the peasant commune was the typical attitude of the Russian liberals (excluding the liberal Slavophiles, such as Iurii Samarin and Alexander Koshelev): It was recognized as a retardative factor in agrarian development:

The argument presented by the economists for the superiority of private property founded on the premise that man is born a property-owner [affirmed Kharlamov] is at least equal to the argument of the Slavophiles that a man is born a member of a family.[3]

But for the time being it was irreplaceable as the guarantor of peasant obligations. It was agreed in principle in the committee that transfer from collective to private land-holding should be left to the peasant commune itself, and the right to leave the commune should be left to the individual peasant. However, this latter possibility was made very remote by the requirements involved: payment of his share of the redemption debt by the departing peasant or the securing of a replacement.[4]

The last major item on the committee's agenda also produced general agreement among its members. The question of the

[1] *Ibid.*, III, 87.   [2] *Ibid.*, II, 179.   [3] *Ibid.*, p. 187.   [4] *Ibid.*

household serfs (*dvorovye liudi*), of whom there were about 20,000 in the province, was raised in the session of 13 January and was resolved with remarkably little difference of opinion. A large majority agreed that the household serfs should be freed promptly, with the *pomeshchiki* receiving remuneration only for the 'revision souls' among them (that is, no payment was to be made for women). This remuneration was to be borne not by the household serfs themselves, but by the state. The committee agreed on a payment of 60 rubles for each 'revision soul'.[1]

Final conflicts and the closing of the committee

The relative concord within the committee following its temporary adjournment soon came to an end. On 20 December a turn to voting on the post-emancipation rights of the gentry had called forth the old and bitter arguments about redemption. And in the next meeting, as the committee neared the end of its deliberations, a 'petition' addressed to the committee by a group of local gentry was received. It was to be followed by many more. This first petition, written by one V. N. Kudriavtsev in the name of the 'gentry of Torzhok *uezd*', expressed a conservative reaction against the doings of the committee. The petition condemned obligatory redemption and the committee's 'arbitrary' determination of allotment and obligation rates for the peasantry, and demanded that the local gentry be consulted directly on both these matters. The petition asserted that the committee's measures, if effected, would ruin the gentry: 'Losing a little, the gentry will sacrifice; losing half, it will be ruined.'[2] The petition was repudiated by the committee, which declined even to recognize it as the work of the 'gentry of Torzhok *uezd*', since it was signed by only twenty-five persons. The following sessions, beginning 7 January 1859, saw a rapid increase in the flow of such petitions from groups of local gentry to the committee. Most of them, signed by a few persons only, were markedly alike. Their general burden was objection to obligatory redemption and to the arbitrary allotment and obligation figures established by the

[1] *Ibid.*, III, 57–8. [2] *Ibid.*, p. 235.

committee. They demanded that the committee 'return to the letter of the government program'. Some of these petitions, perhaps all of them, were written on the initiative of opposition members within the committee itself.[1] Not only petitions, but gentry deputations began to appear before the committee, and to produce considerable disorder in its affairs. On 8 January, amidst much excitement, a deputation of thirty-nine gentry from Tver *uezd* appeared before the committee to read a petition (similar to all the others) and to express their thanks to their deputy, A. S. Verevkin, 'for defense of gentry rights'. This petition was signed by some of the same gentry who, in February 1858, had signed the resolution of the Tver *uezd* assembly approving Unkovskii's redemption plan.[2] In all, the committee received petitions from eight of Tver's twelve *uezdy*. On 13 January the committee received notice from the Ministry of Interior forbidding the presence of 'outsiders' at committee sessions,[3] and with this the procession of gentry deputations and petitions ceased.

It is impossible to determine exactly to what extent this series of petitions and deputations was the result of a concerted effort to block final passage of the committee's program, as it hurried to this end in the last sessions before the approach of the six-month termination date. But the chronological coincidence of the petitions, their marked similarity, and the fact that some of them were directly linked to opposition members in the committee, suggest that opposition members probably provoked the whole campaign. In any case, the campaign failed. The committee majority did not veer from the course it had set. The governor, who had received complaints from gentry groups about the actions of the committee, defended the majority position against these gentry attacks. The plans of the committee majority, he affirmed, 'fully correspond to the Imperial orders and to the amendments on them of the Minister of Interior'.[4]

---

[1] *Ibid.*, III, 40–41.   [2] *Ibid.*, p. 44.

[3] *Sbornik pravitel'stvennykh rasporiazhenii*, vol. I, section IV, item 54. This directive was published 5 January and sent to all provincial committees still in session. There is no evidence that it was made specifically in response to events in the Tver committee. It was probably based on numerous complaints from committee chairmen about interference by gentry groups with the work of their committees.

[4] *Zhurnaly*, III, 84.

Golovachev's attitude to these gentry apprehensions about the future of their class was characteristically expressed in his brief reply to the petition of the Torzhok gentry: 'It seems to me that the gentry can preserve its significance in the present age only when the nobleman becomes a rich peasant.'[1]

The regular sessions of the Tver committee terminated on 19 January 1859. From that date until 7 February 1859, the articles of the committee's formal draft project, which had been drawn up by the 'editing commission', were read and passed upon with minor revisions. The project in its final form was unconditionally approved by 15 members of the committee. The remaining members of the committee either contributed to a 'minority project', signed by nine members, or composed individual projects.

The writing of minority projects had been allowed by the Ministry of Interior, in a directive of 29 December 1858, where it was provided that the committees could present, in addition to the majority, or official, project, one or more minority projects, depending on the individual committees. And it was later ordered (9 May 1859) that of the two deputies to be sent to Petersburg for consultations with the Main Committee, one must represent the signers of the minority project, if such existed in the committee. (Most committees presented only one minority project, but a few presented two, and thus sent three deputies to Petersburg.)[2] The effect of these rulings was to equalize the significance of majority and minority projects: both would receive equal attention from the government and would be equally represented in Petersburg. The aim of the Ministry was fairly obvious: In most of the provincial committees the proponents of emancipation appeared to be in a minority. Seeking support in the committees for its emancipation plans, the government effectively destroyed the binding nature of majority decisions in the committees by giving equal voice to the minorities. Only in Tver, where the unequivocal proponents of emanci-

---

[1] *Ibid.*, II, 228.
[2] *Ibid.*, p. 50: *Sbornik pravitel'stvennykh rasporiazhenii*, vol. I, section IV, item 72.

pation were in a majority, this tactical device backfired. This action of the government in relation to the committees' projects did not leave much room for doubt about the government's attitude toward the legislative efforts of the gentry.

The conflict within the Tver committee did not end abruptly with the formal termination of its activities. The dominating role played by Unkovskii and Golovachev in the activities of the Tver committee naturally gave rise to the accusation that the reform plan for Tver province had been forced on the gentry in general and on the committee itself. N. P. Miliukov, a member of the committee whose antipathy to emancipation was thinly disguised, sent to the government after the closing of the committee what Unkovskii called 'a deceitful denunciation against me and several other members of the committee'.[1] Miliukov claimed that the majority project, besides being in obvious contradiction to the government's instructions, had been repudiated by the gentry of all the province. The committee, he declared, had consisted of two completely opposed 'factions', and the majority project was ' . . . a project of a majority of fourteen members, a forced project, concealing . . . the seeds of the most pernicious anarchy'.[2] The 'tyranny of a majority of one' led by Unkovskii had, claimed Miliukov, abused the rules of procedure, and had not given the minority a fair hearing. He therefore requested that the minority be given a special hearing before the government, in order to ' . . . justify itself before its electors, the gentry of the whole province, which unanimously shares its opinions'.[3] Unkovskii replied to this attack in a letter to the governor, with the request that it be put before the Main Committee to counteract Miliukov's accusations. Denying that the project was 'the affair of a faction of fourteen members', Unkovskii challenged each of Miliukov's assertions. The committee's actions, he declared, were neither irregular nor in contradiction to the government's instructions; they were known to and approved by the government. Conceding that only fourteen

---

[1] *Proekt polozheniia Tverskogo komiteta.* 'Otnoshenie predsedatelia Tverskogo gubernskogo komiteta . . .', p. 10.

[2] *Ibid.,* 'Mnenie Miliukova', p. 10.   [3] *Ibid.,* p. 6.

members consistently advocated land-redemption, Unkovskii pointed out, quite rightly, that the final project consisted of 'many resolutions passed by the Tver committee' either unanimously, or 'by a large majority of all members of the committee without distinction'.[1] (Miliukov himself, Unkovskii noted, had voted for two important measures of the project: the four-*desiatina* allotment maximum, and the evaluation plan offered by M. Vorob'ev.) Unkovskii's rebuttal was approved in the Ministry of Interior, and Miliukov's request was left unanswered.[2]

Unkovskii denied that the committee had been composed of two opposing factions. He described the committee in the following way:

Do not think [he wrote to Dzhanshiev] that the thirteen members who did not sign the majority project were all opponents of emancipation or of land-allotment for the peasants. Such, like Verevkin, Miliukov and Kudriavtsev, were very few. Most of them feared only a too-rapid transformation of the economy, and did not believe in the possibility of immediate redemption because of the enormity of the financial operation involved. That is, they were our opponents out of short-sightedness . . .[3]

The main argument in the committee, declared Unkovskii, was over the necessity of obligatory redemption:

That is what we argued about in Tver with the minority . . . Among the thirteen members who did not sign the project I can name three who were for reform no less than we were: The deputy from Bezhetsk *uezd* Modest Vorob'ev, Zmeev (Kashin *uezd*) . . . and Zubkov (Zubtsov *uezd*).[4]

Summary of the committee's projects

A look at the most important points of the majority and minority projects will serve to summarize the two main positions on reform developed in the Tver committee. Each of these projects was composed of ten chapters, according to the outline provided by the

[1] *Ibid.*, 'Otnoshenie predsedatelia . . .', p. 3.
[2] *TsGIAL, f.* 1180, no. 35, pp. 223–4.
[3] Dzhanshiev, *A. M. Unkovskii*, p. 95.   [4] *Ibid.*, p. 96.

government program of 21 April 1858, plus a 'review of principles' on which the provisions were based. The majority project, which was signed by the original 14-member majority favoring obligatory redemption and P. A. Izmailov (deputy from Ves'e-gonsk, replacing N. A. Ushakov), provided for a 'temporary-obligatory' period to last no more than three years, after which emancipation was to be fully implemented. All peasant families were to have the right then to leave the commune, provided they had proof of acceptance into another peasant commune or another official 'estate', and had paid fifty rubles per soul to the local treasury. The household serfs were to have the right to leave immediately after the emancipation proclamation (that is without remaining in a temporary-obligatory status), but only if they, too, had arranged to enter a peasant commune or another 'estate'. For each 'revision soul' among the household serfs the government would provide a 60 ruble redemption to the former master.

All buildings, moveable property and livestock of the peasants were to remain their inalienable property. The *usad'ba* on which they lived could be redeemed prior to the redemption of their field lands, on private terms supervised by a mediatory commission (This arrangement was provided in the majority project to satisfy the government's demand that the redemption of the *usad'ba* and of field land be the subjects of separate provisions. The majority thereby avoided having to compose two separate projects: one for usage, and one for redemption.) The measures for redemption of field land by the peasants were set forth in chapter 5 of the project, 'Land allotment for the peasants'. The land, besides the *usad'ba*, which was to come under permanent peasant control 'both for the temporary-obligatory period and for the following period', was to be restricted to *field lands* properly speaking, that is lands seeded or lying fallow, and was not to exceed four *desiatiny* for each peasant.[1]

The peasant commune [read the project] has the right to redeem in property all lands allotted to it under the terms of this project, but not

---

[1] The proposal made by Unkovskii, Golovachev, and several other members of the majority that special provisions be made to ensure a certain amount of pasture lands for the peasantry—in recognition of the importance of cattle and fertilizer in the peasant economy—was not realized in the project.

otherwise than with *usad'ba* lands, by paying to the *uezd* treasury the designated sum, of which six percent would equal a general yearly *obrok*.

The project provided the following measures relating to peasant obligations: From 1 November following the Act of Emancipation, all labor and natural obligations were to cease, to be replaced by the following yearly *obrok* for each soul:

For the first *desiatina* of the allotment .... 5·10 rubles
   ,,   ,,   second   ,,   ,, ,,   ,, ... 1·80   ,,
   ,,   ,,   third   ,,   ,, ,,   ,, ... 1·20   ,,
   ,,   ,,   fourth   ,,   ,, ,,   ,, ... 0·60   ,,

or a yearly payment of 8 rubles, 70 kopecks for a maximum allotment. How land redemption was to be achieved was described in chapter 10 of the project, 'Ways and means for implementing the new status': Following the Act of Emancipation a joint-stock company was to be opened in Tver for financing the redemption of peasant lands. The provincial committee (in its 'second phase' of activity) would announce the sale of shares, to which the gentry of the province would have first access. The government was to guarantee the company's income (based on the peasant payments) for forty-two years. The company's notes, backed by the peasant payments and guaranteed by the government, would be given as remuneration to the gentry (who could also take part or all of their capital in company shares). These notes were to be accepted by the state credit institutions in payment for debts on gentry estates.

The most detailed legislation, and the most extensive departure from the dictates of the government program was written into the eighth chapter, 'The organization of peasant administration', which, despite its title, provided a system of *general* local administration based on the plan offered by Golovachev. The basis of peasant organization, according to the project, was to remain the peasant commune, which was to be internally independent. Above the commune was to stand an all-class *volost'*, as the lowest common denominator of local self-government, Right to participate in the *volost'* assembly was to belong to all members of the hereditary gentry with lands within the boundary of the *volost'*, to all other holders of at least 50 *desiatiny* of land, and to representatives elected by the peasant communes. To the *volost'* and its chairman (a member of the hereditary gentry) were to belong the function of review and appeal over the decisions of the peasant communes. Above the *volost'* was to stand the *uezd* administration, consisting of three organs: executive, police, and judicial. The first was to consist of an *uezd* assembly, like the *volost'* headed by a member of the local gentry. All the gentry of the *uezd*, representatives of the merchantry, representatives of the peasant communes, and representatives from the *volost'* assemblies in the *uezd* were to make up the *uezd* assembly. This was to have control over fiscal measures pertaining to the *uezd*, review of action taken by the *volost'* administration, and general administration power in the *uezd*. An 'executive agent' for the *uezd* was to be chosen from among the assembly's gentry membership every three years. Police authority was to be placed in the hands of the 'commandant of *uezd* police', who was to be appointed by the provincial administration, but whose budget was to be controlled by the *uezd* assembly. The judicial functions were to be entrusted to a new *uezd* civil court for all classes. Criminal cases were to be the province of a 'criminal jury-court'. The judicial first instance in the *uezd*, for petty suits, was to be the 'Justice of the Peace' (*mirovoi sud'ia*), chosen from among the hereditary gentry or persons with university education and at least 500 *desiatiny* of land.[1]

The majority project, together with its 'review of principles', thus presented a program for the general reform of Russian political and economic life on the local level.

The minority project, which was presented in the name of nine members of the Tver committee,[2] was in many details identical to that of the majority. It's signers were not, however,

---

[1] *Proekt polozheniia Tverskogo komiteta*, pp. 1–57.
[2] The nine signers of the minority project were: Zmeev, Vorob'ev, Obol'ianinov, Kardo-Sysoev, Korbutovskii, Kaliteevskii, Litvinov, Kudriavtsev, and Zubkov.

in agreement with the opinion of the majority ... 'about the necessity of obligatory alienation of *pomeshchik* land as the property of the peasants for the organization of their welfare.'[1] Nor did they accept the possibility of including in their project legislation pertaining to anything beyond the 'temporary-obligatory status', to which they therefore restricted their project in accordance with the government program. Thus the minority project did not touch upon the question of land-redemption (except to allow it by mutual agreement) or any other final solution of the land question. Nor did it contain any mention of *general* administrative changes.

The 'temporary-obligatory period' was to endure, according to the minority project, for twelve years, after which peasant families could leave the commune under the same conditions provided in the majority project (payment, however, was to be 130 rubles, instead of the 50 rubles proposed by the majority). Provisions for the emancipation of the household serfs were identical to those of the majority project. The *usad'ba* was to be presented in property to the peasants. Field lands were to be left in peasant usage, up to a maximum allotment of three *desiatiny*, but were to remain the property of the *pomeshchiki*.

Again as in the majority project, all personal dependency, all natural obligations, and obligatory labor were to cease immediately after the Emancipation Proclamation. Peasant obligations were to be paid only in money. Redemption of the *usad'ba* was to be arranged by free agreement, or failing that, by a special commission, but in no case were obligations to be paid for the *use* of the *usad'ba* by the peasants. Obligations for the use of field lands were to be determined by a complicated system based on local grain prices and subject to periodic revision. They promised to be significantly higher than the obligations provided for the majority project.[2]

The *volost'*, according to the minority project, was to be an exclusively peasant organization, though its 'guardian', or executive, was to be chosen from among gentry candidates. And

---

[1] *Proekt polozheniia Tverskogo komiteta*, p. 58.

[2] *Proekt polozheniia Tverskogo komiteta. Proekt men'shinstva*, p. 13.

the same was to be the case for the 'Justice of the Peace'. *Uezd-*level administration or judicial instances above the Justice of the Peace were not touched upon in the minority project. The minority's provisions for changes in peasant administration were based on the following principle: 'Rights and responsibilities of administration and justice, which have lain up to the present on each *pomeshchik*, are transferred to the entire gentry class of each *uezd*'.[1]

Conclusions

The passing of the Tver majority project was a *tour de force* by Unkovskii and Golovachev. Together they wrote the 'plan of work' for the committee, almost all the major arguments for the majority position and, finally, the draft project itself.[2] They succeeded in including virtually the entire program of their *zapiska* in the project, excluding only Unkovskii's scheme for separating the redemption of the peasants themselves from that of the land. And that plan Unkovskii and Golovachev abandoned probably more for tactical considerations *vis-à-vis* the government than because of lack of support for it in the committee. They succeeded as well in winning the government's permission to write a project containing a plan of land-redemption for the peasantry, permission which was subsequently extended to other committees. They continued in the committee the line of argument which they had pursued in the *zapiska* of December 1857, and, in fact, added relatively little to it.

Unkovskii had been correct in denying Miliukov's allegation that the committee had been composed of two rigidly opposed factions. But Miliukov's objections were not entirely fanciful. The membership of the committee, despite a wide range of opinions on numerous questions, did tend to polarize into two camps, as the result of several factors: The Imperial Rescripts and especially the government program of 21 April 1858, tended from the beginning to create a division in the committee between those insistent on accepting these directives as orders to be followed to the letter, and those inclined to give them a looser interpreta-

---

[1] *Ibid.*, p. 24.   [2] Dzhanshiev, *A. M. Unkovskii*, p. 95.

tion. The opponents of obligatory redemption, the major issue before the committee, naturally tended to unite around the former position. Unkovskii and Golovachev came to the committee with a reform plan already formulated, and devoted all their energies there to securing its realization in the committee's project. Their pursuit of this end, which was greatly facilitated by the power exercised by Unkovskii as committee chairman, made the discussion of their program the primary activity of the committee, and therefore adherence to it or rejection of it, became the main dividing line there. Also, the government's decision to admit minority projects and to receive deputies from the minorities of the provincial committees naturally tended to crystallize opinions in most committees into two positions. This decision forced most members of the Tver committee who had not already done so to subjugate the multiplicity of their views to a unified program which would have the advantage of being an effective means either for opposition to or advocacy of an important position. In the Tver committee the minority united essentially around opposition to obligatory redemption.

In general, the majority in the Tver committee was united on the principles of land-redemption for the peasants, free labor, capitalist production and local reform. It was far from united on important questions of land-allotment and peasant obligations, and on a number of questions concerning peasant administration and future relations between the gentry and the peasantry.

If differences existed within the majority, there were more considerable differences within the minority, which was organized on an essentially negative platform. It contained both the most obvious reactionaries (though very few), and members who were in broad agreement with the majority in their political, economic and social views, but who remained fearful of obligatory redemption. The minority contained members (again very few) who were jealous of relinquishing even the *barshchina* obligations of their peasants, and others who were among the committee's most energetic advocates of free labor and capitalist production. The minority contained several members who were insistent on retaining the *pomeshchik's* 'patrimonial powers', and many others who advocated their immediate abolition, the institution of an all-class *volost'*, and all the local reforms proposed in the majority project.

In fact, most of the gentry deputies in the Tver committee were convinced of the necessity of peasant emancipation. Differences of opinion were many. The minority project not only rejected obligatory redemption, but also promised a less generous settlement for the peasantry, in matters of allotment and obligations, than did the majority project. But these differences were, on the whole, matters of degree, of ways and means, not the differences between champions of reform and 'reactionaries'.

A study of the Tver committee provides little evidence to suggest that the variety of views on peasant reform expressed there can be related in some direct fashion either to regional differences within the provinces or to the personal economic circumstances of the committee's members. In the Tver committee no consistent regional pattern existed in relation to the basic issues debated there: representatives of the majority and minority positions, liberals, moderates and conservatives alike, came from all parts of the province. There was in fact little possibility that such a regional pattern could have taken shape there, for the simple reason that—unlike some provinces which straddled sharply differing economic regions, such as the black soil and non-black soil belts—Tver province, though extensive in territory, was a remarkably homogeneous region. Although the five northernmost *uezdy* were somewhat poorer in soil than the others, there were no sharp differences within the province in soil, land tenure, or farming methods. Nor had the province, by 1858, been subjected to extensive internal economic differentiation as a result of commercial and industrial development.

The personal economic circumstances of the committee's members also fail to contribute much to an understanding of the differing views on emancipation expressed there. This was a remarkably homogeneous group of *pomeshchiki*, at least from the point of view of land and serf-holding: Most of them were 'middle gentry' masters of from 150 to 300 souls, whose obligations were fulfilled partly by *obrok*, and partly by *barshchina*.[1]

Certainly economic conditions left their imprint on the work of the Tver committee, especially on its details. This was true everywhere. And the pecularities of the region were by no means ignored: The poor soil and low productivity of agriculture may have made loss of land by the *pomeshchiki* generally less regretted than in the black soil regions (while also making remuneration for peasant labor and *obrok* an article of faith for all members of the committee); and the widespread existence of *otkhodnichestvo* obviously influenced concern expressed in the committee about the future availability of labor in the province and helped produce the nearly universal recognition that the peasants must be left 'tied to the land'. But neither the principles on which the majority project was based nor the major differences of opinion within the committee can be accounted for primarily in terms of local economic conditions. How can it be explained, in such terms, why one middling *pomeshchik* of Tver province, like Unkovskii, was convinced that emancipation without obligatory redemption would lead to the ruin of agriculture and the gentry, while another middling *pomeshchik* of the same province, like Zmeev, was equally convinced of just the opposite?

The answer to this question, at least in relation to the majority position in the committee, is fairly certain: Unkovskii and his colleagues were not simply responding to local economic conditions. On the contrary, they were applying to local conditions convictions they had gotten elsewhere. And these were the convictions expressed in the liberal reform program which was the common property of most 'educated opinion' in Russia.

Perhaps more than anything else, the success of the Unkovskii-Golovachev program among the Tver gentry before the founding of the provincial committee and later in the committee itself

[1] Ia. A. Korbutovskii, of Oshtakov *uezd*, owned the smallest number of serfs, 110 souls; the biggest serf owner in the committee was M. V. Neronov, of Kaliazin *uezd*, who owned 833 souls, almost twice as many as any other member of the committee possessed. (Data on the estates of the committee members have been drawn from numerous sources, but mostly from the journals of the committee and from the statistics on gentry estates published by the government in 1860.)

reflected the liberal abolitionist sympathies of a younger and better-educated group of gentry in the province, of which Unkovskii and Golovachev were outstanding, if not typical, representatives. Themselves young and university-educated, Unkovskii and Golovachev, upon retiring to Tver province, immediately found support for their activities among the 'younger generation' in the gentry. Unkovskii's election as gentry marshal seems to have been largely the result of the active support of 'young *pomeshchiki*'. In the committee, Unkovskii and Golovachev found their most devoted supporters among its younger members (Perukhov was a notable exception). The outstanding members of the minority were, for the most part, men of an older generation.[1]

The project presented by the Tver committee's majority proved to be the most progressive and far-reaching plan for peasant emancipation to come from a provincial gentry committee. The provisions of the project which made it such were essentially six in number: (1) Obligatory redemption of field lands by the peasants; (2) complete abolition of *barshchina* and all natural obligations; (3) a reasonably generous land allotment for the peasantry, in return for moderate obligations; (4) the granting of full civil liberties to the peasantry and, relatedly, formation of an all-class *volost'* and general reform of the local administration; (5) immediate abolition of all 'patrimonial control' by the *pomeshchik* over the peasants; (6) rapid transition to fully emancipated status for the peasantry, by-passing completely or restricting to the shortest possible time any 'temporary-obligatory' status. Taken together, these demands can be called the program of the liberal gentry opposition, which began to take shape as soon as the main features of the government's own final project for peasant reform became clear.

The Tver gentry, in presenting its reform project, did not, however, occupy an isolated position. The demand for obligatory land-redemption had been widespread in the press, and the Tver committee had not been the first to raise this demand: The

[1] Zmeev, Kardo-Sysoev, Kudriavtsev, Vorob'ev and Verevkin were all born before 1816.

provincial committee of Kovno province had first brought the question of land-redemption before the government, and the gentry of Nizhnii Novgorod had requested land-redemption in their original petition for the creation of a provincial committee there (and repeated their intention to draw up a project based on redemption in their committee in October 1858).[1] Besides the Tver committee, the majority projects of Kaluga, Kharkov and, with some reservations, Samara, provinces all stipulated land-redemption as the necessary outcome of the emancipation. Numerous minority projects also contained this proposition.[2] Nor was the Tver committee alone in providing for the immediate abolition of *barshchina* and all natural obligations; the Iaroslavl majority project and several minority projects provided for the same.[3] In fact, most of the views on reform expressed by the Tver committee were shared to some extent in other committees.[4]

The following chapter is devoted to consideration of the liberal gentry program elsewhere in Russia.

[1] Solov'ev, 'Zapiski', xxxi, p. 10.
[2] *Redaktsionnye komissii, Materialy*, iv, 263–8.
[3] Kornilov, *Ocherki*, pp. 269–70.
[4] The Tver committee alone, however, wrote a majority project providing for an all-class *volost'* and granting full civil rights to the peasantry. *Ibid.*, pp. 290–2. On the perennial question of why the Tver gentry were the most 'liberal' of all gentry groups, see the conclusion to chapter 5 below.

5

The Liberal Program Elsewhere in Russia

NON-BLACK SOIL PROVINCES

Kaluga

The liberal program set forth by Unkovskii and his followers in the Tver committee found its closest adherents among a minority of the Kaluga committee. The material and economic conditions of that province, located due south and some fifty miles from the border of Tver province, were for the most part similar to those described in chapter 4. The land, a sand-clay mixture typical of Central Russia, was probably as grudging as the land of Tver province, although considerably more of it (some 54 per cent in all) was under cultivation than in the latter province. The gentry economy was heavily dependent on peasant labor, both as a source of income through the *obrok* payments of the peasants, and as a source of cheap agricultural labor, without which profitable agricultural production in the province would have been impossible. The percentage of *obrok*-paying peasants in Kaluga was considerably higher than in Tver, and factory and non-agricultural production was also more developed.[1]

The Kaluga gentry's first reaction to the government's announced decision to proceed with reform was one of considerable reluctance, a characteristic they shared with most of the Russian gentry. However, their apprehension—which was directly

---

[1] Ignatovich calculated that 44·49% of Kaluga's landlord's peasants were on *obrok*, 41·15% on *barshchina*, and 14·35% on mixed obligations. Ignatovich, *Pomeshchich'i krest'iane*, pp. 290–1. Many of the peasants on *obrok* worked in iron-forging and steel-working plants in the province, which employed some 8,500 workers, or in cloth- and paper-manufacturing, which employed probably as many more. The average *obrok* per *tiaglo* (2·31 persons) was about 26 rubles a year on the eve of emancipation. Kornilov, 'Krest'ianskaia reforma v Kaluzshkoi gubernii', pp. 132–42.

related to the vagueness of the government's intentions—gradually gave way to acceptance of the necessity of reform.[1] Essentially two main ideas on the impending reform were gradually developed among the Kaluga gentry: The idea that the reform should be based on the redemption by the peasants of their allotments through government assistance. (This idea was based on recognition of the necessity of a complete abolition of the serf economy: Once deprived of serf labor, it was reasoned, the gentry would be compelled to adapt to intensive agricultural practices, to a 'farm economy', which demanded capital. And the conviction, expressed by the more articulate of the gentry's representatives, that it would not be harmful to alienate a part of the land to the peasants—in return for the necessary capital. If the land granted to the peasants was not to be in generous amounts that was because the gentry feared making the peasants too independent economically and thereby uninclined to hire out as laborers on gentry lands.[2]

The activities of the Kaluga provincial gentry committee passed through two phases: A first phase, during which the committee incorporated the fundamental views just mentioned into its draft statutes and defended them before the government; and a second phase, in which a minority of the committee's members, who were inspired by a broader view of the reform, broke away from the majority to draw up its own reform project. The main points of difference between the majority and minority concerned the questions of peasant allotments and obligations.

Two moderate groups constituted the working majority of the Kaluga committee: The 'moderate liberals' (seven members), cautious but confirmed proponents of reform; and the 'moderate conservatives' (four in number), who were aware of the inevitability of reform and determined not to oppose the basic policies of the government. To the right of the majority stood an 'aristocratic fronde' led by two great landowners, D. A. Chertkov and

---

[1] For a time the government considered the gentry of Kaluga to be among the most reactionary of gentry groups because it was one of the last to request permission to open a provincial committee (on 24 June 1858).

[2] *Ibid.*, pp. 144–6.

D. N. Potulov, who were followed more or less regularly by seven members. The 'aristocratic fronde' advocated landless emancipation of the peasants and retention of considerable direct authority over the peasants for the *pomeshchiki*. To the left of center stood the liberal minority of five members which later produced its own project. To this group belonged: Prince A. V. Obolenskii, a legal scholar and graduate of the juridical faculty of Moscow University at the end of the 1840s; the Decembrist P. N. Svistunov;[1] N. S. Kashkin, a former 'Petrashevets'; A. A. Muromtsev and A. P. Plemiannikov, both university educated young *dvoriane*.[2]

The Kaluga committee got underway very late, in January 1859. By this time the Tver gentry had succeeded in winning government approval for their intention to draw up a project based on land-redemption, and this news was warmly received by the Kaluga committee, which promptly decided in favor of a project of obligatory land-redemption including a government-sponsored financial operation. 'Voluntary redemption', ruled the committee, 'could never be realized . . ., many peasants would be satisfied with only personal freedom, and would add to the number of proletarians.'[3]

Receiving government permission to develop plans for redemption, the committee proceeded directly to questions of allotments and obligations. The committee, in near unanimity, concluded that the redemption price to be paid by the peasants should include 'the combined remuneration for everything alienated [from the *pomeshchik*]'. This meant just what it had signified in the Tver committee and elsewhere: remuneration for the loss of the peasant's labor value as well as for the 'real' value of the land. Such 'combined remuneration' was imperative,

---

[1] Svistunov (1803–89) had been a young guards-officer and member of the Northern Society of Decembrists. Convicted after the 14 December 1825 uprising, he returned to European Russia from Siberia only in 1856, after the general amnesty granted in that year.

There was one other Decembrist in the Kaluga committee, G. S. Batenkov (1793–1863), also a former member of the Northern Society. Batenkov is well known in Russian historiography as the chief assistant to Speranskii during the latter's reform of the Siberian administration in the early 1820s. In the Kaluga committee Batenkov adhered to the 'moderate liberal' faction.

[2] Kornilov, 'Krest'ianskaia reforma', pp. 147-9.   [3] *Ibid.*, p. 232.

argued the Kaluga committee, if the gentry economy were to be saved, if the gentry were to pay their debts and to set up 'the arrangement of their new economic life'.[1] The moderates and liberals concurred on a figure of about two and one-third *desiatiny* as an acceptable allotment for each peasant soul.[2]

On the question of establishing the 'combined remuneration', however, the majority and the liberal minority were unable to agree, and in June 1859 (one month before the committee's closing date), the liberal minority officially announced its intention to present a separate reform project.[3] This decision was announced as soon as it was learned that the government intended to receive representatives of committee minorities in Petersburg on the same basis as representatives of committee majorities. Presented with this opportunity, the liberal minority of the Kaluga committee decided to withdraw from its compromise with the majority and to present its own reform project. And the majority, released from the necessity to compromise with the liberal minority, proceeded to revise its project in a conservative direction.

A single plan for implementing redemption was nevertheless accepted by both majority and minority: The *pomeshchiki* were to receive immediately 5 per cent interest-bearing notes for the entire redemption sum. Payment on these notes was to be guaranteed fully by the government, which would set up state banks for the purpose of carrying out the entire operation of payments and collections from the peasants, and gradual retirement of the peasants' debt.[4] In their plans for the temporary-obligatory period, and the determination of peasants' obligations and allotments, the majority and minority differed greatly: The

---

[1] *Ibid.*, pp. 232–3.

[2] The reactionaries opposed this because they wanted an emancipation without land. Prince Obolenskii, alone among the liberals, also opposed it because he insisted on the retention of the peasants' previously existing allotments. The proposed 2.3 *desiatiny* allotment represented a considerable reduction from the existing average allotment, which was about 3.4 *desiatiny*. Ignatovich, *Pomeshchich'i krest'iane*, pp. 294–5.

[3] The majority proposed evaluation of the peasant allotment at 150 rubles. The minority proposed 120 rubles. The 'aristocratic fronde' thought both figures ruinous for the gentry. Kornilov, 'Krest'ianskaia reforma', pp. 234–5.

[4] The majority's evaluation of peasant obligations was, however, considerably higher than the minority's; only the system was identical.

majority allowed for the separate redemption of the *usad'ba* at a very high price (480 rubles per household). And for an allotment of 2·3 *desiatiny*, a yearly *obrok* of 11·20 rubles was to be paid. The majority project allowed for the continuation of *barshchina* during the temporary-obligatory period, and it accordingly provided for the retention of a considerable part of the traditional *pomeshchik* authority over the peasants. Finally, the majority provided that if the peasants did not undertake to redeem their allotments by the end of the twelve-year transition period, all lands would revert to the *pomeshchiki*.

The minority provided that the temporary-obligatory period was to be terminated only through redemption by the peasants of their allotments. No separate evaluation of the *usad'ba* was, therefore, necessary. *Barshchina* was to be immediately abolished and replaced by an *obrok* not to exceed six percent of the total value of the allotment; or for an allotment of 2·3 *desiatiny* a yearly *obrok* of 7·20 rubles per soul. All direct authority of the *pomeshchiki* over the peasants was to be immediately abolished.[1]

Both parties in the Kaluga committee refused to be limited in their proposals for administrative reform to the peasant administration alone. Their plans, which were expressed most extensively in the minority project, proposed the creation of *uezd* and provincial committees for the general economic administration of the province.[2] The minority project did not stop at this, but went on to demand a series of reforms, including: (1) The reform of the army-recruiting system; (2) the merger of all peasants into one rural class; (3) reform of the courts—public and verbal court procedures, formation of a bar association, and the introduction of trial-by-jury; (4) accountability of all bureaucrats before the courts; (5) elimination of the Table of Ranks; (6) expansion of literacy and primary education; (7) improvement

---

[1] Kornilov, 'Krest'ianskaia reforma', 238–40.

[2] The Kaluga minority, unlike the Tver committee, did not propose the creation of an all-class *volost'* organization. It also opposed the creation of a strictly peasant *volost'*, on the grounds that it would become a tool of gentry control over the peasants. Prince Obolenskii, as the minority's representative in Petersburg, later joined with Unkovskii in demanding an all-class *volost'*. *Ibid.*, p. 246.

of roads and the expansion of railway construction; (8) elimination of the spirits concession and other procedures 'hindering freedom of trade'.[1]

The composition of the Kaluga committee was remarkably similiar to that of the Tver committee: a 'radical-liberal' minority of five, a group of seven 'moderate liberals'; several 'moderate conservatives' and a fluctuating reactionary nucleus. The essential difference between the two committees was the fact that in Tver the 'radical-liberals' (Unkovskii, Golovachev, Bakunin and several others) gained a majority in the committee through the support of the 'moderate liberals'; the 'moderate conservatives' drew up the minority project, and the reactionaries remained in relative isolation. Had the devoted liberals in the Kaluga committee had the leadership, or even consistent support of the chairman (as had been the case in Tver), they may well have gained the upper hand in the committee. But the chairman of the Kaluga committee, F. S. Shchukin, was a vain old man who, though not opposed to reform, was primarily interested in preserving his position as gentry marshal. In the committee Shchukin maintained good relations with the government and tried to observe order and fairness in the committee's work, but never went out of his way to endorse the liberal program, for fear of offending some significant group of his electors.[2]

The reform plans proposed by the liberal minority in the Kaluga committee were essentially the same as those of the Tver majority.[3] To a considerable extent this coincidence must be attributed to the direct influence of the Tver liberals: in general, by the Tver committee's successful attempt to win government approval for a project based on land-redemption; and in particular through close acquaintance with the activities of the Tver committee: The journals of the Tver committee were regularly

---

[1] *Ibid.*, pp. 240–1. 　　　　　　[2] *Ibid.*, pp. 167–8.

[3] The Kaluga minority, however, was less generous in its economic settlement with the peasantry than the Tver majority. Its proposed allotment of 2·3 *desiatiny* was a significant reduction from the existing average allotment (3·38 according to Ignatovich). The maximum allotment proposed by the Tver majority was nearly as large as the existing average allotment. (4·41 *desiatiny*, according to Ignatovich.) (It should be noted, however, that in Kaluga, where *obrok* was significantly more prevalent than in Tver, a smaller proportion of the land had been retained in the direct 'landlord's tillage'.)

sent by Unkovskii to the Kaluga committee, and other correspondence relating to the peasant question was regularly exchanged by the two committees.[1]

Vladimir

In the province of Vladimir the liberal reform program was set
forth in the projects of two minority groups in the provincial
committee.

Agricultural conditions in Vladimir were also very similar to
those prevailing in Tver province, which was located immediately
to the west. The percentage of landlord's peasants on *obrok* in
Vladimir was, however, much higher than in Tver: more than
70 per cent for the province as a whole.[2] The majority of gentry
estates in Vladimir were operated on an entirely *obrok* basis, and
most often with all lands given over to peasant usage. Absentee
landlordism was very widespread among the gentry owners of
those *obrok* estates where the 'landlord's tillage' no longer existed.[3]

The Vladimir gentry received the government Rescript with
acquiescence, if not with enthusiasm, a fact which allowed the
provincial governor to report sanguinely that the overwhelming
majority of the gentry accepted the government's plans and
recognized the need for reform.[4] By the time the provincial

---

[1] Unkovskii regularly exchanged journals and other news with the committees of many
provinces. In a letter of 29 July 1858, sent to each of the gentry marshals of nine non-black
soil provinces (Novgorod, Pskov, Smolensk, Iaroslavl, Kostroma, Vologda, Vladimir,
Moscow and Kaluga) Unkovskii suggested 'a constant exchange of ideas' among the
committees of these provinces which were 'more or less alike in climatic and economic
conditions'. Such an exchange would serve, he wrote, 'as the best means for a thorough
examination of the question ... and the most correct understanding of all subjects
connected with it'. *GAKO, f.* 59, no. 3767, pp. 39–40a and ff. This exchange, undertaken, by all evidence, entirely on Unkovskii's initiative, was regularly maintained
between the individual committees and the Tver committee. Cf. Trubetskaia,
Materialy dlia biografii Cherkasskogo, I, *prilozhenie,* 111–13 (Letter of Unkovskii to A. I.
Koshelev, 18 September 1858.)

[2] Ignatovich, *Pomeshchich'i krest'iane,* pp. 290–1. According to Ignatovich, 72·61% of the
landlords' peasants in Vladimir paid *obrok* only; 7·93% owed *barshchina* only; and
19·46% owed 'mixed obligations'.

[3] V. G. Zimina, *Krest'ianskaia reforma 1861 goda v Vladimirskoi gubernii* (unpublished
dissertation, Moscow, 1956), pp. 51–63.

[4] *Ibid.,* p. 206. Even during the confusion immediately following publication of the
Nazimov Rescript the governor had been able to report that 'certain *pomeshchiki ...*
sympathize with the proposals of the government. They fully recognize the present

committee opened in December 1858, a considerable body of opinion had developed among the gentry which, as the local gendarme officer reported, was:

... Convinced that for the successful outcome of the reform it would be most beneficial to shorten the [duration of] the transition status, and further ... to completely eliminate any influence of the *pomesh-chiki* over the peasants ...[1]

The Vladimir provincial committee proceeded with its work with remarkably little friction among its members—though not in a spirit of unanimity—and produced, in April 1859, three projects of emancipation:[2] The *majority* of the Vladimir committee presented a typically conservative project for the transition period only. Its proposed economic settlement for the peasantry was extraordinarily unfair (high obligation rates, and a 50 percent reduction in peasant land allotments). *Barshchina* and the bigger part of the authority of the *pomeshchiki* were to be left intact during this period, according to the majority's project.[3]

The *first minority*, of six members, presented a project for the redemption of peasant allotments to be carried out during a three-year transition period. Peasants were to retain their existing allotments, providing they did not exceed three *desiatiny*; yearly *obrok* was to be based on the existing average. According to this plan of redemption, the government was to organize the entire operation, giving the *pomeshchiki* immediately the entire redemption sum. All obligatory relations between *pomeshchik* and peasants were to be immediately abolished.[4]

The *second minority*, composed of five members, also presented a plan based on land-redemption, but with an economic settlement more generous for the peasants than that of the first minor-

necessity of reforms and hope that with it the strong discontent among the servile class, which they have remarked for some time, will abate; and that the relations of the landowners to the peasants ... will be more clearly defined, and thereby that the *pomeshchik* estates, far from declining, will be able to increase in value with improved farming.' *Ibid.*, p. 202.   [1] *Ibid.*, p. 217.

[2] Zimina attributes the lack of friction in the committee to the general similarity in the economic circumstances of the committee's members (as in Tver they were mostly owners of from 1–300 serfs owing 'mixed obligations'), and to the relative economic homogeneity of the province. *Ibid.*, pp. 218–19; 266–9.

[3] *Ibid.*, pp. 238–9.   [4] *Ibid.*, pp. 239–53.

ity. (Retention of the existing allotment was proposed with a maximum allotment of $4\frac{1}{2}$ *desiatiny* per soul).[1] Redemption, according to this project, could be financed either by the government or by private means with a government guarantee. Full administrative independence was to be granted the peasants in their communes. At the basis of general local self-government was to lie an all-class *volost'*; the judicial first instance was to be the justice of peace. Police authority in the *uezd* was to be entrusted to a general police officer (*Zemskii pristav*). All these organs were to be organized in a manner identical to that provided in the Tver project. The project as a whole was, in fact, modelled directly upon the project of the Tver majority.[2]

Nizhnii Novgorod

The projects of the Nizhnii Novgorod committee provide an interesting comparison of gentry views within one province. Situated immediately to the east of Vladimir, the province of Nizhnii Novgorod comprised two basic economic regions. The northern half of the province was rather typical of the 'central industrial region'; there *obrok* prevailed, peasant crafts flourished, and the land alone was little valued.[3] Absenteeism among the owners of estates in this area, many of which were quite large, was almost a general rule.[4]

---

[1] This maximum allotment was higher than the existing *average* allotment of 3·81 *desiatiny*.

[2] *Ibid.*, pp. 256–66. The project of the Vladimir minority did not, however, extend its plan of general administrative reform to the *uezd* level. In most other respects the two projects were identical. The Tver committee finished its project well before the Vladimir minority wrote its own, and the journals of the Tver committee were regularly received by the Vladimir committee. (See p. 158 above, footnote.) Little is known about the individual participants of the Vladimir minorities, whose leaders were D. P. Gavrilov and I. S. Bezobrazov, respectively. Zimina suggests that they were representatives of the 'capitalizing' or 'embourgeoisified' gentry. Three of the six members of the first minority were engaged in extensive cultivation of their demesne lands, where they had introduced machinery (threshing machines) and crop rotation. Two of them employed hired laborers. Two of the representatives of the second minority were 'members from the government'. *Ibid.*, pp. 24–45; 256–8.

[3] F. Chebaevskii, 'Nizhegorodskii gubernskii dvorianskii komitet 1858g', *Voprosy istorii*, no. 6 (1947), p. 86.

[4] According to the minority representatives in the Nizhnii Novgorod committee 'barely a fifth, and at times only a tenth of the *pomeshchiki* lived in the country'. Kornilov, 'Gubernskie komitety', no. 5, p. 72.

The Liberal program elsewhere in Russia

The southern half of the province consisted partly of the north-eastern reaches of the black soil zone. There and in the neighboring *uezdy*, *barshchina* prevailed on the *pomeshchik* estates.[1] Gentry holdings in this area, generally smaller than in the north, were for the most part directly exploited by the *pomeshchiki*, who often supplemented the *barshchina* of their serfs with hired peasant labor.[2]

The gentry of the former territory, relatively secure with the largely extra-agricultural income afforded by their *obrok* peasants, tended to conservatism. It was among the gentry of the fertile southern region that more considerable support for peasant emancipation was found. The result of this dichotomy of gentry views and interests was a severe conflict in the provincial committee which was finally resolved only by the direct intervention of the central government.

The initial response of the Nizhnii Novgorod gentry to the government's Rescript was enthusiastic. In a general assembly of the gentry a large majority of the assembled *pomeshchiki* and all the gentry marshals vowed to 'fulfill the Emperor's sacred will'. With the encouragement of the liberal governor A. N. Murav'ev,[3] the gentry sent off its request to open a provincial gentry committee. The request expressed the added desire to grant land to the peasants in return for redemption.[4] It was the first spontaneous gentry response to the Rescript and the Nizhnii Novgorod gentry were the first to open a provincial committee (on 10 February 1858).[5]

---

[1] Chebaevskii, 'Komitet', p. 86. Ignatovich's statistics show that for the province as a whole, 68% of the landlord's peasants paid *obrok*, 32% acquitted *barshchina*. Ignatovich, *Pomeshchich'i krest'iane*, p. 52.

[2] Chebaevskii, 'Komitet', p. 86. ('Direct exploitation by the *pomeshchiki*' refers of course to maintenance of demesne, not necessarily to personal direction of the landlord.)

[3] A. N. Murav'ev had been one of the founders of the pre-Decembrist society the 'Union of Salvation' in 1816. Although he ceased to be active in the secret societies in 1819, he was exiled to Siberia after the Decembrist uprising. There he began a career as an administrator, and in the beginning of Alexander II's reign was appointed governor of Nizhnii Novgorod. A friend of Lanskoi (both had been 'proto-Decembrists' and members of the 'Union of Prosperity'), Murav'ev was placed in Nizhnii Novgorod as a governor who could be relied upon to carry through with the preparation of reform there. In this respect his appointment was one of a kind with those of Baranov in Tver, Artsimovich in Kaluga, and Grot in Samara. Kornilov, 'Gubernskie komitety', no. 2, pp. 221–2; Chebaevskii, 'Komitet' p. 87.

[4] Chebaevskii, 'Komitet', pp. 86–7.   [5] *Ibid.*, pp. 87–8.

Differences of opinion existed in the Nizhnii Novgorod committee from the very beginning. A significant number of deputies favored land-redemption and the removal of all seigneurial authority, but the government instructions had not provided for either of these possibilities, and a majority in the committee opposed their consideration. The majority of the committee, consisting mainly of deputies from the northern, *obrok* regions, proposed restriction of the legislation to the twelve-year transition period, and opposed redemption either of allotments or of the peasant *usad'ba*. The majority also insisted that the committee's project should include explicit terms for remuneration for the labor and persons of the peasants. After violent conflicts in the committee, culminated by the resignation of the chairman (Boltin) and the entire minority of eleven members, order was restored by the direct intervention of the central government: The majority was given a strong reprimand for departing from the government's instructions (in its rejection of redemption of the *usad'ba*, and in its attempt to receive undisguised redemption for the peasants themselves); the minority, supported by the governor and the committee chairman, were assured of the 'Tsar's grace' and asked to carry on the work of the committee.[1]

Finally the majority, consisting of thirteen members, presented a project for the twelve-year transition period only. According to this project, the peasants in their communes were to remain under the direct authority of the *pomeshchiki*. They were to be granted, in use, an allotment of two *desiatiny* per soul, for a yearly *obrok* of eight rubles. The *usad'ba*, to the redemption of which the majority had been forced to agree, was evaluated at the extraordinarily high price of 480 rubles per *desiatina*.[2] According to the majority project, wrote governor Murav'ev: 'Serfdom is abolished only in words, but in fact remains with all its consequences'.[3]

---

[1] *Ibid.*, pp. 89–92; V. Snezhnevskii, 'Krepostnye krest'iane i pomeshchiki nizhegorodgskoi gubernii nakanune reformy 19 fev. 1861 i pervye gody posle nee', *Nizhegorodskaia gubernskaia uchenaia arkhivnaia komissiia. Sbornik statei, soobschenii, opisei i dokumentov*, III (Nizhnii Novgorod, 1898), 76–8.

[2] Chebaevskii, 'Komitet', p. 92; Skrebitskii, *Krest'ianskoe delo*, III, 659. By Ignatovich's calculations, the average existing peasant allotment in the province was about 3·83 *desiatiny*. Ignatovich, *Pomeshchich'i krest'iane*, pp. 296–7. [3] Chebaevskii, 'Komitet', p. 92.

The minority of the Nizhnii Novgorod committee, consisting of nine members (most of whom represented the southern *uezdy* of the province),[1] presented a separate project. This project proposed a six-year transition period, to be followed by the redemption of the peasants' allotments. The allotment norm which had been decided upon by the majority this group found too large, and proposed in its stead an allotment of $1\frac{1}{4}$ *desiatiny* per soul.[2] The obligations proposed by this group were, however, considerably lower than the majority proposals: 4·80 rubles yearly *obrok* for the normal allotment. The *usad'ba* was also evaluated much lower.[3]

Unlike many projects favoring land-redemption, that of the Nizhnii Novgorod minority was equivocal about totally abolishing the *pomeshchik's* seigneurial authority. In principle, abolition of the *pomeshchik* authority was recognized by the minority:

...With the new status of the peasants [declared the minority] executive and administrative authority in the rural communes cannot and must not be placed on the *pomeshchiki*, because, on the one hand, *the pomeshchik is an independent individual who lives where he likes and occupies himself with what he likes;* and on the other hand, the peasants and the *pomeshchiki* will constitute two commercially-contracting parties, and it would be unjust to place one of them under the direct police authority of the other.[4]

'Therefore', declared the minority project, 'the peasants *in their internal economic administration* must be administered by themselves, by the commune [*mir*]'.[5] Nevertheless, the minority provided that the *pomeshchik, if he wished,* could receive the authority of 'head of the community'. The *pomeshchik*, in other words, was relieved of the *obligation* but not the right to wield some authority over the peasants living on his estate.[6]

The projects of the Nizhnii Novgorod committee reflect a curious *mélange* of *pomeshchik* views: The majority at first aspired

---

[1] Cf. Kornilov, 'Gubernskie komitety', no. 5, p. 73, fn.
[2] Such an allotment would have meant a reduction, on the average, of about 60% from the amount of land previously held by the peasantry, as compared to about 37% as a result of the proposal of the majority project. Chebaevskii, 'Komitet', p. 93.
[3] *Ibid.* Skrebitskii, *Krest'ianskoe delo*, III, 660.
[4] Kornilov, 'Gubernskie komitety', no. 5, p. 71.
[5] *Ibid.*, p. 72.   [6] *Ibid.*

to the retention of the peasant *usad'ba*[1] and direct remuneration for the peasants themselves. Failing this, they sought to gain as much compensation as possible through high evaluation of the *usad'ba*. Their main concern, in other words, was to gain somehow compensation for their peasants' *obrok*, which to a large extent represented non-agricultural income. Restricting the size of the allotments left to peasant usage was not, apparently, an all-important consideration.

To the representatives of the minority, redemption of *some* land by the peasants meant a source of capital with which the gentry could (in the words of the committee chairman) 'organize their economies on solid and profitable conditions, adapted to the new order of things'.[2] But the allotment of land which these *pomeshchiki*—representatives of the fertile *barshchina uezdy*—were willing to grant to the peasants was not generous; the more so because these gentry, like their counterparts in Kaluga and nearly everywhere in Russia, feared making their peasants economically independent on their allotments and therefore uninclined to hire out as agrarian laborers or to rent additional lands.[3] The allotment proposed by the minority of the Nizhnii Novgorod committee made both these possibilities extremely remote.

Moscow

The proposals of the Moscow committee afford a marked contrast to some of the other committees of the *obrok*-dominated black soil region where a considerable willingness to consider the redemption of peasant lands was displayed.

The government, aware of the political significance of the Moscow gentry corporation (as the home of many of the country's great aristocrats and, relatedly, as the center of gentry political

[1] It is worth noting that in general, on *obrok* estates, the peasant *usad'ba* constituted the heart of the peasant economy: The peasants' dwellings, their other immovable and movable property were concentrated there; the *usad'ba* was the source of all-important fertilizer; and, on many *obrok* estates, the site of peasant crafts and trades. For the *pomeshchik* whose peasants were on *obrok*, retention of the peasant *usad'ba* often seemed the only way to retain the income from that *obrok*.

[2] Chebaevskii, 'Komitet', p. 89.

[3] Kornilov, 'Gubernskie komitety', no. 5, p. 73.

awareness), had been anxious to get the Moscow gentry to be the first, along with their peers in Petersburg, to respond to the Nazimov Rescript. But in Petersburg it had had to resort to a fabrication, and in Moscow it took behind-the-scene prodding of the Governor-General, Count Zakrevskii, by the Minister of Interior to produce similar results.

The Moscow response finally came on 7 January 1858: Five hundred gentry, the Moscow address to the Emperor announced, had expressed the desire to 'undertake the improvement of the landlords' peasants', but with certain conditions attached— namely, that the projected Moscow committee should have the right to 'free discussion of the principles which would lay at the base of the project' for accomplishing this; and that the committee's deliberations should not be restricted to a six-month period. The gentry, in short, would agree to consider the reform only on their own terms.

Alexander II, however, responded only with the usual rescript, and with the additional cool reminder that the Moscow committee would be obliged to adhere to the same principles and operating procedures as all the other committees.[1]

Once gathered, the Moscow committee, whose members came armed with directives from their *uezd* assemblies, displayed the usual factionalism—a number of conservative deputies bent on changing things as little as possible, and in particular opposed to the government program because of its prescribed alienation of gentry property; the 'moderate conservatives', generally inclined in the same direction, but committed to observance of the governmental instructions; and the adherents of the liberal reform program.[2]

The distribution of views in the committee produced a working majority somewhat to the right of center. The most energetic and able representative of this position was Prince A. S. Menshi-

---

[1] *Materialy*, I, 276–8.

[2] The positions taken by the committee membership on the major issues debated are identified in N. M. Druzhinin, 'Moskovskoe dvorianstvo i reforma 1861 goda', *Izvestiia akademii nauk SSSR. Seriia istorii i filosofii*, v, no. 1 (1948), 62–78. (The article is incorporated, with some additions and deletions, in Akademiia nauk SSSR, *Istoriia Moskvy*, IV [Moscow, 1954], ch. 1.)

kov (1787–1869), a one-time favorite of Nicholas I, ex-commander-in-chief of the Crimean Army, and currently a member of the State Council.[1] Menshikov, who wrote the bigger part of the majority project in the committee, was concerned to give up as little land as possible and to retain as much as possible of gentry authority over the peasants within the limits dictated by the government instructions.

The liberal reform minority was led by the young provincial procurator D. A. Rovinskii, a modest *pomeshchik* of Zvenigorod *uezd* with a background (and future) as a lawyer-humanitarian.[2] Rovinskii and his followers (including the other deputy from Zvenigorod, Gvozdev, two deputies from Dmitrovo *uezd*, Pal'chi-kov and Danilov, and, on some issues, the chairman of the committee, Voeikov) worked for acceptance by the committee of the liberal reform program: full emancipation with land for government-guaranteed redemption (they also argued for the retention, in principle, of existing allotments), immediate abolition of *barshchina*, and complete elimination of direct *pomeshchik* authority over the peasants.

In its draft project, the Moscow majority refused to consider the redemption of any of the land, even of the *usad'ba*, whose redemption was called for in the government instructions. It provided only for the 'permanent use' of the *usad'ba* by the peasants, with the question of its redemption left up to 'mutual agreement' between peasants and *pomeshchiki*. And the dimensions of this *usad'ba* prescribed by the majority were such that they would have restricted it virtually to the land underneath the peasant buildings, removing thereby all gardens, cattle yards and

---

[1] *Materialy*, I, 303–4; Druzhinin, 'Moskovskoe dvorianstvo', pp. 64, 67.

[2] Son of the Moscow Chief of Police, Rovinskii (1824–95) had studied in the Petersburg Law Institute and then entered government service in Moscow (Ministry of Justice). Before the emancipation, Rovinskii had already gained a considerable reputation as a defender of peasant interests. After 19 February 1861, he, like A. M. Unkovskii, became a publicist champion of judicial reform and was one of the most influential advocates of the introduction of the jury system. In 1862 he was called to Petersburg to participate in the planning of the judicial reform, and after its promulgation in 1864 he served in a number of posts in the reformed system. In 1870 he was appointed to the Senate. In his later years Rovinskii acquired a reputation as an historian of art and Russian culture. Cf. the biographical sketch by A. F. Koni in *Entsiklopedicheskii slovar'* (Brok-gauz-Efron), LII, 870–3; and Dzhanshiev, *Epokha velikikh reform*, pp. 658–71.

the like.[1] Providing a three-category system of allotment norms
for the twelve-year transition period only, the majority project
prescribed plots of from 1½ to 4 *desiatiny* per *tiaglo* (or a maximum
of a little more than 1½ *desiatiny* per soul), norms which promised
a reduction of from 50 to 75 per cent of most existing peasant
allotments.[2] For these allotments, the peasants were to pay either
barshchina dues or a high *obrok* of 21–25 rubles per household
(depending on allotment size).[3] The majority project also provided for the retention of considerable authority in the hands of
the *pomeshchik*: While recognizing that the *pomeshchik* could no
longer move the peasants about without their permission, control
their property or dictate their marriages, the committee provided
that the *pomeshchik* was to remain 'head of the peasant community' which was to be formed on each estate: Meetings of the
community were to take place only with his permission, and all
decisions of the community (election of officials, choice of
recruits, etc.) had to be confirmed by him as well.[4]

Before the majority project was definitively composed,
Alexander II made a trip to Moscow, in late August 1858,
during which he made a speech to the marshals of gentry. In his
remarks he expressed displeasure with the committee's project:

You remember that I told you, two years ago in this same room, that
sooner or later it would be necessary to proceed with the abolition of
serfdom, and that it was necessary to being rather from above than
from below . . . When, after the appeal of Petersburg and the Lithua-

---

[1] A majority of the deputies at first refused to include any land in the *usad'ba*, defining it,
in violation of the government's definition, only as peasant buildings and equipment.
Those in the committee, like Menshikov, who argued for at least formal observance of
the government instructions succeeded in reversing this definition, but a majority was
not found for recognition of the peasants' right to redeem the *usad'ba* (also called for
in the instructions). V. I. Picheta, 'Vopros ob usadebnoi osedlosti v Moskovskom
gubernskom komitete', *Uchenye zapiski instituta istorii (RANION)*, v (Moscow, 1928),
430–59.
[2] Druzhinin, 'Moskovskoe dvorianstvo', p. 67. The average existing peasant allotment
in the province under serfdom was about 2·6 *desiatiny* per soul.
[3] *Barshchina* dues were set at 80 days each of 'male' and 'female' labor per year (65 of
which were to be fulfilled during the sowing and harvesting period). The burden of the
obrok payment demanded by the majority can be compared to that of the Tver committee, which required a maximum *obrok* of 22·50 rubles per *tiaglo* for an allotment more
than twice the size of the maximum proposed by the Moscow committee. Kornilov,
'Gubernskie komitety', no. 4, p. 82.
[4] Druzhinin, 'Moskovskoe dvorianstvo', p. 72.

nian provinces, my rescripts were sent out, I, I confess, anticipated
that the Moscow gentry would be the first to respond; the Nizhnii
Novgorod gentry responded, but Moscow province was not the first,
nor the second, nor even the third . . . I gave you the principles and
from them I will not retreat . . . I love the gentry, I consider it the first
support of the throne. I desire the general welfare but I do not wish
that it be achieved at your cost; I am always ready to stand up for you;
but you, for your own benefit, must make an effort for the welfare
of the peasants. Remember that all Russia is watching Moscow province. I am always ready to do for you what I can; give me the
possibility to defend you. Do you understand, gentlemen? I hear that
the committee has already done much: I have read extracts from its
proceedings; there is much that seems to be good. I have noticed one
thing written about the *usad'by*. I understand as the *usad'ba* homestead not alone the buildings but all the *usad'ba* land. I repeat once
again, gentlemen, act in such a fashion that I can stand up for you.
With this you will justify my faith in you.[1]

Following the Emperor's intervention, the committee, on
the initiative of its chairman, elected a subcommittee to revise the
majority project: the peasants were given the right to redeem the
usad'ba, and some of the higher obligation norms were revised
downward.[2]

The liberal minority argued for adoption of the liberal reform
program in the committee, but in vain. Following the visit of
the Emperor, they did succeed in gaining 14 votes (against 15)
for the addition of a supplementary redemption project—that
is, allowing the *pomeshchik* to choose between 'permanent usage'
and redemption—but only at the price of accepting for this
project the majority's allotment and obligation figures. (Ultimately, Rovinskii and his colleagues sent their redemption project to the Ministry of Interior independently, after the closing
of the committee.)[3]

The poor showing of the liberal program and the character of
the committee's majority proposals in general can be attributed
in part to economic circumstances prevailing in Moscow province.
Although the pattern of gentry landholding and the character of

[1] *Materialy*, I, 374.
[2] Druzhinin, 'Moskovskoe dvorianstvo', p. 75.　　　[3] *Ibid.*

peasant obligations in Moscow province were in most respects typical for the 'central-industrial' region in general,[1] economic conditions of the province, and within them the circumstances of many gentry landholders, were considerably different from surrounding areas. The province was comparatively heavily-populated (with three times as many inhabitants, but one-third the territory, of Tver province, for example); commerce and industry were more developed than in the surrounding provinces. Handi-crafts and other non-agricultural pursuits were widely developed among the peasants, mainly due to the demands of the populous capital; and for the same reason agricultural prices were high and the production of foodstuffs for the market was carried on on many gentry estates. 'Mixed obligations' were frequent on gentry estates, but it was especially through high *obrok* rates that the gentry profited from the economic vitality of the province.[2] Land prices were high, too, and promised to be even higher after the emancipation.[3]

These circumstances, which were well understood in the com-mittee, produced a strong movement there to keep as much of the land as possible for the gentry. The prospect of furnishing the large agricultural market, which turned the committee's attention to the problem of the continued availability of peasant labor, re-enforced this tendency (by the familiar argument that if the peasants were given too much land they would not hire out) and also made the liberal proposal for the abolition of labor rent unattractive to the committee majority. The desire to retain access to the considerable sources of non-agricultural peasant income, hitherto tapped by high *obrok* obligations, was equally in evidence in the committee's deliberations.

These conditions were reenforced by a number of political circumstances. Moscow (at the same time that it was the center of abolitionist publicism) was the home-base of an unusually

[1] Cf. Druzhinin, 'Moskovskoe dvorianstvo', p. 63.
[2] *Ibid.* About 15% of the landlord's peasants in the province fulfilled 'mixed obliga-tions', but in some areas much greater percentages of peasants did so, a fact which confirms the thesis, stated in chapter 2, that economic development before 1861 generally led the *pomeshchiki* to increasingly flexible exploitation of the existing modes of peasant obligations. [3] *Ibid.*, p. 68.

large number of great aristocrats, and, with this, the center of gentry political self-consciousness. In general, it was in Moscow (along with Petersburg, for identical reasons) that the government's reform plans provoked the most pretentious reactions of injured class sensibilities, references to the state's 'illegal' attack on the gentry's 'historic' rights and privileges, and ultimately (as will be seen in succeeding chapters) a counter-attack in the form of an 'aristocratic constitutionalism' calling for the creation of a Russian version of the English House of Lords. Considerable responsibility for the character of the Moscow committee's proposals can be attributed to Count Zakrevskii, the Governor-General. Far from supporting the liberal faction, at least within the limits dictated by the office, as had Baranov in Tver, Murav'ev in Nizhnii Novgorod, Artsimovich in Kaluga, or Grot in Samara,[1] Zakrevskii sympathized with and apparently directly encouraged the right wing of the committee which was intent on rejecting the government's instructions.[2] He also was responsible for appointing as members-from-the-government men who were unsympathetic to the liberal position: Prince V. A. Menshikov and N. A. Volkov.[3] The Governors-General of the capital cities and their provinces, in contrast to the ordinary provincial governors, were generally political appointments from among the high aristocracy, and were thus men (most often of military background) whose political orientation was usually conservative. Zakrevskii was no exception to this rule.

[1] See below, pp. 183–9.
[2] A courtier of Nicholas' reign like Menshikov, Zakrevskii was also a landowner of Moscow province, where he had three estates. In preparation for Alexander's visit to Moscow in August 1858, Zakrevskii prepared a memorandum for the Emperor on the subject of emancipation in general and the questions discussed in the Moscow committee in particular. Here he supported the right-wing objection to the redemption of the *usad'ba*, as well as to the alienation of any gentry land, arguing on the grounds of gentry rights and the threat of economic and political disaster. He also proposed that the 'temporary-obligatory' period last no less than 24 years. He ended by urging the Emperor to allow the gentry committee to discuss the reform as it saw fit, without external hindrances. Druzhinin, 'Moskovskoe dvorianstvo', pp. 72–4.
[3] V. A. Menshikov was the apparently somewhat prodigal son of Prince A. S. Menshikov. According to the editors of the *Materialy* (I, 303–4), Zakrevskii appointed him to the committee as a favor to his father, who wanted in this way to prevent his going abroad. Apparently this plan failed, because Menshikov was replaced as member-from-the-government by one N. N. Pavlov. Volkov died before the committee closed and was replaced by A. F. Tomashevskii (*Ibid.*)

The Liberal program elsewhere in Russia

The activities of these committees and the fortunes of the liberal reform program in them were greatly influenced by three men: Iurii Fedorovich Samarin, Aleksandr Ivanovich Koshelev, and Prince Vladimir Aleksandrovich Cherkasskii. They served, respectively, as members-from-the-government in the committees of Samara, Riazan, and Tula provinces. A considerable literature exists on these three men, sometimes called (along with Ivan Aksakov) the 'liberal Slavophiles', who were among the most brilliant and influential champions of peasant reform to be found anywhere in Russia during the 1850s.[1] In the present context they will be considered as members of provincial gentry committees without extensive reference to their numerous activities elsewhere.

Koshelev, the oldest of the three, was born in 1806, the son of a notable member of the Moscow gentry who had studied at Oxford in his youth. After matriculating briefly at Moscow University (1821-2) Aleksandr Koshelev entered service in the archives of the Foreign Ministry (as did Unkovskii later) where he became acquainted with Prince V. F. Odoevskii and was one of the founders of the 'Society of the Lovers of Wisdom', an early landmark in the history of Idealist philosophy in Russia. In the late Twenties Koshelev became one of the 'original' Slavophiles, under the influence of A. S. Khomiakov. Following experience in several branches of government service, and several journeys abroad (during which he became acquainted with many of the major intellectual figures of the time) Koshelev acquired by purchase a large estate (of more than 3,000 souls) in Riazan province and retired to it in the early 1830s. There he undertook to become a 'model *pomeshchik*' and 'rational farmer', and engaged in the state spirits concession (which he later condemned

---

[1] Much of their writings and mutual correspondence have been published: O. Trubetskaia (ed.), *Materialy dlia biografii kniazia V. A. Cherkasskogo*, vols. I-II (Moscow, 1901-4); A. I. Koshelev, *Zapiski, 1812-83* (Berlin, 1884); Iu. F. Samarin, *Sochineniia*, vols. I-X (Moscow, 1877-1911).

and for the abolition of which he propagandized).[1] In the late 1840s Koshelev began actively to advocate peasant emancipation, and took a leading role in the Lebedianskoe Agriculture Society, one of the numerous organizations established in this period for the propagation of rational farming methods. After the war, in 1856, Koshelev became editor of the new journal of Slavophile orientation, *Russkaia beseda*, and in 1858, when some measure of initiative was granted to the press in the discussion of the 'peasant question', he founded a supplement to that journal, called *Sel'skoe blagoustroistvo*, which was devoted entirely to articles (mostly written by gentry landowners) on that subject. In 1857, he composed his memoir (mentioned in chapter 2) arguing for immediate emancipation of the peasants with land.[2]

Samarin's background was not unlike Koshelev's. Born into a wealthy and highly-placed gentry family in 1819, he took a degree in philosophy at Moscow University, where he became engrossed in Idealist philosophy and the history of Russian theology, also as a disciple of Khomiakov. Completing his studies in 1844, he entered government service, where his tour of duty in the Baltic Provinces and in the Ukraine made of him an ardent Great Russian nationalist and imbued him with lasting suspicion of the landed gentry. In 1853, Samarin resigned from service and retired to the country, where he began to turn serious attention to the question of emancipation, beginning with an extensive study of agrarian reform in Prussia (later published, in 1858, in Koshelev's *Sel'skoe blagoustroistvo*), and his own memoir on emancipation for Russia, which he finished in 1856. In the same year he began active participation in the publication of

[1] The spirits concession was without doubt the greatest bureaucratic scandal in mid-century Russia. A system for the 'farming-out' by the government of the production and sale of alcoholic beverages (created by Peter the Great), it provided the government, in 1858, with more than 30% of its regular revenues, and involved nearly fabulous graft and corruption. It naturally, therefore, drew the fire of anti-bureaucratic, free-trade oriented liberal opinion. The pressures on the rural population by the concessionaires, whose revenues grew much more rapidly than those of the state in this business, finally provoked a rather widespread 'sobriety movement' among the peasantry. The concession was abolished in 1863 and replaced by a state monopoly. Cf. V. A. Fedorov, 'Krest'ianskoe trezvennoe dvizhenie 1858–1860 gg.' *Revoliutsionnaia situatsiia v Rossii v 1859–61 gg.* (Moscow, 1962), pp. 107–26.

[2] Koshelev, *Zapiski, prilozhenie* 5.

Russkaia beseda, and subsequently contributed to *Sel'skoe blagous-troistvo*.

Prince Cherkasskii, of even more illustrious background, was born in Tula in 1824. He graduated from the juridical faculty of Moscow University (1844) with a silver medal for his thesis, 'A History of the Rural Class in Russia'. Unlike his two colleagues, Cherkasskii did not enter service as a young man, but retired directly to Tula province, where he soon took up serious study of the peasant question and produced his first project of emancipation in the mid-1840s. At the same time he undertook to free his *obrok* peasants (for payment of redemption), and took part in a group of local *pomeshchiki* who were preparing projects of emancipation for their peasants to be presented to Nicholas I.[1] These plans were cut short in 1848. Cherkasskii, unlike Koshelev and Samarin, had not been converted to Slavophilism, and became closely acquainted with the Slavophiles only during the Crimean War, in Moscow. (Indeed, his relations with the liberal Slavophiles Koshelev and Samarin, which began at this time, were never based on philosophical agreement, but rather on practical approaches to the problem of reform, especially peasant reform. In no religious or philosophical sense was Cherkasskii a Slavophile. His identification with Slavophilism [often made in the historical literature] apparently rests entirely on the fact of his cooperation with Koshelev and Samarin, which lasted through the period of their activities as deputies to the provincial committees in 1858–9).[2] Cherkasskii began his activities as an abolitionist publicist in the projected (but never published) Slavophile organ *Moskovskii sbornik* (1851). After the armistice, he became, along with Koshelev and Samarin, a main contributor to Koshelev's journals. In January 1857, his memoir, 'On the Best Means for the Gradual Abolition of Serfdom', was presented to Lanskoi.[3]

[1] See above, p. 31.
[2] This 'triumvirate' began to fall apart as soon as political questions (primarily questions about the relation between government and gentry in the legislating on reform) came to the fore. Cf. R. Wortman, 'Koshelev, Samarin and Cherkassky and the Fate of Liberal Slavophilism', *Slavic Review*, June 1962, pp. 260–79.
[3] Trubetskaia, *Materialy*, II, *prilozhenie*, 15–67.

The provincial gentry committees, 1858–9

These extraordinary *pomeshchiki* were drawn together by the common cause of emancipation, and their championing of that cause secured their appointments as members-from-the-government in their respective provinces (these are the three best examples of the government's general policy). From the beginning of their duties in the provincial committees, Koshelev, Samarin and Cherkasskii conducted a three-cornered correspondence by which they maintained an essential unity of aims. These aims, at the time they undertook their duties in the committees, were somewhat less far-reaching than those of the Tver liberals. They consisted of the following essential propositions: Emancipation of the peasants with their *usad'by* and with their existing allotments left in their inalienable use. Redemption of land by the peasants was to be the final outcome of the emancipation, but not necessarily the immediate and obligatory outcome (that is, they admitted the possibility of a transition period). Further than this they did not, at that time, proceed, at least so far as their practical aims were concerned. In their general views on broader questions of reform, however, they stood close to the Tver liberals and most of the educated public of the time, as this comment written by Samarin to Cherkasskii on 18 November 1857, reveals:

Ce qu'il y a de plus triste, c'est qu'on semble ne pas comprendre qu'un échec politique comme celui que nous avons subi, et que nous nous subissons encore, oblige entrer franchement dans la voie du progrès à l'interieure, qu'il ne s'agit pas seulement de reparer quelques injustices criantes, ou de distribuer quelques aumones, mais bien d'éveiller toutes les forces productives du pays, les forces morales et intellectuelles, comme les forces materielles, en abolissant le servage (*kazennoe i pomeshchich'e krepostnoe pravo*) en rendant la parole a l'eglise, en donnant une base plus large à l'enseignement public, en reformant notre système d'impot personnel et notre mode de recruitement. En un mot, il faut un plan arrêté, il faut savoir ce que l'on veut et ne pas vivre d'expedient, au jour le jour. Maintenant toute mesure projetée, bonne ou mauvaise, a les mêmes chances de succès.[1]

On the immediate question of emancipation, their views were nearly in accord with those of the government as expressed in

[1] Trubetskaia, *Materialy*, I, 86.

the Rescripts and the government program.[1] In general, Koshelev, Samarin and Cherkasskii accepted the government's initiative warmly, and with little criticism. This attitude may have been largely due to the nature of their appointments and their hope of being given positions of influence in the further elaboration of the reform, a hope which they realistically maintained as well-known advocates of reform with highly-placed acquaintances in government circles.[2] In any case they tended to look upon the government's program differently from those gentry abolition-ists, in Tver and elsewhere, who regarded it as nothing but a hindrance. In their committees, circumstances were such that they found it better to rely on the program as a guarantee of a minimum platform—in effect they found themselves using the program as a shield against attacks from the right, in particular against advocates of a landless emancipation.[3] In the process they found themselves involved in some of the most dramatic events to have occurred anywhere in the provincial committees: All three were constantly plied with poison-pen letters; Koshelev was driven out of the Riazan committee at one point; Cherkasskii was censured by the gentry assembly of Tula and challenged to a duel (which was eventually averted); and Samarin for a time wore a pistol in his belt and was accompanied by serf bodyguards while attending the committee meetings in Samara. And as deputies from the government, all three were accused of being traitors to their class, operating on secret orders from the government.[4]

[1] They objected initially only to the formal distinction made in the Rescripts between the *usad'ba* and the remainder of the peasants' holdings. Cf. Kornilov, 'Gubernskie komitety', no. 3, p. 117.

[2] Cherkasskii, for example, was at this time a close confidant of the Grand Duchess Elena Pavlovna.

[3] On 4 July 1858, Koshelev wrote to Samarin and Cherkasskii about the program: 'I do not think that the program should be departed from at the very beginning. However bad it is, our gentry are one hundred times worse, and therefore we have to catch hold of [the program], especially at first.' Trubetskaia, *Materialy*, I, 117. Samarin replied in agreement: '... Our voice in the committee will be able to have some meaning only on the condition that we firmly hold to [the program] and depart from it as little as possible.' *Ibid.*, p. 119.

[4] Cf. *Ibid.*, I, 233.

The Riazan committee

Riazan province was roughly bifurcated by the line separating the black soil zone of central Russia from the non-black soil region to its north. *Barshchina* dominated in the province among the land-lords' peasants. A very high percentage of smallholding *pomesh-chiki* lived in the province (a fact which led to the elaboration of extensive special rules by the provincial committee to safeguard their interests). The gentry of Riazan, according to the report of the provincial marshal, Selivanov, apparently accepted the news of the Nazimov Rescript with relative equanimity, but to the idea of losing any property they generally reacted with hostility.[1]

In the Riazan committee, which opened on 26 August 1858, Koshelev soon found himself in a minority of two with the other member-from-the-government, D. F. Samarin (brother of Iurii Samarin), although Koshelev himself declared that at least eight members of the committee were sincere proponents of emancipation.[2] At the end of its stormy activities, the Riazan committee presented two projects to the government: a majority project, and a minority project written by Koshelev and Samarin. (In addition the two deputies of Ranenburg *uezd* appended comments to the majority project which, while not constituting a separate project, allowed them subsequently to send a repre-sentative to Petersburg for consultation with the government.)

The committee majority produced a project for the transition period alone (as called for in the government program), with the added stipulation that after the twelve-year transition period the peasants were to lose the right to purchase their *usad'by* and any further arrangements (apparently for all the land) were to be made by 'free agreement of the *pomeshchik* with the peasants'. The majority established norms of allotment of from one to three *desiatiny* per soul (excluding the *usad'ba*), for which the

---

[1] Cf. A. Povalishin, *Riazanskie pomeshchiki i ikh krepostnye* (Riazan, 1903), pp. 305–6; V. N. Eliseeva, 'Podgotovka krest'ianskoi reformy 1861 g. v Riazanskoi gubernii (Ria-zanskii gubernskii dvorianskii komitet 1858–59 gg.)', Riazanskii gos. pedagogicheskii institut, *Uchenye zapiski*, no. 11 (1953), pp. 70–5.

[2] In a letter to his correspondents, Koshelev divided the Riazan committee's members into the following categories: 'Blacks'–14; 'Greys'–5; 'Reds'–8. (Trubetskaia, *Materialy*, I, 177.)

peasants were to pay an *obrok* of approximately 9 rubles per year per soul, or *barshchina* obligations amounting to thirty working days a year. In the majority project for administrative reorganization, the *pomeshchik* was to be left considerable power over the peasant community, as its 'guardian' (*popechitel'*), while plans were drawn up for district (*okrug*) administration to consist of an assembly of all hereditary gentry and any other landowners with holdings in excess of 200 *desiatiny*. This plan was extensively embellished with general comments on the virtues of local self-administration and the separation of powers).[1]

Koshelev and Samarin made proposals significantly different from the majority in several respects: They put no limit on the transition period, except to affirm that it was to be terminated *only* by redemption of the allotments by the peasants. (No distinction was to be made in this respect between the allotments as a whole and the *usad'ba*.) They also advocated retention of existing peasant allotments, but at the same time proposed 'limits' which differed little from the norms established by the majority.[2] As for obligations, Koshelev and Samarin proposed *barshchina* duties about the same as the majority had proposed. *Obrok* obligations stipulated by them were, however, considerably lower than the majority proposal.[3] In matters of administration, Koshelev and Samarin proposed independent self-administration for the peasant communities and institution of an *okrug* administration which would include both the local gentry and representatives from the peasant communes.[4]

Koshelev may have been right in asserting that the committee majority (the fourteen members he designated as 'Blacks') was opposed to emancipation, but there is reason to believe that the animosity he encountered in the committee was not entirely due

---

[1] Povalishin, *Riazanskie pomeshchiki*, pp. 336–40.

[2] Koshelev and Samarin proposed maximum allotment limits of from one to three *desiatiny* (depending on local soil conditions). But even these were considerably lower than the actual existing allotments. The government later established maximum limits of $2\frac{3}{4}$–4 *desiatiny* in the province. Povalishin, *Riazanskie pomeshchiki*, pp. 330–1.

[3] Koshelev and Samarin proposed a yearly *obrok* of 8–10 rubles, but their figure included obligations for both *usad'ba* and field lands which they refused to consider separately. (The majority had demanded a separate sum of 350 rubles for the average *usad'ba*. *Ibid.*, pp. 327–8.) [4] *Ibid.*, pp. 336–40.

to hostility toward reform. Moreover, the project of the majority might well have been less inconclusive and more 'liberal' had it not been for several specific circumstances.

The animosity toward Koshelev, which resulted in his temporary ejection from the committee, was generated not alone by general antipathy toward his pro-emancipation views, but by a specific incident. It arose from the appearance of two articles written by Prince Cherkasskii, in which the latter had defended the temporary retention of corporal punishment for the peasants in the hands of the *pomeshchiki* during the transition period. This article became something of a *cause célèbre* and Ivan Aksakov felt himself called upon to defend the motives of Cherkasskii and the editor of *Sel'skoe blagoustroistvo* and *Russkaia besda* where the articles had appeared (that is, Koshelev). Writing in *Moskovskie vedomosti* (No. 130, 1858), Aksakov praised them as true friends of the peasants and emancipation, who were presently battling against reactionary forces. He closed his defense with reference to their 'victory over the arrogant pretensions of obdurate ignorance and self-interest'. The majority of the Riazan committee took this, not without reason, to be a reference to themselves, and demanded an explanation from Koshelev. (They wanted a refutation from Koshelev to be printed in *Moskovskie vedomosti*). Koshelev refused, in a tactless manner, and the committee voted to remove him from its deliberations. At this point Koshelev voluntarily withdrew, but not for long. He went to Petersburg and saw his old friend Lanskoi, who begged him (according to Koshelev) to stay on.[1] In short order (at the beginning of December 1858), the committee received an Imperial order through the Ministry of Interior demanding the reinstatement of Koshelev.[2]

In this, as in other affairs, the chairman of the committee had tried to steer a middle course between the sentiment of the committee majority and the government's policy. There is little doubt that had he been more decisive, one way or the other, the

---

[1] Koshelev, *Zapiski*, pp. 99–100. In return, Koshelev obtained the appointment of Samarin as the other member-from-the-government, replacing the original appointee who had sided with the conservative majority.

[2] The entire episode is recorded in Povalishin, *Riazanskie pomeshchiki*, pp. 314–18.

committee's project would have turned out considerably different than it did. For example: Several attempts were made during the course of the committee's work, from within the majority, to adopt the solution to the land question which had been devised in the Tver committee. Early in the committee's proceedings, it was decided on the initiative of the deputy F. S. Ofrosimov to form a special commission to develop the 'general principles' on which the committee's work should be based (a proposal identical to that made in Tver by Unkovskii). This was done, and a majority of three in the commission (of five), led by Ofrosimov, made two significant proposals: (1) That redemption of the peasant's labor value should be borne 'not by the peasants themselves, but by the state, that is by all classes in the state or the government'. (2) That if redemption were the Emperor's will, then 'it should be arranged for both *usad'ba* and for field land simultaneously, with the assistance of the government'.[1] These proposals were cardinal components of the liberal gentry program. The chairman, however, refused to allow acceptance of these propositions, on the grounds that they contradicted the Rescripts.[2]

A similar confrontation arose somewhat later as a result of the proposal of the deputy A. M. Afanas'ev. During the discussion of the peasant *usad'ba*, Afanas'ev proposed the definition which had been taken earlier by the Tver committee: 'It is possible to include in the *usad'ba*, first, the land under habitation with all its structures, and secondly, it is useful to include in the *usad'ba* subject to redemption all the land, both *usad'ba* in the narrow sense, and field land as well'' Once again the chairman declared this proposal out of keeping with the government's directives. This time the chairman's decision led to a personal altercation that ended in Afanas'ev's removal from the committee by order of the Ministry of Interior.[3]

Thus, in contrast to Tver, where these propositions had been forwarded by the committee's chairman and defended against

---

[1] This proposition was introduced by the curious phrase: 'Presentation of the land for redemption is impossible, but if it must be done by the unchangeable will of the Sovereign . . .' *Ibid.*, p. 313.
[2] *Ibid.* [3] *Ibid.*, pp. 318–22.

the government's rulings, in Riazan they were made from the sidelines and defeated by the chairman relying on the letter of the directives and the direct authority of the Ministry.

The Tula committee

In the Tula committee Prince Cherkasskii headed a minority[1] in one of the bitterest struggles to have taken place in any of the provincial committees. Unlike Samarin's opponents in the Samara committee,[2] Cherkasskii found that committee majority constituted:

... Besides two fools, all people who are not at all stupid, and some who are positively very intelligent; almost all impossibly stubborn, well-off and cruel conservatives.[3]

Tula province, located immediately to the west of Riazan, possessed nearly the same economic characteristics as the southern, black-soil, region of that province: an overwhelming domination of *barshchina* over *obrok* on gentry estates, fertile land, and a fairly abundant peasant population; in short, a typical province of the central black soil region. The main issue in the Tula committee was clearly the question of land.

Against a majority which fought against peasant land redemption (and for a time refused even to recognize the government-ordered redemption of the *usad'ba*), and for retention of direct *pomeshchik* authority over the peasant communities, while requiring redemption of peasant labor value, Cherkasskii and the Tula minority proposed the liberal solution of land-redemption for the peasants. The minority also proposed an immediate end to *pomeshchik* authority over the peasants, and an allotment and obligation settlement (for the temporary status) which was considerably more generous to the peasants than the majority project.[4]

---

[1] 'Our minority', Cherkasskii wrote to Koshelev at the opening of the committee, 'consists of 10 persons, not completely in agreement among themselves, and in the best circumstances will grow to 12, against 15 or 17.' Trubetskaia, *Materialy*, I, 148. (In the end, the minority project was signed by only six members.)

[2] See below, p. 184.   [3] *Ibid.*, p. 175.

[4] The majority proposed a maximum peasant allotment of about one *desiatina* per soul. The minority figure was two *desiatiny*. Peasant obligations, which were defined by the Tula minority in accordance with the gradation system established by the Tver committee, were reasonably moderate. Cf. Skrebitskii, *Krest'ianskoe delo*, III, 701–3.

The Liberal program elsewhere in Russia

Cherkasskii had to make considerable compromises in order to gain a following in the committee for a more generous land allotment. His personal inclination was the same as that of his correspondents—to defend the existing peasant allotments; in the committee he agreed to a two *desiatiny* allotment norm (per soul) for fear of desertion by his supporters to the majority.[1] (This was noticeably less than the existing average allotment, which was about 2·6–2·8 *desiatiny*.) Like other gentry liberals, Cherkasskii believed in the necessity of presenting the allotments to the peasants for redemption, with the first step of immediately transferring all peasants to *obrok*. At the same time he was more pessimistic than some about the possibility of promulgating an immediate, state-wide program of obligatory redemption.[2]

Gentry support for redemption in Tula province was not inconsiderable: At the gentry assembly held preliminarily to the election of the deputies to the provincial committee (1 September 1858), 105 out of 415 gentry present signed a statement declaring that the peasants of Tula should be presented with their land in property by means of a state financial operation, and that all obligatory relations between *pomeshchiki* and peasants should be abolished immediately.[3]

In the Tula committee, however, the majority was definitely not in favor of this proposal. Cherkasskii, in his struggle with the majority, resolved—like his correspondents—to follow the government program, and accordingly tried to gain acceptance in the committee for the composition of two parallel projects, one with redemption arrangements (as allowed by the government in its decision on the Tver arrangement).[4] Failing that, he

[1] ' . . . I think', Cherkasskii wrote to Koshelev (20 February 1859), 'that the two *desiatiny* allotment supported by the minority has more chances of success than the 2½ *desiatiny* allotment supported by me alone. If I were to act differently, the whole minority would be prepared to go over to the majority . . .' Trubetskaia, *Materialy*, I, 307.

[2] *Ibid.*, p. 294.

[3] Among the signers of this statement were Ivan Turgenev, Leo Tolstoi and A. S. Khomiakov—all Tula *pomeshchiki*. Trubetskaia, *Materialy*, I, 229–30; V. I. Krutikov, 'Tul'skii gubernskii dvorianskii komitet 1858–9 gg.', Tul'skii gos. pedagogicheskii institut, *Uchenye zapiski, vypusk* III (1952), p. 31. (This declaration was subsequently published in *Russki vestnik. Sovremennaia letopis'*, XVII, 339.)

[4] Trubetskaia, *Materialy*, I, 232.

presented to the committee a 'project for redemption by means of a local credit society', which was eventually appended to the minority project.[1]

Cherkasskii clearly saw himself as the leader of abolitionist forces in the province pitted against reaction and self-interest. He reported to his correspondents, not without a certain satisfaction, perhaps, that he was receiving daily unsigned, insulting letters.[2] In November 1858, he wrote that 16 members of the majority had presented to him and P. F. Samarin (another brother of Iu. Samarin and the other member from the government, who had been appointed at Cherkasskii's request)[3] a request, demanding to know if they were receiving 'secret instructions from the government'.[4] Somewhat later, the majority in the committee tried to have Cherkasskii called before a court of peers at the provincial assembly (December 1858), for having offended the local gentry. This action was provoked by the publication of Aksakov's defence of Cherkasskii and Koshelev, which Cherkasskii, like Koshelev, refused to condemn. This led to the signing of a petition of censure and to a general uproar that led the provincial marshal (a supporter of Cherkasskii) to close the assembly temporarily. The episode ended without any definite action being taken. Cherkasskii, on his part, was not without defenders among the gentry. He was given a dinner attended by a third of the gentry present at the assembly (82 out of 280), where he was toasted and hailed as an enlightened product of Moscow University:

First greeting to you, Prince, [so spoke one guest, A. V. Novosil'tsev], from all your university comrades. Moscow University, as the main seed-bed [*rassadnik*] of humanitarian ideas in our society, has the right to take pride in those of its students who, like you, devote their strength to this honorable and humanitarian cause.[5]

---

[1] *Ibid.*, p. 263.   [2] *Ibid.*, p. 232.   [3] *Ibid.*, p. 148.

[4] *Ibid.*, pp. 232–3. It was in connection with this suspicion on the part of the majority that Cherkasskii was challenged to a duel by one of its members, who berated him for 'not sympathizing with the gentry'. Cf. Trubetskaia, *Materialy*, I, 316–17. (Cherkasskii was convinced that the affair had been pre-arranged by the majority in an effort to frighten him out of the committee.)

[5] *Ibid.*, p. 273.

The Liberal program elsewhere in Russia

To this Cherkasskii replied with the following toast:

... I am firmly convinced that I will find agreement from each of you when I propose a toast for the consolidation and development of enlightenment in our beloved fatherland.[1]

The festivities ended with a general toast 'to [our] unforgettable teacher, T. N. Granovskii'.[2]

The Samara committee

In Samara, Iurii Samarin was faced with a situation considerably different from that confronting Koshelev in Riazan or Cherkasskii in Tula. In this huge steppe province located between the Volga and the Urals, the economic and social circumstances of the landed gentry were considerably different from those prevailing in the more centrally-located provinces. In terms of settlement and agricultural patterns, Samara province was still at this time very much a frontier.[3] And in this sparsely-populated region, a marked shortage of labor colored the fears and expectations of the local landowners, 80 per cent of whose peasants were on *barshchina*. This was made clear by the governor, K. K. Grot, in his reply to Lanskoi's inquiry about the response of the local gentry to the news of the Nazimov Rescript:

The first impression produced by the reading of the Imperial rescripts on the *pomeshchiki* was [he wrote] most unsympathetic. They saw in these decrees their ruination and the loss of their property. At the present time, although they have begun to look on the matter more calmly and to become accustomed to the idea of the necessity of undertaking the improvement of the peasant's lot, sympathy toward this question is still not noticeable. The main fear is that because of the large quantity of good free lands of the State Properties and *Udel*

[1] *Ibid.*, p. 274.   [2] *Ibid.*, p. 276.

[3] It is noteworthy that the *zalezh* system of cultivation—repeated intensive cultivation followed by long-term fallow—was still common here in the mid-nineteenth century, a sure sign of sparse population and extensive availability of land. It had long since been abandoned in central Russia. Cf. I. P. Krechetovich, *Krest'ianskaia reforma v Orenburgskom krae (po arkhivnym dannym). Tom I. Podgotovka reformy* (n. p./n. d, but Moscow, 1911), p. 199.

administrations here, which are rented for a cheap price on an *obrok* basis—the peasants upon receiving personal freedom will settle on these lands and leave the *pomeshchiki* without a labor force, as a result of which their incomes will inevitably decrease . . .[1]

The bulk of the local gentry in this frontier province, moreover, were notable for their comparative rudeness and low level of education. This fact was also remarked by Grot, in the same report:

. . . I consider it my obligation to add that there are very few enlightened and knowledgeable gentry in the province entrusted to me, and therefore the majority of their judgments are based on egoism, personal interests and the accidental circumstances of the estates and peasants belonging to them. Impartial judgments, founded on recognition of state and popular needs I have yet to hear.[2]

Samarin, describing his opponents in the provincial committee in a letter to Cherkasskii (9 October 1858), was more blunt:

There is no intelligent, sensible and literate opposition, and one can't be expected . . . We are dealing not with conviction, nor with the interest[s] of people who are aware of their needs and rights, but with savage ignorance, mediocrity, dullness, sloth, and lack of practice in thought and work.[3]

Samarin found himself in a minority of four members in the committee:

Of us, so-called liberals or *extrème gauche*, there are four. Of the moderate . . . and undecided—three; and of the desperate conservatives—nine.[4]

Nevertheless, much of the heightened feeling and hostility which prevailed in the Samara committee—whose details need not be dwelt upon—were due, as they had been in Riazan with Koshelev, to Samarin's undisguised scorn for the 'retrogrades', and to the fact that at every turn he had the support of the liberal governor

---

[1] *Ibid.*, pp. 70–71. [2] *Ibid.*, p. 71.

[3] Quoted in N. Solov'eva, *Liberal'noe dvorianstvo v period podgotovki i provedeniia krest'-ianskoi reformy 1861 g. (Iu. Samarin.)* (Unpublished dissertation, Moscow, 1950), p. 162.

[4] Trubetskaia, *Materialy*, I, 170. (In the end, the minority led by Samarin constituted five persons.)

(and also of the Governor-General of Orenburg Region, Katenin).[1] The committee majority felt themselves abused by the 'bureaucracy' and its 'government man', Samarin.[2]

Despite prevailing circumstances and considerable arguments in the committee, Samarin in the end very nearly had his own way. He wrote the minority project, and was largely responsible for the composition of the articles of the majority project as well, whether as a result of the inability in such matters of the majority (as Samarin claimed) and lack of time, or because of the persuasiveness of his arguments, is not entirely clear.[3] As a result there was little substantive difference between the majority and minority projects of the Samara committee. The minority project proposed somewhat larger land allotments for the peasants than did the majority project, but neither departed significantly from the existing average allotments in the province, as nearly as they could be determined according to several sub-regions. Similarly, the *obrok* payment proposed by the minority was somewhat smaller than the majority proposal (23 as opposed to 25 rubles per year for the average *tiaglo* allotment). Both allowed for reductions in the *barshchina* obligations of the peasants.[4]

In addition to these differences in material arrangements, the

---

[1] The nature of this support included the defence of Samarin by both Grot and Katenin before the *Chef de Gendarmes*, Dolgorukov, whose agent in Samara, one colonel Andreev, plied him with reports about Samarin's 'democratic manifestations' in the committee. (Dolgorukov also received at least one anonymous letter accusing Samarin of having proclaimed in the committee 'the necessity of overthrowing the ruling dynasty'.) Through their intervention, Andreev was removed from his post in June, 1859. (The author is indebted to the late Boris Nicolaevsky for having made available from his personal archives copies of the Grot-Katenin-Dolgorukov correspondence on the 'Andreev case'.)

[2] A detailed account of the committee's activities is given by Krechetovich, chapter 9, pp. 151–236.

[3] Early in the committee's activities, Samarin described his tactic to Koshelev: 'I want to get them to chatter and to introduce a finished project toward the end, when they will be worried about the composition [of a project] and will see that there is no possibility of making anything sensible out of all their resolutions. Then, as almost the sole literate person in the committee, I will have a big advantage.' (Trubetskaia, *Materialy*, I, 120.) Samarin's rather arrogant plan was largely realized (the committee in fact ran out of time and had to petition for an extension), and both the minority and majority projects bore the imprint of Samarin's views, as the governor testified in his assessment of them. (The actual author of the majority project was the other 'government man' on the committee, Mukhanov.) Krechetovich, *Krest'ianskaia reforma*, pp. 227, 235–6 fn.

[4] Krechetovich, *Krest'ianskaia reforma*, p. 232.

majority and minority projects differed in the statutes dealing with the peasant communities: Samarin's minority project quite plainly favored the retention of communal control over all peasant property, allowing for the possibility of land-redemption, for example, by the community alone; whereas the majority in effect left such issues up to the peasants themselves.[1]

There were other less important differences. More significant were the matters on which both the majority and minority projects concurred, and these reflected a clearly liberal orientation. While declining to declare for an immediate cessation of *barshchina*, both majority and minority projects sought to facilitate the transition to *obrok* status for the peasants. Both departed from the government instructions in declining to reserve for the *pomeshchik* the position of 'head of the peasant community', although they did reserve for the *pomeshchik* 'the right to punish [*podvergat' vzyskaniu*] those peasants failing to properly fulfill their obligations to the proprietors'.[2]

Still more significantly, the Samara committee as a whole approved a separate project (following the instructions on this subject which had originally been devised for the Tver committee) on the redemption by the peasants of their allotments.[3] This was, moreover, a retreat from an earlier formulation by the committee, which had simply presented the peasants the right to redeem their allotments: On 2 December 1858, the committee had approved the following proposition as part of the main statute on peasant allotments:

The rural community is presented the right to redeem in full and unrestricted property the peasant land in its entirety; for the determination of the redemption due for this land the *obrok* shall be capitalized at 6 per cent.[4]

In other words, the committee had originally approved the right (but not the necessity) of the peasants to redeem their land without the agreement of the *pomeshchik*, but later removed this from the main statute and made it the subject of a separate project as ordered by the government.

[1] *Ibid.*, pp. 229–30. [2] *Ibid.*, p. 231.
[3] *Ibid.*, p. 177. [4] *Ibid.*, pp. 228–9.

Whether the majority of the committee's members were not sincere in the endorsement of their own project (as Krechetovich asserts),[1] or whether both majority and minority, as according to Grot in his official assessment of the projects, 'worked hard for the genuine improvements of the conditions of the *pomesh-chiks'* peasants';[2] both had in fact 'found it necessary to present to the peasants the right to redeem all the land placed in their use, with the subsequent elimination of obligatory relations of the peasants to the *pomeshchiki'*.[3]

A great deal of the responsibility for the outcome of the Samara committee clearly lay with Samarin, without whom, in the words of Grot (who had appointed him), the committee would not have composed even 'a remotely respectable project'.[4] Samarin recognized the need for the gentry's gradual retreat from dependence on *barshchina* in this labor-scarce province, and thus would not, or could not, propose an immediate end to the practice nor the immediate obligatory redemption of the peasant allotments. He was, apparently, convinced that he had gone as far as possible without seriously jeopardizing the interests of the gentry:

In general [he wrote, in March 1859], if not the whole committee, then at least the minority to which I belong, has gone to the limit of those concessions which the gentry can make without subjecting themselves to complete ruin, and the state to social bankruptcy. In other words we have done everything that could be done ... by way of proper legal reforms, not revolutionary measures.

Let it be said between us that our losses will be enormous ..., but will the people be satisfied with our sacrifices?[5]

Koshelev, Samarin and Cherkasskii were the leaders of abolitionist opinion in their respective provinces. They were, however, unable and, to some extent, unwilling to acquire acceptance in their committees of projects for the complete and immediate emancipation of the peasants with land such as had been done in Tver. Generally speaking, they worked for acceptance

[1] *Ibid.*, p. 236, fn.   [2] *Ibid.*, p. 232.   [3] *Ibid.*, p. 229.
[4] *Ibid.*, p. 234.   [5] Trubetskaia, *Materialy*, I, 309.

of the government program and for acceptance by their committees of reasonably generous allotments and reasonably moderate obligations. In part, their position may have been related to their appointment as members-from-the-government (although other holders of this post, such as Nicholas Bakunin in Tver, were not restrained from departing from the letter of the government program). So, too, especially in relation to the practical matters of allotments and obligations, their outlook was influenced by particular circumstances prevailing in their provinces: the predominance of *barshchina*, land values, population, and the like (this was particularly evident in Samarin's recognition of the need for a transition period which would allow for the gradual abolition of *barshchina*). Most of all, perhaps, their support of the government program is to be explained by their personal views, experience and expectations. All three of them, as their struggle with the conservative gentry majorities continued, became progressively more discouraged about the possibility of expecting positive results from the gentry committees in particular and the provincial gentry in general.[1] Conversely, their hopes in the central government grew apace.[2] All three were, by this time, well-known 'experts' on the peasant question, who entertained hopes of being called by the government to play a major role in the drawing up of the final legislation. And, indeed, early in 1859, Samarin and Cherkasskii, at least, were summoned to Petersburg to sit on the 'editing commissions' which had been established for that purpose.[3]

Their views had always been cautious and colored with 'statism', in the sense of an awareness of the problems facing the government, a receptiveness to governmental modes of thought, and a tendency to look to Petersburg as the only source of change.[4]

---

[1] Cf. Trubetskaia, *Materialy*, I, 230–2.   [2] *Ibid.*, II, 6.

[3] Koshelev was left out, much to his surprise and disgust (and to the surprise of Samarin and Cherkasskii as well). Koshelev, who of the three came nearest to the liberal program's advocacy of state-financed land redemption, may have been rejected because his views were considered too extreme by the government. At the time, Cherkasskii surmised that Koshelev had been rejected because he was editor of a journal and had been having trouble with the censors. Cf. Trubetskaia, *Materialy*, I, 326–8.

[4] An illustration of this, as well as a commentary on his views of the Tver project, is contained in Koshelev's letter to Cherkasskii (February 1859): 'I am sending you . . . the

No doubt this was due mainly to their personal backgrounds as bureaucrats and influential gentry who were accustomed to sharing their views with statesmen and even with members of the Imperial family. Now, as before and later, Samarin, Koshelev, and Cherkasskii proved themselves to be true products of the gentry's tradition of state service.

THE FERTILE SOUTH: KHARKOV

The provincial committee of Kharkov province was one of only three (along with Tver and Kaluga) in all of Russia to produce a majority project based exclusively on obligatory land-redemption. The work of the Kharkov committee, representing the gentry of a southern black soil province, provides an interesting comparison to what is known of the gentry committees of such 'industrial provinces' as Tver, Kaluga, and Vladimir.

The redemption project of the Kharkov committee[1] was in most respects identical to the project of the Kaluga committee and may have been copied after it.[2] In its prescription for the transition period, however, the Kharkov committee was more explicit than the Kaluga project, repeating the provision that had been made by the Tver committee: The temporary-obligatory period was to last no longer than three years, and the redemption operation was to get underway within one year after declaration of emancipation.[3]

Along with these provisions the Kharkov committee ruled

journals and draft statutes of the Tver committee. The project is finished. It is beneficial for the *pomeshchiki* and for the peasants, but for the government—oi, oi, oi! The former receives 145 rubles per soul for four *desiatiny*, or an *obrok* of 8·70 rubles per soul from the *treasury*. The peasants receive four *desiatiny* each and pay 8·70 rubles each. For the manor serfs the *pomeshchiki* receive from the government 60 rubles for each revision soul. *Pas mal!* God grant the government good health and a general's rank.' (Trubetskaia, *Materialy*, II, 293.)

[1] The project of the Kharkov committee was approved by 18 of its 25 members. A minority, though existent, did not present a separate project or send a deputy to Petersburg. N. Tikhonov, 'K kharakteristike dvorianskoi ideologii nakanune padeniia Krepostnogo stroia (Iz istorii Khar'kovskogo gubernskogo komiteta)', *Naukovi zapyski naukovo-doslidchoi katedri istorii ukrain'skoi kultury*, no. 6 (1927), pp. 228–35.

[2] See above, pp. 152–8; and Kornilov, 'Gubernskie komitety', no. 4, 62–4.

[3] Tikhonov, 'K Kharakteristike', p. 228.

that following emancipation the right to buy and dispose of land was to become the right of all classes of the population. All obligatory relations between *pomeshchiki* and peasants were to be immediately terminated—labor rent was to be abolished, and all *pomeshchik* authority over the peasant commune was to cease promptly. The *pomeshchik* was not to be named 'head of the peasant community' (as provided in the government program),

... Because, in the first place, this position would serve the *pomeshchiki* as a new occasion for the continuation, although in another form, of the former arbitrariness; and in the second place, because in Kharkov province two-thirds of the peasants belong to rich *pomeshchiki* who for the most part do not live on their estates.[1]

This situation, the committee declared, would lead to the ruination of peasants and *pomeshchiki* alike, through the corruption and abuse of their powers by the estate-managers of these absentee landlords.[2]

The committee did not propose further, general, changes in local administration, but its deputies, A. G. Shreter and D. A. Khrushchov, who in August 1859 travelled to Petersburg to present their views to the government, adopted outright Unkovskii's plan for an all-class *volost'* and other reforms on the *uezd* level. They then proposed the creation of a 'provincial assembly of representatives' as well.[3]

What explanation did these *pomeshchiki* of a fertile southern province give for their readiness to put an end to serfdom, to part with their seigneurial rights and a portion of the lands of their estates?

Although the committee [read the official commentary to the project of the Kharkov committee]—in order to comply with the [April] program—did not abolish but only shortened as far as possible the transition period, it firmly hopes that the Father of our land, having pronounced first the word of freedom for the peasants . . ., will not neglect . . . the sacrifices and needs of the other class, and by redemption of the lands will perform the good deed for both sides . . .[4]

[1] Kornilov, 'Gubernskie komitety', no. 5, p. 58.
[2] *Ibid.* For the brief transition period the committee proposed administrative control of the peasantry by special officials to be elected (one for each *uezd*) by the local gentry.
[3] See below, pp. 256–9.   [4] Tikhonov, 'K. Kharakteristike', p. 228.

In redemption the Kharkov committee sought 'the full guarantee of the property of the gentry, not only preserving his means of livelihood, but presenting to him *the possibility to begin a new, secure existence*'.[1] What was being described was the new 'farm economy': 'With the abolition of serfdom the decrepit *pomeshchik* economy must disappear and be replaced by a farm economy promising, with the life-giving force of free labor, immeasurably more advantages'.[2]

To create this new economy, argued the Kharkov committee, labor rent must not be allowed to continue, even for the shortest time, for free peasants cannot be made to perform obligatory labor and the *pomeshchiki* would therefore be ruined.[3] The landowner must, however, be assured a settled *labor force*, hence peasant allotments should not be too large, but kept small enough so that the peasants would feel the need to hire out their labor and to rent the lands of the *pomeshchiki*. The prime necessity of the gentry was, of course, capital.[4]

The economic settlement with the peasantry provided by the Kharkov committee was, in accordance with these demands, far from generous. An allotment of from $1\frac{1}{2}$ to $1\frac{5}{6}$ *desiatiny* per soul was proposed, with a money obligation set at 7·20 rubles per soul.[5] For redemption, the committee asked not less than 50 rubles for each *desiatina* of arable land, plus 150 rubles for the *usad'ba*.[6] These figures were plainly meant to include compensation not only for the land, but for the peasants themselves, unremunerated loss of which the Kharkov gentry felt they could ill-afford.[7]

---

[1] *Ibid.*, pp. 229–30. Emphasis added.   [2] *Ibid.*, p. 231.

[3] 'It has [been] demonstrated throughout Germany [stated one declaration of a group of Kharkov gentry] that obligatory labor of a personally free peasant produces less benefit than the servile labor of a Negro driven by the fear of punishment.' *Kolokol*, June 1858, no. 16, p. 132.   [4] *Ibid.*

[5] Skrebitskii, *Krest'ianskoe delo*, III, 667–8; Tikhonov, 'K. Kharakteristike', pp. 239–40. The existing *average* allotment was about $2\frac{1}{2}$–3 *desiatiny*. (As in all other *barshchina*-dominated provinces, peasant allotments were considerably smaller than where *obrok* predominated.)

[6] *Materialy redaktsionnykh kommissii. Prilozhenie. Otzyvy chlenov gubernskikh komitetov*, II, 879.

[7] 'Almost all our estates are in mortgage to the state agencies [proclaimed the gentry of Sumy *uezd*], and that inconvenient situation robs us of any possibility of making this sacrifice . . .' Reference was specifically to the prospect of unremunerated loss of peasant labor. *Kolokol*, no. 16, p. 132.

The Kharkov committee's project may have reflected primarily the views of the gentry of the northwestern area of Kharkov province, where the population was denser and the land richer than in the southeast, which merged with the great steppe area to the north of the Caucasus Mountains. In the northwest land-holdings were relatively small, labor-surplus existed, and *obrok* and non-agricultural work among the peasantry were fairly common (though by no means prevalent: According to Ignato-vich's statistics less than 10 percent of the peasants in the province were on *obrok* before emancipation).[1] There is even some sug-gestion that this area was, in terms of the existing mode of agricultural production, over-populated; the peasants had become a burden to many *pomeshchiki*, who therefore showed a desire to be 'emancipated from the peasants' and to turn to hired labor.[2]

In the southeast by contrast, the steppe-borderlands were underpopulated, a labor shortage was chronic, and the *pomesh-chiki* had regularly to import workers for the harvest season to supplement the *barshchina* of the indigenous peasant population. Hired labor, accordingly, cost dearly in that region.[3] The local gentry tended to place much importance on *barshchina* for their economies, and would probably have favored a lengthy transition period in order to 'preserve [their] economies by means of the introduction . . . of the necessary radical changes'. These gentry must have feared the loss of their serf labor and were apprehensive of expensive hired labor.[4]

But these contrasting gentry circumstances were not fully reflected in the Kharkov committee, where the majority had adherents from the southeastern as well as the northwestern areas of the province.[5] It is generally remarkable that the gentry from

[1] Tikhonov, 'K. Kharakteristike', p. 243; Ignatovich, *Pomeshchich'i krest'iane*, pp. 292–3.
[2] Tikhonov, 'K. Kharakteristike', pp. 239–43.   [3] *Ibid.*, p. 245.
[4] This bifurcation of the province according to population and economy was clearly recognized by the conservative minority of the Kharkov committee, which wrote: The *pomeshchik* farms, primarily of the southern *uezdy*, are by their nature able to exist only with a significant number of yearly [hired] workers, whom, with the new relations, it will be impossible to find for a long while . . .' *Ibid.* Accordingly these deputies tended to favor retention of *pomeshchik* authority over the peasants for the duration of the transition period. *Ibid.*, pp. 235–46.
[5] *Ibid.*, pp. 246–50.

one of the southernmost extremities of the black soil region should have been moved, apparently, by the same fundamental considerations as certain of their counterparts in such provinces as Tver, Kaluga, and Vladimir.

GENERAL CONCLUSION TO CHAPTERS 4 AND 5

In the committees, the economic interests of the gentry were, on the whole, clearly reflected. This was particularly true in relation to the dichotomy in the Russian agrarian economy between the grain-producing black soil provinces and the non-black soil 'industrial provinces'. Patterns of economic interest were most clearly observable in the manner in which the committees dealt with the questions of land-allotments and peasant obligations. Other issues, especially the question of land-redemption and the question of peasant administration, followed these patterns much less closely. This was largely because most committees followed the directions of the government program which, within rather narrow limits, allowed for no expression of local differences on these questions.[1]

In the northern and central non-black soil regions where not land, but the *obrok* of the peasant most often represented the major source of *pomeshchik* income, most committees proposed relatively minor reductions in the existing peasant land-allotments.[2] Proposed obligations for these generally reduced allot-

---

[1] As mentioned earlier, the April 1858 program gave the following essential instructions to the committees: All committees were to write projects for the temporary-obligatory status only (therefore redemption projects and other 'final solutions' were not allowed); the *usad'ba* was to become the property of the peasant; some land beyond the *usad'ba* was to remain permanently in peasant usage; and the *pomeshchik* was to retain the powers and title of 'head of the peasant commmunity'. Skrebitskii, *Krest'ianskoe delo*, I, xxxvi–xxxii.

[2] Only four committee majorities accepted the 'previously existing allotments' as a general guide for the determination of future allotments: Smolensk, Tver, Mogilev and Samara. They were followed by several minority projects. They set maximum limits for the allotments which approximated the existing *average* allotment size. Kornilov, 'Gubernskie komitety', no. 4, p. 69. All other projects set *norms* for this purpose. Of these a very few more or less approximated previously existing allotments. *Ibid.*, p. 70. As Skrebitskii concluded, 'the significant majority of committees leaving the existing allotment size belong to the non-black soil provinces'. Skrebitskii, *Krest'-ianskoe delo*, II, pt. 1, 12.

ments were, however, noticeably increased.[1] In the black soil regions the provincial committees proposed, by and large, smaller peasant allotments, while the obligations asked of the peasants were usually more moderate than those proposed by the committees of the non-black soil area.[2] In between those two general tendencies were the projects of several committees of the fertile, but lowly-populated regions of 'New Russia' (the steppe lands to the north and east of the Black Sea), and the eastern reaches of the black soil belt near the Volga. In these areas the gentry's land-hunger was restrained by the urgent need to retain a peasant labor-force.[3]

The retention of *barshchina* (i.e. labor rent) as a mode of fulfilling peasant obligations during the 'temporary-obligatory period', was approved by all but four committee projects (Tver,

---

[1] A few projects accepted existing *obrok* obligations as a guide to establishing the new rents. Most used schemes based on land prices or profits gained from the land. *Of all the projects of the non-black soil region, only that of Tver province maintained what was essentially the same ratio of obligations to land-quantity as had existed previously.* All other committees proposed obligations increased either relatively to the quantity of land or absolutely. These increases were usually the product of extremely high evaluation of the peasant *usad'ba*, the general practice for achieving compensation for the loss of peasant labor, in the face of the government's refusal to allow it outright. Kornilov, 'Gubernskie komitety', no. 4, pp. 79–82.

[2] In absolute terms they were generally lower than existing obligations, but there, too, because of the large reduction in peasant allotments proposed by these committees, they were almost universally higher—in relation to quantity of land—than previously. In Kharkov, for example, for an allotment of 7·5 *desiatiny* (for one household) peasants paid an average *obrok* of 23·25 rubles. In the project of the Kharkov committee the maximum allotment for one household was defined as 5·4 *desiatiny* in three *uezdy*, and 4·5 in all other *uezdy* of the province. *Obrok* for these allotments was fixed at 21·60 rubles. Had the previously existing ratio between *obrok* and allotment-size been retained, *obrok* for 5·4 *desiatiny* should have been 16·74 rubles, and 13·95 rubles in the remaining *uezdy*. (*Ibid.*, p. 83.) There were numerous exceptions to this general pattern. Some of the most severe reductions in allotments were recommended by committees of the non-black soil *obrok* provinces, including Moscow, Vologda, Novgorod, Kostroma, Olonetsk and Viatka. (*Ibid.*, pp. 70–3.) Similar observations could be made about committee rulings on peasant obligations: Several committees of the black soil region evaluated peasant obligations at least as highly as the committees of the central-industrial region.

[3] The committees of the 'New Russian' provinces of Kherson, Ekaterinoslav and The Tauride proposed a 'voluntary' solution to the land question at the end of the transition period, and for that time offered an extremely meager allotment to the peasants. They demanded, however, obligatory redemption of the peasant *usad'ba*, for the obvious purpose of preventing an exodus of the labor force. In the eastern borderlands (in provinces like Samara and Saratov) the committees tended to favor comparatively large allotments for the peasants with the retention of labor rent and a good deal of authority for the *pomeshchiki*. *Ibid.*, pp. 58, 72.

Iaroslavl, the minority of Kaluga, and the project of five members of the Vladimir committee).[1] In most committees where obligations in *barshchina* were established, the existing average obligation of three days labor per week was replaced by a two-day *barshchina* obligation.[2] This represented an absolute reduction in the labor obligations of the peasantry, but in many cases it did not represent a sufficiently great reduction to correspond to the accompanying decrease in the size of peasant land-allotments. This was particularly true in many provinces of the black soil region, where proposed reductions of the peasant allotments were especially significant.[3]

The manner in which the provincial committees approached the question of *land-redemption* was to a large degree determined by the government's refusal—until the end of 1858, by which time most committees had either closed or had virtually completed their work—to allow consideration of the final solution of the peasant reform. Even so, most of the committees at least approached the question of redemption in their projects. Only four, in fact, let it be unequivocally known that they were against redemption in any form.[4] A minority of the committees proposed the facilitation of voluntary redemption agreements between *pomeshchiki* and peasants. The remaining committees, those not openly favoring redemption, belonged to one of two groups: Those committees which, to a great or lesser degree, favored a *landless emancipation* of the peasants (the majority of these were from the black soil provinces);[5] or those committees proposing *indefinite usage* of the land for the peasants, with the retention of obligatory relations between the classes.[6]

---

[1] Several other projects did provide for the gradual transition from *barshchina* to *obrok* during the course of the transition period. *Ibid.*, p. 74.

[2] *Ibid.*   [3] *Ibid.*, pp. 74–9.

[4] Ekaterinoslav, Kherson, Kostroma and Simbirsk. *Ibid.*, p. 60.

[5] Voronezh, Tambov, Riazan, Kursk, Orel, Poltava, Ekaterinoslav, Kherson, The Tauride, Simbirsk, Kazan, Nizhnii Novgorod, Kostroma, Vologda, Perm, Viatka, and Astrakhan. *Ibid.*, p. 57.

[6] Petersburg, Moscow, Pskov, Olonetsk, Iaroslavl, Vladimir (majority project), Saratov, Mogilev, Chernigov, Tula, and the minority projects of Novgorod, Vologda, Tver, Nizhnii Novgorod, Simbirsk (minority of two), Riazan (minority of three). Similar terms were provided in the projects from several White Russian and Ukrainian provinces. *Ibid.*, p. 64.

The provincial gentry committees, 1858–9

Projects favoring redemption were compiled in the committees of fourteen provinces.[1] Of these, 'projects which recognized (obligatory) redemption of their allotments by the peasants as the one correct solution of the peasant question' were presented in the following committees: Tver (majority project), *Kaluga* (maj. proj.), *Kharkov* (maj. proj.), *Vladimir* (two minority projects), *Riazan* (minority project of two members), and *Simbirsk* (minority project of five members).[2] All these projects of obligatory redemption provided for the indivisibility of the *usad'ba* from the allotment as a whole. The projects of the committees of Kaluga, Kharkov, Tver and Vladimir (project of six members) also proposed immediate compensation for the *pomeshchiki* through the establishment of state-insured redemption banks. The Simbirsk project provided for redemption with or without government guarantee or participation.[3]

Of the provinces expressing general preference for redemption eight belonged to the non-black soil region.[4] But a significant number of such projects came also from the black soil and steppe provinces: a majority project for obligatory redemption from Kharkov; minority projects for obligatory redemption from Riazan and Simbirsk; and projects generally favoring redemption from Penza, Saratov, Samara and Simbirsk.

The question of peasant administration was, for the committees, intimately related to the problem of land-redemption. So long as the peasants were to remain in a 'temporary-obligatory status', living on lands which continued to belong, in theory, to the *pomeshchik* (who was therefore to be the recipient of rent, either in labor or money, from the peasants), it was only natural that considerable authority over the peasants would have to be left to the *pomeshchik*. This was explicitly recognized in the government's 'April Program' which provided that the *pomesh-*

[1] Tver (maj. proj.), Kaluga (maj. and min. projects), Novgorod (maj. and min. projects), Iaroslavl, Kharkov, Saratov, Samara, Penza, Mogilev and in minority projects from Nizhnii Novgorod, Vladimir (2), Riazan, Moscow, and Simbirsk. *Ibid.*, p. 61.

[2] *Ibid.*; *Materialy redaktsionnykh komissii*, 11, 1–85.

[3] Kornilov, 'Gubernskie komitety', no. 4, pp. 61–4.

[4] Tver, Kaluga, Novgorod, Iaroslavl, Nizhnii Novgorod, Vladimir, Moscow and Mogilev.

chik was to become the 'head of the peasant community' for the
duration of the temporary-obligatory period, but giving little
indication of the limits to this authority.

It was therefore to be expected that the majority of provincial
committees should have proposed retention of *pomeshchik*
authority over the peasants, and in some cases to have proposed
specific additional authority for the *pomeshchik* in order to combat
trouble in what was generally anticipated would be a time of
unrest among the peasantry. More than thirty committees
followed the government program in presenting to the *pomeshchiki* the title and duties of the 'head of the peasant community'.[1]
To be sure, none of the committees read into this title the effective retention of serfdom, including the power to sell peasants,
to remove them arbitrarily from the land, to dictate their marriages or to deny them the right to own property or goods. But
the government's directive was, at this point, sufficiently vague
to allow for the writing into the majority of projects very
considerable powers for the *pomeshchiki* over the peasants (especially those who would continue to owe labor rent), including:
the right to accept or reject the elections and decisions of the
peasant communities; the right to punish peasants (by fine,
arrest or corporal punishment) for failure to fulfill their obligations or for abuses committed against the *pomeshchik* or his family;
and, in a few cases, even the right to send peasants into the army
for failure to fulfill obligations or other transgressions.[2]

Conversely, it was only in committees where redemption
projects were composed that the patrimonial rights and authority of the *pomeshchiki* were completely disavowed.[3]

---

[1] The majority of these committees represented the black soil regions where *barshchina*
dominated. But there were exceptions to this rule, including that of St Petersburg
province, whose gentry defended the patrimonial authority of the *pomeshchiki* not on
grounds of economic necessity—*barshchina* was not widespread in the province—but
strictly on 'aristocratic' grounds: the gentry must be guaranteed guardianship over the
peasantry and general dominance in local affairs. *Ibid.*, no. 5, pp. 55–7.

[2] *Ibid.*, pp. 57–8.

[3] Primarily in the committees of Tver, Kaluga, Kharkov and Smolensk. Similar rejection
of 'obligatory relations' were included in the minority projects from Vladimir
and Novgorod, and in the alternate redemption plans of Penza and Saratov. *Ibid.*,
pp. 52–3. The Smolensk committee, which clearly renounced the authority of the
pomeshchik over the peasants, was an exception because it had not composed a project

Although the government had expressly forbidden the committees to consider general aspects of local administration, a few of them refused to consider the reform of peasant administration apart from the reform of local administration in general. Plans for an all-class *volost'* were devised in the project of the Tver majority, the Vladimir minority, in the Riazan minority, and in an alternative redemption project presented by the Saratov committee. In both majority and minority projects of the Kaluga committee there were included plans for the creation of assemblies on both the *uezd* and provincial levels for the general economic administration of the province. These assemblies, according to the Kaluga projects, were to consist of representatives from the gentry, the peasantry, and the urban classes.[1]

Having undertaken an analysis of the projects of the provincial gentry committees, Kornilov concluded that these projects reflected a 'distinct and clear understanding by the *pomeshchiki* of their own advantages and interests'.[2] They therefore differed among themselves, he found, mainly in relation to differences in local economic conditions. The most important of these differences Kornilov discovered to be related to the fact that some committees belonged to the black soil region and others to the non-black soil region.

In the black soil provinces, where the main value of *pomeshchik* estates consisted of the land, the lord's tillage flourished, and *barshchina* was of great importance, Kornilov concluded that most *pomeshchiki* feared the abolition of *barshchina* and the loss of any land. Knowing, however, that the government would not permit a landless emancipation, these *pomeshchiki* tried, in their committees, to reduce the peasant allotments as much as possible.

based on obligatory redemption. It had, however, asked permission to compose such a project, only to be refused by the government; and it included a provision for voluntary redemption in its final project. (Because the Smolensk project contained a clause providing for the use by the peasants of their allotments for the temporary-obligatory period *only*, Kornilov mistakenly added Smolensk to the list of committees advocating landless emancipation. Cf. V. S. Orlov, *Otmena krepostnogo prava v Smolenskoi gubernii* (Smolensk, 1947), pp. 84–99.

[1] *Ibid.*, pp. 61–2.
[2] A. A. Kornilov, *Obshchestvennoe dvizhenie*, p. 49.

Their fear of losing *barshchina* they expressed by insisting on a 'temporary-obligatory period' and by demanding the retention of strong *votchina* authority for the *pomeshchiki*.

In the non-black soil provinces, where the income of the *pomeshchiki* derived largely from the non-agricultural wages and crafts of their *obrok* peasants, the committees feared especially one thing, according to Kornilov: deprivation by the abolition of serfdom of that income which the *pomeshchiki* received from the earnings and crafts of their peasants. Uninterested for the most part in the retention of *barshchina*, the *pomeshchiki* of these provinces realized that it would be difficult to continue to collect *obrok* from the peasants once the peasants had been declared personally free. The retention of *votchina* police authority would be of little help in this, they believed. Therefore, Kornilov continued, the *pomeshchiki* preferred 'immediate and full liquidation of serf relations, but not otherwise than on the condition that they receive money redemption for the loss in the value of the estates belonging to them'.[1] In other words, they demanded redemption not only for the land, which was generally of little value in the non-black soil region, but for the persons of their peasants as well. Because the government had proclaimed un-compensated abolition of personal serfdom these *pomeshchiki* sought this recompensation through very high evaluation of the peasant *usad'ba* and very high *obrok* rates. Land allotments they willingly gave, but allotments small enough so that the peasants would not be able to get by without hiring out their labor on the *pomeshchik's* estate or renting lands from the *pomeshchik*.[2]

Such was Kornilov's now classic generalization. But Kornilov's own work and particularly subsequent, more detailed, studies of individual committees show that this general picture is much oversimplified.

Kornilov's observation that two dominant tendencies existed among the provincial committees—the one toward a landless emancipation, retention of *barshchina* and extensive *pomeshchik* authority over the peasants; the other toward emancipation with land (for redemption) and termination of all obligatory relations

---

[1] *Ibid.*, p. 51. [2] *Ibid.*, pp. 49–51.

between *pomeshchik* and peasants—was a correct one. But his rather strict identification of these tendencies with the committees of the black soil and non-black soil provinces, respectively, is misleading and lacks support by the evidence, as an American historian has recently observed.[1]

What Kornilov identified as the preferences of the committees of the non-black soil provinces *in general* were, in fact, expressed by only a minority of them. Land-redemption, for example, was clearly preferred by the committees (or committee minorities) of only fourteen provinces, and of these only eight were of the non-black soil region. In fact, as shown above, most committees—in the non-black soil region as well as elsewhere—demonstrated no evident interest in abolishing *barshchina*, in giving up all authority over the peasants, or in losing part of their lands to the peasants. Of those few that did, a considerable proportion belonged to the black soil and steppe regions.

Some Soviet historians who have made detailed studies of individual provincial committees have remarked the impossibility of according the variety of committee proposals to the general scheme proposed by Kornilov. Their solutions to this problem have nevertheless generally been true to Kornilov's thesis that the committee projects reflected, above all, local economic conditions and 'the clear and distinct understanding by the *pomeshchiki* of their advantages and interest'. Kornilov erred, in other words, only by spreading his generalizations over too large a territory. They have accordingly replaced his macroeconomic generalizations with their own microeconomic explanations: The diversity of committee proposals directly reflected a diversity of economic conditions.[2]

To a certain extent such conclusions have indeed been justified. Studies of several committees have revealed, for example, the

[1] Blum, *Lord and Peasant in Russia*, p. 583.

[2] Such studies include, *inter alia*: V. S. Orlov, *Otmena krepostnogo prava v Smolenskoi gubernii* (Smolensk, 1947); V. I. Krutikov, 'Tul'skii dvorianskii komitet 1858–9 gg.', *Uchenye zapiski Tul'skogo ped. instituta*, III, 25–64; F. Chebaevskii, 'Nizhegorodskii, gubernskii dvorianskii komitet 1858 g', *Voprosy istorii*, no. 6 (1947), pp. 86–94. N. Tikhonov, 'K kharakteristike dvorianskoi ideologii nakanune padeniia krepostnogo stroia',' *Naukovi zapyski naukovo-doslidchoi katedri istoriï ukraïn'skoï kultury*, no. 6, 1927.

existence of bloc-voting by deputies on basic issues, and these
blocs of deputies have been connected with distinct areas within
the provinces involved.[1] And, in a more general way, other
studies have shown the diversity of conditions within individual
provinces. It is, indeed, becoming increasingly clear as more
regional studies are published that the traditional black soil—
non-black soil dichotomy is virtually meaningless.

It is impossible, moreover, to explain the variety of gentry
views in general or the specific propositions of the provincial
committees in terms of regional economic differences alone.
This has been recognized by some scholars. Druzhinin, for
example, came to the conclusion after a study of gentry publicism
in the reform period that the 'liberal solution' was not representative of the interests of the *pomeshchiki* of any particular
region, but was the desire of most articulate gentry. These he
identified with the 'capitalizing' or 'embourgeoisified' 'middling
gentry' of the Great Russian provinces as a whole:[2]

The *pomeshchiki* of the industrial non-black soil belt and the *pomeshchiki*
of the fertile black soil center were bound together by the unity of the
internal market, by the bond of money exchange, by a community
of new capitalistic relations and a new enterprising spirit. In the
presence of all the varied local differences they proceeded from the same
premise and came to the same final conclusions.

Another Soviet scholar has recently made a detailed study of
370 published and unpublished gentry 'memoirs and projects'
on reform written between 1854–61. His conclusion about those
projects proposing emancipation with land for redemption is
the following:

The estates of these *pomeshchiki* were located, as we see, in various
provinces of Russia. Their material situations were also varied; therefore it is impossible in this case to explain the position of the *pomeshchiki* on the question of allotment of land for the peasants only by the
character, size, or territorial location of their estates.[3]

[1] The studies by Chebaevskii and Tikhonov have been particularly successful in this
respect.
[2] 'Zhurnaly zemlevladel'tsev', II, 309.
[3] N. S. Bagramian, 'Pomeshchich'i proekty osvobozhdeniia krest'ian. (K probleme
krizisa verkhov)', in *Revoliutsionnaia situatsiia v Rossii v 1859–61 gg.* (Moscow, 1962),

The provincial gentry committees, 1858–9

While granting that the gentry were influenced by what they considered to be their own best interests (indeed often by plain greed), the assertion of Kornilov, repeated by other scholars, that they had a 'clear and distinct understanding' of these interests is open to serious question. It is likely that a large proportion of the landed gentry, including many of the committee deputies (who were generally among the best-informed *pomeshchiki*), had very uncertain ideas about the economic realities of their own estates. How much *obrok* did the peasants pay? How much did the land produce? Few knew the answers to these questions, for few kept careful records of their operations. Even those who did, according to the testimony of a contemporary like Kavelin and the later researches of Confino and others, had little idea of the real costs of production and tended to equate gross income with profit.[1]

Quite aside from this question, gentry views of their 'own best interests' were never determined solely by their understanding, however imperfect, of their personal economic circumstances. The *pomeshchiki*, and the committee deputies, were members of a self-conscious class, aware (to varying degrees) that their individual circumstances were related to the general social and legal system (and in this respect, the circumstances of all *pomeshchiki*, whatever the location and size of their holdings, were essentially identical—they all depended on the institutionalized exploitation of the serf population). They all shared, to one degree or another, certain attitudes toward the institution of serfdom (as they all shared, to some extent, a common system of values), and such questions as the relationship of the gentry to the

---

p. 28. The author's tentative explanation of this situation, in keeping with the theme of the collection of articles to which he was contributing, was: 'Evidently, the determining influence on their decision of the land question was the peasant movement, which was growing in intensity with each year; and also the desire of the *pomeshchiki* to hold the peasants in the village with small allotments, as a cheap labor force'. (*Ibid.*)

[1] As Kavelin wrote in his memoir, the *pomeshchiki*, because they were provided with free labor, 'calculate their profits or losses only by the harvest and the commercial prices on grain, but do not take into account, indeed cannot, how much they have spent on the production of their income'. Kavelin saw this as the 'built-in' and primary cause of the economic decline of the gentry under serfdom. Essentially the same view has been argued by Confino. Kavelin, *Sobranie sochinenii*, II, 27. Confino, *Domaines et seigneurs*, ch. 3, especially p. 176.

land and the peasantry, the position of the gentry, as a class, in rural life and in the state, had meaning for all the gentry and were not considered—could not have been considered—on the basis of local conditions alone.

In narrower terms, the provincial committees were not free to simply 'reflect the interests' of the local gentry, because they were constrained, to one extent or another, by the government's directives. In addition, the committees did not act in isolation, but watched one another for guidance in the novel undertaking. The committees communicated among themselves, and their projects and opinions were mutually known, circulated, and often borrowed upon.[1]

In a phrase, the committee projects should not be considered the fortuitously coinciding or conflicting responses of the *pomeshchiki* of various provinces. This was particularly true of the liberal minority of projects: These projects were drawn up in (greater or lesser) accordance with the liberal reform program which was the common property of most 'enlightened public opinion' in Russia. It was this circumstance which Solov'ev had in mind when he identified abolitionist sentiment in the provinces with a 'progressive party' of enlightened *pomeshchiki*:

In all the provinces there was a more or less numerous progressive party which desired emancipation of the peasants, and elaborated in conversations proposals on the means of emancipation long before the announcement of the government measures.[2]

Solov'ev described the gentry who constituted this liberal minority in the following way:

This element consisted of persons who, with European education, were yet full of true patriotism, and who were convinced that all our failures in the last two years of the reign of Emperor Nicholas[3] were

[1] The most influential journals and projects were those of the Tver committee. Another remarkable example of the sort of borrowing that was carried on between committees was provided by the Astrakhan committee which, despite the great contrast in local conditions, borrowed extensively from the project of the Petersburg committee. Kornilov, 'Gubernskie komitety', no. 4, p. 71.

[2] Solov'ev, 'Zapiski', xxxi, 6–7.

[3] This was the required euphemistic way of referring in print to the loss of the Crimean War.

the result of our internal disorder, and that the root of this failure lies in serfdom. For the appearance of these people in the ranks of our society we were indebted to our universities and in part to several . . . other institutions of higher learning.

With their understanding acquired from university lectures, from the reading of progressive foreign and Russian literature, and from their mutual exchange of ideas, they spread throughout the whole Russian land. These people, without any open or secret societies, formed a net of those *intelligent* circles which covered the native Russian provinces.[1]

In other words, the liberal solution was the product of a whole climate of opinion, deeply influenced by liberal European thought, which was publicized and debated in educated society. It was partly in reference to this situation that Paul Miliukov once remarked that Russian liberalism was 'intellectual', representing 'not class opinion, but general public opinion'.[2] The degree of success enjoyed by the liberal reform program in one or another province depended in large measure on the presence of certain individuals who fought for its acceptance—from governors sympathetic to the liberal position to chairmen and other members of the committees.

It is obviously true that gentry liberal opinion reflected dissatisfaction with the state of the *pomeshchik* economy under serfdom, and thus the gentry proponents of the liberal solution appeared as the spokesmen of 'capitalist relations' in agriculture— and many plainly identified themselves as such. In doing so, however, they were not moved simply by their 'economic experience', as Druzhinin suggested.[3] If that were the main criterion, it could be argued with equal logic that the true representatives of 'capitalist relations' in agriculture were not these people at all, but rather the great commercial-producing landholders of the black soil and steppe provinces. It was they, generally, who most successfully survived the emancipation, and in this period most of them were advocates of landless emancipation, if not enemies of reform altogether.

[1] Solov'ev, 'Zapiski', xxxiv, 128–9.
[2] *Russia and its Crisis* (Chicago-London, 1906), p. 226.
[3] 'Zhurnal zemlevladel'tsev', ii, 309.

The Liberal program elsewhere in Russia

If the distribution of progressive gentry opinion depended, as is suggested here, less on the regional pecularities of the *pomesh-chik* economy than on 'enlightenment', it can be assumed that, in general, the views expressed in the projects of the provincial committees were not fixed, but were susceptible to change. That this was in fact the case was demonstrated in the months immediately following the deliberations of the provincial gentry committees.

PART III

THE GENTRY VERSUS THE BUREAUCRACY, 1858–61

At the present time of struggle between the bureaucracy and the gentry which threatens the latter with complete annihilation, it seems to us that the necessary and only possible thing for the gentry to do is to sacrifice for a moderate price a part of its land to the peasants with a guarantee by the government of punctuality of payments. Then, having dealt with the peasantry on a fair basis and in keeping with the personal desire of the Sovereign Emperor, to assert its own rights to participation in the administration and the economic direction of the area; whereas, as long as there remains even a shadow of seigneurial authority, the interference of the bureaucracy, with its present development and centralization, will be inevitable and will bring after it the enslavement of all classes of the people by the sovereign bureaucrats.

Letter of the Riazan Deputies
Volkonskii and Ofrosimov
November 1859

6

The Government and the Gentry, April 1858–November 1859

Ia. Rostovtsev and the editing commissions

The program of April 1858, which had been devised for the guidance of the provincial gentry committees, was far from being the government's last word on reform. In fact it was only the first of a rapid series of changes leading to the final emancipation legislation. In creating the provincial committees, the government forced itself to proceed quickly with an elaboration of detailed reform plans; it could not leave major questions undecided and expect anything but confusion from the gentry. As seen earlier, the government's first, and somewhat panicky, effort after the creation of the committees was the 'April Program', the product of the government's fear that the projects of the provincial committees would significantly depart from the goals indicated and desired by the government itself.

But the 'April Program' was only a stop-gap measure, designed to bridle the energies of the provincial committees by directing their efforts to the pondering of legislation on the 'temporary-obligatory' status. The government could then, presumably, proceed to work out its own plans for the ultimate solution of the peasant question, without having those of the gentry forced upon it. Aside from restricting the committee to legislation on the 'temporary-obligatory' status, the program introduced nothing new about the ultimate outcome of the reform. The land question in particular was left undefined: The program both affirmed that allotments were to be left in the permanent usage of the peasants, and that 'inviolability of the property-rights of the *pomeshchiki* to all the land' was to be respected.[1]

The basic decision represented by the 'April Program'—to disallow any wide-ranging initiative by the gentry on the fundamentals of peasant emancipation—was never reversed by the government. Before long, however, it was realized that the program tended to tie the hands of the government's true allies in the committees—those advocates of an effective abolition of serfdom who sought this in redemption of land by the peasants and in by-passing, so far as possible, the 'temporary-obligatory' status.

As noted in chapter 4, on 15 July 1858, the Main Committee announced the government's intention to invite two members from each provincial committee to Petersburg 'for the presentation to the central government of all information and explanations which it deems necessary to have for the final discussion and examination of each project'.[2] For the purpose of undertaking a preliminary examination of the committees' projects, a 'special commission' was created in the Main Committee. Its members were: Lanskoi, Panin, Murav'ev and Rostovtsev. The Main Committee was shortly thereafter adjourned for the summer months, and its members dispersed.

In the course of the summer, which he spent taking the waters in various German resorts, one member of the special commission, Rostovtsev, composed four letters on the peasant question and sent them to Alexander II. These letters were instrumental in establishing the new, and essentially final, course of the government's reform plans.

Rostovtsev's letters introduced two new ideas into the government's reform plans: (1) The idea that the government should encourage and facilitate the redemption by the peasants of their land-allotments; (2) the principle that the patrimonial powers of the *pomeshchiki* (until then positively supported in the government's announcements) must be curtailed. 'The *pomeshchik*', wrote Rostovtsev 'shall have relations with the community only, not with individuals'.[3]

---

[1] Skrebitskii, *Krest'ianskoe delo*, I, xxvi–xxxii.   [2] *Materialy*, I, 265.
[3] Skrebitskii, *Krest'ianskoe delo*, I, 908–25.

On 18 October 1858, when the Main Committee had re-convened, Alexander II personally called the Committee's attention to these letters and directed that their main conclusions be adopted as general guides for all further preparations of the reform.[1] Accordingly, the Main Committee produced, on 4 December 1858, a new set of basic principles of reform, which were to serve as guides for all further work of the Main Committee, including the examination of the projects to be presented by the provincial committees. The most important of these principles were the following:

1. With the publication of the new legislation on the landlords' peasants, these peasants shall be presented the rights of free rural classes; personal and property rights and the right of complaint.

2. These peasants shall enter the general status of a free rural class in the state.

3. The peasants shall be ascribed to rural communities, which must have their communal administration. [Where communes were not already existent, such units would be instituted for administrative functions only.]

4. Authority over the person of the peasant in connection with the fulfillment or violation of his responsibilities as a member of the community shall be concentrated in the commune and its elected officials.

5. The *pomeshchik* must have relations only with the community, not with individuals.

6. The community shall answer with mutual responsibility [*krugovaia poruka*] for each of its members in connection with the fulfillment of its fiscal responsibilities and its responsibilities to the *pomeshchik*.

7. An effort must be made to transform the peasants into property owners. For this it will be necessary: (a) To decide exactly what means can be offered by the government to help the peasants redeem their field lands; (b) to define the conditions for the termination of the temporary-obligatory status of the peasants. The Emperor also ordered: (a) That beginning in 1859 all increases in the income from the State Properties over the existing [income]

be used to facilitate the redemption of their lands by the peasants; (b) that the commission [attached to the Main Committee] shall consider if it is possible to define the termination of the temporary-obligatory status in the following manner: The temporary-obligatory status shall cease for the community in general, and for the peasant individually, when [the peasants] either in the entire community or individually, redeem that land from the *pomeshchik* which, in accordance with the Imperial Rescripts, will be allotted them in use, or when the peasant redeems from the *pomeshchik* those lands which, on the basis of the same Rescripts, can guarantee his proper payment of taxes and obligations.

8. With the publication of the legislation it shall be ruled that unpopulated lands belonging to the gentry may be purchased . . . by persons of all classes. If there are peasants living on the land, then persons, at present without the right to own populated estates, may purchase such lands as well; with the provision that at the time of purchase of the estate, the peasants living on the estate shall receive their *usad'by*, field lands and other lands for redemption, by mutual agreement . . .[1]

These principles reflected a considerable evolution in the government's official intentions as compared with the vague declarations incorporated in the original Rescripts. The aim of the government was made explicit: *emancipation of the peasants with land*. Although *obligatory* redemption was not advocated,[2] and the details on just how the government planned to achieve this aim were not dwelt upon,[3] the aim was made unmistakably clear in the Emperor's suggestion that 'temporary-obligatory status shall cease . . . when the peasants . . . redeem that land from the

---

[1] Skrebitskii, *Krest'ianskoe delo*, I, lix–lxi.

[2] 'The redemption of the [peasants'] from the *pomeshchiki* by the government', wrote Rostovtsev, 'would cost it a billion silver rubles. The government has not got even a small part of such fabulous riches. The issuing of bonds or loans for such a sum would produce a financial revolution in Russia.' *Ibid.*, p. 910. Obligatory and immediate redemption were therefore out of the question in his view.

[3] The government was very cautious about committing itself financially to a redemption operation. As late as March 1859, in a communique to the Kaluga committee, it was announced that the government 'had not yet come to a final decision: Could it, and to what extent, guarantee redemption'. *Ibid.*, p. xlvi.

pomeshchik which . . . will be allotted them in use'. The gentry were to be served notice that any hopes that the *pomeshchik* would regain all the land after the expiration of the transition period were to be dismissed. So too were many dreams about the gentry's retention of direct patrimonial authority over the individual peasants.

With these new principles officially approved, the Ministry of Interior took a number of steps expressly designed to encourage progressive, pro-redemption elements in the provincial gentry committees. The first and most important of these was the favorable ruling on the Tver committee's petition seeking the right to draw up a redemption project.[1] This ruling was repeated several times subsequently in answer to similar petitions, and was finally sent to all committees still in operation, in March 1859. Of the same intent were the rulings allowing committee minorities to draw up separate projects (29 December 1858), and to send their own representatives to Petersburg for consultations with the government (9 May 1859).[2]

At the same time the government undertook to elaborate the machinery with which to process the projects of the provincial committees and to produce the final reform legislation. The first step in that direction had been the creation of the 'special commission' in the Main Committee in July 1858. It was then the government's intention that all these tasks be retained within the Main Committee, and in October 1858 further procedural refinements were prescribed: The projects of the provincial committees, upon receipt by the central government, were to

---

[1] This ruling in fact preceded the formal announcement of principles, which was made 4 December 1858. It was after the decisive meeting of 18 October, however. (It was communicated to the Tver committee on 5 November 1858.) It is interesting to note that the delegation led by Unkovskii from the Tver committee to demand acceptance of its plan of obligatory redemption arrived in Petersburg only a short while before the 18 October meeting of the Main Committee. It may be (though no mention was made of the Tver petition in the official records of the 18 October session of the Main Committee) that the Tver demands directly helped to precipitate the government's decision to come out for redemption.

[2] Of the same intent were the instructions of 5 and 11 January 1859, which respectively prohibited public attendance at the meetings of the provincial committees, and affirmed that the committees need not adhere to the wishes of gentry assemblies. (In some committees proposals had been made to submit their finished projects to the gentry assembly for general ratification.) Cf. *Zhurnaly sekretnego i glavnogo komiteta*, I, 316–18.

be turned over first to the Ministry of Interior, which would scrutinize each project to determine if it contained 'any kind of departures from the principles and directives Imperially approved for the . . . peasant question', or 'departures in general from the spirit of State legislation'. The Ministry was also to report if and how the individual projects 'really improved the conditions . . . of the peasants'.[1] Thus annotated, the projects would be sent on to the Main Committee. The Main Committee was to have the task of 'compiling one statute for all of Russia', with the necessary addenda, changes and particular regulations for the various localities. During the final revision of all the regulations the Main Committee was to 'take into consideration all useful ideas of the provincial committees'. For this purpose deputies of the committees were to be called before the Main Committee.[2]

These procedures were never in fact followed. On 17 February 1859, Alexander II approved a plan for the creation of a new institution, the Editing Commissions (*redaktsionnye komissii*), to be created under the chairmanship of Rostovtsev. By this act all further consideration of the reform, and the entire task of dealing with the provincial projects and drawing up general legislation, were effectively removed from the hands of the Main Committee and given over to a temporary body outside the general state apparatus and responsible through its chairman directly to the Emperor.[3]

The February decree provided that there be created 'two Editing Commissions . . . for the compilation of systematic digests from all the projects of the provincial gentry committees and for the drawing-up of projects of general legislation'. One of these commissions was to concern itself with the statutes of general legislation, the other with local provisions 'adapted to

---

[1] These tasks were concentrated in the Rural Department (*Zemskii otdel*) of the Ministry, which had been created in March, 1858, as a general clearing-house for 'all matters . . . concerning rural economic organization in the Empire', including relations with the newly-created provincial committees. The Rural Department was the stronghold of the 'liberal bureaucrats' Ia. Solov'ev and N. Miliutin. *Materialy*, I, 264.

[2] *Sbornik pravitel'stvennykh rasporiazhenii*, I, section II, 34–40.

[3] N. P. Semenov, *Osvobozhdenie krest'ian v tsarstvovanie Imperatora Aleksandra II*, I (St Petersburg, 1889), 14–16.

the peculiarities of each region and [to be] published together with the general provisions'. As chairman and direct supervisor of these commissions Rostovtsev was to have complete authority regarding the organization of their work, the number of members in them, etc. Funds for the business of the Editing Commissions were to be supplied to Rostovtsev, who was to be accountable for them only to Alexander II himself.[1]

The commission for general legislation was to consist of bureaucrats from the Ministries (Interior, Justice and State Properties),[2] to be appointed by agreement between the Ministries and the chairman of the Commissions. The other commission was to consist of representatives from the Ministries of Interior and State Properties (appointed in the same fashion) and 'experts' to be appointed by the chairman 'from among the members of provincial committees, or other experienced *pomeshchiki*, according to his judgment'.

To the two commissions a third was subsequently added: a special Finance Commission. Also presided over by Rostovtsev, the Finance Commission was to consist of persons, appointed by him, 'who had specially studied the financial sciences and [who had] a practical knowledge of Russia', as well as of representatives of various government agencies. The special task of the Finance Commission was to be the examination of 'projects on financial measures for facilitating the redemption of their field lands by the peasants, and for the discussion of what means might be provided by the government for helping the peasants with redemption'.[3] The Finance Commission was directed to observe the following principles: (1) Redemption was to remain voluntary, that is to be undertaken only with the consent of both peasants and *pomeshchiki*; (2) Redemption could be accomplished either by private arrangements, or by means of government-financing of arrangements approved by the government. In the second case the government would issue credit certificates to the *pomeshchiki* backed by the state properties; the peasants would

---

[1] *Materialy*, II, 6–11.
[2] And from the Second Section of the Imperial Chancellery.
[3] Skrebitskii, *Krest'ianskoe delo*, I, lxxxi–lxxxii.

pay six percent of the capital sum of the certificates annually (such payments were not to exceed existing peasant obrok rates).[1]

The Editing Commissions came into existence on 4 March 1859, as planned, but the dual structure of the Commissions was not maintained. The two commissions were merged into one 'Editing Commission', and all its members, local experts and bureaucrats alike, took part in the elaboration of both general and local legislation. This Commission was divided into three departments: (1) The Judicial Department concerned with legislation on the rights and obligations of peasants and *pomeshchiki*; (2) an Administrative Department, responsible for legislation on the organization of peasant administration; (3) an Economic Department, with the largest task of producing the legislation for the *usad'ba*, land-allotments and obligations of the peasantry. The Finance Commission remained as a fourth department, essentially, with the specific task of preparing legislation on redemption.[2]

The reports of the several departments became in fact the drafts of the articles of emancipation. These were presented in regular plenary sessions of the Editing Commissions (the plural designation was retained), where they were approved, rejected or modified by a simple majority vote. The work of the Editing Commissions was divided into three periods. In the first period (4 March 1859–5 September 1859), the projects of the provincial committees were studied and initial drafts of the emancipation legislation were written. It was, essentially, in this period that the entire emancipation project was written in its general outlines. In the second period (23 September 1859–5 March 1860), representatives from 21 of 43 provincial committees were called before the Editing Commissions, and the statutes of emancipation were then re-examined in the light of the information provided by these representatives. The third period, beginning 5 April 1860, was devoted to consultation with the representatives of the

---

[1] Of this payment of six percent, one percent was to go to capital reduction, and five percent to interest payments on the credit certificates. *Ibid.*, pp. lxxxii–lxxxiii.

[2] Semenov, *Osvobozhdenie krest'ian*, I, 50–51.

remaining provincial committees and to final codification of the legislation. The last plenary session of the Editing Commissions met on 10 October 1860.

The Editing Commissions consisted, in all, of 36 members: 18 'member-experts'; 11 'government men'; and seven members of the Finance Commission.[1] Thanks to the initiative enjoyed by Rostovtsev in the appointment of members, the overwhelming majority of these members, both 'experts' and 'government men', were devoted proponents of peasant emancipation.[2] Among the bureaucratic representatives appointed to the Commissions were some of the outstanding figures in the history of Russian administration: Ia. Solov'ev, Nicholas Miliutin and A. K. Giers from the Ministry of Interior; V. I. Bulygin from the Ministry of State Properties; M. Kh. Reitern from the Ministry of Finance; and M. N. Liuboshchinskii, Procurator of the Senate. Among the 'member-experts' were Iu. Samarin and Prince V. A. Cherkasskii, A. P. Zablotskii-Desiatovskii (the biographer of Count Kiselev), and N. Kh. Bunge (future Minister of Finance). Most of the 'member-experts' were drawn from the progressive minorities of the provincial committees.[3]

If any point of time between the government's first public announcement of its intention to free the serfs in November 1857, and the fulfillment of that intention on 19 February 1861, could be pointed to as the moment when the proponents within the administration of an effective emancipation definitely gained control of the reform preparations, that moment would be when the Editing Commissions took the entire operation over from the Main Committee. Previous to that development, abolitionist forces in the central government had been concentrated almost exclusively in the Ministry of Interior. Until the creation of the Main Committee, in January 1858, the Ministry had enjoyed a virtual monopoly of action *vis-à-vis* the peasant question. From

[1] The Finance Commission contained *nine* members, but two of them (Pozen and Miliutin) belonged to the main staff of the Editing Commissions also.

[2] Solov'ev, 'Zapiski', XXVIII, 342. Solov'ev, a 'government man' in the Commissions, estimated that less than one-third of the members were 'conservatives'.

[3] The oustanding exceptions were the appointments of Count P. P. Shuvalov (gentry marshal for Petersburg province), V. V. Apraksin (gentry marshal of Orel province), M. P. Pozen, and Count F. E. Paskevich.

the beginning of 1858 the influence of the Ministry had seemed to be on the wane, and that of the Main Committee, the majority of whose members were at least unenthusiastic about emancipation,[1] on the rise. The spring and summer of 1858—during which time the April Program was promulgated, the Main Committee was dismissed for a lengthy vacation, and rumors were spread by certain members of the Main Committee to the effect that the reform plans were unlikely to be soon realized[2]—was seen by the progressive bureaucrats in the Ministry of Interior as a time of increased influence by conservative elements near the throne; influence which in their view still threatened, despite all the Rescripts and provincial committees, a possible dead-end for the reform plans.[3]

With the rise of Rostovtsev to the position of *generalissimo* in charge of preparation of the reform and the creation of the Editing Commissions under his leadership the cause of reform in the central government seemed triumphant. The views expressed in Rostovtsev's letters from abroad and later adopted as the official principles of reform were essentially identical to those which had been developed by the 'enlightened bureaucrats' in the Ministry of Interior.[4]

Historical hindsight makes it appear that the creation of an

[1] The progressive bureaucrats in the Ministry of Interior counted only the Grand Duke Konstantin Nikolaevich, Rostovtsev, Lanskoi, and K. V. Chevkin (Director of Communications) to be sincerely in favor of emancipation. Solov'ev, 'Zapiski', xxxiii, 229–33.

[2] Butkov and Murav'ev travelled about several provinces in the summer of 1858. They let it be known in talks with the local gentry that there need be no hurry with reform, hinting that the government was unlikely to carry out its plans as announced. Both received reprimands from Alexander II in the fall of 1858 for these efforts. Levshin of the Ministry of Interior evidently engaged in some similar talks with groups of provincial gentry at the same time, and also received a reprimand for his efforts. *Materialy* I, 361–6.

[4] The progressive bureaucrats in the Ministry also saw in the creation of the 'special commission' attached to the Main Committee (July 1858) a reactionary scheme to take the entire matter out of the hands of the Ministry of Interior. (A reasonable suspicion, since the 'special commission' was given the task of reviewing the projects of the provincial committees, a job which had originally been given the new Rural Department of the Ministry.) Solov'ev, 'Zapiski', xxxiv, 106–9.

[4] These views expressed two essential principles: (1) Emancipation of the peasants with land by means of a voluntary government-financed redemption operation; and (2) elimination, as far as possible, of the arbitrary power of the *pomeshchiki* over the peasants.

independent body like the Editing Commissions, responsible directly to the Emperor through a trusted *confidant,* was an inevitable necessity for the successful realization of the emancipation. At least the creation of the Commissions was clearly the way out of a serious dilemma: Now that preparation of the reform had reached the stage at which the serious work of codification and the processing of nearly 50 draft statutes from the provincial committees had to be undertaken, it was obvious that the Main Committee was unequipped to handle such a task. It was unequipped both temperamentally and technically: Many of its members were plainly unsympathetic to the government's reform plans; moreover, such a small and unspecialized group of men could not possibly have accomplished the enormous task of codification, a task demanding the extensive technical knowledge and bureaucratic skills of a large number of trained personnel.

The only obvious existing alternative would have been to turn the job over to the bureaucracy, namely to the Ministry of Interior. This alternative was, however, unacceptable to the Emperor for political reasons: From the moment of the government's first hesitant steps toward reform the Ministry of Interior had been the object of resentment from conservative elements in the government and at court. The specific object of this resentment was Nicholas Miliutin and his fellow career-bureaucrats in the Ministry, with whom the initiative for reform lay. Highly-placed conservatives like Prince Orlov (chairman of the Secret Committee) and M. N. Murav'ev (Minister of State Properties) argued, in the Emperor's hearing, that Miliutin and his cohorts were 'red democrats' intent on forcing a constitution on Russia.[1] The connection between serfdom and autocracy—and corollarily between abolitionism and 'constitutionalism' (that is a political threat to the autocracy)—had been drawn many times by supporters of the autocracy, a line of reasoning which had been

[1] Murav'ev, Orlov, and others tried, early in the period of reform preparations, to secure Miliutin's removal from the Ministry. These attempts failed, mainly because of the intercession of Lanskoi and the Grand Duchess Elena Pavlovna, whose *protégé* Miliutin was. Dzhanshiev, *Epokha velikikh reform,* pp. 622–5; M. A. Miliutina, 'Iz zapisok', XCVII, 64–5.

explicitly expounded by Uvarov, among others.[1] And the Emperor himself, who had received numerous letters denouncing the whole plan of reform as a democratic plot by the 'communists and democrats' in the Ministry, was perhaps half-inclined to believe such arguments. At least he could not afford to subject the preparation of reform to the criticism it would provoke from his aristocratic counselors if it were left entirely to the Ministry.[2] Moreover, he was suspicious of the empire-building tendencies of the bureaucracy and was plainly hesitant to turn such an important task as peasant emancipation over to its single control.[3]

The rise of Rostovtsev to the position of general arbiter of the reform and the creation of the Editing Commissions under his supervision were the results of Alexander II's mistrust of both the 'liberals' in the Ministry of Interior and the 'conservatives' in the Main Committee. He therefore followed a well-established precedent and put things in the hands of a man he could personally rely upon. Rostovtsev was the perfect choice: He was a close friend of the Emperor; his devotion was complete and tested; he was of sufficiently illustrious position (member of the Com-

[1] 'The question of serfdom is closely linked to the question of autocracy and even monarchy.

These are two parallel forces which have developed together.

Both have the same historical beginning; both have equal legality . . .

Serfdom, whatever one may think of it, does exist. Abolition of it will lead to the dissatisfaction of the gentry class, which will start looking for compensations for itself somewhere, and there is nowhere to look except in the domain of autocracy. . . . Peter I's edifice will be shaken . . .

Serfdom is a tree which has spread its roots afar: it shelters both the Church and the Throne.' (Barsukov, *Zhizn' i trudy M. P. Pogodina*, ix, 305–8; quoted and translated by N. V. Riasanovsky, in Vucinich (ed.), *The peasant in nineteenth-century Russia*, p. 275.

[2] When Miliutin was appointed Assistant Minister (March 1859) he had to explain personally to Alexander II that he was not a 'red revolutionary', but an 'enlightened bureaucrat.' Revolution was out of the question, he explained, because the government was 'more liberal than society'. Miliutina, 'Iz zapisok', xcvii, pp. 64–5. In Russian court society of the 1850s 'red', 'democrat', and 'communist' all referred to one thing: the threat of a constitution.

[3] When Lanskoi objected to the plan for creating temporary Governors-General in the provinces (see below, p. 222 fn.), Alexander replied (August 1858): '[The critique] was not of course written by *you*, but by some of your departmental or chancellery directors, who don't at all like the proposed new institution *because it would weaken their power and that position which they have become accustomed to enjoy and frequently abuse*'. *ORLB, f.* 327, 1, 16/20, p. 1.

mittee of Ministers, member of the State Council, member of the Secret and Main Committees); and he was unencumbered by any aristocratic allegiances (he was not even of gentry background, nor did he own any serfs).[1]

Rostovtsev lacked one, very important, attribute, however: he had no knowledge of rural Russia. This shortcoming was overcome by leaving the technical work of the Editing Commissions in the hands of the Ministry bureaucrats, essentially in Miliutin's hands, whose views on reform Rostovtsev had come to share.[2] Rostovtsev willingly bowed to Miliutin's superior knowledge and ability, and their cooperation in the Editing Commissions was virtually complete.[3]

The 'conversion' of Rostovtsev to the views held in the Ministry of Interior signified the evolution of government policy toward acceptance of a definitive solution of the peasant problem. Serious proponents of peasant emancipation in the government, including Alexander II, had never considered the possibility of a landless emancipation for the peasants, or of an indefinite 'regulated status'. The one and the other, as Rostovtsev pointed out, were unacceptable primarily because they were

[1] There is no need to recount the details of Rostovtsev's biography here, for they are well-known and easily accessible. Rostovtsev, whose family was of merchant origins (his father had gained gentry status by rising in the Table of Ranks), had spent all his life previous to the reform period in the military. Rostovtsev first drew Imperial attention by informing Nicholas I of the treasonable intentions of his fellow members of the Northern Society in December 1825 (after first honorably warning them that he was going to do so). His career subsequently blossomed, and he eventually became director of Russia's military schools and a close friend of the future Emperor Alexander II. When Alexander assumed the throne, Rostovtsev immediately gained entrance to the highest councils of state. Cf. V. Ia. Bogucharskii, 'Iakov Ivanovich Rostovtsev', *Velikaia reforma*, v, 62–7; N. P. Semenov, 'Deiatel'nost' Ia. I. Rostovtseva v Redaktsionnykh komissiiakh po krest'ianskomu delu', *Russkii vestnik*, LIII–LIV (1864).

[2] A brief account of Miliutin's work in the Commissions is given by P. Leroy-Beaulieu, *Un homme d'état russe (Nicholas Miliutine)* (Paris, 1884), pp. 37–62.

[3] Just how it came about that Rostovtsev's attitude toward reform progressed from hesitant disinterest (when he was first appointed to the Secret Committee in 1857) to identification with the aims of the Ministry of Interior is not clear. It seems most likely that Rostovtsev, a faithful servant of Alexander II who had acquired some statesmanlike ambitions because of his recent appointment to high offices, devoted himself to emancipation once he had become convinced of Alexander II's intentions. Lacking many of the class prejudices of his fellow *sanovniki*, he followed what appeared to him to be the only reasonable path toward effective reform. On this subject see: Unkovskii, 'Zapiski', *Russkaia mysl'*, no. 7 (1906), pp. 98–9; Kovan'ko, *Reforma 19 fevralia 1861 goda* pp. 120–6.

thought likely to lead to peasant uprisings, to a *Pugachevshchina*.[1] The real questions with which the government had to deal were those concerning the possible methods for effecting emancipation with land and with compensation for the gentry, and the question of how rapidly the process was to be completed. Once the government had announced its intention to emancipate the peasants, and especially once the gentry had been called in to discuss the matter, the government had no choice but to proceed rapidly with the solution of these questions.

In all probability, it was this logic of the situation based on the firm recognition of the necessity of emancipation with land which led to the decisions taken by the government in late 1858. Some historians have argued that these decisions were taken under the direct pressure of mounting peasant disturbances;[2] others that they were taken under the pressure from the liberal minority of the gentry.[3] It would appear that neither of these views is correct. The former appears to be based on a preconceived notion of the nature of political change in nineteenth-century Russia and on a tendency, specifically, to relate political change in a mechanical way to quantitative fluctuations in the frequency of peasant 'disturbances'. We know that government officials in general, and Alexander in particular, profoundly feared the possibility of a peasant rebellion in this period. But these fears appear to have been based on general considerations—memories of the Pugachev Rebellion; recent impressions, such as the Galician peasant rebellion of 1846 and the disorders among the Russian peasantry in the last years of the Crimean War;[4] and

[1] The fear of such an eventuality, which Rostovtsev in the Editing Commissions specifically linked to landless emancipation (cf. Semenov, *Osvobozhdenie krest'ian*, II, 254), progressively obsessed the government (and the Emperor in particular) as the preparations for reform advanced. One outstanding symptom of this fear was the plan advanced by Rostovtsev in the spring of 1858 for the creation of special military Governors-General, who would be given extraordinary powers during the period of promulgation of the reform. This plan was not realized, mainly because of opposition from the Ministry of Interior, but it was provisionally approved by Alexander II, who greatly feared the possibility of peasant uprisings. Cf. Dzhanshiev, *Epokha velikikh reform*, pp. 39–42.

[2] This is the unifying thesis of the recent collections of articles on the 'revolutionary situation' (*Revoliutsionnaia situatsiia v Rossi v 1859–61 gg.*, vols. I–IV (Moscow, 1960–5)).

[3] Cf. Gerschenkron, 'Agrarian Policies and Industrialization', p. 726.

[4] In 1854–6 peasant unrest took on a special and acute form, provoked by the government's call for volunteers to serve in the navy. This call produced rumors among the peasants

apprehensions about the response of the peasantry to emancipation
—rather than on the immediate state of the peasantry: Numerous
contemporaries and official government reports testified to a
remarkable and unexpected passivity of the peasantry throughout
the period of the reform preparations (1857–61).[1] The latter
argument—to the effect that a segment of the gentry compelled
the government to take the 1858 decisions—fails to take into
consideration the fact that emancipation with land had long been
the government's aim, and, more immediately, that the government had been gradually approaching the solution announced
in late 1858 for some time.[2] The liberal gentry minority undoubtedly encouraged the government to take the decision for
redemption—albeit 'voluntary redemption'—and may have
provided the support which was necessary before such a decision
could have been taken. It would be wrong, however, to conclude
that the liberal minority compelled the government to take that
decision.

that if they volunteered they would be freed at the end of the war. These rumors resulted
in large-scale fleeing from estates, which was combatted by arrests and armed conflicts.
Hundreds of thousands of peasants are thought to have been involved in this movement
in one way or another. (Cf., Zaionchkovskii, *Otmena krepostnogo prava v Rossii*, p. 50.)
(On the behavior of the peasants in the period immediately preceding the reform see
the author's article, 'The peasant and the emancipation'.)
   The Galician rebellion both frightened the government and provided a lesson in the
benefits of a 'peasantophile' policy, such as the Austrian government had instituted in
response to that rebellion (by abolishing labor duties). The Russian government's
introduction of the 'inventories' in the Southwestern provinces (1847) was a direct
response to these developments. Cf. I. Ignatovich, 'Otrazhenie v Rossii krest'ianskogo
dvizheniia v Galitsii 1846 goda', pp. 161–208.

[1] Thus the official annual report of the Third Section for 1858, the year in which these
decisions were taken: 'Not one disorder has taken on significant proportions or continued for long. Although the instances of disobedience were in sum rather many, in
the vast empire they are scarcely noticeable ... One can say that general calm has been
preserved, and that incomparably fewer disorders have so far taken place than was
expected and predicted'. *TsGAOR, Otchet III otdeleniia za 1858 g.*, p. 129.

[2] On 18 September 1858, Unkovskii wrote to Koshelev: ' ... There is no need to expect
any hindrance from Petersburg. At the end of August I met with the Minister of
Interior and spoke with him about our propositions. He agreed with them fully. ...
From him I learned that the government, apparently, is itself coming to the conviction
that the only solution to the problem can be the redemption of land as the property of
the peasants, and as a result of this the central committee [the Main Committee] is
discussing projects of financial operations which have been presented to it.' (Trubetskaia, *Materialy*, I, *prilozhenie*, 111–13.)

Sources of conflict with the gentry

With the stewardship of the reform lodged in the Editing Commissions and guided by principles in most respects identical to those professed by the gentry liberals; with many of the members of the Editing Commissions recruited from the 'liberal minorities' of the provincial gentry committees, it would seem likely that the central government should now have found considerable support from the liberal gentry.[1] In fact, the Editing Commissions almost immediately found themselves confronted with a united gentry opposition evidently intent on usurping initiative in the preparation of reform from the Commissions. This turn of events was the result of essentially two developments: (1) The elaboration by the government, in 1858 and early 1859, of new plans for a general reform of local administration; and (2) an attempt by the government, in 1859, to reduce gentry participation in the preparation of the peasant reform to a bare minimum.

(1) *Government plans for administrative reforms.* The government understood as well as the Tver liberals that peasant reform could not be promulgated in a vacuum and would have to be accompanied by extensive changes in the general administration. But its view of the nature of the needed administrative reforms was almost diametrically opposed to that of the liberal gentry. The latter demanded administrative reforms that would grant a large measure of local self-government in which the landed gentry could play an important, if not dominant, role. The government, on the contrary, proceeded on the assumption that administrative reform was an affair of its own, and that its main task was to *remove*, as far as possible, gentry influence in local administration and to replace it with administration more or less directly under the control of the bureaucracy.

Local administration as a whole was not treated in the legislation on emancipation, and the provincial committees were

---

[1] The elevation of Rostovtsev and the founding of the Editing Commissions were, indeed, initially looked upon by proponents of emancipation as signs that the government was at last getting down to the problem of reform in a serious fashion. Cf. Trubetskaia, *Materialy*, I, 239.

explicitly informed that all discussion about 'the organization of local administration and police in the *uezdy*' was strictly beyond their competency.[1] The government intended to retain a complete monopoly of initiative in this area, and simultaneously with the preparation of the emancipation it began its own plans for administrative changes. In May 1858, the Ministry of Interior put forth a tentative plan for the reform of local administration, a plan for removing the independent status of the old gentry-elected *zemskii ispravnik* and placing the *uezd* administration under the control of an *uezdnyi nachal'nik* (*uezd* chief), a strictly bureaucratic appointment under the direct control of the provincial administration.[2] This plan, which was not made public—it was submitted only to the provincial governors for comments—became known, nevertheless, to the gentry. They produced general protests, which were reflected in the comments of the governors: they were unanimously negative.[3]

Abandoning this plan, the *Zemskii otdel* of the Ministry drew up a new plan, whose principles were given Imperial approval on 25 March 1859. These principles were the following: (1) Unification of rural and city police administration under the command of an *uezdnyi ispravnik*, appointed by the government; (2) Separation of the investigatory organs (procurators, etc.) from the police and their reorganization under the Ministry of Justice; (3) Creation of a special 'class' or 'self-administration' for local economic functions, and the creation of temporary institutions for the promulgation of the emancipation, which were to be staffed by gentry representatives elected by gentry and peasants alike.[4]

A commission headed by Nicholas Miliutin (actual author of both the above plans) was appointed to develop the details of administrative legislation, and by Senate *ukaz* of 16 June 1860, some of these principles were implemented. Most significantly, the post of *zemskii ispravnik*, until then held by officials elected by the gentry, was taken out of the hands of the gentry and made

---

[1] *Sbornik pravitel'stvennykh rasporiazhenii*, I, section IV, 147–8.   [2] *Ibid.*, pp. 176–89.
[3] Solov'ev, 'Zapiski', XLI, 243–52.
[4] *Sbornik pravitel'stvennykh rasporiazhenii*, I, section II, 52–62.

a government appointment through the provincial governor.[1] Thus the basic aim of the first plan—removal of the chief authority in the *uezd* (which was the *zemskii ispravnik*) from the hands of the gentry—was accomplished. The gentry were thrown a sop in the form of a minor concession to the principles of the 'separation of powers' (the reorganization of the investigatory organs) and self-administration (the plan, then left unrealized, for the creation of local organs of economic self-administration),[2]

(2) *Government plans for further gentry participation in the preparation of reform*. Immediately following these developments, at the end of July 1859, Lanskoi presented a secret memorandum[3] to the Emperor. It was devoted to the provincial committees, the projects of which had by that time been reviewed by the Rural Department of the Ministry. The concluding assessment of the work of the committees was not charitable: ' . . . *The committee projects do not decide the peasant question, but only acquaint us with how the majority of the gentry look on it'*. Gentry views on the question, wrote Lanskoi, could be grouped into three basic currents of opinion:

The first opinion is that of those who have shown little sympathy to the emancipation of the peasants, prompted by the personal material interest of the *pomeshchik* . . .

. . . Finally convinced of the impossibility of counteracting the emancipation of the peasants, they concern themselves only with how to transform the abolition of serfdom into an operation profitable for themselves.

The second opinion . . . This is the tendency of *class interest*. It found supporters most of all among our notable and wealthy *pomeshchiki*. Putting in first place the class interests of the gentry, they wish to create in Russia a noble landed aristocracy, similar to the English, and in the place of present privileged property based on serfdom, to introduce another, no less privileged, on feudal foundations . . . The

---

[1] *Materialy*, ii, 463–68. The Miliutin Commission began the work which eventually led to the *zemstvo* reform of 1864. Its work continued until 1861, when Miliutin was removed from the Ministry, at which time it was renamed the Valuev Commission after its new chairman. The Valuev Commission prepared the legislation for the *zemstvo* reform. [2] *Ibid.* [3] N. P. Semenov, *Osvobozhdenie krest'ian*, i, 826–34.

real aim, pursued by persons of this opinion quite consciously and persistently, is emancipation of the peasants without land.

The third opinion belongs to those wishing full abolition of serfdom. They comprise, although far from the majority, a significant part of the Russian gentry. . . . Sympathizing with the views of the government concerning the protection of the individual peasant from arbitrariness, and the peasants' solid security with land, they do, however, differ among themselves on many particular questions. *But their opinions . . . though differing in details, unanimously defend the complete abolition of pomeshchik authority, and the redemption, obligatory or voluntary, of all or part of the peasant allotment in full property, on conditions as moderate as possible.*

The aim of the memorandum was made clear in its conclusion: The deputies of half the committees were momentarily expected in Petersburg, Lanskoi reminded the Emperor, and the majority of them certainly belonged to the followers of the first two opinions. They would try, he warned, to join together and force the government to change those of its principles with which they disagreed. About this, something would have to be done:

The main concern should be that the opinions which have been independently expressed in the various committees should not be united into harmonious, and so far non-existent, parties of various colorations, which would be disastrous for the government and for the people. Therefore the aspiration toward the formation of parties must be excluded from the very start. In accordance with your Imperial Majesty's order, the deputies chosen by the committees are being summoned 'for presentation to the government of the information and explanations which [the government] considers it necessary to have'. It is useful for the government to obtain opinions from them, not about fundamental principles, which have been affirmed as unchangeable; nor about their elaboration, which belongs solely to the government itself; but exclusively about the adaptation of the projected general rules to the particular conditions of each locale. *Therefore dreams must not be allowed to develop about the deputies . . . being summoned for the decision of any kind of legislative questions, or for changes in the State system.* The abolition of serfdom is a task already decided in the salubrious thought of your Majesty, which cannot be liable to any change.[1]

---

[1] *Ibid.* Emphasis added.

This memorandum was sent to Alexander II, who returned it with the comment: 'I find this view completely correct and in accordance with my own convictions. Please communicate it to Adjutant-General Rostovtsev.'[1] Lanskoi, who feared acutely that the memorandum might become known to the gentry, chose to communicate it orally to Rostovtsev.[2]

The next step was obvious: A set of instructions was composed in the Ministry of Interior for the deputies of the provincial committees, who were due to arrive in Petersburg toward the end of August 1859. The deputies were to be informed that they had been summoned to provide, individually, 'local information and explanations' in accordance with the function which had been assigned their provincial committees: 'The adaptation of the [already accepted] general provisions to the peculiarities of each province'. To this end the deputies were to answer in written form those questions put to them by the Editing Commissions. Upon invitation, it was further explained, individual deputies would be presented for oral interviews with the Commissions. These duties were to be performed in a month's time, after which the deputies were to disperse to their various provinces. *No formal meetings among the deputies were to be allowed.*[3]

Lanskoi's memorandum pointed to the antipathy towards emancipation and the potential for political opposition existing among the gentry as justification for removing the deputies

[1] N. P. Semenov, *Osvobozhedenie krest'ian*, I, 834, fn.

[2] *Ibid.*

[3] Skrebitskii, *Krest'ianskoe delo*, I, cxii–cxiv. The preparation of these instructions was evidently asked for by Alexander II himself after he had read the memorandum. They were prepared by Nicholas Miliutin with the help of Ia. Solov'ev and discussed in a secret meeting (20 August 1859) with several members of the Editing Commissions (Rostovtsev purposely did not involve himself in this matter in order to avoid embarrassment before the gentry deputies). Several representatives of the Editing Commissions (especially P. P. Semenov and Iu. Samarin) objected to the restrictions to be put on the deputies, arguing that there was not much danger of a united opposition being created among the deputies, whose interests varied widely. More dangerous, they claimed, would be the impression created by the restrictions.

Miliutin and his colleagues prevailed, however, by arguing that the majority of the deputies were intent on 'bringing the whole enterprise to naught', and that there was great danger of their being joined by *sanovniki* seeking the same end. P. P. Semenov-Tian-Shanskii, *Memuary*, III (Petrograd, 1915), 285–90; N. P. Semenov, *Osvobozhdenie krest'ian*, I, 612–13.

from any substantive role in the legislative work of the government. The progressive bureaucrats in the Ministry of Interior especially feared a possible union between aristocratic-oligarchic elements in the gentry (the adherents of the second opinion described in the memoir) and certain high dignitaries in Petersburg.[1] Such a development could lead, they believed, to an attempt by the gentry to undertake an overt political move of some sort, or at least to direct pressure on the Emperor to abandon the newly-accepted principles of reform.[2] The immediate aim of the aristocratic-oligarchic party, declared Nicholas Miliutin, was to 'replace the legislation . . . with some kind of defined rules, so that emancipation would remain only in words without the solution of the most vital economic questions'.[3]

In fact, the Ministry bureaucrats considerably exaggerated the political potential of the aristocratic-oligarchic elements among the gentry, as later events were to prove. In the summer of 1859, however, they were the only gentry elements that had shown any sign of developing into an opposition party or movement.[4] The first notable stirrings in that direction had occurred in the winter of 1858–9, as the provincial committees were closed and large numbers of gentry marshals and wealthy *pomeshchiki* flocked to Petersburg to await further developments. The first efforts to form something like an aristocratic opposition occurred there, and were connected with the activities of Senator A. M. Bezo-

---

[1] They had in mind especially Count V. F. Adlerberg (Minister of Court), Count M. N. Murav'ev (Minister of State Properties), Prince V. A. Dolgorukov (Head of the Third Section), Count A. F. Orlov, General K. V. Chevkin, Count V. N. Panin (Minister of Justice), Adjutant-General A. E. Timashev, Secret Councillor V. P. Butkov, Baron P. K. Meyendorf, Prince A. S. Menshikov, Prince P. P. Gagarin, 'and many other influential people'. *Materialy*, II, 159; Solov'ev, 'Zapiski', XXX, 754–6. Orlov, Adlerberg, Gagarin, Panin, Dolgorukov, Murav'ev and Chevkin were all members of the Main Committee.

[2] The Emperor was warned of this danger in the memorandum: 'The champions of this tendency [the aristocratic-oligarchic] have found sympathy both among the backward gentry and, perhaps, among certain personages of high rank close to You, Sovereign; and among several members of the Main Committee.'

[3] Semenov, *Osvobozhdenie krest'ian*, I, 612–13.

[4] The liberal gentry, who represented a potential 'left opposition', had been chary of attacking the government's handling of the reform preparations, especially after its endorsement of land-redemption. The transfer of initiative from the Main Committee to the Editing Commissions was also greeted by them as a step in the right direction. Cf. Trubetskaia, *Materialy*, I, 239.

brazov and his two sons[1] who held regular 'evenings' at their town house in Petersburg:

... A friend of mine [a member of the Editing Commissions wrote to Nicholas Miliutin] accidentally called on Michael Bezobrazov the other evening, at the house on the Fontanka that you know. There were present those already well-known for their *pomeshchik* exploits: Blank, Prince Gagarin, ... Orlov from Vologda, and others. There they berated the reds, Rostovtsev, you and your colleagues—all of whom should be destroyed. As a means to this end they read the draft of an address to the Emperor on the destruction of the works of the provincial committees and the Editing Commissions, and on the acceptance of one main principle: *personal emancipation of the peasants without land.* It is further attested in the address that the reds are traitors, and that the throne and the fatherland can be saved only by the faithful gentry who have signed the address. They plan to gather up to 10,000 signators through various members of the provincial committees, from among whom they ask the Emperor to form a special commission in Petersburg in place of the Editing [Commissions]. They talk of Shuvalov and Paskevich as of representatives of this opinion and have placed great hopes in them.[2]

Such an address was indeed composed. The bureaucracy, claimed its authors, had distorted the original Rescripts and had interfered in the work of the provincial committees, which had thus been rendered worthless. The bureaucrats, declared the address, have 'deprived the people and the Tsar of direct, close and salutary union'. The bureaucrats cannot know the needs of the land, for they are 'gentry and *pomeshchiki* by name only', a foreign element in the state. Disaster can be averted, the address continued, only if the government agreed:

[1] The Bezobrazovs, wealthy gentry of Petersburg and Moscow provinces, were already notorious opponents of the government's reform plans. N. A. Bezobrazov had published a brochure in 1858 (in Berlin) in which he argued that the peasant question could be solved by the refinement of existing legislation alone. (*Ob usovershenii uzakonenii, kasaiushchikhsia do votchinnykh prav dvorianstva.*) The Bezobrazovs were relatives of Prince Orlov, chairman of the Secret Committee.

[2] Miliutina, 'Iz zapisok', xcvii, 583–4. Count P. P. Shuvalov and Count F. E. Paskevich, as members of the Editing Commissions, categorically objected to the idea of making emancipation dependent on land-redemption. Both were influential aristocratic proponents of the 'English solution'. Semenov, *Osvobozhdenie krest'ian*, i, 148–56.

... To allow the election of two representatives from each province with full authority from their class, and to create with them an assembly of the gentry for the examination of the legislation prepared by the Editing Commissions and the Main Committee ...

This assembly shall be given the right to elect, from among the *sanovniki* surrounding the throne, a chairman who shall have direct access to Your Majesty. The examined and discussed legislation shall be presented to the judgment of Your Imperial Majesty through the State Council.[1]

The address failed, however, to attract a large number of signatures; and although it was known to the government, it was never formally presented to the Emperor.[2]

One other document to come from this same group of opposition-minded aristocrats attracted the government's attention at about the same time. This was the polemical letter sent by Count V. P. Orlov-Davydov[3] to various high government officials in the spring of 1859. Orlov-Davydov's attack was reserved mainly for the Editing Commissions, which had, he wrote, exceeded their proper function, which was merely to compile a digest of the statutes produced by the provincial committees. Therefore Orlov-Davydov also demanded the calling of a gentry assembly for the final solution of the peasant question, which was, he claimed, the responsibility of the gentry alone. Terminated by verbose denunciations of the bureaucracy and praise for English 'self-government', Orlov-Davydov's letter was rightly taken by the bureaucrats as an expression of the 'desire for a constitutional-aristocratic form of government'.[4]

---

[1] *Materialy*, II, 106–7, 109.   [2] *Ibid.*, p. 96.

[3] Count V. P. Orlov-Davydov (1809–82) was the model of the aristocratic anglophile described in Lanskoi's memorandum. A wealthy landowner with large estates in Simbirsk province and elsewhere, he was a graduate of Edinburgh university and an erstwhile diplomat who had seen service in the Russian embassy in London. He also was a much-travelled amateur *littérateur* and classicist who in his lifetime wrote various works, including a book of travel impressions from a trip to Greece and Asia Minor (1839–40) and a two-volume biography (1878) of his maternal grandfather (Count V. G. Orlov, whose name and title he took by permission of the Emperor in 1856). He was an honorary member of the Academy of Sciences. In 1862 he was elected provincial gentry marshal in Petersburg province.

[4] 'Ne serait-il pas prudent de dérober l'autorité à l'influence de ce hazard [wrote Orlov-Davydov in reference to bureaucratic caprice] et de lui donner un cours légal dans toutes les régions plus rapprochées du trône, d'où elle puisse s'écouler graduellement et

Both the Bezobrazov address and the Orlov-Davydov letter angrily condemned the government's latest plans for local administrative reform as a new effrontery by the overweening bureaucracy. 'Why take from the gentry', demanded Orlov-Davydov, 'the right to elect the police-officers, who constitute the first level of self-government?'[1] It would appear that Orlov-Davydov, and presumably others like him, had specific plans for the gentry deputies selected to gather in Petersburg. P. D. Stremoukhov, one of these deputies, has left the following account of a chance encounter with Orlov-Davydov in mid-1859:

> Once, meeting me at a reception at the house of Minister Lanskoi, the well-known anglomaniac Count V. P. Orlov-Davydov ... began to assert dogmatically that the deputies not only have the right, but are obligated to band together in a cooperative opposition force against the government, whose actions in the peasant reform were clearly leading to the undermining not only of the material welfare of the gentry, but of its political significance, as a class which had served as the immemorial support of the throne. [He also asserted] that an opposition organized in that fashion would have the character of his majesty's opposition, similar to the English parliamentary opposition which, serving as the protector of the royal power against the mistakes, errors and, in general, bad policies of its ministers, deservedly called itself 'Her Majesty's opposition'.[2]

The Ministry of Interior had struggled long for the cause of peasant emancipation. It had seen its efforts consolidated and its goals raised to the rank of first principles by the creation of the Editing Commissions. At that point the Ministry came to the conclusion—evidently shared by Alexander II—that the government's intentions about emancipation had advanced considerably beyond the wishes of the mass of landed gentry. Thus in August 1859, its gains seemed threatened by the possible united opposition

---

également dans les classes inférieures de la société.' *Ibid.*, p. 113, fn. (The letter was published in Paris under the title *Lettre d'un deputé de Comité à M. le Président de la Commission de rédaction, aide-de-camp Général Rostovtzeff.*)

[1] *Ibid.*, p. 112.

[2] P. D. Stremoukhov, 'Zametka odnogo iz deputatov pervogo prizyva', *Russkaia starina*, CII, p. 141.

of its old enemies the conservative *sanovniki* and the gentry deputies. The 'enlightened bureaucrats' in the Ministry, led by Miliutin, were deeply distrustful of the gentry and their distrust was compounded by the fact that virtually all demands for increased gentry participation in the reform had so far come from conservative, aristocratic circles. In their view, gentry demands for participation in the solution of the peasant question had only one source—narrow class interests; and one aim—obstruction of the government's reform plans.[1]

In the same view, demands for administrative reforms and participation by the gentry in general administrative functions were also looked upon as aristocratic pretensions:

Infected with aristocratic ideas, or, it would be better to say, love of power and swaggering, some of our fine gentlemen dream of a boyar *duma*, that is, of oligarchial rule. Others praise the English arrangement and demand class self-rule. They are joined by some of the provincial gentry, far from aristocrats by their birth, education and social position, but also demanding gentry representation.[2]

The Ministry's opinion of such gentry pretensions was succinctly expressed in a second memorandum presented by Lanskoi to the Emperor in August 1859:

The gentry as a class has not demonstrated in any way its administrative knowledge and abilities. On the contrary, all affairs which have so far been entrusted to the class administration of the gentry have been conducted extremely badly.[3]

---

[1] 'Never, never, so long as I am in power', Miliutin was reported to have said about that time, 'will I allow any pretensions whatever [of the gentry] to the role of initiators in matters concerning the interests and needs of the people as a whole. Concern with them belongs to the government; to it and it alone belongs any initiative in any reform whatever for the welfare of the country. *Tout pour le peuple, rien par le peuple.*' N. Barsukov, *Zhizn' i trudy M. P. Pogodina*, XVII (St Petersburg, 1903), 132. (Miliutin may never have uttered these words; it is of sufficient significance that they were attributed to him.)

[2] From a memorandum presented by Lanskoi to Alexander II in August, 1859 (actually written by Miliutin), quoted in N. I. Iordanskii, *Konstitutsionnoe dvizhenie 60kh godov* (St Petersburg, 1906), p. 50; Miliutina, 'Iz zapisok', XCVII, pp. 105–13.

[3] Iordanskii, *Konstitutsionnoe dvizhenie*, p. 52. At the same time, however, Lanskoi claimed to recognize the need to grant the gentry at least limited participation in local administration. In his memorandum on the provincial committees, Lanskoi had explicitly

The gentry versus the bureaucracy, 1858–61

Convinced of the fundamental immaturity of Russian society, believing the government to be 'more liberal than society', the bureaucrats in the Ministry of Interior were intent on retaining a full government monopoly in all areas of reform.[1] The gentry, however, were unwilling to accept this judgment, as their deputies demonstrated in Petersburg.

THE FIRST CONVOCATION OF GENTRY DEPUTIES, AUGUST–NOVEMBER, 1859

The conflict with the government

The first group of representatives from the provincial committees, 44 deputies from 21 provinces, arrived in Petersburg during the third week of August. Of the 21 provinces represented, eleven were north-central and western non-black soil provinces,[2] six were of the black soil region,[3] and four were of the outlying regions of the Empire.[4] Nine of the assembled deputies represented committee minorities.

On the twenty-fifth of August 1859, these deputies were called together and presented the list of instructions that had been prepared for them in the Ministry of Interior. The deputies, most of whom had expected at least some form of collective consultation with the Main Committee, were predictably out-

recognized this: '... In order to reward the gentry for the loss of *pomeshchik* authority, they should be presented with leadership in local economic administration; and in order to give them the possibility of moral influence on the local inhabitants their direct participation in the appointing of justices of the peace and other responsible officials, general for both classes, ... would be useful.'

[1] In an audience with Alexander II early in 1859 Miliutin defended himself against charges of 'constitutionalism' with the following words: '... Of this [a constitution] one could dream in one's youth and under entirely different circumstances. Now ... I have had time to grow grey in the struggle with the arbitrariness and immaturity of the higher strata of our society, which with a constitutional rule would create the despotism of an oligarchy in our country; that I certainly do not desire for my fatherland now, when the government is more liberal than society and includes in its program the emancipation of the peasants.' Miliutina, 'Iz zapisok', XCVII, p. 64.

[2] Nizhnii Novogorod, Petersburg, Kostroma, Moscow, Vitebsk, Tver, Pskov, Minsk, Vladimir, Novgorod and Iaroslavl.

[3] Simbirsk, Kharkov, Voronezh, Tambov, Saratov, and Riazan (a border-province, but predominantly of the black soil region).

[4] Chernigov, Astrakhan, Viatka, Poltava. (A list of the provinces and the deputies of the first convocation is located in Semenov, *Osvobozhdenie krest'ian*, II, 909–11.)

raged.[1] Their immediate response was to call a meeting, which was held the next day in the spacious townhouse of Count P. P. Shuvalov (now acting as deputy from the Petersburg committee). There an address to the Emperor was composed (its actual authors were Shuvalov, Koshelev, and Unkovskii) in which the object of their outrage was clearly identified. The Emperor, it was claimed in the address, had promised that the deputies of the provincial committees would be called 'for meetings in the Main Committee and for general examination of the projects...' (a reference to Alexander's speech to the Tver gentry in August 1858). But *the bureaucracy* could not allow that:

... Distorting over the course of many years all the best ideas of the Tsar, and poisoning the most noble feelings, could the bureaucracy allow such a union, in which the Tsar could hear the voice of his people otherwise than through the lying mouth [of the bureaucracy]?

Our sorrow, Sovereign, is inexpressible! We have seen many times in the course of this affair how Imperial orders have been set one against the other or violated by the bureaucracy; but its boldness has never reached the extent that it has at present.

The journals of the Editing Commissions and all the administrative measures are full of harmful, fatal, principles. We see them, but are deprived of the possibility of exposing them.

Therefore, concluded the address, the deputies requested the following:

... Let all the deputies elected by the committees ... gather in meeting with the Main Committee and there proceed with a general, loyal

---

[1] Semenov, *Osvobozhdenie krest'ian*, 1, 607; *Materialy*, 11, 124. The only more or less detailed account of the activities of the deputies in Petersburg (as distinct from their written commentaries for the Editing Commissions, which will be discussed later on in this chapter) was written by Koshelev. As a deputy from the Riazan committee, Koshelev became one of the most active gentry opponents of the 'tyranny of the Editing Commissions', and thus found himself opposed to his former close associates Samarin and Cherkasskii, who were both members of the Editing Commissions. Koshelev's polemical account of the struggle of the deputies against the Editing Commissions was published in Leipzig in 1860 under the title *Deputaty i redaktsionnye kommissii po krest'ianskomu delu*.

examination, collation and correction of the draft statutes of the committees, under Your personal chairmanship, Sovereign, or that of one of the members of the Imperial family.[1]

The deputies, however, did not dare to formally present their address to the Emperor, and ended by requesting Rostovtsev, as chairman of the Editing Commissions, only to allow 'general assemblies' of the deputies, and to see to it that the considerations of the deputies were presented directly to the 'supreme authority'.[2] In reply, the deputies were informed that no official meetings of the deputies would be allowed, and that they were to adhere strictly to the instructions they had received.[3]

'Private meetings' of the deputies were, however, allowed, and they continued to gather regularly. The deputies soon formed three informal circles (*kruzhki*). One of these groups was led by Unkovskii:[4]

To this group [Stremoukhov recalled] belonged the most energetic reformers. Here, in connection with the peasant reform, there took place a broad discussion of the question of the reorganization of the courts and the administration, reforms upon which the beneficial results of the peasant reform itself depended. And here the question of freedom of the press was also put forth with special persistence. Such a broad and essentially radical program gave to the meetings of this group a particularly political coloration.[5]

As far as the peasant question, narrowly conceived, was concerned, this group was united by the demand for obligatory redemption.

A second group was constituted by deputies also favorably disposed to redemption, but with differences of opinion on whether or not it should be obligatory. Unlike the Unkovskii circle, this group apparently restricted itself to discussion of the peasant reform as such, but here too 'politics' entered the picture

[1] Semenov, *Osvobozhdenie krest'ian*, I, 614–17.
[2] *Materialy*, II, 129–30.   [3] *Ibid.*, pp. 131–2.
[4] To this group belonged (in addition to Unkovskii and the other deputy from Tver, Kardo-Sysoev) the deputies from Iaroslavl, Kostroma, Vladimir, and Kharkov. *Ibid.*, p. 135. These deputies were generally considered 'the most energetic reformers'. Barsukov, *Zhizn' i trudy Pogodina*, XVII, 131.
[5] Stremoukhov, 'Zametka', p. 141.

by the demands of some of its members that the peasant question be resolved by the summoning of 'class representatives'.[1]

A third group of more conservative inclinations, according to Stremoukhov of a 'completely aristocratic character', gathered at the house of the Petersburg marshal, Count Shuvalov, another well-known aristocratic anglophile, who 'doctrinarily defended the idea of the preservation for the *pomeshchiki* of full property rights to all the land'.[2] The first two of these circles met regularly, and their members collaborated in the writings of the responses to the questions put to them by the Editing Commissions.[3]

By the time the deputies had finished their work, which consisted essentially of writing answers to the questions of the Editing Commissions and commentaries on the legislative drafts already completed by the Commissions, they had produced some 4,000 pages, or three large volumes of writings.[4] Despite the productivity of their stay in Petersburg, the deputies' conviction that their presence there was a mere formality grew steadily stronger, and many of them hurried to finish their work and to leave the capital. Some, including the two deputies from Tver, scorned personal appearances before the Editing Commissions.[5]

Several general meetings of the deputies were held in mid-October, when it was once again decided to draw up an address to the Emperor, this time with the request that the gentry deputies be allowed to examine the final drafts of legislation prepared by the Editing Commissions, and subsequently to have meetings with the Main Committee.[6] Before a final version of this address could be prepared, however, numerous deputies lost courage and refused to sign. As a result the deputies eventually

[1] *Ibid.*, p. 142.   [2] *Ibid.*

[3] *TsGIAL, f.* 1180, no. 133, pp. 45–6a; *Materialy*, II, 136–7. To the second group belonged the deputies from Riazan (including Koshelev), Tambov, Saratov, one deputy from Voronezh, one from Chernigov, and the single deputy from Moscow.

    The third circle contained the deputies from Poltava, Petersburg, Pskov, Novgorod, and one deputy each from Voronezh, Simbirsk, and Chernigov. A few other members took little or no part in these circles.

[4] *Materialy redaktsionnykh komissii. Prilozhenie k trudam redaktsionnykh komissii . . . Otzyvy chlenov gubernskikh komitetov*, vols. I–III (St Petersburg, 1859–60).

[5] *TsGIAL, f.* 1180, no. 133, pp. 103–4a, 110a. In all, deputies from only 14 of the 21 committees actually put in personal appearances before the Editing Commissions.

[6] Semenov, *Osvobozhdenie krest'ian*, II, 933–4.

presented three addresses to the Emperor: (1) An emasculated version of the original address, signed by 18 deputies; (2) an address presented by the deputy from Simbirsk, D. N. Shidlovskii, and (3) an address presented by the members of the 'Unkovskii circle'.[1]

The first address (which was signed by all deputies remaining in Petersburg except those who had presented separate addresses) avoided any strict demands, referring only to the 'general conclusion that the projects of the Editing Commissions do not, in their present form, correspond to the general needs'; and requested only that the deputies 'be allowed to present [their] comments on the final works of the Editing Commissions before their transmission to the Main Committee'.[2]

Shidlovskii's address was much bolder. It accused the Editing Commissions of pursuing the 'obvious intention of destroying the class- and property-significance of the gentry'. Shidlovskii's demands reflected the same 'aristocratic pretensions' as the Bezobrazov address had earlier in the year:

. . . The fusion of the autocracy with the gentry, as the first and most natural defender of the throne and fatherland, is obligatory . . . Sovereign! Allow there to be called to the foot of thy throne special elected representatives from the gentry; and complete, under thine own chairmanship, Sovereign, the cause which will be the glory of thy reign.[3]

The address presented by Unkovskii and other members of his circle[4] was of an entirely different nature. Avoiding any demands for a review of the legislation by gentry representatives, the address restricted itself to making four concrete demands:

. . . Knowing your intent, Sovereign, that Russia follow the path of peaceful development; convinced that the peasants have the hope . . . to receive full freedom and land in property, and that the conditions

---

[1] *Ibid.*, pp. 934–9.   [2] *Ibid.*, pp. 934–5.   [3] *Ibid.*, pp. 937–9.

[4] The author of the final version of this address was not Unkovskii, but Shreter, deputy from Kharkov. It was signed by only five members of the 'Unkovskii circle', because the remaining members (Kardo-Sysoev and the deputies from Vladimir and Kostroma), at the time of its composition, had already departed from Petersburg. *Materialy*, II, 171; Dzhanshiev, *Unkovskii*, pp. 132–4.

of the classes cannot be improved without the reform of the existing order of administration, police and the courts, we dare humbly beg of Your Imperial Majesty the following:

1. To grant the peasants full freedom, with the allotment of their land in property by means of immediate redemption, at a price and on conditions not ruinous for the *pomeshchiki*.[1]

2. To form economic-executive administration [*khoziaistvenno-raspor-iaditel'noe upravlenie*] common for all classes, and based on the elective principle.[2]

3. To create an independent judiciary authority, that is jury courts, and civil court institutions independent of the administrative authority; with the introduction of public and verbal legal procedure; and with the subordination of local officials to direct responsibility before the court.

4. To allow society, by means of freedom of the press [lit: *pechatnaia glasnost'*], to bring to the attention of the central government [lit: *vysshaia vlast'*] the insufficiencies and misuses of local administration.[3]

The 'address of the five deputies' was, then, a repetition of the basic demands of the liberal gentry program as expressed in the Unkovskii-Golovachev *zapiska* of January 1858, in the Tver provincial committee, and elsewhere.[4]

The government left these addresses unanswered. Their authors, however, were variously dealt with: Shidlovskii and Unkovskii were given strong reprimands and placed under police surveillance in their respective provinces. The four co-signers with Unkovskii of the 'address of the five deputies' and the 18 signers of the main address were given reprimands through

[1] 'The peasants will only then feel their condition improved [it was noted in the preface to the four demands] when they will have escaped from all obligations to their masters, and when they will have become property-owners. For personal freedom is impossible without freedom of property'. Semenov, *Osvobozhdenie krest'ian*, II, 936.

[2] 'In the obligatory relations established [by the proposals of the Editing Commissions] between personally-free peasants and *pomeshchiki*, deprived of social significance and any part in the administration of the people, lie the seeds of a dangerous struggle between the classes.' (From the preface to the four points.) *Ibid.*

[3] *Ibid.*, pp. 935–7.

[4] To these general demands the address added the specific complaint that the Editing Commissions were planning 'an increase of the land-allotment for the peasants ... and an extreme reduction in [peasant] obligations in most provinces'; a plan which, if realized, would be ruinous for the gentry. This complaint probably reflected the views of the Kharkov deputies especially, for they had specific quarrels in this area with the Commissions. Unkovskii had no such quarrel. (See page 248 below.)

the governors of their provinces. The initiative for these actions came from the Ministry of Interior, where the danger of gentry opposition was most strongly feared.[1]

The addresses, and all that had taken place between the government and the deputies in Petersburg, confirmed the earlier fears of the Ministry of Interior that the gentry deputies, by and large, intended to wreck the efforts of the Editing Commissions and to take the matter into the hands of the gentry.[2] In a meeting of the Main Committee devoted to the deputies' addresses, Lanskoi presented a report maintaining that *all* the addresses contained two essential elements: '(1) General rejection of the works of the Editing Commissions. (2) Solicitation that the draft legislation . . . be subjected to final discussion by gentry plenipotentiaries.'[3] The gentry, argued Lanskoi, had had every opportunity to express their opinions: in *uezd* meetings, in the provincial committees, and now in Petersburg. But the deputies, instead of criticizing the specific work of the Editing Commissions, had devoted themselves almost exclusively to condemnation of the basic principles accepted by the central government and followed by the Commissions.[4]

All this, and the demands for gentry representation, explained Lanskoi, was the result of the fact that the bigger part of the deputies had succumbed to the influence of 'certain persons' in Petersburg who entertained aristocratic pretensions.[5] Such

---

[1] *Materialy*, II, 187. Shidlovskii was given special treatment because his address was considered particularly offensive; Unkovskii because he was a provincial gentry marshal. *TsGIAL, f.* 1180, no. 133, p. 194.

[2] 'It is evident [wrote Lanskoi in an answer to Koshelev's attack on the Editing Commissions] . . . that the sincere wish of the deputies who came here in the first convocation was to create from among themselves a state institution which would definitely decide the peasant question.' *ORLB, f.* 327, 1/11/8, pp. 1–2.

[3] *ORLB, f.* 327, 1/22/6, 1.

[4] *Ibid.*, p. 5.

[5] Lanskoi had in mind mainly the Bezobrazov group. Simultaneously with the addresses of the deputies, M. A. Bezobrazov had presented an address of his own. Like the Shidlovskii address, this one condemned the work of the bureaucracy and demanded the calling in of gentry representatives. ('The right of the Russian land to have representatives for consultation with the [Emperor] exists now as it did formerly. No one can take it away. It is a right born with the origins of the Russian people.') Bezobrazov's condemnation of the bureaucracy was fanatical. It had, he intimated, actually seized power from the Emperor, who was thus no longer autocrat. The aim of the bureaucracy in undertaking the emancipation?—to undermine the very foundation of

'illegal aspirations' should be curbed to protect the 'general state interest', Lanskoi warned. As for further participation by the gentry in the resolution of the peasant question:

... The further participation of these deputies, or of other pleni-potentiaries from the gentry, in the solution of the peasant question would be, evidently, superfluous, harmful, and for the solution of the question itself—useless.

The final solution of the question, which has such a great state sig-nificance, belongs only to the central government, which alone can impartially weigh and reconcile the interests of both classes.[1]

Even aspirations of the gentry toward 'independent participation in general affairs, or so-called "self-rule"' was not to be tolerated:

... Such pretensions obviously cannot be tolerated, and it is therefore necessary to watch vigilantly that they not find encouragement even in general and abstract discussions of questions of state law.[2]

Copies of the reprimands to the deputies who had signed the addresses were widely circulated. They produced great irritation among the gentry, who began to complain that the bureaucracy, not content with taking the serfs and the land away from them now wanted to rob them of their traditional right to present collective petitions to the Tsar.[3] The situation, as described at that point by Koshelev, was extremely tense:

Formerly . . . the gentry were dissatisfied with certain actions of the government related to the peasant question; but at least the enlightened minority of *pomeshchiki* stood on the side of the government and

the state in order to clear the way for a constitutional order. Semenov, *Osvobozhdenie krest'ian*, 2, 940–53.

This address, which was presented to Alexander II through Bezobrazov's friends in the Third Section, had a profound effect on the Emperor. 'He has completely convinced me [Alexander wrote on the margin of the address] of the wish of the likes of him to set up an oligarchic rule in Russia.' *Ibid.*, p. 952. Bezobrazov's address undoubtedly helped to convince the government that the activities and addresses of the deputies represented an essentially aristocratic opposition. Bezobrazov's case was brought before the Main Committee, which ruled that he be removed from service (he was then a *chinovnik* in the Ministry of Interior and a *kamerger dvora*) and be deprived of the right to enter either of the capitals. *Materialy*, II, 221.

[1] *ORLB, f.* 327, 1/22/6, 10–10a.
[2] Miliutina, 'Iz zapisok', XCVIII, 119.
[3] *Materialy*, II, 191.

fought strongly on its part. Now these latter have had their mouths shut, for there is nothing to be said in justification of the government. It itself acts in almost revolutionary fashion; from others it demands blind and silent obedience. It takes the initiative in everything itself, and that which exists has not, in its view, any preferential rights to further existence. To others it does not permit even...a word in their defense. *Dissatisfaction, even bitterness of everyone against the bureaucracy, in Petersburg, in Moscow, and in the provinces of Russia, grows not by the day but by the hour.*[1]

Not content with reprimanding the gentry deputies, the government proceeded to act on Lanskoi's warning that no further gentry participation in the peasant question should be permitted. On 9 November 1859, the Main Committee approved an order for transmission to the gentry marshals, providing that: ... *The gentry in their assemblies must not enter into any discussions of subjects connected with the peasant question in general.*[2]

By its hostile reception of the gentry deputies the government had created a momentarily united opposition of those deputies, in which the aristocratic Count Shuvalov joined with the liberal Unkovski in denunciation of the bureaucracy. By its further actions directed toward altogether removing gentry participation in the preparation of the reform, the government managed to drive virtually all elements of the gentry into opposition. Gentry assemblies were due to convene during the winter of 1859–60 in several provinces (Vladimir, Novgorod, Orenburg, Orel, Riazan, Iaroslavl, and Tver—December, 1859; Vologda, Kostroma, Estland, and Bessarabia *oblast'*—January, 1860).[3] The government awaited these assemblies with apprehension.

[1] *Ibid.*, pp. 191–2.

[2] *Ibid.*, p. 260. In point of fact this directive, which originated in the Ministry of Interior, was not new. It had already been sent (in the winter of 1858–9) to the marshals of several provinces where it had been anticipated that the gentry assemblies would try to interfere with the work of the provincial committees in those provinces. It was not then, however, made into a general order (despite the wishes of the Minister of Interior) and did not produce any particular response among the gentry. *Zhurnaly sekretnego i glavnogo komiteta*, I, 317–18; TsGIAL, *f.* 1180, no. 37, pp. 6–37a.

[3] *Materialy*, II, p. 258. Gentry assemblies were always held in the winter, either in December or January. Because regular assemblies were held only once in three years, in any given year only a dozen or so provinces were likely to have assemblies.

The government and the gentry, 1858–9

Views of the gentry deputies on reform

Before turning to the 'gentry assembled' in the winter of 1859–60 (the subject of the following chapter), a somewhat closer examination of the views and activities of the gentry deputies in Petersburg will be necessary—necessary because the comments of the gentry deputies indicate that considerable changes had taken place in gentry thought about reform since the time of the provincial committees.

The most striking of these changes was reflected in the deputies' views on *land-redemption*. It has been mentioned earlier that very few provincial committees had proposed land-redemption in their projects. Of the fourteen committees in which projects (either majority or minority) obviously favoring redemption had been produced, ten were represented in the first convocation of deputies in Petersburg.[1] The large majority of deputies gathered there, however, represented committees which had taken no stand on the redemption question. Nevertheless, most of the deputies departed from the projects of their respective committees and advocated land redemption before the Editing Commissions. All but a few individuals among the deputies did so,[2] and a majority of them unequivocally demanded obligatory redemption.[3]

There is no need to dwell on the arguments of the deputies in favor of land redemption. They are mostly familiar from the arguments of the Tver liberals and other proponents of redemption in the provincial committees. The reasons offered by the deputies for immediate land redemption were conveniently

---

[1] Tver, Novgorod, Iaroslavl, Nizhnii Novgorod, Vladimir, Saratov, Riazan, Moscow, Kharkov, and Simbirsk.

[2] Probably opposed to redemption were: Shidlovskii (Simbirsk), Prince Gagarin (Voronezh), Count Shuvalov, and Count Levashov (Petersburg), and the deputies from Saratov, Shcherbatov and Oznobishin. Skrebitskii, *Krest'ianskoe delo*, IV, 318–54. It is impossible to be certain, for the general demand for redemption was so great among the deputies that few dared to take an outright stand in opposition.

[3] Among them, deputies from Astrakhan, Vladimir (2), Vitebsk (2) Voronezh, Kostroma, Minsk (2), Nizhnii Novgorod, Novgorod, Poltava (2) Riazan (3), Tambov (2), Tver (2), Kharkov (2), Chernigov, and Iaroslavl (2). (The figures in parentheses indicate the number of deputies from a given province who took this position; the absence of such figures indicates that only one deputy from the province favored obligatory redemption.)

summarized by the staff of the Editing Commissions in the following way:

First—The disadvantages of the temporary-obligatory status because of the unsteadiness of the order established by it, as a temporary arrangement; the incompatibility of obligatory labor with the freedom of the peasants; the undefined nature of rights to the land belonging to the *pomeshchiki*, but being in peasant usage, and also the unreliability of the proper fulfillment of obligations in the absence of full authority for the *pomeshchik*.

Second—The disadvantages accompanying the redemption of the *usad'ba* alone; namely, inadequate guarantee of the welfare of the peasants ...; inevitable losses for the *pomeshchik* farms with the removal of the *usad'ba* plots from the general land complex, and the difficulties in the economic organization of the community without presentation to it of an adequate and irrevocable land allotment.

Third—All the results to be gained from the acquisition of landed property by the peasants, such as: a genuine improvement in their material welfare with the guaranteeing for them of the fruits of their centuries-long labor; protection of the interests and rights of the *pomeshchiki* by the payment for the land of redemption capital, necessary for the transformation of *pomeshchik* farming; finally, the possibility of a better administrative organization, encompassing all classes of the agricultural population.[1]

Where did this evidently new enthusiasm for land-redemption come from? To some extent, of course, it was not new. Much more support for redemption would have been forthcoming in the provincial committees had not the government expressly forbidden its consideration. And by the time the government itself came around to accepting redemption and granting the committees the right to draw up plans of redemption, most of the provincial committees had already closed.[2]

Yet, to an even greater extent there also existed an undoubtedly new enthusiasm. By mid-1859 the gentry had gained considerable experience in contemplating emancipation and its possible consequences. The question had by that time been under public

[1] Skrebitskii, *Krest'ianskoe delo*, IV, 399.
[2] Kornilov, 'Gubernskie komitety', no. 4, p. 60.

discussion for some 18 months, and the gentry, through their work in the provincial committees and the gradual clarification of the government's intentions, had come, by and large, to realize both that the government was steadfast in its intentions to free the serfs with land, and that the reform was not going to be a wildly radical departure in which gentry interests would be neglected. In ever-growing numbers, therefore, the *pomeshchiki* gradually retreated from hysteria to more rational thoughts of self-interest; and these thoughts increasingly led to the conclusion that land-redemption was the only feasible method of gaining some reasonable compensation and preserving social peace among the peasantry. This movement was clearly remarked by Lanskoi in his August 1859 memorandum:

In step with the development of the peasant question the idea of redemption [wrote Lanskoi] has increasingly taken root and is becoming a general conviction.... At present committees of the most opposite ends of Russia and of the most contradictory tendencies... have united on the idea of redemption.[1]

By the end of 1859, the government press could state that from among the gentry 'very few objections against redemption have been forthcoming'.[2]

The periodical press probably had a significant influence on this evolution of gentry thought. During 1858 and part of 1859, when considerable freedom of discussion of the peasant question was allowed, the most important journals in which the question was discussed—*Sovremennik, Russkii vestnik, Sel'skoe blagoustroistvo*, and others—carried on energetic propaganda for the acceptance of land-redemption. Especially after November 1858 (when, after the government's decision to accept land-redemption, the press was allowed for a time to advocate even a government-financing of redemption), many articles appeared pointing out the advantages for the *pomeshchiki* of immediate redemption, and the dangers of a temporary-obligatory period. The advantages of free labor and the gentry's need for capital were especially

[1] Semenov, *Osvobozhdenie krest'ian*, I, 832.
[2] Ivaniukov, *Padenie krepostnogo prava*, p. 184, fn.

stressed in these articles.[1] In *Kolokol*, of course, Herzen had been advocating obligatory land redemption since 1857.

On the deputies' demand for immediate *obligatory* redemption the government turned a deaf ear. The Editing Commissions had from the beginning operated on the principle that redemption was a necessity; the only question remaining was whether it should be voluntary or obligatory. Despite its recognition that the 'significant majority of comments by the deputies from the provincial committees is inclined to favor obligatory redemption', the government refused to undertake obligatory redemption. Its objections to obligatory redemption, as expressed by the Finance Commission of the Editing Commissions, were essentially two: (1) It would be impossible to effect immediate elimination of *barshchina* and its replacement by *obrok*, the necessary preliminary to redemption; and (2) the objection that 'obligatory redemption would demand the immediate issue of credit bonds in enormous quantities, which would produce the most disastrous results both for internal credit and for the land-owners themselves'.[2]

Rostovtsev and the members of the Finance Commission were aware of the dangers and injustices likely to be present in a 'temporary-obligatory period', and steps were taken toward what was thought would be a shortening of that period.[3] But the Finance Commission sought to provide only the machinery which would allow the *pomeshchiki*, in the event of a voluntary agreement, to receive guaranteed compensation, and permitting the peasants to purchase the land on a long-term credit basis.[4] In fact the government anticipated a rapid progress of redemption on a voluntary basis. Its central concern was to maintain controls in order to keep the operation from getting out of hand in the first few years, and then to encourage its rapid completion.[5] The entire system, as ultimately constructed by the Finance Com-

[1] The articles written by Unkovskii and Golovachev (discussed in chapter 4, pp. 110–14 above) were outstanding examples of this type of article. A discussion of the redemption question in the contemporary press is to be found in Ivaniukov, *Padenie*, pp. 122–9.
[2] Kovan'ko, *Reforma 19 fevralia*, p. 147.
[3] *Ibid.*, pp. 130–1; Skrebitskii, *Krest'ianskoe delo*, IV, 253.
Kovan'ko, *Reforma 19 fevralia*, pp. 137–9.   [5] *Ibid.*, p. 155.

mission, was designed to encourage the *gentry* to take up redemption. The peasantry, it was thought, would take it up readily. (This assumption proved to be, by and large, erroneous: the gentry rushed to undertake land-redemption, and the peasantry held back.)[1]

In matters relating to the determination of the size of peasant allotments and peasant obligations the deputies tended to be much more conservative; for the most part they defended the judgment of their respective committees. A wide variety of opinions on these subjects therefore existed among the deputies. One thing, however, the deputies shared in virtual unanimity: bitter dissatisfaction with the proposals on allotments and obligations made by the Editing Commissions.

The Editing Commissions had proposed a solution to the allotment problem based on the following essential principles: (1) Retention of existing average peasant allotments, with (2) the establishment of uniform limits, both maximum and minimum, on the size of allotments;[2] and (3) the retention for the *pomeshchik* of at least one-third of the total of his estate regardless of these norms. The minimum allotment-limit was finally established at one-third the size of the maximum limit in a given area.[3] The maximum and minimum norms were established by the Editing Commissions on the basis of the information on landed estates (of 100 souls or more) provided by the provincial committees, and also to some extent on statistical information gathered by the state tax-collecting agencies. While proclaiming retention of existing peasant allotments, this system of imposing maximum limits on the size of allotments ultimately resulted in the removal of very significant quantities of land from peasant usage—about 16 per cent of the total land previously held

[1] *Ibid.*, p. 89. (This subject will be discussed in a later chapter.)

[2] For this purpose Russia was divided into seven basic 'zones', the most extensive of which were the 'black soil', 'non-black soil', the 'steppe zone', and the 'New Russian zone'. Each of these zones was further subdivided into 'locales', 38 in all, for each of which special maximum norms were established. Cf. Zaionchkovskii, *Otmena krepostnogo prava v Rossii*, attached map.

[3] The Editing Commissions had originally proposed a minimum allotment of two-fifths the size of the maximum norm, but in the end reduced it as a concession to gentry opinion. An excellent discussion of this complicated subject is included in chapter seven of Ivaniukov, *Padenie krepostnogo prava*.

by the peasants in Russia as a whole (excluding the western provinces).[1]

A few of the deputies had no quarrel with these plans of the Editing Commissions. Unkovskii, for example, could not argue with a scheme which was nearly identical to that of his own committee and which established a maximum allotment nearly identical to that proposed in the Tver project.[2] Most, however, complained that the Editing Commissions' allotment scheme provided for 'extreme inequality of losses falling on the *pomesh-chiki*'. Almost half the deputies were opposed to the setting of any lower limits on the peasant allotments; and all but a few were in favor of guaranteeing for the *pomeshchik* not one-third of his lands, but a *full two-thirds*.[3] Even the few deputies who were not, in principle, opposed to retention of existing allotments objected that the scheme of the Editing Commissions would be ruinous for large numbers of *pomeshchiki*, because of the arbitrary establishment of maximum and minimum limits. Koshelev, who recognized the existing allotment in principle and even advocated raising the minimum peasant allotment to two-thirds that of the maximum, nevertheless was convinced that the allotment norms arrived at by the Editing Commissions were altogether too arbitrary, and accused the Commissions of neglecting the projects of the provincial committees and the statistics compiled by them.[4]

---

[1] The amount of what came to be known as 'cut-offs' varied greatly in various regions. In the central non-black soil region it was relatively small: For Tver, for example, 5·2 per cent. In the black soil regions it was much larger: In Saratov, for example, 38·1 per cent. The figures for the maximum norms *originally* proposed by the Editing Commissions were subsequently revised downward, under gentry pressure, but even the original figures would have resulted in considerable loss of land for the peasantry. Zaionchkovskii, *Otmena krepostnogo prava v Rossii*, pp. 206–7; Ivaniukov, *Padenie krepostnogo prava*, pp. 258–60.

[2] The allotment norm proposed by the Editing Commissions was the same as that proposed by the majority of the Tver committee itself (four *desiatiny*), for all but the five northernmost *uezdy* of the province, for which the Commissions proposed a four and one-half *desiatina* allotment. With this revision Unkovskii had no quarrel either. He did agree with most of his fellow deputies, however, that in many parts of Russia the loss to the *pomeshchiki* as a result of acceptance of the allotment norms proposed by the Commissions would be considerable, and on *barshchina* estates even enormous. Dzhanshiev, *Unkovskii*, pp. 132–4.   [3] Ivaniukov, *Padenie krepostnogo prava*, p. 273.

[4] *Ibid.*, pp. 275–6. One of the chief complaints against the Editing Commissions' norms was that they took no cognizance of the differences between *obrok* and *barshchina* estates, the former being often entirely in peasant usage.

In short, the deputies generally wanted greater reduction of the peasant allotments than the Editing Commissions were willing to provide (though this was not their only complaint). This only served to convince Miliutin ibid the other leaders of the Editing Commissions of the necessity to hold fast against the greedy pretensions of the landed gentry.

The story was the same in regard to the question of *peasant obligations*. The Editing Commissions proposed to establish peasant obligations on the basis of existing average *obrok* obligations. To this principle the Commissions attached the system of gradations invented by M. A. Vorob'ev in the Tver committee.[1] Obligations were to remain unchangeable[2] and, in principle, previously existing obligations were nowhere to be exceeded.

Though agreement among the deputies was widespread concerning the principle of the retention of previously existing obligations, objection to the manner in which the Editing Commissions proposed to determine obligations according to that principle was nearly universal among them. The bigger part of the obligation norms proposed by the provincial committees exceeded those established by the Editing Commissions by 100 percent or more![3] Most of the deputies defended the proposals of their committees, and once again accused the Editing Commissions of acting arbitrarily and neglecting the recommendations of the provincial committees. They maintained that the arrangement provided by the Editing Commissions would be ruinous for the gentry. In other words, the level of peasant obligations proposed by the Commissions was too low.[4]

Questions of local administration and political demands among the deputies. 'In their struggle with the bureaucratic principle', Kornilov wrote of these deputies, 'that social teaching which to this day constitutes the basis of our *zemstvo* liberalism was

[1] See above, pp. 133–4.
[2] The Editing Commissions subsequently—again under the pressure of gentry criticism—allowed for a revision of obligation rates after 20 years. Skrebitskii, *Krest'ianskoe delo*, III, 114.
[3] Kornilov, 'Gubernskie komitety', no. 4, p. 84.
[4] Skrebitskii, *Krest'ianskoe delo*, III, 729–53. 850–959. The deputies' objections concerned mainly money obligations; Differences between the deputies and the Commissions on the question of *barshchina* obligations were less severe. *Ibid.*, pp. 973–5.

matured and given a clear and firm foundation.'[1] The political process of which Kornilov wrote in fact occupied the bigger part of the deputies' time and efforts in Petersburg. The political demands which arose from the deputies' confrontation with the bureaucracy were expressed with particular clarity in the deputies' critique of the Commissions' proposed reform of peasant administration. The deputies' written 'commentaries' on the draft statutes of the Commissions were devoted primarily, often exclusively (with the exception of the answers to the specific questions put to the deputies by the Commissions), to the question of general political and administrative reforms. As a student of the period has remarked, several of these commentaries count among the outstanding political tracts of the period.[2]

The government's views on the organization of peasant administration had undergone, by the time the Editing Commissions were created, a considerable evolution from the aims announced in the original Rescripts. According to these first statements of government intention, the *pomeshchiki* were to be left effectively in charge, after the reform, of the peasant community. By the end of 1858, as noted earlier, this policy had been replaced by one based on the intention of removing so far as possible all gentry influence over the post-reform peasant community. This change of policy had been intimately related to the government's decision to adopt land-redemption as the final solution of the peasant question. The Editing Commissions carried this new policy to its logical conclusions.

In the preliminary draft, the peasant community (*krest'ianskoe obshchestvo*) was to be the basic *economic* unit of peasant organization, a self-governing unit with its officials elected from its own midst.[3] The basic *administrative* unit of peasant organization was

---

[1] Kornilov, 'Gubernskie komitety', no. 5, p. 63.

[2] Iordanskii, *Konstitutsionnoe dvizhenie*, p. 73.

[3] Its tasks were to remain those of the traditional commune: Controlling the use and distribution of land, mutual responsibility for peasant obligations, selection of army recruits, etc. It was assumed apparently that the communities would be territorially coextensive with the already-existing communes and their elected administrations (the *obshchina* and the *mir*), and thus that the organizational machinery would be there, ready-made. The fact that this often was not the case proved to be the source of much confusion after 1861—a problem that cannot be dwelt upon here.

to be the *volost'*, consisting of one or more communities (it was intended to be roughly equal in size to the traditional parish). This, too, was to be an exclusively peasant affair, controlling the community and responsible in general for the civil affairs of the peasantry, their relations with the state, etc.[1] The *volost'* assemblies were to be presided over by a peasant-elected *starshina* (elder). Their membership was to consist of elected delegates from the communities and their elders: Within the *volost'*, so far as the peasants were concerned, the *starshina* was to be the general administrative authority, invested with considerable police and administrative functions and fulfilling the orders of the higher administrative authorities. Attached to the *volost'* administration was to be a *volost'* court for small claims cases among the peasantry.[2]

Within this administrative complex the *pomeshchik* was to have no function. His relations with the community were to be confined to the elder, to whom all complaints about peasant conduct were to be made. The elder, in turn, was to be responsible for the preservation of order and the property of the *pomeshchik* so far as the peasants were concerned.[3]

Questions of general administration on the local level were not considered by the Editing Commissions.

Gentry reaction to these measures was universally negative. Among the provincial committees the tendency to preserve 'patrimonial authority' had been clearly observable, a natural tendency when the prescribed goal of the reform was a 'temporary-obligatory' status. Conversely, advocacy of land-redemption included, as a corollary, opposition to the retention of obligatory relations between the classes. It is not surprising, therefore, that the majority of gentry deputies in Petersburg were opposed to the retention of the 'patrimonial authority' of the *pomeshchik* in any form.[4]

The argument of the deputies with the Editing Commissions

---

[1] Among its functions: general economic and social control in the area of the *volost'*; maintenance of *volost'* schools; charitable functions; maintenance of grain stores; distribution of state obligations among the communities.

[2] Skrebitskii, *Krest'ianskoe delo*, I, 331–565.   [3] *Ibid.*, pp. 683–5.

[4] *Materialy redaktsionnykh kommissii*, XII, 1–4.

was not, then, over the question of whether or not to preserve this patrimonial authority. The deputies joined in unanimous condemnation of the government's plans for the reorganization of local administration. They saw in these plans, including the projects of the Miliutin Commission for the reorganization of the *uezd* administration, a bureaucratic effort to remove gentry influence altogether from local affairs, and to replace it with 'petty governmental tutelage over the entire life of the people'.[1] This vision united most of the deputies against the common enemy: bureaucratic centralization; and their attack was not only against projected administrative changes, but against the existing order as well. In short, they developed a counter-plan comprising a complete overhaul of local administration:

The majority of the members of the first convocation, in subjecting the faults of the existing system of administration to detailed examination, find that they are the result of petty government tutelage over the entire life of the people; the unification of all administration in the hands of one non-responsible executive authority; and the complete absence of an independent judiciary.

Because of these basic faults, all our administration, they say, constitutes an entire system of abuses, which can be removed only by radical reform of the administration. At the basis of this reform, in the opinion of all the deputies of the provincial committees, there must be placed: publicity [*glasnost'*]; the creation of an independent, autonomous court common for all classes; the accountability of officials before the court; strict separation of the judiciary, administrative, and police authority; and the self-administration of society in economic [*khoziaistvennye*] affairs. Whereas, moreover, with the abolition of servile dependency, there is no longer any rational reason to retain the separation of the rural inhabitants, with their subordination to various departments; and whereas the interests of the gentry are inextricably bound up with the interest of other rural inhabitants, *economic-administrative organization* [*upravlenie*] *should be common, and elective, for all classes*. A new administration must be swiftly organized on these principles, otherwise complete arbitrariness of the *chinovniki* awaits Russia, leading to disturbances and uprisings. As a result of this, while recognizing the unconditional impossibility of leaving any longer

[1] *Materialy redaktsionnykh komissii*, XII, 1–4.

252

authority over the rural community to the *pomeshchiki*, these same members find it necessary to give the gentry the right of participation in local administration, for the preservation of their moral authority and their importance as landowners.[1]

This summation (written by the staff of the Editing Commissions) shows plainly that the political views formerly expressed by a few of the provincial committees—most forcefully by the Tver committee—were subsequently espoused by the deputies of most of the provincial committees. If the argument and even the language of the Editing Commissions' summation recall the Unkovskii-Golovachev memorandum of January 1858, and the projects of the Tver committee, that is because the summation quoted extensively from the most substantive and influential of the deputies' commentaries, that of Unkovskii himself.[2]

The most important arguments from Unkovskii's lengthy commentary have been mentioned, so they need not be dwelt upon here.[2] Unkovskii's commentaries were devoted mainly to elaboration of the evils of the existing system of arbitrary bureaucratic rule and to the argument for the necessity of accompanying the emancipation with general administrative reforms which would be common for all classes, as set forth in the summary quoted immediately above. Two points of his argument are here particularly noteworthy: (1) His insistence that the necessary reforms could not be entrusted to the bureaucrats; and (2) his reservation of an influential role for the gentry within the proposed all-class administration.

Promulgation of administrative reforms, Unkovskii argued, must be taken out of the hands of the bureaucrats:

[1] *Ibid.*, pp. 1–3.
[2] Unkovskii's commentaries were completed on 15 October 1859, and immediately received wide circulation. They were copied in large quantities and were published in 1860, in their entirety, by Herzen and Ogarev, as the ninth and final volume of *Golosa iz Rossii*. In a preface, in which they apologized for printing it without the author's permission, Herzen and Ogarev explained that they were printing the document because 'its appearance is useful. In it is heard the voice of good sense, in the cause of the social good.' The commentaries were first published, along with those of the other deputies, in the Materials of the Editing Commissions, but these were printed in very limited quantities—for distribution only to officials and members of the Commissions—because it was decided that their strongly oppositionist character made them unfit for public distribution. PD, f. A. I. Skrebitskogo, no. 284, 3814. 3815/xxb 138/.

The correct development of these principles would be best of all assured if it were entrusted not to officials but to men of science, who are less prejudiced than others . . , and in part to inhabitants of various locales who have experienced themselves all the inconveniences of the existing order of things . . .

If the projects of reform will be devised only by administrative personnel, then they will likely not fully correspond to their goals, and most likely will be restricted to certain changes aimed at still greater strengthening of the power of local officials, the restricting of their responsibility, and the facilitating of their labors.

This declaration was aimed directly at the Editing Commissions' plan to establish a separate peasant administration under the aegis of the provincial administration; and at the reforms of the *uezd* administration then being planned by the Miliutin Commission.[1] In the view of Unkovskii, and of the other deputies, these schemes represented a two-sided attack—from below (the level of peasant administration), and from above (the level of *uezd* administration)—on the position of the gentry in local affairs. Its aim, they believed, was to remove the gentry from all participation in local administration, and to replace it with the bureaucracy. Far from envisaging a reform which promised to limit the arbitrariness of the bureaucracy, these plans, in the view of the deputies, promised nothing but a further, and final, extension of the bureaucracy's power into the *uezd* and even into the peasant villages—provinces which had so far remained, by and large, the preserves of the landed gentry.

As a representative of the liberal wing of gentry opinion, Unkovskii stood for land-redemption and the complete abolition of the *pomeshchik*'s '*votchina* authority' over his peasants. However, he and other gentry of like mind had no intention of removing the gentry from relations with the peasantry altogether.

[1] As an example of the ineffectuality of attempts by the bureaucracy to reform itself Unkovskii specifically mentioned the recently developed plan of the Miliutin Commission for the separation of investigatory functions from the police apparatus. This was arranged, Unkovskii argued, to no end: The new officials are also under the direct authority of the provincial governors and their chancelleries, all remains in the hands of the executive authority. *Materialy redaktsionnykh kommissii. Prilozhenie k trudam. Otzyvy chlenov gubernskikh komitetov*, II, 682.

In arguing for the participation of all rural classes at the lowest levels of administrative organization, Unkovskii clearly reserved first place for the gentry:[1]

The landed gentry, most enlightened of all the rural classes, alone can guide and instruct the people in the fulfillment of government directives...

... I am convinced that this participation in the common affairs of local inhabitants cannot be considered humiliating for the gentry, especially in the event that they be given first place in the public assemblies and preferred right to the occupation of offices, as was proposed by the Tver committee.[2]

As for the privileges of the gentry, they cannot harm the independence of the peasants, for the lower class of the people is in any case and everywhere more numerous than the upper [class], and preference in the occupation of public offices for more educated persons serves as the best guarantee of the rights of the entire population.[3]

Unkovskii's critique of the bureaucratic administration and his demands for its reform found general agreement among the other gentry deputies. His commentaries were, in effect, raised to the level of an opposition program for the deputies as a whole. This was recognized, as noted earlier, by the Editing Commissions which, in summarizing the deputies' views on administrative questions simply quoted, from Unkovskii's commentaries.[4] Unkovskii's positive program was included in the 'address of five deputies' and widely repeated in the commentaries of other deputies.[5]

---

[1] Unkovskii did not refer in his commentary to the details of self-administration at the *uezd* level. He did note, however, in referring to the duties of the *volost'* assembly, that one of these duties was to be 'the election of representatives for participation in *uezd* assemblies'. *Ibid.*, pp. 697–8.

[2] Although Unkovskii did not elaborate on the details of gentry privileges in local administration, he obviously had in mind the system elaborated by the Tver provincial committee. Cf. above, chapter 4, pp.143–4.

[3] *Materialy redaktsionnykh komissii. Prilozhenie k trudam. Otzyvy chlenov gubernskikh komitetov*, II, 661–98.

[4] See above, pp. 252–3.

[5] Unkovskii's colleague from the Tver committee, Kardo-Sysoev, supported this program fully and gave his own critique of the existing administration in his commentaries. *Materialy redaktsionnykh komissii. Prilozhenie k trudam. Otzyvy chlenov gubernskikh komitetov*, II, 765–78.

A striking example of this were the commentaries of the deputies from Riazan, Ofrosimov and Volkonskii, of which many pages were copied directly from Unkovskii's argument.[1] Repeating Unkovskii's positive program for local reforms ('And so everything depends on freedom of expression; on the foundation of an independent court; on the responsibility of officials before the court; on the strict separation of powers and on self-administration of the classes in the economic sphere')[2] they at the same time took more care than had Unkovskii in spelling out the manner in which the gentry would be allowed to play a dominant role in local administration. Agreeing with Unkovskii that the *volost'* 'should embrace all inhabitants of the area without any separation of classes and estates', they proposed specifically that the *volost'* assembly should be constituted by:

(1) All hereditary gentry with property in the *volost'*.[3]
(2) All other landowners with property of no less than 300 *desiatiny* in the territory of the *volost'*.
(3) Deputies elected by the communes in the *volost'* (One representative for each 100 peasant electors).[4]

Khrushchov and Shreter, deputies from Kharkov and co-signers with Unkovskii of the 'address of five deputies', produced much the same argument, also extensively laced with paragraphs from Unkovskii's commentaries:

... At the basis of the answers to the following questions [wrote Khrushchov and Shreter] we suppose:
(1) Judiciary institutions completely independent from the executive authority, dispensing justice publicly, verbally and conscientiously; that is, a jury court.
(2) Justices of the Peace[5] also independent of administrative authority, and:

---

[1] Compare *ibid.*, pp. 96–106 and 665–95.   [2] *Ibid.*, p. 100.
[3] Or, as they called it, district (*okrug*), in order to distinguish it from the *volost'* for peasant affairs prescribed by the Editing Commissions.
[4] *Ibid.*, p. 109.
[5] The question of Justices of the Peace (*mirovye sud'i*) provided yet another insult to the gentry, and more evidence of the bureaucracy's intention to force the gentry entirely out of local affairs. The original plan put forth in the Ministry of Interior had been to create a 'Justice of the Peace' for the purpose of mediating between the *pomeshchiki* and peasants immediately after emancipation, in arguments arising from the terms of

(3) Direct responsibility before the court of the executive officials of local administration.[1]

Like many other deputies, Khrushchov and Shreter linked the success of a financial program for land-redemption to prompt promulgation of administrative reforms:

In Russia, there is no trust in the government at all, because with the existing organization of administration, police, and judiciary, the implementation of the laws is in no way guaranteed; as the result of which no one is assured of the protected enjoyment of his personal and property rights.

On the other hand, with a good organization of the administration, based on the elective, not on the bureaucratic, principle . . ., not only is redemption of the land possible, but fundamental changes of the way of life of the classes and the greatest and most decisive financial operations are fully realizable.[2]

Following Unkovskii, Khrushchov and Shreter prescribed an all-class, elective local self-administration. In their commentaries

the emancipation. This office was to have been elective (by the peasants) from among gentry candidates. In the Miliutin Commission this principle was revoked, on the grounds that the gentry could not be allowed such potentially great influence in peasant affairs, and that the peasants were too immature to be entrusted with such an important responsibility as election of the Justice of the Peace. The result was that the Justice of the Peace, or Peace Mediator (*mirovoi posrednik*) as he came to be called, was appointed by the provincial governor from among the local gentry.

Besides being a 'mediator', the Peace Mediator was in general responsible for the promulgation of the reform and was, as well, a sort of 'commissioner for peasant affairs', with nearly dictatorial powers over peasant self-administration. The communal and *volost'* elders, themselves something like police-officers, were directly responsible to the Peace Mediators, and thus indirectly to the provincial administration. Skrebitskii, *Krest'ianskoe delo*, I, 686–8, 706–9, 715–17, 725–9; *Krestianskaia reforma v Rossii 1861 goda. Sbornik zakonodatel'nykh aktov* (Moscow, 1954), pp. 136–151.

[1] *Materialy redaktsionnykh komissii. Prilozhenie k trudam. Otzyvy chlenov gubernskikh komitetov*, II, 780–1.

[2] This same argument was made by other deputies, perhaps most notably by Kosagovskii, majority deputy from Novgorod: 'The adoption of a correct elective basis [of administration], reform of the courts, strict separation of . . . powers, and finally, personal responsibility of officials before the courts and the law . . ., those are the conditions in which the supreme government can count on the cooperation of society in all its decrees. If, in addition to all this, freedom of the press will be allowed, the larger part of abuses will be, if not completely eliminated, at least not hidden and therefore they will not go unpunished. The above conditions will inevitably increase the trust of society in the government; this trust is more necessary at the present time than ever before, because the peasant question will not be solved without significant financial undertakings on the part of the government.' *Ibid.*, I, 772–3.

they also carried these principles even further than had Unkovskii: Together with Kosagovskii and Bezobrazov (deputies from Novgorod and Vladimir, respectively) they produced a plan of administrative reorganization from the communal to the provincial level.

According to this plan, the lowest common denominator of administration for both peasants and *pomeshchiki* was to be the *volost'*; its assembly was to be constituted by: (1) All local gentry owning property in the territory of the *volost'*; (2) other persons having 'higher education' or owning at least 50 *desiatiny* of land; (3) representatives from the peasant communes. The executive of the *volost'* was to be a member of the local gentry, elected by the *volost'* assembly and subject to its general control.[1] The rural police authority was to be vested in the rural police-officer (*zemskii pristav*) and two helpers (for each *volost'*). He was to be appointed by the *uezd* police authority, and subject to the local courts. The court of first instance, according to this plan, was to be the 'Justice of the Peace', elected from among the local gentry.[2]

The *uezd* administration prescribed by this plan was to consist of an *uezd* assembly (all landed gentry of the *uezd*, 'honorary citizens' and merchants of the 1st and 2nd guilds, representatives of other urban classes, and deputies from the *volost'* assemblies). Police power in the *uezd* was to be vested in the 'head of *uezd* police and his helpers', appointed by the governor. In each *uezd* a reformed court was to be formed of two branches, civil (court and magistrate) and criminal (judge, two assessors, procurator and a twelve-man jury).

Provincial administration, according to this plan, was to consist of the *provincial assembly* and the *provincial board of administration*. The former was to include: All gentry; all 'honorary citizens' and merchants of the first and second guilds; representatives of other urban classes (one per 1,000 electors); and deputies, one each, from the *volosti*. This assembly was to meet once every three years. The board of administration comprised: The pro-

---

[1] *Ibid.*, pp. 773–4; Skrebitskii, *Krest'ianskoe delo*, I, 763–6.
[2] The exact means of election of these officials were not mentioned in this project. Other than gentry, persons with higher education or 500 desiatiny of landed property were eligible. Skrebitskii, *Krest'ianskoe delo*, I, 764.

vincial marshal of the gentry and a deputy from each *uezd*. The duties of this board were to include: 'The entire economic-administrative direction of the province...' The governor, according to this project, 'as the superior government official supervising peace and order in the entire province', and as head of the police for the province, was to *offer his measures* on econo-mic-administrative questions to the board of administration. In case of disagreement with the board, the governor could turn to the central authorities.

Finally, an *appellate* court was to be created for every three or four provinces, with appropriate criminal and civil divisions. These courts, the plan's authors quite immodestly declared, could replace the State Senate in this function.[1]

The commentary of the liberal Slavophile deputy Koshelev also differed little from that of Unkovskii. Like Khrushchov, Shreter, and others, he proposed a three-level organization of local self-administration:

In Russia improvement of internal administration is possible only on the condition of its transfer, within possible limits, to local public participation. This participation must not be confined within the narrow circle of the classes. In the district [or *volost'*] it must belong to the entire rural population, to the landowners of all designations, who must all fuse into one whole ... In the *uezdy* the entire rural and urban population must also have one assembly, one administration, one court. The same must be said for the higher instance, the province.[2]

In this arrangement Koshelev, like all his colleagues, gave first place to the gentry:

As individuals [the *pomeshchiki*] cannot retain either command, *vot-china* police authority, or higher justice over the peasant communities; otherwise serfdom would be resurrected, and in an even worse form. But the gentry, as the most educated class and as the main landowner, must, for the welfare of the entire region, preserve a preferential voice there ...[3]

[1] *Materialy redaktsionnykh komissii. Prilozhenie k trudam. Otzyvy chlenov gubernskikh komitetov*, I, 773–9; 2, 816–19; Skrebitskii, *Krestian'skoe delo*, I, 759–819.
[2] *Materialy redaktsionnykh komissii. Prilozhenie k trudam. Otzyvy chlenov gubernskikh komitetov*, II, 196.
[3] Skrebitskii, *Krest'ianskoe delo*, I, 780.

17-2

Conclusions

The developments described in this chapter were of the greatest importance in the evolution of relations between the government and the gentry. They raise, moreover, numerous questions about the nature of Russian political thought which demand some consideration in historical perspective. (It is clear, for example, that the attitude toward the bureaucracy revealed by the gentry deputies was not a new one; and the two political responses produced by the deputies—the 'aristocratic' and the liberal—also conformed to historical precedents.) These questions will be considered at some length in the general conclusion to Part Three. The following comments are limited to the immediate context of the events considered in the preceding pages.

The few commentaries introduced above illustrate what were generally-held views among the deputies. These deputies had come to Petersburg from all parts of Russia, representing committees which had made often widely differing proposals about peasant reform. They departed Petersburg in a spirit of united opposition, at least in their attitude toward the bureaucracy: The reform, they were convinced, had been taken over completely by the bureaucracy which was intending to exploit the emancipation in order to expand its authority to the very villages of rural Russia, driving out in the process all gentry influence there. The point of fundamental difference between the deputies and the Editing Commissions consisted, as Koshelev wrote, of the fact that, in the plans of the Editing Commissions,

. . . Bureaucratic interference had been established in rural affairs, and that the influence of the gentry on the peasants had been completely eliminated. Although the future organization of the local police and of the justices of the peace had been carefully concealed from the deputies, nevertheless rumors about the appointment of these *chinovniki*, not by selection by the rural population in general, but by the arbitrariness of the governors; rumors about the purely bureaucratic organization of the entire *uezd* administration and courts —[these rumors] greatly disturbed the members of the provincial committees . . .

... The deputies had, together, to stand against the Editing Commissions, to point out energetically their errors and to inform the government that their conclusions not only destroy the significance of the gentry as landowners, but strengthen, perhaps against their wish, that which is most hated in Russia—Bureaucratism [*Chinovnichestvo*]. This the deputies conscientiously did.[1]

Few of the provincial gentry committees had proposed general administrative reforms. Nearly all the deputies in Petersburg did. Indeed, for these deputies reform of local administration became the central issue. Though compelled by the government to present their commentaries individually, a majority of the deputies met together and produced a common critique of the bureaucratic administration, and a common program of administrative reform based on local, elective, self-administration. This program had been formulated earlier by several provincial committees, most clearly by the Tver committee; and in Petersburg it was developed most thoroughly by the deputy from Tver, Unkovskii. The views which he developed in his commentaries were generally accepted by the deputies of the first convocation.[2] A liberal gentry opposition had been formed from among the gentry deputies.

The gentry opposition created among the deputies of the first convocation was in fact a temporary union of a majority of liberally-oriented proponents of emancipation with a conservatively-inclined minority. This union was made possible by the common conviction of the two groups that the bureaucracy's conduct of the reform was wrong and harmful, a conviction which (as Iordanskii pointed out) the more conservative gentry had held for some time but which—and this is most noteworthy—the liberal gentry deputies acquired only through their confrontation with the Editing Commissions.[3] By and large, liberal gentry in the provincial committees had been optimistic about the government's conduct of the reform. They had been given support by the government against the conservatives in their

[1] *Materialy*, I, 198–9, 208.
[2] Cf. A. A. Garmiza, *Podgotovka zemskoi reformy 1864 goda* (Moscow, 1957), pp. 59–60.
[3] Iordanskii, *Konstitutsionnoe dvizhenie*, p. 71.

committees on numerous occasions, and thus had had no reason
to assume an oppositionist attitude. The creation of the Editing
Commissions, it will be recalled, was looked upon by the liberal
gentry as a progressive step. It was only when, as deputies, they
were called to Petersburg that they became disenchanted with
the government's conduct of the reform preparations.

In concrete terms, the liberal gentry opposition came into
existence primarily in reaction to the government's attempt to
deprive the gentry of any significant participation in the preparing
of the reform; and to the government's plans for the bureaucratic
reorganization of local administration. The immediate object
of the deputies' enmity was the Editing Commissions, and the
most important issue at stake was the administrative question.
Therefore the most objectionable of the Commissions' proposals
was the plan for the creation of a separate peasant administration.

But the deputies' quarrel with the Commissions was not
limited alone, as Garmiza has suggested,[1] to questions of administrative reform and the political future of the gentry. This dissatisfaction of the deputies was also clearly evident in relation to
other questions specifically concerning the peasant question in a
narrower sense. The majority of the deputies wanted an emancipation with immediate and obligatory redemption, not the
voluntary arrangements proposed by the Editing Commissions.
To be sure, the deputies' demand for immediate and obligatory
redemption, like their foreswearing of seigneurial authority, was
full of political implications: a transition period during which even
greatly diminished seigneurial authority would have to be
retained would, in the deputies' view, provide an opportunity to
the bureaucracy to extend its control over rural Russia. Only by
a complete untying of relations between the classes could the
bureaucracy be kept out. That is why, basically, advocacy of
land-redemption was always accompanied by insistence on the
need to abolish the seigneurial authority of the *pomeshchiki*. Thus
it was to the Editing Commissions' plans for voluntary redemption and a transition period of undetermined length, as well as to
specific administrative plans, that Koshelev referred when he

---

[1] Garmiza, *Podgotovka zemskoi reformy*, p. 57.

wrote that 'bureaucratic interference had been established in rural affairs'.

Moreover, most deputies were profoundly disturbed by the arrangements for allotments and obligations elaborated by the Commissions. These points of disagreement with the Commissions, no less perhaps than fear of the bureaucracy's administrative plan, made the deputies unwilling to accept estrangement of the gentry from further participation in the reform.

Perhaps the view of many of the deputies was best summed up by Unkovskii, in a letter written many years after the reform:

As I, so all my closest colleagues and...all the best and most intelligent party of the gentry...were prepared for significant sacrifices, not only personal, but class; but not otherwise than on the condition of the abolition of serfdom, *not only for the peasants alone, but for the entire people*...Instead, in the Editing Commissions the whole business came to nothing but economic calculations, and none of the members of the Commissions began, or even allowed us to begin, a serious discussion about the change in the order of administration, even though only local....Thus, in the autumn of 1859 the whole business took such a turn that for a long time the entire serf order with *barshchina* and *obrok* (without redemption) remained, and was modified only by political and property-losses for the gentry—mainly by leaving in force the former arbitrariness, both in local and state administration.[1]

It is worth noting once again at this point that the gentry's relationship to the several proposed solutions to the peasant questions was a dynamic one which can only be understood 'historically', that is through study of the ongoing rush of events—in particular the development of relations between the government and the gentry in the preparation of reform—and not alone by means of static generalizations about certain group or regional interests. The confrontation of the gentry deputies with the Editing Commissions in 1859 was of particular importance in this dynamic process.

What the deputies called opposition to Bureaucratism, the Ministry of Interior and the leaders of the Editing Commissions saw as an attempt to wrest the reform out of the government's

[1] Dzhanshiev, *Unkovskii*, pp. 132–3. Emphasis added.

direction and to resolve it in a manner profitable for the gentry alone; plus unacceptable political demands of an aristocratic-oligarchic coloration, reaching even to demands for a constitution or for 'permanent representatives in the higher governmental administration'.[1]

Lanskoi and Miliutin were justified in their prediction that the deputies would strive to create a united opposition to the government's conduct of the reform. The nature of this opposition, was, however, profoundly misrepresented by them. The Ministry bureaucrats claimed that the opposition of the gentry deputies represented those aristocratic-oligarchial groups which had earlier been the only vocal critics of the government's plans. The motivation of the deputies, they thus implied, was general opposition to peasant emancipation. The fact was that the majority of the deputies were advocates of the *liberal gentry program*, and their chief spokesman was not Count Shuvalov, but A. M. Unkovskii.

Thus the argument of the Ministry that the deputies were intent on forcing an aristocratic constitution on the government, an intent which they extrapolated from the demands of Orlov-Davydov and Bezobrazov, was much exaggerated. Despite many rumors current in Petersburg during the presence of the deputies there,[2] the liberal gentry opposition made no such demands. It demanded not an aristocratic consitution, but a *Rechtsstaat*.

The deputies departed the capital convinced that the work of the provincial committees and their own efforts had been completely ignored by the Editing Commissions.[3] While still in

---

[1] Miliutina, 'Iz zapisok', XCVIII, 106.

[2] On 23 October 1859, A. V. Nikitenko made the following notation in his diary: 'They say that there are great disagreements on the peasant question between the Commissions and the deputies. The latter, incidentally, are supposedly striving openly for a constitution'. A. V. Nikitenko, *Dnevnik*, II (n.p., 1955), 100.

[3] The question of to what extent, if any, the Editing Commissions utilized the projects of the provincial committees and the commentaries of their deputies is a complicated one. Koshelev's lengthy diatribe, referred to above, reflected the view of the large majority of deputies. Primarily in an attempt to refute Koshelev's accusations, the 'enlightened bureaucrats' in the Editing Commissions compiled the *Materialy dlia istorii uprazdeneniia krepostnogo sostoianiia*. The main purposes of these materials, an invaluable collection of documents in their own right, were two: (1) To counteract anti-bureaucratic propaganda in general, by presenting the bureaucracy as the guardian of reform locked in battle with reactionary dignitaries and greedy *pomeshchiki*; and (2), to refute specific accusations made by Koshelev. (The three volumes of the *Materialy*

Petersburg, they had attempted in several petitions to make their objections known to Alexander II, for which they received only censure. Their next attempt would be through the forthcoming provincial gentry assemblies.

were published anonymously, but have generally been ascribed to Senator D. P. Khrushchov, in 1856–7 Assistant Minister of State Properties. There is some evidence, however, that the real editor of the *Materialy* was Prince Cherkasskii, assisted by Nicholas Miliutin and Khrushchov. Cf. P. A. Zaionchkovskii (ed.), *Dnevnik P. A. Valueva*, I (Moscow, 1961), 369 (Editor's comment no. 57.))

The editor[s] of the *Materialy* took pains to show that all the materials presented by the gentry committees and their deputies were minutely examined by the Editing Commissions and even published along with the other materials of the Commissions. They also pointed out that virtually all legislative provisions made by the Commissions had appeared in one or another of the projects of the provincial committees (*Materialy*, I, 145–63). Strictly speaking, these assertions were correct. However, on major questions of policy the Editing Commissions followed previously established government principles and were not at all deterred by overwhelming gentry disagreement. In general the Editing Commissions looked on the projects of the provincial committees as 'useful materials from which much could be borrowed, but which did not at all give them directing and mandatory orders'. Kornilov, *Obshchestvennoe dvizhenie*, p. 53.

7

The Provincial Gentry Assembled and the Second Convocation of Gentry Deputies in Petersburg (December 1859–April 1860)

THE PROVINCIAL GENTRY ASSEMBLIES, DECEMBER 1859–MARCH 1860

The Tver provincial assembly

The first provincial gentry assembly to gather after the return of the deputies to their provinces met in Tver on 8 December 1859.[1] With more than 250 *pomeshchiki* in attendance, the Tver assembly proved from the first moment to be a dramatic affair.

The first sessions of the Tver assembly witnessed an attempt by a group of conservative opponents of Unkovskii to prevent his re-election as gentry marshal (his three-year term was expiring), and, in a more general way, to demonstrate general disapproval of the reform plans for which Unkovskii and the majority of the Tver provincial committee stood. The plan of these *pomeshchiki*—led by Ozerov (the former provincial marshal whom Unkovskii had helped to drive from office), Khvostov (former marshal of Tver *uezd*), Prince Shakhonskii and Miliukov (Unkovskii's old opponents from the Tver committee)— was to implicate Unkovskii in the misuse of gentry funds

---

[1] The authors of the *Materialy*, in presenting some of the materials connected with the gentry assemblies of 1859–60, introduced the Riazan assembly as the first to get underway and to attract the government's attention. As a matter of fact, the Riazan gentry convened later than the Tver gentry (on 10 December). Though they were, strictly speaking, the first gentry group to send an address to Alexander II (on 12 December), this address was discussed simultaneously with the address of the Tver gentry (written on 14 December) in the Main Committee on 17 December 1859.

which had been allotted for the construction of a schoolbuilding in Tver.[1]

In accordance with this plan, several members of a control commission which had been created to check on the work of the building committee (consisting of Unkovskii, the *uezd* marshal and several deputies) accused Unkovskii and the committee of misuse of funds; they also hinted at bribe-taking and general corruption. Unkovskii easily refuted these charges, and was given a vote of thanks by the assembled gentry for his work on the building project. The five members of the control commission who had made the accusations were driven from the assembly in disgrace; one of them, Dolgolov, was literally thrown out. On Unkovskii's urging they were formally excluded from the gentry assembly.

The result of this episode, terminated on 11 December, was the opposite of that hoped for by Unkovskii's opponents: Unkovskii now had the firm support of the assembly, a majority of whose members had earlier been critical of his views on peasant reform.[2]

This crisis past, the Tver gentry proceeded to the discussion of other matters, the most urgent of which was, of course, the peasant question. It was suggested that Unkovskii and Kardo-Sysoev (whose remarks before the Editing Commissions had been lithographed and circulated among the gentry) be heard from on that subject. At this point Unkovskii was compelled to read the ruling of the Minister of Interior, which forbade discussion of the peasant question by the gentry assemblies (Unkovskii had received this ruling from the governor of Tver on 13 November, 1859).[3]

The result of the reading of the order was general confusion in the assembly, followed by protests that the gentry's rights were

---

[1] This construction project, still unfinished when Unkovskii was elected marshal, had been begun in the 1840s. As marshal, Unkovskii uncovered misdoings by the contractors and the former marshal (Ozerov) and informed the gentry of this. He eventually finished the building and saved the gentry treasury several thousand rubles from the originally estimated cost of construction. Unkovskii was to account for expenditures on this project at the 1859 assembly.

[2] *TsGAOR, f.* 109, no. 11, part 14, pp. 1–7a; *GAKO, f.* 59, no. 3833, pp. 26–32a.

[3] *GAKO, f.* 59, no. 3747, p. 145a.

being violated. Some members proposed that the government ruling be ignored. At that point a *pomeshchik* of Bezhetsk *uezd*, A. I. Evropeus, interrupted to protest such action. The gentry, Evropeus pointed out, had to proceed according to law:

At the present time [he argued] only our consultative assembly has the legal right to enter into discussion of questions of public welfare and it serves as the only legal guarantee against the arbitrariness of the bureaucracy ... which has in view only its own private interest, diametrically opposed to the interests of all society and the will of the Sovereign Emperor. ... Let us not imitate in our actions this bureaucracy, which for the sake of its interests distorts the laws with its circulars.[1]

Evropeus proposed that the assembly be temporarily adjourned while a telegram was sent to the Minister of Interior seeking clarification of the law: Did not the Minister's ruling violate the rights of the gentry? This proposal was accepted by a vote of 186–54 in the assembly.[2]

Unkovskii, as marshal, passed this request on to the governor for transmission to the Minister. The governor, however, refused to send the telegram, repeating the argument of the government ruling to the effect that the gentry had already received sufficient opportunity to discuss the peasant question. The gentry if it liked, the governor wrote to Unkovskii, could send such a telegram on its own behalf. In the meantime the assembly was to continue and to proceed to the election of its officials.[3]

The gentry assembly received this communication on 14 December. A few members opposed any further action, but a large majority proposed that a petition be sent directly to Alexander II. The main proponents of this measure were Evropeus and Golovachev.[4] A petition was accordingly drawn up and approved by a vote of 231–56 (24 abstaining) the same day. Brief, and couched in expressions of loyalty, the petition asked only one thing:

[1] *TsGAOR, f.* 109, no. 11, part 14, pp. 52–3a.
[2] *TsGAOR, f.* 109, no. 11, part 14, pp. 11–12a. The specific legal question involved articles 112 and 135 of the ninth volume of the Code of Laws (1857 edition), which gave the gentry assemblies the right 'to discuss the needs and welfare of the gentry'.
[3] *Ibid.*, pp. 13–15a.
[4] *Ibid.*, pp. 24–5a; *Materialy*, II, 277–8.

' . . . Permission for the Provincial Gentry Assembly to undertake discussion of the needs and welfare [of the gentry], without
being hindered by possible propinquity with the peasant question'.[1] This petition was sent to the Emperor on 15 December,
and was also lithographed and distributed among the local
gentry.[2]

In Petersburg the petition of the Tver gentry was discussed in
the Main Committee on 17 December. The Main Committee
directed that the petition be left 'without further action', *and
that Unkovskii be immediately removed from his post as gentry marshal.*
The Tver assembly, the Main Committee concluded, was to get
on with its elections and disperse within the time allotted by law
(fifteen days in all).[3]

The government order, read before the gentry assembly on
20 December, was greeted by a dead silence. Ordered to proceed
with the election of their marshals and to close the assembly by
22 December, the gentry responded by refusing to elect a new
provincial gentry marshal; they also declined to elect marshals
for eight of Tver's twelve *uezdy.*[4] Before closing the assembly
the gentry voted to honor Unkovskii by creating twelve 'Unkovskii Stipends' at the University of Moscow, the recipients
to be chosen by Unkovskii himself. And on the closing day of
the assembly the gentry called on Unkovskii and presented him
an official address of thanks. Contributions were also collected to
commission an engraved portrait of Unkovskii.[5]

---

[1] *TsGIAL, f.* 1180, no. 37, pp. 43–8. See Appendix II. Although approved by 231 votes,
the petition received only 155 signatures.

[2] *TsGAOR, f.* 109, no. 11, part 14, pp. 18–19a.

[3] 'In view of the fact [read the decision of the Main Committee] that the Tver provincial
marshal and the gentry indicated above should not have petitioned about the retraction
of the Imperial order so positively expressed, His Imperial Majesty has ordered: That
their most loyal petition be left without further action.

'Moreover, the Emperor has seen fit to order: That the Tver Provincial Marshal,
Collegiate Assessor Unkovskii, having allowed the passing of the proposal of the gentry
for the presenting of such a petition, and even having been the first to sign it, be immediately removed from the post of Provincial Marshal'. *TsGIAL, f.* 1180, no. 37,
pp. 52–4.

[4] *TsGAOR, f.* 109, no. 11, part 14, pp. 46–8a. This was accomplished by the refusal of
candidates to stand for balloting, or, in cases where candidates did stand, their failure
to receive the required number of votes.

[5] *Ibid.,* pp. 49–9a, 64–5a, 69–70a. The portrait in question, an engraving, was made in
Moscow in January 1860, in 150 copies for subscribers among the Tver gentry.

In this way the Tver gentry informed the government of their attitude toward its decision to remove Unkovskii. The assembly at large did not, however, escape punishment either: The Senate, which subsequently reviewed the activities of the Tver gentry assembly, condemned the exclusion of the members of the control commission who had tried to implicate Unkovskii in the misuse of funds and ordered that all signers of the motion approving their exclusion from the assembly be fined 150 rubles each, plus 50 more from the *uezd* marshals and 60 more from Unkovskii.[1]

Following the government's refusal to allow discussion of the peasant question in the gentry assembly and its dismissal of Unkovskii from the post of provincial marshal, a number of gentry leaders, led by Unkovskii, decided to gather privately to draw up a plan for the foundation of a private land bank for the financing of land-redemption. At the time of the gentry assembly Unkovskii, Golovachev and Nicholas Bakunin had talked frequently about a land-redemption operation (had discussion of the 'peasant question' been allowed at the assembly, Unkovskii would almost certainly have used the occasion to gather support for obligatory land-redemption, a situation of which the central government was of course aware). All agreed that there would be nothing dangerous in such an operation. If the government would not undertake the operation, they decided, it could be accomplished by private means.

Accordingly and on Unkovskii's suggestion, a number of gentry leaders—including Unkovskii, Golovachev, Evropeus, Bakunin and several other ex-marshals of *uezdy*—began to gather regularly at Unkovskii's apartments in Tver and at the house of the director of the Tver gymnasium, Rzhevskii, for the purpose of discussing plans for a private land bank.[2]

The plan for founding a land bank was not original with the Tver gentry. On 16 April 1859, all loans by the state credit institutions on gentry estates had been stopped. This move by

---

[1] Rozum, *Tverskie liberaly*, pp. 298–301.
[2] Unkovskii, 'Materialy k biografii', pp. 24–5a; Unkovskii, 'Zapiski', no. 6, pp. 57a–8; no. 7, pp. 89–90.

the government and its endorsement of (voluntary) land-redemption prompted much discussion among the gentry, and in the government itself, about the creation of new credit agencies for the financing of redemption. The Ministry of Finance announced (in the summer of 1859) that for this purpose 'land banks, with sufficient means and organization conforming to the new economic conditions' would have to be created. To this end a special commission attached to the Ministry of Finance was formed, with the task of elaborating the principles upon which such banks could be created.[1]

The meetings in Tver were, however, obviously an affair of the disgruntled, and were promptly reported by Unkovskii's enemies—Klokachev (recently appointed temporary provincial marshal by the governor), the members of the control commission who had been excluded from the gentry assembly,[2] and others[3]—as the plotting of revolution. Meeting together, these *pomeshchiki* prepared a denunciation of Unkovskii, Golovachev and Evropeus and delivered it, in Klokachev's name, to the vice-governor, Ivanov, at the end of January 1860.

All the troubles which had occurred in the provincial assembly, they declared in their denunciation, were caused by 'several persons in the province who in general aspire to fundamental political transformations'.[4] Many gentry followed these few, the denunciation explained, not from conviction but 'only from fear of falling behind such so-called progressive people'. Once their

[1] Trubetskaia, *Materialy*, II, 99–101.
[2] Shakhonskii, leader of this group, had called Unkovskii to a duel after the closing of the assembly. The duel never transpired, thanks to the intervention of the governor. Rozum, *Tverskie liberaly*, p. 297.
[3] The main participants in this affair were: Klokachev; Mashkov (president of the Tver civil court, a former friend of Unkovskii who became his enemy because of Unkovskii's criticism of his activities in court); Khvostov (former provincial marshal and marshal of Tver *uezd* who had been called to court for misuse of gentry funds; an outspoken opponent of the Tver provincial committee, and a personal enemy of Unkovskii); and Turin (a former *chinovnik* and close friend of Klokachev). Among their close supporters were: Verevkin, Ozerov (the former marshal exposed by Unkovskii), the members of the control commission (Gembel', Opukhin, Shakhonskii, Dolgolov, Tyl'nov), Preferanskii (a *chinovnik* in the provincial administration and a personal enemy of Unkovskii), Porokhovshchikov (also a *chinovnik* in the provincial administration and an enemy of Unkovskii who had accused him of graft), and one Krivtsov. *TsGAOR*, f. 109, no. 11, part 14, pp. 204a–11a.
[4] *TsGAOR*, f. 109, no. 11, part 14, p. 79.

scheme had been discovered by the government, which promptly effected the removal of Unkovskii from his post, these same leaders had organized a demonstration which had resulted in the refusal by the gentry to elect new marshals and other officials. This 'party', announced the denunciators, had not stopped at that: It was now planning a meeting of the gentry for 7 February 1860. Such a meeting, they warned, could have dangerous consequences, consequences which could be avoided only by 'the temporary removal from Tver province of the main leaders of this party'.[1]

Ivanov, acting head of the provincial government during the temporary absence of Baranov, was an official of much less liberal inclinations than his superior. He immediately reported this denunciation to the Minister of Interior (30 January 1860), adding a number of details of his own: The 'secret gathering with unknown aims' scheduled for 7 February was to consist of no fewer than 120 persons, he reported, and had been called expressly by Unkovskii, Golovachev and Evropeus (who was, Ivanov noted, already under police surveillance as a former *petrashevets*).[2] Evropeus and Golovachev had prepared special speeches—of unknown content—for that meeting, the aim of which, Ivanov

[1] *Ibid.*, pp. 79a–80a.
[2] Aleksandr Ivanovich Evropeus (b. 1827) belonged to an old Tver gentry family. He was educated in the Tsarskoe Selo *lycée* and the Alexandrine *lycée* in Petersburg and was a student in the former school at the same time as his contemporary, Unkovskii. Following graduation from the *lycée*, Evropeus worked for a year as a *chinovnik* and then went on leave to continue his studies at St Petersburg University in political economy. As a student in the university Evropeus was widely acquainted in literary and scholarly circles, and was especially close to the editorial staff of the journal *Sovremennik*.

As a university student, Evropeus also became acquainted with Petrashevskii and joined his 'circle'. In 1849 he was arrested with the other members of the Petrashevskii circle (at twenty-two he was the third youngest member). He was charged with 'propagating the pernicious system of Fourier' and sent into the ranks to serve in the Caucasus. In 1855 he was raised to the rank of a junior officer for bravery in a campaign against the mountain tribes, and in May 1856 made a lieutenant. In 1857 Evropeus was allowed to retire from the army, but was kept under secret surveillance. In mid-1858 he was allowed to travel abroad, where he evidently married (his wife was an Englishwoman). Before and after that he had lived on his mother's estate in Bezhetsk *uezd*.

At the questioning after his arrest in 1849, Evropeus was asked 'who particularly had an influence on the development in [him] of socialistic or liberal ideas?' He replied: 'I am a Fourierist, not a liberal. My ideas about fourierism were developed directly from the reading of the *Théorie de l'unité universelle.*' *Ibid.*, pp. 16–17, 33a; *Delo Petrashevtsev*, III (Moscow, 1951), pp. 175–88; E. Zhukovskaia, *Zapiski* (Leningrad, 1930), p. 145.

predicted, was: ' . . . to discuss and carry out immediately the announcement to the peasants of the abolition of *barshchina*, and the granting to them of personal freedom'.[1] Ivanov also confided that his undercover agents had reported that several gentry had made dark hints, after the closing of the assembly, about peasant revolution.[2]

The central government was greatly disturbed by this report. It was expressly feared that Unkovskii might serve as a focal point for a concentrated opposition movement among the gentry. He had been under surveillance since his dismissal from the post of provincial marshal. The watch on him was now doubled.[3] The Third Section headquarters promptly notified the gendarme officer in Tver, Simanovskii, of the meetings of Unkovskii and his friends and of the meeting planned for 7 February. These events were to be followed closely and reports on them were to be sent daily to Petersburg.[4]

Now under the double surveillance of the civil police and the local gendarme staff, Unkovskii and his associates continued to plan for the 7 February meeting. The gendarme officer proceeded to make daily reports, to speculate about the place of meeting and about the possible participants, and to record the arrival in Tver of all strangers. These reports were read daily by the Emperor himself.[5] Vice-governor Ivanov hinted, in his reports, that the Unkovskii group was composing some sort of

[1] *TsGAOR, f.* 109, no. 11, part 14, p. 142.   [2] *Ibid.*

[3] *TsGAOR, f.* 109, no. 11, part 14, pp. 66–70a. Special attention was paid to Unkovskii's journey to Moscow on 19 January for the purpose of having his portrait made and for consultation with I. K. Babst and other specialists about his land bank plans. (Babst, a former student of Granovskii, was professor of political economy in Moscow University at the time. An expert in bank credit and monetary exchange, Babst was also a well-known advocate and popularizer of classical economic liberalism in the years immediately preceding the peasant reform). The gendarme officer in Moscow reported that the dismissal of Unkovskii had produced a very bad impression on the Moscow gentry, among whom Unkovskii had many supporters. These supporters were thought to be planning a testimonial dinner for Unkovskii, either in the English Club or the Gentry Assembly, an event which was likely, warned the officer, to produce some sort of 'extraordinary occurrence'.

Unkovskii's brief stay in Moscow passed uneventfully, however (Unkovskii, aware that he was under surveillance, refused to take part in such a dinner or even to accept private invitations). The gendarme officer was left to report conversations overheard in the cafe of the Bolshoi Theater.

[4] *Ibid.*, p. 71a.   [5] *Ibid.*, pp. 77–8a, 94–9a.

radical manifestoes which were being sent to all corners of Russia. He also surmised that the group was in contact with a correspondent of Herzen's *Kolokol*.[1]

On 7 February the meeting in question took place as planned, in the house of Rzhevskii, director of the gymnasium. It was preceded by a banquet in the local hotel. Twenty-seven persons participated in the dinner and meeting, including most of the members of the majority of the former provincial committee and a number of other Tver *pomeshchiki* (Evropeus, the two younger brothers of Nicholas Bakunin, and others). Also in attendance were Simanovskii and the governor of Tver himself.[2] The purpose of the meeting, as announced beforehand to the governor, was 'to agree upon the organization of a private land bank'. The main item on the agenda was to be the reading of a charter for the proposed bank, written by Unkovskii.[3]

According to the gendarme's report, the dinner proceeded in orderly fashion. The most noteworthy occurrence there was the proposal of Kudriavtsev (*pomeshchik* of Torzhok *uezd*) for the founding of an 'agricultural society' in Tver province, which was unanimously approved by the persons attending.[4] 'Of political matters or matters concerning the government decree, or even about the peasant question [Simanovskii reported], there was not a word'.[5] In the meeting following the dinner only the matter of the land bank was discussed. Adjourning late at night without having finished the discussion of Unkovskii's project,

[1] This last surmise may have been correct. The events of the Tver gentry assembly were reported in great detail in *Kolokol*, by an eyewitness who must have been a member of the gentry assembly. (Cf. *Kolokol*, nos. 65–6, 15 March 1860). The denunciation of Unkovskii, Golovachev, Evropeus and others for being in contact with 'agents of Herzen' was fairly common in those days, and had begun earlier during the days of the provincial committee. (*TsGAOR, f.* 109, no. 37, part 14, p. 26). In November 1861, after the emancipation, the wife of Evropeus was discovered while returning from Western Europe to possess 'forbidden works and letters disclosing her close relations with the traitors Herzen, Ogarev and Dolgorukov; a letter of Dolgorukov [prince Petr] to the husband of Evropeus in which Dolgorukov asked to carry on a correspondence with him, and inviting Unkovskii to do the same, drew especial attention'. *TsGAOR, f.* 109, no. 11, part 14, pp. 323–4a.
[2] *TsGAOR, f.* 109, no. 11, part 14, pp. 126–8. Members from the former provincial committee in attendance were: Unkovskii, Vel'iashev, Bakunin, Kishenskii, Kharlamov, Chagin, Vul'f, Miachkov, Panafidin, Balkashin, Neronov and Golovachev.
[3] *Ibid.*, p. 123.   [4] *Ibid.*, p. 125.
[5] *Ibid.*, p. 124a.

the participants agreed to meet the next day to finish it. This was done, in the presence of the governor, and the participants then dispersed, with the agreement to meet again on 29 February for the signing of the bank project, after which it was to be presented to the government for approval. A resolution for the founding of an agricultural society in Tver was also drawn up for presentation to the governor.[1]

The meeting thus ended without untoward incident. In the meantime, *Chef de Gendarmes* Dolgorukov, aroused by Ivanov's report of 'the existence of a secret society',[2] had dispatched, on 8 February, Adjutant-General Iafimovich to Tver to make special investigation of these allegations, as well as to investigate allegations about improper proceedings at the recent gentry assembly.[3]

Arriving in Tver on 9 February, Iafimovich undertook, in the following five days, an investigation of the matter and found the accusations of Klokachev and Ivanov about the meetings to be totally false. In short, his findings coincided with those of Baranov and Simanovskii, who had disputed Ivanov's accusations even before the meeting of 7 February.[4]

In spite of this, Iafimovich, in his final report from Tver (14 February), came to the following conclusions about the 'disturbances' in Tver: Unkovskii was guilty of two transgressions: (1) He had allowed Evropeus to take part in the gentry assembly, a right the latter did not have as a person who had been judged in the Petrashevskii affair; this had resulted in Evropeus' 'producing disturbances in the assembly'. (2) Unkovskii had illegally made use of a lithograph during the assembly for the printing of the petition to the Emperor. Golovachev was guilty of having insulted the acting gentry marshal Klokachev in a letter. And Evropeus, though having committed no specific legal offense,

---

[1] *Ibid.*, pp. 125a–6a, 130–30a.   [2] *Ibid.*, p. 117.   [3] *Ibid.*, pp. 113–14a.

[4] *Ibid.*, pp. 131–3a. The Third Section was particularly worried by rumors which had circulated in Tver before the meeting to the effect that Babst, the Moscow banker Mamontov, the millionaire merchant Kokorev, the railway entrepreneur Glazenap and other influential people from outside the province were planning to come to the 7 February meeting. None of them did—all participants were Tver *pomeshchiki*. Unkovskii had received a pledge of 100,000 rubles from Kokorev for the proposed bank. Unkovskii, 'Materialy k biografii', p. 25a.

18-2

Iafimovich found guilty of 'being, so to speak, the cause of the disorders which took place during the recent assembly'.[1]

These three persons, concluded Iafimovich,

> ... If left in their places of residence after their ill-intentioned actions, can serve as examples for the disturbance of the general peace. Therefore I would consider it necessary to send the designated *Unkovskii, Golovachev* and *Evropeus* away for a time ... to locations in distant provinces to be named by the government; with the institution of close secret police surveillance over them there. *This measure would seem necessary, in my opinion, in order to let them understand that illegal actions do not remain unpunished, and also as an example to others.*[2]

On 20 February 1860, Lanskoi informed Dolgorukov that Unkovskii and Evropeus were to be sent into administrative exile, the former to Viatka, the latter to Perm. Unkovskii was conducted to Viatka on 24 February; Evropeus left for Perm on 28 February under escort.[3]

Golovachev was left in the hands of the local court where a suit brought against him by Klokachev was pending. Klokachev, who had been the object of nearly unanimous scorn among the local gentry since his willing acceptance of the post left vacant by Unkovskii, had refused to register the gentry's motion for the founding of twelve 'Unkovskii stipends' in Moscow University, on the grounds that one of the *uezd* marshals had not signed the motion. He also took several other steps to prevent the effecting of the resolution.[4] This action of Klokachev had given Golovachev the opportunity to address to him (at the end of January 1860) a scornful letter written in the vitriolic style Golovachev so liked to employ. Golovachev accused Klokachev of having had no right to delay the registering of the resolution. Completing his formal accusation, Golovachev proceeded to epithets. Klokachev's behaviour, he wrote, was nothing but 'outrageous insolence':

> I think [he wrote] that the cause of this was only pitiful, low and vile envy, envy of a man who has earned universal respect not only in our

---

[1] *TsGAOR, f.* 109, no. 11, part 14, pp. 149–9a.
[2] *Ibid.,* pp. 149–50. Emphasis added.   [3] *Ibid.,* pp. 175a, 178.
[4] *Ibid.,* pp. 83–6a.

province, but in all of Russia. This envy caused you to find any captious objection in order to prevent the Tver gentry from immortalizing the memory of the beneficent activity of a person esteemed by them. . . . You have only found the means to demonstrate clearly and positively what sort of person you are; you found the means to cover yourself with shame in the eyes of every decent person, and nothing more.

Knowing you well, I expected nothing better from you; but now all know to what baseness you are capable of descending. . . . A man capable of behaving as you have does not have the right to take offense at any remarks whatever. However, I am prepared to answer for my remarks before any court in which you may wish to bring charges . . .[1]

Golovachev, whose aim was to get Klokachev involved in a lawsuit and thereby to expose publicly his activities, sent copies of this letter to all the gentry marshals and to the governor. Klokachev addressed a complaint against Golovachev to the central government, seeking administrative measures against him. Although such a case, involving a provincial marshal, was indeed liable to administrative action by the Senate, the government found it unwise to handle the case administratively, fearing that it would be presented as an 'act of arbitrariness on the part of the government'.[2] Klokachev's case was therefore directed to the regular courts by the Ministry of Interior, which arbitrarily caused the suit to be brought immediately before the *uezd* court. That court obligingly sentenced Golovachev to six months' stay in a mental sanitarium [*smiritel'nyi dom,*] but the sentence was overruled by the appellate court on complaint by Golovachev that the *uezd* court had tried him without bringing formal charges against him. The case was buffeted about in the courts from that time until the court reform of 1864, when it was cancelled altogether. Golovachev thus escaped exile and was never punished for his letter.[3]

The formal charges against Unkovskii (the only one of the three against whom formal charges were made) were upheld by the Committee of Ministers. They were, for the most part, of specious coinage. In answer to a demand for an explanation

---

[1] *Ibid.*, pp. 87–8a.   [2] *Ibid.*, p. 75.
[3] Cf. Dzhanshiev, *Epokha velikikh reform, pp.* 140–2, fn.

of why Evropeus was admitted to the gentry assembly (a demand made by the Ministry of Interior before the investigation of Iafimovich), Unkovskii replied that the assembly had had no reason to exclude him: It was known that he had been sent into the ranks, but he had not been deprived of gentry status, and had subsequently been 'rehabilitated' by being raised to officer status. He was a registered *pomeshchik* of Bezhetsk *uezd* and fulfilled all qualifications for participation in the assembly.[1] To this explanation the government had no reply.

Unkovskii's use of a lithograph to print the petition of the assembly presented a more complex problem. Unkovskii had the personal permission of the Emperor for the use of a lithograph, but presumably only for the purpose of printing the journals of the provincial committee. Unkovskii argued that even so the use of the lithograph was only for making official papers available to members of the assembly, not for public distribution, and therefore was not subject to permission from the censors. Moreover, Unkovskii reminded the government that official papers had traditionally been reproduced in the gentry assemblies and in the office of the provincial gentry marshal without the permission of the censors.[2]

In any event, these charges, and the charges against Evropeus, were never formally registered by the government, on the remarkable grounds that Unkovskii and Evropeus had, by the Emperor's order, already received sufficient punishment by being exiled![3]

The open charges against Unkovskii and the others were accompanied by numerous clandestine denunciations.[4] In the

---

[1] *TsGAOR, f.* 109, no. 11, part 14, pp. 135–6.

[2] M. Lemke, *Ocherki osvoboditel'nogo dvizheniia 'shestidesiatykh godov'* (St Petersburg, 1908), p. 455.

[3] 'Although on the exact basis of the law [Lanskoi wrote to Dolgorukov, 21 February 1860] Collegiate Assessor Unkovskii would be subject to the jurisdiction of the Ruling Senate for allowing these disorders, in view of the fact that by Imperial order of the 18th of February Unkovskii and Evropeus have both received punishment already by their exile—the one to Viatka and the other to Perm—I have subsequently proposed to the Governor of Tver province that the aforementioned matter be left without further execution.' *TsGAOR, f.* 109, no. 11, part 14, pp. 167–7a.

[4] Aside from those already mentioned, one of the most persistent of these accused Unkovskii of having celebrated the anniversary of the Decembrist uprising with the

end, however, the government had few illusions about the secret plans and secret societies alluded to by Klokachev and the vice-governor, Ivanov. There was not a shred of evidence of their existence, and these accusations were steadfastly denied by Baranov and the local gendarme officer, Simanovskii, both of whom were on friendly terms with Unkovskii and his colleagues and knew the accusations to be false.[1] Their affirmations were fully confirmed by Iafimovich.

The real reason for the exile of Unkovskii and Evropeus was clearly stated in Iafimovich's recommendation: They were to serve as examples to other gentry that the government was not inclined to tolerate such disorders as had been going on among the Tver gentry. The gentry were to be warned against proceeding with discussion of the peasant question—in or out of their assemblies—and proposing their own independent solutions. Iafimovich's recommendation was speedily approved in the Main Committee where Panin, Minister of Justice, and Lanskoi evidently particularly insisted on the exile.[2]

The news of the exile of Unkovskii and Evropeus scandalized the Tver gentry. Even the 'lower classes', Simanovskii reported, were moved to feelings of sympathy for Unkovskii.[3] All agreed that Evropeus and Golovachev had been picked by the government as scapegoats, as the most able—and reckless—of the participants in the assembly (Unkovskii, as gentry marshal, was of course chief scapegoat).[4] The gentry showered hostility on the

Decembrist Matvei Murav'ev-Apostol who lived in Tver. This was a false accusation. Murav'ev-Apostol was not in the province at the time in question. Unkovskii, 'Materialy k biografii', 27–8.

[1] Simanovskii was, in fact, a good friend of Unkovskii, and regularly supplied him with his copy of Herzen's *Kolokol*. When the news came of the decision to exile Unkovskii and Evropeus, Simanovskii warned them in time to allow them to put their papers in order before their quarters were searched. *Ibid.*, pp. 26–9a.

[2] *Ibid.*, pp. 26, 91. Unkovskii, who had access to the papers of the case some years later, wrote that Count Panin 'simply announced that my exile was necessary at all costs because the court could not accuse me of anything illegal, but that my presence in society was dangerous'. (*Ibid.*, p. 91.) Unkovskii thought the decision originated in the Main Committee or the Committee of Ministers. He did not know of Iafimovich's recommendation, thinking Iafimovich had given him and Evropeus a complete acquittal in his investigation. *Ibid.*, pp. 26–8.

[3] *TsGAOR, f.* 109, no. 11, part 14, pp. 191–91a.

[4] *Ibid.*, pp. 196a–7.

denouncers of Unkovskii, Evropeus and Golovachev, including the vice-governor Ivanov, whose role in the affair was attributed by the gentry to a desire to injure Unkovskii and to satisfy his personal antipathy toward Baranov. To placate gentry opinion, the government shortly afterward removed Ivanov from his post and replaced him with another career bureaucrat, M. E. Saltykov (Saltykov-Shchedrin).[1] Klokachev was removed as temporary provincial marshal and replaced, in August 1860, by Brovtsyn (marshal of Staritsa *uezd*).

In spite of considerable fear by the Tver gentry that other exiles would follow (rumors to that effect were widely circulated in the province),[2] the supporters of the land bank project met again on 29 February and signed the project which had been written by Unkovskii. It was then entrusted to one of the signers for presentation to the Ministry of Finance for approval.[3] Several more meetings were held in the course of the year, capital was accumulated, and after the Emancipation Proclamation the project was approved by the government.[4]

The petition seeking permission to create an agricultural society in Tver was, however, rejected by the Ministry of Interior because it had been signed by the 'ill-intentioned persons' Unkovskii, Golovachev and Evropeus.[5]

In August 1860, special *uezd* assemblies of the gentry were held—by government order—for the election of *uezd* marshals. The gentry proceeded with these assemblies unwillingly, and in five *uezdy* they refused again to elect marshals.[6] New elections were held in these *uezdy* at the end of the year. By the time of the emancipation (19 February 1861) no marshals had yet been elected in two *uezdy* (Vyshnii Volocheck and Tver).[7]

From Viatka, where he was not uncomfortably ensconced in the

[1] *Ibid.*, pp. 195–6a. [2] *Ibid.*, pp. 202–2a.
[3] *Ibid.*, pp. 182–2a. The project was signed by thirty-one persons.
[4] *Ibid.*, pp. 303–4.
[5] *Ibid.*, pp. 219–20, 232–2a. This decision was appealed to the Senate by Nicholas Bakunin, Miachkov and Kudriavtsev. The Senate overruled the decision of the Ministry of Interior, and the petition was passed on to the Ministry of State Properties for consideration.
[6] *Ibid.*, pp. 271–2a (Tver, Korcheva, Torzhok, Vyshnii Volochek, and Ves'egonsk).
[7] *Ibid.*, pp. 238–42, 226–7a, 245–456a, 271–2a, 297–9a.

society of the provincial governor and his wife, Unkovskii addressed a letter to Alexander II, protesting his innocence of the charges brought against him.[1] Neither he nor the gentry, wrote Unkovskii, had had any secret or overly-ambitious aims:

I never thought [he insisted] that the problem of peasant emancipation could be decided by the gentry or its representatives; but I have always been convinced that for the success of this transformation the conscious, sincere cooperation of the gentry is necessary . . .[2]

The charges brought against him and the other gentry were, Unkovskii wrote, the inventions of enemies of emancipation. The only way that such unfounded denunciations and rumors could be stopped, he argued, was to make the preparations of the reform fully public.[3]

Unkovskii and Evropeus remained in exile only about seven months. They were allowed to return to Tver in September and October, 1860, respectively.[4] Their exile was obviously intended to be more a warning to the gentry than severe personal punishment.

The Riazan provincial assembly

It will be recalled that the provincial gentry committee of Riazan, a province located on the borderline separating the central-industrial region and the central black soil area, had in its majority project flatly opposed land-redemption for the peasants. The committee drew up a project for the transition period alone. After the twelve-year transition period the peasants, according to this project, were to lose the right of usage of their allotments and all further arrangements were to be made by 'free arrangement of the *pomeshchik* with the peasants'. The committee was also very un-generous in its proposed economic settlement with the peasantry, and its administrative proposals left much authority over the peasants directly in the hands of *pomeshchiki*.

---

[1] Unkovskii sent his letter on the advice of governor Baranov, who delivered it for him. Unkovskii, 'Materialy k biografii', pp. 57–7a.
[2] Lemke, *Osvoboditel'noe dvizhenie*, p. 453.   [3] *Ibid.*, pp. 452–3.
[4] *TsGAOR, f.* 109, no. 11, part 14, pp. 248, 250–1.

The gentry liberal program had been represented in the committee by Koshelev and D. F. Samarin, members appointed by the government. They proposed land-redemption, self-administration for the peasants in their communes, and other local reforms (as proposed by Koshelev before the Editing Commissions; see above, p. 259). Koshelev and Samarin were followed by several other members of the committee in supporting land-redemption and complete elimination of obligatory relations, primarily by the deputies from Ranenburg *uezd*, Prince Volkonskii and Safronov.[1]

In Petersburg all the deputies of the Riazan committee—Koshelev (representing the minority), Ofrosimov (majority representative) and Prince Volkonskii (representing the special opinion of the Ranenburg deputies)—had sided fully with the liberal opposition. Ofrosimov and Volkonskii presented a common commentary borrowed mainly from the remarks of Unkovskii.[2] All three joined in signing the address of eighteen deputies, for which they received official reprimands.

Returning to Riazan in a state of high indignation in November 1859, Volkonskii and Ofrosimov,[3] like their Tver colleagues, distributed lithographed copies of their commentaries among the local gentry. These were accompanied by special letters in which the deputies explained that the government had deprived them in Petersburg of their right to consult with the higher authorities and had restricted them to contact with the Editing Commissions alone. The Commissions had prepared their own project, the deputies explained, which had nothing in common with those of the provincial committees. The aim of the Commissions' project, they vowed, was none other than to:

... Drive the *pomeshchiki* to the sacrifice of the lands given over to the peasants ... for a trifling cost, by means of the usage by the peasants of the lands ... for obligations, never changeable ... and unguaranteed by anything concrete.

[1] See above, pp. 176–80.
[2] See above, p. 256.
[3] Koshelev remained in Petersburg where he had been appointed a member of the special commission for considering legislation on land banks. Trubetskaia, *Materialy dlia biografii kn. Cherkasskogo*, II, 99–101.

Moreover, they complained,

The quantity of land designated by the Commissions for such usage and for redemption is so great, that it threatens not only the complete ruin of the *pomeshchiki* but the destruction of agriculture in the entire State.[1]

Volkonskii and Ofrosimov reported that as representatives of their class they had felt unable to submit to the instructions of the Editing Commissions, whose obvious aim was 'to remove the gentry from the affair and subjugate all the inhabitants to their arbitrariness'.[2] The bureaucrats had, however, prevented the truth from reaching the throne and the deputies had, in the end, to present their commentaries to the Editing Commissions.[3] Their commentaries had been based on the following considerations:

At the present time of struggle between the bureaucracy and the gentry which threatens the latter with complete annihilation, it seems to us that the necessary and only possible thing for the gentry to do is to sacrifice for a moderate price a part of its land to the peasants with a guarantee by the government of punctuality of payments. Then, having dealt with the peasantry on a fair basis and in keeping with the personal desire of the Sovereign Emperor, to assert its own rights to participation in the administration and the economic direction of the area; whereas, as long as there remains even a shadow of seigneurial authority, the interference of the bureaucracy, with its present development and centralization, will be inevitable and will bring after it the enslavement of all classes of the people by the sovereign bureaucrats.[4]

Thus had Ofrosimov, former leader of the conservative majority of the Riazan committee, changed his views. Faced in Petersburg with the government's firm intention to alienate a part of the gentry's lands to the peasantry, Ofrosimov chose what appeared to him the only alternative: *Obligatory* redemption to guarantee

---

[1] Povalishin, *Riazanskie pomeshchiki i ikh krepostnye*, p. 376. [2] *Ibid.*
[3] *Ibid.* The deputies also maintained that their presence in Petersburg had been a mere formality, for no attention had been paid to their commentaries.
[4] *Ibid.*, p. 377.

remuneration for the gentry; and abolition of seigneurial rights, to prevent the bureaucracy from using some sort of regulated status in order to interfere in local affairs and to prevent the gentry from taking their rightful part in them.[1]

While the commentaries and letter of the deputies were circulating among the Riazan gentry, the government order prohibiting discussion of the peasant question was communicated to the provincial marshal. As in Tver, the gentry began by disputing the legality of such a ruling, maintaining that the gentry's right to address the Emperor about their grievances could be revoked only by formal changes in the law. The governor, N. P. Murav'ev, warned the government on 7 December that the gentry were likely to ignore the ruling, and that in such a case he intended to close the gentry assembly.

The Riazan gentry assembly opened on 10 December. The gentry proceeded immediately to a discussion of the government ruling, which they unanimously found to be in violation of their basic rights.[2] On 12 December the gentry composed an address to Alexander II and sent it off to Petersburg. Essentially, the address was the same as that sent by the Tver assembly: The gentry pleaded that discussion of any of the gentry's needs without reference to the peasant question would be impossible. The address therefore begged permission to ignore the government ruling of 9 November.[3]

This address was discussed in the Main Committee on 17 December 1859, along with the address of the Tver assembly. The request of the Riazan assembly was summarily dismissed by the

---

[1] On 20 December, Volkonskii and Ofrosimov were given a banquet by the gentry, where they were presented with a testimonial statement signed by 186 *pomeshchiki*. 'Honorably have you fulfilled your task [it proclaimed]; unswervingly have you understood the intentions of the gentry . . .' (*Materialy*, II, 262.)

[2] The governor claimed that the gentry were impelled to this conclusion by two articles which had appeared in the Moscow newspaper *Russkaia gazeta* on 9 December. These articles (written by two *pomeshchiki*, one of them an *uezd* marshal from Orel province) called upon the gentry to exercise their right to petition the Emperor in order to protest the excesses of the bureaucracy and to urge further reforms ('publicity of all judiciary processes and investigation . . ., replacement of the spirits-concession . . ., permission to organize local administration from persons responsible to the control of public opinion'). *Russkaia gazeta*, 9 December 1859, pp. 2–3; *TsGAOR, f.* 109, no. 11, part 17, pp. 7–9; *Materialy*, II, 264–5.

[3] *TsGAOR, f.* 109, no. 11, part 17, pp. 10–10a. See Appendix II.

Main Committee; the assembly was informed by telegram of this decision and instructed to proceed to its elections.[1]

When word of the Main Committee's decision reached Riazan some members of the assembly proposed following the tactic which had been pursued in Tver: A boycott of the gentry elections.[2] The governor, however, called in all the *uezd* marshals and managed to convince them to proceed with the elections.[3] On the nineteenth of December the government's reply to the address was officially read before the assembly. The deputy from Zaraisk *uezd*, Rzhevskii (the director of the Tver gymnasium, who had come directly from Tver for the assembly), then proposed that the gentry, while respecting the order not to discuss the peasant question in the assembly, draw up a special petition to the Emperor *outside the assembly* and present it through the provincial gentry marshal after the closing of the assembly. This proposal was accepted by a vote of 191–36, and the gentry retired from the assembly hall to compose the petition.

The petition of 19 December, signed by all the gentry participating in the Riazan assembly (156 signatures) contained two main requests: (1) The request that complete emancipation be carried out immediately, in view of the fact that the 'undefined position in which the *pomeshchiki* and the peasants are [according to the project of the Editing Commissions] is harmful in both the economic and the moral sense'; the incomplete abolition of serfdom threatened to place both classes in mutually hostile relations threatening to the social order. (2) The request that emancipation be carried out 'not otherwise than by means of obligatory redemption of the lands allotted to the peasants', on the basis of the allotment norms established by the Riazan committee; and that for this purpose a local land bank be organized by the gentry, utilizing the food-reserve funds of the province, amounting to a million rubles. The government, assured the

[1] *TsGIAL, f.* 1180, no. 37, pp. 20a, 50–1.
[2] *TsGAOR, f.* 109, no. 11, part 17, 20–5a; *TsGIAL, f.* 1180, no. 37, p. 86. The chief proponents of this tactic, according to the local gendarme officer, were Ofrosimov, Volkonskii, Rzhevskii (Unkovskii's associate from Tver, a *pomeshchik* of Zaraisk *uezd* in Riazan province), and several other deputies to the assembly.
[3] *Ibid.*

petitioners, would thus not be forced to participate in a financial operation.

On the basis of these principles the gentry asked permission to draw up an emancipation project and a plan for the organization of the redemption bank.[1]

The gentry elections were completed and the Riazan assembly closed on 22 December without further incident.[2]

The petition of the Riazan gentry was taken by the provincial gentry marshal to the governor in January 1860, after the closing of the assembly. Forwarded by the governor to Petersburg, the petition was discussed in the Main Committee on 29 February. Relaying the decision of the Main Committee to the governor of Riazan, Lanskoi wrote only that the government had already taken all necessary measures. As for the question of the land bank, the Main Committee had ruled that 'reserve capital, according to the existing laws, has a defined purpose and cannot be used for other purposes'.[3] The provincial gentry marshal was given a reprimand for his efforts.[4]

The Iaroslavl provincial assembly

The gentry assembly convened in Iaroslavl on 10 December, the same day as in Riazan. The activities of the gentry there closely paralleled events in Riazan and Tver.

[1] *TsGAOR, f.* 109, no. 11, part 17, pp. 26–7. See Appendix II. (Povalishin, *Riazanskie pomeshchiki i ikh krepostnye*, pp. 381–5, discovered among the personal papers of Ofrosimov the text of such an emancipation project and a plan for a land bank. For some reason, Povalishin concluded that these documents were sent to the government along with the petition. The archival evidence and the reply of the Main Committee to the petition—*Zhurnaly sekretnego i glavnogo komiteta*, I, 490–1—indicate that only the petition was sent to the government. The project introduced by Povalishin may have been a preliminary draft prepared by Ofrosimov in the event that government permission were granted.)

[2] This was happily reported by the local gendarme officer to Dolgorukov. Despite tense moments, when the gentry seemed likely to be carried away by news of events in Tver and Orel (where assemblies were also underway) and by the influence of Ofrosimov, Volkonskii and others, the gentry had proved, he wrote, that 'in a calm state they are able to judge such individuals by their worth and readily prefer to them calm and well-intentioned men'. (The government feared not only boycott of elections but also the possible election of some of these troublemakers.) 'Thank God', Alexander II pencilled in the margin of this report. *Ibid.*, pp. 24a, 29.

[3] *Zhurnaly sekretnego i glavnogo komiteta*, I, 490–1; Povalishin, *Riazanskie pomeshchiki i ikh krepostnye*, p. 386.   [4] *Materialy*, II, 267.

The provincial gentry assembled, 1859–60

The gentry of Iaroslavl had not distinguished themselves in their provincial committee, where they had presented a typically conservative project following the rules of the April program. The deputies of the Iaroslavl committee in Petersburg, however, had come out emphatically for the liberal program and joined with Unkovskii and the deputies of the Kharkov committee in signing the 'address of five deputies'.

Returning to Iaroslavl for the assembly, the deputies—Dubrovin and Vasil'ev[1]—like their colleagues in Tver and Riazan, gave an accounting of their activities in Petersburg to the gentry. On the evening of the opening of the gentry assembly they gathered with more than a hundred gentry in the local hotel and there read their commentaries for the Editing Commissions.[2] According to the local governor the deputies received 'praises and universal enthusiasm' from the assembled gentry for their activities in Petersburg, including their signing of the address of five deputies.[3] After the reading of the commentaries the gentry repaired forthwith to the gentry club, where they composed and signed a vote of thanks to the deputies for their efforts in Petersburg. In so doing, the Iaroslavl gentry, as represented by their most influential members, fully endorsed the liberal reform program.[4]

Moved by the account of Dubrovin and Vasil'ev, the gentry discussed the possibility of sending a protest against the activities of the Editing Commissions to the Emperor. The protest did not, however, materialize, for lack of support by the gentry of several *uezdy*.[5] But when the governor, on 15 December, announced that the gentry were not to be allowed to discuss the peasant question, the majority of the assembled gentry immediately com-

---

[1] D. V. Vasil'ev was the natural son of some house servants of a local *pomeshchik*, who adopted him. From his adopted father Vasil'ev received gentry status and an estate of some 200 souls. He had no formal education.

P. N. Dubrovin was the son of a local *pomeshchik*, and a Frenchwoman (a governess?). Dubrovin had studied in Moscow University. A poor *pomeshchik*, his estate counted no more than 60 souls. *Materialy*, II, 298.

[2] *TsGIAL, f.* 1180, no. 37, p. 61a.

[3] *Ibid.*; *TsGAOR, f.* 109, no. 11, part 18, pp. 1–1a.

[4] *Ibid.*, p. 2a. The representatives of only one *uezd*—Myshkin—refused to sign the commendation to the deputies.

[5] Myshkin, Uglich and Rostov *uezdy*.

posed a petition to the Emperor which was in most respects identical to the 'address of the five deputies'. This action was, however, stopped by the governor before the petition could be completed.[1]

In indignation, the gentry then took the following steps:

(1) They persuaded the provincial marshal to present their demands to the Emperor over his individual signature. These demands, or 'wishes' as they were referred to in the marshal's letter to Alexander II, were the following: (a) creation of an all-class provincial and *uezd* administration for 'economic matters'; (b) liberal court reform, and accountability of officials before the courts; (c) freedom of the press.[2]

(2) Proceeding to the gentry elections, the provincial marshal, P. Bem, and all the *uezd* marshals refused to stand for election to the post of provincial marshal, in order to allow the election of Vasil'ev and Dubrovin, who, in spite of their initial refusal, were voted in as provincial marshal and candidate, respectively, by a large majority vote in the assembly.[3]

The petition of the Iaroslavl gentry, presented by the provincial governor on 17 December, was officially ignored by the government. Bem was given a severe reprimand.[4] Vasil'ev and Dubrovin were refused confirmation in office by the government, which appointed the Iaroslavl *uezd* marshal to the post. With that the elections ended and the gentry departed from Iaroslavl, apparently without further incident.

The Orel provincial assembly

The Orel gentry, also meeting in mid-December, proceeded in less dramatic fashion than their counterparts in Tver, Riazan and Iaroslavl, perhaps because the Orel gentry had not yet sent representatives to Petersburg. Nevertheless, when the gentry heard the ruling forbidding discussion of the peasant question in the assembly, they responded by composing a resolution:

[1] *Ibid.*, pp. 9a–10. [2] *TsGIAL, f.* 1180, no. 37, pp. 59–60a. See Appendix II.
[3] *TsGAOR, f.* 109, no. 11, part 18, p. 3.
[4] *TsGIAL, f.* 1180, no. 37, p. 59.

To inform the SOVEREIGN most loyally that the gentry with deep regret, see in this prohibition a sign of distrust ... [The gentry] consider that it is their sacred duty to bring to the MOST GRACIOUS attention [of the Emperor] the fact that the prohibiting of the discussion of the peasant question has deprived the gentry of one of their most essential rights to speak and inform the government of the needs of the region, which at the present time are almost all intimately connected with this question.[1]

In accordance with this resolution, the provincial gentry marshal and the marshals of eleven of the province's twelve *uezdy* (Briansk *uezd* abstaining) sent an address to the Emperor. The Orel gentry assembly had obeyed the government order prohibiting discussion of the peasant question, explained the address,

... But they also requested us, as their representatives, to present directly to YOUR IMPERIAL MAJESTY a special resolution expressing the general regret which echoed deeply in the hearts of the gentry, who recognized in the aforementioned prohibition MONARCHIAL distrust in their proven faithfulness and devotion to the throne of YOUR IMPERIAL MAJESTY.[2]

The protest of the Orel gentry went no further, and their elections were carried out in orderly fashion. Their address received only the marginal comment of Alexander II: 'In my opinion this does not deserve any attention'.[3]

Unlike the assemblies of Tver, Riazan and Iaroslavl, the activities of the Orel assembly had definitely conservative and aristocratic overtones, which were remarked by the government with some apprehension. Both Count Orlov-Davydov, author of the letter to Rostovtsev, and S. I. Mal'tsev,[4] one of Russia's

---

[1] *Ibid.*, pp. 70–4. [2] *Ibid.*, pp. 68–9a. See Appendix II.
[3] *Ibid.*, p. 68.
[4] Sergei Ivanovich Mal'tsev (1810–93), *pomeshchik* of Orel and Kaluga provinces, owner of more than 200,000 souls, was probably the most extraordinary *pomeshchik* in prereform Russia. Raised in the highest court circles, where he had many family ties, Mal'tsev began a brilliant military career but left it in 1849 to devote himself to industrial enterprises. In this field he enjoyed incredible success: He founded numerous metallurgical, arms, and chemical factories, employing more than 3,500 workers in Kaluga alone (he also had factories in many other provinces). His factories produced the first rails in Russia, the first Russian steam-engine, and Russia's first screw-propelled vessel.

greatest landowners and industrialists, played prominent roles in the Orel assembly. Well-known as advocates of 'aristocratic constitutionalism', Orlov-Davydov and Mal'tsev spoke in the assembly on the necessity of introducing gentry representatives into the governmental system. Mal'tsev even presented a memoir, in the name of the Briansk gentry, advocating the presence of permanent gentry representatives in the central government.[1] Their propositions were not accepted, however, by the gentry assembly.

The Vladimir provincial assembly[2]

Convening on 17 January 1860, the Vladimir gentry proceeded directly to the question of the gentry's 'needs and welfare'. The government ruling prohibiting discussion of the peasant question provoked a stormy protest in the assembly, led by I. S. Bezobrazov[3] and P. A. Protopopov.[4]

Mal'tsev formed cartels for the furnishing of his factories and carried on independent trade-relations with foreign countries, including Rumania, Bulgaria and Turkey. He had his own ships and a private railway on his lands, at a time when his railway comprised one-tenth of the entire rail network in the country.

Although known for enlightened treatment of his factory workers, Mal'tsev was a harsh master to his peasants and an enemy of emancipation. Mal'tsev nurtured a violent hatred of the Ministry of Interior and the bureaucracy in general. In 1858 he wrote a memoir which enjoyed wide distribution. In it Mal'tsev professed to see a direct parallel between contemporary Russia and France in 1789, and relied heavily on Tocqueville's new book *L'Ancien régime* (published in 1856) in his attacks on the bureaucracy. The fatal error of Louis XVI, wrote Mal'tsev, had been his view of the nobility as a rival. Mal'tsev therefore proposed an end to ministerial arbitrariness by calling into the central government two gentry representatives from each province. The Tsar would then rely on the gentry, which would properly rule the 'people'. In this interpretation, blaming all of Russia's troubles (including the loss of the Crimean War) on misguided reforms conceived by the overweening bureaucracy, and denying the necessity of emancipation, Mal'tsev essentially shared the views of Bezobrazov. Cf. N. V. Sakharov, 'Iz vospominanii o V. A. Artsimoviche', *V. A. Artsimovich. Vospominaniia, kharakteristika* (St Petersburg, 1904); Kornilov, 'Gubernskie komitety' no. 2, pp. 218–20. *TsGAOR, f.* 109, no. 61, pp. 2–10 (the memoir).

[1] *Materialy*, II, 347.
[2] See above, pp. 158–60, for an account of the activities of the Vladimir provincial commitee.
[3] Bezobrazov had been the leader of the second minority in the Vladimir provincial committee which produced a project modelled after the Tver majority project. As a deputy to Petersburg he joined the liberal opposition and was a member of the 'Unkovskii circle' there.
[4] Protopopov had also been a member of the provincial committee, an adherent of the majority position, where he had been given a reprimand for being a troublemaker. Like Golovachev in Tver, Protopopov had a predilection for writing insulting letters and getting himself involved in libel suits. *TsGAOR, f.* 109, no. 11, part 4, pp. 94–9a.

Speaking before the assembly, Bezobrazov declined to violate the government order. Instead, he declared, he would address himself to the 'representation of [the gentry's] future situation':

... Where is the guarantee of the desired future? What if, in exchange for the ready sacrifices of the gentry, it is excluded from general self-administration, it is left isolated, it is deprived of the possibility of merging with the people.... What if ... they take away from us definitive participation in the administration of the country? The rule of the *chinovniki* will suppress everything and the Russian gentry, which for so many centuries was the support of the throne and was not sparing of lives for the good of the fatherland, will perish in the chaos of the new administration![1]

Bezobrazov concluded his speech by summoning the gentry to inform the Emperor of this dangerous situation.

Protopopov's speech repeated many of these same ideas. The gentry, he insisted, had the right and duty to discuss their needs and to petition the throne about them. To these comments he added a specific list of necessary reforms: (1) 'Free and general elective principles ...; (2) the strictest protection of the inviolability of rights and moral respect for human dignity by every official; (3) strict and equal accountability of all officials before the courts and the law for failure to fulfill their responsibilities; (4) public court procedures; and (5) trial by jury.' Without such preliminary changes, Protopopov warned, the gentry would 'move backward forever and exclude [themselves] from the mass of the ... population, in some kind of removed upper class completely without significance':

Let us ourselves sacrifice our conceited charters, our geneological tables [*barkhatnye knigi*], our aristocratic title, for a new and resurrected life; and for all this former proud and vainly useless grandeur of ours let us most loyally request ... one common title with all the classes: free citizens, fully recognizing the autocratic authority and the common legal responsibility of every individual, not before administrative arbitrariness, but before public justice and a general, elective jury court![2]

[1] *Materialy*, II, 303–6. [2] *TsGAOR*, f. 109, no. 11, part 4, pp. 23–5a.

This extraordinary proposal of class-abnegation received only one explicit objection from among the assembled *pomeshchiki*![1]

Aroused by the speeches of Bezobrazov and Protopopov, the gentry appointed a committee to draw up an address to Alexander II. The address, composed after a draft by Bezobrazov, was duly accepted by a vote of 186–34 and sent directly to the Emperor.[2] By far the most detailed and the boldest of the gentry addresses of the winter of 1859–60, the Vladimir address first gave an 'Unkovskiite' critique of the existing administration and argued the impossibility of retaining it after emancipation. This was followed by the concrete proposals which constituted the main body of the address:

MOST GRACIOUS SOVEREIGN, the Gentry consider it their sacred duty to call to YOUR MAJESTY'S most gracious attention that for the peaceful and successful conclusion of the imminent reform and for the realization of YOUR beneficent designs, the following, according to our sincere and deep conviction, are necessary:

(1) Strict separation of powers: Administrative, judicial and police.

(2) Common administration for all classes.

(3) Economic-executive administration elected from all classes and responsible only before the courts and the public; and with elected officials confirmed in office not by the administrative authority, but only by correctness of the electoral process.

(4) Government appointed police administration, organized in a purely protective spirit, and acting exclusively in accordance with the law.

(5) Public civil legal procedure guided only by the law, and public criminal justice based on conscience and the law; that is, a jury court.

(6) Direct responsibility of each and all before the courts.

(7) Personal accountability of all officials for failure to fulfill their responsibilities, without the right to refer to the orders of their superiors.

(8) The establishment of new, firm and strict measures for the support of private and State credit.[3]

[1] *Ibid.*, pp. 13–16a. V. Solominskii objected that the assembly had no right to consider the surrender of gentry privileges without full participation of Vladimir's 2000–3000 *pomeshchiki*.   [2] *Ibid.*, p. 13; *Materialy*, II, 315. See Appendix II.
[3] *TsGAOR, f.* 109, no. 11, part 4, pp. 11–12.

The provincial gentry assembled, 1859–60

The address of the Vladimir gentry, not restricted to a mere expression of disappointment (as in Orel) or with merely requesting the right to discuss the gentry's 'needs and welfare', thus went much further than the addresses presented by their colleagues in Tver or elsewhere. *It was in fact the first presentation of the essential demands of the liberal gentry program made not by individuals but in the name of the gentry of an entire province.*[1]

The Vladimir address, and news of the activities of the Vladimir assembly in general, were received in Petersburg with great dissatisfaction. The speeches of Bezobrazov and Protopopov, in particular, were considered revolutionary. The address was discussed in the Council of Ministers on February 11 under the personal chairmanship of Alexander II. Some there—especially Lanskoi—proposed that severe measures be taken against the Vladimir gentry, but it was finally decided (perhaps as a result of the Emperor's insistence) to restrict punishment to a 'most severe reprimand' to the provincial marshal for allowing the gentry to compose such an address and for appending his signature to it:

It is not allowed by any law [read the government decision on the Vladimir address] to discuss questions concerning the general state organization at gentry assemblies, and all the less to interfere in them [that is, in such questions]. In [expressing] these views, the solicitation of the Vladimir gentry . . . is completely contrary to the spirit of our state organization and cannot be tolerated. The gentry who participated in the signing should not have allowed themselves to undertake such a petition. To deter them from this unallowable action was the direct responsibility of the former provincial marshal . . . Bogdanov.[2]

The *uezd* marshals were also given reprimands. Protopopov, elected marshal of Pokrov *uezd* at the assembly, was refused confirmation in this office by the government. Bezobrazov, however, was allowed to retain his position of marshal of Kovrov *uezd* (to which he had been re-elected).

The gentry took fright at the government's actions. Many

---

[1] The address presented in the name of the Iaroslavl provincial marshal also made similar specific demands, but it was not an official presentation of the assembled gentry.

[2] *Kolokol*, 15 May 1860.

proceeded to protest that they had not understood the import of what they had signed, insisting that, in any case, they had considered it not an address, but a petition (*proshenie*). According to the gendarme officer, Bezobrazov and Protopopov continued for some time to 'speak loudly and freely' among the gentry, but the gentry took no subsequent steps.[1]

The St Petersburg provincial assembly

The last significant demonstration of gentry opposition to occur among the assemblies of 1859–60 took place in Petersburg itself.[2] Events there were watched by the government with particular apprehension.

The role of the Petersburg gentry in the preparation of the peasant reform was particularly significant. The influential and active members of the Petersburg gentry were an extraordinary group of aristocrats, many of them closely connected to the court and higher government offices: Generals, senators, ministers and other high dignitaries who lived permanently in the capital. The provincial marshal in these years, P. P. Shuvalov, belonged to the highest level of court society.[3]

---

[1] *TsGAOR,f.* 109, no. 11, part 4, 50–1a. Protopopov protested his non-confirmation in office in a letter to the Emperor, but to no avail. *Ibid.*, pp. 71–8a.

[2] The remaining assemblies meeting in the winter of 1859–60 proceeded in less excited fashion. The Novgorod and Orenburg gentry made no formal protestations to the government during their December meetings. Of the several assemblies meeting in January, the most eventful was that of the Kaluga gentry, where opponents of the former provincial committee came out in force. After much arguing, the assembly failed to agree on the contents of an address to the Emperor, and none was ever sent. The Vologda gentry, also meeting in January 1860, sent an address to the Emperor, but it contained only a complaint against the provincial governor, not a general protest about the peasant question. In Nizhnii Novgorod, where there was no assembly, an informal meeting of gentry marshals drew up a petition asking: (1) Lowering of the allotment norms set by the Editing Commissions; (2) immediate redemption of field land by means of a government financial operation; (3) immediate abolition of 'all obligatory relations between the *pomeshchik* and the peasants'; (4) reform of the local administration. This petition, signed by numerous gentry, was officially ignored by the government because of its irregular origin. *Materialy*, II, 303, 326; Kornilov, 'Krestian'skaia reforma v Kaluzhskoi gubernii', pp. 249–60; Chebaevskii, 'Nizhegorodskii gubernskii komitet 1858 g.', *Voprosy istorii*, no. 6 (1947) p. 94.

[3] Shuvalov's father had been a lieutenant of Suvorov and an adjutant to Alexander I. His brother, A. P. Shuvalov, was a noted publicist. His close relative, P. A. Shuvalov, had held numerous high posts, and after the emancipation became head of the Third Section and *Chef de Gendarmes*.

The provincial gentry assembled, 1859–60

Because of the extraordinary position and influence of the Petersburg gentry, the government, from the beginning of its reform preparations, placed much hope on their cooperation, knowing that they would be looked upon as exemplars by the gentry of other provinces. The government accordingly had arranged for the Petersburg gentry to be the first in the Russian provinces to request a rescript for the founding of a provincial committee.

From the beginning, the Petersburg gentry, while well aware of the need for peasant reform, had tended to favor an aristocratic solution to the peasant question. In practical terms, they advocated a reform based on the inventory system already existing in the nearby Baltic provinces—not a landless emancipation, but a *Bauerland* solution of controlled usage and obligations. At the time of the Rescripts, this position had more or less converged with the government's announced principle of 'permanent usage' for the peasantry and full retention of property rights for the gentry. The honeymoon with the government soon ended, however, when it became clear that the Petersburg gentry passionately opposed even the redemption of the peasant *usad'by*.

Eloquent defenders of gentry privileges, their deliberations were habitually accompanied by demands for increased political rights for the gentry and general reform of local administration 'on the English model'.[1] The Petersburg provincial committee stood for retention of the seigneurial rights of the *pomeshchiki* and general tutelage in local affairs by the gentry as a class.[2] While objecting to obligatory redemption of the peasant *usad'ba* the committee nevertheless granted a comparatively generous allotment *in usage*, for modest obligations.[3]

These views were upheld by Shuvalov as a member of the Editing Commissions.[4] As a deputy to the Editing Commissions from the Petersburg committee, Shuvalov (along with Count N. V. Levashov) sided with the majority of deputies in political

---

[1] Kornilov, 'Gubernskie komitety', no. 2, p. 220.
[2] *Ibid.*, pp. 220–1; no. 4, pp. 64–6; no. 5, p. 55.
[3] *Ibid.*, no. 4, p. 65.
[4] Semenov, *Osvobozhdenie krest'ian*, I, 257–66.

matters but spoke out against the creation of an independent peasant *volost'* and against obligatory redemption.[1]

As presiding officer in the Petersburg assembly, meeting in March 1860, Shuvalov tried to prevent disturbances, and especially to prevent the presentation of an address to the Emperor, an action which, in view of the news from other provinces, was widely anticipated. The main stimulus to anti-government demonstrations in the assembly came from the Tsarskoe Selo marshal A. P. Platonov and the conservative pamphleteer N. A. Bezobrazov, both of whom were considerably less flexible in their attitudes about gentry rights and privileges than was Shuvalov.[2]

In order to avoid the instigation of untoward incidents by the ultra-conservatives in the assembly, Shuvalov sought, and obtained in a personal audience with Alexander II, permission for the gentry to hold unofficial meetings *outside* the assembly on the subject of the peasant question.[3] When the time came for the assembly to discuss the 'needs and welfare' of the gentry (16 March), Platonov and Bezobrazov presented a lengthy memoir which was in fact a projected address. Avoiding all direct discussion of the peasant question, it followed the pattern of argument already customary with the Bezobrazovs: a pseudo-historical analysis of the origins, rights and privileges of the gentry class. Its purpose was clearly to excite the assembly into presenting an address of a completely conservative nature to the Emperor, demanding preservation of the sacred rights of the gentry.[4] A counter-project for an address was presented by A. P.

---

[1] *Materialy redaktsionnykh komissii. Prilozhenie. Otzyvy chlenov gubernskikh komitetov,* II, 311–94.

[2] Platonov had such a reputation from the Petersburg committee. Bezobrazov had incurred imperial disfavor for his part in the 'Bezobrazov address' presented in the summer of 1859.

[3] As a result of this unofficial discussion the gentry produced an amendment to the project of the Petersburg provincial committee (a unique occurrence). The amendment's main idea was the creation of a three-year period, immediately following emancipation, for the conclusion of free agreements between the *pomeshchiki* and peasants. After this period, a normal peasant allotment (of 9 *desiatiny* per *tiaglo*) was to be put into effect on those estates where agreements had not been reached. *Materialy,* II, 316–17; 447, fn.

[4] *Ibid.,* pp. 317–18. The actual author of the memoir was undoubtedly Bezobrazov.

Shuvalov, brother of the provincial marshal. This project also contained a request for the preservation of gentry rights, but a request of more moderate tone, in that it referred mainly to the gentry's rights of electing officials (it was in fact directed primarily against the proposals of the Miliutin commission), and not to the seigneurial and property rights of the gentry.[1]

The assembly debated the relative merits of both projects and finally, after much argument, approved a compromise project by a vote of 200–90 and sent it to the Emperor through the Minister of Interior. This address expressed two main ideas: (1) Objection to the Miliutin Commission's intended incursion on the gentry's right to elect administrative officials on the provincial and *uezd* levels; (2) assurance that 'the guarantee of the future well-being of all classes in the state [the gentry see] in the preservation and proper development, under the shelter of the Autocratic power, of the principles of local self-government which have existed in Russia since ancient times'.[2]

Alexander II received this address with anger, but was subsequently calmed by being assured that the gentry, in using the words 'self-government', were only expressing their desire to retain the right to elect the *zemskii ispravnik* in the *uezdy*.[3] The address was finally left without response by order of the Emperor.[4] True to their aristocratic inclinations, the Petersburg gentry had presented an address, the intent of which contrasted in striking fashion with the addresses presented by the other gentry assemblies in 1859–60. In Tver, Riazan, Iaroslavl and Vladimir the gentry had been moved to present addresses to the Emperor out of a desire to see a definitive reform legislation providing for immediate obligatory redemption and the institution of other liberal reforms, including local administration for all classes based on elective principles. In the address of the Vladimir assembly and of the provincial marshal of Iaroslavl these political demands had been spelled out in specific terms; and in Vladimir the gentry had even talked of abolishing gentry titles, and of the creation of 'one common title for all classes'.

[1] *Ibid.*, pp. 318–21.   [2] *Ibid.*, pp. 321–4. See Appendix II.
[3] *Ibid.*, pp. 324–5.   [4] Garmiza, *Podgotovka zemskoi reformy*, pp. 62–3.

The gentry versus the bureaucracy, 1858–61

In Petersburg the gentry responded in unison with their counterparts in Vladimir, Tver and elsewhere in denouncing bureaucratic arbitrariness. Beyond this point their paths diverged. Indeed the address of the Petersburg gentry was as much a rejection of the proposals of the gentry of Vladimir and other provinces as it was a response to the bureaucratic offensive. The first words of the Petersburg address strictly denounced tampering with any gentry privileges:

Your Imperial Majesty branded as 'lie and slander' rumors concerning the decline of royal trust in our estate. . . .

These words are deeply imprinted in our hearts.

They constitute our bulwark against any encroachment upon the rights and welfare of the gentry as defined by the wisdom and force of the Charter to the Gentry.[1]

With the closing of the Petersburg assembly the wave of gentry protests subsided. The government held fast to its prohibition of further gentry discussion of peasant reform: In less than six months the Editing Commissions completed their legislative projects and turned them over to the scrutiny of the Main Committee. In less than a year the projects, basically unchanged, were officially ratified by the State Council, signed by the Emperor, and the emancipation was proclaimed.

Before proceeding to some conclusions about the significance of the gentry assemblies of 1859–60 it will be necessary to consider briefly the final effort at consultation between the government and the gentry before emancipation—the second convocation of gentry deputies, which gathered in Petersburg from February to April 1860.

THE SECOND GENTRY DEPUTATION TO ST PETERSBURG,
FEBRUARY–APRIL 1860

Soon after the gentry assemblies of January, and before the convening of the Petersburg assembly, the 40 deputies from the remaining 22 provincial committees began to arrive in the

[1] *Materialy*, II, 322.

capital for consultation with the Editing Commissions.[1] The deputies were officially received by Alexander II on 21 February.[2]

The convocation of these deputies had been awaited in Petersburg with perhaps even greater apprehension than the arrival of their colleagues of the first convocation, a fact of which the deputies themselves were well aware:

The deputies of the second convocation [wrote the editors of the *Materialy*] arrived in Petersburg with perhaps even greater hostility against the Editing Commissions than their predecessors. . . . The latter had willed to them all the irritation with which they had left Petersburg after their unsuccessful efforts and the reprimands they had received. The majority of the new representatives . . . were witnesses to everything that had recently transpired in the gentry assemblies as a result of the circular of the Minister of Interior. On them lay, as it were, the obligation to take revenge against the government for all the injuries suffered by the gentry.[3]

The terms of the will left by the deputies of the first convocation were drawn up by Koshelev, who had become the prolific, though unofficial, pleader of the deputies' case against the government. In a 'letter from a deputy of the first convocation to a deputy of the second convocation'[4] Koshelev gave counsel to the new group of representatives:

Accept . . . with obedience the position which the famous instruction [of 11 August 1859] has arranged for the deputies; but in private meetings try to achieve unanimity; that is most important of all. . . . Do not digress to right or left . . ., do not stand rigidly for your personal convictions; disregard even local interests . . . You are obliged to direct and concentrate your blows on several main, most vital propositions on which the whole edifice constructed by the Editing Commissions rests.[5]

---

[1] The following committees were represented: The Vilno General Commission (with the task of drawing up a common project for the three western provinces of Vilno, Kovno and Grodno), Vologda, Ekaterinoslav, Kazan, Kaluga, Kiev General Commission (representing Kiev, Podolsk and Volynia), Kursk, Mogilev, Olonetsk, Orel, Orenburg, Penza, Perm, Samara, Smolensk, The Tauride, Tula, Kherson, and the Don Cossack lands. Semenov, *Osvobozhdenie Krest'ian*, III, pt. 1, pp. 437–8.

[2] *Materialy*, II, 428–31. [3] *Ibid.*, pp. 393–4.

[4] *Pis'mo deputata pervogo prizyva k deputatu vtorogo prizyva* (Leipzig, 1860).

[5] *Materialy*, II, 403.

According to Koshelev, these propositions were the following: (1) The proposition for 'granting *pomeshchik* lands to the peasants in permanent usage for unchangeable obligations'. This must be replaced, wrote Koshelev, by obligatory redemption of the peasant plots via a government-financed credit operation. (2) The scheme of maximum-minimum norms for establishing allotment sizes. The differences between the maximum norm and minimum norm were too great. The Commissions, moreover, had employed unreliable statistics on land-holding; and their normal figures, and the geographical divisions to which they applied were therefore arbitrary and untrustworthy. Koshelev urged the deputies to insist that a new survey of land-holdings be made *in the localities* in order to establish reasonable allotments for natural geographic units. The same applied to obligations: They had been arbitrarily set in Petersburg and must be brought into line with local differences. (3) The Editing Commissions had undertaken to undermine 'popular customs' by proposing legislation which threatened to facilitate destruction of the peasant communes.[1] The communes, argued Koshelev, must be protected 'like the apple of our eye'.[2] Their destruction promised only bureaucratic interference in the life of the people. (4) Finally, the deputies were to fight against the bureaucracy's attempt, made evident in the work of the Commissions, to exploit the reform in order to extend its power and to crush the significance of the gentry ... The deputies must unite to demand:

Presentation of the right of local self-government, representing not one, but all classes ...; responsibility of officials not to the distant government, but to the population about them as well; and the organization of public and verbal court procedure ...[3]

The deputies came near to following Koshelev's advice about the need for unanimity and concerted effort. Gathering together in specially arranged quarters, they drafted their commentaries for the Editing Commissions as if they were a legislative assembly. The commentaries by the large majority of the deputies on the

---

[1] Here Koshelev referred to the proposal giving individual peasant families the right to redeem their *usad'by* separately and allowing the exit of the peasants from the commune.
[2] *Ibid.*, p. 418.　　　　　　　　　　[3] *Ibid.*, p. 425.

several sections of the Commissions' draft project were presented in common, over the collective signatures of the deputies, instead of separately for each province as the 11 August instructions had directed. Permission for these procedures was granted by the government with the calculation that a more conciliatory policy toward these deputies than had been used toward their predecessors would prevent them from undertaking open manifestations or presenting addresses.[1]

In most other respects, however, the second convocation of deputies rejected Koshelev's counsel and departed widely from the proposals of their predecessors. The most striking point of difference between the deputies of the second convocation and their predecessors was the former's nearly unanimous rejection of obligatory land-redemption. They joined with the deputies of the first convocation in rejecting the 'permanent usage' principle which had been adopted by the government,[2] but their alternative was not the one urged on them by Koshelev. Their preference they described in the following way:

The principle of voluntary agreement, divorced from any obligatory decrees and based on the mutual relation between supply and demand, presents, without any doubt, the best means for the solution of all economic questions in general.[3]

In short, the deputies frankly proposed that the land question be solved by 'voluntary agreement' between *pomeshchiki* and peasants, or what Lanskoi, in his August 1859, memoir, labelled 'landless emancipation':

Renouncing their feudal rights [declared the deputies] the gentry do not consider it possible to take upon themselves beyond that any kind of sacrifices in land.[4]

The deputies proposed that the announcement of emancipation should be followed by a three-year preparatory period, during

[1] *Ibid.*, pp. 394–5.
[2] 'We cannot in any circumstances [declared the commentary of 32 deputies on the propositions of the economic department of the Commissions] recognize as just the permanent right of usage by free peasants of the *pomeshchik*'s landed property without the consent of the owner.' *Materialy redaktsionnykh komissii. Prilozhenie. Otzyvy chlenov gubernskikh komitetov*, III, book 2, p. 66.
[3] *Ibid.*, IV, book 2, pp. 3–4.   [4] Semenov, *Osvobozhdenie krest'ian*, III, part 1, p. 483.

which peasant obligations were to be limited by law and peasants and *pomeshchiki* were to have the right to enter into voluntary agreements concerning the quantity of land to be granted the peasants in use or for redemption and the obligations to be paid. The government was to provide the credit machinery for effecting redemption in case of mutual agreement.[1] Redemption was to be founded on the 'real value of the land' (that is, on land-sale values or average *obrok* rates). At the end of the three-year period, on those estates where voluntary arrangements had not been reached or where the *pomeshchiki* were unwilling to accept redemption on terms established by the government, the peasants were to be given the right to move to state lands or to private lands where voluntary arrangements could be made.[2]

Thus the deputies, using the same argument of the superiority of hired labor and capitalist production as their colleagues of the first convocation, rejected the solutions proposed by the Editing Commissions and their predecessors alike. The former, they argued, promised only a continuation of obligatory relations and an extension of bureaucratic control. The latter was inimical to free relations and the principle of private property.

Anticipating the objection that *their* solution threatened undue exploitation of the peasants by the *pomeshchiki* and the creation of a landless proletariat, the deputies replied that the free market would prevent such developments: The *pomeshchik* would be forced to offer his peasants favorable conditions in order to keep them from leaving the estate. Far from expanding the size of his own tillage after emancipation, the need for greater capital investment in his own operation (for hired labor, machinery, etc.) would force the *pomeshchik* to decrease it.[3]

The deputies' proposals on administrative questions also departed significantly from those of their predecessors, and especially from the Slavophile inclinations of Koshelev. Far from defending

[1] *Ibid.*, p. 488. The deputies also proposed the creation of local banks or credit institutions in each province for facilitating redemption.
[2] *Ibid.*, pp. 486–8. These proposals bore a close resemblance to the special project drawn up by the Petersburg gentry assembly at about the same time (see above, p. 296 fn.) and may have been modelled upon that project. Cf. *Materialy*, II, 434–5.
[3] Semenov, *Osvobozhdenie krest'ian*, III, part 1, p. 484.

the peasant commune from the designs of the Editing Commissions as Koshelev had urged, they predicted and approved its extinction. 'Communal use of the land', they declared, 'is not in the nature of the peasants. An aspiration toward individualistic farming [*fermerstvo*] is noticeable among them.'[1] After emancipation, they predicted, communal use of the land would not long survive, for the peasants who had not bought land would be transformed from bound laborers [*tiaglovye*] into free renters of land.[2] This development they fully approved: ' . . . The right of exit from the commune [read the commentary of 36 deputies] should, as far as possible, be facilitated, and the power exercised by the *mir* should be significantly diminished.'[3] Here, as elsewhere in the deputies' statement, there spoke the voice of doctrinaire *laissez-faire*, of capitalist relations in agriculture. It is once again made clear that capitalist, or 'bourgeois', interests cannot simply be equated with the liberal program and its upholders. To be sure, many defenders of the liberal solution would have accepted, in principle, these statements about the commune, for they were concerned with it only as a practical device for the maintenance of social and fiscal control over the peasants. This concern was apparently absent from the thoughts of the authors of the second deputation's statement.

For all their insistence on free relations between *pomeshchiki* and peasants, however, the deputies demanded that the *pomeshchiki* should be made heads of the peasant *volosti*. This was, they affirmed, the only solution to the problem created by the immaturity of the peasants and the threat of extensive bureaucratic interference in local affairs. For the same reasons, they declared, the gentry should be given 'direct participation in local administration'.[4]

Such were the main arguments of the deputies of the second convocation. Advocates among them of the solution proposed by the deputies of the first convocation were very few. The most outstanding of these was Prince A. V. Obolenskii, deputy from

---

[1] *Materialy redaktsionnykh komissii. Prilozhenie. Otzyvy chlenov gubernskikh komitetov*, III, book 1, p. 243.

[2] *Ibid.*, book 2, p. 84. [3] *Ibid.*, book 1, p. 187. [4] *Ibid.*, pp. 184–7.

the minority of the Kaluga committee which had produced a project based on the proposals of the Tver committee.[1] In Petersburg Obolenskii continued to advocate obligatory redemption, creation of an all-class *volost'* administration and other proposals made by the first convocation. In his commentaries Obolenskii announced his complete agreement with the opinions expressed by Unkovskii.[2]

In mid-April the deputies left the capital, leaving behind them a 'concluding statement' (signed by 36 of the 40 deputies) which reiterated their objections to the Commissions' proposals and their advocacy of 'voluntary arrangements'. Unlike their predecessors, they departed without having presented any addresses; nor had they demanded either general reforms or the summoning of gentry representatives for the final codification of the legislation. The implications of their opinions were, therefore, considerably less radical than those of their predecessors, in spite of their rejection of many of the proposals of the Editing Commissions. Politically they had presented few threats to the government, whose conciliatory policy toward them thus seemed justified.

What was responsible for the considerable divergence of opinions between the first and second groups of gentry deputies in Petersburg? To a considerable extent the differences between them seem to have been related to their origins: The majority of provincial committees which had earlier shown preference for obligatory redemption and expansion of local self-government on an all-class basis had been represented in the first convocation. In the second convocation such committees were represented only by the deputies from Kaluga and the minority representative from Samara. The majority of the deputies in the second convocation represented some of the most fertile grain-producing areas in the Empire: Ekaterinoslav, Kherson, The Tauride; and other black soil provinces: Kazan, Kursk, Penza, Samara, Tula

---

[1] See above, chapter 5, pp. 152–8.
[2] *Ibid.*, p. 133; book 2, pp. 131–2; IV, book 1, pp. 49–63. Obolenskii was followed, at least in his advocacy of obligatory redemption, by I. A. Pushkin, deputy from Tula (minority), and by the deputies from Kherson province, Kasinov and Sokolov-Borodnin. Cf. *ibid.*, III, book 2, pp. 115–20, 395.

and Orel. The remaining provinces represented were not of the non-black soil *obrok* regions (with the exception of Kaluga), but outlying areas of the Empire and non-Russian regions: the western provinces, the Ukraine, Vologda, Perm, Orenberg and the Don Cossack lands.

Forceful representatives of the liberal solution to the peasant question were almost totally lacking in the second convocation (Obolenskii and Samarin were the only representatives of this orientation), and leadership of the collective efforts of the second convocation was largely in the hands of representatives of the grain-producing and *barshchina* provinces: Miklashevskii from Ekaterinoslav, Khvostov from Orel, and Ivanov from Smolensk.[1]

The particular interests of the gentry of the fertile, *barshchina* provinces were revealed in many of the commentaries made by the deputation, most especially in their unwillingness to lose field land irretrievably to the peasants. Their emphasis on the free market and hired labor, their scorn for the peasant commune, seem to have reflected the interests of *pomeshchiki* who envisaged capitalist agricultural production for the market as an easily realizable goal. Their lack of interest in the commune as a device for ensuring the proper acquittal of peasant obligations,[2] their failure to specifically demand remuneration for peasant labor, even their relative disregard of the problem of existing gentry debts,[3] seem to reflect the interests of solvent *pomeshchiki* of fertile *barshchina* areas.

Just as with the first gentry deputation, however, the position taken by the deputies of the second convocation was not influenced alone by their origins and general views. The second deputation affords yet another proof that gentry attitudes toward

---

[1] *Materialy*, II, 427-8.

[2] The deputies' proposal that the *pomeshchiki* be made heads of the peasant *volosti* was of course born of the intention that the gentry should retain general authority in the countryside; but it does not reflect that direct concern about the fulfilment of peasant obligations which was mainly responsible for the advocating of strict retention of the commune by the deputies of the first convocation.

[3] These deputies proposed that upon redemption all gentry debts on their estates should be collected by the state immediately out of the redemption sum. This practice (which was in fact put into effect by the final legislation) was widely criticized among the gentry because it often left the owners of heavily-indebted estates without any operating capital. Semenov, *Osvobozhdenie krest'ian*, III, part I, p. 488; II, 85, 921-7.

the solution of the 'peasant question' can be properly understood only by approaching them dynamically, that is, within the context of ongoing events and, in particular, within the framework of government-gentry relations in the preparation of the reform. Attention must be directed to the circumstances in which the second convocation of deputies met.

The arrival of the deputies in Petersburg coincided with a crisis in the government's handling of the reform preparations which had been precipitated by the death of Rostovtsev, chairman of the Editing Commissions, on 6 February 1860.[1] Rostovtsev's death inevitably created a crisis in the government's reform plans, because the very principles of reform had until then depended on an understanding between Rostovtsev and Alexander II: They had been elaborated by Rostovtsev in his letters of the summer of 1858, and their pursuit in the Editing Commissions had been assured by putting that body under Rostovtsev's complete discretionary control and by making Rostovtsev responsible to the Emperor alone. In other words, the chairmanship of the Editing Commissions was the seat of policy control and the only formal link between the machinery of policy implementation and the supreme authority.

The appointment of the Minister of Justice, Count V. N. Panin, as Rostovtsev's successor seemed to indicate a new departure. Panin was a notorious reactionary, and had been one of the

[1] Rostovstev, who had been the main target of the gentry's rage against the Editing Commissions, had fallen ill in October 1859. His illness, a carbuncular infection of the neck that became gangrenous, may have been provoked by the pressures exerted on him by the confrontation of the deputies of the first convocation with the Commissions. From mid-October, Rostovtsev had to absent himself from the Commissions. Although he returned for a brief time in November (and continued to control the Commissions from his sick-bed) his condition soon worsened.

It was ironical that Rostovtsev should have had to bear the brunt of gentry antagonism against the bureaucracy. Caught in the middle of this struggle, Rostovtsev had from the beginning been conciliatory toward the gentry position, and had awaited the arrival of the deputies with optimism. Even after the conflicts began, Rostovtsev retained a higher, and more accurate, opinion of the deputies of the first convocation than did Lanskoi and Miliutin. The majority of these deputies, he wrote to the Emperor on 23 October 1859, wanted either immediate obligatory redemption and a quick separation of the gentry and peasants, or the same via gradual and voluntary redemption. These deputies, he declared, 'are in agreement with the Imperially sanctioned main principles and sincerely wish full emancipation of the peasants.' (Semenov, *Osvobozhdenie krest'ian*, II, 928–30.)

opponents of the progressive bureaucrats in the Main Committee. His appointment was universally assessed by contemporary observers as a reactionary move, possibly a decision on the part of Alexander II to abandon the principles of reform followed until then by the Editing Commissions.[1] This impression, current in Petersburg following the appointment of Panin, encouraged the deputies of the second convocation to challenge the proposals of the Editing Commissions, from which it seemed likely that authority would be withdrawn.

Specifically, the new lack of certainty about the government's intentions encouraged the majority of these deputies to follow their inclinations as black soil *pomeshchiki* in objecting to any compulsory alienation of their lands—either for 'permanent usage' as the Commissions proposed, or for obligatory redemption as their gentry predecessors had demanded. Evidence that the deputies' departure from the position occupied by their predecessors on the crucial land question was directly related to this situation is the fact that when the deputies first arrived in Petersburg—before the appointment of Panin—a majority of them (27) explicitly favored obligatory redemption. Only later did they abandon their advocacy of redemption, 'as a result [the editors of the *Materialy* affirmed] of the rumors current in March about the closing of the Editing Commissions and the alleged change of the Emperor's views on the peasant question'.[2]

Thus, the views of the deputies of the second convocation on the land question further attest to the truth of the observation made in the preceding chapter: Gentry advocacy of obligatory redemption bore a direct relation to the government's position. As it became ever clearer in the course of 1858–9 that the government was intent on freeing the peasants *with land*, gentry advocacy

---

[1] A detailed account of the reaction to Panin's appointment in various circles can be found in Barsukov, *Zhizn' i trudy Pogodina*, XXVII, 161–82. It was the progressive bureaucrats who were especially shocked by Panin's appointment: Miliutin prepared to resign, and was apparently restrained from doing so only by Lanskoi, who confided to him that Panin had been appointed 'à la condition de ne rien changer à la marche des affaires ni au personnel'. (Leroy-Beaulieu, *Un homme d'état*, p. 55, fn.) Herzen, in *Kolokol*, called the appointment 'a premeditated humiliation of public opinion and a victory for the planters' party', and called upon the members of the Commissions to resign at once, (*Kolokol*, no. 65, 15 March 1860.)

[2] *Materialy*, II, 427–8.

20-2

of obligatory redemption of the peasant lands (preferable to 'permanent usage' for all the reasons pointed to by Unkovskii and others) rapidly grew. The temporary confusion about the government's aims that was created by the death of Rostovtsev and the appointment of Panin provoked the deputies of the second convocation to beat a fast retreat on this issue *when it seemed possible that the government might change its policy on this question.*

The fears, and expectations, were not justified. Although it was not generally known at the time, Alexander II had appointed Panin with the explicit understanding that he would make no changes in the membership of the Commissions and would not interfere with the majority opinion there.[1] He was also made to promise strict adherence to the principles established for the Editing Commissions as reaffirmed in a final memoir written by Rostovtsev not long before his death.[2]

Panin's appointment was one more example of the kind of conciliatory policy that Alexander II had been pursuing all along in the preparation of the emancipation—the policy which had led to the foundation of the secret committee while maintaining the initiative in the reform elsewhere, and later to the creation of the Editing Commissions under Rostovtsev. The task at hand was to find someone who could preside over the completion of the work of the Commissions—already finished in rough fashion—and to guide their projects through review by the Main Committee in the face of opposition from Ministers, court dignitaries, Petersburg aristocrats, the deputies of the second convocation and the gentry in general.[3] Alexander II (who alone made the decision) saw in Panin the best possible choice: He was at once a well-

---

[1] Semenov, *Osvobozhdenie krest'ian*, II, 634–5.

[2] *Ibid.*, p. 694. (For the text of the memoir, which also included the latest plans for implementing emancipation and outlined the tasks remaining for the Commissions, see *ibid.*, pp. 968–73.)

Even many years afterward, the first historian of the emancipation, Ivaniukov, thought that the nomination of Panin represented a profound shift toward reaction by the government, and that the reform was carried out only because the preparations had gone too far and had been too well publicized to be discarded. (*Padenie krepostnogo prava*, pp. 373–5.) Events were put in their proper perspective only when Semenov published the details of Panin's appointment (in volume II of his *Osvobozhdenie krest'ian*).

[3] Semenov, *Osvobozhdenie krest'ian*, II, 629–35.

known conservative Minister, a great aristocrat, a wealthy *pomeshchik* (owning more than 20,000 souls in various provinces), and a man who could be counted on to sacrifice his personal convictions to the will of the Emperor.[1] His appointment, in short, would allow the continued pursuit of the original course of reform while serving to mollify conservative opinion, especially influential aristocratic opinion in Petersburg. More generally, it was designed (in the words of one contemporary) as 'a warranty to the landowners that their interests would be observed'.[2] The extent to which Panin's appointment served to mollify conservative opinion is problematical; it is a fact that Panin did not seriously interfere with the completion of the reform legislation as scheduled and in accordance with the established principles.[3]

CONCLUSION TO PART THREE

The activities of the Russian gentry in 1859–60, described in some detail in this and the preceding chapter, constituted an unprecedented development in the history of that class and, indeed, in the history of the modern Russian state—the transformation of the previously lifeless formal class organization of the gentry into a vehicle for the expression of the independent interests of an important segment of Russian society; and, at the same time, the crystallization of a critically-minded body of public opinion founded upon a concrete social base.

As remarked in Chapter 1, the Russian gentry, prior to the reign of Alexander II, had exercised virtually no authority in the political life of the country through their provincial class organization. Their activities had been restricted to self-administration, as a class, and to a begrudging role in the general administration of the provinces and the *uezdy*. The transformation began with the invitation to the gentry to participate in the discussion of peasant

---

[1] *Ibid.*   [2] Barsukov, *Zhizn' i trudy Pogodina*, XVII, 176.

[3] There were some changes made in the peasant statutes while Panin was chairman, including some changes in allotment and obligation norms and a provision for revising peasant obligations at the end of twenty years, but all these measures (which were concessions to complaints by the gentry deputies) were independently introduced by the departments of the Commissions and were approved by a majority of the Commissions' members. Semenov, *Osvobozhdenie krest'ian*, II, 705; III, part 2, pp. 629–32.

reform in 1857—which immediately revived, or, more correctly, instilled life into the gentry institutions—and culminated in the assemblies of 1859–60, when the gentry turned to the central government with demands for administrative and political reforms.

The summons to form provincial committees was the first occasion since the organization of the gentry into provincial estates on which they had been called upon to discuss questions of national significance. It was also Russia's 'first experience in more or less public discussion, by elected bodies, of social and state questions'.[1] From the beginning of this discussion, the gentry understood that the peasant problem concerned not only their material welfare, but their political and social status, and the general political, social and administrative structure of the state as well. Thus the gentry, once called upon to consider peasant reform, proceeded swiftly to consideration of far broader questions concerning the future of the gentry as a class and, indeed, the general political, social and administrative order in the country.

The government, however, in creating the provincial committees, sought essentially only approbation from the gentry for its emancipation plans. It was this motive, and to some extent the need to rely on the gentry for information about rural conditions, which had impelled the government to turn to the gentry. But the government refused to give the gentry the authority they sought in deciding the peasant question—in part out of a reasonable apprehension that acceptance of the gentry's proposals for emancipation would be disastrous for the peasantry (and thus for the economic and political stability of the state); and in part out of that hesitancy, characteristic of bureaucratic polities, to foster any independent action by 'society'.[2]

This authority was variously understood among the gentry: To many it meant the plain authority for the provincial com-

[1] Solov'ev, 'Zapiski', XXXIII, 245.
[2] For a stimulating discussion of relations between state and society in bureaucratic polities (with relevance to nineteenth-century Russia, although evidence is taken mainly from pre-modern systems), see S. N. Eisenstadt, 'Political Struggle in Bureaucratic Societies', *World Politics*, IX, no. 1 (1956), 15–36.

mittees to draw up the terms of emancipation for their provinces with only a minimal amount of 'editing' by the central government. To others the need for general legislation, which would not be simply a legislative *collage* of the gentry projects, was clear. (Nevertheless, even the most liberal of gentry representatives, while disclaiming that the gentry alone should decide the reform, did expect and demand that they at least be entrusted to decide the basic questions of land and obligation norms for the peasantry.) In the end, the solid rock of contention between the government and the gentry was the question of a land settlement for the peasants. The two poles of gentry opinion—the one advocating 'voluntary arrangements', the other obligatory redemption— equally rejected the 'permanent usage' doctrine of the Editing Commissions. In addition to the question about the character of the land settlement, the quantitative question was also of great importance: The gentry representatives—the provincial committees and the deputies to Petersburg—almost unanimously proposed significant reductions in the size of the existing peasant allotments (whose retention was defended in principle in the Commissions), or otherwise disputed the norms of allotments and obligations established by the government. This fact provided the ultimate rationale to the progressive bureaucrats in the Editing Commissions for rejecting decisive participation by the gentry in the preparation of peasant reform.

In practice, the government's rejection of the gentry was a gradual process, which took the form of a step-by-step limitation of gentry initiative, beginning with the program of April 1858, proceeding to the strict delimitation of the duties of the gentry deputies in Petersburg, and culminating in the outright prohibition of further gentry discussion of the peasant reform in November 1859.

As the government's refinement of its reform plans progressed, its tolerance of public discussion of these plans decreased in a direct ratio. The gentry, however, refused to accommodate themselves to the whim of the central government. Indeed, as emancipation evolved from a subject of general discussion to one of imminent realization, gentry demand for substantive participation in the reform preparations and for consideration of further reforms—particularly administrative reforms—grew in inverse proportion to the government's efforts to restrict gentry initiative. When it was discovered that the government intended to retain a monopoly on the consideration of further administrative reforms and was, moreover, planning legislation designed to replace the administrative authority of the gentry in local affairs by a system of officials directly controlled by the provincial bureaucracy, virtually all articulate members of the landed gentry went into opposition. The bureaucracy, they claimed, was exploiting the peasant reform in order to extend its authority into all levels of Russian life.

The gentry opposition developed political demands to counter the expansion of this bureaucratic absolutism. They demanded (to use a phrase current at that time) 'political privileges in return for the gentry's loss of seigneurial privileges'. The gentry opposition produced essentially two alternatives to the expansion of bureaucratic authority: An 'aristocratic' alternative, and a liberal alternative.

The 'aristocratic' alternative demanded enfranchisement of the gentry alone. The gentry were to retain their traditional position as a privileged class. The gentry were not to be forceably deprived of their lands; the land question was to be solved by 'voluntary agreement'. (Some advocates of the aristocratic position maintained that even after emancipation only the gentry should have the right to own populated lands.) The aristocratic political alternative to bureaucratism contained two primary elements: the organization of local self-government in the hands of the landed gentry, with retention of considerable authority over the peasantry; and promulgation of an 'aristocratic constitution'—that is, the introduction of gentry representatives into the central governmental apparatus.

The aristocratic response to the crisis created by the imminence of emancipation and the threat of bureaucratic absolutism advocated the 'restoration' of something that had never existed in Russia: It stood in defense of 'historic' gentry rights and privileges, and demanded the 'revitalization' of the political role of the gentry in the life of the state which, formerly effective, had been undermined (so declared Bezobrazov, Orlov-Davydov and other ideologues of the aristocratic party) by the overweening bureaucracy.

The political program of the gentry liberals—who proposed obligatory redemption as the solution of the peasant problem— remained, up to the time of the emancipation, essentially that which had been formulated by the Tver gentry and by the 'address of five deputies' in Petersburg: Separation of powers; local, elective self government common for all classes; and judicial reform, including the responsibility of officials before the courts. While recognizing the necessity of granting the gentry a position of influence in local government, the gentry liberals on the whole called for termination of the gentry's privileged status and the creation of a legally unified citizenry, in which property qualifications would become the sole index of political responsibility. They did not propose limitation of the autocracy, 'constitution', or other fundamental changes in the central state structure.

The gentry liberals chose the path of the *Rechtsstaat* and the liberal reforms which had been pursued, in Western Europe and England, primarily by the commercial and industrial bourgeoisie. It has often been remarked that liberalism, despite its traditional association with the struggle of the bourgeoisie against feudal privilege, has on numerous occasions in European history been taken up by the nobility in its struggle against its traditional enemy, bureaucratic absolutism. The history of Russia in the reform period appears to confirm this generalization. The gentry liberals repeated time and again that the retention of feudal estates and privileges could lead only to the atomization of Russian society and thus to the perpetuation of bureaucratic domination.

The liberal gentry opposition movement was born of the conflict between the gentry deputies and the Editing Commissions in 1859. Before that time the most vocal and—from the government's point of view—the most dangerous opposition to the government's reform plans had come from conservative, mainly aristocratic, opponents of emancipation. Sincere gentry proponents of emancipation, for the most part, had reserved strong criticism of the government's actions, from the conviction that it was, after all, headed in the right direction and had to be defended against attack from the enemies of emancipation both within and outside the government.

In the first deputation to Petersburg, the deputies experienced a profound disenchantment with the government's intentions—both in relation to the immediate question of emancipation and the more general questions involving the future political and administrative structure of the state. The deputies then undertook an attack against the imperial bureaucracy. Following the dismissal of the gentry deputation, the opposition was carried into the provinces to the gentry assemblies, meeting in the winter of 1859–60—in some cases directly, by deputies returning from the capital.

Seething with feelings of class-humiliation and rage against the bureaucracy, the assemblies, for the first time since their creation, took on the attributes of the 'estates' after which they had been modelled. They gave voice to the opposition mood of the gentry. The assemblies most actively inclined toward opposition—Tver, Riazan, Iaroslavl and Vladimir—endorsed the liberal program: They called for immediate obligatory redemption, termination of compulsory relations between the classes, and the other reforms already enumerated in the 'address of five deputies'. The address of the Vladimir gentry was the first formal adoption of the liberal program by the gentry of an entire province, and the first presentation by a gentry assembly of the political program of gentry liberalism to the central government.

Unkovskii and others, in provincial committees and elsewhere, had argued the advantages of the liberal program from the beginning. It took the confrontation of the gentry deputies with the bureaucracy in 1859, however, to open the eyes of many gentry to these lessons. The extent to which they were learned was revealed by the commentaries of these deputies and by the assemblies of 1859–60. The most important causes of the growing gentry acceptance of the liberal program for emancipation were two: (1) Gradual realization by ever larger numbers of *pomesh-chiki* in 1858–9 that the government fully intended to realize its goal of emancipation of the peasants with land; and (2) growing understanding among the gentry that the *pomeshchiki*, unless they abandoned their claims to all the land and exclusive privileges, were inviting fatal interference of the bureaucracy in local affairs.

The liberal call for obligatory redemption, though it won many adherents, was never accepted in the years before emancipation by a majority of the gentry; and its fortunes continued to depend, to a considerable extent throughout this period, on the government's intentions: This was shown by the second deputation of gentry representatives to Petersburg, whose rejection of the liberal solution was prompted primarily by the belief that the government was about to renounce its intention of emancipating the peasants with land. For the majority of gentry, perhaps, the proposal of obligatory land redemption was attractive only as an alternative preferable to the 'permanent usage' solution espoused by the Editing Commissions.

The projects for political reform put forth by aristocrats and liberals alike had their antecedents. The 'aristocratic-constitutionalist', or *Ständestaat*, position can be traced back to the equally Anglophile 'senatorial party' of the early reign of Alexander I, and perhaps even to aristocratic groups in the reign of Catherine II —as the response of certain educated and politically important gentry to the growth of bureaucratic absolutism. The liberal response, on the other hand and perhaps paradoxically, owed a considerable debt to what has been called the 'bureaucratic approach' to Russia's political problems[1]—a rationalist belief, engendered by the Enlightenment, in the progressive possibilities of the unlimited autocracy. This tradition can be traced directly to the activities of Michael Speranskii, the great reforming bureaucrat of the reign of Alexander I.

The apparent paradox arises, of course, from the fact that the

---

[1] M. Raeff (ed.), *Plans for Political Reform in Imperial Russia, 1730–1905* (Englewood Cliffs, N.J., 1966), Editor's Introduction, p. 29.

main enemies of the liberal gentry were just those progressive bureaucrats (of whom Nicholas Miliutin was the outstanding example) who were certainly the direct heirs of Speranskii. The fact remains that the gentry liberals, like the progressive bureaucrats, were suspicious of the 'reactionary' proposals of the aristocrats, and continued to display a considerable faith in the reforming potential of the autocracy. (One may recall Chicherin's comments, cited in Chapter 2, about the role of the state in progressive change, as an example of this point of view.) It was to become clear, in the succeeding few years (as will be seen in the remaining chapters of this book), that this faith was then in the process of disintegration—precisely because of the experience with the government in the reform period—but the debt to the tradition of progressive bureaucratism remained great until this time among the liberal gentry, and that was the reason why they made no effort, before 1861, to introduce formal limitations on the autocracy.[1]

The political dichotomy within the gentry indicated by the 'aristocratic' and liberal proposals was, in some respects, a superficial one: Both represented attempts to make of Russia a state ruled by law, within the context of the autocracy. Both represented, in other words, responses to bureaucratic arbitrariness produced by articulate and increasingly 'independent' members of Russian society—the one by calling for the formulation of the rights and privileges of the various 'estates' (with emphasis, of course, on the first estate), and the other by calling for structural and operational changes in the administrative machinery as such.

Both solutions proposed by the gentry were based upon preservation of the autocracy, while being directed against its 'bureaucratization', and both thus approached the solution to the political problem in terms of the necessity of a 'union of tsar and people', that traditional theme in Russian political history since the Time of Troubles at the beginning of the

---

[1] By far the best analysis, although extremely brief, of the political currents of this period is P. N. Miliukov's: *Russia and its Crisis* (Chicago and London, 1906), ch. 5. See also Raeff, *Plans*, pp. 26–30.

seventeenth century: 'The tsar is good, but his advisors are bad', or, in the modern context, 'The Emperor is prevented from exercising his autocratic authority for the national weal by the bureaucracy, which is corrupt and ruled by its urge for self-aggrandisement.' It was the importance of this concept for the gentry which had made the prohibition on discussion of the peasant question by the gentry assemblies appear to be a major attack on the one formal channel of contact between 'tsar and people' that existed—the right of petition by the gentry directly to the autocrat. All concurred in condemning this action. The aristocratic party proposed to rectify the situation by introducing permanent gentry council into the framework of the central government; the liberals had no such conciliar plan, insisting only on the legal limitation of bureaucratic arbitrariness.

In short, in nineteenth century Russia, as in other centralized bureaucratic societies, there were political issues that cut across social and economic lines to unite the gentry and, indeed, Russian 'society' in general. Among these were those *desiderata* usually identified, in the European political tradition, with *Rechtsstaat* liberalism. As formulated by S. N. Eisenstadt, these included attempts to legalize:

(a) autonomy [that is, the right to be 'left alone' or to achieve some limited measure of autonomous participation in political life]; (b) more general legal rights, *e.g.*, due process of law, non-violation of property, etc; (c) autonomy of independent legal bodies and courts of law; and (d) general, 'universal' human or political rights.[1]

By the 1850s, especially after the experience of the regime of Nicholas I, there had developed in Russian society a general desire for the affirmation of these rights.

Following emancipation, officially proclaimed on 19 February 1861, the gentry opposition movement did not die, but entered a new stage of development in which demands for political and

[1] *The Political System of Empires* (New York 1963), p. 213. Or, in Miliukov's words: 'Autonomy, self-government, publicity, an effective control of society over bureaucracy—such was at that time the general cry of public opinion', *Russia and its Crisis*, p. 265.

administrative reforms—before emancipation necessarily auxiliary to the peasant question—became predominant. The gentry opposition movement in this period was concentrated in the provincial gentry assemblies, and is the central subject of the remaining chapters.

PART IV

THE GENTRY
AFTER EMANCIPATION, 1861–5

Assuming even the full preparedness of the government to promulgate reforms, the gentry are deeply convinced that the government is not capable of realizing them. The free institutions to which these reforms lead can come only from the people and otherwise will be merely a dead-letter and will place society in an even more strained position.

Therefore the gentry do not turn to the government with a request for the carrying out of these reforms, but recognizing its failure in this matter, restrict themselves to indicating that path onto which [the government] must venture for the salvation of itself and of society. This path is the gathering of representatives from the entire people without distinction as to class.

Protocol of the Tver Provincial
Assembly, 2 February 1862

8

Promulgation of Emancipation and the Tver Gentry in 1861-2

PROMULGATION OF EMANCIPATION AND THE PEASANTS' RESPONSE

With the closing of the Editing Commissions on 10 November 1860, their legislative drafts were turned over to the Main Committee, where they were approved without major changes,[1] and passed on to the State Council on 14 January 1861. There the project, to which a majority of the Council proved hostile, was pushed through under the personal chairmanship of Alexander II, after only one significant change—the introduction of the so-called 'Gagarin' or 'beggar's' allotment. (According to this provision a peasant could, with permission of the *pomeshchik*, choose to receive without obligation an allotment one-fourth the size of the official norm.)[2] The State Council concluded discussion of the project on 17 February 1861, and on 19 February (the anniversary of his coronation) it was signed into law by Alexander II.

According to the emancipation legislation (which in form and content constituted the projects of the several departments of the Editing Commissions), the landlords' peasants were freed, with their *usad'by* and with allotments of field land left in 'permanent usage'. Freed in their communities, their obligations (both for the

---

[1] The Grand Duke Konstantin, appointed chairman for that specific task, gathered a majority in the Main Committee in favor of the Commissions' projects, at the price of some juggling of allotment and obligation figures in favor of the *pomeshchiki* of certain regions. The conservative members Murav'ev and Dolgorukov remained adamantly opposed to the project to the end, and had ready a counter-project based on the 'inventories' system (written by P. A. Valuev, soon to be Minister of Interior and at that time serving under Murav'ev in the Ministry of State Properties.) A. Popel'nitskii, 'Delo osvobozhdeniia krest'ian v Gosudarstvennom Sovete 28 ianvaria–17 fevralia, 1861 g. Istoricheskaia spravka po neizdannym istochnikam', *Russkaia mysl'.*, no. 2 (1911), p. 140.
[2] *Ibid.*, pp. 135–7.

321

land and for other responsibilities, such as general taxes and recruitment) were guaranteed by the mutual responsibility (*krugovaia poruka*) of all the peasants in one community. The *pomeshchik* was deprived of direct authority over the peasants, and, as the gentry deputies to Petersburg had feared, was entirely isolated from the peasants administratively: The *volost'*, constituting several communities (from 300–2,000 souls) was created as the basic administrative organization of strictly peasant self-government. And the peasants were subjected to the authority of the government-appointed peace mediators (*mirovye posredniki*), who exercised wide powers, both defined and *ad hoc*, over the organs of peasant administration; and to other government officials.[1]

Full entrance into the 'temporary-obligatory' status provided by the legislation was to be preceded by two preliminary stages: For two years after the Emancipation Proclamation, the peasants were to remain essentially under the old order, until land charters (*ustavnye gramoty*) could be drawn up on each estate according to the established rules. And, until nine years after emancipation (1870), the peasants were to be obliged to remain on their allotments, paying *obrok* or *barshchina* for their use (unless redemption arrangements had been concluded in the meantime).

Land-redemption, which was to be the only exit for most peasants from the temporary-obligatory status, was given no time-limit in the original legislation. Redemption was voluntary for the *pomeshchik*, but obligatory for the peasants if the *pomeshchik* opted for it. Redemption was guaranteed by the state, which upon the conclusion of redemption agreements, was to pay 80 percent of the capital value of the redeemed allotments (75 percent for less than maximum allotments) to the *pomeshchiki* in interest-bearing bonds and credit paper.[2] The peasants were to pay the remainder directly to the *pomeshchik* by private agreement, *if re-*

---

[1] Only those aspects of the legislation which have direct relevance to the present discussion are mentioned here. For a detailed description of the legislation, in English, see Liashchenko, *History of the National Economy*, pp. 376–402.

[2] About one-third of this sum was to be paid to the *pomeshchiki* in 'five-percent state bank bonds', immediately exchangeable for cash upon demand. The remainder was to be paid in 'redemption certificates' (also interest-bearing), which were to be replaced by the bonds gradually over a fifteen-year period.

demption had been agreed to by the peasants. If not, the *pomeshchik* had to be content with the part provided by the government: the remainder could not be exacted from the peasants. They were to redeem their allotments with payments to the state extended over a period of forty-nine years.

This was the manner in which the government intended to sever the ties of personal servitude and to set out on the path toward eventual creation of a landowning peasantry without overstraining state finances or disturbing social tranquillity, and at the same time providing for the gentry.

The response of the peasants to the emancipation is a vast and complex subject lying beyond the necessary confines of this study.[1] A few comments about the immediate reaction by the peasants to the Emancipation Proclamation—publicized throughout Russia in the first weeks of March 1861—are nevertheless indispensable.

Unlike the gentry, the peasants had not been prepared in any way by the government for the reform. Expectation of liberation had been, however, everywhere in evidence among the peasantry: Rumors of liberation had figured importantly in peasant disorders throughout the second quarter of the century, and had become extremely widespread during and immediately after the Crimean War.[2] After the public announcement of the government's intention to abolish serfdom, the imminence of liberation was generally expected among the peasants, and, indeed, the notion that it had already been proclaimed by the Emperor but was being withheld by the *pomeshchiki* and *chinovniki* was widely subscribed to.

With at least some regard for the dangers involved in generalizing about the thoughts of 22 million individuals, there is little reason to doubt that most peasants anticipated that emancipation

---

[1] See the author's 'The Peasant and the Emancipation', in Vucinich (ed.), *The peasant in 19th Century Russia*, where an attempt has been made to describe the general characteristics and dynamics of this process.

[2] There is little doubt but that these rumors had their origin in the government's efforts at piecemeal emancipation, begun under Alexander I, and in the continuing 'secret' discussion of peasant reform during the reign of Nicholas I. The Crimean War was productive of innumerable rumors about the possibility of gaining liberation through volunteering for service in the army or navy; and immediately after the war rumors that freedom could be gained by migrating to the devastated Crimea were very widespread and produced many peasant run-aways.

would give them all the land, free of any charges or obligations, and would bring an end to all responsibilities, not only toward the *pomeshchiki*, but toward the state as well.[1] The gap between peasant expectations and the terms of emancipation (as described very generally, and confusingly, in the manifesto read to the peasants by their parish priests) was, therefore, abysmal. For the individual peasant, it must have seemed that little, if anything, had changed: He remained tied to the land and the commune, and was told he would have to go on paying *obrok* or *barshchina* obligations, as well as fulfilling other responsibilities, and in about the same quantities. Moreover, he was told that things were to remain as before for two more years; the prospect of being relieved of redemption obligations in forty-nine years could hardly have been reassuring.

Immediately following the proclamation, peasant disorders on an unprecedented scale began to be reported from practically all the provinces. For the first five months of 1861, more than 1,300 disturbances of one sort or another were reported throughout the Empire, some 700 of which led to armed intervention by government troops.[2] This was a greater number of disturbances than had been reported for all the preceding years of Alexander's reign, combined. To be sure, the disturbances arising from this situation in the first weeks and months after the proclamation were not organized movements, nor did any of them produce 'revolutionary' demands. They rarely involved violence and for the most part, in fact, constituted passive refusal by peasants to carry out their *barshchina* obligations—clearly, for the peasants 'emancipation' had meant first of all abolition of *barshchina*.

These disturbances were the product of what the governor of Kaluga, in a contemporary report, described as the 'heavy incomprehension and sorrowful disenchantment' of the peasants.[3] Rumors circulated widely among the peasants that the 'real freedom' had indeed been granted them by the tsar, but was

---

[1] Cf. V. A. Fedorov, 'Trebovaniia krest'ianskogo dvizheniia v nachale revoliutsionnoi situatsii', in *Revolutsionnaia situatsiia v Rossii v 1859–61 gg.* (Moscow, 1960), pp. 133–48.

[2] *Krest'ianskoe dvizhenie v Rossii v 1857–mae 1861 gg. Sbornik dokumentov* (Moscow, 1963), p. 736.

[3] P. A. Zaionchkovskii, *Provedenie v zhizn' krest'ianskoi reformy 1861 goda* (Moscow, 1858), p. 64.

being concealed by the *pomeshchiki* and *chinovniki*. (And this idea gave rise in turn to the rumored existence of a 'golden charter', *zolotaia gramota*, bearing the message of true liberation.) Being the product of temporary confusion, this wave of disturbances rapidly passed. The period of greatest difficulties with the peasants was March–May 1861. Thereafter, the number of disturbances declined swiftly, as the terms of emancipation came gradually to be understood (and the realization that the publicized terms were the 'real thing' took hold), especially after the beginning of work by the peace mediators, the government-appointed officials who were charged with implementing the reform at the local level. They were active in most areas by mid-1861. There then followed the still relatively unstable period during which the charters defining peasant obligations and allotments were drawn up. This task was largely completed by the beginning of 1863, after which time the rate of peasant disturbances fell rapidly and continued to decline throughout the 1860s.[1]

Short-lived though it was, this wave of peasant disturbances, and especially several remarkable incidents—such as the tragic affair of Bezdna, Kazan province, in which 61 peasants were killed[2]—produced a profound impression on the government and

---

[1] According to the most recent and most complete collection of statistics, the rate of peasant disturbances in the 1860s, beginning in 1861, was the following:

Year	Total no. of disturbances in Russia
1861	1,859 (1,340 from Jan. 1–June 1)
1862	844
1863	509
1864	156
1865	135
1866	91
1867	68
1868	60
1869	65

As 'disturbances' were counted: ' ... Refusal [of peasants] to fulfill *barshchina*, obligations and non-submission to *pomeshchiki*; resistance against the authorities and army commands; seizure of lands and property of the *pomeshchiki*, etc.'. *Krest'ianskoe dvizhenie v Rossii v 1857–mae 1861 gg.*, p. 736; *Krest'ianskoe dvizhenie v Rossii v 1861–69 gg.* (Moscow, 1964), pp. 798–800.

[2] In April 1861, a local peasant, Anton Petrov, attracted several thousand peasants from surrounding villages by claiming that the emancipation legislation had provided immediate freedom for the peasants, an end to all obligations, and the ownership of

all of Russian society. To many it seemed that the fears of social disorder which had been haunting them since discussion of reform began were being realized. To many *pomeshchiki* in particular, fears of economic disaster, of lands left unworked, seemed about to come true.[1] And throughout the two-year waiting period between 1861 and 1863, the persistent circulation among the peasants of the rumor that 1863 would bring the 'real freedom' they desired gave rise to predictions in various quarters that the prevailing relative calm was only temporary and would certainly be followed by serious disorders, if not a general holocaust.[2]

GOVERNMENT POLICY AND THE GENTRY AFTER THE EMANCIPATION PROCLAMATION

The political struggle surrounding the preparation of the peasant reform had shown that the Russian government shared with other bureaucratic regimes the urge to 'control . . . the main centers of power in the society, and to minimize the possibility that any of these centers or groups [would] be able to monopolize influence and power within the society and determine the goals of the polity'.[3]

The government, by undertaking to abolish serfdom, had, however, awakened new forces in public opinion and had called forth public discussion not only of peasant reform, but of other

nearly all the land. When the local authorities tried to arrest Petrov, the peasants refused to allow it, by surrounding the house he was in. After ordering the peasants to disperse, a local military command fired into the crowd, which then quickly fled; 61 peasants were killed instantly by the firing, 41 died later from wounds, and 71 others were wounded. (Zaionchkovskii, *Otmena krepostnogo prava*, pp. 152–4.) In all respects, save the amount of bloodshed involved, which was uniquely great, the Bezdna affair was typical of the disturbances that occurred in the first months after emancipation as a result of confusion about its terms.

[1] A. Kornilov, *Krest'ianskaia reforma* (St Petersburg, 1905), pp. 168–9.

[2] This rumor, which was most frequently associated with the slogan *slushnyi chas* (the promised hour), was reported by the agents of the Ministry of Interior to be common belief among the peasantry at large in many provinces. The rumor that the 'real freedom' would arrive after two years apparently arose from the belief that the proclaimed terms of emancipation were applicable only to the two-year waiting period. Cf. Emmons, 'The peasant and emancipation', pp. 63–4.

[3] Eisenstadt, 'Political Struggle', p. 22.

extensive reforms and all manner of social and political questions. In its efforts to prepare the public (in particular the gentry) for peasant reform, it had even facilitated these developments, by calling on the gentry to discuss the peasant question and also by granting the press unprecedented freedom from censorship: For a time, roughly between the publication of the Nazimov rescript and early 1859, the press had been free to discuss nearly all aspects of the 'peasant question'. And throughout the first years of Alexander's reign, 'exposé literature' (*oblichitel'naia literatura*), ridiculing administrative corruption and other unsightly aspects of Russian life, had played a significant role in domestic journalism.

Those who saw in these developments a promise that the autocracy was about to transform itself into a liberal monarchy were sadly mistaken: the government had never intended giving free rein to 'public opinion' or to the public discussion of affairs of state, and as independent aspirations within Russian society rapidly grew, the government became increasingly fearful that this movement had gotten out of hand. Accordingly, it had begun to restrict this movement even before the proclamation of emancipation. This process had begun in serious fashion by early 1859, and was related then, in its immediate context, to the government's desire to protect its plan of reform from criticism and attack. Its application to the gentry has been discussed in some detail. Also, the relative freedom of discussion of the peasant question in the press began to be withdrawn: In early 1859, for example, Koshelev had had to terminate publication of *Sel'skoe blagoustroistvo*, one of the main organs of liberal and liberal-Slavophile commentary on the peasant question, and toward the end of that year *Russkaia beseda* was also closed.[1] Severe restrictions were placed as well on the publication of exposé literature.

[1] The first major step in this direction was a new government ruling in January 1859, which provided that all articles on the peasant question had to be submitted for preliminary approval to all Ministries concerned with their contents (previously articles had been subjected to the review of the Ministry of Interior alone). The effect of this ruling was to make the timely publication of articles on peasant reform virtually impossible. *Sbornik postanovlenii i rasporiazhenii po tsenzure s 1720 po 1862 g.*, I (St Petersburg, 1862), 440–1.

The gentry had responded to these developments with a strenuous attack against the bureaucracy. The attack was well-aimed, to the extent that it recognized that preparation of the emancipation (and other reform plans) had been given into the hands of the reforming bureaucrats. But it was ill-placed, to the extent that it was based on a belief that the Emperor had become the captive of these bureaucrats. The Russian state had become bureaucratized, but it had not become a 'bureaucratic state' if such a term implies that it is the bureaucracy which rules. Russia was, rather, a 'bureaucratized autocracy', in which the monopoly on political power was jealously guarded by the autocrat himself, not only from 'society', but from the bureaucracy as well. This was as true of Alexander II as it had been of Nicholas I: Alexander had on numerous occasions shown his mistrust of the political inclinations of the reforming bureaucrats, and of the 'empire-building' urges of the bureaucracy in general. And his reliance during the reform's preparation on extraordinary bodies—such as the Secret Committee and the Editing Commissions—and on individuals directly answerable to him—such as Rostovtsev and Panin—perpetuated the practices of his father.[1]

If one self-appointed task of the autocrat was to play off the bureaucracy against 'society' in maintaining his political monopoly, then the Emancipation Proclamation signaled the time to shift the scales in favor of 'society', that is, the gentry. With the legislation completed and its promulgation underway, Alexander II undertook, at the expense of the reforming bureaucrats, a series of moves designed to mollify gentry opinion; that is, to reconcile the gentry to the reform and thereby to neutralize the gentry opposition. The first step was the removal of Lanskoi and Miliutin from their posts in April 1861. This action had one definite purpose: It was meant to provide, as Alexander's official biographer succinctly and correctly put it,

... Demonstration of the Emperor's wish to take into consideration the rightful interests of the gentry in the further direction of the peasant affair, and also to erase that disturbing impression which had

[1] See above, pp. 218–21; 306–9. See also the comments by Rieber, in *The Politics of Autocracy*, especially pp. 54–5.

been produced on the majority of landowners by the distrustful and even somewhat neglectful behavior of the administrative organs toward the landed gentry.[1]

Thus did Alexander II reward his most assiduous servants.[2] Though undertaken primarily to placate conservative gentry opinion, the removal of Lanskoi and Miliutin could also be expected to assuage the liberal gentry. Miliutin especially had been blamed in liberal circles for the measures taken against Unkovskii and other members of the Tver gentry in the spring of 1860.[3] Other leading figures from the Editing Commissions, having made their contributions, were also sacrificed to gentry opinion: Samarin, Cherkasskii and others among them left government service, at least temporarily. There could be no mistaking the seriousness with which the government looked upon the gentry opposition.

Named to replace Lanskoi as Minister of Interior was P. A. Valuev, who had an appropriate reputation as an opponent of the bureaucracy's attempt to remove the gentry from the direction of local administration, and as a critic of the arbitrary tendencies of the Editing Commissions.

On the way out, Miliutin had declared that 'the real struggle will now be not here [in Petersburg] but in the localities'.[4] He

---

[1] Tatishchev, *Imperator Aleksandr II*, I, 360. The reason for the dismissals was made quite clear to Miliutin, who wrote in a letter to Prince Cherkasskii immediately after his removal: 'They have removed Lanskoi and me from the Ministry without waiting our initiative. We were informed that this is necessary for reconciliation with the gentry, and it seems that they seriously think that such a modest sacrifice will console the gentry class. . . . It seems doubtless that the tragicomic *quid pro quo* . . . between the Emperor on the one hand and his domestics [*dvornia*] on the other is starting once again.' Trubetskaia, *Materialy*, II, 277.

[2] Lanskoi and Miliutin were not disgraced or removed from government service. Lanskoi was placated by being made a count; Miliutin was 'kicked upstairs' to the Senate, but with a long leave of absence for foreign travel.

[3] In a letter to Herzen (16 April 1860), Ivan Aksakov wrote of the Tver events: 'The Emperor is terribly disturbed by the behavior of the gentry. He sees in it constitutionalist strivings. He proclaims that he is obligated to hand power over to his heir in the same condition that he received it from his papa [*papen'ka*], and so on. Unfortunately, I must add that not only does all public opinion accuse Nicholas Miliutin, but there is positive evidence that he, having made the banner of the bureaucrats his own, became involved in the struggle and is responsible for the biggest part of the oppressive measures.' *ORLB, f.* 69 (*Gertsen-Ogarev*), no. ix/3 (*Pis'mo Aksakova k Gertsenu*).

[4] Trubetskaia, *Materialy*, II, 277.

was right, and Valuev's policy for conciliating the gentry concentrated on the manner in which the reform was applied in the
countryside. Every attempt was made to appease gentry interests
in the concluding of economic arrangements with the peasantry.

The first step in the pursuit of this policy was the removal of
those progressive governors who had received previously, during
the preparation of reform, full government support in their
struggle against gentry interference in the work of the provincial
committees. A. N. Murav'ev (Nizhnii Novgorod), Grot (Samara)
Artsimovich (Kaluga), and other progressive governors were
removed from their posts before the end of 1862.[1]

The second step involved the peace mediators who had been
appointed for the promulgation of the reform legislation.[2] These
officials (several in each *uezd*) were given the real task of carrying
out the reform—the composition, together with the peasants and
pomeshchiki, of the charters delineating the land settlement, and
the setting of obligations. In addition to this central task (which
was to be completed within the initial two-year period of
moratorium), the mediators had the job of educating the peasantry about the emancipation legislation, setting up the new
organs of peasant administration (the *volosti*), serving as arbiters
in disputes between peasants and *pomeshchiki*, and in general
serving, temporarily, as the fundamental administrative and
judicial authority in the countryside.[3]

Because of the enormous importance of the peace mediators
for the successful realization of the reform, the Editing Commissions had taken pains to ensure that persons of good faith,
with sympathy for the peasants' interests, were appointed to these
posts (the mediators were appointed by the provincial governors

[1] Kornilov, *Krest'ianskaia reforma*, pp. 177–8; cf. also, Kornilov, 'Krest'ianskaia reforma v
Kaluzhskoi gubernii', chapters 6–9.
[2] The legislation created a hierarchy of institutions for promulgation of the reform. At the
highest level stood the 'Main Committee on Peasant Affairs', a post-reform replacement
of the old Main Committee. General purview over the course of reform promulgation
in the provinces was entrusted to 'Provincial Offices on Peasant Affairs'. Under them
were the '*Uezd* Peace Assemblies', and at the lowest level the peace mediators (the
mediators of each *uezd*, sitting with the *uezd* marshal of gentry and a representative of
the government, comprised the '*Uezd* Peace Assembly').
[3] *Krest'ianskaia reforma v Rossii 1861 goda*, pp. 133–58.

from among the gentry of each *uezd*).[1] The most devoted abolitionists among the gentry, especially the former liberal members of the provincial committees, almost all became peace mediators. So, too, did many young and idealistic *pomeshchiki* recently out of university. As a result, these offices were filled, at least in those provinces where the governors paid serious attention to the appointment of good mediators, by men who were uninclined to neglect the welfare of the peasantry.[2]

In the provinces, such as Samara, Tver, and Kaluga, where the mediators were recruited primarily from among convinced abolitionists, a situation soon developed which in many ways resembled the relations that had earlier existed between the provincial committees (or their progressive minorities) and the gentry at large: In Tver province, the gentry of several *uezdy* collectively accused their mediators of being socialists, intent on the ruin of their class, and demanded their removal.[3] In Kaluga, the majority of the provincial gentry rose up against the mediators, denouncing their 'extreme democratic and socialistic intentions'. They also demanded the removal of the governor, Artsimovich, who supported the mediators, his proteges.[4]

Although the peace mediators, who had been appointed before Valuev became Minister, enjoyed considerable immunity from administrative authority, Valuev nevertheless undertook a purge of the mediators, seeking to remove those who called forth gentry protests. Before he could carry out his plan, however, most of the charters had been drawn up and the crucial task of the mediators thus completed.

While taking these steps to mollify gentry opinion, the government showed no inclination to admit participation by the gentry or any other segment of the public in the preparation of the further reforms to which it now turned its attention. As if having learned a lesson from its conflicts with the gentry over the peasant

---

[1] Kornilov, *Krest'ianskaia reforma*, p. 171; A. N. Kulomzin, 'Vospominaniia mirovogo posrednika', *Zapiski otdela rukopisei biblioteki im. Lenina*, vyp. 10 (pp. 9–32), p. 10. In many cases, Miliutin himself apparently had arranged for these appointments.

[2] Kornilov, *Krest'ianskaia reforma*, pp. 178–9.

[3] *GAKO, f.* 59, no. 4023, pp. 10–13, 17–21; N. V. Zhuravlev, *M. E. Saltykov-Shchedrin v Tveri, 1860–62* (Kalinin, 1961), pp. 149–50.

[4] Cf. Kornilov, 'Krest'ianskaia reforma v Kaluzhskoi gubernii', chapters 6–9.

reform, the government now jealously guarded its monopoly in the preparation of those other reforms which most vitally interested the gentry: The *zemstvo* reform (that is, reform of local administration) and the reform of the judiciary. They were promulgated, respectively, in January and November 1864, on the basis of drafts prepared by special bureaucratic commissions, without participation by the gentry or other formal representatives from 'the public' (although 'experts' of various backgrounds were called in).

The government, however, had been made well aware of the gentry's interest in further reforms, especially reform of local administration, by the gentry assemblies of 1859–60. And in order to ward off gentry criticism and to avoid the probably explosive results of an outright ban on the discussion of administrative reform, the Ministry of Interior, in December 1860, had issued a series of questions to a number of gentry assemblies for their discussion. These questions, five in number, solicited gentry comment:

1. On the views and proposals of the gentry about the examination of the presently acting statutes on service by election [that is, official functions performed by gentry-elected officials].
2. On provincial gentry obligations, the organization of their administration and the expenditures from this source which ought to be realized.
3. On the organization of land credit by means of the creation of banking institutions corresponding to present needs.
4. On the organization of medical institutions, with the purpose of increasing the number of doctors and hospitals now existing in the provinces; and of the distribution of medical facilities in keeping with local conditions.
5. On the means of bringing new settlers to *pomeshchik* lands by voluntary arrangements; and also on the rules for the hiring of laborers for *pomeshchik* farms who are not members of neighboring communities.[1]

While all these questions were of obvious concern to the landed gentry, only the second one invited some discussion of local administrative reform.

[1] Garmiza, *Podgotovka zemskoi reformy*, p. 64.

To some extent these questions were designed to provide the government with information for its legislative endeavors. The primary object of their composition, however, was explicitly stated by Valuev in an official memorandum:

The initial thought of presenting to the regular provincial gentry assemblies the right to discuss certain administrative questions indicated and defined by the government was called forth by news received from various quarters about addresses allegedly being prepared for presentation to the Emperor. *This measure was taken primarily with the aim of diverting, as far as possible, the declaration of proposals and pretensions not in keeping with the aims of the government; and especially to avoid such declarations in the form of addresses to the Emperor.*[1]

The activities of the gentry assemblies meeting in 1861 and early 1862 proved that the reports which Valuev had received 'from various quarters' were accurate. They also demonstrated that the government's attempts to mollify and divert gentry discontent had not been successful.

The first gentry assemblies to be held after the eventful meetings of 1859–60 convened in the following winter—December 1860–January 1861—shortly before the proclamation of emancipation. In the several assemblies of that winter no extraordinary events occurred: The gentry occupied themselves, by all evidence, with their routine affairs and with the discussion of the 'five questions', which had recently been submitted to their attention.[2] In the following winter, however, in the first assemblies to meet after the proclamation, the gentry were once again bristling with protests and busy with plans for sending addresses to the Emperor.

THE TVER GENTRY IN 1861–2

The most radical and outspoken reaction to the government's emancipation, and the one which went furthest in the direction from which the government had tried to divert attention, was

[1] *TsGIAL, f.* 1275, no. 22, pp. 85–6, quoted in Garmiza, *op. cit.*, p. 65. Emphasis added.
[2] Not all gentry assemblies were presented the 'five questions' for discussion. Evidently, answers were solicited from only thirteen provinces: Nizhnii Novgorod, Kharkov, Pskov, Voronezh, Kursk, Smolensk, Moscow, Tula, Vladimir, Tambov, Simbirsk, Petersburg and Orenburg. (Cf. Garmiza, *Podgotovka zemskoi reformy*, p. 68, fn.)

that of the Tver gentry. By discussing in some detail the activities of the Tver gentry in 1861–2—a process which cannot be repeated for all the provinces, for reasons of space and available information —some appreciation of the relationship between the various issues—economic, social and political—raised by the gentry in this period can be had. And with the issues defined, in a sense, by study of the Tver gentry, the manner in which they were approached by the Russian gentry at large can then be described in more analytical fashion.[1]

Background to the Tver provincial assembly of February 1862

Following the proclamation of emancipation, most of the Tver liberals who had been active in the provincial committee and elsewhere took posts as peace mediators to help implement the reform legislation.[2] Many of these liberal peace mediators soon found themselves accused by local *pomeshchiki* of favoritism to the peasantry. On 1 July 1861, 48 *pomeshchiki* of Bezhetsk *uezd*, led by their marshal of gentry, condemned the actions of three local mediators. They, declared the Bezhetsk gentry, were prejudiced in favor of the peasants to the detriment of gentry interests, with the result that their actions were 'dividing the

[1] No attempt will be made in the following chapters to consider all the gentry assemblies meeting during the period in question. Attention is paid to those in which significant events (especially the presentation of addresses) and/or debate occurred. To a great extent this process of selection is pre-determined by the available evidence: The primary source of information about the gentry assemblies are the reports of the Third Section, which naturally tended to pay attention only to those activities which it considered to be of some significance for the central government.

[2] A few of them refused to accept such appointments, on the grounds that any post in the existing system of administration was unacceptable. Among them was Unkovskii, who refused a job as mediator and an appointment to the provincial office on peasant affairs. He declared that he would hold no post until an independent judicial system was instituted in Russia: 'Not fear of indictment and persecution prevent me from accepting an official position,' he wrote, 'but the deep conviction that in the absence of a real court, no civil servant can enjoy real independence or true moral influence.' (Quoted in Rozum, *Tverskie liberaly*, p. 318.)

Refusing an official position, Unkovskii became a *krest'ianskii poverennyi*; that is, a representative of peasant interests in various cases arising from disputes over land-division during the promulgation of the land charters. He won 18 cases before being deprived, by administrative decree of the Minister of Interior, of the right to represent peasants before the mediating institutions. Cf. Dzhanshiev, *A. M. Unkovskii*, pp. 152–67.

classes more and more, with every day that passes'.[1] The Bezhetsk gentry demanded their removal and replacement by persons 'enjoying the confidence of the gentry'.[2] Similar complaints were brought against mediators in three other *uezdy* of Tver province in the summer and fall of 1861.[3]

To these attacks against the peace mediators, the Tver liberals responded in a collective letter to the provincial marshal.[4] Signed by 83 *pomeshchiki*,[5] the letter dismissed the attacks as the 'egotistical attempts of certain gentry to remain, even though temporarily, on the former basis of servile arbitrariness'. The peace mediators, the letter declared, 'should be governed by their personal convictions alone, without being placed in dependence on the wishes and views of their electors'. Their point of view and the tasks of the peace mediators were described in the following way by the authors of the letter:

We affirm that the task of the institutions operating in connection with the peasant reform consists mainly in the development of independence and consciousness by the peasants of the right to lay a sound foundation to our union with all the classes in that solid and uniform mass with which the future lies. Having in mind this main goal, we do not find that the preservation of exclusive class privileges and advantages has constituted for us a significant question; and we know certainly that persons attracted by the benefits of the moment to the injury of genuinely common interests represent an insignificant minority among the gentry of our province.[6]

One of the prime instigators of this letter, and perhaps its main author, was M. E. Saltykov, who had been appointed vice-governor of Tver in mid-1860. Saltykov had been engaged in a polemic in the press since April 1861, over the responsibilities of the peace mediators, in which he had argued that the mediators

---

[1] *GAKO, f.* 59, no. 4023, pp. 10–13, 17–21.   [2] *Ibid.*
[3] Zhuravlev, *M. E. Saltykov-Shchedrin v Tveri*, p. 149.
[4] *TsGIAL, f.* 445, no. 46, p. 2. Undated, this letter was written sometime in late 1861.
[5] Among the signers were Unkovskii, Evropeus, the four brothers of Michael Bakunin (Nicholas, Aleksei, Pavel and Il'ia, all *pomeshchiki* of Tver province, where the Bakunin family estate was located), most of the former members of the liberal majority of the Tver provincial committee, and the vice-governor of Tver, M. E. Saltykov (Saltykov-Shchedrin), himself a local *pomeshchik*.
[6] *TsGIAL, f.* 445, no. 46, pp. 2–3.

must not be responsible to the *pomeshchiki* who had nominated them, but must rather be responsible to the law and the provincial authorities, and to the public at large. And to this end he had proposed, in an article published in *Moskovskie vedomosti*, the organization of periodic provincial conferences of peace mediators, where they could exchange experiences and also present accountings of their action for publication.[1]

The reference to 'union with all classes' was not meant as a pious generality. Some of the signers of the letter had already undertaken to effect such a union. On 17 June 1861, a group of nine Tver *pomeshchiki* led by Unkovskii addressed a remarkable petition to the provincial office on peasant affairs. This request, the original statement of the 'repentant noblemen' of the 1860s, was the following:

To the Tver Provincial Office on Peasant Affairs: Petition of the undersigned gentry of Tver province.

Under serfdom the populated gentry estates were assessed with state taxes and obligations according to the number of male inhabitants living on them, and were paid out of the general sum of the income of *pomeshchiki* and peasants. Whether the taxable individuals[2] or the owners of the estates paid these taxes, in any case, with the unlimitable right of the masters to place any *obrok* and obligations on the peasants, and with the inescapable obligation of the *pomeshchiki* to protect the peasants from ruin, all the burden of state taxes and obligations lay not on the peasants alone, but on the income of the masters themselves. The law took the entire populated estates as indivisible taxable units.

At the present time, with the separation of part of the land for the permanent use of the peasants freed from servile dependence, these taxable units are cut into parts; however, all the burden of state taxes and obligations is not divided, as justice would demand, among the newly formed sections, but is carried over in full sum on the peasants alone; from the *pomeshchiki*, in whose control part of the land is left, all obligations for the indemnification of state and local expenditures are removed entirely.

On this basis the peasants have received a social organization separate from the landowners, and are invested with special local

[1] 'Ob otvetstvennosti mirovykh posrednikov', *Moskovskie vedomosti*, no. 91, 27 April 1861. [2] That is, the peasants.

1   The Tver provincial committee majority (1858–9)
Front row center: A. M. Unkovskii; second row center: A. A. Golovachev

self-administration; the landowners remain excluded from this self-administration of the people, like foreigners who are of no use to the country, but enjoy the benefits of the state system at the expense of others. It goes without saying that it is wrong to enjoy public rights without having any public obligations.

Fully understanding the awkwardness of our insulting situation as citizens without rights or obligations, and desiring to enjoy the rights of local self-administration equally with the peasants, we the undersigned address to the Tver Provincial Office on Peasant Affairs the most respectful request to take the necessary steps for attaching us to the peasant volosti nearest our places of residence, with the right to vote in the volost' assemblies equal to their other members, and with the obligation to pay taxes and obligations together with the peasants who have been freed from our dependency.

To this we find it necessary to add that until special action by the government on this matter, we obligate ourselves to designate a part of the taxes and obligations due from the lands left in our control, by voluntary agreement of each of us with the peasants freed from his dependency; and in cases where such agreement is not forthcoming, to submit to the jurisdiction of the Peace Mediators and to the final decisions of the *uezd* Peace Assemblies.[1]

Similar petitions were made in the summer and fall of 1861 by several other groups of Tver gentry, and by several individual *pomeshchiki*. One petitioner even asked to be registered as a 'temporarily-obligated peasant' and attached to a peasant commune.[2] These demands and the arguments behind them were publicized by Saltykov in an article which appeared in *Russkii vestnik* in October 1861.[3] The similarity of all these petitions suggests that they were designed as a coordinated protest against the separate administration of the peasantry, and as a demand for reforms instituting general local self-administration.

The dissatisfaction of the Tver liberals with the terms of emancipation was not limited to questions of administration alone. Perhaps on the suggestion of Saltykov, an extraordinary provincial conference of peace mediators was held in Tver on

---

[1] *GAKO, f.* 484, no. 82, pp. 1–2a. (The petition was not passed upon by the provincial office). *Ibid.*, pp. 3–3a. Emphasis added.

[2] *Ibid.*, pp. 4–6a.

[3] 'Gde istinnye interesy dvorianstva?' *Russkii vestnik. Sovremennaia letopis'*, XLII (1861).

11–13 December 1861, under the chairmanship of Nicholas Bakunin.[1] Here numerous amendments to the emancipation legislation were proposed in the name of the conference as a whole. Among them were:

2. The necessity of redemption, as the only means of eliminating obligatory relations.
3. ... The calling of ... peasants to participation in the election of the Peace Mediators.
4. ... The election to offices of rural administration and justice of persons of all land-owning classes by the peasants.
5. ... Obligatory transfer of the peasants from *barshchina* to *obrok* within half a year.[2]

Points 3 and 4 of this protocol were based on the proposition 'that participation of the peasants in the election of the peace mediators will increase the beneficial influence of the latter on the successful progress of the common cause' and 'that the elective principle, common for both classes, will greatly facilitate their rapprochement'.[3]

The decisions of the extraordinary conference of peace mediators were discussed in *uezd* meetings of the gentry throughout the province. A week later, on 20 December the gentry of Korcheva *uezd* unanimously declared that good relations between the two 'hostilely-divided classes' could be achieved only by immediate redemption of the peasant allotments. The Korcheva gentry proposed that the Minister of Interior be petitioned to permit an extraordinary assembly of the Tver gentry for discussion of the subject.[4]

In the first week of January 1862, the gentry of Torzhok *uezd* presented a similar declaration:

---

[1] This conference was called on the initiative of five members of the provincial office on peasant affairs (Bakunin among them). Such gatherings, while not formally provided for in the legislation, were not unknown in other provinces. Such a conference had been held, for example, in Kaluga during July 1861.
[2] *GAKO, f.* 59, no. 4038, pp. 5–6a.
[3] *Tverskie gubernskie vedomosti*, no. 1, 1862. Quoted in I. V. Kniazev, 'M. E. Saltykov-Shchedrin i krest'ianskaia reforma', in *Revoliutsionnaia situatsiia v Rossii v 1859–61 gg.* (Moscow, 1963) (pp. 445–57), p. 455.
[4] *GAKO, f.* 59, no. 4093, pp. 95–6a.

The experience of the last eight months has shown and definitely confirmed the conviction in society that redemption of the peasant lands presents the only true and satisfactory escape from the present unstable situation.[1]

Redemption was progressing slowly, the Torzhok gentry continued, because of the nature of the legislation: The peasants would never agree to be bound to payments for forty-nine years; and the *pomeshchiki* would not agree to lose twenty percent of their capital by forcing redemption on the peasants; nor would they trust payment in notes issued by a government already known to be in bad financial straits. Only immediate and simultaneous redemption could rectify the situation. However, warned the Torzhok declaration, the remedy could not be provided by the customary bureaucratic means:

... Such a reform cannot be satisfactorily executed by bureaucratic means, a fact to which the very legislation of 19 February serves as evidence; as do all other attempts of this sort to improve the judiciary, finances, and education.

Only through the active participation of society through its elected representatives can a satisfactory solution of these problems, on which the welfare of the whole nation depends, be expected.[2]

And on 30 January, the gentry of Tver *uezd* endorsed a protocol which expressed the same conclusion about the necessity of redemption, but with an added argument: 'Gentry property', declared the Tver gentry, 'has been placed in a completely impossible situation.' Redemption had in effect become obligatory for the gentry, 'under threat of losing the bigger part of their property'. The Tver gentry therefore concluded that the government guarantee of only 80 per cent of the redemption sum was unjust, and should be replaced by fully-financed obligatory redemption.[3]

All the proposals made by the Tver gentry from the time of emancipation to January 1862—for legal unification of the classes, for immediate and obligatory land-redemption, and finally for

---

[1] *Ibid.*, pp. 29–9a.   [2] *Ibid.* Emphasis added.
[3] ORLB, *Arkhiv Cherkasskikh*, I 26/11, pp. 1–3a.

participation by popular representatives in further legislative undertakings—were taken up in the extraordinary provincial gentry assembly which met in Tver on 1 February 1862.

The Tver Gentry Assembly, 1–4 February 1862

With the co-operation of the vice-governor, Saltykov, the Tver gentry had gained permission to hold an extraordinary assembly for the ostensible purpose of discussing a land bank. Convening on 1 February 1862, the assembly immediately turned to the question of land redemption, declaring, by a vote of 113 to 22 that 'obligatory presentation to the peasants of land with government assistance represents the only means of guaranteeing the social and proprietary interests of the gentry'.[1]

The assembly then heard the proposals of E. A. Kardo-Sysoev, former deputy, with Unkovskii, to the Editing Commissions. In a prepared speech Kardo-Sysoev announced his intention of 'clarify[ing] the abnormal and dangerous situation of society'.[2] Several needs were predominant, he declared, and first among them was the need of 'immediate elimination of obligatory relations between the *pomeshchiki* and peasants by means of immediate redemption, as the Peace Mediators announced in their provincial assembly of 12 December 1861'. Second, in Kardo-Sysoev's view, was the need to stabilize credit by introducing publicity and public accounting of state finances. The third primary need, said Kardo-Sysoev, was the 'institution of an elective basis, for all classes, for economic self-administration, and the unification of all classes in relation to administration and justice'.[3]

Kardo-Sysoev concluded his speech with the following proposition:

Do the gentry find such an opinion sound, and do they find it useful and necessary to disturb the SOVEREIGN EMPEROR with a most loyal request for permitting the discussion of all the questions arising from the above-mentioned social situation in a *consultative assembly of representatives elected by all classes* . . .?[4]

Kardo-Sysoev's proposals were all accepted by the assembly.[5]

---

[1] *TsGIAL, f.* 1282, no. 1104, p. 18.   [2] *GAKO, f.* 59, no. 4079, p. 2.   [3] *Ibid.*, pp. 2a–4.
[4] *Ibid.*, pp. 6a–7. Emphasis added.   [5] *Ibid.*, pp. 1–1a.

The assembly then entrusted the composition of a report on these subjects to a special editing commission.[1] The report, or protocol, of the commission was subsequently endorsed by the assembly at large. It contained five points. The first three points dealt with the necessity of immediate promulgation of redemption of the peasant allotments 'with the assistance of the entire state'. Only in this way, declared the Tver protocol, could Russian finances be firmly stabilized. To the same end other measures were required, including: 'Reorganization of the financial system . . ., so that it will depend on the people and not on arbitrariness; institution of an autonomous public judiciary . . .; introduction of complete publicity into all branches of state and public administration.'[2]

Besides all these reforms, there is needed the elimination of those hostile relations between the classes which are the result of the legislation of 19 February 1861, *which raised the question of emancipating the peasants, but did not finally solve it.* Elimination of class antagonism can be achieved only by [the classes'] complete fusion. The gentry, deeply aware of the immediate necessity of escaping from this antagonism and wishing to eliminate any possibility of reproach that they constitute a barrier on the path of the general welfare, proclaim before all Russia that they renounce all their class privileges, in accordance with the protocol of the assembly for 2 February;[3] and do not consider obligatory presentation to the peasants of land in property, with remuneration of the *pomeshchiki* through the assistance of the entire state, to be a violation of their rights, in accordance with the same protocol.[4]

The assembly concluded its protocol with a fifth point:

The realization of these reforms is impossible through those government measures by which our public life has so far been moved. *Assuming even the full preparedness of the government to promulgate reforms, the gentry are deeply convinced that the government is not capable of realizing*

[1] The commission consisted of Unkovskii, A. Bakunin, V. N. Kudriavtsev, P. D. Kishenskii and A. N. Nevedomskii, *TsGIAL, f.* 1282, no. 1104, pp. 22–2a.

[2] *Ibid.*, pp. 20–20a.

[3] The gentry had decided, by votes of 111–38 and 123–22, respectively, to 'renounce [their] class rights . . . in relation to the gathering and expenditure of taxes and the fulfillment of natural obligations . . .', and 'to abolish the gentry class elections . . .' *Ibid.*, pp. 35–5a.

[4] *Ibid.*, pp. 20a–1. Emphasis added.

them. *The free institutions to which these reforms lead can come only from the people,* and otherwise will be merely a dead-letter and will place society in an even more strained position.

Therefore the gentry do not turn to the government with a request for the carrying out of these reforms, but recognizing its failure in this matter, restrict themselves to indicating that path onto which [the government] must venture for the salvation of itself and of society. *This path is the gathering of representatives from the entire people without distinction as to class.*[1]

On the basis of this protocol, following the proposal of Kardo-Sysoev, the assembly voted 'to present to HIS IMPERIAL MAJESTY a most loyal petition ... about all that concerns changes in gentry rights and privileges, and about the means which afford the possibility of improving the conditions of the classes and of the people for the benefit of Russia'. The same commission was entrusted with the composition of this petition.[2] The result was the 'address of the repentant noblemen', one of the most famous documents of the 1860s:

The Manifesto of 19 February [so the address began, after the usual obsequies] in proclaiming freedom to the people, improved somewhat the material welfare of the peasants, but did not free them from servile dependency; nor did it eliminate all the lawless actions resulting from serfdom. The common sense of the people cannot accord the freedom proclaimed by YOUR MAJESTY with the existing obligatory relations toward the *pomeshchiki*, nor with the artificial division of the classes. The people see that they, in time, can free themselves from obligatory labor, but must remain eternal payers of *obrok*, transferred to the authority of those same *pomeshchiki*, called peace mediators.

SOVEREIGN! We sincerely admit that we ourselves do not understand this situation.

Such an enormous misunderstanding places all of society in a hopeless situation, threatening the state with destruction.

What prevents its elimination?

[1] *Ibid.*, p. 21. Emphasis added. This article of the protocol was also based on voting in the assembly on 2 February, on the proposition: 'Do the gentry recognize the necessity of calling elected representatives from the entire people, without distinction as to class, for the solution of all private and state questions raised by the present critical state of affairs?' The proposition was approved by a vote of 126–27.
[2] *ORLB, Arkhiv Cherkasskikh,* I, 26/11, 20–20a.

In obligatory presentation of land in property to the peasants we not only do not see a violation of our rights, but consider this the only means to guarantee the tranquillity of the land and our own material interests.

We ask that this measure be swiftly put into effect by means of the general resources of the state, without placing the entire burden only on the peasants, who are least of all responsible for the existence of serfdom.

The gentry, by virtue of class advantages, have so far escaped fulfillment of the most important public obligations. SOVEREIGN, *we consider it a grievous fault to live and enjoy the benefits of the public order at the expense of other classes.* Unjust is that order of things in which the poor man pays a ruble and the rich man pays not even a kopeck. This could be tolerated only under serfdom; but now it places us in the position of parasites who are completely useless to their fatherland. *We do not wish to have such a disgraceful privilege, and we do not accept responsibility for its further existence.*

We most loyally request YOUR MAJESTY *to be allowed to take upon ourselves a part of the state taxes and obligations, according to the circumstances of each of us.*

Besides property privileges, we enjoy the exclusive right to provide persons for the administration of the people. In the present day we consider the exclusiveness of this right a transgression, and ask that it be extended to all classes.

MOST GRACIOUS SOVEREIGN! We firmly believe that YOU sincerely desire the well-being of Russia, and therefore consider it our sacred duty to state frankly that between us and YOUR IMPERIAL MAJESTY'S government there exists a strange misunderstanding which hinders the realization of YOUR good intentions.

Instead of that actual realization of freedom promised to the Russian people, the dignitaries have invented a temporary-obligatory status which is unbearable for peasants and *pomeshchiki* alike. Instead of simultaneous and obligatory transformation of the peasants into free and independent property-owners, they have invented a system of voluntary agreements which threatens to lead both peasants and *pomeshchiki* to extreme ruin. Now they find necessary the preservation of gentry privileges, whereas we ourselves, who are more than anyone concerned in this matter, desire their abolition.

This universal dissension serves as the best evidence that the reforms now demanded by extreme necessity cannot be accomplished bureaucratically.

We ourselves do not undertake to speak for the entire people, in spite of the fact that we stand nearest to them; and we are firmly convinced that good intentions alone are insufficient, not only for the satisfaction, but even for the [understanding] of the people's needs.

We are convinced that all reforms remain unsuccessful because they are undertaken without the permission or knowledge of the people.

The summoning of elected representatives from all the Russian land represents the only means for the satisfactory solution indicated, but not effected, by the legislation of 19 February.[1]

The assembly appointed Brovtsyn (acting provincial marshal) and Unkovskii to present its address directly to the Emperor. The Emperor, however, refused to receive the Tver representatives and the address, read in the State Council on 15 February, was left 'without further action' by order of Alexander II.[2]

Aftermath of the Tver assembly: the 'affair of the thirteen peace mediators'

The unprecedented boldness of the Tver address, with its blanket rejection of all the government's reform efforts, could not have failed to arouse governmental displeasure. The immediate response was merely rejection of the gentry's address and expression of 'imperial disfavor'. Soon, however, the government was presented with an opportunity to make a more serious response to the bold and improper demands of the Tver liberals. The opportunity was provided by Nicholas Bakunin, who, on 8 February 1862, presented a statement signed by himself and twelve other officials from the mediating institutions to the provincial office on peasant affairs.

In December 1861, this statement declared, the peace mediators of Tver province had recognized that immediate obligatory redemption was the only solution to the existing difficult situa-

---

[1] *GAKO, f.* 59, no. 4081, pp. 1–4. (Original draft.) Emphasis added. This address was printed in *Kolokol*, but with several errors. The most nearly correct published copy of the address is to be found in Lemke, *Ocherki osvoboditel'nogo dvizheniia*, pp. 447–9. The address was signed by nine *uezd* marshals, the acting provincial marshal Brovtsyn, and 103 gentry. (About 140 gentry participated in the assembly.) (*TsGAOR, f.* 109, no. 123, p. 4.)

[2] The Emperor's ruling stated: 'The most loyal petition, constituting a request that goes beyond the sphere of those judgements which are by law presented to the gentry assemblies, and is therefore baseless and out of place, shall be left without further action.' Zhuravlev, *M. E. Saltykov-Shchedrin v Tveri*, pp. 162–3.

tion. They had, nevertheless, continued to act in accordance with the legislation, not then knowing the views of the public on this question. The views of the public had subsequently been clarified in the gentry assembly of 1–4 February, and had confirmed the convictions earlier expressed by the peace mediators—namely:

1. The failure of the legislation of 19 February.
2. The necessity of presenting to the peasants their land in property.
3. The insolvency of class privileges.
4. The failure of the government to satisfy the public needs and [the necessity of] summoning representatives of the entire people, without distinction as to class.[1]

The thirteen officials therefore declared that they considered it their duty 'to accept these convictions as the only guide to their activities, and declare[d] that any form of activity contrary to these conviction they consider harmful to society'.[2]

Although the import of this declaration—that its authors, as officials of the mediating institutions, no longer considered the legislation of 19 February to be binding—was clearly understood by the provincial office, no action was taken there except to remind the petitioners that they were bound to observe the existing laws.[3] The provincial procurator (an *ex officio* member of the office) objected, however, insisting that such a declaration was a 'violation of service responsibilities' and should be prosecuted. He accordingly notified the Ministry of Justice.[4]

The government's response was not long in coming. By order of the Emperor a member of the State Council, Adjutant-General Annenkov, was dispatched to Tver on 14 February 1862, together with several gendarme officers, to arrest the thirteen signers of the declaration. The arrests took place between 16–21 February. The arrested peace mediators were transported to Peter-Paul fortress in Petersburg, where they remained until

---

[1] *TsGAOR, f.* 109, no. 123, pp. 11a–12.
[2] *Ibid.* The thirteen signers of the declaration were: Nicholas Bakunin (member of the provincial office on peasant affairs); A. Bakunin and S. Balkashin (*uezd* marshals, *ex officio* members of the '*uezd* peace assemblies'); P. Glazenap, N. Kharlamov, N. Poltaratskii, M. Lazarev, A. Likhachev, A. Nevedomskii, V. Kudriavtsev, A. Kishenskii, A. Dem'ianov (all peace mediators); and L. Shirobokov (candidate peace mediator).
[3] *Ibid.*   [4] *Ibid.*, pp. 33–6a.

decision of their case by the Senate in July 1862. According to the Senate decision, the thirteen peace mediators were deprived (ironically) of certain class privileges and sentenced to confinement in the Petersburg mental sanitarium. The last part of the sentence was not, however, carried out: On 21 July, the prisoners were granted imperial grace and released.[1]

The 'affair of the thirteen peace mediators' drew wide attention in Russian society, mainly because it was the first significant punitive action to have been taken against a group of gentry since the emancipation.[2] Rumors circulated in Petersburg that similar measures would soon be taken against other oppositionist-minded gentry. Valuev, whose general policy toward the gentry had been one of mollification, had previously avoided any such sharp confrontations, and the government's response to various gentry addresses had been noticeably mild and perfunctory. Bismarck, at that time Prussian ambassador in Petersburg, reported that Valuev was reputed to have been opposed to the punitive measures taken against the peace mediators, even to the extent of offering his resignation.[3] Count Panin, however, was said to have convinced Alexander to take action against the peace mediators (a hypothesis lent weight by other sources).[4] Whoever was responsible, the extraordinarily severe treatment of these Tver gentry was clearly related to the fact that they were not simply *pomeshchiki*, but government officials who were obviously

[1] *TsGAOR, f.* 109, no. 123, pp. 37–289. (In fact, the prisoners did spend several days in the Petersburg mental sanitarium, having been transferred there from the fortress on 18 July, three days before the rendering of the Senate decision and the expression of imperial grace.)

[2] Probably the most extraordinary response to the arrest of the Tver peace mediators was made by V. V. Bervi, then serving as a *chinovnik* attached to the Senate (and later, in 1869, author of the famous book *The Situation of the Working Class in Russia*). Bervi sent a letter to the Emperor, another to the English ambassador, and addressed yet another to the marshals of the gentry, protesting the action taken against the peace mediators. If the government would not give in to progress, he wrote in these letters, a terrible revolution would inevitably occur. 'Let it be known to the English people,' he wrote to the English ambassador, 'that not everyone in Russia will put up silently with such arbitrariness.' For his efforts, Bervi was confined in a mental institution for six months and then exiled to Astrakhan. *TsGAOR, f.* 109, no. 139, pp. 1–2a, 11–19a, 34 and ff. Cf. also, L. F. Panteleev, *Iz vospominanii proshlogo* (Moscow, 1934), p. 238, fn.; and F. Venturi, *Roots of Revolution* (New York, 1960), pp. 487–8.

[3] B. E. Nol'de, *Petersburgskaia missiia Bismarka, 1859–62* (Prague, 1925), pp. 257–8.

[4] Cf. Barsukov, *Zhizn' i trudy Pododina*, XIX, 31–5.

heading toward open insubordination. Considering the crucial role of the peace mediators in the promulgation of the reform, the government must have been apprehensive about the possibility of similar oppositionist activities by others among them. They were all, after all, *pomeshchiki*.

In their response to the emancipation, the Tver gentry raised issues which can be classified under the following three headings: (1) Rejection of the 'temporary-obligatory status' provided by the state legislation; (2) views on the future of the gentry class and local administration; (3) 'constitutionalism'.

The Tver liberals had been predicting disastrous consequences for anything but complete emancipation through universal obligatory redemption ever since the debate on peasant reform had begun. The sudden proliferation of peasant disorders immediately following the emancipation proclamation, and the nearly universal difficulties connected with the fulfillment of *barshchina* and *obrok* apparently served to convince the large majority of Tver *pomeshchiki*—as indicated by the address of the Tver assembly—of the correctness of the liberal analysis.

The protocol and address of the 1862 assembly revealed that the Tver liberals had modified their original conditions for obligatory redemption in one significant respect: When Unkovskii had first raised the question in his 1857 *zapiska*, he had called for redemption of serfdom itself (i.e., peasant labor-value) by the state as a whole, and redemption of the land by the peasants (with the aid, to be sure, of a government financial operation). But this distinction had not been preserved either in the Tver committee's project or in the general legislation. In the 1862 address, Unkovskii's original proposal was revived and carried further: It was now proposed that the entire redemption burden be borne 'by the general resources of the state'.

The second major innovation of the Tver address was its dramatic renunciation, in the name of the gentry, of class privileges, and the voluntary assumption of taxation and other state obligations on an equal basis with the peasantry. This pronouncement probably had little to do with the feelings of 'grievous fault' on which it was allegedly based. Rather, it was directly related to the views which the Tver liberals had expressed long before in arguing against the separate administration of the various classes. All these renunciations of class privileges, requests by *pomeshchiki* to join peasant *volosti*, and demands for peasant election of peace mediators are best understood as dramatic demands for the reform of local administration on the basis of effective self-government common for all classes of the population.

The third and final major request of the Tver address was for the 'summoning of elected representatives from all the Russian land'. According to the address and the protocol upon which it was based, such an assembly of elected representatives would be called for the specific purpose of completing the peasant reform and promulgating other necessary, and related, reforms. The address and its predecessors, especially the assembly protocol, the speech of Kardo-Sysoev and the earlier proclamation of the Torzhok gentry, all insisted that no useful reforms could be accomplished by 'bureaucratic means' alone. Some historians have seen constitutionalist demands in these declarations of the Tver gentry.[1] Strictly speaking, no such demands were made: There was no mention of a written constitution, nor of a permanent representative element in the central state institutions. That the Tver gentry, however, envisaged more than a commission of elected representatives to assist the government was stated quite clearly in the assembly protocol: 'Assuming even the full preparedness of the government to promulgate reforms, the gentry are deeply convinced that the government is not capable of realizing them. The free institutions to which these reforms lead can come only from the people . . .' And Kardo-Sysoev, in the concluding remarks of his speech to the Tver assembly, had hinted strongly at the necessity of permanent popular representation:

Is not the conscious desire of society to take part in the solution of the most important questions and to help the government in these matters indicated . . .? Is it not now obvious that any separation of the govern-

[1] Cf. Iordanskii, *Konstitutsionnoe dvizhenie*, ch. x.

ment's actions from society can have fatal results? Is it not, finally, obvious that the powerful development of centralization and bureaucratic principles has outlived its historical epoch with the abolition of serfdom . . .?[1]

Political traditions die hard. The Russian liberal tradition of faith in the progressive possibilities of 'enlightened despotism' and mistrust of the aristocratic implications of 'constitutionalism' apparently remained sufficiently strong to prevent the Tver liberals from employing the word 'constitution'. But it is clear that this faith had by now undergone a process of serious decay.

The Tver gentry rejected the government's emancipation because they expected it to be economically disastrous for themselves; because they considered it a threat to peaceful relations between the classes; because it provided for the administrative isolation of the gentry from the peasants—an arrangement they considered dangerous for all the reasons already mentioned by the deputies in 1859 and the assemblies of 1859–60. In their disappointment with the emancipation they drew conclusions about the reforming capabilities of the government in general, and were thus led to demand the participation of public representatives for the correction of the peasant reform and for the proper promulgation of the other administrative reforms which had been demanded since the early days of discussion of the peasant question.

[1] *GAKO, f.* 59, no. 4079, p. 5a.

9

The Variety of Gentry Views and the 'Constitutionalist Campaign' of 1861-2

In some respects the Tver address was a unique phenomenon: The Tver gentry alone made renunciation of class privileges the subject of a formal address to the Emperor; and they alone went so far as an outright rejection of the emancipation legislation, and explicit denial of the government's competency in legislating reforms. But all the issues raised by the Tver gentry were raised elsewhere by the gentry in the winter of 1861-2, and on some of them a surprising unanimity of views was to be found.

THE CRITIQUE OF THE 'TEMPORARY-OBLIGATORY' STATUS

The evidence of the other gentry assemblies meeting in the first year after emancipation indicates that the landed gentry throughout Russia were deeply dissatisfied with the terms of emancipation: They too testified unanimously to the unsatisfactory state of affairs in rural Russia which, in the words of one of the first addresses to the Emperor, signed by more than 500 gentry of Tula province (December 1861), threatened 'to upset the economy, sow destructive discord between the peasants and the *pomeshchiki*, and cause incalculable harm to agriculture'.[1] They attributed this state of affairs—which, they predicted, promised imminent ruin for the *pomeshchiki*—primarily to the failure of the peasants to properly acquit *barshchina* and other obligations, and to the *pomeshchik*'s lack of capital necessary to set up farming operations on a hired-labor basis.

[1] *TsGAOR, f.* 109, no. 11, part 3, p. 7. See Appendix III.

350

In their protocol, the gentry of Voronezh province, meeting in early 1862 (10–26 January) laid particular emphasis on the first of these two conditions:

The law of 19 February 1861 [read the protocol] while observed by the *pomeshchiki*, is not being observed by the peasants. Obligations are not being fulfilled, because the rural population, knowing that the land will not be taken from those in arrears, becomes ever more convinced of the apparent illegality of all obligations for the land.[1]

The Voronezh protocol went on to describe the details of the situation which was threatening the gentry with imminent ruin: Fields were already lying idle, and cattle and forests were rapidly disappearing.

The financial straits of the gentry were described in illuminating detail by the protocol of the Riazan gentry assembly, drawn up on 28 February 1862:

1. ... The *pomeshchiki* are faced with the organization of farms based on free labor, attended by the purchase of various equipment and machines, beasts of burden, and by many other substantial outlays.
2. ... The *pomeshchiki* lack capital.
3. ... Most *pomeshchiki* have private debts as well as debts to the [state] credit insitutions.
4. ... All ... loans from the state have ceased.[2]
5. ... The income of the *pomeshchiki* has significantly decreased, but their expenditures for the hiring of necessary laborers, for drayage, etc., have doubled and trebled ...[3]

The same conditions were described in the addresses and protocols of most of the other gentry assemblies gathering in the winter of 1861–2.

The situation as a whole was summed up in telegraphic fashion by the Moscow gentry assembly, in a petition sent to Alexander II in January 1862:

At all levels of society a species of discontent reigns; the laws are not being observed in their strict sense; neither person nor property is protected from the arbitrariness of the administration; the classes are

---

[1] *TsGIAL, f.* 1282, no. 1091, p. 17.
[2] It will be recalled that all loans to gentry estates had ceased on 16 April 1859.
[3] *ORLB, Arkhiv Cherkasskikh,* I 26/14, 1.

set against each other, and the antagonism between them grows incessantly in consequence of those actions of administrative officials which do not satisfy local needs. Moreover, a complete lack of money; fears of a State financial crisis, expressed in the instability of the currency; the complete absence of credit; and finally, a multitude of false rumors. .... Such, in a few words, is our present situation.[1]

More remarkable than the unanimity with which the assembled gentry decried the situation created by the government legislation was the near-unanimity of their alternative demands: All (excluding a few conservative fanatics like N. A. Bezobrazov)[2] now rushed to demand immediate abolition of *barshchina*—that is transfer of all *barshchina* peasants to *obrok*—and rapid implementation of obligatory redemption of the peasant allotments. This development was attested to in the annual report of the Third Section (1862):

Although certain *pomeshchiki* have themselves retarded the progress of the peasant reform for the extraction of benefits from their former quantity of *barshchina* obligations, and partly from fear of disorders accompanying the promulgation of the charters, the majority [of *pomeshchiki*] unanimously desire the most rapid termination of relations with the peasants, even agreeing to significant losses on their part.[3]

And in demanding immediate promulgation of redemption, the gentry assemblies, one after another, demanded (as had the gentry of Tver *uezd*) that the government undertake financing of the entire sum, so that the gentry would not be faced with the loss of 20–25 per cent of the redemption price in those cases where the peasants did not agree to redemption, as well as other measures designed to make credit readily available to the *pomeshchiki*.

Thus the Tula assembly, in its address to the Emperor, demanded: (1) Immediate cessation of *barshchina* (which was, the

---

[1] *TsGIAL, f.* 1282, no. 1092, pp. 28–8a. See Appendix III.
[2] In January 1862, Bezobrazov presented a draft address to the Emperor for approval of the Moscow assembly in which, among other things, he once again condemned the emancipation legislation as a violation of the rights of the gentry, in particular their property rights. His proposals were not accepted by the Moscow gentry. *TsGAOR, f.* 109, no. 302, pp. 23–5.
[3] *TsGAOR, Otchet III otdeleniia za 1862,* p. 92.

2 The thirteen peace mediators (1862). Seated, second and third from left: Nicholas and Aleksei Bakunin

gentry had found, unfulfillable, and led to daily conflicts with the peasants); (2) sale to the state treasury of peasant allotments by *pomeshchiki* who wished to sell them, but whose peasants would not agree to redeem them, and for the full price; (3) transfer to the peasant allotments of debts on the estates, so that the land left in gentry hands could be sold or mortgaged freely.[1]

The Moscow assembly petitioned the Emperor, asking for:

Elimination of hostile relations between the gentry and the peasantry by means of obligatory, rapid separation of lands simultaneously with the granting of the land charters [*ustavnye gramoty*]; guarantee of *obrok* by the Government and redemption with guarantee not of 80 percent, but of the entire sum.[2]

The Pskov gentry, also meeting in January 1862, proposed:

[1]. Obligatory transfer of the temporarily-obligated peasants to *obrok* on demand of the *pomeshchik*, and . . . guaranteeing of *obrok* by the Government.

[2]. Redemption of the allotment-lands of the temporarily-obligated peasants . . . at ruble-for-ruble value, and with payment by five per-cent bonds guaranteed by the lands . . ., rather than by credit certificates.[3]

The Riazan assembly, meeting at the end of February 1862, called in a protocol for:

1. Carrying out separation of peasant lands from *pomeshchik* [lands] immediately, without waiting for the expiration of a two-year period.
2. Obligatory redemption of peasant lands, with ruble-for-ruble payment . . .

---

[1] This provision had two purposes: (1) Avoidance of direct responsibility for debt pay-ments by the *pomeshchiki* during the period before redemption would be undertaken; and (2) permission of free sale or mortgaging of those lands left to the *pomeshchiki*. Transfer of the debt (as proposed by the Tula gentry and other assemblies) was not demanded as an attempt to absolve the gentry of responsibility for the debts—they would have to pay, either through preliminary deduction from peasant obligations, or, when redemption occurred, through deduction of the debt from the capital sum paid over by the state.

[2] *TsGIAL, f.* 1282, no. 1092, pp. 28a–9.

[3] *TsGAOR, f.* 109, no. 33, part 2, pp. 23–4. See Appendix III. 'Ruble-for-ruble value' referred to full government guarantee of the redemption sum; replacement of credit certificates by bonds meant rejection of payment in any form not immediately nego-tiable at face value for cash. (Approximately two-thirds of the sum payable by the government was to be in the form of credit certificates, according to the legislation.)

3. Loans against obligatory redemption, in part payment of the redemption sums due the *pomeshchiki*, at 150 rubles for each allotment, in order to present to the *pomeshchiki* the possibility of organizing farming on the basis of free hired labor.

4. Removal to the lands transferred to the peasants of the debts to the [state] credit institutions.[1]

Essentially similar demands were made in the addresses or protocols of the gentry of Voronezh, Petersburg, Kherson, and Simbirsk provinces, where provincial assemblies also gathered in 1862.[2]

There is every reason to believe that the large majority of the landed gentry were agreed about the necessity of the immediate transfer of peasants to *obrok* and the rapid implementation of redemption. In short, the analysis of the current situation and the resulting demands of the gentry assemblies in 1861–2 apparently confirmed the correctness of the liberal reform program.

GENTRY VIEWS ON THE FUTURE OF THEIR CLASS AND THE REFORM OF LOCAL ADMINISTRATION

Nearly as universal as the demand for redemption of the peasant allotments were the demands of the gentry assemblies for further reforms. The common goal of all these demands was the elimination of the existing system of arbitrary bureaucratic administration. All the gentry assemblies now followed the Vladimir assembly of 1860 in demanding: judicial reform, including the introduction of public, verbal court procedure, independence of the judiciary, and, for the most part, a jury system; personal responsibility of all government officials before the courts; reform of state finances, mainly in the direction of making the state budget public; and an end to press censorship.[3] Finally, and

[1] ORLB, *Arkhiv Cherkasskikh*, 1 26/14, 5–6.

[2] *TsGIAL, f.* 1282, no. 1091, pp. 17a–18a; *TsGAOR, f.* 109, No. 33, part 4, pp. 11–13. P. Zelenyi, 'Khersonskoe dvorianstvo i khersonskaia guberniia v 1862 godu', *Severnyi vestnik*, August 1889, pp. 65–6; *TsGIAL, f.* 1341, no. 59, pp. 51–2. See Appendix III.

[3] Thus, for example, the Moscow gentry's petition to the Emperor (approved by a vote of 306–58) called for 'protection of personal and property rights of all citizens of the State by the introduction of verbal and public court procedure and a jury court . . .', 'publication of state revenues and expenditures, as a means of calming fears about

foremost, the gentry in one voice demanded the institution of local self-government.

The gentry's demand for the reform of local administration was not, of course, a new one. The question of administrative reorganization had been inevitably raised by the discussion of peasant emancipation. During preparation of the peasant emancipation, the demand for local self-administration had been made by the Tver provincial committee, by numerous deputies of the 'first convocation', and by the gentry assemblies in 1859–60. The government had hesitatingly begun consideration of local administrative reorganization in 1858 and then taken it up in formal and serious fashion by the creation of the 'Miliutin commission' in 1859. Government recognition of the gentry's demand for *self*-administration was indicated in Lanskoi's August 1859, memoir, in terms of a 'reward' for the gentry. And the Miliutin commission proposed to include in its plans for local administrative reform the principle of 'participation of every class in economic [*khoziaistvennoe*] administration'.[1]

After 19 February 1861, discussion of local administrative reform was taken up with a new intensity by the government, the gentry and public opinion at large. Although no direct public participation in the preparation of the *zemstvo* reform was permitted, the 'five questions' did give the gentry some opportunity to express their opinions on that subject. And, just as before 1861 with the specific question of emancipation, these opinions were expressed within the context of an ongoing discussion by 'society' at large, at least part of which found its way into print. To be sure, most serious political questions were off-limits for the censored legal press. But their published discussion could be, and was, carried on abroad and 'underground'.

a financial crisis...', and 'public discussion in the press of questions concerning changes in all fields which the Government is planning in connection with forthcoming administrative and economic reforms'. (*TsGIAL, f.* 1282, no. 1092, pp. 28–9a.) And the Riazan assembly, in a protocol, demanded 'introduction of publicity into the administration of finance...', 'organization of public and verbal court procedure, and independence of the judiciary...', and 'organization of proper police authority, with responsibility before the courts'. (*ORLB, Arkhiv Cherkasskikh,* 1 26/14, pp. 5–6.)

[1] Garmiza, *Podgotovka zemskoi reformy*, p. 131.

The gentry after emancipation, 1861–5

In the domestic press, Katkov's *Russkii vestnik* (where Unkov-skii, Golovachev and other gentry liberals had published their views on emancipation before 1861) took the lead in proposing the abolition of caste distinctions. Katkov himself, at that time still in the liberal anglophile stage of his political development, argued in a number of commentaries published in 1861–2 that caste distinctions, indeed the gentry class itself, were not 'Russian', and identified them as German imports.[1] In his view, the gentry, now that emancipation had been executed, while ceasing to be a closed estate, could take the place in Russia of a middle class. In short, as his intellectual biographer has written, Katkov, while militating against 'artificial' social divisions, accepted as natural the tendency of society to coalesce into groups of common interest, and this meant primarily *property* interests. Thus on the *zemstvo* question he proposed that local self-government be based on property qualifications.[2]

It was also in *Russkii vestnik* that Saltykov-Shchedrin published his articles proposing an end to gentry class privileges and calling for the 'union of the classes' by the gentry's voluntary entrance into the peasant communes and *volosti*.

The debate in the legal press over gentry privileges got underway in serious fashion in early 1862, at the time when most of the gentry assemblies (and especially such politically important assemblies as Moscow, Petersburg and Tver) were meeting for the first time after the emancipation. It was launched by Ivan Aksakov. Writing in his paper *Den'* (*The Day*) on the occasion of the opening of the Moscow assembly (6 January 1862), Aksakov urged the gentry to request 'that the gentry be allowed to perform, solemnly and before all Russia, the great act of abolishing itself as a class; that gentry privileges be modified and extended to all classes in Russia'.[3] The gentry, Aksakov argued, no longer stood apart either by privilege or by origin: They had lost their essential privilege, on which all their other privileges had depended, that of owning serfs; and their origins were not by blood—the Table

---

[1] *Sovremennaia letopis'*, no. 15 (1861).
[2] S. Nevedenskii, *Katkov i ego vremia* (St Petersburg, 1888), p. 158.
[3] I. S. Aksakov, *Sochineniia*, v (Moscow, 1887), 218.

of Ranks had changed that.[1] The retention or addition of other
privileges for the gentry would lead, warned Aksakov, only to
curtailment of the rights of other classes and to division between
the upper and lower strata of society.[2]

In Aksakov's view, the gentry was bound to disappear as a
separate class; the *pomeshchiki* would 'enter the general status of
private landholders, formed freely and naturally from persons
of all classes, completely equal in rights, without distinction as
to origin, and without any property qualifications'.[3] The private
landholders were not, in Aksakov's opinion, to form a privileged
class with advantages over the peasants. Private and 'communal'
landholders alike were to gather in common assemblies where
they would choose their common representatives.[4]

Aksakov's article immediately became a *cause célèbre* in Russian
society.[5] Although Aksakov's open invitation to the gentry to
abolish itself as a class was not again repeated in the domestic
press of the period, his opinion that the gentry were fated to merge
into the 'general status of private landholders' was almost generally
accepted in contemporary journalistic opinion. His recommendation that all property qualifications also be abolished was not.[6]

Aksakov's proposal to the gentry was actually taken up by
some of the gentry assemblies, most dramatically by the Tver
assembly. Whether or not we attribute the initiative for the Tver
gentry's act of self-abnegation primarily to Aksakov's article, it
remains certain that these 'class-nihilists' were acting within a
definite political context, and could be sure that their act would
be comprehended by their contemporaries.

Shortly after the appearance of Aksakov's article, a brochure
written by the indefatigable publicist A. I. Koshelev began to
circulate in the capitals and among the gentry. Published in
Leipzig under the title *What Exit for Russia from the Existing
Situation*,[7] Koshelev's brochure foreshadowed most of the con-

---

[1] 'More than half the gentry', Aksakov wrote, 'are the sons of merchants, priests, *mesh-chane*, and even peasants'. *Ibid.*, p. 217.
[2] *Ibid.*   [3] *Ibid.*, p. 219.   [4] *Ibid.*
[5] Cf. B. N. Chicherin, *Vospominaniia. Moskovskii universitet*, pp. 66–8; Garmiza, *Pod-gotovka zemskoi reformy*, p. 83 and ff.; Sladkevich, *Ocherki istorii obshchestvennoi mysli*, p. 128.   [6] On this question see below, pp. 367–8.
[7] *Kakoi iskhod dlia Rossii iz nyneshnego polozheniia?* (Leipzig, 1862).

conclusions of the forthcoming Tver gentry assembly. Koshelev began his argument with an analysis of the 'existing situation' which was in most respects identical to the complaints of the gentry assemblies; 'Everywhere—,' wrote Koshelev, 'in Petersburg, in Moscow, in the interior of Russia, north south, east and west—all are dissatisfied, all feel confined, insulted, and poverty-stricken. All are convinced that Russia cannot long remain in such a state.' The gentry were disgruntled and dissatisfied with the terms of emancipation; the peasantry thought itself deceived by the gentry; the merchantry was confused and consequently curtailing credit and hoarding its capital; writers, scholars professors, students—to their complaints against the censorship and various restrictions on learning there was no end.[1]

Koshelev's plan for remedying the critical situation contained several points. For the gentry, he proposed—following Aksakov —an end to special privileges:

The gentry must emancipate themselves from all the privileges by which they have so far separated themselves from other citizens. The sooner and the more willingly that they do this, the more will be not only their honor, but the more will be their advantages. To bind oneself to that which is impossible of retention is stupid. Now, by timely renunciation of false privileges, we can raise ourselves in the eyes of the people and acquire genuine rights. [The people] have need of us; they fear the bureaucracy even more than we; now we can become their leaders . . .[2]

K. D. Kavelin, in a brochure called *The gentry and the peasant emancipation* (published abroad in 1862, but written in May 1861), had also favored elimination of legal class distinctions and privileges, arguing that the gentry would flourish while undergoing a gradual transformation into a class distinguished only by land and property.[3]

The approving prediction that the gentry were fated, as Aksakov put it, to merge into 'the general status of private landowners', although generally accepted in the predominantly

---

[1] *Ibid.*, pp. 1–2. [2] *Ibid.*, pp. 16–17.
[3] *Dvorianstvo i osvobozhdenie krest'ian*, in *Sobranie sochinenii K. D. Kavelina*, II (St Petersburg, 1898), 126–8.

liberal press, did not go unchallenged. Count Orlov-Davydov, a participant in the January 1862 Moscow assembly, responded to Aksakov's proposition with the argument, published in *Nashe vremia*, that:

Needs and opinions should be expressed by each class separately, in its own language and from its own personal point of view, even if with a smattering of class prejudices and passions. . . . If, on the contrary, such a mixing [of classes in a representative assembly] were to take place, then all the civil classes would fuse into one democratic chaos, impermissible in any well-structured monarchy. Each class has its own high and responsible calling and proper circle of activities in the elaboration of social and state welfare; therefore in a monarchial system no one class has the right to repudiate its rights or related obligations, to annul the essence of its calling, in a word—to destroy itself. It is obvious that such self-destruction of one class will lead to the destruction of all other classes, and therefore of all the conditions for the existence of the monarchy.[1]

But it was not only from within the 'aristocratic' camp that the Aksakov proposition was criticized. In his articles, first published in *Nashe vremia* in 1862, Boris Chicherin also argued against destruction of the gentry as a distinct legal estate. In his opinion, only the gentry was capable of performing the functions of a 'political class', which it would have to continue doing until a middle class (so far non-existent in Russia) was able to assume the task. The peasants, though they were the government's main concern, were not capable of political thought.[2] Chicherin therefore also opposed elimination of the gentry or its unification with other classes. He went only so far as to propose opening gentry status to university-educated persons owning at least 500 *desiatiny* of land.[3]

Superficial as it has been, this brief glance at the views professed in Russian publicism on the question of gentry privileges reveals

---

[1] Barsukov, *Zhizn' i trudy Pogodina*, XIX, 5–6.

[2] 'There has developed in the gentry', Chicherin wrote, 'a consciousness of rights which does not exist in the other classes. And this, together with education, makes the gentry the only possible political actor in Russia.' Chicherin, *Neskol'ko sovremennykh voprosov* (Moscow, 1862), p. 90. Chicherin pointed out that this meant, first of all, the need for gentry dominance in local administration. (*Ibid.*, p. 258.)

[3] *Ibid.*, pp. 85 ff. This proposal Chicherin borrowed from a proposal made in the Moscow gentry assembly in January 1862.

the three basic positions put forward on this subject: The majority, 'classical-liberal' view, which proposed an end to all caste distinctions and saw the gentry's future as a group of property holders; the more conservative, but essentially liberal, view which was skeptical of the simple efficacy of property as a criterion for political influence and thus, corollarily, concerned to preserve for the gentry, as the most 'enlightened' segment of the population, a special role in local administration; and the outright conservative view which wanted to preserve the pre-1861 class distinctions more or less intact. All of these views found their reflection in the opinions expressed in the gentry assemblies in 1861–2.

On the whole, gentry discussion of local self-administration after the emancipation can be distinguished from the pre-emancipation discussion by its primary concern with the details of the *zemstvo* reform—with questions of representation, property qualifications, and the like. Before emancipation, the discussion for the most part, had involved broader questions concerning limitation of bureaucratic arbitrariness and the general principles of self-administration.

As Garmiza has observed, the majority of the gentry assemblies considering the government's questions restricted themselves to 'laconic protocols concerning the organization of *zemstvo* obligations'.[1] Moreover, few of the assemblies (even of the more liberally-inclined among them) ventured to define the function of the proposed *zemstvo* institutions in any wider terms than the strictly economic functions of composing budgets for the collection and expenditure of the taxes and obligations which were part of the general *zemstvo* funds.[2]

It is a remarkable fact that all the gentry assemblies accepted, as a matter of course, the principles that local self-government was to be participated in by all classes, and was to be founded on an elective basis.[3] (In Moscow, Pskov and Petersburg as in Tver, the gentry also proposed in this regard the election of peace mediators to replace the existing system of bureaucratic appointments.) The crucial subjects of debate among the gentry were:

---

[1] Garmiza, *Podgotovka zemskoi reformy*, p. 71.   [2] *Ibid.*   [3] *Ibid.*

The question of what was to become of gentry privileges and gentry class-organization with the institution of general local self-administration; and especially the question of what sort of electoral system was to be instituted—to what extent if any were the gentry to be assured a preferential position in the new institutions. These were the main subjects of debate in the gentry assemblies; a debate so strong that important questions concerning the competence of the proposed institutions and their relation to the central government were often hardly touched upon.[1]

The gentry's response to these issues was complex and represented many points of view. On the whole, however, gentry views adhered to the liberal-conservative dichotomy which had already been established in gentry opinion on peasant emancipation. The most extreme expression of the liberal position was provided by the Tver gentry, whose renunciation of their class privileges included renunciation of the gentry's class organization and all their administrative functions. These were to be absorbed, in the view of the Tver liberals, by local institutions of general self-government representing a legally and fiscally unified citizenry. The Tver gentry did not present a detailed plan for the organization of local self-government. It is, accordingly, impossible to define exactly the views of the Tver liberals on such important questions as representation and property qualifications. It seems certain, however—on the basis of such documents as the Tver committee's plan for administrative reform and Unkovskii's Commentaries—that the Tver gentry did not envision a total democratization of local self-government, on the principle of 'one man—one vote'. Like all gentry liberals of the time, they probably counted on some property qualifications to ensure a significant position in local self-government for the gentry (the 'educated class'); the gentry as landholders, not as members of a privileged class, were to have a voice in local affairs. One can be equally certain that the Tver liberals envisioned general executive-administrative competency for the *zemstvo* institutions, as well as the 'housekeeping' functions then being planned for them by the government.

[1] *Ibid.*, p. 82.

Closest to the Tver assembly in their views on this subject were the Kherson gentry, who met in provincial assembly in the fall of 1862. Here, in a draft protocol approved by the majority of deputies, the Kherson gentry made the following remarkable declaration:

In the entire nation we see general mistrust, a fall in trade and the economy, general ferment of thought. It could not have been otherwise. The elimination of one of the main bases of the civil structure draws after it the necessity of general reform.

With the abolition of serfdom the Sovereign Emperor, immortalizing himself, dealt the decisive blow to the former order of things. Now, so far as we are able to understand, His Majesty has summoned us to new participation in his further labors, desiring to know our sincere opinion about the basic reforms which are necessary for Russia.

The opinion of the Kherson gentry will not be wordy.

Having in mind the welfare of the fatherland, convinced that without the unification of the entire people into one whole no changes are realizable, we renounce all our exclusive legal rights, preserving among them only the right—undefined by law—to be, as the most enlightened class and that which has made the comparatively largest sacrifices to the fatherland, the moral representatives of the people.[1]

The old class-organization, the protocol continued, must be replaced by 'regional self-governments' of 'elected representatives from all classes, with the greatest possible reduction in property qualifications'.[2] No other assemblies solved the problem of reconciling gentry privileges and administrative functions with the proposed institution of self-government for all classes by formally renouncing all gentry privileges and advocating the abolition of gentry institutions.

[1] Zelenyi, 'Khersonskoe dvorianstvo', pp. 65–6.
[2] *Ibid.*, p. 66. In the end, the protocol was not endorsed by the provincial assembly in this form. The marshal, E. A. Kasinov, fearing controversy and the wrath of the government, persuaded acceptance of the protocol without the bold words 'we renounce'. That paragraph was replaced by the statement: 'We propose that application of the elective principle to regional self-administration is the best means for unification of the public interests of all classes.' And with that change the protocol was unanimously accepted. (*Ibid.*, pp. 73, 76.) Other reforms proclaimed urgent by the protocol included: '1. The necessity of full publicity of judicial procedure, with a jury system; 2. Full and equal responsibility before the law of all members of society . . .; 3. Abolition of the law on obligatory service'. (*Ibid.*, p. 66.)

The remainder of the assemblies differed among themselves mainly over questions concerning the arrangement of property qualifications, representation, and other matters directly concerning the organization of the *zemstvo* institutions. A few assemblies were of the same general inclination as the Tver and Kherson assemblies, and were also more explicit than the latter in their prescriptions for the structure and competence of the *zemstvo* institutions. Noteworthy in this respect were the proposals of the Nizhnii Novgorod and Petersburg gentry.

The Nizhnii Novgorod gentry had been among the first to respond to the government's 'five questions' (in December 1860). They then proposed the creation of *zemstvo* institutions (assemblies and executive committees) on the *uezd* and provincial levels. Election to these institutions was to take place in three *curiae* (of landholders, urban population and peasant communes, respectively). Within the *curiae*, representation was to be strictly in proportion to the land taxes, without distinction as to class. The provincial assembly—according to the gentry's proposal, by far the most authoritative of the proposed institutions—was to contain at least 50 per cent peasant representatives, about one-third representatives from the landholding *curia*, and one-sixth from the urban population. This was by far the most considerable representation allowed the peasantry by any of the detailed gentry projects.[1]

The Petersburg assembly, traditional bastion of the 'aristocratic' position, had not passed on the details of local administrative reform in their January 1862 meeting, but they had heard then the proposals of A. P. Platonov, gentry marshal of Tsarskoe Selo *uezd* and a former close associate of N. A. Bezobrazov. He proposed participation of the population in local self-administration not by classes, but in accordance with regional principles: *uezd* assemblies were to consist of representatives of the towns and *volosti* of the *uezd*; provincial assemblies (*dumy*) were to be constituted by representatives of the *uezd* assemblies, and so forth. Platonov did not, however, propose the reduction of gentry representation to the same level as peasant representation.

[1] *Trudy komissii o gubernskikh i uezdnykh uchrezhdeniiakh*, part II, book 2 (St Petersburg, 1863), appendix, pp. 1–3; Garmiza, *Podgotovka zemskoi reformy*, pp. 72–4.

Popular representation should be arranged, he declared, 'so that enlightened citizens would have a voice, preferential in comparison to their number, over those citizens of inferior means whose education has not yet reached the same level of development'.[1] Platonov's plan thus provided that representation be proportioned according to property qualifications, with the added retention of a hereditary factor: 'Enlightenment', he contended, tended to be passed from generation to generation, a situation which merited proper reflection in popular representation.[2]

Though warmly received in the Petersburg assembly, Platonov's proposals were not officially endorsed as the basis of a protocol or petition.[3] The gentry did agree, however, in official protocol, to end the exclusiveness of their class organization by admitting 'all landowners to the gentry assembly, for activities pertaining to the general interests of the rural population'.[4]

Meeting a year later, in March 1863, the Petersburg gentry proceeded to elaborate a detailed plan for *zemstvo* reform. According to this plan, the *zemstvo* institutions were to include—beside the *uezd* and provincial assemblies and their executive bodies—an '*uezd* electoral congress', which was to consist of persons from all classes without division into electoral *curiae*. Its members were to include: persons with direct right of participation (owners of landed property valued at not less than 15,000 rubles); representatives elected by persons or groups holding not less than 750 rubles in property; and peasant representatives, one from each *volost'*. This congress was to elect: deputies to the provincial assembly, the chairman and other members of the

---

[1] *TsGAOR, f.* 109, no. 33, part 4, p. 22. [2] *Ibid.*, pp. 22–3.

[3] *Ibid.*, p. 5.

[4] *Ibid.*, p. 3. This provision was a compromise between two extremes of opinion in the assembly, the one—led by the ubiquitous N. A. Bezobrazov—demanding total retention of gentry exclusiveness, the other—led by the representatives of Petersburg and Iamburg *uezdy*—proposing elimination of exclusive gentry organizations altogether. According to this compromise solution, the gentry were to maintain a separate organization for their 'class affairs'. (*Ibid.*, pp. 8–9a, 42–52a, 53–6a: The proposals of Bezobrazov and the Petersburg and Iamburg gentry.)

A similar declaration, advocating 'participation in elections [i.e., gentry assemblies] and in the administration of local affairs by persons of all the other classes', was made by the Simbirsk gentry in 1862. *TsGIAL, f.* 1341, no. 59, pp. 51–2.

provincial executive committee, and the peace mediators and other officials of the *uezd*. The functions of the *zemstvo* assemblies were carefully spelled out by the Petersburg assembly. Although for the most part strictly 'economic', they also included election of officials for certain 'judicial and administrative posts', and the right to 'petition about the economic needs and welfare of the province'.[1]

The Pskov gentry, meeting in January 1862, carried on an animated discussion of the future of their own class organization, a discussion prompted by the government's 'five questions'. On this issue the Pskov assembly split into two clearly opposed parties. One party, comprising a large majority in the assembly, demanded abolition of gentry class-exclusiveness and proposed unification of all classes along the lines which had recently been advocated by Ivan Aksakov in *Den'*.[2] This party was led by a group of young *pomeshchiki*, including a Baron Medem, V. V. Golenishchev-Kutuzov and (in the words of the local gendarme officer) 'many other more or less enlightened persons'.[3] 'You speak of our rights', declared Baron Medem, 'but what kind of rights are these . . ., granted us by some woman . . .?[4] We must unite with the people and stand at their head, for only then will we be sufficiently strong to put a stop to arbitrariness and government-by-decree'.[5]

The minority party in the assembly, reported the gendarme officer, consisted of 'men of old gentry convictions, and belonging, for the most part, to high society'. They stood for 'class exclusiveness, and solemnly protested against the new ideas'.[6]

The Pskov assembly exploited the right of response to the government's questions to present a detailed plan for the organization of local self-administration. 'Local . . . institutions must receive the

---

[1] *Trudy komissii o gubernskikh i uezdnykh uchrezhdeniiakh*, part II, book 2, appendix, pp. 29–37.
[2] See above, pp. 356–7.
[3] Medem was a young *pomeshchik* who had been educated in the Alexandrine *lycée*. Kutuzov, 'intelligent, educated and scholarly', had been under attack by many local *pomeshchiki* for his actions as a peace mediator. *TsGAOR, f.* 109, no. 33, part 2, pp. 6a–7.
[4] That is, Catherine the Great—a slighting reference to Bezobrazov's memoir, which praised the 'immortal Catherine' as author of the Charter to the Gentry.
[5] *Ibid.*, pp. 12–12a. This phrase betrays the influence of Koshelev's summons.
[6] *Ibid.*, p. 7.

right [declared the protocol of the assembly] of direct and immediate participation in the expenditure of all general [*zemskie*] sums . . . The confirmation of budgets and control must be the right of all classes'.[1] For this purpose the Pskov gentry proposed the creation of provincial and *uezd zemstvo* assemblies of representatives elected from all classes of the population. The gentry, as such, were to receive no separate representation in these institutions, being incorporated into the general classification of 'landholders' (in which practically, of course, the gentry would remain the nearly exclusive participants). Primary influence in the *uezd* assemblies was assured for the 'landholders' by property qualifications: All owners of 500 *desiatiny* of land or more were to have the right of direct participation; the peasants were to have one representative from each *volost'*. The provincial assembly was to consist of two deputies from the 'landholders' of each *uezd*, and one deputy each from the peasantry and urban classes of each *uezd*.[2] Similar in its emphasis on high property qualifications for direct participation in the projected *zemstvo* institutions was the project of the Kursk gentry, which proposed an all-class, elective *zemstvo* organization with high qualifications for landowners (equal to the qualifications for participation in the gentry assemblies), and very restricted representation for the peasantry and urban population. According to the Kursk proposals, the gentry marshals were to be chairmen of the *zemstvo* assemblies and their executive committees.[3]

Of more unequivocally conservative sympathies in their proposals concerning gentry privileges and the projected representative institutions were the gentry of Orenburg, Kaluga and Novgorod. The Orenburg gentry, meeting in late 1862, formally proposed retention of gentry privileges alongside the new *zemstvo* institutions, and restriction in the latter of the 'democratic element'. The Kaluga gentry (meeting in January 1863) made

[1] *Trudy komissii o gubernskikh i uezdnykh uchrezhdeniiakh*, part II, book 2, appendix, p. 8.
[2] *Ibid.* Gentry influence was also guaranteed by the provision that the gentry marshals act as chairmen of the executive committees of the assemblies. Two of the four members of the provincial executive committee were to be gentry representatives, as was at least one of the four members of the *uezd* executive committees.
[3] Garmiza, *Podgotovka zemskoi reformy*, pp. 70–1.

similar proposals, especially in relation to retention of gentry assemblies and other organs of gentry class organization. So too did the Novgorod gentry, who proposed participation by the gentry in the *zemstvo* institutions as a class prerogative, independent of property qualifications.[1]

The gentry responses to the government's 'five questions' and the available information about the gentry assemblies of 1861–2 permit a generalization about gentry views on the important questions of gentry privileges and local self-administration. These views may be arranged in a spectrum with the following characteristics: At the 'left' end of the spectrum were the views of a small yet significant minority of *pomeshchiki* (the Tver gentry, the Kherson gentry, and significant groups in several other assemblies) which frankly demanded abolition of gentry privileges and separate gentry administration. In its most far-reaching application—that of the Tver gentry—this demand was extended to the problem of emancipation, by the proposal that all classes share in the burden of redemption. The Tver gentry, preceded by the gentry of Petersburg and Iamburg *uezdy*,[2] also explicitly proposed that the gentry—as landowners—shoulder their share of the general tax burden in the state. In this view, the social and political future of the landed gentry lay with the assimilation of the gentry into a general class of landed proprietors, open to all segments of the population. The influence of the landowning class would be maintained through an effective system of local self-government, in which its significance would be assured by giving it approximately one-third of total representation.

The broad middle segment in the spectrum of gentry opinion in fact shared much of this view. While hesitant, or unwilling,

---

[1] *Ibid.*, pp. 69–70.
[2] A draft of an address to the Emperor presented to the Petersburg assembly in January 1862 by a group of gentry from Iamburg and Petersburg *uezdy* proposed, *inter alia*, that all taxes and obligations be transferred from the peasants personally to the land, including gentry land. Apparently this draft was not voted upon by the assembly (although Herzen published it in *Kolokol*—1 March 1862—under the title 'Address which the Petersburg gentry composed, but feared to present to the Emperor', thus implying that it was accepted by the assembly as a whole). *TsGAOR*, f. 109, no. 33, part 4, pp. 53–6a.

to part with all gentry privileges, and unattracted by the prospect of sharing the burdens of redemption and general taxes, it also accepted the classic liberal proposition that property, not formal class distinctions, should be the basic denominator for political influence. Accepting this proposition, it proposed, on the whole, a position of greater influence in local affairs for landed property than did the representatives of the gentry 'left'.

Finally, the 'right' extreme of the spectrum of gentry opinion was occupied by a conservative minority which—although accepting the principle of all-class, elective self-administration—explicitly defended retention of separate gentry organization, and demanded formal recognition of the gentry's privileged status in the system of *zemstvo* representation.

None of the gentry assemblies supported any one of these views in unanimity. Rather, each of them was, to one or another degree, a microcosm of the general spectrum of gentry opinion.

'CONSTITUTIONALISM': THE CAMPAIGN FOR POPULAR REPRESENTATION

As events in Tver province showed, the government's hopes that solicitation of gentry opinion on a few questions concerning local affairs would forestall consideration by the gentry assemblies of broader political questions and the presentation of addresses with political demands proved to be in vain. It was not only in Tver that these hopes were disappointed: In almost all the gentry assemblies meeting in 1861–2, broader political questions were raised, above and beyond the specific question of local administrative reform. Gentry demands raised in the gentry assemblies reflected differing political views, but in one essential aspect they all had a common goal: The calling in by the government of public representatives for reconsideration of the emancipation legislation and for effective participation in further reform legislation. Although the gentry nowhere demanded institution of a formally constitutional regime, their demands were generally considered 'constitutionalist' by contemporaries, and the more extreme among them (such as the Tver address) certainly did contain constitutionalist implications, in so far as they advocated participation by representatives of the public in all major legislative undertakings then being considered. (It is with these considerations in mind that the terms 'constitutional' and 'constitutionalist' will be used henceforth.)

The origins of the constitutionalist campaign

The 'constitutionalist campaign' mounted by the gentry in the winter of 1861–2 was begun by Russian publicists writing abroad or 'underground'.

The most explicit, and for the gentry probably the most influential, argument connecting the possibility of further reforms, and in particular of meaningful local self-administration, and popular representation at the center was made by A. I. Koshelev, in the same pamphlet in which he had advocated the abolition of gentry privileges. Continuing his negative assessment of the current situation after proposing an end to gentry exclusiveness, Koshelev proposed other remedies, beginning with immediate redemption of the peasant allotments.[1] The possibility of any basic improvements or changes was, however, blocked by the bureaucracy. Koshelev concluded that there was only one way to overcome the bureaucracy and escape from the current critical situation:

Only united concerted union of the living forces of the country can afford the necessary strength and resources for the peaceful and true escape from the present critical situation. In former times, on difficult occasions, the Tsars summoned elected representatives for advice from the whole Russian land. When, if not now, should this pacifying and fruitful means be resorted to? *The summoning of a duma of the land in Moscow, the heart of Russia, far from the bureaucratic center, is, in our extreme conviction, the only path to the solution of the great problems facing our time.*[2]

---

[1] *Kakoi iskhod*, p. 15.

[2] *Ibid.*, pp. 37–8. Emphasis added. Koshelev accompanied his proposal with a concrete plan: In each *uezd* there were to be formed assemblies for discussion of local problems, consisting of one deputy from each peasant *volost'* and an equal number of deputies (for the *uezd* as a whole) from private landholders. The urban classes were to have representatives in numbers comparable to the others in regard to population, but not to exceed the number of representatives from either one of the other groups. Each

Koshelev proposed that 'those crucial problems, the solution of which is so necessary for Russia', be presented to the decision of the *duma*. 'Here,' he concluded, 'the peasant problem will be decided easily and finally . . .'[1]

True to his Slavophile principles, Koshelev protested that the *duma* which he was advocating had nothing to do with parliaments, constitutions or limitations on the autocracy. It was to be a strictly consultative body. To his protestations, however, Koshelev appended the following significant comment:

What does constitution mean? If this word implies a charter, with two houses, with an artificial balance of powers, with transformation of the Sovereign into a reigning puppet, then such a constitution, it is firmly hoped, we will never have. *But, at the same time we are deeply convinced that with time—not now—the Tsar, having learned of the genuine needs of the country through the dumy of the land, will grant to Russia a state charter [gosudarstvennaia ustavnaia gramota] that will guarantee us all those rights which are crucial for the individual citizens, and which in other lands have been gained by struggles and force.*[2]

Local self-government, argued Koshelev, was good and necessary for Russia, but would remain useless and ineffectual if the central administration were left unreformed. 'It is necessary', he wrote in another brochure published later in 1862, 'to change the system of higher administration; without this no new local institutions can succeed. This change can be produced only by a *Duma* of the Land . . .'[3]

Koshelev's reasoning that the government was incapable of carrying out the necessary reforms, and that this could be accomplished only by an assembly (or *duma*) of elected representatives was repeated in February by the Tver gentry. It is not possible to say to what extent the Tver gentry, in drawing up their protocol and address, were indebted to Koshelev's brochures; but that the extent was considerable seems indicated by the fact

uezd assembly would send from three to six deputies to a provincial *duma*, which in turn would elect from three to six deputies to the *duma* in Moscow. In the provincial and central *dumy* no distinction as to the origin of the deputies was to be made. *Ibid.*, pp. 40–41.

[1] *Ibid.*, p. 41.   [2] *Ibid.*, pp. 38–9. Emphasis added.
[3] *Konstitutsiia, samoderzhavie i zemskaia duma* (Leipzig, 1862), pp. 38–9.

that Kardo-Sysoev's analysis of current conditions—on which the assembly's protocol was based—was in large part borrowed directly from Koshelev's brochure.[1]

A significant role in the campaign calling for a *zemskii sobor* was also played by the editors of *Kolokol*.

To a remarkable degree the views and proposals of Herzen and Ogarev in the years immediately preceding and following the proclamation of emancipation had followed the same evolution as those of the liberal gentry, and of the Tver liberals in particular. The reform program advanced by *Kolokol* in the pre-emancipation period was essentially identical to the liberal gentry reform program. And in the period following publication of the government Rescripts and the publication of its own first program, *Kolokol's* position remained firmly in line with the gentry liberals. Like Unkovskii, Herzen and Ogarev urged redemption of the peasants' labor value by 'all classes of Russia in accordance with wealth, like "income tax".'[2] And later—but also before emancipation—Herzen and Ogarev preceded (and perhaps provoked) the 1862 proposal of the Tver gentry by advocating participation of the whole state in redemption not only of peasant labor, but of peasant lands as well.[3]

Following the gentry assemblies of 1859–60, and evidently influenced by them, *Kolokol* began to advocate the creation of land banks,[4] and to urge the further liberal reforms which had been proposed in the gentry assemblies. In an article entitled 'Letters to a Compatriot' (1 August 1860), Ogarev described these reforms as: (1) '. . . Emancipation of the peasants with land immediately'; (2) ' . . . Emancipation of Russia from bureaucratic administration . . .' (3) '. . . Development of the elective principle and of rural and urban self-administration'; (4) '. . . Pub-

---

[1] Kardo-Sysoev's review of the state of the various classes repeated, almost word-for-word, the introduction to Koshelev's pamphlet. *GAKO, f.* 59, no. 4079, pp. 5–5 a.

[2] *Kolokol*, nos. 42–3, 1–15 May 1859, p. 342.

[3] *Kolokol* proposed 'capital reimbursement to the *pomeshchiki* out of the general state revenues, without any special collection from the peasants beyond the customary taxes paid by all for the general welfare'. B. S. Ginsberg, 'Otnoshenie A. I. Gertsena i N. P. Ogareva k krest'ianskoi reforme v period ee podgotovki (1857–60 gg)', *Istoricheskie zapiski*, no. 36 (1951), p. 214.

[4] *Kolokol*, nos. 77–8, 1 August 1860, pp. 643–4.

licity for the courts and emancipat[ion] of the common popular court from bureaucratic formalism'.[1] Although the editors of *Kolokol* were considerably distressed by fluctuations in the progress of the government's reform plans (especially by the crisis created by the death of Rostovtsev), they refrained in the period preceding emancipation—like the gentry liberals—from any explicitly political demands.

Following the Emancipation Proclamation, *Kolokol* at first responded with enthusiasm, though not to the neglect of its further demands.[2] Its tone, however, soon changed. In the issue of 15 June 1861, an analysis of the emancipation legislation was begun by Ogarev, who described it as 'a misshapen state of affairs'. *Kolokol's* main objections to the government's legislation were the following: The peasants had not been freed from obligatory labor; redemption of land had not been instituted; the separate peasant administration placed the peasants in 'serfdom to the *chinovniki*'; and finally, *obrok* had been increased, but peasant lands reduced.[3] The causes of this state of affairs, wrote Ogarev, were two:

1. The government is *not sincere* in the emancipation of the people; that is, essentially, the Emperor does not want any kind of emancipation.

2. [The government] is completely *incapable*; that is, it is incapable of *understanding* anything, or of *doing* anything.

Ogarev finished the article with the following words: 'The old serfdom has been replaced by a new one. In general, *serfdom has not been abolished. The people have been deceived by the Tsar*'.[4]

In mid-1861, Herzen and Ogarev, in their disenchantment with the emancipation and the general course of Russian politics (they were especially disturbed by the government's policy toward Poland), set out on two new ventures: They began to circulate their demand for a 'real emancipation' in articles, printed in *Kolokol* and elsewhere, which were designed for consumption by the peasants and other 'common people' in

---

[1] *Ibid.*, p. 643.   [2] *Kolokol*, no. 95, 1 April 1861, p. 797.

[3] *Kolokol*, nos. 101, 103–6, 15 June–1 September 1861.

[4] *Kolokol*, no. 101, 15 June 1861, pp. 845, 848.

Russia;[1] and they began to campaign for the calling of a *zemskii sobor*.[2]

The calling of a *zemskii sobor* had first been mentioned in the pages of *Kolokol* in January 1861, in an article called 'On the new year'.[3] And in July 1861, Ogarev outlined in *Kolokol* a system of self-government culminating in an assembly of elected representatives from all the provinces 'to decide what obligations and taxes should be paid by the people for needs of the state'.[4]

Inside Russia, the constitutionalist campaign was taken up by at least two underground proclamations in 1861. The first of these, Shelgunov's *To the Younger Generation* (*K molodomu poko-leniiu*), was written early in 1861, shortly after the proclamation of emancipation.[5] Addressed to 'the younger generation of all classes', it has been called the 'most typical document of revolutionary populism'.[6] 'Populist' it certainly was—it contained lengthy theoretical forays on the possibility of avoiding capitalism in Russia, and on the virtues of the peasant commune ('our rural *obshchina* is the basic cell, the union of such cells is Rus''). But despite occasional sneers at 'constitutionalist tendencies' and apparent advocacy of an end to private landed property and of the monarchy, its positive program was not revolutionary, but essentially 'constitutionalist' and reformist, in so far as it proposed concrete reforms designed to introduce the rule of law and the limiting of the arbitrary central authority. Among its positive demands were the following:

We want freedom of speech, i.e. abolition of all censorship.

We want the development of that principle of self-government which already partly exists in our people . . .

We desire that all citizens of Russia enjoy equal rights, that privileged classes not exist, that the right to higher office be granted by ability

---

[1] *Kolokol* had not previously engaged in popular propaganda. Cf. *Kolokol*, no. 102, 1 July 1861; nos. 122–3, 15 February 1862; also *Literaturnoe nasledstvo*, XXXIX–XL (Moscow, 1941), 328–36.

[2] Both these ventures seem to have been undertaken primarily on the initiative of Ogarev. Cf. *Literaturnoe nasledstvo*, XXXIX–XL, 310.

[3] *Kolokol*, no. 89, 1 January 1861, p. 751.   [4] *Kolokol*, no. 102, 1 July 1861, p. 855.

[5] M. Lemke, *Politicheskie protsessy v Rossii 1860-kh gg.* (2nd ed. Moscow-Petrograd, 1923), pp. 62–80. The proclamation was printed in 600 copies by the Free Russian Press in London and distributed in Russia in September, 1861.

[6] F. Venturi, *Roots of Revolution* (New York, 1960), p. 247.

and education, not by birth ... We do not want a nobility and titled personages. We want equality of all before the law, equality of all in state burdens, in taxes and obligations.

We desire ... that the government give the people an accounting of the money collected from them.

We want public and verbal courts ...

We want abolition of the transition status of the emancipated peasants. We desire that redemption of all personal landed property be immediately effected.[1]

Also in the course of 1861 (June–October), there appeared three numbers of the clandestine publication *The great Russian* (*Velikoruss*), which proclaimed an openly constitutionalist program. Of all the underground proclamations of the early 1860s, *The great Russian* was by far the most widely known, and was in particular well-known among the gentry.[2] Addressed 'to the educated classes' in general, *The great Russian* defined three major tasks for Russia: 'A better solution of the peasant question, the liberation of Poland, and a constitution'.[3] The proper solution of the peasant question, declared the proclamation, consisted of granting the peasants all the land they had previously used, and the 'liberation of [the peasants] from any special payments or obligations for redemption, taking [redemption] upon the entire nation'.[4] A constitution was to ensure 'responsibility of ministers, voting of the budget, a jury-court system, freedom of religion, freedom of the press, abolition of class privileges, and self-administration in regional and communal affairs'.[5]

According to *The great Russian*, the government could not be expected to grant on its own a constitution or otherwise reform itself. The Emperor, however, could be compelled to accept these changes without a bloody revolution. Therefore, it de-

---

[1] Lemke, *Politicheskie protsessy*, pp. 74–8.

[2] *Velikoruss*, in *Proklamatsii 60kh godov* (Moscow-Leningrad, 1926), pp. 27–38. (Also published in *Kolokol* in late 1861). See also Sh. M. Levin, *Obshchestvennoe dvizhenie v Rossii v 60–70e gody XIX veka* (Moscow, 1958), p. 189. The authorship of *The great Russian* has not been ascertained with certainty. There is some evidence to suggest that Chernyshevskii may have been involved in its publication. *Ibid.*, pp. 191–3 and E. S. Vilenskaia, *Revoliutsionnoe podpol'e v Rossii* (*60–e gody XIXv.*) (Moscow, 1965), pp. 84–9.

[3] *Kolokol*, no. 109, 15 October 1861.

[4] *Ibid.*   [5] *Ibid.*

clared, 'the educated classes must take the handling of affairs from the incapable government into their own hands'.[1] The writing of a constitution was to be entrusted to a representative assembly. *The great Russian* accordingly produced a draft-address for submission to the Emperor. It declared:

Only the government, relying on the free will of the nation itself, can realize those reforms without which Russia will be subjected to a terrible revolution. Call, Sovereign, representatives of the Russian nation to one of the capitals . . . so they may draw up a constitution for Russia.[2]

The great Russian urged that this address be publicized by the gentry assemblies and other established bodies, and that signatures be collected for it. 'If', the proclamation warned, 'the educated classes do not form a peaceful opposition which will force the government to eliminate the causes for an uprising before the spring of 1863, the people will irresistibly rise in the summer of 1863'.[3] The 'educated classes' clearly meant the gentry.

The gentry campaign

The call to the gentry was not in vain. In the assemblies of 1861–2 the gentry opposition movement reached an unprecedented height, and the 'constitutionalist campaign' among the gentry was for the first time elevated from the private demands of a few conservative activists like Mal'tsev, the Bezobrasovs and Count Orlov-Davydov to the level of official gentry declarations. The constitutionalist demands raised in the gentry assemblies of 1861–2 no longer represented a single political outlook, but consisted, primarily, of two currents of political thought: the continuation of the 'aristocratic-constitutionalist' outlook which had first been elaborated in conservative circles in the capitals in 1859–60, during the gentry's struggle with the Editing Commissions over the

[1] *Ibid.*, no. 107, 15 September 1861. [2] *Ibid.*, no. 115, 8 December 1861.
[3] *Ibid.* The fear of an uprising in 1863, shared by gentry, intelligentsia and government alike, was based on the observation of the extremely widespread belief among the peasants that the two year 'waiting period' provided by the legislation would be followed by the 'real freedom' they had anticipated.

preparation of the peasant reform; and a new 'liberal-constitu-tionalist' trend.

The aristocratic case was pleaded most eloquently in 1861–2, as it had been before the emancipation, by N. A. Bezobrazov, and the center of his operations were the two assemblies of Moscow and Petersburg which had traditionally been most closely associated with the aristocratic position.

Appearing before the Moscow assembly on 10 January, Bezobrazov read a memoir containing proposals for presentation to the Emperor: in the manner to which he was accustomed, he expatiated at great length on the inalienable historic rights of the Russian gentry. In spite of grandiloquent affirmations about the necessity and justice of emancipation ('with joy we can greet each of our peasants with the title of citizen'), Bezobrazov's arguments were essentially reactionary: The emancipation legislation, he declared, had violated the terms of the Charter to the Gentry in its incursions on the property rights of the gentry. *Personal* emancipation, Bezobrazov affirmed, was no violation of the Charter, but the legislation must be revised to remove incursions on the right of the *pomeshchik* to do with his land as he saw fit. (Bezobrazov did not go so far as to demand for the *pomeshchik* the right to simply drive all the peasants from the land, but in the draft petition for presentation to the Emperor with which he finished his speech, the Emperor was asked 'to confirm the basic right of the *pomeshchiki* to confirm or reject ... in the bounds of [their] estate[s] the elections and decisions of the communes', and 'to confirm the irrevocable right of every *pomeshchik* to remove from his estate and to present to the jurisdiction of the government any ... peasants who have not fulfilled their legal obligations ..., granting the peasants at the same time the right to move from one estate to another').

In calling for these changes, and others, Bezobrazov requested the Emperor, in his draft petition:

MOST GRACIOUSLY to permit the gentry to elect from among themselves representatives, two from each province, with the res-ponsibility ... of correcting the new legislation on the *pomeshchiks'* peasants in its detail, with the aim of according it with the unshakeable principles granted in the Charter to the Gentry. To allow these gentry representatives to gather in one of the capitals, as a general or state assembly. To permit this assembly to appoint, from among its members, a chairman, spokesmen and secretaries; and with the presentation of its work for IMPERIAL ratification through the State Council, to permit this assembly to send its appointed members for explanations and representation . . .

He further proposed:

To . . . extend the two-year period defined by the Manifesto of 19 February for the retention of the former order until completion of the . . . work of the state gentry assembly.[1]

Bezobrazov's memoir and petition were circulated simultaneously among the members of the Pskov assembly, and were presented by Bezobrazov personally to the Petersburg assembly (of which he was also a member) a week later (16 January).[2] The call for summoning a gentry assembly was not however adopted by any of these assemblies. In only one case, that of the Voronezh gentry, was the demand for a strictly gentry assembly made the subject of an official assembly protocol (January 1862). Here the Voronezh protocol referred to:

The need of a stabilizing element (*élément de stabilité*) in Russian legislation, which the Voronezh gentry see in . . . the participation of two gentry from each province in the state institutions.[3]

Bezobrazov's proposals, when put to the vote in the Moscow assembly, were, however, approved by a majority of 194–167, and failed to be adopted officially only because they failed to get the two-thirds majority required for confirmation of such petitions in the gentry assemblies.[4] But despite this considerable support, the Moscow gentry ended by giving their enthusiastic approval (by a vote of 306–58) to an address of quite different character.

[1] *TsGAOR, f.* 109, no. 302, pp. 23–5.
[2] *TsGAOR, f.* 109, no. 33, part 2, pp. 1–1a; 8–9a, 42–52a.
[3] *TSGIAL, f.* 1282, no. 1091, p. 17a. It may be that the address of the Tula gentry, which called for 'a general commission . . . in which there [would] be appointed at least several property owners from each province' for participation in further reform legislation, should be placed in the same category. *TsGAOR, f.* 109, no. 11, part 3, pp. 7–12. See Appendix III.
[4] Barsukov, *Zhizn' i trudy Pogodina*, XIX, 4. (Barsukov's recording of the vote differs slightly from the record of the III Section).

This petition, presented to the assembly in the name of the gentry of Podol'sk *uezd*, was introduced by Sergei Golovin (a *pomeshchik* of Podol'sk *uezd*) with a plea that the gentry exercise, in this critical moment of their existence, 'that noble moderation which is one of the characteristics of the gentry class'.[1] In contrast to Bezobrazov's petition, this one made no mention of gentry rights, but called for rapid completion of obligatory redemption of the peasant plots, and other reforms. It concluded by proposing the summoning of a special provincial gentry commission, to be succeeded by a 'general assembly' of all the land:

The Moscow gentry most loyally request YOUR IMPERIAL MAJESTY to permit them to elect from among themselves a committee for discussion of the main principles which should lie at the base of future regulations on elections; for review of the statute on general obligations; and for discussion of the question of rural credit and local needs, with participation in its labors of deputies from other classes, since these questions concern the entire rural population; the works of the committee, reviewed in a general assembly of elected persons from all classes of the State called from the provinces to Moscow, that city being the heart of Russia, to be submitted to the good judgement of YOUR IMPERIAL MAJESTY.[2]

The Moscow gentry, in calling for a 'general assembly of elected representatives from all classes of the state', presented the first formal gentry request for the summoning of an 'assembly of the land', a *zemskii sobor*. Traditional defenders of gentry privilege, the Moscow assembly had rejected the principle of gentry exclusiveness. It would appear that the considerable approval initially given to Bezobrazov's draft petition was provoked not by approval of his defense of gentry exclusiveness and certainly not by his implicit rejection of obligatory redemption, but rather by the simple fact that it was a political challenge to the government.

The Petersburg gentry, like the Moscow gentry before them, demonstrated in their assembly (which opened on 16 January

[1] *TsGIAL, f.* 1282, no. 1092, pp. 144–6; *TsGAOR, f.* 109, no. 33, part 1, pp. 17a–18.
[2] *TsGIAL, f.* 1282, no. 1092, pp. 28a–9a. Essentially the same combination of a gentry commission followed by a general assembly was called for by the Tambov assembly in the same month. *TsGIAL, f.* 1341, no. 59, pp. 51–2.

1862) that their views, too, had undergone some changes. Here Bezobrazov's proposals were rejected by a vote of 148–64.

Much more sympathy in the assembly was shown for the speech of A. P. Platonov. The burden of Platonov's speech (the same in which he had proposed local administrative reforms) was the following: The main cause of deficiencies in the reform legislation was the fact that it had been elaborated without the participation of the people. 'All this', claimed Platonov, 'destroys the faith of the people in the government, shakes the devotion of the subjects to the Emperor, and undermines his supreme power'.[1] There was, Platonov concluded, only one way to ensure the inviolability of the autocracy, while assuring that the 'voice of the people' would reach the throne:

... Participation of the civil classes in the state administration, and in the institution of a general popular representation by means of the union of elected representatives from all parts of the state in one state *duma* of the land.[2]

Platonov's proposal for the summoning of a '*duma* of the land' (*zemskaia duma*), made in the language and adorned with the argumentation of Slavophilism, was essentially identical to the request of the Moscow assembly for the summoning of a 'general assembly of elected representatives from all classes of the state'.[3] Platonov specifically insisted that the 'voice of the people' as a whole, not of the gentry alone, should reach the throne.

Only the Tver and Moscow assemblies presented formal addresses to the Emperor asking for the summoning of 'a general assembly of elected representatives from all classes of the state', but essentially similar demands, although not in the form of addresses, were also made by the Tambov gentry (January 1862), who called for 'the summoning of elected representatives from all classes for participation in legislative affairs';[4] and by the Riazan gentry (February 1862), who proposed 'the calling to

[1] *Ibid.*, pp. 17–17a.   [2] *Ibid.*, p. 17a.
[3] Referring to Russian history, Platonov argued that elective representation of the land in affairs of state was the historic right of the Russian people, having been exercised from the time of Ivan the Terrible to the end of the reign of Peter the Great (in the old *zemskie sobory* and later in the Senate created by Peter). *Ibid.*, pp. 15–15a.
[4] *TsGIAL, f.* 1341, no. 59, p. 52.

[Moscow] of persons elected by all the classes', for the purpose of 'final collective discussion' of all necessary reform measures.[1] And the Tula gentry, in the first address calling for a central elected representative body (December 1861), had proposed the calling of 'a general commission . . . in which there [would] be appointed at least several property owners from each province' for participation in further reform legislation.[2]

The 'aristocratic constitutionalists' demanded the summoning of a central gentry assembly or *duma*[3] in one of the capitals, variously for the amendment of the emancipation legislation, for participation in further reform legislation, and for general consultation. The goal of the 'aristocratic constitutionalists' remained as earlier the securing for the gentry of a formal voice in affairs of state. The fundamental force which raised 'aristocratic-constitutionalist' proposals from the drawing rooms of Petersburg and Moscow to open advocacy in numerous gentry assemblies was the growing conviction among the gentry that the emancipation, as effected, and the government's plans for local administrative reorganization threatened the very existence of the gentry class. Although the demand for the calling of a central gentry assembly or *duma* was not, in 1861–2, formally championed by the gentry assemblies of the two capital provinces, there could be no doubt that the source of the movement was to be found in the aristocratic circles of Petersburg and Moscow.

'Liberal gentry constitutionalism' was a new phenomenon. It will be recalled that before the emancipation gentry liberals had carefully dissociated themselves from any proposals for limiting the autocracy, or for the calling of special representatives to the capital, mainly for the reason that such demands were then generally associated with conservative opposition to emancipation; in short, for fear of deflecting the government from its reformist undertakings. The new gentry demand for a general assembly, or, as it was often called, a 'gathering of the land'

[1] *ORLB, Arkhiv Cherkasskikh*, I 26/14, pp. 5–6.
[2] *TsGAOR, f.* 109, no. 11, part 3, p. 12.
[3] In the Pskov assembly, one Okunev had proposed that the government be requested 'to found a *duma* of deputies from the gentry in St Petersburg'. *TsGAOR, Otchet III otdeleniia za 1862 g.*, pp. 78a–9.

(*zemskii sobor*), was raised after the moratorium which ended with the Proclamation of Emancipation.

Although only a minority of the gentry went so far as to add to the call for popular representation a renunciation of their class privileges, the poor showing of the 'aristocratic' program in the gentry assemblies would seem to indicate that a majority of the landed gentry had come to realize that the potentialities of the Charter to the Gentry had disappeared along with serfdom; that maintenance of class exclusiveness could only lead to the gentry's social and political isolation in the face of the expanding bureaucratic administration; and that the best alternative for the landed proprietors was to make a bid for political influence on the basis of the classic liberal principle of property ownership.

ECHOES OF THE GENTRY CAMPAIGN FOR A
ZEMSKII SOBOR

If the taking up of the campaign of addresses for further reforms and the summoning of a *zemskii sobor* by the Tver gentry and other assemblies in the winter of 1861–2 was, to some extent, a response to the appeals of Herzen, Ogarev, Koshelev and the underground publicists, the gentry assemblies in turn provoked a flurry of similar appeals, directed to the Emperor by various members of the intelligentsia—some of them well-known and influential, such as Herzen, Ogarev, Chernyshevskii and Nicholas Serno-Solov'evich; and others who have remained anonymous. Their response is one of the best measures of the political significance accorded by contemporaries to the gentry assemblies.

It was Chernyshevskii who made the most explicit statement about the political significance of the gentry opposition movement. As editor of *Sovremennik* in the period 1857–61, Chernyshevskii had joined the rest of the abolitionist press in publicizing the liberal reform program—that is, emancipation of the peasants with the redemption of their existing allotments through a government-financed operation.[1] Following the proclamation of

---

[1] Cf. Sladkevich, *Ocherki istorii obshchestvennoi mysli*, pp. 56–86. To be sure, Chernyshevskii differed in his general philosophical and political views from the Russian liberals. His 'real' or 'ultimate' *desiderata* in relation to the peasant reform, which he could not,

emancipation, Chernyshevskii joined the chorus of complaint against the incompleteness of the reform and continued to make common cause with the liberal gentry opposition, whose aims he endorsed in his remarkable *Letters without address*. In the *Letters*, written in February 1862—apparently under the immediate impression of the recent Tver gentry assembly[1]—Chernyshevskii denounced the terms of emancipation as nothing more than a superficial touching-up of the old order. He predicted (as had *The great Russian* before him) that an anarchic popular uprising would soon follow if the legislation were left unchanged. Chernyshevskii also drew the by now familiar conclusion—that the failure of the legislation lay in its having been devised in a purely bureaucratic manner, and that, therefore, nothing could be expected so long as the existing bureaucratic system remained unchanged. In this situation, the gentry—who had actually gotten little out of the reform and were no more satisfied than the peasants, despite the government's intentions—had turned away from the government and had taken up the general cause of reform as their own, feeling themselves, like the other classes, to be suffering at the hands of the bureaucratic administration. This development Chernyshevskii fully approved:

... With the abolition [of serfdom] the overwhelming majority of the gentry have already completely made peace, as with an irrevocable fact.... In thoughts about reform of the general administration and justice on new bases, about freedom of expression—the gentry are only the representatives of all the other classes.[2]

of course, propagate in the press, have been variously reconstructed by historians. According to the most radical reconstruction, the predominant view in Soviet historiography, they included: Unremunerated confiscation of all *pomeshchik* lands, and nationalization of the land with preservation of the communal system of land-usage. (Cf. *Ibid.*, p.86).

In *Sovremennik*, however, Chernyshevskii's differences with the liberals had been reflected primarily in the polemic over the peasant commune, which Chernyshevskii defended, from a utopian-socialist point of view, as the seed of future socialism and the key to the avoidance of capitalism and a proletariat. His main opponent in this debate was Vernadskii's *Ekonomicheskii ukazatel'* (*Economic Index*), which was the most dogmatic purveyor of classical economic liberalism in the period, and which, accordingly, had little sympathy for the idea of retaining the peasant commune.

[1] Cf. Kornilov, *Krest'ianskaia reforma*, pp. 184–5. The *Letters*, which were in fact addressed to the Emperor, were not passed by the censor and were first published abroad only in the 1870s. [2] N. G. Chernyshevskii, *Polnoe sobranie sochinenii*, x (Moscow, 1951), 100–1.

The gentry, Chernyshevskii noted, were the people's representatives not because they desired reform more than other classes, but because they had the organization that allowed them to be heard. Chernyshevskii here made no specific demands of the Emperor, but the general implication of the *Letters* was to urge acceptance of the reform demands of the gentry assemblies.

Also in the spring of 1862, Nicholas Serno-Solov'evich drew up a draft-address which he apparently planned to present to the Emperor along with a letter (these documents were seized by the authorities at the time of his arrest along with Chernyshevskii in July 1862). In it, he presented an outline of a constitutional project which provided 'supreme [executive] power' in Russia to the Emperor, and legislative power to a central 'Popular Assembly' and to provincial assemblies to be elected by all classes through *curiae*. The usual freedoms and a reformed judiciary were also provided. The peasants were to receive their allotments in property immediately, paying obligations to the state equal to those of the state peasants, and the Popular Assembly was to decide on proper remuneration for the gentry landowners.[1]

Similar demands for reforms and the convocation of an assembly of popular representatives were made in March and April 1862, respectively, in the anonymously-published short proclamations *To the Officers* (*K ofitseram*) and *Zemskaia duma*. Condemning the government as 'the armed insurgent against peaceful Russia, now shooting the people without need, now whipping and sending them into *katorga*, now filling the prisons with students, now seizing peaceful [*sic*] mediators', *To the Officers* declared:

Every Russian knows that for the welfare of his homeland it is necessary: to free the peasants with land, giving the *pomeshchiki* remuneration; to free the people from the *chinovniki*, from whips and lashes; to give all classes the same rights to the development of their well-being; to give society the freedom to arrange its own affairs; to institute a public court system, and to give everyone the right to express his thoughts freely . . .[2]

[1] N. A. Serno-Solov'evich, *Publitsistika. Pis'ma* (Moscow, 1963), pp. 178–87.
[2] *Materialy dlia istorii revoliutsionnogo dvizheniia v Rossii v 60-kh gg.* (Paris, 1905), p. 69.

Zemskaia duma, printed clandestinely in Petersburg, proclaimed that a party—*Zemskaia duma*—had been formed with the goal of changing the existing form of administration, which—being founded on force and arbitrariness—was ruining Russia and corrupting her people. The aims of the party, which evidently existed only in the imagination of the proclamation's author(s),[1] were:

Full emancipation of the peasants with all the land in their use, and: Calling of a *duma* of all the land, of elected representatives from all classes, for the composition of a new 'Law Code' ['*Ulozhenie*'], and for defining the size and means of remuneration for the *pomeshchiki* by means of the resources of the entire state.[2]

In London, the address of the Tver assembly impelled Ogarev to return to the theme of a *zemskii sobor* which he had been the first to raise. In 1862 this became one of his main concerns and he composed a number of draft-addresses to the Emperor on that subject.[3] One of these addresses, in the composition of which Herzen also took part, was actually distributed for signatures among the authors' acquaintances abroad. It was designed mainly to solicit gentry support.[4] Composed in mid-1862, this address began with an assessement of current Russian conditions, primarily the situation of the peasants and the gentry. After the familiar declaration that the government had proved itself incapable of undertaking meaningful reforms, the address continued:

We, the undersigned . . . turn to you, Sovereign, we beg and. . . desire, implore and demand that the people be consulted about the general needs through their elected representatives and called to a general *Zemskii Sobor* for the decision of how and with what institutions to save, calm, renew and exalt the Russian people and all its tribes [*plemena*], the Russian land and all its regions.

[1] There is some evidence that N. I. Utin was involved in its composition, and it appears to have been printed on the same press as *Velikoruss*. Cf. I. Miller, 'Vokrug Velikorussa', in *Revoliutsionnaia situatsiia v Rossii v 1859–61 gg.* (Moscow, 1965) (pp. 84–123), p. 110.
[2] *Materialy dlia istorii revoliutsionnogo dvizheniia*, pp. 67–8.
[3] Cf. *Literaturnoe nasledstvo*, LXIII (Moscow, 1956), 107–20.
[4] V. P. Baturinskii, *A. I. Gertsen, ego druz'ia i znakomye. Materialy dlia istorii obshchestven- nogo dvizheniia Rossii* (St Petersburg, 1904), pp. 183–4.

Therefore we request:

(1) That *volost'* and town meetings for the election of deputies to a general *Zemskii Sobor* be called in all provinces.

(2) That all adult people elect, without distinction as to class, religion, or [other] schemes, but by number [alone] . . .

(3) That, for the removal of mistrust on the part of the peasants, the gentry be registered in any *volost'* of their *uezd* for *voting* . . .

(4) That the gentry, in voting, not have any privileges by class or rank.

Continuing with the organization of voting (points 5–11), the address concluded:

(12) That in this *Zemskii Sobor*, following the resolution of the order of sessions and voting, the following be publicly discussed and resolved: The rights of property ownership . . ., the remuneration of the gentry in keeping with their sacrifice of land; the means of organizing elective administration of village, *volost'* and town; the union of *uezdy* in districts [*oblasti*] and the means of organizing district self-government; the nature and size of taxes and obligations . . . [and] the budgeting of state expenditures and income; the organization of courts, civil and criminal; the organization of church parishes; the organization of village, *volost'*, district and state credit institutions. And in general that all questions be discussed and resolved which the *Zemskii Sobor* may consider necessary . . .[1]

Conclusions

Looking back at the proclamations and addresses of 1861–2, one cannot fail to be impressed by the general similarity of the demands expressed in them, whether they came from the assembly hall of the Tver or Moscow gentry, the Free Russian Press in London, or a clandestine press in a Petersburg basement. The call was for completion of the emancipation through immediate state-financed redemption, legal and fiscal unification of the classes, an independent court system, freedom of speech, freedom of the press, popular representation in government at the center, and the institution of local self-government in the provinces. Without forgetting there were, among the authors of these documents, adherents of 'Russian socialism', the proclama-

---

[1] Iordanskii, *Konstitutsionnoe dvizhenie*, pp. 127–9.

tions and addresses of 1861–2 were calling for *liberal* reforms, for the *liberalization* of Russian life and politics, not for revolution. The one significant exception in this regard was P. G. Zaich-nevskii's *Young Russia (Molodaia Rossiia)*[1] which appeared in May 1862, and attracted instant notoriety because its appearance coincided (quite accidentally) with the outbreak of the great Petersburg fires. *Young Russia* called for immediate, violent social revolution, the goal of which would be 'a social and democratic Russian republic' in which landed property would be socialized, marriage and the family abolished, women emancipated, etc. It is a measure of the contemporary mood of the radical intelligent-sia that its most influential representatives, including Cherny-shevskii, Herzen, and even Bakunin, strongly condemned *Young Russia* as an irresponsible and immature act.[2]

Three observations in particular should be made about the campaign for the summoning of a *zemskii sobor*: (1) It was, in every case, based on the affirmation that the bureaucratic adminis-tration had proved itself, in its preparation of the emancipation legislation, incapable of carrying out meaningful reforms. Al-though few of the proclamations and addresses spoke specifically of a 'constitution' or of the detailed structure of a permanent political order (*Velikoruss* and Serno-Solov'evich's project were notable exceptions), they were all 'constitutionalist' in so far as they advocated participation by representatives of the public in the major legislative undertakings then being considered. (2) All of the addresses calling for liberal reforms and the summoning of a *zemskii sobor* expressed, in the very fact of their composition, apparent belief in the possibility of a 'union of tsar and people', by-passing the bureaucracy to finish the emancipation and liberalize the state *without fundamental social or political upheavals*. (3) The proclamations, and especially the addresses devised by the intelligentsia, were composed, in part at least, with the specific intention of encouraging and supporting the opposition move-ment underway among the landed gentry. It is noteworthy that

[1] *Materialy dlia istorii revoliutsionnogo dvizheniia*, pp. 56–63.
[2] Cf. B. P. Koz'min, *Iz istorii revoliutsionnoi mysli v Rossii* (Moscow, 1961), pp. 266–71; Levin, *Obshchestvennoe dvizhenie*, pp. 201–3.

all the documents cited in the preceding pages advocated not simply giving all or any part of the land to the peasants, but its *redemption*. And the addresses produced in 1862 under the impact of the gentry opposition movement regularly made a point of referring specifically (in the words of Ogarev's address) to 'the remuneration of the gentry in keeping with their sacrifice of land'. The attention paid to the situation and welfare of the gentry in these addresses was based on recognition of the fact, most explicitly stated by Chernyshevskii, that the gentry opposition movement represented at that time the most powerful progressive political force in the country. 'The gentry', Chernyshevskii declared, were 'the representatives of all the other classes' because they possessed the organization which allowed them to be heard. The addresses were designed to encourage this movement, in the hope that the gentry opposition could persuade the Emperor to summon a *zemskii sobor* and grant the liberal reforms. The authors of the proclamations and addresses indeed thought this a distinct possibility—a fact which explains Herzen's vehement rejection of Zaichnevskii's revolutionary appeal: he feared that such proclamations would frighten the government into reaction.

Although these hopes may appear in retrospect to have been unrealistic, they did not appear so at the time. Gentry discontent was intense; the government was faced with the possibility of a flood of gentry addresses containing political demands, and with the potential widespread disaffection of the peace mediators on whom the success of the emancipation's promulgation depended.

In a broad sense, all the gentry political demands were provoked primarily by deep dissatisfaction with the terms of emancipation. The Tver address was the culmination of a gentry campaign which sought to persuade the autocratic government to submit its emancipation legislation to review and amendment by representatives of Russian society (or some part of it), and to permit participation by these same representatives in all further reform efforts. To be sure, this campaign contained widely varying proposals—from the demand by the ubiquitous Bezobrazov and the Voronezh gentry for a strictly gentry assembly on the one extreme, to the democratically-oriented proposal of the Tver assembly on the other. Considered in terms of the gentry as a class, it was nevertheless a single campaign or opposition movement, united by intense dissatisfaction with the terms of emancipation and an intense desire to see the rapid promulgation of other reforms through some measure of public participation in the legislative process. It was certainly so viewed by the government.[1]

The immediate origins of this oppositionist campaign lay in the confrontation of the gentry with the Editing Commissions in 1859, and extended through the stormy gentry assemblies of the winter of 1859–60. The campaign itself began with the address of the Tula gentry in December 1861, the first formal gentry demand for public participation in the government's legislative undertakings. During the winter of 1861–2, the gentry opposition movement reached its greatest intensity, as reflected in several addresses, numerous protocols, and general discussion, and then swiftly subsided; The Tver address was essentially its last, and most radical, expression. No addresses and protocols like those described and quoted in the preceding pages were forthcoming from the gentry assemblies which gathered in the following winter. Nearest of all to a resuscitation of the previous year's demands came the Petersburg gentry, who met in extraordinary assembly in March 1863, to discuss the government's 'five questions'. There the gentry once again listened to Platonov's proposal for the calling of a 'duma of the land', as well as to several more conservative propositions, including one for 'a general meeting of three deputies from each province for the solution of the question of *zemstvo* institutions'.[2] Nothing, however, came of these proposals in the Petersburg assembly, and little more was heard from the gentry assemblies before the promulgation of the *zemstvo* reform.

The story of the 'constitutionalist campaign' of 1861–2 would not be complete without noting that it was by no means un-

---

[1] See below, pp. 394–402.
[2] *Otechestvennye zapiski. Sovremennaia khronika*, 1863, no. 47 (1863), p. 33.

animously supported within the ranks of reform-minded public opinion. Some of Russian liberalism's outstanding spokesmen—including most significantly Kavelin and Chicherin—actively opposed it.

In a brochure called *The gentry and the peasant emancipation* (published abroad in 1862, but written in May 1861), Kavelin agreed with the 'constitutionalists' that 'just allotment of land, the quickest possible transfer to *obrok*, conscientious and honest conclusion of the land charters, [and] quickest possible transfer of the peasants to redemption with land' were absolutely necessary.[1] So too, he wrote, were 'inviolability of person and property ...; a proper budget...; a good administration and police, responsible before the courts; ... intelligent and wise criminal and civil laws ..., the broadening of public [court] procedure, development of public education ...; and administrative decentralization'.[2] Kavelin, however, argued that these reforms were inevitable, and would come without a constitution or any limits on the autocracy. In fact, he declared, political guarantees were unrealizable at the present time, for Russia lacked 'developed elements of representation in the people':[3]

The component popular elements in Russia are two [Kavelin continued]: the peasants and the *pomeshchiki*; of a middle class there is nothing to be said. ... As for the mass of the people—of course no one knowing them even slightly would consider them a prepared, developed element of representative government. May God grant that these illiterate, for the most part poor, undeveloped masses, only yesterday emerging from slavery, will be able to exercise as they should their civil rights and that meager dole of self-administration which has been presented them by the law.

There remains the gentry. In our time it is difficult to imagine an exclusively gentry constitution. Thank God we do not live in the middle ages, nor in barbaric times, when it was possible.[4]

Therefore, declared Kavelin, 'The gentry must not seek the solution to their present difficult situation in fruitless dreams

[1] *Dvorianstvo i osvobozhdenie krest'ian*, in *Sobranie sochinenii K. D. Kavelina*, II (St Petersburg, 1898), p. 133.
[2] *Ibid.*, pp. 137, 142.   [3] *Ibid.*, p. 139.   [4] *Ibid.*, p. 140.

about representative government'.[1] The gentry's role, he continued, was elsewhere:

To make provincial life not only possible and bearable, but even pleasant and comfortable—that is the immediate task of the gentry ... Russia is still in all respects a sorry wasteland; *she must be developed by beginning at the bottom, not at the top.*[2]

This was Kavelin's answer to the demand for a *zemskii sobor.* Chicherin, in a series of articles also published in 1862, came to essentially the same conclusions, showing himself, if anything, to be more content with the government's current reform efforts than was Kavelin.[3] As the just-quoted passage suggests, the 'anti-constitutionalist' arguments of Kavelin and Chicherin were apparently directed primarily against then-current conservative plans for a 'gentry constitution'. In the view of Kavelin and Chicherin this was the dominant element in the constitutionalist movement then underway among the gentry,[4] rendering it compromised and, in their opinion, dangerous. Kavelin frankly expressed fear that an attempt to introduce a gentry constitution might result in a peasant uprising.[5]

In their anti-constitutionalism, Kavelin and Chicherin remained true to the views which they had outlined in Herzen's *Voices from Russia* some years before. They had then decided that the current period of reform was not the time for talk of basic political changes.[6] Until 1861, this view and their program for peasant

[1] *Ibid.*, p. 141.   [2] *Ibid.*, p. 142. Emphasis added.
[3] B. N. Chicherin, *Neskol'ko sovremennykh voprosov* (Moscow, 1862), pp. 85–132, 249–64.
[4] Referring (in his memoirs) to the Moscow gentry assembly of January 1862, which had called for an assembly of representatives from all classes, Chicherin wrote: 'Hiding under the mantle of liberalism, sighing about the old order of things, the gentry thought in this way to take power into their own hands and turn matters to their advantage.' Chicherin, *Moskovskii universitet*, pp. 66–7.
   Kavelin and Chicherin, together with Ivan Turgenev, had objected vociferously to the circulation by Herzen and Ogarev of the address calling for a *zemskii sobor* (see above, pp. 384–5). Turgenev in particular directly accused its authors of trying to capitalize on the discontents of the reactionary gentry (Baturinskii, *A. I. Gertsen*, p. 186). On this issue, friendly relations between Kavelin and Chicherin on the one side, and Herzen on the other, were completely severed.
[5] 'This play at constitution frightens me so that I can think of nothing else', Kavelin wrote to Herzen (April 1862). 'The gentry are going to provoke the *muzhiki* to the last limit.' *Pis'ma K. D. Kavelina i I. S. Turgeneva k A. I. Gertsenu* (Geneva, 1892), p. 47; quoted in Sladkevich, *Ocherki*, p. 111.
[6] Chicherin, *Moskva 40-kh godov*, pp. 153–63.

emancipation kept them in the forefront of the liberal abolitionist movement. After the Emancipation Proclamation, their views led them away from Herzen and that element of gentry opinion represented most consistently by the Tver gentry. After 1861 the attitude of Kavelin and Chicherin toward the terms of emancipation and the government's general efforts at reform remained on the whole tolerant and optimistic. To some extent this was probably due to their circumstances as professional scholars and university professors, who, despite their gentry ties and origins, were relatively independent of most of the concerns of the rural *pomeshchiki*. It was also the product of their general views on Russian history and politics. As representatives of the 'State School' of Russian historical thought, their appreciation of the role of the state in Russia's historical development was especially great. Much of this view shows through their conclusions about the primitiveness and lack of independence of Russian society. Although Kavelin and Chicherin probably had no lower an assessment of the capabilities of the Russian *muzhik* than any of their liberal *pomeshchik* contemporaries, they shared an acute conviction that the social basis for political liberalization in Russia was extremely weak.

A critique of gentry constitutionalist plans remarkably similar to Kavelin's was given in a manuscript circulated in mid-1862 by Iurii Samarin, the leading intellectual among the liberal Slavophiles.[1] In contrast to the plan for 'crowning the edifice' which had been advanced by his fellow-Slavophile Koshelev, Samarin insisted on 'laying the foundation' first. Russian society, he declared, was not ready for a constitution:

A popular constitution cannot be for the time-being in Russia; and a constitution not of the people; that is, the rule of a minority, acting without the confidence of the majority, is a lie and a deceit.[2]

A lie, concluded Samarin, because it would in fact increase centralization ('Petersburg as the center of autocracy is burdensome for Russia; Petersburg as the center of a constitutional government would crush her finally'); a deceit, because the

---

[1] 'Po povodu tolkov o konstitutsii' ('Concerning talk about a constitution') (first published in *Rus'*, no. 29, 30 May 1881).　　[2] Nol'de, *Iurii Samarin*, p. 178.

popular mass would perforce remain outside the new system. The needed reforms, Samarin insisted, could be accomplished without a constitution. This was essentially the same argument which Kavelin had used against the aristocratic party.

Samarin's opposition to the gentry's constitutionalist plans was more than the product of his Slavophile convictions. In it was to be seen that dismay with the capabilities of the landed gentry which he had carried from his struggles in the Samara provincial committee, an attitude reinforced by his observations of the gentry's behavior in Samara province in the months immediately following the emancipation.[1] Samarin's colleague Prince Cherkasskii was of like mind, and joined him in the debate with Koshelev.[2]

Those of liberal persuasion who objected to the campaign for a *zemskii sobor* also opposed, by and large, the idea of immediately granting to the projected *zemstvo* institutions any extensive political authority. This attitude became especially noticeable after the publication, in the fall of 1862, of the government's basic plan for the *zemstvo* reform, which provided strictly economic, 'housekeeping', functions for the *zemstvo* institutions.[3] Chicherin promptly pronounced himself fully satisfied with the scope of competency planned for the *zemstvo*.[4] The discussion of the *zemstvo* institutions by the Petersburg gentry (March 1863), in which the conservatives among the gentry appeared to be the most liberal politically—demanding wide competency for the *zemstvo*[5]—while their 'liberal' colleagues refused to make poli-

---

[1] *Ibid.*, pp. 144–5, 178–9. Also like Kavelin, Samarin was much less displeased with the reform legislation than were many. He favored from the beginning a transition period preceding redemption. (Cf. Trubetskaia, *Materialy* I, 281–2.)

[2] Cherkasskii's mistrust of the gentry's constitutionalist strivings seems also to have been largely the heritage of his disenchantment with the gentry in his work on the preparation of peasant reform.

[3] See below, pp. 400–2.

[4] *Neskol'ko sovremennykh voprosov*, p. 252.

[5] Here Platonov once again played a leading role, by presenting a second version of his 1862 proposals. On 18 March he presented a memoir to the assembly calling for 'the necessity of expanding the self-administration of the *zemstvo*' (an obvious reference to 'crowning the edifice'). He also proposed the summoning of popular representatives for participation in the deliberations on the *zemstvo* and judicial reform legislation. V. I. Semevskii, *Krepostnoe pravo i krest'ianskaia reforma v proizvedeniiakh M. E. Saltykova* (Petrograd, 1917), pp. 42–6.

tical demands in connection with the proposed institutions of self-government, drew wide attention in the press. The liberal journal *Otechestvennye zapiski* delivered a typical analysis of this apparently puzzling situation from what it called the viewpoint of the 'moderate liberal':

This situation[1] has given rise to confusion in a certain part of the public, and has given occasion to think that toward the end of the debates the conservatives became liberals, and the liberals—cowardly conservatives and bureaucrats. We do not share this error, and think that the defenders of class privileges have remained completely true to their convictions even when they have pleaded for the broadening of the political rights of the *zemstvo*. Indeed, in their opinion, dominance in the *zemstvo* ought all the same to remain with the gentry. It is natural that the granting of political rights to the *zemstvo*, with such a formulation of the question, would lead only toward strengthening the gentry and increasing their privileges. The majority of the [Petersburg assembly's editing] commission objected to political rights for the provincial [*zemstvo*] assemblies, not at all to the detriment of liberalism.[2]

There was thus displayed a divergence in liberal-oriented opinion over the constitutionalist and other specifically political demands put forth in the immediate post-emancipation period. Some Russian liberals associated the constitutional campaign primarily with conservative and exclusively gentry interests. And it may be that this consideration, plus a general fear of frightening the government off the path of reformism altogether, was responsible for the silence in 1861–2 of at least several gentry assemblies on the question of popular representation in affairs of state.[3] In short, they displayed the same attitude toward political demands as they had during the period of preparation of the emancipation. Other liberals refused any longer to be moved by these considerations and joined in the constitutionalist campaign, having come to the conclusion that the past and present performance of the government in its reformist undertakings was hopelessly inadequate.

[1] That is, the seeming reversal of roles by liberals and conservatives in the Petersburg assembly.

[2] *Otchestvennye zapiski. Sovremennaia khronika*, XLVII (1863), p. 35.

[3] Cf. B. Veselovskii, *Istoriia zemstva za 40 let*, III (St Petersburg, 1910), pp. 31–2.

10

Government Response to Gentry Demands and the Decline of the Gentry Opposition Movement

The two years, 1861–2, immediately following the emancipation proclamation constituted an important period in the history of Russian political development. They saw the first gropings by the radical intelligentsia toward the formation of a secret society— the first *Land and Liberty* (*Zemlia i volia*); the great student disturbances in Petersburg and Moscow in the fall and winter of 1861; followed by the notorious Petersburg fires (May 1862), and the arrest and incarceration of Chernyshevskii, Pisarev and Nicholas Serno-Solov'evich (July 1862). In the tradition of Soviet historiography this period marks the beginning of the *raznochinets*-Populist stage of the revolutionary movement. And the mounting of the constitutionalist campaign by the gentry and the intelligentsia has led one historian to christen it as the time of 'modern Russia's first constitutional crisis'.[1]

THE GOVERNMENT RESPONSE

The evidence suggests that the widespread criticism to which the emancipation legislation was subjected, the circulation of political demands and, under these circumstances, consternation about where to proceed next on the path of reform produced considerable confusion and something like a collective loss of nerve in the higher circles of government. Commenting in his diary on 13 April 1861 about a recent session of the State Council, Valuev, the Minister of Interior, wrote:

[1] Nol'de, *Iurii Samarin*, p. 172.

The decline of the gentry opposition movement

The general impression is, as in the previous session, most sad. We are as if in a dead-end with no way out in sight. The Emperor does not see that there lies before him the dilemma: Either to guide affairs along a new path, or not to guide them at all. His advisors either do not see this themselves, or have not the spirit to tell him.[1]

Bismarck, then in Petersburg as Prussian ambassador, wrote in the same month that:

Parties, or even individual influential state dignitaries who would consider it desirable or possible to preserve the existing institutions of the Russian Empire evidently do not exist . . .[2]

In the Ministries and the State Council, anticipation of extensive reforms and even of formal constitutional limitations on the autocracy was extremely widespread. Even Murav'ev (the conservative Minister of State Properties), so Valuev reported in mid-1861, was 'already testing the wind and . . . preparing to be a member of a constitutional ministry'.[3] Bismarck again confirmed Valuev's observations, writing that:

In the notion that 'all must change', all unite: the aristocrat, the democrat, the panslavist, and the orientalist; and the existing order can scarcely find a few defenders among the old bureaucrats, for the most part without influence or ambitions, primarily Germans. . . . If the times be peaceful, I hope to live long enough to hear a speech by Gorchakov before the Russian notables. . . . Gorchakov dreams, when he gives rein to his fantasy, of speeches which will overwhelm the dumbfounded senators, be published in Paris, and sold on the streets. The higher gentry dreams of the position of the English peers and of the successes of Mirabeau.[4]

By mid-1862, after the gentry assembly meetings of the preceding winter, Valuev began to compose his memoir outlining a plan for limited political representation in the central government, with the professed aim of forestalling more extensive limitations on the autocracy.[5] The generous sentiments for reform

---

[1] *Dnevnik P. A. Valueva, ministra vnutrennikh del*, I (Moscow, 1961), 97–8.
[2] Nol'de, *Petersburgskaia missiia Bismarka*, pp. 254–6.
[3] *Dnevnik Valueva*, I, 117.   [4] Nol'de, *Peterburgskaia missiia Bismarka*, pp. 255–6.
[5] *Vestnik prava*, no. xxv, book 9 (1905), pp. 225–33. Though presented to the Emperor only on 13 April 1863, the memoir was based on plans elaborated by Valuev as early as June 1862. (Cf. *Dnevnik Valueva*, I, 31–4, commentary by the editor, P. A. Zaionchkovskii.)

in Russian society, Valuev argued, needed to be kept under control, through firm central direction. The demand for 'participation in legislative affairs or in the general state administration' had been made and would continue to be made in the *zemstvo* assemblies soon to be created. 'It will be difficult', he continued, 'to refuse such requests. If it will be difficult to refuse them, would it not be better to forestall them.' 'A little participation in matters of legislation and general state financial affairs', he concluded, 'does not constitute a threat to the autocratic authority.'[1]

Valuev presented his plan to the Emperor, but that was the extent of such innovations in the government. Valuev himself had remarked in the spring of 1861 that:

The Emperor not only does not venture to show agreement to the gradual development of constitutional forms, but has even decisively spoken out in the opposite sense not long ago, and has not, evidently, changed his views on this question.[2]

Alexander did not change his mind under the impact of the constitutionalist campaign. He and a majority of his advisors rejected Valuev's plan.[3]

Alexander's intolerance of 'constitutional' plans did not, however, preclude sensitivity to the gentry's demands. To be sure, the government gave notice to the gentry that it was reserving for itself all considerations of further reforms. After two sessions (on 16 February and 10 May 1862) devoted to 'the improper resolutions of the gentry assemblies' of the preceding months, the Council of Ministers drew up the following communique for transmission to the gentry by the Minister of Interior:

Concerning the petitions and proposals dealing at one and the same time with local needs and general legislative questions, the Minister of Interior is directed to inform the Gentry that these latter questions cannot be subjected to unilateral resolution by proposals of one or another individual provincial assembly, but constitute a subject of general concern for the central Government; and that at the present

---

[1] *Vestnik prava*, pp. 228–9. Valuev's plan provided for participation by representatives of the (future) *zemstvo* institutions in the State Council.
[2] *Dnevnik Valueva*, I, 101.   [3] *Ibid.*, pp. 36–7.

time they are not only under consideration, but are being subjected to careful and encompassing discussion in the relevant administrative and legislative instances.

Concerning the questions which the Gentry Assemblies had no legal right to raise or discuss, the Ministry of Interior shall inform the Gentry of the provinces concerned that their proposals and petitions are being left without further action, since they go beyond the sphere of subjects presented to their discussion by law. [The Ministry shall also inform the Gentry] that the Government, at present concentrating all its attention on the reforms in various parts of the administration for the general welfare, reserves for itself the further conduct of these reforms toward their ultimate goal.[1]

These and other, on the whole mild, warnings were accompanied by the arrest and incarceration of the thirteen peace mediators of Tver province, a lesson which could not have been lost on the gentry of other provinces.

At the same time, however, the government reacted to the gentry's complaints about the emancipation and the bureaucratic administration with a series of concessions. These began with the elaboration of a number of amendments to the emancipation legislation which did considerably facilitate the pace of redemption and provided the gentry with more ready access to operating capital.

The nearly universal gentry demand for redemption of the peasant allotments was not directly acceded to by the government (obligatory redemption was put into effect only in 1881, after the death of Alexander II). It did, however, take certain ameliorative measures. It will be recalled that the government's plan for a system of voluntary redemption had been based on the assumption that the peasants would readily agree to redemption, but that the *pomeshchiki* would not. When the reverse proved to be true, the government took several steps to facilitate redemption for the *pomeshchiki*. The most important of these measures was the law of 27 June 1862, which allowed redemption to be undertaken on *barshchina* as well as on *obrok* estates.[2] The

---

[1] *TsGIAL, f.* 1341, no. 59, pp. 51a–52a.

[2] According to the original legislation, redemption could be undertaken only on *obrok* estates, meaning that peasants on *barshchina* or partly *barshchina* estates had first to be

gentry demand for full government financing was not acceded to, but a law of 10 May 1862 did allow *pomeshchiki* whose peasants currently paid less *obrok* than provided in the legislation to receive the full redemption sum from the state treasury. The government also rapidly acceded to gentry demands for the creation of land banks. By a circular of 21 May 1861, the gentry of all provinces were permitted to gather to consider the foundation of such banks, for which charters were soon made available.[1] Gentry demands for freeing their remaining lands from debt were answered by the government with the laws of 12 February 1862, and 10 July 1863, which provided for the transfer of the state debts of the *pomeshchiki* to the peasant allotments.[2] The great majority of debts were thus transferred in the first years after emancipation (in the first eleven years, 85 per cent of the entire outstanding gentry debt was transferred to peasant lands),[3] and the land left in gentry hands was legally freed from debt.

With these encouragements from the government, the gentry and peasants gradually began to solve the problem of redemption: By the beginning of 1864 nearly a million peasants (959,892 'souls') had been transferred to redemption, almost 75 percent of them by mutual agreement. Within ten years after emancipation (by 19 February 1870), a full two-thirds (6,679,344 'souls') had been transferred to redemption status.[4] Although just beginning, the pace of redemption agreements was already rapid by mid-1862, and its continuous progression robbed the gentry demand for obligatory redemption of a good deal of its urgency.

transferred to *obrok* before redemption could be undertaken. This ruling had been devised to prevent too sudden a drain on state finances, since the preliminary transfer of estates to *obrok* would necessarily have been a time-consuming process. Kovan'ko, *Reforma 19 fevralia*, p. 147.

[1] *Ibid.*, pp. 292–3.

[2] *Ibid.*, pp. 294–5. This did not, of course, mean that the gentry were absolved of these debts and the peasants burdened with them. Debt payments were deducted by the state directly from the peasant *obrok* payments during the transition period, leaving the *pomeshchik* lands free of debt (and thus capable of being mortgaged or sold), but also leaving the *pomeshchiki* with smaller *obrok* payments. When redemption was undertaken, the debt, in full, was deducted before reimbursement to the *pomeshchik*.

[3] *Ibid.*, pp. 296–7.

[4] Zaionchkovskii, *Otmena krepostnogo prava v Rossii* (2nd ed., Moscow, 1960), pp. 48–9; Zaionchkovskii, *Provedenie v zhizn' krest'ianskoi reformy*, p. 316.

The decline of the gentry opposition movement

Less explicitly of a concessionary character, but bearing that
mark nevertheless, were the reformist activities of the government in other fields of administration, activities to which Valuev
had referred in his circulars to the gentry marshals.[1] So far as the
gentry were concerned, the most important reforms under
preparation in the immediately post-emancipation period were
the *zemstvo* reform and the reform of the judicial system. Both
were officially promulgated in 1864, but the general terms of
each of them, significantly, were made public in 1862.

In January 1862, Alexander II ordered the State Chancery to
'develop in general features . . . views on those main principles
the undoubted virtues of which are presently recognized by the
science and experience of European states, and in accordance
with which the judicial organs of Russia must be reformed'.[2]
From this date, preparation of the judicial reform, which lay in
the hands of a special committee composed of bureaucratic
experts and professional jurists, proceeded rapidly, though by an
entirely 'bureaucratic' process. The result was a radically reformed judiciary, unquestionably the most thorough, enlightened
and well-planned of all the Great Reforms. Its provisions, which
met virtually all the requirements of the most severe gentry critics
of the old judicial system,[3] included: Courts common for all classes,
legal equality of all citizens, and independence of the courts from
the general administration. A modern jury system was introduced
for the criminal courts, and court procedure in general under the

---

[1] The most significant reforms promulgated by the Russian government in the 1860s
following the peasant emancipation were: The new charter for the universities (18 June
1863); the reform of state financial administration (1862–6, including abolition of the
notorious spirits concession in 1863); the *zemstvo* reform (1 January 1864); the judicial
reform (20 November 1864); and the press laws (6 April 1865).

[2] Dzhanshiev, *Epokha velikikh reform*, p. 381.

[3] Unkovskii and Golovachev, among others, greeted the judicial reform with genuine
enthusiasm. Unkovskii, between 1861 and 1864, became one of Russia's outstanding publicists on questions of judicial reform. Among his activities was the translation (partly hired,
partly his own) of five books on western jurisprudence—primarily Anglo-American—
and their publication in Russia. After the judicial reform Unkovskii joined the St
Petersburg bar and became a trial-lawyer, remaining there the rest of his life. Subsequently Unkovskii was involved in some of the most famous trials of the second half
of the nineteenth century, including the Pypin-Zhukovskii case in 1866 (concerning
the closing of the journal *Sovremennik*), and the defense of the assassins of Alexander II
(Unkovskii defended Rysakov). Golovachev, *Desiat' let reform*, pp. 396–7; Unkovskii,
'Materialy k biografii', pp. 33–4a; 'Zapiski', no. 7, pp. 106–10.

reformed system was public and verbal, with formal and just rules of procedure and evidence.[1]

The 'Main Principles' of the *zemstvo* reform, as developed by the Valuev commission, were published in the autumn of 1862, after their discussion in the Council of Ministers and their confirmation by the Emperor. These principles provided for the creation of *zemstvo* institutions—*uezd* and provincial assemblies and their executive organs—for the administration of strictly local economic [*khoziaistvennye*] affairs.[2] The organization of the *zemstvo* was to be an 'all-class' one, with representation not by classes, strictly speaking, but according to property qualifications. The Valuev commission frankly recognized, however, the desirability of preserving primary influence in these institutions for the landed gentry,[3] a situation assured by a curial system of election to the assemblies: Election was to be by three *curiae*. The first two (of landholders and urban population, respectively) were to be formed according to property qualifications; the third (the peasant *curia*), by class alone. In the first *curia* there were to be included all landowners of a defined quantity of land, and the owners of industrial and other rural enterprises. The property qualifications for members of the gentry class within this *curia* were only half as great as for other land- and property-holders. Gentry influence was also to be retained by making the gentry marshals chairmen of the *uezd* and provincial assemblies.

Over the *zemstvo* institutions, the government—primarily

---

[1] Generally, two shortcomings of the reformed court system, as it was originally instituted, have been noted: It was not given jurisdiction over cases of offenses against the state, certain matters relating to the press, and certain administrative offenses; and the independence of judges, especially at the higher levels, was potentially threatened by retention for them of a system of bureaucratic awards and honorifics. In the large literature on the court reform, two of the most useful introductions are I. Gessen, *Sudebnaia reforma* (St Petersburg, 1905), and M. Shubinskii, 'Sudebnaia reforma', in *Istoriia Rossii v XIX veka* (Granat), III, 231–68.

[2] Among them: administration of the traditional '*zemstvo* obligations'; administration of financial, grain, and other reserves for popular provisioning in time of famine or disaster; matters relating to public charity and welfare; care for local trade and industry; distribution of the state fiscal burden within the provinces; and the right to petition the government about local needs.

[3] 'It is necessary,' wrote Valuev in a report accompanying the reform project, 'while summoning all classes to participation in the affairs of the *zemstvo*, to preserve for the gentry that significance which in reality belongs to it.' (Garmiza, *Podgotovka zemskoi reformy*, p. 175.)

through the governors and the Ministry of Interior—was to retain a general purview and the right of intervention: The governors and the Minister had the right to veto all measures passed by the *zemstvo* which they found to be 'contrary to the law or the general state welfare'.[1]

Subsequently, in discussion of the project in the State Council (December 1863), significant amendments—especially in the electoral system—were made: Differences in property qualifications between gentry and other property-holders were abolished, and the number of representatives from the peasant *curia* were made equal to those of the landholders' *curia*.[2] Competence of the *zemstvo* was also widened to include initiative in popular education and medical care (later, two of the outstanding fields of *zemstvo* activity). Nothing, however, was changed in regard to the general sphere of competence for the *zemstva* or their position in relation to governmental authority.[3]

The government's project for *zemstvo* reform undoubtedly failed to satisfy anyone completely. Among the gentry, the greatest dissatisfaction was that of the democratically-inclined liberals who, like the Tver gentry, condemned the retention of class privileges reflected in the project.[4] And some conservative

---

[1] *Istoriia Rossiia v XIX veka*, III, 205.

[2] *Ibid.*, p. 229. In the first *zemstvo* elections, held in 33 provinces, the total number of electors was 13,024, of whom 6,204 were 'landholders', 5,171 were from the peasant *curiae*, and 1,649 were from the town populations.

[3] The government's general view of the *zemstvo* was that these institutions, while reflecting some degree of 'self-government and decentralization of authority', were in general an extension or elaboration of the state authority, made necessary by the abolition of serfdom. Thus, many of the tasks of the *zemstvo*, especially those concerning the administration of provisions and the collection and distribution of fiscal obligations, were pointedly declared obligatory for the *zemstvo*. This concept was clearly stated by Valuev in his report of 22 February 1862: 'The *zemstvo* administration is only a special organ of one and the same state authority, and receives its rights and authority from it . . .' (*Dnevnik P. A. Valueva*, I, 34.)

[4] 'The *zemstvo* legislation', wrote Golovachev (in a review of the reform written in 1872), 'parades under the banner of classlessness; that is, the abolition of hereditary privileges, but at the same time it preserves privileges for the landowning class. And since the landowning class consists almost exclusively of gentry, essentially these privileges have remained with the gentry.' 'Thus,' he concluded, 'in the place of certain privileges, others have been created.' In fact, Golovachev declared, as a result of the *zemstvo* legislation, the number of official positions exclusively in the hands of the gentry now exceeded the number of such positions which had formerly depended on election by the gentry assemblies. *Desiat' let reform*, pp. 390–1.

opposition registered complaint that the peasant voice would be too powerful in the *zemstvo*.[1] However, the principle if not the exact terms of a 'classless' *zemstvo* which yet retained a place of significant influence for the gentry through a system of property qualifications was undoubtedly acceptable to the majority of gentry, including most of their liberal representatives.[2]

THE DECLINE OF THE GENTRY OPPOSITION AND THE LAST ECHOES OF GENTRY CONSTITUTIONALISM

The high point of the constitutionalist campaign had been passed by the summer of 1862. The possibility of a constitutionalist movement representing not only the landed gentry but broad segments of the educated public and the intelligentsia had been destroyed by the scandal surrounding the Petersburg fires in late May 1862.

The fires in Petersburg began on 16 May, and in the following days several large blocks of buildings were destroyed. Evidence was found that these fires, or some of them, had been deliberately set, and this news circulated rapidly. Rumors about their origins spread among the population of Petersburg, which was in a state of general panic. Rumors circulated that the Poles, or even the gentry (presumably out of rage over the emancipation) were responsible, but the popular mind soon decided—under the impression of the recent student disturbances at Petersburg University and the appearance of the underground proclamations[3]

---

[1] Thus a minority of the Petersburg assembly meeting in March 1863 proposed that only gentry and large landholders be admitted to direct participation in the projected *zemstvo* assemblies.

[2] Cf. Garmiza, *Podgotovka zemskoi reform*, chapter 3. The elaboration of the *zemstvo* reform project, while effected by purely bureaucratic means, was a complex process, representing a compromise between many points of view held among government representatives. This process has recently been studied with thoroughness by Garmiza (especially in chapters 4 and 5 of his book). Two excellent pre-revolutionary discussions of the reform and its preparation are: S. Tseitlin, 'Zemskaia reforma', *Istoriia Rossii v XIX veke*, III, 179–231; and A. Kizevetter, *Istoricheskie Otkliki* (Moscow, 1915), pp. 269–314 ('Bor'ba za zemstvo pri ego vozniknovenii').

[3] In this situation, Zaichnevskii's *Young Russia*, which had proclaimed the existence of a revolutionary committee and had called for violent revolution, drew special attention.

—that the students had started the fires in the hope of fomenting revolution.[1] Although no firm evidence for this conclusion existed, it soon became general conviction in Petersburg society and was given currency in the press.

The government, already disturbed by the appearance of the proclamations, seized upon the situation to undertake an offensive against the leaders of radical opinion: A 'special investigatory committee' was created to look into the origins of the proclamations and other activities of the radical intelligentsia, and in July a number of persons suspected of conspiring in the publication of the proclamations were arrested. Among them were Chernyshevskii, Serno-Solov'evich and Pisarev.[2]

The immediate effect of these developments was to bring an abrupt end to the intelligentsia's participation in the constitutionalist campaign. By mid-1862 the outstanding representatives of that part of intelligentsia opinion which had been involved in the publication of the proclamations had either been arrested or were in the process of becoming true revolutionaries.[3] The constitutionalist campaign, if it were to be continued, would once again have to be an almost entirely gentry affair.

As it turned out, however, the force of the gentry opposition movement had been largely spent in the winter of 1861-2. The government's concessions, particularly those which facilitated redemption and reduced the gentry's financial distress, together with the publication of its plans for the *zemstvo* and judicial

---

[1] Cf. L. F. Panteleev, *Iz vospominanii proshlogo* (Moscow, 1934), pp. 238–47.

[2] Levin, *Obshchestvennoe dvizhenie* pp. 197, 205. Some arrests had been made earlier: Mikhailov, as author of the proclamation *To the younger generation*, and N. Obruchev, accused of distributing *The great Russian*, had been arrested in April.

[3] The effect of the government's repressive measures against the intelligentsia was exemplified by the case of Zaichnevskii. He wrote *Young Russia*, the first openly revolutionary summons, in prison, after having been arrested (in July 1861) for his activities as a leader in student demonstrations. In *Young Russia*, Zaichnevskii condemned the limited constitutionalist program of *The great Russian*, with whose publication he himself had formerly been associated. (*Ibid.*, pp. 198–9.)

On the extremely cloudy history of the proclamations and the activities of the intelligentsia 'underground' in this period, see the recent monographs which sum up Soviet research in these areas: Ia. I. Linkov, *Revoliutsionnaia bor'ba A. I. Gertsena i N. P. Ogareva i tainoe obshchestvo 'Zemlia i volia' 1860 kh godov* (Moscow, 1964); and Vilenskaia, *Revoliutsionnoe podpol'e v Rossii*.

reforms, had robbed the gentry's demands of a good deal of their urgency. So, too, did the fact that the terms of emancipation were not immediately producing the disastrous results predicted by the gentry.

The gentry assemblies of 1861–2 furnished ample evidence that the wave of peasant disturbances which immediately followed the Emancipation Proclamation produced profound fear and excitement among the landed gentry. However (as shown in Chapter 8), the wave of peasant unrest proved to be a temporary phenomenon, the product, primarily, of confusion about the terms of emancipation. Although it was not immediately noticed by contemporaries, the crest of this wave had passed as early as June 1861, and, even at its crest, serious disorders had never involved more than four percent of the total number of Russian villages.[1]

Numerous gentry complaints about fields lying unworked for lack of labor—i.e. because of improper acquittal by the peasants of their *barshchina* obligations—were certainly founded on some degree of fact, especially in 1861. Very little statistical information exists on this question, but the available evidence suggests that the situation was on the whole much less grave than many gentry claimed. In Kaluga province, where gentry predictions of economic ruin were exceptionally numerous in 1861, a senatorial investigation conducted at the end of the 1861 harvest season found the gentry agricultural economy to be in no serious danger.[2] And in weekly reports, the Minister of Interior did note some complaints coming in from the provinces about the progress of the harvest in 1861, but these were not judged, in most cases, as serious problems and the assessment of the progress of the harvest and the fulfillment of peasant obligations was in general optimistic: He argued, in fact, that those instances in which planting and harvest were not proceeding as well or as rapidly as usual were to be explained less by peasant recalcitrance than by bad weather and by the fact that peasant labor obligations had

[1] Zaionchkovskii, *Provedenie v zhizn' krest'ianskoi reformy*, p. 131.
[2] Kornilov, 'Krest'ianskaia reforma v Kaluzhskoi gubernii', pp. 366–9; Cf. also M. Naidenov, *Klassovaia bor'ba v poreformennoi derevne (1861–3 gg.)* (Moscow, 1955), pp. 234–6.

been placed within strict limits by the legislation.[1] (In other words, the *pomeshchiki* had a smaller labor reservoir on which to draw.)[2]

The crucial year of uncertainty was clearly 1861, when peasant refusal to fulfill *barshchina* obligations reached its height during the planting season. Gentry fears must have been considerably allayed by early 1862, when the results of the 1861 harvest season became relatively evident. Some uncertainty about agrarian relations certainly remained until the charters defining peasant obligations were drawn up. This task was largely completed by early 1863.

The early winter of 1862–3, the beginning of the traditional season of gentry assembly meetings, did not see the resumption of the campaign of addresses which had reached its height the preceding winter with the Tver declaration. If any such plans were afoot, they were cut short by the outbreak of the Polish insurrection, which began on 10 January 1863.

The 'Polish question' had occupied Russian public opinion for some time, in a serious fashion at least since the beginning of active Polish demonstrations for independence in June 1860. From that time until the open insurrection in January 1863, demonstrations, often ending in armed intervention by Russian troops, grew more frequent despite a Russian policy which was, on the whole, conciliatory to Polish nationalistic demands.[3] During this period of increasing tension, the Polish patriots received the nearly universal support of educated Russian opinion. Such important figures in Russian journalism as Kavelin, Pogodin, Samarin, Aksakov, and even Katkov favored independence for Poland within the bounds of the Congress settlement while

---

[1] *Otmena krepostnogo prava. Doklady ministrov vnutrennikh del o provedenii krest'ianskoi reformy 1861–2* (Moscow-Leningrad, 1950), p. 68.

[2] The head of the Third Section was less optimistic in his report for 1861. While agreeing that 'in general the granting of rights to the former serf population did not produce, with few exceptions, such great disorders as many *pomeshchiki* feared', he claimed that many peasants had either shunned their obligations or worked carelessly and as a result some grain remained unharvested and the planting for 1862 was reduced, 'in some places by a third', and in Riazan and Samara provinces by half the customary quantity. E. A. Morokhovets (ed.), *Krest'ianskoe dvizhenie 1827–69. Vypusk II* (Moscow-Leningrad, 1931), p. 22. The more detailed and encompassing reports of the Minister of Interior indicate, however, that these were exceptional cases.

[3] Tatishchev, *Zhizn' i tsarstvovanie Aleksandra II*, 1, 389–439.

letting it be known that they were opposed to open insurrection.[1] Radical opinion, including Herzen's *Kolokol*, adopted the cause of Polish independence as a major part of its political program in this period; and most of the clandestinely-published proclamations of 1861–2, beginning with *The great Russian*, included demands for the liberation of Poland. In 1862 the first proclamation calling upon Russian soldiers and officers in Poland to turn their arms against the Russian government made its appearance. This call was repeated in *Kolokol* in October 1862.[2]

The Russian government was rescued from the failure of its Polish policy—which had failed to stem in any way the growing Polish revolutionary movement—by the extraordinary burst of Russian patriotic sentiment which followed upon the outbreak of the Polish insurrection. This seizure of patriotic feeling, which seems to have enveloped virtually all elements of the gentry as well as all the liberal and liberal-Slavophile publicists who had formerly sympathized with Polish aspirations, was called forth by the massacre of Russian soldiers in their Warsaw barracks (the event which opened the insurrection), and was reinforced by fear of foreign intervention (primarily from France and England) and rumors that this intervention would result in the removal from the Empire of Lithuania, Belorussia, and parts of the Ukraine.

The gentry rushed to present Alexander II with patriotic addresses. The first to do so were the Petersburg gentry, who declared:

The pretensions toward the possessions of Russia provoked by the Polish disturbances arouse in us both sorrow and anger. Those envious of us think that the period of reforms undertaken by You for the welfare and prosperity of the state facilitates their aims against the unity of the Russian state. But their attempts would be in vain! Experienced in devotion and self-denial, the gentry, sparing neither effort nor sacrifices, will stand up to the defense of the boundaries of the Empire in close union with all the classes. May the enemies of Russia know that the powerful spirit of our ancestors by which the state unity of our beloved fatherland was founded lives in us still.[3]

---

[1] Kornilov, *Obshchestvennoe dvizhenie*, pp. 131–6. [2] *Ibid.*, p. 133.
[3] Tatishchev, *Zhizn' i tsarstvovanie Aleksandra II*, I, 427–8.

The Moscow gentry also hurried to present their address, which was written in language of nearly abject devotion:

Sovereign, we are all behind You as one man. All troubles are stilled and fall before the all-powerful summons of the fatherland. The enemies who have stirred up the western region of your holdings seek not the good of Poland, but the destruction of Russia, which has been called by You to a new historical life. Sovereign, your right to the Kingdom of Poland is a strong right. It has been purchased with Russian blood, spilled many times in defense against Polish craving for power and Polish treachery.... Rely on the tested devotion of your gentry. As ever, they will be in front, where danger threatens. At the head of Russia, which You have liberated, You are mighty, Sovereign, You are mightier than your predecessors. Trust ... in your righteousness and in the love felt for you by all Russia.[1]

On 17 April 1863, Alexander received deputations from various classes and regions of Russia, who came bearing similar patriotic addresses. Among them were the provincial gentry marshals of Tver, Novgorod, and the Baltic provinces. More followed in succeeding weeks.[2]

There is little doubt that the wave of patriotic sentiment and anti-Polish feeling represented by the gentry addresses and by the Russian press led by Katkov in *Moskovskie vedomosti* helped greatly to inspire the government to resist western diplomatic pressures and persevere in its crushing of the Polish revolt, which, from a purely military point of view, had been doomed to failure from the start.[3] Within a few months the rebellion was effectively crushed and the Russian government set out on a policy of russification in Poland.

The effect of the Polish insurrection on Russian public opinion was profound. The radical intelligentsia was completely discredited in the eyes of the educated general (i.e. largely gentry) public, having already been seriously compromised by its suspected connection with the Petersburg fires. The 'nihilists' were now denounced as fomentors of revolution in Poland, a conclu-

---

[1] *Ibid.*, p. 429.
[2] *Ibid.*, p. 431.
[3] Kornilov, *Obshchestvennoe dvizhenie*, pp. 159–60.

sion lent weight by the pro-Polish demands of the proclamations. The same fate befell Herzen's *Kolokol*.[1]

Thus, the last significant effort of that segment of gentry opinion which stood ready to join an 'all-class' constitutionalist campaign was the proclamation of the Tver gentry in February 1862. More conservative gentry aspirations of a constitutionalist character, though subsiding for the most part also in 1862, did not disappear so abruptly. They were heard from at least once in 1863—in the Petersburg assembly in March, where a conservative proposal for 'crowning the edifice' of the *zemstvo* institutions received considerable support[2]—and were given their final expression two years later in a petition addressed to the Emperor by the Moscow gentry. The revival by the Moscow gentry of political demands related to the *zemstvo* institutions was provoked primarily by the impending first convocation of *zemstvo* assemblies. The petition, made by the Moscow gentry assembly on 11 January 1865, already after the passing of the new *zemstvo* legislation, was the last manifesto of the aristocratic-constitutionalist movement, after which it disappeared forever. It was, also, chronologically, the last formal demand for the calling of popular representatives to come from a gentry assembly. The Moscow address called for the 'crowning of the *zemstvo* edifice', and more:

The *zemstvo* called by YOU, SOVEREIGN, to new life is fated, in its full development, to consolidate forever the glory and solidarity of Russia.

Complete, SOVEREIGN, the STATE edifice which YOU have founded, with the summoning of a general Assembly of elected representatives from the Russian land *for discussion of the common needs of the entire State*. Enjoin YOUR faithful gentry, *for this same purpose*, to elect from among themselves their best representatives. The gentry have always been the solid support of the Russian Throne . . .

---

[1] The circulation of *Kolokol* in Russia rapidly fell in 1863 from over 2,000 copies to less than 500, and the emigre journal never again regained its former powerful influence on Russian opinion. (Cf. *ibid.*, p. 161; and *Literaturnoe nasledstvo*, XXXIX–XL, 31.)

[2] See above, pp. 392–3.

The decline of the gentry opposition movement

... By this path, SOVEREIGN, YOU will know the needs of our fatherland in their true colors, YOU will renew faith in the executive authorities, YOU will achieve correct execution of the laws by all alike, and their application to the needs of the country.

The Truth will reach YOUR throne unhindered, and external and internal enemies alike will fall silent when the people, in the person of their representatives surrounding the throne with devotion, will constantly watch that treachery will nowhere penetrate...[1]

Although the decision in the Moscow assembly to present this address to the Emperor was nearly unanimous,[2] the terms of the address represented a compromise solution to a lengthy debate. The two major positions put forth in this debate were those which had been heard in the 1862 Moscow assembly: The first of these was the position—on the whole a liberal one—which had dominated in 1862, when the gentry had petitioned the Emperor requesting the convocation of an assembly of representatives from all classes of the population. Essentially the same petition—but calling now for a permanent central assembly of representatives from the newly-created *zemstvo* institutions—was proposed in the 1865 assembly in the name of the gentry of Podol'sk and Zvenigorod *uezdy*.[3] The other major position was, of course, that of the indefatigable N. A. Bezobrazov. In several speeches, Bezobrazov repeated his proposals of 1862, demanding strict observance of the Charter to the Gentry, and calling for the summoning of 'two [gentry] representatives from each province for the convocation in one of the capitals of a State Gentry Assembly'.[4]

Both these proposals enjoyed considerable support in the assembly. The equally indefatigable Court Orlov-Davydov proposed a compromise solution incorporating features of each of them. He called for the convocation in the capital of dual assemblies—one of elected representatives from the *zemstvo*; the other of gentry representatives.[5] This solution, with some modi-

---

[1] Kornilov, *Obshchestvennoe dvizhenie*, p. 172.
[2] The address was approved by a vote of 270–37 in the assembly.
[3] *Le vote de la noblesse de Moscou. Débats d'une adresse à L'Empereur Alexandre* (Paris, 1865), pp. 37–8, 42.
[4] *TsGAOR, f.* 109, no. 11, pt. 1, p. 17a.
[5] *Le vote de la noblesse de Moscou*, pp. 62–9.

fications, was finally accepted by the assembly as the basis for its address.

In presenting their address, the Moscow gentry, while rejecting Bezobrazov's proposal for a strictly gentry assembly, nevertheless clearly approved the preservation of exclusive gentry organizations alongside the new *zemstvo* institutions. The Moscow gentry had participated in the 1862 campaign for the calling of an all-class assembly of representatives. They betrayed no inclination, however, of following their Tver neighbors in proposing the abolition of gentry privileges and separate class organization.[1]

The government's response to the Moscow address showed clearly that the political situation in the country had changed. The time had passed when the constitutionalist campaign among the gentry represented a powerful political force. The government now was little inclined to tolerate such gentry demonstrations.[2] The Moscow gentry were never given the opportunity to present their address formally: On 16 January, the Moscow assembly was dissolved by Senate *ukaz*, all its resolutions were declared null and void, and the Moscow gentry were deprived of the right to petition the Emperor concerning their needs.[3] Alexander II, who in 1861–2 had left the task of reprimanding and disciplining the gentry to the Minister of Interior, now showed himself to be in no mood to tolerate such gentry demands. In a rescript on 29 January 1865, which was sent to 'all Governors-General and Governors of those provinces where there are gentry assemblies or *zemstvo* assemblies are to be founded', Alexander declared (in direct reference to the Moscow address):

The reforms which have been successfully completed during the ten years of M Y reign and those reforms even at present being completed

---

[1] The speeches of Bezobrazov, Orlov-Davydov and Golokhvastov, all of which were filled with attacks against the bureaucracy and the 'traitors to their class' (*Ibid.*, p. 56) who advocated abolition of gentry privileges, were greeted in the assembly with thunderous applause. (*TsGAOR, f.* 109, no. 11, pt. 1, pp. 23–23a.)

[2] Evidence that the government was no longer acutely concerned with the machinations of the gentry is afforded by the annual reports of the Third Section. Whereas in 1861 and 1862, much of these reports were devoted to the gentry assemblies, since 1863 the Third Section's attention had been consumed by the Polish revolt and the revolutionary movement. (*TsGAOR, Otchety III otdeleniia, otchety za 1863, 1864.*)

[3] This right was returned to the Moscow gentry only in 1888. (Veselovskii, *Istoriia zemstva*, III, 98.)

by MY orders sufficiently attest to MY constant concern to improve and perfect in so far as possible . . . the various branches of the state structure. The right of initiative in the main aspects of this gradual improvement belongs exclusively to ME, and is indissolubly bound to the autocratic power entrusted to ME by GOD. The past, in the eyes of all MY subjects, must be the guarantee of the future. To none of them is it allowed to give prior notice to MY incessant care for the well-being of Russia, or to decide beforehand questions about the basic principles of her state institutions. No class has the right to speak in the name of other classes. No one is called to take upon himself before ME petitions about the general welfare and needs of the state. Such departures from the order established by existing legislation can only hinder ME in the execution of MY aims, in no case facilitating the achievement of that end to which they might be directed. I am firmly convinced that in the future I will no longer be confronted with such hindrances on the part of the Russian gentry, whose centuries-long services to the Throne and fatherland are always in my memory, and in whom my trust has always been and is now unshakeable.[1]

The government's response to the Moscow address and the Emperor's rescript displayed an abruptness which had been markedly absent in the government's relations with the gentry assemblies in 1861–2. Then the government's response to the gentry's addresses had been, on the whole, mild, in an apparent effort not to offend gentry sensibilities. (The one significant exception to this policy had been the treatment of the thirteen Tver peace mediators, who were not, of course, officially connected with gentry class organization.)

If the government's behavior in 1865 reflected (as it most

[1] *TSGIAL, f.* 1341, no. 59, pp. 32–3. While in Moscow in September 1865, Alexander had a remarkable conversation with Golokhvastov, who had been one of the most outspoken proponents of the address in the Moscow assembly. The conversation, as related by Tatishchev, was the following: "'What did this prank mean [Alexander demanded, referring to the Moscow address] . . . What did you want, a constitutional form of government?" Hearing the affirmative reply of Golokhvastov, the Emperor continued: "And now you are, of course, convinced that I do not want to part with my rights out of petty vanity! I give you my word, that I am prepared right now, on this table, to sign any kind of constitution, were I convinced that this were for the good of Russia. But I know that if I were to do that today, Russia would break to pieces tomorrow.'" (Tatishchev, *Zhizn' i tsarstvovanie Aleksandra II*, 1, 492.)

probably did) a belief that gentry opposition was no longer a problem of vital concern for the government, it nevertheless betrayed apprehension lest the forthcoming *zemstvo* assemblies put forth demands similar to those of the Moscow assembly. This apprehension was also revealed in further government actions: The governors and gentry marshals were instructed to remind not only the gentry assemblies, but the *zemstvo* deputies as well, of the legal limits to gentry activities.[1] And the weekly journal *Vest'* was closed down for eight months for having greeted the Moscow address and published it and a speech which had been given by Orlov-Davydov before the assembly.[2]

But such demands were not forthcoming in the initial *zemstvo* gatherings. In the first meeting of the Petersburg *zemstvo*, A. P. Platonov (now a deputy in the provincial assembly) renewed his proposal that a petition calling for a 'central *zemstvo* assembly' be made by the Petersburg *zemstvo*. But although this proposition met with wide favor in the provincial *zemstvo* assembly, a majority of that body decided to refrain from any disturbing demands, and Platonov's proposal was accordingly left unacted upon.[3] According to the historian of the *zemstvo*, Veselovskii, most 'progressive *zemstvo* men' in the first years after the institution of the *zemstvo* shared a belief in the desirability of creating a central assembly, but insisted that the *zemstva* restrict themselves to their legal limits, while pressing for as much independence as possible within these limits, and preparing public opinion for the idea of 'crowning the edifice'. On the whole, the *zemstva* did not overstep the bounds prescribed for their activities in their first meetings. Only a few assemblies even mentioned widening the independence of the *zemstvo*'s activities from administrative control.[4]

---

[1] Veselovskii, *Istoriia zemstva*, III, 98–100.
[2] *Vest'*, published between 1863–5 in more than 3,000 weekly copies, represented a conservative point of view roughly identical to that of Count Orlov-Davydov, who frequently wrote in that organ. *Vest'* propagandized, by implication, the promulgation of an 'aristocratic constitution'; on the *zemstvo* question, *Vest'*, like Orlov-Davydov, called for a *zemstvo* dominated by the gentry, with participation by large landholders of non-gentry status. (Kornilov, *Obshchestvennoe dvizhenie*, pp. 165, 171; Garmiza, *Podgotovka zemskoi reformy*, pp. 104–5.)
[3] Veselovskii, *Istoriia zemstva*, III, 99–101.   [4] *Ibid.*

The decline of the gentry opposition movement

The revival, in 1865, of political demands related to the *zemstvo* organization proved to be a temporary phenomenon, provoked primarily by the first convocation, in that year, of the *zemstvo* assemblies. These political demands, although not entirely illiberal, came from traditionally conservative gentry quarters. As in 1862, the origins of these demands caused many liberals to hesitate in their espousal. The latter chose instead, as Iurii Samarin had predicted in 1862, 'to concentrate all their energies on the *zemstvo* institutions, as the preparatory school for the political education of the masses'.[1] To the extent, therefore, that the government's policy reflected the attitude that the *zemstvo* reform was primarily 'a means to buy off a constitution', that policy was a success. But a success only for the time being. Eventually, Valuev's prediction that persistent and unignorable constitutionalist demands would arise from within the *zemstva* themselves was realized, in Russia's 'second constitutional crisis' following the Russo-Turkish war in the late 1870s. It then became clear that the *zemstva* had succeeded the gentry assemblies as the focus of political liberalism in Russia.[2]

[1] *Ibid.*, pp. 31–2.

[2] In this development, the Tver *zemstvo* became one of the centers of '*zemstvo* constitutionalism'. The center of liberal gentry opposition in Tver had been largely dispersed by the events of 1859–62. The first elections in Tver to the new *zemstvo* institutions (1865) yielded a conservative majority, both in the *uezd* assemblies and in the provincial *zemstvo*. Only Maksimovich and Golovachev, from among the well-known gentry liberals, took an active part in *zemstvo* affairs. The rest of them were either gone from the province (like Unkovskii), or had been deprived of the right to participate in *zemstvo* affairs (the thirteen peace mediators). In following elections, however, the liberals gradually gained control of the Tver *zemstvo*: In 1874 the famous liberal *zemstvo* figures P. P. Petrunkevich and E. V. De-Roberti made their appearance on the executive committee of the Tver provincial *zemstvo*, and in 1877 the liberal Olegin was elected chairman of the provincial assembly.

In the following year, in answer to Alexander II's appeal to the *zemstva* for help in combating terrorism, the Tver *zemstvo* made its historic plea for a constitution. This was one of the opening signals of the *zemstvo* constitutionalist movement, which led to Russia's 'second constitutional crisis' and Loris-Melikov's 'dictatorship of the heart'. (Kornilov, *Obshchestvennoe dvizhenie*, p. 246; Rozum, *Tverskie liberaly*, pp. 358–64.)

Conclusion

Russia provides ample confirmation of Tocqueville's classic observation that 'the most perilous moment for a bad government is one when it seeks to mend its ways'. The emancipation was probably the greatest single piece of state-directed social engineering in modern European history before the twentieth century. Its ultimate aim was to fortify social and political stability; in fact it produced serious stresses and strains, of both a short- and a long-term character, in the social and political fabric.

The political ferment resulting from the raising of the emancipation issue makes it clear, in retrospect, why Nicholas I had so feared taking that step: He rightly foresaw that it would give rise to a political challenge to the autocracy. We have followed here the rise and decline of that challenge. Totally unaccustomed to taking directives from without, the government assumed the initiative in preparing the emancipation and a series of related reforms, with no intention of allowing public interference in its deliberations. In order, however, to prepare the gentry for emancipation and to acquire their cooperation in its preparation and implementation, the government was compelled to invite the gentry, and to some extent the public at large, to discuss the impending changes.

The government itself provoked the challenge, for it sought the unattainable: acquiescence and cooperation without a share of responsibility. Confronted with a confused and noisy response to its November 1857 invitation to the gentry, the government, in reflex action, began to circumscribe the terms of its invitation. This in turn provoked opposition, which led the government, in a series of moves in 1858–9, to withdraw entirely its invitation to gentry and public discussion: The gentry assemblies were forbidden to further discuss the 'peasant question', and the vise of censorship was once again tightened on the press. The government's retreat further stimulated the opposition and led to the

414

raising of political demands in the gentry assemblies of 1859–60. But the government held fast and promulgated its emancipation with only minimal recognition of the gentry's criticisms.

In the tense atmosphere surrounding the proclamation and initial implementation of the reform, the gentry, in a state of outrage and fear for the future, set underway their 'constitutionalist campaign' in the assemblies of 1861–2. The government responded with a number of concessions to gentry complaints about the terms of emancipation, and some recognition of public opinion was reflected in the further reforms already under preparation. But it also ceased experimenting with public discussion of its reform plans. These concessions, time, and some fortuitous circumstances allowed the government to weather the crisis, which was clearly over with the outbreak of the Polish insurrection in January 1863.

It is only in terms of this pattern of events that the much-debated question of gentry attitudes toward emancipation can be resolved. Generalizations about static group or regional interests, about the black soil—non-black soil dichotomy, are plainly insufficient. The only adequate approach to the problem is through analysis of the dynamics of gentry attitudes; and the key to this analysis is to be found in the development of government-gentry relations in the preparation of the reform.

Another observation which can be made about periods of reform is that they afford particularly good vantage points for studying the structure and functioning of social and political systems. In this they are perhaps excelled only by the Tocquevillian vantage point of looking back at the old regime through the prism of revolution. Looking back at the events discussed in this book, several points worth stressing in conclusion can be discussed within the context of three problems, which will be called: (1) The autocracy; (2) Russian liberalism; (3) the gentry.

1. The autocracy. The Russian autocracy had come by the mid-nineteenth century to a political crossroads, and the turn it chose there determined, to a great extent, the subsequent character of internal state politics.

Conclusion

The day had passed when a Peter the Great could institute sweeping reforms in the life of the state with only sporadic reactions from a fragmented and inarticulate society. By the reign of Alexander II it had become clear—abundantly so in the years 1857–62—that there had come into existence in Russia a 'public opinion', ultimately the product of the expansion of education and the means of communication, and that the autocracy, if it were to undertake significant changes, would henceforth be confronted by this 'public opinion' in one way or another. The government, by announcing its intention to emancipate the serfs, opened the door to a wide-ranging movement for the liberalization of the autocratic system, a movement in which the gentry played the leading role. The autocracy learned from the confrontation in this period that attempts at reform give rise to demands for public participation in affairs of state. Having no intention of relinquishing undivided political authority, the autocracy drew a profoundly conservative conclusion; namely, that all change is dangerous. At the same time, for good or ill, it received a brief education in the politics of minimal compromise, and this lesson was not forgotten.

The opposition movement of the 1860s did not wring a 'constitution' from the autocracy, but it did win concessions. As Witte later argued in his pamphlet *Autocracy and the zemstvo*, the *zemstvo* reform, as devised, was a concession to gentry opinion.[1] Reform of local administration, to be sure, was made necessary by the emancipation, but it was pressure from the gentry which brought the government to admit an element of popular representation into the reorganized administration, instead of proceeding, as it had originally intended, with a simple extension of the bureaucratic apparatus. It is similarly noteworthy that the most radical and best-organized of the reforms—the judicial—embodied most of the principles of judicial organization which had been repeatedly and universally demanded by all the gentry and Russian 'society' at large. Thus, the reforming activities of the autocracy in this period were to some extent in

---

[1] S. Witte, *Samoderzhavie i zemstvo. Konfidentsial'naia zapiska ministra finansov stats-sekretaria S. Iu. Vitte (1899 g.)* (St Petersburg, 1907.)

the 'logic of things', dictated by the initial step of emancipation and the concerns that had led to that step. They bore, however, the stamp of political concession and were carried through by the momentum of the opposition movement. The attrition to which these reforms, especially the *zemstvo* reform, were subsequently subjected is indicative of the extent to which the political atmosphere of the early 1860s was responsible for their original character.

The politics of emancipation show clearly that the government of the 'bureaucratized' autocracy was far from being a genuine bureaucratic system of the type described by Max Weber.[1] The autocrat retained undivided political authority and intervened systematically in the workings of the government administration —by disallowing effective inter-ministerial communications; by appointing personal favorites to higher administrative offices; by handling such important affairs of state as the emancipation outside the regular bureaucratic channels; by playing various elements of society off against the bureaucracy and *vice versa*. The 'personal character of political authority'[2] remained very strong in Russia in the middle of the nineteenth century. Ironically, this was indicated by the very insistence of the gentry—conservatives and liberals alike—that this was no longer so, that the monarch was the slave of a sovereign bureaucracy.

2. Russian liberalism. The 'union of tsar and people' was in fact a notion that pervaded Russian political thought from right to left, reflecting both the survival of pre-modern political conceptions (often nestled among the latest western doctrines) and prevailing political conditions. This fact, together with the broadly voiced demand for the *Rechtsstaat* which was raised in the reform period, provokes numerous questions about the nature and history of Russian liberalism.

Paul Miliukov distinguished two periods in the history of Russian liberalism. In the first period, according to him, the history of liberalism had been the history of 'public opinion'

---

[1] H. Gerth and C. Wright Mills (eds.), *From Max Weber: Essays in sociology* (New York, 1962), pp. 196–204.

[2] Raeff, *Plans for political reform*, p. 9.

Conclusion

(in the sense that it was essentially an intellectual movement, possessing neither a clearly-defined class orientation nor an organized political party). Its practical goal was emancipation, and the social milieu in which the struggle for emancipation developed was the educated gentry. The heroes of the first period had been Novikov, Radishchev, the Decembrists, and the liberal minority of the gentry who had helped the autocracy to carry through the emancipation. The second period, which began after the goal of the first period—emancipation—had been achieved, was the history of a political party and its goal was political liberty, a constitutional order. The heroes of the second period were the *zemstvo* liberals and, increasingly as time passed, people of non-noble origin, men of the 'liberal professions'. In the second period, Miliukov observed, it was in the *zemstva* that the liberal 'political party' elaborated its system of practical politics and organized itself.[1]

It is apparently true that in Russia the emancipation was a prerequisite for the development of political parties in general. Before that event, the elaboration of practical programs by different segments of political opinion had been subordinated to the common goal of emancipation. This study shows, however, that it was even before emancipation, specifically in the period of its preparation, that the practical program and further goals of political liberalism began to be defined. That is to say, these goals were initially elaborated not in the *zemstva*, but by the gentry assemblies in their confrontation with the government in the period 1857–62. The platform of *zemstvo* constitutionalism was initially formulated then, and most explicitly by the Tver gentry in their 1862 assembly.

If it is, nevertheless, clear that the political-constitutionalist phase of Russian liberalism belongs essentially to the post-emancipation period, what can be said about liberalism in the pre-emancipation period beyond noting that it was a set of values very broadly shared in educated society? In so far as it

[1] Miliukov, *Russia and its crisis*, chapter 5. On the post-emancipation evolution of Russian liberalism, see G. Fischer, *Russian liberalism: From gentry to intelligentsia* (Cambridge, Mass., 1958).

aimed at eliminating administrative arbitrariness and establishing certain fundamental 'civil' rights for the individual, the entire anti-bureaucratic opposition of the immediately pre-emancipation years could be called liberal. Within this opposition, however, there were elements which, in almost any other context, could not be called liberal—the 'aristocratic' party and the proto-Populist radicals, to mention the two most obvious cases. The conflict between the government and the gentry over the peasant emancipation revealed, sociologically and intellectually speaking, who the direct antecedents of the *zemstvo* liberals were: The people who made up the liberal gentry opposition, as described in the preceding pages.

Like the English utilitarians, Russian liberals passed through a phase of infatuation with enlightened despotism. It was a long infatuation. Belief in the progressive potential of the autocracy had characterized the activities of a number of brilliant reforming bureaucrats, among them Speranskii and Nicholas Miliutin, and was to continue to do so after the emancipation, as the careers of Dmitrii Miliutin, Witte, and others demonstrate. This outlook, however, was by no means the peculiar property of a bureaucratic elite set off in opposition to the public in general and the gentry in particular. Indeed, the very existence of a bureaucratic elite, socially and intellectually distinct from the educated elite as a whole, is a matter open to serious doubt. The gentry still constituted the social basis of the bureaucracy, and the views of a Miliutin were by no means peculiar to career bureaucrats.[1] In

---

[1] Miliutin certainly did mistrust the gentry. But so, too, did many 'gentry', including Cherkasskii, Samarin and Koshelev. Cherkasskii, no career bureaucrat, wrote many of the statutes of the editing commissions against which his peers fulminated, while Koshelev's whole career is almost a caricature of the absence of a gentry-bureaucratic polarization: He had spent much of his early life both in government and playing the role of a gentleman farmer. When he was not invited to participate in the editing commissions, he became one of the most outspoken critics of 'bureaucratic arbitrariness' (while serving at the same time, 1859–60, on a government commission for organization of local banks). Shortly afterward, he accepted an offer to participate in the Russian administration of Poland, where he served for some time (1861–3) as its director of finance. Many other *pomeshchiki* who had, or were to have, important administrative careers also wrote bitter denunciations of 'bureaucratic arbitrariness' at this time, including Dmitrii Tolstoi, future Minister of Education and Minister of Interior. (*ORLB, Arkhiv Cherkasskikh. Zapiska D. A. Tolstogo protiv redaktsionnykh komissii.* 1860.)

any case, events of the early reform period show clearly that faith in the reforming capabilities of the autocracy was shared by much of the educated public at large, including many of the landed gentry. And it was for this reason that gentry-based liberalism had not been constitutionalist-oriented before 1861.

Probably the single most important political result of the struggle between the government and the gentry over emancipation was the disintegration of this faith and the turn by many to the belief that the desired reforms could come only through popular participation in government. More often than not, this belief was expressed in traditional Russian terminology, but its aim was constitutional monarchy. Russian liberals turned in 1861 from civil rights to political rights, from *Rechtsstaat* liberalism to constitutional liberalism. As with the radicals, the liberals' faith in the reforming powers of the autocracy, which had been most explicitly stated by Boris Chicherin in 1856, remained intact until the emancipation was proclaimed, and then began to disintegrate. It disintegrated most rapidly among those liberal gentry who had been most involved in the preparation of the reform.

3. The gentry. The epoch of the great reforms was a decisive moment in the history of the Russian landed gentry.

It may be said that in this brief span of time there occurred both the birth and death of the provincial gentry as a political force in the state. As mentioned in chapter 1, it was only in the 1850s, when the provincial gentry were called upon to participate in the preparation of emancipation, that their provincial institutions were given the breath of political life on a significant scale, and the gentry began to utilize them for clearly political purposes. Some of the provincial assemblies then rose to demand a role for the gentry in affairs of state. But it was an ironical fact in the history of that class that its provincial institutions were also politicized for the first time for the express purpose of demanding the abolition of gentry privileges and the elimination of these institutions themselves. The liberal gentry, who had no interest in the organs of gentry administration for their own sake, utilized them because they were the only available means of bringing political pressure to bear on the central government.

Conclusion

The emancipation and accompanying administrative changes—n particular the creation of the exclusively peasant communes and *volosti*—served to destroy such bonds of common interest as had existed between landlord and peasant, and the *zemstvo* reform, which was in large part a concession to the gentry demand for political participation, at the same time destroyed the exclusive significance of the local gentry institutions.

The emancipation dealt the gentry class an economic blow from which it never recovered. The glowing promises of the liberal abolitionists about the future of the gentry as commercial farmers was never realized for most of them. The economic plight in which the gentry found themselves immediately after emancipation—mainly their lack of capital to adapt to the 'new order of things'—was not solved by their wholesale turn to redemption. Most *pomeshchiki* had been living on credit since long before the emancipation, maintained by loans from the state and the availability of 'free' labor. The emancipation brought them to a reckoning with their debts—preliminarily deducted from the redemption payments made to them—which left few of them with enough capital to set up farming on a hired-labor basis. (By 1881, these deductions amounted to about 303,000,000 rubles out of a total sum of about 750,000,000 rubles paid for redemption.) And those credit certificates which were received after deduction of debts were subjected to rapid and drastic devaluation (a process itself reflecting the gentry's dire need for cash). The gentry thus turned to renting the lands left them, and increasingly to selling them—an alternative which became progressively more attractive as land prices rose (under the pressure of peasant land-hunger) but grain prices declined throughout the last third of the nineteenth century. The results are too well-known to bear detailed recounting: Now that private landholding was no longer the virtual monopoly of the gentry, land passed out of the hands of that class at an accelerating rate, so that by the First World War the gentry were left with probably less than half the land with which they had emerged from the emancipation settlement. Measures taken by the state to arrest this process led, for the most part, only to a reaccumulation of the extensive indebtedness that had been liquidated in the emancipation.[1]

Thus the liberal abolitionists were mistaken in their expectations for the future of gentry landholding. There were, of course, factors which they could not reasonably have been expected to foresee: the lack of practical experience and the psychological inadaptibility of the *pomeshchiki*; the failure of a cheap labor force to materialize; economic fluctuations; the appearance of competitors in the European grain market and other factors leading to the continuing depression of grain prices. It would appear, however, that their basic miscalculation was the failure to appreciate the extent of gentry indebtedness and the results which the reckoning with the state credit institutions would bring. A few were heard to insist that these debts somehow ought to be taken care of independently of the emancipation settlement, so that the gentry could receive the full redemption sum. But most, anxious to allow escape from credit payments, insisted that the debts be liquidated in the way that they in fact were. On the whole, conservative fears that the emancipation would bring the gentry to economic ruin were profoundly justified.

However faulty, the predictions of the liberal gentry abolitionists about the economic prospects of the gentry were, of course, sincere. Sincere, but essentially of secondary importance. These were not capitalist entrepreneurs on the make, but men who saw in the existence of serfdom the fundamental barrier to the development in Russian life of those liberal values and institutions of which they, along with many other educated Russians of their generation, dreamed.

The reform produced no immediate, dramatic changes in the social and economic order—the peasants were released from their state of thralldom in a highly cautious and incomplete fashion, in accordance with the government's essentially conservative aims. But in a negative way—for what it failed to do—the emancipation was largely responsible for the social and economic crisis that resulted in the Russian Revolution. To the extent that it was

---

[1] G. Pavlovsky, *Agricultural Russia on the eve of revolution* (London, 1930.)

the relatively undifferentiated peasant masses, goaded on by the pressure of rapid population growth and the burden of state-directed industrialization and war, which provided the elemental force for the destruction of the old regime, the emancipation contributed heavily to the Revolution's coming. By retention of the commune and various other restrictions, it hindered the creation of conditions that could have led to the social and technological modernization of rural Russia. The emancipation also removed the possibility that the impetus for such change might have come from the landed gentry.

APPENDIXES

BIBLIOGRAPHY

INDEX

Appendix I

Excerpts from the Memorandum of A. M. Unkovskii and A. A. Golovachev, presented to Alexander II in December 1857, in response to the Imperial Rescript.[1] *TsGAOR, f.* 109, no. 1960. *(Zapiska Golovacheva, A. A., i Unkovskogo, A. M. 1858).*

[GOLOVACHEV:] ON THE WEAKENING OF PATRIARCHAL FOUNDATIONS AND THE NECESSITY OF EMANCIPATION

The necessity of emancipation is obvious. One need only compare peasant-*pomeshchik* relations of twenty years ago to those of today, and any unprejudiced person will be convinced that the patriarchal foundations on which these relations are based are weakening with every day that passes. May God help us if they disappear and we make no attempt to replace them with new and more rational foundations.

To what, then, should this weakening of patriarchal foundations, formerly so firmly binding, be attributed: Here time and enlightenment are of great importance. There are epochs in the historical life of nations when a certain trend is possible, which is

---

[1] '(Golovachev) wrote the first, critical, part [recalled Unkovskii in his memoirs], in which he gave a detailed criticism of all the instructions which had come from above. I wrote the second part, of almost the same size [each was about 90 handwritten pages in length], in which our views about the basis on which the peasants could be freed were enunciated. In this part I demonstrated that the question could be solved in no other way than by granting all [the peasants'] land as property, for redemption.' Unkovskii, 'Materialy k biografii', p. 45a. The part of the memoir written by Unkovskii was published, first by Herzen in *Kolokol* (no. 39, 1 April 1859), and later by Dzhanshiev (*A. M. Unkovskii*, pp. 59–71), though never in full. The part written by Golovachev has never been published and is, to the author's knowledge, unknown in the historiography of the peasant reform (Dzhanshiev knew that Golovachev had taken some part in the writing of the memoir, but, thinking the Unkovskii half to be the complete document, assumed that Golovachev had collaborated with Unkovskii in its composition).

impossible in others. The way of life, the character, the customs, the needs of a people all change, and with them changes the nature of national labor [*narodnyi trud*]. The dependence of one private individual on another is a universal phenomenon in the youth of nations [*mladencheskie epokhi narodov*]. But however enslaved a people may be, a part of that people gradually free themselves over a certain period of time, and free labor appears alongside obligatory labor. This free labor, unable to compete with obligatory labor in one and the same industry is transferred to other forms of activity. Thus, in a given industry, provided with sufficient gains by obligatory labor, no effort is made toward improvement and everything proceeds by routine. The antediluvian order and ignorance remain undisturbed and form and insurmountable barrier to any progress. In other spheres of activity, however, the entrepreneur, lacking the certain security afforded by the unfree laborer, tries to better his lot with improvements of every kind.

These are the reasons why our agriculture is on such a low level compared with other branches of industry. Success in other branches of activity creates the necessity for improvements in the backward industry and gives rise to the opinion that obligatory labor is harmful.

It was mentioned above that enlightenment also has its importance here. Enlightenment cannot progress at an equal pace at all levels of society. The *pomeshchiki*, as person of greater means, necessarily had to advance far ahead of their peasants and to begin a completely new way of life. Formerly they had led a life which, if not identical to that of the people subjected to them, was at least close to it. They had much in common with them. Now, as a result of education, these two classes are constantly growing further apart and are coming to understand each other less and less. Together with this phenomenon, civilization is also penetrating into the lower levels of society. As it develops, it creates in these classes a consciousness of the injustice of existing relations, a process aided by the proximity of free classes.[1] And

[1] [Reference is evidently to non-peasants and perhaps also to the peasantry of the Baltic Provinces, Western Ukraine and Galicia.]

just as this proximity is a necessity, so too is the consciousness of injustice, and this grows with time.

These are the internal historical, necessary causes of the weakening of those foundations upon which serfdom rests. But if they weaken the ties, they do not yet produce antagonism. There are other, external, causes arising from the conscious action of society itself or of the Government. Recognition of unjust dependency and a desire to protect the dependent person to some extent from arbitrariness and violence give rise to a series of legislative measures which have already clearly provoked antagonism. This antagonism, as a result of the necessity of the measures themselves, is in turn a necessity. So far in the historical life of the people there has been no struggle although attempts at it do appear in certain places. On the other hand, the festering sores of social demoralization are beginning to do their work. An enserfed man, with almost no rights in relation to his master, in need of the necessities of life, remains in ignorance, and against authority can only resort to lies and deceit, thievery and tricks. The serf-owner, who has both police and judicial authority on his estate, is obliged, in frequently confronting these vices, to resort to corporal punishment, the repetition of which causes him to lose all respect for the person of the serf. Obliged to serve the State, the serf-owner carries this disrespect for the individual over into his bureaucratic activity. Guided by arbitrariness in his relations with his serfs, he unfortunately resorts frequently to unjust and unlawful demands, which he by force of habit also continues to do in the State service. Thus serfdom gives rise, by a natural process, to dishonesty among the bureaucrats, and consequently to popular distrust of them. Even the free classes have no sympathy for the gentry class and, being closer in level of education and way of life to the serfs, they naturally gravitate more toward them. These are the results of the present state of things, which directly give rise to the necessity of emancipating the serf class.

Few doubt this, and these few rarely exert themselves to ponder over the existing situation. They are accustomed to the everyday order, and the presence of any idea outside this order gives rise to fear for the future. This fear is forgivable, because society has not the faintest idea of the principles by which the Government will be guided in the economic, financial and administrative life of the State. The choice of a path for the transition and a sincere exchange with the Government should remove all misgivings.

ON THE IMPOSSIBILITY OF GRADUAL EMANCIPATION

The question now arises: By what path to arrive at the new order of things. Is a gradual transition, as the Government proposes, possible, or is it necessary to terminate dependency completely? At first glance it appears that a gradual transition, without destroying all the economic relations of the landowner to the laborer, is better; but the deeper we penetrate into the existing order and future relations of these two classes, the more we are convinced of the opposite.

We saw above that half-measures for restricting the *pomeshchik*'s authority and guaranteeing the necessities of life to the peasant give rise to antagonism, for they implant in the peasant the conviction that the Government desires [his] emancipation, but that the *pomeshchiki* raise all possible obstacles to it. This disposition of the peasants is so strong, and their ignorance of the laws so great, that the most baseless pretexts, lacking even the shadow of common sense, are taken by them as decisive reasons for seeking freedom, and with this there occurs complete disobedience. It is sufficient for the peasants to submit some kind of petition for emancipation and they are completely convinced that obedience to the *pomeshchik* will deprive them of freedom and constitute an offense against the person of the SOVEREIGN EMPEROR. Anyone who has witnessed the admonition of such peasants has of course heard the following words: 'Why, I will be against the GREAT SOVEREIGN if, after troubling him with a petition, I oblige myself to obey the *pomeshchik*'. And no explanations, not only from the local authorities, but even from persons sent out by IMPERIAL command, will make him believe that he is obliged to be obedient. He will lie down with a cross beneath the birch rod, repeating that the Saints suffered more. When measures of severity exceed human endurance, then, and only then, will the peasant submit to necessity. Such an attitude is the fruit of the half-measures taken in recent years by the Government, and although it can be said that war does not yet exist between the gentry and the peasants, it is nevertheless ready to begin. The transitional status which the Government proposes to introduce will provoke everywhere what now occurs in rare instances and will lead to complete anarchy. Hatred between the two classes, which are obliged to live together, and on whose mutual cooperation the entire welfare of the State must be based, will take firm root. To reconcile freedom and slavery, the police and administrative authority of the *pomeshchik* and the independence of the peasant—this is an utterly impossible task. And it is this task which lies at the base of the idea of a gradual transition from dependency to freedom. The peasants in the transitional state must receive the right to file complaint against the *pomeshchik*, but at the same time must be subjected to his police authority. To what will this right of complaint lead? Is it possible to expect an impartial judgment when justice will be in the hands of *chinovniki* who are also *pomeshchiki*? Is it indeed possible to conceive of an impartial judgment when authority and subordination will remain even after the judgment? Morever, rumors have long been circulating among the people that they are to be freed. They sense that the time has come when they can hope for a better lot. They await this calmly and with the firm conviction that it is inevitable. Place them now in a state of semi-dependency and explain to them the necessity of this semi-dependency in terms of administrative aims, and they will understand neither these aims nor their necessity; and, what is worse, they will not believe that this has IMPERIAL sanction. They will be disappointed in their expectations and their dissatisfaction as a result of this disappointment will be turned once again against the *pomeshchiki*, whom they will regard as their persecutors. The result of such a state of affairs will inevitably be the destruction of the entire economic order—the very thing [the Government] wanted to strengthen by effecting gradual emancipation; and, moreover, not temporary destruction which will pass as soon as discontent subsides—no, destruction born of hatred, and therefore long-lasting, if not permanent . . .

. . . From all this it is clear that gradual emancipation presents dangers which should not be risked. An entirely different matter would be a decisive transition that would leave no relations between the peasant and the *pomeshchik* except those that could be established by means of mutual agreement . . .

EMANCIPATION WITH *USAD'BA* LAND ALONE PROVIDES NO GUARANTEE OF THE FREEDOM OF THE PEASANT

[This section begins with a detailed argument, whose main points can be summarized as follows: Freeing the peasants with their *usad'ba* alone would leave them as much the pawns of the landowners as before. During the transition period they would have to pay obligations for use of farmland according to the arbitrary decision of the *pomeshchik* or of a committee. Following this, the peasants would still have to accept terms offered them if they wished to remain on their homesteads, for as settled farmers they would have to use the land immediately surrounding their homesteads. Only there could they pasture their cattle and replenish the soil.]

In such a state of affairs the peasant will be forced to choose one of two [alternatives]: Either to remain a cultivator and come to complete ruin; or to sell his cattle and all his agricultural implements and turn to trade, handicraft, or wage-work, even with the loss of his garden. It goes without saying that he will choose the latter means, and will he then remain a farmer [*zemledelets*]? No, he will become that very homeless rural proletarian, subjected to all those misfortunes of a wandering life which the Government wishes to eliminate. One can say with complete conviction that the *usad'ba* land alone cannot provide sufficient guarantee that the peasant will preserve his settled way of life. Let us imagine ten million revision souls, or twenty million rural inhabitants, who do not have the slightest provision for their means of existence nor any common interests with the rest of the Russian population. Will not such a state of affairs destroy the entire economic order which the Government is trying to support? And will it not give the peasant a most burdensome bondage instead of freedom? Such a state of affairs will change the entire character of our peasant. It will kill the farmer in him and will turn him into a city dweller or a homeless rural proletarian. We must add to all this the fact that our peasant has become accustomed to consider himself an owner of land. The causes of this must be sought in the entire historical life of the people: Let us only recall that a significant portion of our peasants entered the serf class with land that belonged to them [several words missing]. Will it be easy, indeed possible, for them to renounce this conviction which has penetrated the entire character of their way of life, and has become completely fused with their existence? Only emancipation of the peasant with enough land to assure him at least the means to feed himself will enable him to preserve that mode of life which provides a sound guarantee for the future prosperity of Russia; and will reconcile him with the Gentry with whom he will have to have many common interests, as a small landowner with a large one. Instead of a struggle between these classes, a union will be formed from which the life of the State will draw new strength on the road to enlightenment and progress.

INSUFFICIENT GUARANTEES OF THE INTERESTS OF THE *POMESHCHIK*

We have seen the disadvantages for the peasants of such an emancipation. Now let us see to what extent it provides for the interests of the *pomeshchiki*. The *pomeshchik* retains property rights to all the land, excluding the *usad'ba*, but the peasant receives [other land] in perpetual usage. How can these two concepts be reconciled? The property-owner is obliged to surrender his property to the use of another without any possibility of ever regaining it for himself. The most essential indicator of property is its use. And moreover he is not even able to determine the amount of remuneration for this concession, for the amount of *obrok* and labor is determined by a committee. If it is assumed that this situation will remain permanent, then any idea of property-rights to the land held by the peasants must vanish. The right of property necessarily assumes the freedom to dispose of property as one sees fit. To destroy this freedom means to create the very same disadvantages for the landowner as for the peasant . . .

. . . But not all *pomeshchik* land will be turned over to peasant usage. Half of it, at least, will remain in the possession of the *pomeshchiki*. We ask: What will they do with it? Let no one think that we fear a labor shortage, or a disproportion of price between agricultural products and hired labor, or other objections to which the defenders of serfdom resort. No, we ask what the *pomeshchik* will do with the land because in any industry in which production is by hired labor there must be working capital: There must be buildings to house the workers; agricultural implements and machines (especially the latter in order to lower the cost of production); work animals; money for paying the workers' wages and for maintaining them. This capital is considerable and necessary, both at the very beginning of the establishment of the operation and later, especially in the event of crop failure or other calamities, in order to maintain operations in the usual way. Every industrial enterprise has need of reserve funds, and all the more so agriculture, where a greater part of success and failure is beyond all human calculations . . . Thus [without capital] the economy continually worsens, and we have good reason to say that the *pomeshchik* can do nothing with the land left to him. He does not have the capital to establish an economy based on hired labor. One can say with certainty that only one out of ten *pomeshchiki* has the necessary capital. Are nine-tenths of the *pomeshchiki* to be completely ruined? . . .

[UNKOVSKII:] In our opinion, emancipation of the Russian peasant can be reconciled with the security of direct State taxes and the property of the *pomeshchik* by only two methods: Personal emancipation without any allotment of land; or complete separation of the peasants from their owners, with allotment to them of a strictly necessary amount of *usad'ba*, plow, meadow, and pasture land, and with remuneration of the *pomeshchiki* in return for this.

In the first case, the freedom of the peasant is indisputable and the right of the proprietor to the land is completely guaranteed, for the latter has the unconditional right to dispose of his property, which also serves as the guarantee of direct State taxes. We do not defend this method of emancipation, and therefore we will not expand upon it, but simply indicate its possibility. Our Great Russian peasant has never experienced feudal dependency or homeless slavery. He long ago became accustomed to live in his own house in his native village commune, and to possess the land directly. He is deeply convinced of his right to the land. It is sufficient to cast a swift glance at the historical origin of serfdom and the present condition of *pomeshchik* estates in Great Russia to understand to what an extent laws and customs have encouraged the development of this conviction. Always and everywhere the commune of Russian peasants was 'bound to the land', and had in fact the irrevocable right and unlimited opportunity to use as much land as was necessary for its sustenance. Although the *pomeshchik* did have by law the right to take the peasant into his household and use his labor much more profitably, recognition of the right of the peasants to the land was so strong that almost nowhere were there cases in which the *pomeshchiki* deprived whole communities of land; and wherever something of the sort was contemplated rebellions occurred. Thus the peasant commune, whose provisions and obligations were the responsibilities of its owner, was the permanent and sole actual owner of the land it occupied. Even all chance calamities, such as crop failure, fires, etc., had no influence on this right and fell on the *pomeshchiki* alone, who in case of such losses incurred debts and frequently were deprived of their estates, while the peasant commune remained in the same place and was transferred to a new owner, retaining its previous rights to the land. It is quite natural that such an attachment to the land in the course of two hundred years has led the peasants to a *full awareness of their right of possession and no assertions of the Government* or resolutions of provincial committees are capable of shaking this conviction.

Therefore the Great Russian peasant, fully recognizing that his right to the land exists only on condition that he fulfill his obligations to the *pomeshchik* and remain personally dependent upon him, will readily agree to pay a given sum for his emancipation with land, but will never wish to receive freedom communally without an allotment of land to the commune in a quantity sufficient for its economic welfare.

In the second case, assuming emancipation of the peasants with land and their complete separation from the *pomeshchik*; that is, the dissolution of all their mutual obligatory relations, the freedom of the peasants, regardless of their greater or lesser attachment to the land, is indisputable. The *pomeshchik*, receiving for the peasants and for the land capital redemption in money or bonds, is remunerated as fully as possible, and the fulfillment of the peasants' obligations to the Government is guaranteed by the land granted them as property.

Justice demands that in such an emancipation of the peasants the *pomeshchiki* be remunerated both for the land removed from their ownership, *and for the emancipated peasants themselves.*

Considering it inappropriate in the present memorandum to discuss all the details of this question, we do find it necessary to present a general view on the subject and to indicate at least the possibility of this method of abolishing serfdom.

Let us first examine [the questions:] to what extent should the *pomeshchiki* be remunerated for the emancipated peasants and their land; and on whom should the expenses for this remuneration fall. We see that the law on the binding of the peasants to the land as a natural consequence deprived the serfs of personal freedom and made of them a commodity. We see that the *pomeshchiki* bought peasants with land and without land, and took into consideration in making such purchases not only the numbers of peasants, but their individual attributes as well.

In Russia to the present day human beings have been freely bought and sold wholesale, like property. Relying on the force of the law, persons who by law have the right to own human beings have to this day not scrupled to employ capital for the purchase of human beings like property, the possession of which is permitted and protected by the laws. To declare this property illegal and to withdraw it without any remuneration is unjust because persons owning serfs at a given moment cannot answer for the stability of age-old State institutions; and because laws cannot have retroactive force. We do not have the means of determining to what extent the ancient governments of Russia had the right to dispose of lands by distributing them as conditional holdings and as hereditary holdings, because in order to do this we would have to go back to the right of original occupation of the land for each *pomeshchik* estate individually (which is obviously impossible); but we see that the inevitable result of this distribution of lands was the necessity of binding the human being to the land, and consequently depriving him of personal freedom. Moreover, the former governments deprived whole masses of people of freedom, giving them as property to *pomeshchiki* and allowing [the *pomeshchiki*] to buy, sell and mortgage them like objects.

From this it is clear that the value of any populated estate under serfdom consists not only of the land, but of the people as well, for whom the *pomeshchik* must be remunerated as for the land; the more so, because in certain areas uninhabited land has no value at all. Of course, the emancipated peasants must themselves buy the land allotted to them; but who will remunerate the *pomeshchiki* for the personal freedom of the peasants and household people? Is it really possible to allow that in this case the value of human beings be combined with the value of the land and that those same human beings, who were deprived of liberty in the name of the needs of the State, be forced to redeem their own slavery? They themselves are least of all to blame for the existence of serfdom, and have been sacrificed for the general welfare of the State. The laws of universal human justice do not allow that the injured party be forced to make reparations for an injury done to him.

If this rule is overturned, the granting of freedom will not be a just restoration of human rights, and the emancipated people themselves will understand that *they are being sold, not granted, freedom*.

Appendix I

On the basis of unalterable principles of justice, the restoration of violated rights must be the responsibility of those who have violated them. We see that the Russian serf was deprived of his personal liberty and made an object as a result of the decrees of the government of the Russian land, decrees with which the entire people complied and sympathized. We see that serfdom was created by the government itself, for whose actions responsibility must be borne by *all classes* of the State equally; the more so because the decrees of the Government on this subject were in complete accord with the needs, conceptions, and customs of the entire people, and because emancipation of the serfs is in the interest of the entire State.

All the above leads to the irrefutable conclusion that in order to preserve justice the *pomeshchiki* must be remunerated for the people and for the land removed from their possession; and that remuneration for the former must by no means fall only on the emancipated serfs, but on all classes of the State, and on all forms of property without any exception.

There then inevitably follow the questions: How is the quantity of land essential to the peasant for guaranteeing his settled way of life and his liberty to be determined; by what means are the losses of the *pomeshchiki* resulting from such an emancipation of the peasants to be evaluated; and where are the means for their remuneration to be found?

The quantity of land essential to the peasants cannot be determined precisely either by establishing one figure for a given locality, or on the basis of their existing allotments. The first method of determination is decidedly impossible, for the diversity of the basis of the peasants' economic life presents no possibility of determining by one figure this necessary quantity of land, not only for a particular district, but even for two neighboring villages. The second method is completely unsuitable for the following reasons: Determination of the quantity of land presently allotted for the use of the *pomeshchik*'s peasants was made according to the will of *pomeshchiki*, and, since their dispositions depended on accidental circumstances, the present peasant land allotment on the majority of *pomeshchik* estates far exceeds their

438

basic needs. Many *pomeshchiki,* who are called away from their estates by various circumstances and frequently do not visit them in the course of their entire lives, have been content with a certain *obrok* and have made all their land available for peasant usage.

Therefore the present distribution of land cannot be accepted as the basis for future allotments. In our opinion the sole and best method of determining this quantity is voluntary agreement between the *pomeshchiki* and the peasants, established within certain limits in order to control arbitrariness. Although it is impossible to indicate one quantitative unit of land necessary for the peasants in a given locality, it is nevertheless possible to determine a quantity of land *less* than which a peasant of a given *uezd* may not have without the loss of his settled way of life. It is also possible to determine the local average value of land. This minimum will designate the quantity of land which the *pomesh-chik* is *obliged* to relinquish to the peasants . . .

. . . We said that remuneration for the losses of the *pomeshchiki* should consist of two elements: remuneration for the people and redemption of the land removed from their possession; of which the first must fall to the State, and the second to the emancipated peasants themselves. In our opinion this remuneration must be calculated as money capital and issued to the *pomeshchiki* in the form of fully guaranteed, interest-bearing bonds. Such an issuing of capital is essential for the support of the *pomeshchik* economies and their adaption to cultivation by hired hands. Therefore remuneration by permanent annual rent is unsuitable; and any other non-pecuniary remuneration, such as labor obligations, village production, etc., has no place in the present case and is not in accord with conceptions of liberty. Otherwise there will be no room for liberty and serfdom will be replaced by a kind of *perpetual bondage,* unendurable for the people and in no way guaranteeing the rights of the landowners. We have seen that such a determination of obligatory rural duties is impossible, because arbitrariness would reign as formerly with all the force of serfdom and would simply be transferred from the *pomeshchiki* into the hands of Government agents, who would

rule the entire State as if it were their property. Such an emancipation of the peasants is not their emancipation, but only the
reduction of the rights of the gentry to the same level of im-
morality [as those] of the serfs. Moreover, the remuneration of
the *pomeshchiki* must be capitalized, which is possible only if it is
monetary.

There remains a single most important question: Where are
the means for remuneration of the *pomeshchiki* to be found?
Unfortunately, many reject the only judicious method of emancipating the peasants, that which we have set forth, solely because
they are convinced of the insufficiency of our State resources.
This conviction among private persons is founded exclusively on
rumors originating from our State officials; and among these
latter it is founded exclusively on official reports, which always
contradict reality, and on the insufficiency of funds in the budget
of State revenues and expenditures. This conviction receives
considerable support from the fact that we have always been
accustomed to believe rumors and the words of authorities created
by the table of ranks, but never dare look at the reality around
us to verify their words with our own eyes.

The resources of the State exist not exclusively in the building
occupied by the State Treasury, and not exclusively in the figures
of the budget which indicate its revenues. It cannot be doubted
that the gold ingots stored in the Treasury and the estimated
budget revenues hardly suffice to cover annual expenditures.
We are not relying on these resources. The sources of State
wealth of which we speak are scattered throughout our Empire.
They exist in all regions and are visible at every step. In some
places they are even more visible than in the graphs of the
ministerial reports. One need only look attentively around, and
he will see that these resources even exceed needs, but that needs
are frequently unsatisfied as a result of the unprofitable disposition
of resources . . .

. . . Let us examine how great the resources would have to be
for redemption of the peasants with part of the land in Tver
province. The average value of a revision soul with the part of
the land he needs would not, in our opinion, exceed 150 silver

rubles. Peasants alone, with an insignificant quantity of moveable and immoveable property, sell for 50–60 silver rubles. According to the ninth revision, there are 360,557 souls, including serfs and household people, in our province, among which the peasants alone number 338,707 souls.

Therefore, reimbursement for the peasants alone amounts to 21,663,420 silver rubles. If, in the complete absence of available funds, the *pomeshchiki* are issued for this sum four-percent bonds guaranteed by taxes on all classes and all forms of property, the yearly payment on them of five percent, including capital reduction, will be no more than 1,081,671 silver rubles. This amount, which will be distributed among 630,424 revision souls of all the tax-paying classes of the province and on capital and property of all sorts, will comprise an annual outlay two (if not three) times less than the donation made by the *pomeshchiki* and tax-paying classes alone for the volunteers [*opolchenie*] in 1855. Finally, the provincial committees can easily indicate means, other than those included in the revenue budget, which can cover a part of the capital debt for redemption of the people, and thus decrease the amount of annual payments. In this category one can include indications for the reduction of many expenditures; the funds from the rural taxes collected for various building projects, which could easily be postponed until a more favorable time; various public properties which bring no income to the State and could be sold without any inconvenience; and so forth. We hope to indicate many such sources, and to accomplish this the committees need only the right to receive from all localities and officials the necessary information. Finally, the aforementioned annual interest can be lowered at the discretion of the committees themselves. As for remuneration of the *pomeshchiki* for the land removed from their possession, the bonds issued for this purpose can easily be guaranteed by the land comprising the allotment to the peasant communes.

For the implementation of this operation and for the financial management of the peasant communes, banks can be established in every province, on the example of Austria and Prussia. They can be combined with the existing Offices of Public Charity and the Committees on General Taxes, entrusting their administration to persons elected from all classes in the province, with public accountability and personal and material responsibility of the elected officials. This latter is necessary in order to create confidence in the bonds.

In our time no one believes any longer in secret administration and unaccountable *chinovniki*. Numerous experiences have destroyed any illusions about such means of conducting affairs.

Payment of interest on the bonds by the emancipated peasants will be quite easy. According to our calculations the cost of redemption of the lands in Tver province cannot exceed 36,000,000 silver rubles, for which an annual five-percent payment cannot exceed 1,800,000 silver rubles; which will constitute no more than 5 silver rubles annually per soul, or 12 rubles, 50 kopecks from a household—the lightest *pomeshchik*'s *obrok*. With strict measures for collection of arrears and a declaration that debtors will be sent to Siberia for failure to make interest payments within a given period, there will be no arrears.

This is our view on the subject of emancipating the peasants and the sole method for a judicious, just and peaceful solution of the problem. If it is objected that the bonds will not be equal to their declared capital value, we can answer that this can never be, for securities which bear interest and are sufficiently guaranteed never flood the money market and do not lose their nominal value. England serves as an example of this, with her vast quantity of bank notes, which circulate freely . . . The judicious and open administration of this matter renders inconceivable any distrust in the turnover, which is made public and is guaranteed by the property of its administrators.

Therefore we find it absolutely essential that the provincial committees be allowed:

(1) To demand from all institutions and persons all necessary information and to discuss the financial resources of the province.

(2) To discuss essential changes in the structure of the rural administration, the local police and other institutions connected with this subject.

Appendix I

(3) Not to be bound by the narrow framework of [Government] instructions, but to present and discuss *all necessary subjects* with complete frankness. This last is necessary because many questions concerning the public life of the State are connected with the question of peasant emancipation. It is absolutely impossible to isolate it from all other questions and resolve it completely separately.

Appendix II

Documents of the Provincial Gentry
Assemblies, 1859-60

1. Petition of the Tver Gentry Assembly to Alexander II, 14 December 1859. *TsGIAL, f.* 1180, no. 37, pp. 43-8.

YOUR IMPERIAL MAJESTY

MOST GRACIOUS SOVEREIGN

The Gentry of Tver province are deeply aware of the immutability of resolutions issuing from the Supreme Authority. These resolutions fully define the relations of all estates and institutions to those persons who have the good fortune to proclaim the commands of YOUR SUPREME IMPERIAL MAJESTY. Recognizing that the right to discuss their needs and welfare, granted to the gentry by the literal sense of articles 112 and 135, volume IX of the code of laws on the social orders, is, by its direct connection with the peasant question, presently curtailed by the exalted command of YOUR IMPERIAL MAJESTY, proclaimed by the circular order of the Minister of Interior, the gentry of Tver province consider it their sacred duty to follow the indications of the definite statutes, article 177, volume I, part I of the fundamental code of laws and articles 112-113, volume IX of the code of laws on the social orders, and to submit to the most gracious view of YOUR IMPERIAL MAJESTY a most loyal request to allow the provincial gentry assembly to undertake discussion of its needs and welfare, without being hindered by their possible propinquity with the peasant question.

The gentry were indeed summoned to participate in the resolution of this question through the provincial committee. But at present, finding themselves in full complement in the provincial assembly and armed with the practical knowledge

444

which they have received from agricultural experience and from contact with the local administration, [the gentry], by the open exchange of their thoughts alone, could prepare the solution of a significant part of the questions which constitute serious difficulties in the peasant problem. Thereby, the gentry would have a great opportunity to fulfill the promises given personally to YOUR IMPERIAL MAJESTY on the 11th of August, 1858, in the city of Tver.

If the gentry make bold to address themselves directly to YOUR IMPERIAL MAJESTY, they do so as a result of the portentous words spoken by YOUR MOST GRACIOUS SOVEREIGN to the Pskov gentry.

The Tver Provincial Assembly awaits with full hope YOUR IMPERIAL MAJESTY'S authorization of our most loyal petition.

With feelings of deepest reverence, YOUR IMPERIAL MAJESTY'S most loyal servitors: [155 signatures]

2. Address of the Riazan Gentry Assembly to Alexander II, 12 December 1859. *TsGIAL, f.* 1180, no. 37, pp. 34–5.

YOUR IMPERIAL MAJESTY

Meeting for elections, the Gentry of Riazan province heard the order of the Minister of Interior containing the command of YOUR IMPERIAL MAJESTY not to enter into any discussions of subjects touching upon the peasant question in any way.

Being accustomed to the sacred duty to regard with reverence the will of the MONARCHS, and now as always animated by the immutable feelings of loyal subjects, the Riazan Gentry make bold to present most loyally to YOUR IMPERIAL MAJESTY'S gracious attention the fact that the peasant question, especially at the present time, is merged to such a degree with the general interests of the gentry class that [the gentry] foresee difficulty in discussing their own needs without touching at all upon the peasant and attendant questions.

The Gentry, vouchsafed the high and flattering MONARCHIAL trust to participate in the preliminary plans for the reform of the life of both classes and constantly moved by zeal to further the

paternal intentions of YOUR IMPERIAL MAJESTY, submit to
YOUR most gracious attention a most loyal request to be allowed,
at the present gentry assembly of Riazan province, to avail
themselves of one of the fundamental rights granted the Gentry
by the wisdom and benevolence of the MONARCHS: To discuss
their needs and welfare without being hampered by the peasant
question or others with which it is inseparably linked; and without
being restricted to the time-limit set for elections, on account of
the time spent waiting for the decision on this most loyal petition.

With the deepest devotion we have the pleasure to be YOUR
IMPERIAL MAJESTY'S AND MOST GRACIOUS SOVEREIGN'S
loyal subjects: [Signatures]

3. Petition of the Riazan Gentry to Alexander II, December 19
1859. *TsGAOR, f.* 109, no. 11, part 17, pp. 26–7.

[MOST GRACIOUS SOVEREIGN]

Without undertaking an examination of the essence of the
peasant question, whose discussion in the present assembly was
forbidden by IMPERIAL command in response to the most loyal
[address] of the Riazan Gentry, we find it necessary, in conformance with article 135, vol. IX, of the Code of Laws, to
inform the Government of two most vital and urgent needs of
the Gentry; namely:

1. The abolition of serfdom within the shortest possible time,
since the present indeterminate position of both *pomeshchiki* and
peasants is harmful, both economically and morally. Moreover,
serfdom, which has not been abolished but only occasionally
restricted by administrative decrees, places both classes in distres-
sing relations, frequently disruptive of public order.

2. Solution of the peasant question not otherwise than by
means of obligatory redemption of the lands allotted to the
peasants, in conformance with the project of the provincial
committee, for obligatory duties will be just as oppressive to the
peasants as serfdom and will be the cause for even greater clashes
between the two classes. This demand is made all the more
sound by the fact that the Gentry can undertake financing even

without Government assistance, through the organization of a Land Bank, for whose exchange funds there presently exists a capital of nearly a million silver rubles, collected from the *pomeshchiki* and peasants.[1]

Not doubting that the Government will choose to honor the wish of the Gentry, they request that this same class be entrusted to compile the project and rules for the Land Bank, through elected deputies. [156 signatures]

4. Petition of Iaroslavl Provincial Gentry Marshal Petr Bem to Alexander II, 17 December 1859. *TsGIAL, f.* 1180, no. 37, pp. 59–60*a*.

MOST GRACIOUS SOVEREIGN

Relying on article 12, vol. IX of the Code of Laws (1857 edition), which grants the right to the Gentry to address most loyal petitions about their welfare and needs to YOUR IMPERIAL MAJESTY, the Gentry of Iaroslavl province, in their current provincial meeting, wished to submit the following to YOUR most gracious attention:

1. The formation of provincial and *uezd* administration for all classes on an elective basis, with the broad development of influence by local elected authorities on economic [*khoziaist-vennye*] directives, without concerning matters of general administration.

2. The establishment of autonomous judicial authority, independent of the administrative authority and with the introduction of a jury court, public judicial procedures, and personal responsibility of all officials before the courts.

3. The introduction of freedom of the press for the uncovering of judicial and administrative abuses, with responsibility solely before the courts for deliberate distortion of the truth.

The Iaroslavl Gentry were not able to realize these ideas, aroused by the words of confidence with which YOU, SOVEREIGN, in the Imperial Rescripts, gladdened the Gentry who are devoted to throne and homeland. The provincial governor, by

---

[1] [These were funds taken from the general taxes and left in the provincial treasury for the purposes of emergency food purchases and the maintenance of emergency food reserves.]

his memorandum of 15 December of this year, no. 979, based on the circular instructions of the Minister of Interior, 9 November, no. 215, expressing the Imperial order forbidding discussion of subjects touching upon the peasant question, demanded the obligatory postponement of the intention of the Iaroslavl Gentry, which I have summarized above, on the grounds that it involved the peasant question. Seeing no other way of fulfilling the sacred duty to convey to YOUR MAJESTY'S attention the most loyal wishes of the Iaroslavl Gentry, borne by me as the representative of the Iaroslavl Gentry estate, I make bold to submit it to YOUR MONARCHIAL VIEW from my person directly.

YOUR IMPERIAL MAJESTY'S loyal subject, Iaroslavl Provincial Gentry Marshal with the title of *Kamer-Junker* of the Court, State Councillor Petr Bem.

5. Address of the Orel Gentry Marshals to Alexander II, December 1859. *TsGIAL, f.* 1180, no. 37, pp. 68–69*a*.

MOST GRACIOUS SOVEREIGN

In their assembly of 15 December, the Gentry of Orel Province ordered the Provincial and *uezd* Gentry Marshals to assure YOUR IMPERIAL MAJESTY that they are, with unchanging and loyal obedience, always ready to obey YOUR sacred will. Thus the Gentry fulfilled precisely and without contradiction YOUR IMPERIAL MAJESTY'S announced order not to enter into discussions of subjects concerning the peasant question.

Nevertheless they have requested us, as their representatives, to present directly to YOUR IMPERIAL MAJESTY a special resolution expressing the general regret which echoed deeply in the hearts of the Gentry, who recognized in the aforementioned prohibition MONARCHIAL distrust in their proven faithfulness and devotion to the Throne of YOUR IMPERIAL MAJESTY.[1]

YOUR IMPERIAL MAJESTY'S most loyal subject:

[Signed by Provincial Marshal V. Apraksin and 11 of the 12 *uezd* Marshals of Orel province]

---

[1] [These were milder words than those of the directing protocol: '[The Gentry] have fulfilled precisely the will of their Monarch, but at the same time consider that it is their duty to submit to [Your Majesty's] most gracious judgment that the prohibition

6. Address of the Vladimir Gentry Assembly to Alexander II, [19?] January 1860. *TsGAOR, f.* 109, no. 11, part 4, pp. 9–12*a*.

MOST AUGUST MONARCH

Fully supporting the charitable intentions of YOUR IMPERIAL MAJESTY concerning the liberation of the peasants and the closely related improvement of various departments of the administration, the Gentry of Vladimir Province consider it their sacred duty to submit their convictions, dictated by practical experience, to YOUR MAJESTY'S most gracious attention.

Recognizing the full importance of the present time, in which such great reforms are being prepared and our fatherland is being resurrected in a new life, the gentry cannot conceal these sincere convictions, and make bold to set them forth with straightforward candor and full trust in YOUR beneficent concern for the happiness of YOUR people.

MOST GRACIOUS SOVEREIGN, deign to hear YOUR loyal subjects. Entering on the path of epochal legislative reforms in connection with the alteration of the life of the most numerous class in the State, our fatherland lacks sufficient guarantee of the strict fulfillment of the law. Our entire administration is founded on bureaucratic principles, all orders are administered by persons alien to those orders. Moreover, being separated into mutually-isolated estates, with completely secret administration and un-accountability of officials, they are not only unable to aid the Government in achieving its goals, but are not even able to petition concerning their own local welfare. In addition, correct behavior and execution of the laws by the officials are in no way guaranteed, for our courts, obliged to process cases in deepest secrecy and to be guided in their resolution only by the written investigations of the executive authorities and established rules of evidence, but not by the dictates of conscience or their own convictions, are completely dependent on the arbitrary will of the investigators and their superiors. Therefore, they provide none

on discussion of the peasant question has deprived the Gentry of one of their most essential rights: To discuss, and to petition the Government about, local needs, almost all of which at the present time are inseparably linked with this question.' *TsGIAL, f.* 1180, no. 37, p. 70*a*.]

449

of the guarantees necessary for the administration of justice. Finally, all officials, in the event of violation of their legal responsibilities, are subject to trial only when it suits their administrative superiors.

All the above leads to the conclusion that the execution of our laws depends for the most part on arbitrary personal will.

Such a state of affairs has been allowed to exist up to the present because a country in which serfdom was tolerated could not have a correct understanding of legality. But with the abolition of serfdom, the intelligent and unanimous assistance of the local orders in furthering governmental aims and strict fulfillment of the laws is necessary, not only for successful implementation of the reform itself, but also for the realization of YOUR IMPERIAL MAJESTY'S own beneficent goals. For the emancipated peasants, deprived of the protection of the *pomeshchik* and in the absence of justice or responsibility on the part of officials, will be subjected to even greater and unbearable dependence on the arbitrary will of the *chinovniki*; and thereby they may altogether lose respect for genuine legality.

MOST GRACIOUS SOVEREIGN! The Gentry consider it their sacred duty to call to YOUR MAJESTY'S most gracious attention that for the peaceful and successful conclusion of the imminent reform and for the realization of YOUR beneficent designs, the following, according to our sincere and deep conviction, are necessary:

1. Strict separation of powers: Administrative, judicial and police.

2. Common administration for all classes.

3. Economic-executive administration elected from all classes and responsible only before the courts and the public; and with elected officials confirmed in office not by the administrative authority, but only by correctness of the electoral process.

4. Government-appointed police administration, organized in a purely protective spirit and acting exclusively in accordance with the law.

5. Public civil legal procedure guided only by the law, and public criminal justice based on conscience and the law; that is, a jury court.

6. Direct responsibility of each and all before the courts.

7. Personal accountability of all officials for failure to fulfill their responsibilities, without the right to refer to the orders of their superiors.

8. The establishment of new, firm and strict measures for the support of private and State credit.

On these grounds, the Vladimir Gentry make bold to solicit most loyally the proposed changes for all classes which are necessary in the new life of the Russian people. MOST GRACIOUS SOVEREIGN! YOU first awakened this life in the people. In the grandeur of YOUR spirit, YOU will understand the feelings of YOUR most loyal subjects.

[Signed by more than 120 Gentry]

7. Address of the Petersburg Gentry Assembly to Alexander II, March 1860. *Materialy*, II, pp. 321–4.

MOST GRACIOUS SOVEREIGN

With reverential joy the St Petersburg Gentry learned of the most significant words recently pronounced by YOUR IMPERIAL MAJESTY to the Gentry representatives of 24 provinces.

YOUR IMPERIAL MAJESTY branded as 'lie and slander' rumors concerning the decline of Royal trust in our estate, and deigned to command belief only in YOUR words, MOST AUGUST SOVEREIGN!

These words are deeply imprinted in our hearts.

They constitute our bulwark against any encroachment upon the rights and welfare of the Gentry as established by the wisdom and force of the Charter to the Gentry.

Such was, is, and shall be for all the power of the words of the RUSSIAN TSAR.

Following this great precept, the St Petersburg Gentry entrust the protection of their most sacred possession to YOU, GREAT SOVEREIGN, with most loyal confidence. But at the same time the Gentry recognize the obligation, placed upon them by this favor, to be on guard, to point out all the obstacles that might possibly arise to hinder the realization of the good intentions of their Great Protector.

For this reason, they dare to call the most gracious attention of YOUR IMPERIAL MAJESTY to a circumstance which, by its official character, has acquired particular significance.

In accordance with the existing fundamental laws, the filling of the majority of judicial and administrative offices, both provincial and *uezd*, is left to class election. Recently, the composition of preliminary proposals for the reform of these local institutions was entrusted to a special Committee attached to the Ministry of Interior.

Fully recognizing the timeliness of certain changes, the Gentry of St Petersburg province nevertheless consider it their sacred duty to declare solemnly before Throne and Fatherland that they have not so much taken pride in the right of class election as an honorary privilege, as they have valued it as the truest means of safeguarding the public and private weal. To this conviction, founded on a deep awareness of the aspirations of our social life, the St Petersburg Gentry remain true today. And we therefore dare to most loyally submit to the most gracious attention of YOUR IMPERIAL MAJESTY that they see the guarantee of the future well-being of all classes of the State in the preservation and correct development, under the shelter of the Autocratic power, of the principles of local self-government which have existed in Russia since ancient times.

> [Adopted by a vote of 200–90 in the Petersburg provincial assembly.]

Appendix III

Documents of the Provincial Gentry Assemblies, 1861-2

1. Petition of the Tula Gentry Assembly to Alexander II, December 1861. *TsGAOR, f.* 109, no. 11, part 3, pp. 7-12.

MOST GRACIOUS SOVEREIGN!

On the basis of the Imperially-granted right of the Russian Gentry to confer about their needs and to present them most loyally to the MONARCH himself, the Tula Gentry make bold to bring to YOUR IMPERIAL MAJESTY's most gracious attention the situation in which they now find themselves.

The legislation on the temporarily-obligated peasants and household people has so far proven unsatisfactory. The difficulties and conflicts of interest arising from it disturb the economy, sow destructive discord between the peasants and *pomeshchiki*, and cause incalculable harm to agriculture, which constitutes the main source of the national wealth of YOUR MAJESTY's extensive Empire.

The Gentry, deprived of more than half of the land belonging to them in exchange for an *obrok* which does not correspond to its value, are unable to receive income from the land remaining to them because the obligatory labor of free men is unthinkable and in view of the surplus allotment of land to [the peasants], hired [labor] is unprofitable.

As a result, the quantity of grain placed on the market has decreased and will decrease still more in the future. A loss to the State is inevitable, and taking into consideration the rapid destruction of forests which the landowners are incapable of preserving, and the destruction of many factories and various other industrial enterprises for whose continuation there are no means, the damage to the economic strength of the State will be im-

453

measurable. The Gentry class, which has always preceded all other classes on the path of enlightenment and good will, will through no fault of its own come to complete ruin.

In order to relieve such a disastrous situation and to avoid its destructive consequences in the not-far-distant future, the Tula Gentry find no other course than to petition most loyally before the Throne of the magnanimous MONARCH for the following:

1. For permission to transfer the peasants from labor obligations to *obrok* independently of their wishes, with guarantee of this *obrok* by the Government, in order to eliminate daily conflicts as quickly as possible and to establish between *pomeshchiki* and peasants those peaceful relations which are equally necessary for both.

2. For allowing rapid separation of property, without which proper cultivation either by the *pomeshchiki* or by the peasants, and redemption itself, are impossible.

3. For sale of peasant allotments to the Treasury by *pomeshchiki* who so desire, if the peasants themselves do not wish to purchase them. With transfer of the debt to the credit institutions, redemption of a reduced allotment for the full sum determined by the legislation without a 25 percent reduction will not burden the Government, and the debt will be guaranteed by peasant *obrok*. Payment of the remaining sum [to the *pomeshchiki* after deduction of their debts] could be carried out by means of special five-percent notes which would be redeemed through sale of various State properties, as well as by regular means, in place of the certificates legislated for this purpose.

Those same *pomeshchiki* who do not wish to sell the peasant allotments to the Treasury could be allowed to transfer their debts to the credit institutions onto these allotments, freeing the remaining *pomeshchiki* lands from mortgage. Until this is resolved, sale of estates in arrears should be suspended.

4. For rapid provision of financial aid to the extremely needy smallholding *pomeshchiki*, as provided in the legislation; and also for transfer of the peasant allotments [on their estates] to the Treasury, or removal of their peasants to State lands.

Finally, for the sake of the peace and welfare of the State and for the well-being of all YOUR IMPERIAL MAJESTY's most loyal subjects, that inapplicability which has thus far so often been evident in promulgated laws must in the future be eliminated. It is possible to achieve this only by establishing one commission to which there will be named at least a few property-owners elected from each province, together with experts from those sections of the administration to which the statutes under preparation are related, in place of separate commissions working on the composition of projects in various fields of State reforms. Such a commission must have the right to present its legislative drafts directly to the Royal purview of YOUR IMPERIAL MAJESTY. Only in this way will our statutes satisfy the vital needs of the people, facilitate the development of all its moral and material energies, and correspond to the local conditions of the country for which they are intended.

MOST GRACIOUS SOVEREIGN! With a sense of limitless devotion and firm reliance on the good will of the EMANCIPATOR MONARCH, the Tula Gentry most loyally submit their urgent needs to the gracious Royal attention of YOUR IMPERIAL MAJESTY, raising heartfelt supplication to the most high Throne. May our beloved fatherland prosper on the path of the reforms peacefully and legally undertaken by YOUR MAJESTY, to the welfare of Russia and the undiminishing glory of her beloved MONARCH.

YOUR IMPERIAL MAJESTY'S DEVOTED SUBJECTS:
[Signatures]

2. Address of the Moscow Gentry Assembly to Alexander II, January 1862, *TsGIAL, f.* 1282, no. 1092, pp. 28–29*a*.

[MOST GRACIOUS SOVEREIGN]

Moved by love of fatherland, the Moscow Gentry have had the happiness of demonstrating their devotion many times by their services to the welfare of the State during grave moments of trial. The unforgettable year 1812, and the arrival of YOUR MOST AUGUST namesake in the original capital at the time of the unexpected incursion of the enemy into the territory of the Empire, still remain fresh in our memory. Certain of sympathy from Moscow, EMPEROR ALEXANDER I turned at that time to our Gentry, summoning them to the salvation of the Fatherland. The voice of the EMPEROR touched the hearts of his loyal subjects. Within several hours there appeared both money and troops, Moscow rose up and, soon after her, the rest of Russia. Our Fatherland emerged with glory from the struggle, and the State became more powerful than ever before.

But then it was a foreign enemy that threatened [the State]. Now an internal danger, no less potent, threatens it. At all levels of society a species of discontent reigns; the laws are not being observed in their strict sense; neither person nor property is protected from the arbitrariness of the administration; the classes are set against each other, and the antagonism between them grows incessantly in consequence of those actions of administrative officials which do not satisfy local needs. Moreover, a complete lack of money; fears of a State financial crisis, expressed in the instability of the currency; the complete absence of credit; and finally, a multitude of false rumors disturbing the minds of the people. Such, in a few words, is our present situation, and the Moscow Gentry, moved by love of the Fatherland and devotion to the Throne, resolve to speak the whole truth to their SOVEREIGN.

The foundation-stone on which all abuses were based has been removed—serfdom has been abolished, but much remains to be done in order to re-establish the shaken edifice of the State on firm foundations. To root out evil; to march forward behind their SOVEREIGN along the path of peaceful reforms in order to satisfy the needs of society; to institute complete order; to forestall, even for the future, every possibility of disorder—these are the wishes of the Moscow Gentry, and they address themselves to their SOVEREIGN, submitting to his good judgment the following measures capable of removing our Fatherland from its difficult position:

1. The greatest possible expansion of the elective principle in State service, and greater scope to local self-government. With this, strict observance of the laws, not only by subordinates, but by higher officials as well; and strict accountability and responsi-

bility before the law, personally, of each and every official in State service.

2. Protection of the personal and property rights of all citizens of the State by means of the introduction of verbal and public court procedure and a jury court.

3. Elimination of hostile relations between the Gentry and the peasantry by means of obligatory, rapid separation of [their] lands, simultaneously with the granting of the land charters; guarantee of *obrok* by the Government, and redemption with guarantee not of 80 percent, but of the entire sum.

4. Publication of State debts and estimates of State revenues and expenditures, as a means of calming fears of a financial crisis.

5. Public discussion in the press of questions concerning changes in all fields which the Government is planning in connection with forthcoming administrative and economic reforms.

These are the means which can contribute to the well-being of our Fatherland. Many times YOUR IMPERIAL MAJESTY has turned confidently to YOUR devoted Gentry, and they have always responded with alacrity to the call of their SOVEREIGN.

Many times have YOU said, SOVEREIGN: 'I trust you, have trust in ME', and the Gentry have always awaited with confidence the fulfillment of the beneficent undertakings of their TSAR. At the present difficult time they are once again prepared to stand as a firm support around the Russian Throne and to aid their SOVEREIGN with all their strength in the fulfillment of his beneficent intentions. With this aim the Moscow Gentry most loyally request YOUR IMPERIAL MAJESTY to permit them to elect from among themselves a committee for discussion of the main principles which should lie at the base of future regulations on [Gentry] elections; for review of the statute on local obligations; and for discussion of the question of rural credit and local needs, with participation in its labors of deputies from other classes, since these questions concern the entire rural population; the works of the committee, reviewed in a general assembly of elected persons from all classes of the State called from the provinces to Moscow, that city being the heart of Russia, to be submitted to the good judgment of YOUR IMPERIAL MAJESTY.

3. Protocol of the Pskov Gentry Assembly, 18 January 1862. *TsGAOR, f.* 109, no. 33, part 2, pp. 23–6.

Discussing their needs in the Provincial Assembly on 18 January 1862, the Gentry of Pskov Province, in view of the position in which they have been placed by the radical change in the life of the peasants, felt the necessity of petitioning for the change of several statutes directly concerning the interests of the Gentry estate. Deeply aware of the justice of the peasant reform and warmly sympathetic to the new life of the Russian People, it is nevertheless impossible to deny that the new order of things has more or less unfavorably affected the economic position of every *pomeshchik* in the province. Willingly sacrificing their personal material interests to the public welfare, the Gentry are concerned here only with those specific subjects of legislation whose change would protect the interests of the Gentry class within the limits of strict justice, without violating the general concept of the new civil life of the peasants. Firmly trusting that the needs and welfare of all classes of the State are equally near to the heart of the MONARCH-EMANCIPATOR, it has been resolved in the Provincial Assembly to petition through the Minister of Interior concerning the following subjects:

1. Obligatory transfer of the temporarily-obligated peasants to *obrok* on demand of the *pomeshchik*, and the guaranteeing of *obrok* by the Government.

2. Redemption of the allotment-lands of the temporarily-obligated peasants in accordance with the rules laid out in the statute, at ruble-for-ruble value and with payment by 5 percent bonds guaranteed by the allotment-lands of the peasants, rather than by credit certificates.

3. Remortgaging of estates for another 33 years with loans from the credit institutions on the former basis of 4 per cent and $1\frac{1}{2}$ per cent for principle reduction and with the old certificates; and the transfer of this debt to the peasant allotment, freeing the remaining *pomeshchik* land from distraint.

4. The application to our area of those articles of the Code of Laws which are in force in the Baltic Provinces for protection of forests against illegal cutting of timber.

5. In view of the fact that all classes have benefited from the new Statue and that the Gentry alone have suffered losses and will suffer yet new losses with the fundamental transformation of their economy to the new basis of free labor, as yet untried here, the Pskov Gentry, seeking for themselves the privileges granted to all new builders, migrants and settlers, make bold to petition before the person of the MONARCH for the exemption of unpopulated *pomeshchik* lands from all new land taxes, except those presently in existence, for approximately twenty years.

Discussing those changes which could in their opinion be permitted in several articles of the IMPERIALLY-confirmed statute of 19 February without violating the general sense of the legislation, the Pskov Gentry resolved, in their meeting of 18 January 1862, to request the Provincial Gentry Marshal to make presentation to the Minister of Interior for a most loyal report to the SOVEREIGN EMPEROR on the following subjects:

1. Granting to the Gentry of the right to elect Gentry representatives to the Provincial Office on Peasant Affairs in equal number with the Government representatives there. If such a change shall be judged inconvenient, then at least let it be decreed that, in case on any question all three Gentry representatives should unanimously disagree with the five Government representatives, resolution of such a question shall be presented to the Main Committee, without being [previously] acted upon.

In addition, the Gentry request that the Provincial Office on Peasant Affairs conduct public rather than closed sessions.

2. Replacement of the Government representatives by attorneys [*striapchie*] in the *uezd* arbitration conferences, with the aim of decreasing *zemstvo* expenditures.

3. Granting to the Gentry the right to elect candidates to the office of peace mediator, and to the peasants [the right] to elect peace mediators from among them.

4. In conformance with the sense of article 173 of the local Statute [on emancipation], it is necessary to amend article 175 of the same Statute by restricting the right of the Provincial Office on Peasant Affairs to lower the *obrok* of the temporarily-obligated peasants below one ruble per soul.

5. Speedy provision of assistance to the smallholding Gentry, in so far as these persons are in a hopeless situation and are deprived of the ability to continue their operations on the new foundations.

6. Postponement of the issuing of the land charters, in so far as the majority of landowners, due to insufficiency of surveying means, have thus far been unable to delimit the land destined for peasant allotments.

4. Resolutions of the Voronezh Gentry Assembly, 4 February 1862. *TsGIAL, f.* 1282, no. 1091, pp. 17–18 *a*.

Resolution of the Voronezh Gentry

with Appendixes

The appendixes consist of a private opinion (with 29 signatures) of the following import:

The law of 19 February 1861, which has been carried out by the *pomeshchiki*, is not being carried out by the peasants. Obligations are not being fulfilled, because the rural population, knowing that the land will not be taken away from those in arrears, is becoming ever more convinced of the apparent illegality of any obligations associated with it.

The fact of possession has overpowered the law and the juridical foundations of property.

In the future—ruination as a result of debt payments, constant thievery, or unjust redemption (for four-fifths of value and with liquidation of the State debt by redemption at the expense of the *pomeshchiki* alone); in the present—deserted fields, destruction of livestock and forests and a fall of prices on all products because of the high cost of transport; such is the state of Gentry property in Voronezh Province. The personal situation of the Gentry is likewise uncertain: They are isolated from the rural population by property relations; from one another by distance; and from affairs of State by the fact that they participate in them briefly and only once every three years, at the time of assembly.

This gives rise to their powerlessness and the need to define their significance as a class, and, in respect to the State order, their function in the Empire. The significance of the Gentry as a class wanes with every day that passes, and their future function, as a constituent part of the nation, should, it seems, consist of safeguarding the unity of Power [i.e. the autocracy]. For this they are very well suited, by certain of their class characteristics: by their corporate and other habits of life, in part by their established traditions and especially by their higher level of education in comparison with other classes.

Proceeding from causes to actions, the *Resolutions* consist of the following declarations:

1. On the necessity of safeguarding property by fundamental protective law.

The safeguarding of the property of the *pomeshchiki* in particular will be attained only by means of the Land Charters, with the understanding that they must be drawn up *in the very near future* by the Peace Mediators alone, the latter to be supplied with a *special instruction*, drawn up in a spirit of pacification.

2. On the necessity of a source of stability (*élément de stabilité*) in Russian Legislation, which the Voronezh Gentry believe would be provided by admission of two Gentry from each province to participate in State Institutions.

The alterability and the resultant unstable operation of the Laws arise from an insufficient element of restraint (veto) and an absence of control over the executors [of the laws].

3. On the necessity of changing several articles of the Statute of 19 February 1861 on the following subjects [i.e., to provide for]:

(*a*) The right of the *pomeshchiki* to obligatory *obrok* (art. 236–241 of the local statute) and payment to them of the full redemption sum (art. 68 of the statute on redemption).

(*b*) Immediate identification of those State properties by which the redemption certificates are to be guaranteed (art. 142 of the statute on redemption); also, the supplying of smallholders with money instead of certificates.

(*c*) Obligatory acceptance by the peasants of $\frac{1}{4}$ the maximum allotment if the *pomeshchik* grants this to them as a gift (art. 123 of the local statute).

(*d*) Elimination of deadlines for delimitation of peasant allotments, and carrying this out simultaneously with the Land Charters (art. 52 and 65 of the local statute). And together with this, re-examination of section III of the first chapter of the local statute on the transfer of *usad'by*, in a manner which will ameliorate the position of the landowners.

(*e*) Termination of all obligatory relations in nine years. In case of failure to pay *obrok*, the peasants to be deprived irreversibly of that land not paid for in the course of one year (art. 132 of the local statute).

(*f*) Elimination of damage to fields by cattle and illegal cutting of timber by means of mutual responsibility of the [peasant] communities.

(*g*) Termination of sale of estates for overdue payments to the Credit Institutions until resolution of the peasant question.

(*h*) Extension of the deadline for request of assistance by smallholders for one more year (art. 20 of the additional rules on smallholders); and definition of smallholding estates, not as those with 20 souls [or less], but as those with land area equal to 40 maximum allotments [or less].

4. On the rapid termination of special surveying, making it obligatory in those tracts in which $\frac{2}{3}$ of the owners of overlapping land fail to come to any agreement.

5. On the empowering of *Uezd Courts* to draw up deeds for the alienation of property without limit as to sum.

6. On the subjection of all officials to the law and the courts alone, not [solely] to the instructions of their superiors. Revocation of the right of superiors to remove subordinates from their posts without trial.

7. On the necessity of public court procedure and the establishment of a *Common Court* for all Russian subjects, even those in [state] service, without regard to wealth or rank.

8. On [the right to] unrestricted gatherings of the Gentry in the *uezdy*.

9. On the prescription of general and uniform three-year terms for elected officials.

10. On the extremely unsatisfactory state of roads in the Empire.

11. On the expansion of postal communications between Voronezh and neighboring provinces.

12. On permission for Jews to settle freely on *pomeshchik* lands.

Bibliography

This list does not include all the materials consulted in the writing of the book. It contains only materials cited. Therefore it is not meant to be a bibliographical introduction to the subject under discussion.

The organization of the list according to published and unpublished materials is one of simple convenience—to avoid having to make this distinction for each item. The distinction between 'primary' and 'secondary' sources did not appear relevant to most of these materials.

The list of archival collections is not a list of specific documents, but only of the collections—*fondy*—from which documents have been drawn. The addition of a list of contemporary periodicals seemed suggested because of frequent references to them in the book, and because citations from them have sometimes been made without designation of specific authors or articles.

The full titles of archives are given in the 'Key to Abbreviations' at the beginning of the book.

I. ARCHIVAL COLLECTIONS AND OTHER UNPUBLISHED MATERIALS

GAKO - *f.* 59. *Kantseliariia tverskogo gubernskogo predvoditelia dvorianstva.*

f. 148. *Tverskoi gubernskii dvorianskii komitet dlia ulushcheniia byta pomeshchich'ikh krest'ian (1858–1859).*

f. 466. *Tverskoe gubernskoe pravlenie.*

f. 484. *Tverskoe gubernskoe po krest'ianskim delam prisutstvie.*

ORLB - *f.* 69. *Gertsen, A. I., i Ogarev, N. P.*

f. 327. *Cherkasskie, kn. V. A. Cherkasskii i kn. E. I. Cherkasskaia.*

f. 588. *Pogodin, M. P.*

GPB - *f.* 1007. *Unkovskaia, S. A.*

PD - *f.* 265. *Arkhiv zhurnala Russkaia starina.*

f. 284. *Skrebitskii, A. I.*

TsGALI - *f.* 445. *Saltykov, M. E.*

TsGAOR - *f.* 109. *III otdelenie. Sekretnyi arkhiv.*

Otchety III otdeleniia za 1858, 1862, 1863, 1864.

TsGIAL - *f.* 772. *Glavnoe upravlenie tsenzury.*

f. 1180. *Glavnyi komitet po krest'ianskomu delu.*

Bibliography

f. 1282. *Kantseliariia MVD.*

f. 1291. *Zemskii otdel, MVD.*

f. 1341. *Pervyi departament Senata.*

Netting, A. *Russian Liberalism: the years of promise, 1842–1855.* Unpublished dissertation, Columbia University, 1967.

Federov, V. A. 'Mezhevye opisaniia 1850kh godov kak istochniki po istorii krest'ianskogo khoziaistva v Rossii (po materialam Tverskoi gubernii).' Unpublished paper presented at the History Faculty of Moscow State University, 31 October 1962.

Rozum, M. A. *Tverskie liberaly v reformakh 6okh godov XIX veka.* Unpublished dissertation, Moscow, 1940.

Solov'eva, N. *Liberal'noe dvorianstvo v period podgotovki i provedeniia krest'ianskoi reformy 1861g. (Iu. Samarin).* Unpublished dissertation, Moscow, 1950.

Zimina, V. G. *Krest'ianskaia reforma 1861 goda v Vladimirskoi gubernii.* Unpublished dissertation, Moscow, 1956.

II. PUBLISHED MATERIALS

Akademiia nauk SSSR, institut istorii. *Delo petrashevtsev*, vol. III. Moscow, 1951.

Akademiia nauk SSSR, institut istorii. *Revoliutsionnaia situatsiia v Rossii v 1859–1861gg.* 4 vols. Moscow, 1960–5.

Aksakov, I. S. *Sochineniia*, vol. V. Moscow, 1887.

Bagramian, N. S. 'Pomeshchich'i proekty osvobozhdeniia krest'ian. (K probleme "krizisa verkhov").' *Revoliutsionnaia situatsiia v Rossii v 1859–1861gg.* Moscow, 1962.

Barsukov, N. *Zhizn' i trudy M. P. Pogodina*, vols. 17–19. St Petersburg, 1903–5.

Baturinskii, V. P. *A. I. Gertsen, ego druz'ia i znakomye. Materialy dlia istorii obshchestvennogo dvizheniia v Rossii.* St Petersburg, 1904.

Beloff, M. 'Russia.' A. Goodwin (ed.). *The European nobility in the eighteenth century.* London, 1953.

Bermanskii, K. 'Konstitutsionnye proekty tsarstvovaniia Aleksandra II.' *Vestnik Prava*, vol. XXV, book 9, 1905.

Bezobrazov, M. A. *Ob usovershenii uzakonenii, kasaiushchikhsia do votchinnykh prav dvorianstva.* Berlin, 1858.

Bliumin, I. 'Ekonomichheskie vozzreniia dekabristov.' *Problemy ekonomiki*, no. 5–6, 1940.

Bibliography

Ocherki ekonomicheskoi mysli v Rossii v pervoi polovine XIX veka. Moscow-Leningrad, 1940.

Blum, J. *Lord and peasant in Russia from the ninth to the nineteenth century.* Princeton, 1961.

Bochkarev, V. N. 'Dvorianskie proekty po krest'ianskomu voprosu pri Nikolae I.' *Velikaia reforma,* vol. III.

Bogucharskii, V. Ia. 'Iakov Ivanovich Rostovtsev.' *Velikaia reforma,* vol. V.

Chebaevskii, F. 'Nizhegorodskii gubernskii dvorianskii komitet 1858g.' *Voprosy istorii,* no. 6, 1947.

Cherniavskii, M. *Genealogiia gospod dvorian vnesennykh v rodoslovnuiu knigu Tverskoi gubernii s 1789 po 1869 god.* Lithographed, n.p., n.d.

Cherniavsky, M. *Tsar and People: a historical study of Russian national and social myths.* New Haven, 1962.

Chernyshevskii, N. G. *Polnoe sobranie sochinenii,* vol. X, part 2. N.p., 1906.

Chicherin, B. N. *Neskol'ko sovremennykh voprosov.* Moscow, 1862.

Vospominaniia. Moskva 40kh godov. Moscow, 1929.

Vospominaniia. Moskovskii universitet. Moscow, 1929.

Dmitriev, S. S. ''Vozniknovenie sel'skokhoziaistvennykh vystavok v Rossii.' *Voprosy istorii sel'skogo khoziaistva, krest'ianstva i revoliutsionnogo dvizheniia v Rossii. Sbornik statei k 75-letiu Akademika N. M. Druzhinina.* Moscow, 1961.

Druzhinin, N. M. 'Moskovskoe dvorianstvo i reforma 1861 goda.' *Izvestiia akademii nauk. Seriia istorii i filosofii,* vol. 5, no. 1, 1948.

'Zhurnal zemlevladel'tsev, 1858–1860.' Rossiiskaia assotsiatsiia nauchno-issledovatel'skikh institutov obshchestvennykh nauk, institut istorii. *Sbornik statei,* vol. I, 1926; *Uchenye zapiski,* vol. II, 1927.

Dzhanshiev, G. *Epokha velikikh reform.* 8th ed. Moscow, 1900.

Edeen, A. 'The civil service: its composition and status.' C. Black (ed.). *The Transformation of Russian Society. Aspects of Social Change Since 1861.* Cambridge, Mass., 1960.

Eisenstadt, S. N. 'Political struggle in bureaucratic societies.' *World politics,* vol. IX, no. 1, 1956.

The political systems of empires. New York, 1963.

Eliseeva, V. N. 'Podgotovka krest'ianskoi reformy 1861 goda v Riazanskoi gubernii. (Riazanskii gubernskii dvorianskii komitet 1858–1859gg.)' Riazanskii gos. pedagogicheskii institut. *Uchenye zapiski,* no. 11, 1953.

Bibliography

Entsiklopedicheskii slovar' (Brokgauz-Efron), vols. IIIa, X, XIa, XXIa, XXIV, XXVIIIa, LII.

Evreinov, G. *Proshloe i nastoiashchee znachenie russkogo dvorianstva.* St Petersburg, 1898.

Fedorov, V. A. 'Krest'ianskoe trezvennoe dvizhenie 1858–1860gg.' *Revoliutsionnaia situatsiia v Rossii v 1859–1861gg.* Moscow, 1962.

'Lozungi krest'ianskoi bor'by v 1861–1863gg.' *Revoliutsionnaia situatsiia v Rossii v 1859–1861gg.* Moscow, 1963.

'Trebovaniia krest'ianskogo dvizheniia v nachale revoliutsionnoi situatsii.' *Revoliutsionnaia situatsiia v Rossi v 1859–1861gg.* Moscow, 1960.

Fischer, G. *Russian Liberalism. From gentry to intelligentsia.* Cambridge, Mass., 1958.

Garmiza, A. A. *Podgotovka zemskoi reformy 1864 goda.* Moscow, 1957.

Gerschenkron, A. 'Agrarian policies and industrialization, Russia 1861–1917.' *Cambridge Economic History of Europe*, vol. VI, part 2. Cambridge, 1965.

Gerth, H., and C. Wright Mills (eds.). *From Max Weber: essays in sociology.* New York, 1962.

Gessen, I. *Sudebnaia reforma.* St Petersburg, 1905.

Ginsberg, B. S. 'Otnoshenie A. I. Gertsena i N. P. Ogareva k krest'-ianskoi reforme v period ee podgotovki (1857–1860gg.)' *Istoricheskie zapiski*, no. 36, 1951.

Golosa iz Rossii, vols. I–IV, IX. London, 1856–60.

Golovachev, A. A. *Desiat' let reform.* St Petersburg, 1872.

Istoriia zheleznodorozhnogo dela v Rossii. St Petersburg, 1881.

'Po povodu voprosa ob ulushchenii byta pomeshchich'ikh krest'ian.' *Russkii vestnik. Sovremennaia letopis'*, vol. XIV: 1, 1858.

Haxthausen, Baron A. von. *Etudes sur la situation intérieure, la vie nationale et les institutions rurales de la Russie.* 3 vols. Paris, 1847–53.

Iablochkov, M. *Istoriia dvorianskogo sosloviia v Rossii.* St Petersburg, 1876.

Ignatovich, I. I. *Pomeshchich'i krest'iane nakanune osvobozhdeniia.* 2nd ed. Moscow, 1910.

'Otrazhenie v Rossii krest'ianskogo dvizheniia v Galitsii 1846 goda.' *Sbornik trudov professorov i prepodavatelei gos. Irkutskogo universiteta. Vypusk V.* 1923.

'Krest'ianskie volneniia.' *Velikaia reforma*, vol. III.

Il'in, G. *Agrarnaia reforma 1861 goda v Moskovskoi gubernii.* Dissertation abstract. Moscow, 1950.

Bibliography

Iordanskii, N.I. *Konstitutsionnoe dvizhenie 60kh godov.* St Petersburg, 1906.

Istoriia russkoi ekonomicheskoi mysli, vol. I, part 2. Moscow, 1958.

Ivaniukov, I. *Padenie krepostnogo prava v Rossii.* 2nd ed. St Petersburg, 1903.

Kabuzan, M. *Narodonaselenie Rossii v XVIII-pervoi polovine XIX v.* Moscow, 1963.

Kafengauz, B. 'Voina 1812 goda i ee vliianie na sotsial'no-ekonomicheskuiu zhizn' Rossii.' *Voprosy istorii,* no. 7, 1962.

Kavelin, K. D. *Sobranie sochinenii,* vol. II. St Petersburg, 1898.

Kizevetter, A. *Istoricheskie ocherki.* Moscow, 1912.

Istoricheskie otkliki. Moscow, 1915.

Kliuchevskii, V. O. *Kurs russkoi istorii,* vol. II. Moscow, 1957.

Koliupanov, N. 'Pamiati K. D. Kavelina.' *Russkie vedomosti,* no. 123, 7 May, 1885.

Korf, S. *Dvorianstvo i ego soslovnoe upravlenie za stoletie 1762–1855 godov.* St Petersburg, 1906.

Kornilov, A. A. 'Gubernskie komitety po krest'ianskomu delu v 1858–1859gg.' *Russkoe bogatstvo,* nos. 1–5, 1904.

'Krest'ianskaia reforma v Kaluzhskoi gubernii pri V. A. Artsimoviche.' *V. A. Artsimovich. Vospominaniia, kharakteristika.* St Petersburg, 1904.

Krest'ianskaia reforma. St Petersburg, 1905.

Kurs istorii Rossii XIX veka. 2 vols. Moscow, 1912–14.

Obshchestvennoe dvizhenie pri Aleksandre II. (1855–1881). Istoricheskie ocherki. Moscow, 1909.

Ocherki po istorii obshchestvennogo dvizheniia i krest'ianskogo dela v Rossii. St Petersburg, 1905.

Koshelev, A. I. *Deputaty i redaktsionnye komissii po krest'ianskomu delu.* Leipzig, 1860.

Kakoi iskhod dlia Rossii iz nyneshnego polozheniia? Leipzig, 1862.

Konstitutsiia, samoderzhavie i zemskaia duma. Leipzig, 1862.

Pis'mo deputata pervogo prizyva k deputatu vtorogo prizyva. Leipzig, 1860.

Zapiski. (1812–1883.) Berlin, 1884.

Koval'chenko, I. D. 'O tovarnosti zemledeliia v Rossii v pervoi polovine XIX v.' *Ezhegodnik po agrarnoi istorii vostochnoi Evropy, 1963g.* Vilnius, 1964.

Koval'chenko, I. D. and L. Milov. 'Ob intensivnosti obrochnoi ekspluatatsii krest'ian tsentral'noi Rossii v kontse XVIII- pervoi polovine XIX v.' *Istoriia SSSR,* no. 4, 1966.

Bibliography

Kovan'ko, P. L. *Reforma 19 fevralia 1861 goda i ee posledstviia s finansovoi tochki zreniia.* (*Vykupnaia operatsiia 1861g.–1907g.*) Kiev, 1914.

Koz'min, B. P. *Iz istorii revoliutsionnoi mysli v Rossii.* Moscow, 1961.

Krechetovich, I. P. *Krest'ianskaia reforma v Orenburgskom krae* (*po arkhivnym dannym.*) *Tom I. Podgotovka reformy.* N.p./n.d., but Moscow, 1911.

Krest'ianskaia reforma v Rossii 1861 goda. Sbornik zakonodatel'skikh aktov. Moscow, 1954.

Krest'ianskoe dvizhenie v Rossii v 1857-mae 1861gg. Sbornik dokumentov. Moscow, 1963.

Krest'ianskoe dvizhenie v Rossii v 1861–1869gg. Sbornik dokumentov. Moscow, 1964.

Krest'ianskoe dvizhenie v 1861 godu posle otmeny krespostnogo prava. Chast' I i II. Doneseniia svitskikh generalov i fligel'-ad'iutantov, gubernskikh prokurorov i uezdnikh striapchikh. Moscow-Leningrad, 1949.

Krutikov, V. I. 'Tul'skii dvorianskii komitet 1858–1859gg.' Tul'skii ped. institut. *Uchenye zapiski, vyp.* III, 1952.

Kulomzin, A. N. 'Vospominaniia mirovogo posrednika.' *Zapiski otdela rukopisei biblioteki im. Lenina, vyp.* 10. Moscow, 1941.

Lemke, M. *Ocherki osvoboditel'nogo dvizheniia 'shestidesiatykh godov.'* St Petersburg, 1908.

Politicheskie protessy v Rossii 1860-kh gg. 2nd ed. Moscow-Petrograd, 1923.

Leontovitsch, V. *Geschichte des Liberalismus in Russland.* Frankfurt/Main, 1957.

Leroy-Beaulieu, P. *Un homme d'état russe (Nicolas Miliutine).* Paris, 1884.

Levin, Sh.M. *Obshchestvennoe dvizhenie v Rossii v 60–70e gody XIX veka.* Moscow, 1958.

Levshin, A. I. 'Dostopamiatnye minuty v moei zhizni.' *Russkii arkhiv,* no. 8, 1885.

Liashchenko, P. I. *History of the national economy of Russia to the 1917 Revolution.* New York, 1949.

Linkov, Ia. I. *Revoliutsionnaia bor'ba A. I. Gertsena i N. P. Ogareva i tainoe obshchestvo 'zemlia i volia' 1860-kh godov.* Moscow, 1964.

Literaturnoe nasledstvo, vol. XXXIX–XL. Moscow, 1941; vol. LXIII. Moscow, 1956.

Litvak, B. G. 'Ob izmeneniiakh zemel'nogo nadela pomeshchich'ikh krest'ian v pervoi polovine XIX v.' *Ezhegodnik po agrarnoi istorii vostochnoi Evropy, 1963g.* Vilnius, 1964.

Bibliography

Materialy dlia istorii revoliutsionnogo dvizheniia v Rossii v 60-kh gg. Paris, 1905.

Materialy dlia istorii uprazdneniia krepostnogo sostoianiia pomeshchich'ikh krest'ian v Rossii v tsarstvovanie Imperatora Aleksandra II. 3 vols. Berlin, 1860–2.

Miliukov, P. *Russia and its Crisis.* Chicago–London, 1906.

Miliutina, M. A. 'Iz zapisok.' *Russkaia starina*, vols. XCVII–XCVIII, 1899.

Miller, I. S. 'Vokrug Velikorussa.' *Revoliutsionnaia situatsiia v Rossii v 1859–1861gg.* Moscow, 1965.

Moore, B., Jr. *Social origins of dictatorship and democracy. Lord and peasant in the making of the modern world.* Boston, 1966.

Naidenov, M. *Klassovaia bor'ba v poreformennoi derevne (1861–1863gg.)* Moscow, 1955.

'Na zare krest'ianskoi svobody.'*Russkaia starina*,vols. XCII–XCIV, 1897–8.

Nikitenko, A. V. *Dnevnik.* 3 vols. N.p., 1955.

Nol'de, B. D. *Iurii Samarin i ego vremia.* Paris, 1926.

Peterburgskaia missiia Bismarka, 1859–1862. Prague, 1925.

Orlov, V. S. *Otmena krepostnogo prava v Smolenskoi gubernii.* Smolensk, 1947.

Orlov-Davydov, V. P. *Lettre d'un deputé de comité à Monsieur le Président de la commission de rédaction, aide-de-camp, Général Rostovt-zeff.* Paris, 1859.

Otmena krepostnogo prava. Doklady ministrov vnutrennikh del o provedenii krest'ianskoi reformy 1861–1862. Moscow–Leningrad, 1950.

Pamiatnaia knizhka Tverskoi gubernii za 1861g. Tver, 1862.

Panteleev, L. F. *Iz vospominanii proshlogo.* Moscow, 1934.

Pavlov, A. S. 'V. I. Nazimov. Ocherki iz noveishei letopisi severo-zapadnoi Rossii.' *Russkaia starina*, vols. XLV–XLVI, 1885.

Pavlov-Sil'vanskii, N. *Gosudarevy sluzhilye liudi. Proiskhozhdenie russkogo dvorianstva.* St Petersburg, 1898.

Pavlovsky, G. *Agricultural Russia on the eve of Revolution.* London, 1930.

Picheta, V. I. 'Pomeshchich'e khoziaistvo nakanune reformy.' *Velikaia reforma*, vol. III.

'Vopros ob usadebnoi osedlosti v Moskovskom gubernskom komitete.' *Uchenye zapiski instituta istorii (RANION)*, vol. V. Moscow, 1928.

Pis'ma K. D. Kavelina i I. S. Turgeneva k A. I. Gertsenu. Geneva, 1892.

Pokrovskii, V. *Istoriko-statisticheskoe opisanie Tverskoi gubernii.* 2 vols. Tver, 1879.

Bibliography

Popel'nitskii, A. 'Delo osvobozhdeniia krest'ian v gosudarstvennom sovete 28 ianvaria-17 fevralia, 1861g. Istoricheskaia spravka po neizdannym istochnikam.' *Russkaia mysl'*, no. 2, 1911.
'Sekretnyi komitet v dele osvobozhdeniia krest'ian ot krepostnoi zavisimosti.' *Vestnik Evropy*, February–March 1911.

Povalishin, A. *Riazanskie pomeshchiki i ikh krepostnye.* Riazan, 1903.

Pozen, M. P. *Bumagi po krest'ianskomu delu.* Dresden, 1864.

Preobrazhenskii, V. *Opisanie Tverskoi gubernii v sel'skokhoziaistvennom otnoshenii.* St Petersburg, 1854.

Proklamatsii 60-kh godov. Moscow–Leningrad, 1926.

Rashin, A. G. *Naselenie Rossii za 100 let (1811-1913gg.) Statisticheskie ocherki.* Moscow, 1956.

Redaktsionnye komissii dlia sostavleniia polozhenii o krest'ianakh vykhodiashchikh iz krepostnoi zavisimosti. *Pervoe izdanie materialov.* 18 vols. St Petersburg, 1859–60.

Prilozhenie k trudam. Otzyvy chlenov gubernskikh komitetov. 3 vols. St Petersburg, 1859–60.

Prilozhenie k trudam. Svedeniia po pomeshchich'im imeniiam. 6 vols. St Petersburg, 1860.

Rieber, A. J. (ed.). *The politics of autocracy. Letters of Alexander II to Prince A. I. Bariatinskii, 1857-1864.* Paris–The Hague, 1966.

Romanovich-Slavatinskii, A. *Dvorianstvo v Rossii ot nachala XVIII veka do otmeny krepostnogo prava.* St Petersburg, 1870.

Rosenberg, H. *Bureaucracy, aristocracy and autocracy. The Prussian experience, 1660-1815.* Cambridge, Mass., 1958.

Rozental', V. N. 'Pervoe otkrytoe vystuplenie russkikh liberalov v 1855-56 gg.' *Istoriia SSSR*, no. 2., 1958.
'Ideinye tsentry liberal'nogo dvizheniia v Rossii nakanune revoliutsionnoi situatsii.' *Revoliutsionnaia situatsiia v Rossii v 1859-1861gg.* Moscow, 1963.

Rozhkova, M. K. (ed.). *Ocherki ekonomicheskoi istorii pervoi poloviny XIX veka. Sbornik statei.* Moscow, 1959.

Rozov, E. K. 'K voprosu o razlozhenii feodal'no-krepostnicheskoi sistemy khoziaistva i dvizhenii pomeshchich'ikh krestian v pervoi polovine XIX veka (po materialam Tverskoi gubernii).' Smolenskii gos. pedagogicheskii institut. *Uchenye zapiski*, vol. 5, 1957.
'O sushchnosti smeshannoi sistemy ekspluatatsii v Tverskoi gubernii nakanune reformy 1861 g.' *Istoricheskie nauki*, no. 1, 1958.

Bibliography

Razlozhenie foedal'no-krepostnicheskoi sistemy khoziaistva i pomesh-chich'ikh krest'ian v Tverskoi gubernii s nachala XIX veka do reformy 1861g. Dissertation abstract. Moscow, 1858.

Rozum, M. A., 'Podgotovka krest'ianskoi reformy v Tverskom komitete.' Kalininskii pedagogicheskii institut. *Uchenye zapiski,* vol. 10, no. 1. Kalinin, 1945.

Sakharov, N. V. 'Iz vospominanii o V. A. Artsimoviche.' *V. A. Artsimovich. Vospominaniia, kharakteristika.*

Samarin, Iu. 'Po povodu tolkov o konstitutsii.' *Rus',* no. 29, 1881.

Sbornik postanovlenii i rasporiazhenii po tsenzure s 1720 po 1862g., vol. 1. St Petersburg, 1862.

Sbornik pravitel'stvennykh rasporiazhenii po ustroistvu byta krest'ian vyshedshikh iz krepostnoi zavisimosti, vol. 1. St Petersburg, 1861.

Semevskii, V. I. *Krepostnoe pravo i krest'ianskaia reforma v proizvedeniiakh M. E. Saltykova.* Petrograd, 1917.

Krest'ianskii vopros v Rossii v XVIII i pervoi polovine XIX veka. 2 vols. St Petersburg, 1888.

Krest'iane v tsarstvovanie Imperatritsy Ekateriny II, vol. 1. 2nd ed. St Petersburg, 1903.

Semenov, N. P. 'Deiatel'nost' Ia. I. Rostovtseva v redaktsionnykh komissiakh po krest'ianskomu delu.' *Russkii vestnik,* nos. 10–12, 1864.

Osvobozhdenie krest'ian v tsarstvovanie Imperatora Aleksandra II. Khronika deiatel'nosti komissii po krest'ianskomu delu. 3 vols. in 4. St Petersburg, 1889–1892.

Semenov-Tian-Shanskii, P. P. *Epokha osvobozhdeniia krest'ian v Rossii (1857–1861gg.) v vospominaniiakh P. P. Semenova-Tian-Shanskogo.* 4 vols. St Petersburg, 1911–16.

Serno-Solov'evich, N. A. *Publitsistika. Pis'ma.* Moscow, 1963.

Shepukhova, N. 'Ob izmenenii razmerov dushevladeniia pomesh-chikov evropeiskoi Rossii v pervoi chetverti XVIII–pervoi polo-vine XIX v.' *Ezhegodnik po agrarnoi istorii vostochnoi Evropy, 1963g.* Vilnius, 1964.

Shtein, V. *Ocherki razvitiia russkoi obshchestvenno-ekonomicheskoi mysli XIX-XX vekov.* Leningrad, 1948.

Shubinskii, M. 'Sudebnaia reforma.' *Istoriia Rossii v XIX veka* (Granat), vol. III. N.p., n.d.

Skerpan, A. 'The Russian National Economy and Emancipation.' *Essays in Russian History. A Collection Dedicated to George Vernadsky* (edited by A. Ferguson and A. Levin). Hamden, Conn., 1964.

30-2

Bibliography

Skrebitskii, A. *Krest'ianskoe delo v tsarstvovanie Imperatora Aleksandra II.* 4 vols in 5. Bonn, 1862–8.

Sladkevich, N. G. *Ocherki istorii obshchestvennoi mysli Rossii v kontse 50-nachale 60-kh godov XIX veka.* Leningrad, 1962.

Snezhnevskii, V. 'Krepostnye krest'iane i pomeshchiki Nizhegorodskoi gubernii nakanune reformy 19 fev. i pervye gody posle nee.' Nizhegorodskaia gubernskaia uchenaia arkhivnaia komissia. *Sbornik statei, soobshchenii opisei i dokumentov,* vol. III. Nizhnii Novgorod, 1898.

Solov'ev, Ia. A. *Sel'sko-khoziaistvennaia statistika Smolenskoi gubernii.* Moscow, 1855.

'Zapiski Senatora Ia. A. Solov'eva o krest'ianskom dele.' *Russkaia starina,* vol. XXVII, 1880; vols. XXX–XXXI, 1881; vols. XXXIII–XXXIV, XXXVI, 1882; vol. XXXVII, 1883; vol. XLI, 1884.

Sostoianie promyshlennosti Tverskoi gubernii za 1850g. Tver, 1851.

Stremoukhov, P. D. 'Zametka odnogo iz deputatov pervogo prizyva.' *Russkaia starina,* no. 4, 1900.

Struve, P. B. *Krepostnoe khoziaistvo. Issledovaniia po ekonomicheskoi istorii Rossii v XVIII i XIX vv.* St Petersburg, 1913.

'Osnovnye momenty v razvitii krepostnogo khoziaistva v Rossii v XIX v.' *Mir Bozhii,* nos. 10–12, 1900.

Tatishchev, S. S. *Imperator Aleksandr II. Ego zhizn' i tsarstvovanie.* 2 vols. 2nd edition. St Petersburg, 1911.

Tikhonov, N. 'K kharakteristike dvorianskoi ideologii nakanune padeniia krepostnogo stroia.' *Naukovi zapyski naukovo-doslidchoi katedri istorii ukrain'skoi kultury,* no. 6, 1927.

Troinitskii, A. *Krepostnoe naselenie v Rossii po X narodnoi perepisi.* St Petersburg, 1861.

Trubetskaia, O. *Materialy dlia biografii kn. V. A. Cherkasskogo.* 2 vols. Moscow, 1901.

Trudy komissii o gubernskikh i uezdnykh uchrezhdeniiakh, part II, book 2. St Petersburg, 1863.

Tseitlin, S. 'Zemskaia reforma.' *Istoriia Rossii v XIX veke* (Granat), vol. III.

Tugan-Baranovskii, M. *Russkaia fabrika v proshlom i v nastoiashchem.* 7th ed. Moscow, 1938.

Turgenev, N. *La Russie et les russes.* 3 vols. Paris, 1847.

Tverskoi komitet ob ustroistve byta pomeshchich'ikh krest'ian. *Zhurnaly.* 3 vols. Lithographed. Tver, 1858–9.

Proekt polozheniia. Tver, 1859.

Bibliography

Unkovskii, A. M. 'Zamechaniia o neobkhodimosti i pol'ze vykupa.' *Russkii vestnik. Sovremennaia letopis'*, vol. XIX: 2, 1859.

'Zapiski.' *Russkaia mysl'*, nos. 6–7, 1906.

Valuev, P. A. *Dnevnik P. A. Valueva, ministra vnutrennikh del.* 2 vols. Moscow, 1961.

Vasil'chikov, A. *Zemlevladenie i zemledelie v Rossii i drugikh evropeiskikh gosudarstvakh*, vol. I. 2nd ed. St Petersburg, 1891.

Velikaia reforma. Russkoe obshchestvo i krest'ianskii vopros v proshlom i v nastoiashchem. 6 vols. Moscow, 1911.

Venturi, F. *Roots of Revolution.* New York, 1960.

Veselovskii, B. *Istoriia zemstva za 40 let.* 4 vols. St Petersburg, 1909–11.

Vilenskaia, E. S. *Revoliutsionnoe podpol'e v Rossii (60-e gody XIX v.).* Moscow, 1965.

Vil'kins, I. *Chto nuzhno pomeshchich'emu izdel'nomu krest'ianinu dlia bezbednogo soderzhaniia sebia v nechernozemnoi gubernii.* Moscow, 1832.

Mysli i nabliudeniia o polozhenii zemledel'cheskoi promyshlennosti. Moscow, 1843.

Voenno-statisticheskoe obozrenie Tverskoi gubernii. St Petersburg, 1848.

V. A. Artsimovich. *Vospominaniia, kharakteristika. Sbornik, izdannyi v pamiati V. A. Artsimovicha.* St Petersburg, 1904.

Le vote de la noblesse de Moscou. Débats d'une adresse a l'empereur Alexandre. Paris, 1865.

Witte, S. Iu. *Samoderzhavie i zemstvo. Konfidentsial'naia zapiska ministra finansov stats-sekretaria S. Iu. Vitte (1899g.)* St Petersburg, 1907.

Wortman, R. 'Koshelev, Samarin and Cherkassky and the Fate of Liberal Slavophilism.' *Slavic Review*, June 1962.

Zaionchkovskii, P. A. *Otmena krepostnogo prava v Rossii.* Moscow, 1954. 2nd ed., 1960.

Provedenie v zhizn' krest'ianskoi reformy 1861g. Moscow, 1958.

Zelenyi, P. 'Khersonskoe dvorianstvo i Khersonskaia guberniia v 1862 godu.' *Severnyi vestnik*, August 1889.

Zheltukhin, A. 'Proekt osvobozhdeniia krest'ian.' *Zhurnal zemlevladel'tsev*, vol. VI, prilozhenie 6, 1860.

Zhukovskaia, E. *Zapiski.* Leningrad, 1930.

Zhuravlev, N. V. *M. E. Saltykov-Shchedrin v Tveri, 1860–1862.* Kalinin, 1961.

Zhurnaly sekretnogo i glavnogo komiteta. 2 vols. Petrograd, 1915.

Bibliography

III. CONTEMPORARY PERIODICALS

Den' (weekly: Moscow, 1861–5).

Ekonomicheskii ukazatel' (weekly: St Petersburg, 1857–8).

Kolokol (irregular: London, 1857–65; Geneva, 1865–7).

Otechestvennye zapiski (monthly: St Petersburg, 1839–84).

Russkaia beseda (bimonthly: Moscow, 1856–60).

Russkaia gazeta (weekly: Moscow, 1858–9).

Sel'skoe blagoustroistvo (monthly supplement to *Russkaia beseda:* Moscow, 1858–9).

Sovremennik (monthly from 1843: St Petersburg, 1836–66).

Vest' (weekly to 1865: St Petersburg, 1863–70).

Zhurnal zemlevladel'tsev (biweekly: Moscow, 1858–60).

Index

Index

Ekonomicheskii ukazatel', 41 n., 382 n.
Elena Pavlovna, grand duchess, 57 n., 175 n.
Elizabeth I, empress, 5
England, 11, 25; gentry politics and, 226, 233
Englehardt, 79
English utilitarians, 419
Enlightenment, the, 34
Evropeus, A. I., 268, 270–81 passim, 335 n.

Finance Commission, 215–16, 246–7; see also Editing Commissions
Finland, 3 n.
'Five questions', the, 332–3, 355, 367
Frederick II, emperor, 13
Free Economic Society, 21, 36–7
Free labor, propaganda for, 37, 38, 91; discussion in Tver committee, 109, 111, 115, publicism and, 245–6; deputies of second convocation and, 302–3
Free Russian Press, 373 n., 385
Free trade, 37, 115

Gagarin, P. P., prince', 52 n., 229 n., 230
'Gagarin allotment', 321
Galicia, 1846 rebellion in, 30, 116, 222, 223 n.
Garmiza, A. A., 262, 360, 402 n.
Gerschenkron, A., 23 n., 56 n.
Giers, A. K., 217
Glazenap, P., 345 n.
Golenishchev-Kutuzov, V. V., 365
Golitsyn, prince, 86
Golokhvastov, P. D., 410 n., 411 n.
Golosa iz Rossii, see Voices from Russia
Golovachev, A. A., 157, 413 n.; early career and biography, 79, 82–4, 87–9; response to Nazimov Rescript, 89–95, 96, 97, 98, 99; in Tver provincial committee, 100–51 passim, 157; and 1859 Tver assembly, 268–81 passim; and zemstvo reform, 401 n.
Golovin, S., 378
Gorchakov, M., prince, 395

Governors, provincial, 12, 16; and government appointments in reform period, 84, 87 n., 161 n., 330
Granovskii, T. N., 80, 183
Great Russian, The, 374–5, 382, 386, 406
Grot, K. K., 48 n., 161 n., 170, 183, 184, 185 n., 187, 330

Haxthausen, A. von, baron, 10 n., 26 n, 28, 30, 35, 57 n., 60, 119
Herzen, A. I., 35, 274 n.; editor of Kolokol, 43, 48 n., 253 n., 307 n.; on Russia and the West, 119; and the constitutionalist campaign, 371–3, 381, 384, 390 n., 391; and Young Russia, 386, 387; and the Polish revolution, 406, 408
Household serfs, 80, 80 n., 136–7

Iafimovich, adjutant-general, 275, 278, 279
Iamburg uezd, Petersburg province, 364 n., 367
Iaroslavl province, provincial committee of, 151, 193–8 passim; 1859 provincial assembly of, 286–8; deputies to Petersburg from, 287
Ignat'ev, P. N., count, 53 n., 62, 66
Ignatovich, I. I., 23 n., 75–6, 192
Indebtedness, of gentry, 26–9, 30–3, 40, 351, 352, 354, 398, 421–2; see also State credit institutions, Land banks
Industrialization, 48–9, 118–19, 423
Inventory rules, for western provinces, 32, 33, 60
Iordanskii, N. I., 261
Ivan the Terrible, tsar, 379 n.
Ivaniukov, I., 308 n.
Ivanov, S. S., 305
Ivanov, Tver vice-governor, 272–4, 275, 279–80
Izmailov, P. A., 142

Jakob, professor, 37
Judicial reform, 255–7, 259, 277, 291, 313, 332, 341, 354, 374, 383, 385, 389, 399–400, 403

477

Index

Ministry of Interior (*cont.*)
87–8, 90; further directives and rulings, 139–40, 141, 213–14, 217–19, 221, 225–9, 263–4, 278, 280; *see also* Bureaucracy, Miliutin, N. A., Lanskoi, Levshin

Mir, see Commune, peasant

Mirovoi posrednik, see Peace mediator

Mogilev province, provincial committee of, 193–8 *passim*

Moore, B., Jr., 25

Moscow Agricultural Society, 22

Moscow Gentry Institute, 79

Moscow province, gentry assemblies of, 7; provincial committee of, 164–70, 193–8 *passim*; agriculture and economy, 168–9; 1862 provincial assembly of, 351–2, 353, 354 n., 356, 360, 376–9; gentry response to Polish insurrection in, 407; 1865 provincial assembly of, 408–12

Moscow University, 33 n., 80, 83, 171, 172, 173, 276

Moskovskie vedomosti, 178, 336

Moskovskii sbornik, 173

Murav'ev, A. N., 161, 170, 330

Murav'ev, M. N., count, 210, 218 n., 219, 229 n., 321 n., 395

Murav'ev, N. P., 284

Murav'ev-Apostol, M., 279 n.

Muromtsev, A. A., 154

Napoleon, 28

Napoleon III, 51 n.

Nashe vremia, 359

Nazimov, V. I., 52, 60–1, 62

Nazimov Rescript (November 1857), origins of, 51–62; gentry response to, 62–5, 90–5; *see also* entries for individual provinces

Nevedomskii, A. N., 341 n., 345 n.

Nicholas I, emperor, 9, 10, 13, 15, 22, 27 n., 28, 32, 33, 35 n., 41, 42, 47, 49, 55, 78, 87, 88, 118, 166, 173, 203, 317, 323 n., 328, 414

Nicolaevsky, B. I., 185 n.

Nikitenko, A. V., 264 n.

Nizhnii Novgorod province, 6 n.; provincial committee of, 62, 151, 160–5, 193–8 *passim*; agriculture and economy, 160–1; 1860 meeting of marshals in, 294 n.; 1860 provincial assembly of, 363

Nobility, European, 8, 8–9 n.

Novgorod province, provincial committee of, 193–8 *passim*; 1859–60 provincial asembly of, 294 n.; gentry proposals for *zemstvo* reform in, 366–7; gentry response to Polish insurrection in, 407

Novikov, N. I., 34, 418

Obolenskii, A. V., prince, 154, 155 n., 303–4, 305

Obolenskii, M. A., 80

Obrok, role in serf economy of, 22–5, 37; system for rates after emancipation, 132–4, 249; gentry proposals on, 193–4, 199, 249; in final legislation, 322; *see also Barshchina*, entries on individual provinces

Obruchev, N., 403 n.

Obshchina, see Commune, peasant

Odnodvortsy, 15

Odoevskii, V. F., prince, 171

Ofrosimov, F. S., 179, 256, 282–3, 284 n., 285 n., 286 n.

Ogarev, N. P., 253 n., 274 n., 371–3, 381, 384, 387

Okrug, 177

Olegin, Tver zemstvo leader, 413 n.

Olonetsk province, provincial committee of, 193–8 *passim*

Orel province, provincial committee of, 193–8 *passim*; 1859 provincial assembly of, 288–90

Orenburg province, 1859–60 provincial assembly of, 294 n.; 1862 assembly of, 364

Orlov, A. F., prince, 52 n., 219, 229 n.

Orlov-Davydov, V. P., count, 231–2, 264, 289–90, 313, 359, 375, 409, 410 n., 412

Ostashkov *uezd*, Tver province, 96–7

Otechestvennye zapiski, 393

Index

Index

Rostovtsev, Ia. I., member of Secret and Main Committees, 59, 67–8 n.; head of Editing Commissions, 127, 209–24 *passim*, 236, 289, 306, 308, 328, 372

Rovinskii, D. A., 166

Rozum, M. A., 101–2

Russkaia beseda, 172, 173, 178, 327

Russkaia gazeta, 284 n.

Russkii vestnik, 245, 337, 356

Russo-Turkish War, 413

Rzhev *uezd*, Tver province, 96–7

Rzhevskii, Tver school director, 270, 274, 285

St Petersburg, *see* Petersburg

Saltykov, M. E., 280, 335–6, 337, 340, 356

Samara province, provincial committee of, 151, 183–9, 193–8 *passim*, 392; agriculture and economy, 183–4; gentry response to emancipation, 331

Samarin, D. F., 176, 282, 305

Samarin, Iu. F., 136, 419 n.; biographical note, 171–3; and Samara provincial committee, 173–5, 183–9; in the Editing Commissions, 217, 235 n., 329; and the constitutionalist campaign, 391–2, 413; and the Polish question, 405

Samarin, P. F., 182

Saratov province, provincial committee of, 193–8 *passim*

Secret Committee, 51–2, 58, 61–2, 66; *see also* Main Committee

Secret Committee of 6 December 1826, 15

Selivanov, Riazan gentry marshal, 176, 178–80

Sel'skoe blagoustroistvo, 172, 173, 178, 245, 327

Semenov, N. P., 130

Semevskii, V. I., 29 n., 36

Senate, Ruling, 259, 270, 346

Serfdom, as a legal order, 19–20; economic system of, 19–20, 22–5

Serno-Solov'evich, N. A., 381, 383, 386, 394, 403

Service, state, 7–18 *passim*

Shchukin, F. S., 157

Shelgunov, N. V., 373

Shidlovskii, D. N., 238–9, 240 n., 243 n.

Shirobokov, L., 345 n.

Shreter, A. G., 190, 256–9

Shuvalov, A. P., count, 294 n., 296–7

Shuvalov, P. A., count, 294 n.

Shuvalov, P. P., count, 217 n., 230, 235, 237, 242, 243 n., 264, 294–7

Siberia, 3 n., 15

Simanovskii, Tver gendarme officer, 273, 274, 275, 279

Simbirsk province, provincial committee of, 193–8 *passim*; 1862 provincial assembly of, 354

Skerpan, A., 38 n.

Slavophiles, 35, 119, 171, 173, 379; and peasant commune, 41 n., 82, 136

Sluzhilye liudi, 7–8

Smallholders, gentry, 4–6, 15, 16–17 n., 17, 176

Smith, A., 37–9

Smolensk province, 31; provincial committee of, 193–8 *passim*

Society of the Lovers of Wisdom, 171

Solov'ev, Ia. A., and work on reform, 56 n., 217; memoirs, 59 n., 62 n., 203

Sovremennik, 245, 381, 382 n.

Speranskii, M. N., 315, 316, 419

Spirits concession, 171–2

Ständestaat, 315

Staritsa *uezd*, Tver province, 96–7

State Council, 377, 394–5; and reform preparation, 61 n., 321; other rulings, 344, 401

State credit institutions, 26–7; gentry indebtedness to, 26–8, 30–1; abolition of loans by, 270–1; *see also* Indebtedness, Land banks

State Loan Bank, 26

'State School', 391

Stremoukhov, P. D., 232, 236, 237

Struve, P. B., 27

Svistunov, P. N., 154

Szlachta, 9

Index

Index